How Effective Sermons End

How Effective Sermons End

BEN AWBREY

Foreword by Alex D. Montoya

RESOURCE *Publications* · Eugene, Oregon

HOW EFFECTIVE SERMONS END

Resource Publications
An Imprint of Wipf and Stock Publishers
199 W. 8th Ave., Suite 3
Eugene, OR 97401

www.wipfandstock.com

PAPERBACK ISBN: 978-1-6667-4018-9
HARDCOVER ISBN: 978-1-6667-4019-6
EBOOK ISBN: 978-1-6667-4020-2

07/01/22

Special Thanks to LG and T Cordell
For their encouragement to the author
Throughout the years this work was in progress

Contents

Foreword

"Thanks, pastor! I needed that" was a common response of an aged saint in my congregation to many sermons I preached. Upon reading *How Effective Sermons End* I wish to say the same, "Thanks, Dr. Ben Awbrey. I needed that." Dr. Awbrey touches our greatest need as preachers: to end our expositions well. I concur with him both as a preaching pastor and as a former professor of preaching. He nails it when he asserts that the "Church commonly is denied a most valuable aid, that is sermons that end well with true purpose, passion, power, and practical instruction for the hearers."

My dear friend and senior professor of preaching has already helped with two other preaching aids, *How Effective Sermons Begin* (2008) and *How Effective Sermons Advance* (2011). To which he adds perhaps his greatest contribution (in my estimation), *How Effective Sermons End*. The heart of *How Effective Sermons End* is that the sermon conclusion should be the high point of the sermon. Yet for most of us it has become the most neglected part of the sermon. Most of us devote the bulk of our time to the study and exposition of the text of Scripture and either devote little or no time to the crafting of an adequate conclusion. Hence we have here a personal and powerful reminder and exhortation to conclude our expositions of Scripture with purpose, passion and power.

Dr. Awbrey does not uncover new ground in his treatment of conclusions, but rather draws out for our study what was common course in homiletics for the last five centuries in the study of conclusions. The beauty of *How Effective Sermons End* is that in his book Dr. Awbrey presents the material in a thorough and fresh manner that speaks to the modern Biblical expositor, all the while remaining true to his devotion to Christ and the commitment to the divine inspiration of the Holy Scriptures. He never compromises on the supremacy, authority and sufficiency of Scripture, nor does he advocate minimizing, nor dumbing down, nor replacing the priority of Scripture in the preaching and exposition of Scripture. He maintains a high view of Scripture throughout the book. In the preparation of a conclusion Dr. Awbrey simply reminds us that the excellency of God's Word should be accompanied with the excellency of delivery, that the King's message should not be clothed in pauper's rags when better raiment can be secured. Such better raiment we have in *How Effective Sermons End*.

FOREWORD

Dr. Ben Awbrey treats the six elements of effective conclusion in great detail: synopsis, transition, purpose, closing appeal, persuasion, and the Gospel presentation. He does so with thoroughness, scholarship, and an exaltation of Christ and Scripture. He is also a pastor's professor. By this I mean that he speaks as a preaching pastor mentoring pastors in the art of preaching and thus resulting in men of God thoroughly equipped for preaching effective sermons from beginning to end. He writes with a pastor's head and heart, and not as an armchair theologian.

How Effective Sermons End touched me in many ways, among which are these. First, by the selected quotations at the beginning of each chapter which serve to summarize the contents and Velcro the theme to the mind. These pithy statements alone are worth the reader's time. Then we are exposed to the plethora of books used throughout, books rare, old and new, which beg us to read them. There is no doubt that Dr. Awbrey did his homework on how sermons end. Then, I was also captivated by the sections on persuasion and proclaiming Christ, topics not usually emphasized in preaching manuals. In addition, his "how to" sections are excellent examples for preachers young and old on how to prepare good conclusions. All to say as a preaching pastor to preachers and potential preachers, *How Effective Sermons End* will be a helpful resource.

Can you teach an old dog new tricks? Well, this old preacher and professor of preaching was challenged to end his expositions well. From now on I will have my dear friend and professor leaning over my shoulder as I come to the conclusion of my sermon. No longer will it be just a word at the end of my notes: "Conclusion." Now it will include purpose, passion, and power. "Thank you, Dr. Awbrey. I needed this book." May *How Effective Sermons End* revolutionize our exposition of Scripture so that our sermons end in a climax of passion and power, and not in a failed kamikaze conclusion of boredom, fizzle, and lack of purpose! With the help of this book we will learn to "land the plane well."

ALEX MONTOYA

Introduction

"If poor conclusions were a disease, the Church would be suffering a plague of pandemic proportion! However, A sermon conclusion in the preaching ministry of a true pastor who incorporates the Word of God in his closing appeals to God's people so that they may achieve the purpose of the sermon in their lives is poised to provide all that is possible through the means of this most important element of a sermon."

"In this book, the sermon conclusion is characterized as the highpoint of the sermon. As the highpoint of the sermon the conclusion should, and may well be understood as: the essence of earnestness; the peak of passion; the epitome of enthusiasm; the zenith of zeal; the summit of sincerity; the showcase of shepherding; the infusion of insight; the apex of application; the liaison for life-change; the pinnacle of persuasion; the climax of conviction; the crux of correction; the expedient of exhortation; the effulgence of encouragement; the conveyor of comfort; the harbinger of hope; the instiller of inspiration; the means of motivation; the resource of reproof; the revealer of remediation; the restorer of resolve; the refiner of righteousness; the procurer of purpose; and the conclusion includes the giving of the gospel."

To preach well is tough. To conclude well is tougher. This assertion is demonstrated clearly, even by the best preachers, many of whom do great work in preaching until they *attempt to conclude* their sermons, then their sermons simply fall apart and become unglued.

For me, Super Bowl LI will always serve as a fitting analogy of the typical sermon conclusion in preaching. Super Bowl LI was a game in which the Atlanta Falcons snatched defeat out of the jaws of victory more adeptly than any team who had preceded them in Super Bowl history. For the first three quarters the Atlanta Falcons totally dominated the New England Patriots. But the fourth quarter and the initial minutes of the very first overtime period in Super Bowl history defaced the whole game for the Atlanta Falcons. The last 18 minutes and 57 seconds of tragedy negated 45 minutes of triumph! At the end of the third quarter, Patriots 3 and the Falcons 28. At the end of the game, Patriots 34 and the Falcons 28. Thirty-one unanswered points! For the Falcons, what should have been, a Super Bowl Championship, never happened because of how the game was concluded! Many sermons are victimized by the same epic collapse in their conclusions!

For one to do a better job in preaching, generally, and to do a better job in concluding a sermon, specifically, requires one to become more concerned about the craft of preaching. Halford Luccock, in his book, *In the Minister's Workshop*, provides many valuable insights regarding the craft of preaching sermons. He is helpful as he warns about the prospect of falling victim to a distorted preoccupation with technique as he writes, "Personal and professional calamity impends when a means becomes an end. Yet we dare not forget that the end depends on the means. A consideration of ends without attention to means is pure sentimentalism."[1] Although I agree with Luccock's warning and I believe it is well intended and serviceable, we would do well to remember that preaching is a synergistic reality in which its total will always be greater than the sum of its parts. And this is true even when all the parts are crafted with the greatest of care. And yet, great care in crafting sermons is still needed by, even incumbent upon, every preacher of God's Word.

The improvement needed in the craft of preaching sermons is demanded due to the inherent difficulty of preaching. From the beginning of the sermon to its completion, the preaching process is nothing other than an intense struggle. For a preacher, a sermon is like two wrestling matches, simultaneously occurring, one with a text and its subject-matter, and the other with an audience. The great struggle of preaching begins with the tenseness of the initial minutes which determine whether a preacher will get an effective grip on the subject-matter and on his hearers.[2] However, the epic struggle of preaching is in presenting the truth by means of appeals, persuasion, and warning in such a way to "etch itself on the mind" of the hearers so that the goal of preaching—an effective presentation of God's Word which can change the lives of the hearers—can be achieved. Though difficult, this goal "is so great as to deserve any extent of discipline and sacrifice."[3] In the act of preaching, a preacher is on trial and his immediate vindication will come through a demonstration of skilled workmanship in the craft of preaching, a product of "toiling at a craft with intensity."[4] In regard to the concept of skilled workmen, I cannot help but to think about those men described in Joshua 20:16 of whom it was written that they were choice, left-handed men who could sling stones at a hair and not miss. An obvious result of much time and effort in developing their craft. To be sure, such toiling with intensity is never more needed than in the craft of concluding sermons!

In one way, a sermon is like many other things we are familiar with and experience in life. In other words, how something ends is a crucial consideration in determining its value and its effect on the lives of others. We should not overlook the

1. Luccock, *In the Minister's Workshop*, 31.

2. Luccock, *In the Minister's Workshop*, 33.

3. Luccock, *In the Minister's Workshop*, 34.

4. Luccock, *In the Minister's Workshop*, 36.

importance of how something ends. Whether reference is being made to the passing of a friend, the outcome of an athletic competition, the evaluation of a movie, or the culmination of a career, how the matter is brought to conclusion wields significant persuasion as to how we are inclined to view the whole. Such is the case, and particularly so, for sermons.

The bottom line is this—the Church commonly is denied a most valuable aid, that is, sermons that end well with true purpose, passion, power, and practical instruction for the hearers! Doing good work in concluding sermons does not happen naturally for preachers by accruing additional years of service in the ministry of preaching. In fact, the very opposite thing, most likely, will become a reality—he becomes so skilled at doing subpar work that producing poor conclusions has become second nature to him. He can do this very easily and does so routinely. He has become adept at being very bad at concluding his sermons. To do differently will require a different thought process about sermon conclusions and how to go about them.

This book, as an examination of sermon conclusions, advocates six elements[5] which constitute the material to be incorporated by a preacher as he concludes his sermon. Each of the six elements have a proven track record throughout the history of preaching. By this I mean that each element, throughout five centuries[6] in homiletical writings in Europe and America, was part of the instruction of those who trained men to preach, was advocated in many homiletical treatises, and demonstrated by many preachers in their preaching.

However, this does not mean that each of the six elements have been uniformly advocated in homiletical literature and in the practice of preaching throughout the centuries. For each of the six elements, there have been those, in their teaching, writing, and practice of preaching, who were averse to its inclusion in a sermon conclusion. The bottom line is this, there has never been uniform thinking as to what elements a sermon conclusion should incorporate. And it is certain that in these days there will be no uniform thinking as to what a sermon conclusion should include.

Therefore, there can be no doubt about this—there will be many who will take exception to the necessity or benefit of one, or even more, of the six elements advocated in this book as being necessary, or even beneficial, in a sermon conclusion. Every homelitician and preacher must be true to his convictions, in theory and practice, regarding the matter of preaching, generally, as well as the more specific matter of the sermon conclusion.

The overarching argument in this book is that the sermon conclusion should be the highpoint of the sermon. This is nothing new in the theory of concluding sermons. However, the theory and practice of sermon conclusions as the highpoint of the sermon is overwhelmingly absent in these days. For a sermon's highpoint to be the

5. The six elements are: a synopsis, a vital transition, closing appeals, a clinching element of persuasion, the purpose of the sermon achieved, and a presentation of the gospel message.

6. From William Perkins's book *The Art of Prophesying* published in 1606 to present-day texts.

conclusion will necessitate that substantially more content be contained in it than is commonly evidenced in sermons today. In present-day practice, sermon conclusions, when they exist, stand no chance whatsoever of being the highpoint of the sermon. They are too deprived of substance and significance to be anything other than what they are—an insignificant appendage tacked on to the sermon.

If one were to take a random selection of 100 preachers, all of whom are mature, godly men who love the Lord greatly and hold a high view of Scripture, the vast majority of them would have one very significant thing in common regarding their preaching. The unfortunate commonality is this—the most substantial improvement and the most beneficial upgrade in their preaching would be that of improvement in their sermon conclusions. This does not mean that the conclusion is the only thing needing improvement, or substantial improvement in the preaching of these men. Typically, several other elements of preaching would be ripe for a significant upgrade. This does mean, however, that the sermon conclusion is the most significant universal weakness in preaching. If poor conclusions were a disease, the Church would be suffering a plague of pandemic proportion! The sad reality is this—Poor conclusions are endemic in the preaching ministry of the Church.

The argument of this book regarding sermon conclusions is not "more for the sake of more." The argument is more for the sake of the sermons we preach and for the people who hear them! If sermon conclusions are to rise above the low level of present-day practice, then there must be a return to a high view of sermon conclusions, as well as an enriched supplementation of content in their composition.

The marketing jingle of "A Little Dab will Do Ya!" was an effective slogan decades ago for the haircare product, Brylcreem. But the homiletical version of Brylcreem, an enfeebled "little dab" of content marshalled in present-day sermon conclusions will not do if the intent is to provide believers with strategic insights necessary for them to go from "as is" to "as should be" in faithfully living the purpose of the text expounded in the sermon. Additionally, there is need for a clear declaration of the person and work of Jesus Christ so that unbelievers may have a true understanding of Him and, thereby, may receive the free gift of eternal life by repenting of their sins and believing in Him, trusting in the finished work He has accomplished.

If the benefit of a sermon conclusion is to be more than an encouragement to the hearers that they are about to be dismissed, then there is a need for a theory and practice of concluding sermons with substance and strength. Hearers of sermons need to be provided a new reality for how sermons end, so new and so different, that in the hearing of them they will learn to anticipate with great expectancy what the preacher will offer them in his sermon conclusion.

What is needed is a common practice of ending sermons that would be analogous to the marvel of Christ's first miracle performed at a wedding feast in Cana of Galilee where the headwaiter exclaimed to the bridegroom, "Every man serves the good wine first, and when the people have drunk freely, then he serves the poorer wine; but you have kept the good wine until now."[7] How beneficial it would be, no matter how good the earlier fare of a sermon, if the hearers could rightly expect that the best is being saved for the end of the sermon, and then, having heard the conclusion know that their expectation had been realized. This is the result of sermons that end effectively.

Effective conclusions end well because they are composed of effective elements, elements so rich in substance and elements that work so well together that they may truly constitute, and may be deemed as, the best "wine" of the sermon. This is what we want to learn to do—to provide the best for last, that is, to provide the most significant and the most instructive insights of the sermon in our conclusions. Put negatively, what we want to learn to do is to make sure the conclusions of our sermons do not suffer the same unfortunate ending, a colossal collapse, like the Atlanta Falcons supplied to Super Bowl LI.

Ilion T. Jones summarized the matter well with two comments he made about sermon conclusions. He wrote: "Conclusions are consistently the weakest parts of sermons. Far too many sermons ravel out at the ends. Every poor conclusion is a lost opportunity because, there the sermon should come to its final climax, there its main purpose should be achieved, there the preacher's supreme effort should take place. More attention should therefore be given to the problem of how to make conclusions effective."[8] Such attention is desperately needed and long overdue since the most consistent feature about a sermon conclusion in preaching is "the fact that so many ministers seem not to work at the job of learning to do it well."[9]

I believe that we owe it to our Lord, who saved us and called us to preach, and to those who hear us preach to reconsider what we do and how we go about our sermon conclusions. Furthermore, I believe it is incumbent upon us to understand carefully and thoroughly all we can about the elements of a sermon conclusion so that we may learn to conclude our sermons with significant substance and strength.

I believe an important clarification to the reader of this book may be beneficial. I am concerned that any reader of this work may draw two inaccurate conclusions regarding either my intentions or my theological perspective in writing what is presented in the following pages. In the pages of this work the author experienced relentless tension in writing about a preacher's methods, practices, and responsibilities in light of an omnipotent, sovereign God. It is of great significance to the author that the reader understand that this author has the greatest conviction that nothing a preacher does or does not do allows, causes, limits, or prevents God from acting as He so chooses regarding His working and the results of His work in the lives of those who hear His Word preached, regardless of the preaching that occurs. In the writing of this book, I found myself, on very many instances, providing a theological insertion to balance what was being written regarding a preacher's intentions, methods, practices, procedures, and

7. John 2:10.

8. Jones, *Principles and Practice of Preaching*, 160.

9. Jones, *Principles and Practice of Preaching*, 160.

routine in preaching God's Word. This, however, served only to become unprofitable as consistency in this attempt provided numerous insertions to the point that they served as a distraction. Therefore, I left only a few theological balancing insertions along the way to lessen the possibility of the reader concluding that I am not cognizant of God but only man-centered in my approach to all things germane to preaching. I determined, rather, to make this clarification here and hope for the best in reference to a reader's suppositions about my understanding of God's sovereign, omnipotent working through His Word as he reads the content of the chapters of this book.

Secondly, this book was produced as a research project. Though not intended to be a sequential historical development of homiletical thought about sermon conclusions through the centuries of written homiletical works, my intent was to provide substantial references about sermon conclusions that have been advocated by many over centuries of writing. The purpose of this was to provide the reader with the data that substantiates that of all the components of preaching none has been so abandoned in practice as the sermon conclusion. Therefore, rather than advocating my views and convictions about sermon conclusions, I have supplied prodigious references from many sources that have guided and help form my views and convictions. I believe that if I am advocating anything about sermon conclusions that is beyond what has been advocated through the years it is that the closing appeals should be Scripture-based. I do not claim originality in this assertion, only that my advocacy of this practice may be significantly stronger than that which has been previously advocated by others.

1

General Matters about the Sermon Conclusion and Preachers: Part 1

"The preacher, who is not a pastor, becomes isolated. The pastor, who is not a preacher, becomes insignificant. It must never be said about anyone that, he is a preacher, but not a pastor, or that, he is a pastor, but not a preacher."

"The true pastor's preaching is never separated from his love for God's people. The preaching of a true pastor is actual ministry. His love for God's people is apparent through his preaching because he cares for the people to whom he preaches, and his preaching is an act of caring for them. Their spiritual well-being, edification, growth, and sanctification are clearly his concerns. Nothing matters to him more than their grasp and implementation of God's Word."

"The desire of a true pastor in preaching will gravitate naturally to the conclusion of the sermon where his hearers become the focal point of the greatest focus of the sermon, the conclusion. His desire to do his hearers the greatest good in this portion of the sermon, particularly, will also drive him to beseech God's help to affect what he could never do on his own."

"Regardless of the content and tone of the text and the sermon preached from it, in the conclusion of the sermon the content and tone should be positive as correction and remediation become hard targets of the true pastor. In the body of the sermon the true pastor, as a faithful shepherd, feeds God's sheep. In the conclusion of the sermon the true pastor, as a faithful shepherd, tends God's sheep. He desires to tend them. He seeks to correct what is weak, inadequate, and erroneous in their lives. He desires to establish a pathway in the training of their righteousness. He seeks to bind up their wounds. He desires to nurture them. He seeks their healing. God's people

need this ministry, a ministry that is in his heart to provide, and the Word of God contains the substance to make this ministry a perpetual provision."

"How great it is that God's people are benefitted by a preached sermon. But a pastor must only and always be concerned that God's people are fed, not flattered. A faithful preacher must impart truths that will do many things for his hearers, everything except flattering them. But he will say these things anyway because it is necessary for their spiritual health and well-being."

"The mind, will, emotions/affections, conscience, and volition of the hearers must be addressed if the behavior patterns of God's people are to be redirected. There is no other part of the sermon that provides such free opportunity to address God's people in their comprehensive makeup than the sermon conclusion."

"In no small way, it is due to the positive tone of a true pastor that makes his preaching more like a journey than a Sunday drive. Unlike a Sunday drive which is designed to go nowhere, in particular, the journey-like preaching of a true pastor is designed to reach a specific destination. That destination is reachable for all who respond unconditionally to the mandates and instruction of Scripture. Thus, a significant turning-point in life is only a commitment away for all who desire it. This, then, is the basis for a positive tone in preaching."

"The absence of a positive tone is unfortunate, and a critical tone is disastrous. A critical preacher, or a 'pulpit scold,' may be able to proceed, for a season of time, without adverse consequences. However, this will be a brief season. The law of sowing and reaping will quickly become apparent. He simply will not be able to continue as he began without facing the inevitable reality of people tiring of his negativity. . . . He will discover that it is one thing to show men that they are in the wrong, and to leave them there—another thing to show them how to get right."

"The conclusion should be the magnum opus of the sermon. The great work that is the sermon conclusion is not that it is the most extensive part of the sermon but that it is the portion of the sermon that provides the greatest take-away for the hearers. In the conclusion the mind, conscience, emotions/affections, and will of the hearers should be pressed with an earnestness that cannot be denied. If understanding has been gained in the body of the sermon, the conscience, emotions/affections, and the will, especially, must be gained in the conclusion."

"When preaching is accompanied by a lack of earnestness the effort and intent may be directed toward preaching but the result must be other than preaching the Word, namely, misrepresenting the Word. Not misinterpreting the Word but misrepresenting the Word. The interpretation is correct. What gets said should be said because what is said is true, true according to the text that is being preached. The

misrepresentation comes from the fact that what is said, though true according to the text, is not true according to the heart of the one preaching it because there is little conviction in his heart. He has little conviction about what he has rightly interpreted. His hermeneutics are solid gold, but his heart is ice cold! The good thing is that there was no twisting of the Scriptures, he 'cut it straight.' But the bad thing is that what was cut straight never cut his own heart, therefore, the exhibiting of conviction in proportion to the truth, as demanded by the truth, was absent. Correct interpretation minus conviction does not equal preaching! There is a prevailing fault in preaching that must be remedied—the fault of preaching in a cold indifferent tone."

"Conviction in the heart of the preacher is the starting point. As good as it is to have a preacher with convictions about the truth he proclaims, that is not good enough. Those to whom he preaches are to be impacted by the preacher's conviction so that it may become infectious. This is what is needed but this is beyond the preacher's control. He is responsible to have convictions about God's truth, but he is incapable to convict the hearts of his hearers. . . . But, when a preacher's heart is as true as his convictions, upon completing his responsibilities, he can trust God to work as only he can work in the lives of his hearers. . . . He alone can do what no preacher can do, or ever has done—bring conviction to the heart of a man. In God's incredible grace, he has designed to use preachers of the Word as instruments in the work he accomplishes in the lives of men for time and for eternity."

"The positive tone of conviction is an undeniable quality of the preaching of a true pastor in the sermon conclusion. This is the place in the sermon where his hearers will be challenged to respond to God's Word, to implement its truth, and to conform to its requirements in their lives."

"In the sermon conclusion, like no other place in the sermon, the positive tone of conviction is a palpable reality in the preaching of a true pastor. A true pastor will burn and shine in the conclusion of his sermons."

THE TRUE PASTOR AND THE SERMON CONCLUSION

No part of the sermon "defines itself" more definitively, more conclusively, than the sermon conclusion.[1] But it must be recognized equally that no part of the sermon also defines the one who preaches it more definitively, more conclusively, than the sermon conclusion.

The sermon conclusion essentially defines the one preaching by answering this question—To what degree is the man preaching, a true pastor? By true pastor, I mean one who desires to build up God's people predominantly through preaching because

---

1. Phelps, *The Theory of Preaching*, 1882, 456.

preaching is what he is passionate about. To have a low conception of the preaching ministry is crippling to usefulness, like having one's right arm withered. One does not excel in that which fails to command one's utmost respect and does not suffuse one with enthusiasm.[2] By true pastor, I mean one whose spiritual gifts, fulfilment, and effectiveness are related to his pulpit ministry, primarily.

But is the measure of a true pastor limited to his pulpit ministry alone? Certainly not. However, the standard of measure for a true pastor would not be the impressive title of "a great pastor." A man who is known as "a great pastor" is known as such because of the opulent time[3] spent with people in his home, their homes, hospitals, various venues, time spent counseling them, etc. Such men are not inclined to accomplish, and do not take the time to accomplish, the kind of study that can result in an effective preaching ministry. The preaching of "a great pastor" is one of the lesser things he does, it is not something for which he is known. Yet, a true pastor will be a faithful shepherd of God's people. Pastoral ministry will be an important function in his stewardship of serving God's people.

Nevertheless, by true pastor, I mean the kind of preacher that faithfully expounds Scripture thoroughly, not superficially, and in doing so he will certainly denounce sin, sinful behaviors, and sinful accommodations. He reflects God's hatred for sin just as well as God's love for people. Additionally, by true pastor, I mean the "be both" mandate of Phillips Brooks when he says that a preacher needs to be a pastor so that his preaching may be more readily received by his hearers. The preacher, who is not a pastor, becomes isolated. The pastor, who is not a preacher, becomes insignificant. It must never be said about anyone that, he is a preacher, but not a pastor, or that, he is a pastor, but not a preacher.[4] Phillips Brooks's conviction was certain in his admonition to, "Be both; for you cannot really be one unless you also are the other."[5]

So, the sermon conclusion defines the one preaching as it answers the question— Is the man preaching, a true pastor? No part of a sermon evidences a true pastor like the sermon conclusion. The preacher's identity is never more established, and his heart is never more evident than in this portion of the sermon. The sermon conclusion is simply the part of the sermon where the true pastor shines. With the sermon conclusion as "a lampstand" and the true pastor as "a lamp," the true pastor finds himself in the sermon conclusion as one who is positioned to give much needed "light to all who are in the house." In the sermon conclusion, the heart of the true pastor is "a city set on a hill" which "cannot be hidden." As in no other part of the sermon, in the

2. Burgess, *The Art of Preaching*, 1881, 69.

3. I am not saying that such connections with God's people are unnecessary because they are. However, for the sake of a preaching ministry that is a significant ministry of the Word, these activities, at times, must be wisely and lovingly curtailed.

4. Brooks, *On Preaching*, 77.

5. Brooks, *On Preaching*, 77.

conclusion the true pastor's heart is like a "light that shines before men" in such a way that they can see his good works and glorify the Father in Heaven.[6]

In the sermon conclusion the true pastor may do the greatest good for the most people. A sermon conclusion in the preaching ministry of a true pastor who incorporates the Word of God in his closing appeals to God's people so that they may achieve the purpose of the sermon in their lives is poised to provide all that is possible through the means of this most important element of a sermon. In this book, the sermon conclusion is characterized as the highpoint of the sermon. As the highpoint of the sermon the conclusion should, and may well be understood as the essence of earnestness; the peak of passion; the epitome of enthusiasm; the zenith of zeal; the summit of sincerity; the showcase of shepherding; the infusion of insight; the apex of application; the liaison of life-change; the pinnacle of persuasion; the climax of conviction; the crux of correction; the expedient of exhortation; the effulgence of encouragement; the conveyor of comfort; the harbinger of hope; the instiller of inspiration; the means of motivation; the resource of reproof; the revealer of remediation; the restorer of resolve; the refiner of righteousness; the procurer of purpose; and the conclusion includes the giving of the gospel.[7]

This part of the sermon, like no other, calls for an honest, sympathetic dealing with people regarding their lives in relation to the truths of Scripture. Sympathy without truth ushers one into certain heresy and makes for a quick disqualification from the ministry. However, truth without sympathy issues forth from the kind of man whom his hearers "respect but to whom they seldom go and whom they do not care to see coming to them."[8] But where there is sympathetic truth, there may be an acceptance of the truth in the highest order on behalf of the hearers because of the likeability and respectability of the one who preaches to them so acceptably.[9]

Preachers who are true pastors preach not only *to* God's people but *for* them. This result is indicative of the man's character and his relationship with God and with God's people. His desire to shepherd God's people prevents him from being a "pulpit scold" who is always preaching *at* them and always preaching in a denunciatory tone. This is not only a pity, but it is spiritually debilitating for people. Ultimately, it is not advantageous if, when God's people assemble to worship, the preacher dwells on their faults that he so expertly finds in them. Life is difficult for all people, at times with heavy burdens, and many times with bitter sorrows. People need and crave encouragement and comfort[10] beyond the reproof, rebuke, correction and instruction which every

6. The quoted phrases were taken from a portion of Christ's Sermon on the Mount found in Matthew 5:13–16. His phraseology which clearly portrays the lives his followers are to fulfill is apt terminology to describe a true pastor's preaching ministry in his sermon conclusion.

7. The characteristics of the sermon conclusion discussed in the chapters to follow will not, in every instance, be characterized by the alliterized phrases found above.

8. Brooks, *On Preaching*, 78.

9. Brooks, *On Preaching*, 77.

10. Sangster, *The Craft of Sermon Construction*, 197.

preacher of God's Word must supply. Yet, in so doing, it must be recognized that, while only a few hearers are inclined to rebel against the goading or the urging of a preacher for them to act, no one has ever been "scolded out of" one's sins.[11]

For example, consider the Apostle Peter. The Lord had to regather him after his unthinkable threefold denial. Peter was instructed by the Lord to, "Tend My lambs . . . Shepherd My sheep . . . Tend My sheep" John 21:15–17. Peter's sermon on the Day of Pentecost, particularly the conclusion of his sermon, shows that he was involved in the tending and shepherding ministries but also how he accomplished such service in his preaching. Acts 2:14–36 shows Peter providing some very effective and much needed rebuke for the past and present actions of the mockers who had crucified the Lord. In answer to their outcry, "Brethren, what shall we do?" Peter's response reveals the tending ministry of a true shepherd as he said, *"Repent, and each of you be baptized for the forgiveness of yours sins; and you will receive the gift of the Holy Spirit. For the promise is for you and your children and for all who are far off, as many as the Lord our God will call to Himself."* And *with many other words he solemnly testified and kept on exhorting them, saying "Be saved from this perverse generation!"* (Acts 2:36–40). What were the results of Peter's faithful tending and shepherding? *"And that day there were added about three thousand souls."* The souls of 3,000 of Christ's sheep were brought into the fold through the faithful preaching of Christ's under-shepherd.

As it was with Peter, a true pastor so identifies with God's people that when he preaches, he not only preaches to them but for their benefit. The true pastor's preaching is never separated from his love for God's people. The preaching of a true pastor is actual ministry. His love for God's people is apparent through his preaching because he cares for the people to whom he preaches, and his preaching is an act of caring for them. Their spiritual well-being, edification, growth, and sanctification are clearly his concerns. Nothing matters to him more than their grasp and implementation of God's Word. Ultimately, a preacher must study the Scriptures as one who will preach them to God's people on God's behalf. He must not study as if the truth he sought were *only for his own enrichment*.[12] In so doing, two noteworthy results will be his: first, it will bring a deeper and more solemn sense of responsibility in the study of Scripture; second, there will be a greater desire to discover the implications for humanity in every truth, the crucial nexus at which every doctrine touches humanity.[13] Unlike some men who preach with a certain detachment from people, a true pastor's preaching identifies

---

11. Moore, *Thoughts on Preaching*, 1861, 74.

12. My point here is that a preacher should move from studying for his own growth and edification, to studying to prepare a message for God's people. I believe it is a mistake to begin one's time in studying God's Word motivated to fulfill one's preaching responsibility rather than being motivated to study for one's own edification.

13. Brooks, *On Preaching*, 46.

so well with his hearers and there is such obvious concern for them that there is an acceptability, not only to his appeals, but even to his warnings.[14]

The preacher who is a true pastor has a heart for preaching and he has a heart for God's people. This does not preclude the true pastor from praying much about the message he will preach and praying for the ones to whom he will preach. Because the nature of the sermon conclusion is the most significant part of the sermon and the portion of the sermon where the ministry of a true pastor is most apparent, this must be a major concern in prayerful preparation to preach effectively. The effective preaching of a true pastor is not limited to an accurate, in-depth, insightful understanding of a text of Scripture, though this must be the foundation upon which the conclusion is based. However, a true pastor's effective preaching will culminate in a conclusion that helps God's people to implement the purpose of the preaching text in their lives.

Since the best source of the needed help to be offered in the conclusion will be found in other related passages of Scripture, prayerful consideration and a thorough search of the Scriptures are required to supply these inclusions. And, just as it is important to provide significant content in the conclusion, it is equally important that the heart of a true pastor is thoroughly prepared to dispense the biblical counsel. Therefore, a true pastor is no exception to the necessity for the preparation of his heart as well as his sermon.

It is a mistake to preach from a heart that has not been prepared for preaching. Preparing to preach is much more than preparing a sermon. Preparing the sermon is an important part of the preparation, but it is only a part. A man must prepare himself to preach. For this to be done productively, the sermon must be prepared completely. That is why it is such a compromise to leave the preparation of the sermon so late in the week that one is scrambling to complete it just before the time of its delivery.[15]

The desire of a true pastor in preaching will gravitate naturally to the conclusion of the sermon where his hearers become the focal point of the greatest focus of the sermon, the conclusion. His desire to do his hearers the greatest good in this portion of the sermon, particularly, will also drive him to beseech God's help to affect what he could never do on his own. The true pastor is no less dependent upon God than anyone else who preaches. On the contrary, it's just that the sermon conclusion, being the part of the sermon that holds special opportunity for him, will become a special focus of prayer for the true pastor.

THE POSITIVE TONE OF A TRUE PASTOR

The preaching of a true pastor builds up his hearers. Because he is a true pastor, he seeks to build them up. Regardless of the content and tone of the text and the sermon preached from it, the conclusion of the sermon's content and tone should be positive

14. Sangster, *The Craft of Sermon Construction*, 199.

15. Sangster, *The Craft of Sermon Construction*, 203.

as correction and remediation become hard targets of the true pastor. In the body of the sermon the true pastor, as a faithful shepherd, feeds God's sheep. In the conclusion of the sermon the true pastor, as a faithful shepherd, tends God's sheep. He desires to tend them. He seeks to correct what is weak, inadequate, and erroneous in their lives. He seeks to bind up their wounds. He desires to nurture them. He seeks their healing. God's people need this ministry, a ministry that is in his heart to provide, and the Word of God contains the substance to make this ministry a perpetual provision.

Austin Phelps is correct in his comments about preaching as it is found in Scripture that biblical appeals, almost without exception, are expectant in their delivery bearing "a ring of courage and expectation" in them.[16] This is indicative of the true pastor's preaching, as well. A positive tone and an expectant note in preaching, just as expectant appeals in the sermon conclusion, are predicated upon the work that God has accomplished in the preacher's life in his preparation to preach as well as the preacher's dependence upon the Holy Spirit to work in the hearts of his people as he delivers God's Word.

Two obstacles stand in the way of a preacher doing effective work in sermon conclusions—thoughtlessness and self-centeredness.[17] Thoughtlessness and self-centeredness are nearly eradicated in the preaching of the true pastor. Earnest, conscientious preachers can minimize effective sermons, prepared with great care and diligence, by ending them thoughtlessly. This is a grievous and very common obstacle. Much preaching is like delivering information about medicine to sick people but withholding the medicine from them.[18] The information is true, fact-based, and important, but the information "is not medicine." To give the medicine, having provided the information, "is the preacher's duty."[19] The medicine to be provided is not more information but the practical instruction needed to achieve the purpose of the preaching text in the fullest manner.

The preacher's failure to fulfill his responsibility makes him culpable of the indictment of declaring truth for the sake of declaring it only, with no regard "to its results in life."[20] It is in the sermon conclusion where the medicine is administered. A true pastor is inclined to do this since the conclusion provides him with the opportunity to tend God's flock, which he is highly motivated to do. A good shepherd as modeled in Psalm 23 is "aware of the state of the flock. If the sheep need medicine, the sensitive shepherd does not press forward with his plans of giving regular food. If the sheep are hungry and waiting to be fed, the sensitive shepherd does not take

16. Phelps, *The Theory of Preaching*, 1882, 565.

17. Breed, *Preparing to Preach*, 1911, 117–18.

18. Brooks, *On Preaching*, 126.

19. Brooks, *On Preaching*, 126. Of course, in expository preaching the information, the exposition of Scripture, is the medicine not just information about the medicine. However, the conclusion would be the prescription for the medicine so that it could be acquired and administered personally.

20. Brooks, *On Preaching*, 127.

out the medicine and give it as if it were food. If the sheep need mending, the sensitive shepherd does not administer the rod of correction."[21] Scripture is certain about the necessity of a vigilant understanding of the state of and caring for the needs of God's people. Proverbs 27:23 says, "Know well the condition of your flocks, and pay attention to your herds." Paul mandated to the Ephesian elders that they were to "Be on guard for yourselves and for all the flock, among whom the Holy Spirit has made you overseers, to shepherd the flock of God which he purchased with His own blood" (Acts 20:28). The fulfillment of a shepherd's duty requires that he knows God's people so well that he is aware of "where they are in their struggles, their questions, and even in their sins and weaknesses."[22] The sermon conclusion provides a great opportunity to tend to the practical matters of God's people for their everyday living, which is the very thing a true pastor desires to do.

A true pastor will not only tend God's people, but he will do so in a manner that is indicative of his heart and will be most profitable to the ones who hear him preach, that is, he will seek to encourage them. Part of the reason Chuck Swindoll is such an effective preacher and concluder of sermons can be attributed to his determination to conclude his sermons in an encouraging fashion. Early in Swindoll's preaching ministry he forged the following convictions about his sermon conclusions, specifically, and preaching, generally. "I determined never again to end on a negative note. Even if I must correct, reprove, or rebuke sin, I will conclude with hope and encouragement."[23] "The Word of God is both encouraging and empowering. Our messages, if lifted from Scripture, should be no less so."[24] By the implementation of these convictions through decades of preaching, this true pastor has effectively incorporated the shepherd's rod and staff in the lives of God's people in a way that has been of great spiritual benefit to untold millions of believers around the world.

An additional component of thoughtlessness is that much preaching, and even more so sermon conclusions, may be described by the word "petty." Preaching often tries to bypass the misfortunes of life rather than instructing people to meet hardship with endurance by offering inducements to patience in the suggestions of compensation in this life or in the life to come, thus imparting a higher and stronger perspective which teaches people to embrace their sorrows and bear them in a life of true faith and faithfulness. The best help which a preacher may provide those who bear the burdens of life is not to seek to take away his burden but to call on them to appropriate Christ's strength so that they may be able to bear them in a manner that pleases and glorifies God.[25] It is the lack of such effort to awaken a resolute spirit that is deficient in the vast majority of sermon conclusions. Much preaching tries to comfort with consolation,

21. Borgman, *My Heart for Thy Cause*, 144.
22. Borgman, *My Heart for Thy Cause*, 147.
23. Swindoll, *Saying It Well*, 246.
24. Swindoll, *Saying It Well*, 247.
25. Brooks, *On Preaching*, 79.

almost exclusively, without imparting the equally serviceable necessity to fire with resolve and courage.[26] The true pastor not only desires to provide medicine along with giving information about the medicine, but the medicine he administers will be specific to address the needs, problems, and weaknesses of God's people. The true pastor, because of the man he is and preacher he is, is not hindered by the obstacle of thoughtlessness in his sermon conclusions.

The second obstacle standing in the way of effective conclusions is self-centeredness. An effective sermon may be minimized by ending it with a self-aggrandizing rhetorical flourish allowing the preacher to "go out in a blaze of glory." How unfortunate it is when there is a recognizable conclusion, that may be the highpoint of the sermon in actuality, that it should be this type of self-serving product designed to magnify the preacher before the people of God. Rather than supplying practical aid to help God's people live according to his Word, rather than glorifying God as the one who is sufficient and willing to enable them to obey his Word, he is content, in substance and style, to say things that might exalt himself before God's people.

A great sermon is more of a result rather than an intention. The intention of a sermon that is truly great is to glorify God and to grow God's people in a spiritually significant way. The intention to preach a sermon that people would think to be a "great sermon" is a sin of a preacher's ego seeking the flattery of his hearers. How great it is that God's people are benefitted by a preached sermon. But a pastor must only and always be concerned that God's people are fed, not flattered. A faithful preacher must impart truths that will do many things for his hearers, everything except flattering them. But he will say these things anyway because it is necessary for their spiritual health and well-being.

At times the true pastor must accomplish a pulpit version of Jael's dealing with Sisera when Jael took a tent peg and hammered it into Sisera's brain. Rather than merely loosening a few flakes of "dandruff" from his scalp she nailed his "skull to the ground."[27] Brian Borgman provides a fitting exhortation to pastors as he writes, "If preaching is to be searching and lively in application, it must go beyond shaking a few flakes loose, and get to the real business of fastening the truth firmly into the heads of the listeners."[28] Again, a true pastor is not inclined to self-aggrandizement since he seeks to minister to God's people, not impress them. After all, the conclusion is all about the hearers, not the preacher. Neither obstacle should ever become a stumbling block for any preacher. But neither obstacle poses much of a hurdle to the true pastor since thoughtlessness and self-centeredness are not his stock in trade as he preaches.

Though the conclusion of a sermon should be positive, not negative, it should be a message that is left pulsating in the hearts of the hearers. And though the closing words should bring assurance and hope, these must be acceptable to God and the

26. Brooks, *On Preaching*, 80.

27. Borgman, *My Heart for Thy Cause*, 162.

28. Borgman, *My Heart for Thy Cause*, 162.

natural outcome of the text that was expounded. A. W. Blackwood insisted that, if sermons conclude as they should, they lead to decisive action which must, in effect, "sound the call to another holy war."[29] Because Christ called people to this holy war, he was insensitive to men's whims though he loved them and was completely committed to meet their needs. What was absent in Christ, but readily observable in many preachers, is a "sycophancy" which seeks to discern what is desired by his hearers, then provide it at all costs—even if it sacrifices things mandated from Scripture. Such sycophancy cannot prepare God's people to live righteous lives. On the other hand, the more one prizes the spiritual edification of God's people, the more able one will be to oppose "their whims" and to propose what is needful for them to engage the holy war to which they are called.[30]

The life of a Christian in this world is a war, one that certainly is to be lived as a holy war. To this end, believers must be built up by the Word of God to fight this holy war productively, and believers should be encouraged by the one proclaiming the Word to engage this holy war relentlessly. Therefore, a preacher's sermon, generally, and his sermon conclusion, specifically, should be exceedingly functional. The overall thrust of the sermon conclusion must be earnest statements of fundamental truth, designed to accomplish the purpose for which the sermon was preached. More specifically, the last words of the sermon should be intended to bring consolation to the hearers and inspire the hearers toward their personal commencement to apply the truth proclaimed to them.

A commencement for the application of biblical truth, generally, and the accomplishment of the sermon's purpose in the lives of the hearers, specifically, is what the conclusion is to achieve. If this is not achieved in the conclusion, then the sermon may be considered by this standard to have been a failure, even though other valuable results were accomplished. "We have to do not only with a dark intellect that needs to be informed, but with a hard heart that needs to be impressed, and a torpid conscience that needs to be awakened; we have to make our hearers feel that in the great business of religion, there is much to be done, as well as much to be known."[31] The mind, will, emotions/affections, conscience, and volition of the hearers must be addressed if the behavior patterns of God's people are to be redirected. There is no other part of the sermon that provides such free opportunity to address God's people in their comprehensive makeup than the sermon conclusion.

In no small way, it is due to the positive tone of a true pastor that makes his preaching more like a journey than a Sunday drive. Unlike a Sunday drive which is designed to go nowhere, in particular, the journey-like preaching of a true pastor is designed to reach a specific destination. That destination is reachable for all who respond unconditionally to the mandates and instruction of Scripture. Thus, a

---

29. Blackwood, *The Fine Art of Preaching*, 136.
30. Brooks, *On Preaching*, 59.
31. James, *An Earnest Ministry*, 1847, 86–87.

significant turning-point in life is only a commitment away for all who desire it. This, then, is the basis for a positive tone in preaching.

Positive Tone as Essential for Effective Preaching

A positive tone supplied in the sermon conclusion is essential for effective preaching. But this requires that one never sacrifice truth on the altar of receptibility. A preacher must not fail to preach any truth simply because it may not be well-received. Phillips Brooks insightfully asks, "Who are you that you should stint the children's drinking from the cup which their father bid you to carry to them, or mix it with error because you think they cannot bear it in its purity?"[32] Preaching necessitates a constant conviction that "truth is always strong no matter how weak it looks, and falsehood is always weak, no matter how strong it looks."[33]

The absence of a positive tone is unfortunate, and a critical tone is disastrous. A critical preacher, or a "pulpit scold," may be able to proceed, for a season of time, without adverse consequences. However, this will be a brief season. The law of sowing and reaping will quickly become apparent. He simply will not be able to continue as he began without facing the inevitable reality of people tiring of his negativity. If a preacher attempts to preach without a positive note, specifically in his conclusions, "He will discover that, while perhaps he has been cutting up many weeds, he has planted very few trees and some very little corn; so that as autumn after autumn goes by, there is not much fruit ripening in the orchard and there is hardly any crop in the fields. He will discover that it is one thing to show men that they are in the wrong, and to leave them there—another thing to show them how to get right."[34] Showing people how to get right, bringing correction to their present state, is the vital ministry for which the sermon conclusion is intended.

The desirable qualities that a sermon conclusion should possess, among other qualities, are these; personal, specific, positive, and vigorous. In the sermon conclusion the preacher confronts the hearers personally and directly with the truth claims of his message. The hearers must be made to feel that the message is personally applicable. The use of personal pronouns—you, your, yours, we, us, our, ours—are mandatory to make the message warm, direct, and personal. The preacher's heart and attitude are contributing factors, as an asset or a liability, to hearers in their personal response to the sermon. The sermon conclusion is no place for complaining, nagging, or anger on behalf of a preacher since a conclusion should demonstrate an obvious and sincere concern to help the hearers. Through the sermon in general, but particularly in the

32. Brooks, *On Preaching,* 271.

33. Brooks, *On Preaching,* 271.

34. Dale, *Nine Lectures on Preaching,* 1890, 18.

sermon conclusion, the hearers should witness a preacher earnestly desiring to sow in their hearts the seeds of truth and faithfulness.[35]

A positive conclusion yielding insights about how to implement the truth into one's life will appeal to more hearts than a negative one which is critical of past errors, only. People are prone to respond better to affirmative exhortations than to threats and warnings. However, threats and warnings are productive if issued from a preacher who is concerned for his hearers. This means force and emphasis must be an integral part of a sermon conclusion's content, energetically delivered with urgency. Force, emphasis, energy, and urgency are not negative characteristics but are positive characteristics of preaching. These can be viewed favorably and received by one's hearers. But the hearers must feel that what is said in the conclusion of the message can and will make a very real difference to them personally.[36]

The hearers must be convinced that the preacher truly desires for them to respond to God's Word. Therefore, the conclusion of the sermon will be composed of either, inferences[37] or direct appeals. The inferences ought to embody the force of an appeal, and the appeal ought to carry all the weight of inferences. The conclusion should be the *magnum opus* of the sermon. The great work that is the sermon conclusion is not that it is the most extensive part of the sermon but that it is the portion of the sermon that provides the greatest take-away for the hearers. In the conclusion the mind, conscience, emotions/affections, and will of the hearers should be pressed with an earnestness that cannot be denied. If understanding has been gained in the body of the sermon, the conscience, emotions/affections, and the will, especially, must be gained in the conclusion. The final minutes of the conclusion must make a good return on the investment of every minute of the sermon that has preceded them.[38]

A wise and capable preacher will not only expound God's truth, but he will conclude his sermon with application to the needs of the hearers since true theology and true Christian living must not be separated from each other.[39] The commonly recognized inclusions of a sermon conclusion such as exhortation, entreaty, appeal, encouragement, consolation, and warning have been viewed as "therapy."[40] A therapeutic conclusion contains any of the above components and it most often contains several, or more, of them. Even as a sermon conclusion takes the form of warning, it promises at the same time; it sets a warning over against a promise. Every

35. Ellicott, *Homiletical and Pastoral Lectures*, 1880, 81.

36. Brown Jr., Clinard, Northcutt, *Steps to the Sermon*, 123.

37. "Inferences," as a type of application in preaching, was a common term to refer to a certain type of appeal found in a sermon conclusion. Specifically, an inference may be better understood by what is now referred to as an "implication." Whereas a direct appeal is hortatory, in the form of an "you ought" or "you ought not," "you must" or "you must not," an inference is more didactic as they provide a further unfolding of the practical aspects of a truth as it relates to one's living.

38. Blaikie, *For the Work of the Ministry*, 1873, 125.

39. Hall, *God's Word Through Preaching*, 1875, 28–29.

40. Davis, *Design for Preaching*, 194.

inclusion of a sermon conclusion whether appeal, exhortation, entreaty, encouragement, warning, or promise is profitable for, and can be legitimately directed to, those who are followers of Christ.[41]

Since every Christian has need of the profitable effects of all of Scripture—instruction, reproof, correction, and training in righteousness—every sermon must be viewed in the prospect of an effective means of invaluable aid for God's people. A positive tone in preaching is indicative that the profitable effects of Scripture are not being forgotten about in the process of concluding a sermon.

Positive Tone as Conviction

There are charges that should never be brought against a preacher. Being uninteresting, devoid of life and energy when preaching eternal truth is such a charge.[42] When Henry Ward Beecher was asked how he felt when he saw someone asleep in his congregation, did he not feel like sending someone to wake him up? Beecher replied, "No, I think someone should be sent to wake *me* up."[43]

A lack of earnestness in preaching stems from a lack of conviction one holds about scriptural truth as one tries to preach it. Conviction is "an intrepidity born of deep-seated persuasion that the truth for which one speaks brooks no compromise and that it must be stated."[44] When preaching is accompanied by a lack of earnestness the effort and intent may be directed toward preaching but the result must be other than preaching the Word, namely, misrepresenting the Word. Not misinterpreting the Word but misrepresenting the Word. The interpretation is correct. What gets said should be said because what is said is true, true according to the text that is being preached.

The misrepresentation comes from the fact that what is said, though true according to the text, is not true according to the heart of the one preaching it because there is little conviction in his heart. He has little conviction about what he has rightly interpreted. His hermeneutics are solid gold, but his heart is ice cold! The good thing is that there was no twisting of the Scriptures. He "cut it straight." But the bad thing is that what was cut straight never cut his own heart, therefore, the exhibiting of conviction in proportion to the truth, as demanded by the truth, was absent. *Correct interpretation minus conviction does not equal preaching*! There is a too common fault in preaching that must be remedied—the fault of preaching in a cold indifferent tone which "creates a wall of crystal between the preacher and his hearers; some light passes through it but hardly any heat."[45]

41. Davis, *Design for Preaching*, 194–5.

42. Burgess, *The Art of Preaching*, 1881, 208.

43. Breed, *Preparing to Preach*, 1911, 353.

44. McLaughlin, *Communication for the Church*, 71–72.

45. Ellicott, *Homiletical and Pastoral Lectures,* 1880, 82.

Preaching is done by a man who holds convictions about the truth he proclaims as well as being held by the convictions he has about God's truth. John MacArthur is helpful to establish this as he identifies what is the preacher's source and task in preaching. Both, the source and task of preaching are significant factors in preaching with conviction. Referring to the source of preaching MacArthur writes, "Preaching may be popular, but it is not necessarily *powerful*. No one can preach with power who does not preach *the Word*."[46] Of even greater insight is MacArthur's reproof, "No human message comes with a stamp of divine authority—only the Word of God. How dare any preacher substitute another message?"[47] So, how can it be that a preacher could take up the Word of God and preach God's eternal, authoritative Word, but do so without conviction? The answer is that the truth the preacher proclaimed never captivated the preacher.

Regarding the task of preaching MacArthur writes, "As ambassadors for God, our task is not to promote our own ideas but rather to represent our King rightly. That means that all we should be doing is bringing the revealed truth of God to bear on the minds of men."[48] Furthermore, MacArthur insists that, "The preacher's task is not to be a conduit for human wisdom; he is God's voice to speak to the congregation."[49] As I believe MacArthur's comments are incontrovertible, I want to stress that they are no less true for the sermon conclusion. In the sermon conclusion, the preacher must still speak for God. The only way this can happen is if he is still citing and establishing the truths of Scripture. Therefore, the preacher must draw from what God has stored up in the whole counsel of his Word as he preaches the closing appeals of his sermon conclusion for God's people. In other words, the closing appeals of the sermon conclusion should be drawn from other passages in God's Word that relate to the subject-matter, purpose of the sermon, and preaching passage. Greater development will be given to the wider use of Scripture for the closing appeals of a sermon conclusion in chapter seven.

The correct task and source for preaching are integral for preaching with conviction. Those who approach preaching with a good understanding of the correct source and task in preaching can preach with conviction. Not only should such conviction be apparent in the sermon conclusion, but it should be prominent.

Even when the preacher is gripped by conviction about the truth he proclaims, and he feels awed by the sense of God's presence, and he is conscious of his responsibilities before God and man, and he esteems rightly the souls committed to his care,

46. Dever et al., *Preaching the Cross*, from John MacArthur's chapter "Why I Still Preach the Bible after Forty Years of Ministry," 145.

47. Dever et al., *Preaching the Cross*, from MacArthur's chapter "Why I Still Preach the Bible after Forty Years of Ministry," 143.

48. Dever et al., *Preaching the Cross*, from MacArthur's chapter "Why I Still Preach the Bible after Forty Years of Ministry," 150.

49. Dever et al., *Preaching the Cross*, from MacArthur's chapter "Why I Still Preach the Bible after Forty Years of Ministry," 143.

he may yet discover that the apparent result[50] of his pulpit effort was to make no deep impression upon those to whom he preached. This, at times, is an inevitable situation for anyone who preaches. We have certain responsibilities regarding our preaching, many of them, but the result of our preaching is a responsibility we do not have to bear. The affect and effects of preaching lie in the prerogative of God not man. "The secret to powerful preaching lies with God, not man. Skill alone does not make a preacher; God makes the preacher."[51] God alone gets the credit for the results from the preaching of the preachers he makes. A preacher can never be responsible for any measure of success God may allow in his preaching.

But every preacher is responsible for this, that the truth he presents be not dry, but accompanied with some energy, the energy of the Spirit. According to William Arthur, a preacher "is bound to stir up the gift of God within him, to keep his lamp trimmed, and his light burning, and evermore to be replenishing it with holy oil."[52] The source of power in preaching is the Spirit of God in the preacher. This power is not something that can be faked by the preacher or ignored by the hearers.[53] Without a demonstration of the Spirit's power in one's preaching little will be achieved in the lives of his hearers.[54]

A preacher is responsible to meditate upon the portion of God's Word that constitutes the preaching portion of the sermon and to internalize the insights he has discovered and will preach to others. Furthermore, the substance of his message has been applied already in his life, so that he is living what he seeks to see accomplished in the lives of those to whom he preaches. The first and, perhaps, greatest work God does through his Word is in the heart and life of the one who preaches it. This should be the case every time one preaches God's Word.

Conviction is Supplied by the Holy Spirit Alone

Conviction in the heart of the preacher is the starting point. As good as it is to have a preacher with convictions about the truth he proclaims, that is not good enough. Those to whom he preaches are to be impacted by the preacher's conviction so that it may become infectious. This is what is needed but this is beyond the preacher's control. He is responsible to have convictions about God's truth, but he is incapable to convict the hearts of his hearers.

The preaching of the biblical prophet Jonah to the Ninevites exemplifies a preacher's inability to bring conviction to his hearers. Even if he were able to do so,

---

50. Of course, apparent results are just that, results as they appear to be. The actual results of any preached sermon cannot be known, except to God alone.

51. Montoya, *Preaching with Passion*, 21.

52. Arthur, *The Tongue of Fire*, 1859, 274.

53. Arthur, *The Tongue of Fire*, 1859, 274.

54. Piper, *The Supremacy of God in Preaching*, 39.

Jonah would not have brought conviction to these hearers. Jonah relished the destruction of the Ninevites, not their repentant response to his preaching. For the Ninevites to fall under conviction, to repent in sackcloth and ashes, was Jonah's great dread. The fact that the Ninevites responded so resolutely to his preaching cannot be credited to Jonah. Jonah's conviction was in God's lovingkindness and in God's working through his Word. In the prospect of preaching to the Ninevites, these convictions posed a certain threat to Jonah as evidenced by his testimony that to forestall the sparing of the Ninevites he fled to Tarshish knowing that, "You are a compassionate God, slow to anger and abundant in lovingkindness, and One who relents concerning calamity" (Jonah 4:2). Despite his correct theology, the positive tone of conviction was not apparent in Jonah's preaching because his heart was not right. But, when a preacher's heart is as true as his convictions, upon completing his responsibilities, he can trust God to work as only He can work in the lives of his hearers. This should be a delight and a source of great encouragement to every preacher.

Through the perfect precision of the Holy Spirit, preaching is used as a scalpel to do surgery on the hearts of hearers of the Word. Under his sovereign direction, "it locates, lances, and removes the infection of sin."[55] He alone can do what no preacher can do, or ever has done—bring conviction to the heart of a man. In God's incredible grace, he has designed to use preachers of the Word as instruments in the work he accomplishes in the lives of men for time and for eternity.

D. L. Moody emphasized the importance of a preacher's use by God to influence his hearers when he said, "The best way to revive the church is to build a fire in the pulpit."[56] Fire in the pulpit, if the phrase is to be understood in a meaningful way, can only be attributed to a Spirt-filled man of conviction preaching in the power provided by the Holy Spirit of God. Conviction in the heart of a man, the work that God alone does, very often occurs in the context of a Spirit-filled preacher. William Arthur provided three compelling assertions about the preaching of the Apostle Peter on the day of Pentecost which exemplifies that power in preaching can be supplied solely by the Holy Spirit. First, though his natural powers of intellect and speech were unchanged, a powerful command of speech was given to him in preaching God's Word, the effects of which were undeniably apparent.[57] Second, in this sermon Peter simply quoted passages from the Word of God and applied them to his hearers. Yet, the whole multitude was smitten with the conviction of their sins and exclaimed, "Men and brethren, what must we do?"[58] Third, "I will be with thy mouth" was fulfilled here more clearly in the preaching of a common fisherman than in any other instance in which the power of God was displayed through the proclamation of Scripture.[59]

55. Piper, *The Supremacy of God in Preaching,* 95.

56. As cited in Lawson, *Famine in the Land,* 65.

57. Arthur, *The Tongue of Fire,* 1859, 89.

58. Arthur, *The Tongue of Fire,* 1859, 91–92.

59. Arthur, *The Tongue of Fire,* 1859, 93.

The positive tone of conviction is an undeniable quality of the preaching done by the true pastor in the sermon conclusion. This is the place in the sermon where his hearers will be challenged to respond to God's Word, to implement its truth, and to conform to its requirements in their lives.

Just as it is desired by the true pastor for unbelievers, under conviction from the Holy Spirit of God to respond to the gospel message, he also desires believers to respond to the sermon preached for their edification. They too must submit to the Spirit's work of correction that starts with the work of conviction. Changed lives result from changed thinking and changed hearts. Changed thinking and changed hearts, that is, conviction brought about through the Spirit, is the starting point of the Spirit's work in the lives of believers and unbelievers.

In the preaching of John the Baptist and Jesus Christ, the first recorded word from their mouths was the word "Repent," a message directed to the mind, heart, and the will of the hearers.[60] The Apostles Peter and Paul called for repentance, not to feel remorse in the conviction of their sins before a Holy God, but to repent, to change one's thinking and their response to the preached Word of God.[61] The concurrent works of changed thinking and changed hearts, which produce a changed will, are accomplished by the Holy Spirit of God in unbelievers as regeneration, and in the lives of believers as illumination. As the Holy Spirit illuminates a believer's mind, he changes the understanding, heart, and will of the believer. And so, as the Holy Spirit changes the life of a believer, he does so because of a changed understanding of God's Word.

In the sermon conclusion, like no other place in the sermon, the positive tone of conviction is a palpable reality in the preaching of a true pastor. A preacher who is a true pastor will burn and shine in the conclusion of his sermons. As John Piper eloquently stated, "There must be heat in the heart and light in the mind—and no more heat than justified by the light."[62] But, the sermon conclusion of a true pastor will evidence substantial heat, all of it justified by the truth of Scripture and empowered by the Spirit of God.

---

60. In Acts 2:37 records, "Now when they heard this, they were pierced to the heart." The piercing was concurrent with the hearing. Acts 2:41 records, "So then, those who had received his word were baptized." That their volition, or will, was impacted is noted by the facts of receiving his word and, therefore, being baptized.

61. Orr, *The Faith that Persuades*, 91.

62. Piper, *The Supremacy of God in Preaching*, 84.

2

General Matters about the Sermon Conclusion and Preachers: Part 2

"Sin in the lives of believers must be corrected, and this by loving confrontation. As deplorable as sin is in a Christian's life, the correction of such is of utmost value. The closing appeals found within a sermon conclusion should provide a correcting influence for the hearers since one preaches to help God's people to become more faithful followers of Christ."

"Everyone to whom one will preach has need of correction. The only believers who have no need of biblical correction are found in Heaven, not in assembled congregations on Earth. The needed correction to be provided must demonstrate from Scripture how to combat common disorders and leading abuses observable in the lives of God's people."

"To provide correction means that we 'pierce to the heart of things,' that we get to the facts which lie behind appearances, that we get to the root problems which are responsible for observable erroneous attitudes, motives, and behaviors. Therefore, to provide the needed correction in the sermon conclusion, preachers must scour the Word of God to discover the biblical insights which correct the errors of their hearers that will aid in achieving the purpose of the sermon in the hearers' lives."

"Preachers must offer biblical corrections as solutions to the problems hearers have so that they may be persuaded that the corrections are of tremendous benefit. The nature of correction in a preaching ministry is that it not only remedies biblical ignorance and/or disobedience, but it also remediates a lack of spiritual earnestness."

"While probing the errors of his hearers, the true pastor will not fail to indicate how

the errors may be remedied. For correction to be a true remedy, the closing appeals ought to be pointed out by the preacher with such exact precision that the hearers may know clearly what they must do. A true pastor provides the ways and means by which hearers' lives may be corrected. Because of the watchful care of a true pastor, his hearers are furnished with the practical means by which their lives, more than ever before, can be fit for The Master's use. This is the goal of the ministry of correction."

"Not only is it true that a true pastor can provide noncensorious correction but a true pastor, because he is such, can bring correction to God's people that will benefit them because it is intentional, instructional, irresistible, impartial, and invaluable."

"A true pastor, because he is precisely that, is about as apt to withhold a needed word as much as he is willing to provide a malicious, misdirected indictment upon God's people. Neither should be forthcoming, and a true pastor will not be guilty of either of them."

"The mealy-mouthed man poaching on the pulpit, whose real agenda is to maintain favorable approval ratings from his hearers will seldom provide the needed ministry of correction. It will not happen often, if at all. He's just not up for it. He's not in the ministry to do that. This would adversely affect his reputation on behalf of some who hear him preach."

"Without tenderness, the courage would harden into harshness. Without courage, the tenderness would soften into sentimentality. In the combination of the two there is the highest excellence of both, producing the positive tone of correction. Some preachers are all courage, while many are all tenderness. Few preachers combine both in the same sermon, yet this combination is what is most needed in preaching."

"As in no other place in the sermon, the conclusion is where the ministry of correction is most vital for life-change. If the hearers go away admiring the sermon, the preacher has failed; if they go away remembering the sermon because it contained insights to live new lives, he has succeeded immensely. In the final analysis, life-change is the bullseye of the sermon conclusion. A sermon conclusion that results in life-change does so by means of correction. A change in life is preceded by correction."

"A truly pleasing message is one that does true spiritual good to the hearer. That which is entertaining does not result, necessarily, in spiritual good. Spiritual good is not produced by entertainment but by the Word of God. It is one thing for a hearer to be pleased by a man preaching his entertaining sermon. It is altogether different for a hearer to be pleased because God worked through his Word in the life of that hearer who was pleased not because of entertainment but because of the personal benefits brought by God through his preached Word."

"How can a preacher have a preaching ministry in which comfort is a consistent commodity? It must come out of his own life of sympathy, compassion, love, and respect for people. In a word, he must be the recipient of such things from the Lord and being cognizant of them in his week of study, he can freely demonstrate to others that which he has so freely received. This is what makes a preacher sensitive, thoughtful, appreciative, and helpful, so that comfort will be given in his sermon conclusions."

"Believers are not to be left to their disobedience. Disobedience forfeits their comfort in Christ and brings upon them conviction for their sin. Comforting words cannot remedy disobedience. Repentance and obedience remedies disobedience. The only words of comfort for a disobedient believer are a corrective word of how to get right and stay right in their Christian walk."

"Most probably, we have witnessed earnest men whose tone defeated their purpose. This never failed to catch our attention, but for all the wrong reasons. Such a spectacle always has been, and always will be, grievous to behold. The reason for this defeating tone is that the preacher is more delighted to declare the sinfulness of sin rather than the remediation of sin in the lives of believers. The solution to a denunciatory tone is a pure motive and sincere forthrightness which bring biblical solutions to the issues of life. This allows a preacher to preach more effectively because he has discovered helpful insights from God's Word, from which he can speak with love and respect to those whom he seeks to reconcile to God, and to the ways of God."

"To be persuasive preachers, we must be imbued with sympathy and truth. . . . Truth and sympathy are the soul of a persuasive ministry. . . . There must be truth, or sympathy is empty emotion, and there must be sympathy, or truth is cold and heartless."

THE POSITIVE TONE OF A TRUE PASTOR (CONTINUED)

Positive Tone as Correction

The ministry of correction in preaching provides an undeniable sense of gravity to the sermon. John Piper describes the gravity of preaching as an "intensity of feeling, a weightiness of argument, a deep and pervading solemnity of mind, a sense of the power of godliness, a fervency of spirit, a zeal for God."[1] The gravity of preaching not only has impressive characteristics that mark it, but it has significant results as well. Perhaps, the most significant result from the gravity of preaching is the correction brought to those who hear God's Word preached to them.

Believers don't always aspire to receive what is most needed in their lives. This is especially true regarding correction. How many believers attend a preaching service

---

1. Piper, *The Supremacy of God in Preaching*, 50.

hoping to receive some stout correction to their lives? Yet, correction is one of the profitable ministries of the Word of God in the lives of believers so that they "may be adequate, equipped for every good work" (2 Timothy 3:17b).

As the Apostle Paul instructed Timothy, he commanded him to reprove, rebuke, exhort, with great patience and instruction (2 Timothy 4:2b). Paul, not being a man-pleaser, never practiced nor advocated a form of ministry designed to give people what they want, a methodology of ministry that is so prevalent today. As John MacArthur commented, "He did not urge Timothy to conduct a survey to find out what his people wanted. He commanded him to preach the Word—faithfully, reprovingly, and patiently."[2] A true pastor not only practices Paul's instruction to Timothy, but he will demonstrate it in the positive tone of correction that will be part of his typical sermon conclusion. As correction is needed by his hearers, a faithful preacher as a true pastor will supply what is needed in the way it will be beneficial for those who hear it—the positive tone of correction. Steven J. Lawson writes:

> Pastors who are committed to biblical exposition must have a confrontive element in their preaching if they are to emulate the prophets and the apostles. Regrettably, this kind of reproof and rebuke is often missing from present-day preaching. Adrian Rogers mandated boldness in preaching as he insisted that, "It is better to be divided by truth than to be united in error. It is better to speak the truth that hurts them and heals, than falsehood that comforts and then kills. It is not love and it is not friendship if we fail to declare the whole counsel of God. It is better to be hated for telling the truth than to be loved for telling a lie. . . . It is better to stand alone with the truth than to be wrong with a multitude."[3]

Sin in the lives of believers must be corrected, and this by loving confrontation. As deplorable as sin is in a Christian's life, the correction of such is of utmost value. The closing appeals found within a sermon conclusion should provide a correcting influence for the hearers since one preaches to help God's people to become more faithful followers of Christ.[4]

The Need for Pastoral Correction

The true pastor in his preaching ministry fleshes out the truth that ministers exist for churches, not churches for ministers.[5] Everyone to whom one will preach has need of correction. The only believers who have no need of biblical correction are found in Heaven, not in assembled congregations on Earth. The needed correction to be

2. Dever et al., *Preaching the Cross*, from John MacArthur's chapter "Why I Still Preach the Bible after Forty Years of Ministry," 141.

3. Lawson, *Famine in the Land*, 68.

4. Potter, *Sacred Eloquence*, 1868, 255.

5. Dale, *Nine Lectures on Preaching*, 1890, 222.

provided must demonstrate from Scripture how to combat common disorders and leading abuses observable in the lives of God's people specifically, and in our culture generally.[6]

To provide correction means that we "pierce to the heart of things," that we get to the facts which lie behind appearances, that we get to the root problems which are responsible for observable erroneous attitudes, motives, and behaviors.[7] Therefore, to provide the needed correction in the sermon conclusion, preachers must scour the Word of God to discover the biblical insights which correct the errors of their hearers that will aid in achieving the purpose of the sermon in the hearers' lives.

The natural law of homeostasis reveals the fact that organisms stay in balance until acted upon by an outside force. If an outside force causes the status quo to be disrupted, people become out of balance. People rarely act or change until they are out of balance and, therefore, are compelled to do so. Once out of balance, people are open to take proper steps to correct or restore balance. It is our responsibility to correct by providing specific insights from the Word of God that expose error and reveal solutions to these errors.

The Need for Appropriate Pastoral Correction

Preachers must offer biblical corrections as solutions to the problems hearers have so that they may be persuaded that the corrections are of tremendous benefit. The nature of correction in a preaching ministry is that it not only remedies biblical ignorance and/or disobedience, but it also remediates a lack of spiritual earnestness.[8] Thomas Potter offers the needed guidelines of a true pastor's ministry of correction. His four guidelines are as follows: one, indication of error; two, explanation of the remediation offered; three, clarification of what is required for remediation; four, illustration of how remediation is to be implemented.[9]

As with a loving parent toward a child, a faithful pastor will provide correction for common errors once reproof and rebuke have been rendered. A rebuke is a censure, in that, it surfaces blameworthy conduct or behavior and addresses such accurately. A biblically sanctioned rebuke serves as a helpful precursor for the ministry of correction. However, a rebuke is never a use of unnecessary criticism to blame or condemn one's actions or conduct, nor is it a condemnation accompanied by unwarranted anger. Though a biblically sanctioned rebuke is often like a dose of "bitter medicine," the true pastor will temper its bitterness by the considerate tone and language in which he will dispense it.[10]

6. Potter, *Sacred Eloquence*, 1868, 255.

7. Dale, *Nine Lectures on Preaching*, 1890, 297.

8. Dale, *Nine Lectures on Preaching*, 1890, 246.

9. Potter, *Sacred Eloquence*, 1868, 256–58.

10. Potter, *Sacred Eloquence*, 1868, 259.

While probing the errors of his hearers, the true pastor will not fail to indicate how the errors may be remedied.[11] For correction to be a true remedy, the closing appeals ought to be pointed out by the preacher with such exact precision that the hearers may know clearly what they must do.[12] A true pastor provides the ways and means by which hearers' lives may be corrected. Because of the watchful care of a true pastor, his hearers are furnished with the practical means by which their lives, more than ever before, can be fit for The Master's use.[13] This is the goal of the ministry of correction.

Perhaps, the discussion above is being short-circuited by the memory of Christ's eight-fold "woes" directed toward the scribes and Pharisees found in Matthew 23:13–36. However, Christ was not saying anything out of line regarding the scribes and the Pharisees. They were guilty of every condemnation he uttered and there was no unwarranted anger in his expression of their guilt. Though Jesus was The Good Shepherd, he was not the shepherd of the scribes and Pharisees and these men were not his sheep. They were his enemies. As his enemies, Christ spoke to them the truth regarding the egregious hypocrisy of their lives and the damning influence they had upon the lives of many. The ministry of correction was not a possibility for them. In fact, Christ spoke to them the most serviceable thing they could hear, which was a warning to them about their lostness, their separation from God. His question to them in Matthew 23:36 was, "You serpents, you brood of vipers, how will you escape the sentence of hell?" This warning, by way of indictment, was an accurate depiction of the present state and future reality for these men. The hypocrisy and the influence of these men were harsh realities. Only harsh terminology was fitting to address the present and future realities of these men. The appropriately harsh terminology of Christ toward the scribes and Pharisees was censure since a present-day judgment was being passed upon them for their sins, a judgment that foreshadowed what was in store for them when they appear before him in final judgment.

Correction from a True Pastor Is Not Censure

Since Christ's censure of the scribes and Pharisees is completely different from the ministry of correction conducted by a true pastor on behalf of Christ's sheep, let's clarify five concepts about the ministry of correction that, when accomplished by a true pastor, will be effective because they are not offered as, nor will they be perceived as, censure. These concepts are intentional, instructional, irresistible, impartial, and invaluable correction.

One, Intentional correction—The motive is crucial. The motive in correction is to intervene between non-compliance to the truth. The motive in correction is not to complain about the hearer's lack of compliance. The intention is not to speak against

11. Potter, *Sacred Eloquence,* 1868, 259.

12. Potter, *Sacred Eloquence,* 1868, 259.

13. Potter, *Sacred Eloquence,* 1868, 260.

people for being imperfect. Not much is done for people by scolding them, nor telling them "over and over again that they ought to be better." Men are not annoyed into goodness.[14] The intention is towards correcting what is wrong, not just blaming them for the wrong.

Two, Instructional correction—In speaking truthfully about how the hearers may be conducting themselves contrary to the instruction of Scripture, it must be remembered that "mere lamentations will work no deliverance for them."[15] A preacher must consider by what truths, by what method, and by what means God's people may be afforded instruction from God's Word that will help them live lives of obedience. Correction in the form of insightful instruction from Scripture is what is beneficial for them.[16]

Three, Irresistible correction—Phillips Brooks, in the quote that follows offers great counsel. However, this counsel will be implemented only by a true pastor because it requires a selflessness and seeking the best for others—traits that a true pastor possesses. "Never tolerate any idea of the dignity of a sermon which will keep you from saying anything in it which you ought to say, or which your people ought to hear. It is the same folly as making your chair so fine that you dare not sit down in it."[17] Correction that is needed is correction that must be given. Correction that must be given is irresistible, it cannot be kept back from those who need it. Hopefully, the correction that is irresistible on the preacher's behalf will be received irresistibly by the hearers.

Four, Impartial correction—While one must be fearless in the denunciation of sins, care must be taken to not describe an individual sinner as to enable hearers to identify him. People do not mind being preached *to*, but they do not want to be preached *at*, and they loathe to be publicly indicted in preaching. The necessity is to be so insightful about the correction needed that each hearer can make application to himself of the truth which is being preached.[18] The correction to be made public is that which is applicable to and profitable for many, not personal indictments made publicly.[19]

Five, Invaluable correction—Invaluable correction is initiated by one who is faithful to the Lord and to his people by instructing them how to live pleasingly to him. But, even more so, invaluable correction is provided by one who is faithful to God's people by instructing them how to prepare for eternity.[20]

Not only is it true that a true pastor can provide noncensorious correction but a true pastor, because he is such, can bring correction to God's people that will benefit them because it is intentional, instructional, irresistible, impartial, and invaluable.

14. Dale, *Nine Lectures on Preaching*, 1890, 241.
15. Dale, *Nine Lectures on Preaching*, 1890, 242.
16. Dale, *Nine Lectures on Preaching*, 1890, 243.
17. Brooks, *On Preaching*, 150–51.
18. Taylor, *The Ministry of the Word*, 1876, 140.
19. Of course, an instance of church discipline is not in view here.
20. Dale, *Nine Lectures on Preaching*, 1890, 302.

Sycophants Cannot Correct

A true pastor, because he is precisely that, is about as apt to withhold a needed word as much as he is willing to provide a malicious, misdirected indictment upon God's people. Neither should be forthcoming, and a true pastor will not be guilty of either of them. In William M. Taylor's excellent work, *The Ministry of the Word*, the Lyman Beecher Lectures on Preaching delivered in 1876, the renown pulpiteer uttered two statements that every man who enters a pulpit should take the greatest of care to never violate. He said: "We must be careful not to keep back any part of the truth from fear of offending any prominent individual, or provoking 'Demetrius and the craftsmen.' We must preach the truth that God bids us, diminishing not a word, and if men will take offense, we must see to it, that the cause of their indignation shall be in the truth itself and not in our manner of proclaiming it."[21] Again, Taylor provides much needed instruction in his day, and ours, as he exclaimed:

> The timid (man) who is always trying to keep from offense becomes at length an object of contempt; while he who faithfully reproves, rebukes, and exhorts with all long-suffering and doctrine, becomes a power in the community and draws to himself the confidence and affection of his people. The sycophant is despised even by those on whom he fawns, but he who speaks to men in the assurance that God is with him, will secure both their attention and respect, even when he is telling them unpalatable truths.
>
> . . . [It is] our duty to keep back from our hearers nothing that will be profitable unto them; to seek their good, rather than their good opinion; and to set clearly before them the solemn responsibilities of life. This is demanded of us alike by loyalty to God, a regard for the welfare of those who wait upon our ministry, and a consideration of the account which we ourselves must give.[22]

The mealy-mouthed man poaching on the pulpit, whose real agenda is to maintain favorable approval ratings from his hearers will seldom provide the needed ministry of correction. It will not happen often, if at all. He's just not up for it. He's not in the ministry to do that. This would adversely affect his reputation on behalf of some who hear him preach. Why should he do that which would not win for him the approval of man? How about, of course, the ultimate priority of seeking the approval of God? The true pastor, however, because he does seek God's approval and his hearer's benefit, will provide correction but will do so in a positive tone. He will do so because he means to help them.

21. Taylor, *The Ministry of the Word*, 1876, 140–41.
22. Taylor, *The Ministry of the Word*, 1876, 141–42.

Courage and Tenderness Needed for Correction

The positive tone of correction requires the combination of tenderness and courage. It may seem that tenderness is incompatible with courage, but tenderness is the complement of courage in the positive tone of correction. Profitable correction cannot exist without the confluence of both. Just as the Ohio River cannot exist without the confluence of the Allegheny and the Monongahela Rivers, so it is with correction. Without tenderness, the courage would harden into harshness. Without courage, the tenderness would soften into sentimentality. In the combination of the two there is the highest excellence of both, producing the positive tone of correction. Some preachers are all courage, while many are all tenderness. Few preachers combine both in the same sermon, yet this combination is what is most needed in preaching.[23]

The need of correction in preaching is clearly established in Scripture. The Apostle Paul instructed Titus with the following words:

> For the grace of God has appeared, bringing salvation to all men, disciplining us to deny ungodliness and worldly desires and to live sensibly, righteously and godly in the present age, looking for the blessed hope, the appearing of the glory of our great God and Savior Christ Jesus, who gave Himself for us, that He might redeem us from every lawless deed and purify for Himself a people for His own possession, zealous for good deeds (Titus 2:11–14).

This glimpse of God's will for those whom he has saved screams for the need of the ministry of correction. Without this needed ministry, God's design for the salvation of his people is not receiving vigorous aid from the primary means through which it is to be fulfilled—through preaching, specifically through the profitable ministry of correction. God's purpose of salvation is not just to change the eternal destiny of those he saves, but to keep continually changing the temporal lives of those he has saved. The presently continuing, ongoing component of our sanctification is related to the ministry of correction in the lives of Christians—a ministry of a faithful preacher who is a true pastor.

The value of the sermon conclusion, uniquely, lies in its power to impact the lives of the hearers. As in no other place in the sermon, the conclusion is where the ministry of correction is most vital for life-change. If the hearers depart reflecting upon the craftsmanship of the sermon, the preacher has failed; if they go away remembering the sermon because it contained insights to live new lives, he has succeeded immensely.[24] In the final analysis, life-change is the bullseye of the sermon conclusion. A sermon conclusion that results in life-change does so by means of correction. A change in life is preceded by correction.

In a serious concern for, and a conscientious thought process about, preaching, two inevitable, yet oppositely directed questions will arise: How shall preaching be made

23. Taylor, *The Ministry of the Word*, 1876, 145.
24. Abbott, *The Christian Ministry*, 1905, 114.

attractive? and, How shall preaching be made effective? Paul is most helpful in formulating the one and only answer to these questions as he writes to the Corinthian Church, "And when I came to you, brethren, I did not come with superiority of speech or of wisdom, proclaiming to you the testimony of God. . . . And my message and my preaching were not in persuasive words of wisdom, but in demonstration of the Spirit and of power, that your faith should not rest on the wisdom of men, but on the power of God" (1 Corinthians 2:1, 4–5). A. T. Pierson touches on a vital point when he warns, generally, that: "in seeking attractiveness we may sacrifice effectiveness, mixing with God's medicine, to make it more palatable, what destroys its corrective and curative properties." More specifically, Pierson asserted that, the fatal fruit of the forbidden tree of preaching is for preachers to veil the message of Scripture behind "the golden and silver tissues of ornate speech, corrupting the wisdom of God with the wisdom of man."[25]

A common error is for preachers to make the act of preaching an event that is entertaining and pleasing to men. However, a truly pleasing message is one that does true spiritual good to the hearer. That which is entertaining does not result, necessarily, in spiritual good. Spiritual good is not produced by entertainment but by the Word of God. It is one thing for a hearer to be pleased by a man preaching his entertaining sermon. It is altogether different for a hearer to be pleased because God worked through his Word in the life of that hearer who was pleased not because of entertainment but because of the personal benefits brought by God through his preached Word.

The power of God unleashed through his Word is to be evident without any effort of man to tame or weaken its effect. Effective preaching is the unrestrained power of God demonstrated in preaching his Word. The unrestrained power of effective preaching is in every facet of its working, including its corrective ministry in the lives of believers. A true pastor in his sermon conclusion allows God to work freely as he seeks to provide the positive tone of correction in his closing appeals to believers. As he does, he will be in accordance with two points of William M. Taylor's advice: first, "Never forget that they are always needing help; and remember always, that you are the servant of him of whom it was said, 'A bruised reed shall he not break, and the smoking flax shall he not quench;'"[26] second, "If you mean to do good to a man, the very worst course you can take is to begin by insulting him."[27] The faithful preacher as a true pastor supplies the much-needed help of correction, but never in a way that needlessly disparages his hearers since he seeks to benefit them, not to speak poorly about them.

Positive Tone as Comfort and Consolation

In the view of some, the pulpit is a place of frequent failure regarding the ministry of comfort. One of the obvious components of apostolic preaching is the frequency of

---

25. Pierson, *The Divine Art of Preaching*, 1892, 107.
26. Taylor, *The Ministry of the Word*, 1876, 148.
27. Taylor, *The Ministry of the Word*, 1876, 140.

words of encouragement. And, as it was for them, so it is with us. Those to whom we preach populate a struggling and suffering humanity. Tempted, sorrowing men and women are our hearers. "Never is a sermon preached, except it is preached to some hearers who are carrying a load of personal grief."[28] To such people we preach. There is a great need for God's people to be comforted. We must preach to comfort them, and the sermon conclusion is the portion of the sermon where we must not fail them in this needed ministry. A sincere, compassionate tone of tenderness is needed in the sermon conclusion if one is to discharge this part of a preacher's ministry.

How can a preacher have a preaching ministry in which comfort is a consistent commodity? It must come out of his own life of sympathy, compassion, love, and respect for people. In a word, he must be the recipient of such things from the Lord and being cognizant of them in his week of study, he can freely demonstrate to others that which he has so freely received. This is what makes a preacher sensitive, thoughtful, appreciative, and helpful, so that comfort will be given in his sermon conclusions.[29] As John Piper phrased it, gladness and gravity should be woven together in a preacher's life and preaching as to "sober the careless soul and sweeten the burdens of the saints."[30] A sweetened burden is an excellent way to capture the concept of comfort.

Comfort is based upon two ever-available resources to every believer: a relationship with God in one's life; and a working with God in one's life. Regarding their relationship with God, believers are comforted as they are reminded that: they have an eternal standing with God as those whom he has justified; they are those whom he has chosen to be his own before the foundation of the world; they are those whom have received forgiveness of their trespasses according to the riches of his grace which he has lavished upon them; they are those whom are to the praise of his glory, etc.[31] Regarding their working with God, believers are comforted as they are reminded that: they are chosen in him to be holy and blameless before him; they are to be like the Holy One who called them in all their behavior, because it is written, "You shall be Holy, for I Am Holy"; they are his workmanship, created in Christ Jesus for good works, which he prepared beforehand, that we should walk in them; they are those for whom he gave Himself, that he might redeem them from every lawless deed and purify for Himself a people for his own possession, zealous for good deeds; they are to work out their salvation with fear and trembling, etc.[32]

As our being cannot be separated from our doing, and as our justification cannot be separated from our sanctification, so our comfort is only enhanced by being instructed about how our relationship to Christ is to be lived out in this world according

28. Hoyt, *Vital Elements of Preaching*, 1929, 117.

29. Hoyt, *Vital Elements of Preaching*, 1929, 132.

30. Piper, *The Supremacy of God in Preaching*, 52.

31. Rom. 5:1, Eph. 1:4, Eph. 1:7, Eph. 1:12, among other passages that support these truths.

32. Eph. 1:4, I Pet. 1:15–16, Eph. 2:10, Tit. 2:14, Phil. 2:12, among other passages that support these truths.

to his Word. Instruction regarding what it means to walk worthy of our calling, and how we are to walk in obedience to his Word, is not a burden-producing thing. Believers are not to be left to their disobedience. Disobedience forfeits their comfort in Christ and brings upon them conviction for their sin. Comforting words cannot remedy disobedience. Repentance and obedience remedies disobedience. The only words of comfort for a disobedient believer are a corrective word of how to get right and stay right in their Christian walk.

Positive Tone as Commencement

Phillip Doddridge's advice regarding sermon conclusions was, "be sure to close handsomely."[33] To close handsomely, for Doddridge, meant to conclude a sermon that brings consolation to the hearers so that they may begin living in a new way. In the sermon conclusion the hearers should be encouraged to commence living commensurate to the purpose of the text that has been preached to them by means of the insights of related passages of Scripture. The key concept is the newness of life that can now be theirs if they walk according to the truth. Just as in a graduation ceremony, more properly referred to as a commencement ceremony, where the graduates are challenged to leave their institutions of study and chart a different and productive course in life, so it is in a sermon conclusion. The hearers of the sermon need to be addressed regarding the difference, a positive difference, the sermon should have in their lives.

Positive Tone in Purposeful Preaching

It has been said that preaching must be done in fear and trembling before God, "less the tone defeats the purpose."[34] Most probably, we have witnessed earnest men whose tone defeated their purpose. This never failed to catch our attention, but for all the wrong reasons. Such a spectacle always has been, and always will be, grievous to behold. The reason for this defeating tone is that the preacher is more delighted to declare the sinfulness of sin rather than the remediation of sin in the lives of believers. The solution to a denunciatory tone is a pure motive and sincere forthrightness which bring biblical solutions to the issues of life. This allows a preacher to preach more effectively because he has discovered helpful insights from God's Word, from which he can speak with love and respect to those whom he seeks to reconcile to God, and to the ways of God. Such motives make it clear to the hearers that the preacher's desire is to patiently persuade them to respond to Scripture with motives, attitudes, and actions that are obedient to the faith.[35]

33. Doddridge, *Lectures on Preaching*, 1807, 66.
34. Luccock, *In the Minister's Workshop*, 240.
35. Luccock, *In the Minister's Workshop*, 240.

Beyond the necessity to move the feelings of the hearers, it is necessary to consider what ought to be the tone of preaching to persuade men to embrace the truth of God in their lives.[36] It is the prerogative of the preacher not only to challenge the hearers to obey God and to move their feelings so that they desire to obey God, but he must consider carefully how he speaks to his hearers in the process.

To be persuasive preachers, we must be imbued with sympathy and truth. It was said of the Lord's preaching that the common people heard him gladly. Christ's preaching touched hearts, that is, the hearts of people who primarily populated the lower classes of society. In his voice was a tone which was absent from the religious leaders of his day who had no compassion, no love, no concern, no sympathy for others. How very tragic since sympathy colors and tones everything. Truth and sympathy are the soul of a persuasive ministry. According to C. J. Ellicott, there must be truth, or sympathy is empty emotion, and there must be sympathy, or truth is cold and heartless.[37] Neither empty emotion nor cold, heartless truth can provide the positive tone of purposeful preaching. The positive tone of purposeful preaching is not optional in the sermon conclusion.

Positive Tone of Hope

In a preaching ministry of the sermon conclusion, hope cannot be absent if the conclusion has been thought out carefully and prepared properly. To come to the end of a biblical message that does not contain hope is a certain indication of not understanding the preaching passage according to its antithetical prospect (an appropriate declaration that what is in error can and must be remedied) and/or its wider biblical context (an appropriate demonstration from Scripture how what is in error can and must be remedied).

One non-rival to true hope must be considered, namely, fear. Fear legitimately has a place in preaching. Just as there is a legitimate understanding of the fearful reality of eternal Hell for those who are without Christ, there should be a legitimate fear in the hearts of believers who walk in disobedience to God's Word. Such fear would be well-founded in view of: the Heavenly Father's discipline on his children for unrepentant sin; the consequences that will be reaped because of sin in a believer's life; and the loss of opportunities to serve God in faithful obedience forfeited by one's disobedience. Fear is a respectable and profitable reality in the lives of men before a Holy God. Fear is a beneficial aid to a believer to cease and desist from wrong-doing and as a preventative from initiating an act of wrong-doing.

Hope is beneficial to motivate believers to start or keep doing that which is right. Fear and hope are comparable in that both are advantageous. In a contrastive way fear and hope have been distinguished along the following lines: fear is an urgent and

36. Moore, *Thoughts on Preaching*, 1861, 71.

37. Ellicott, *Homiletical and Pastoral Lectures*, 1880, 76.

immediate stimulant to action, but hope is a more noble and enduring stimulant for sustained living, as arguments and appeals addressed in hope find a more permanent lodging in the heart.[38] With no motive or attempt to nullify the rightful role of fear, there must be an acknowledgment of the higher function of hope in the sermon conclusion.

As to hope in preaching, preachers need to commit to end on a hopeful note. Even the most darkly convicting messages exist in the context of the good news of the gospel. Therefore, there can and should be a light at the end of the tunnel. According to Bryan Chapell, "The preacher who leaves a congregation depressed, despairing, and pessimistic about their sin and situation has failed to preach."[39] In like manner David L. Larsen writes, "I do not think we can leave a congregation of hurting souls in the swamp. . . . We cannot leave our people without a word of hope. This may be the last message someone hears. If the text ends in the slough we have every right to view it in its larger context and speak to the ravenous hunger of our people for some affirmation of hope and good news."[40] It is the failure of a sermon conclusion, and the one preaching it, that he would leave God's people in the "slough of despond" without causing them to contemplate the broader message of God's Word. If a preacher has been faithful to the preaching passage that rightly may have brought concern to the hearts of the hearers, should he be any less faithful to show them in the sermon conclusion how they can respond so that they may not fall victim to that which distresses them?

No one should walk away from hearing a sermon preached to its conclusion filled with despair, unless the hearer responds to the sermon with a hardened heart, or an unrepentant heart set on continuing in a path of sin, continuing to live a life of disobedience. Such a hearer is welcome to the hopelessness resulting from a hardhearted response committed to disobeying God's Word! He has rejected the counsel offered to him in the sermon conclusion! The despair of such a hearer is due, not to a preacher who offered no hope, but to himself since he was not interested in the hope that was clearly provided to him!

The purpose of the sermon will not be achieved in the life of every hearer. It is the hearer's responsibility to respond to what is offered in the sermon conclusion. It is, however, the preacher's responsibility to make sure there is needed instruction in the sermon conclusion to which a hearer can respond, and thus fulfill the purpose of the sermon in an optimal manner.

Conclusions should challenge and inspire the heart. It is pointedly asserted that, "No man has a right so to preach as to send his hearers away on flat tires. Every discouraging sermon is a wicked sermon. . . . A discouraged man is not an asset but a liability."[41] Such a liability is averted by the preaching of a true pastor who provides the

---

38. Moore, *Thoughts on Preaching*, 1861, 73.

39. Chapell, *Christ-centered Preaching*, 249.

40. Larsen, *The Anatomy of Preaching*, 129.

41. Demaray, *An Introduction to Homiletics*, 100.

positive tone of hope through the insights of Scripture which bring needed solutions to the failures found in the lives of God's people.

Positive Tone in Christ's Preaching

If a preacher's heart is right, his desire "is not to drive, but to draw; not to irritate, but to soften."[42] With persuasion understood as the ultimate outcome of our preaching, we must be prayerful about the tone in which we speak a word of rebuke. Rebuke is one of the profitable designs of Scripture which is needed in the lives of God's people. Yet, we must not be guilty of being motivated by our fallen nature to administer censure, which it loves to do and does it so unbecomingly. Scripture makes it clear that "the anger of man does not achieve the righteousness of God" (James 1:20).

Earlier in this chapter, we covered the ground that correction is not censure and that a true pastor seeks only to benefit, not berate, God's people because his heart is right. However, there are some who have a fatal facility with censorious words, the prevalence of such is simply a manifestation of one's inner life, an inner life that is bereft of "the seed whose fruit is righteousness which is sown in peace by those who make peace" (James 3:18). To be persuasive, even as we, at times, must be involved in the denunciation of evil, requires that we are filled with "the wisdom from above, which is first pure, then peaceable, gentle, reasonable, full of mercy and good fruits, unwavering, without hypocrisy" (James 3:17). If reproofs and rebukes are based upon the Word of God and controlled by the Spirit of Christ, our tone will be without a needlessly offensive edge as the method, manor, and motive for preaching is conducive for preaching effectively.[43] People want to be treated with sincerity, impartiality, respect, and love. When so treated, they will seldom object to reproof, rebuke, and correction.[44]

Even in the case of making severe warnings or admonitions, no one should be able to miss the preacher's obvious compassion and sympathy. As we find in Matthew 11:20–30, our Lord began to reproach the cities in which most of his miracles were done, because they did not repent. Though we see that he was "uttering woes that were like flashes of divine wrath"[45] toward the people of Chorazin, Bethsaida, and Capernaum, still he provided one of the most compelling invitations found in Scripture. With words of incredible kindness and gentleness, he said: "Come to Me all who are weary and heavy-laden, and I will give you rest. Take My yoke upon you and learn from Me; for I am gentle and humble in heart: and you shall find rest for your souls. For my yoke is easy, and my load is light" (Matthew 11:28–30). Such compassionate sympathy in the face of such brazen hostility and rejection! How scandalous it is for

42. Moore, *Thoughts on Preaching*, 1861, 77.

43. Moore, *Thoughts on Preaching*, 1861, 80.

44. McLaughlin, *Communication for the Church*, 74.

45. Burrell, *The Sermon: Its Construction and Delivery*, 1913, 191.

any preacher, having become the beneficiary of such kindness, not to offer the same to those who have no less need than he once did. In our preaching we must follow the perfect model of Jesus Christ—"who loved while He chided; who pitied, while He blamed; and who, when remonstrance could do no more, continued to plead and pray, 'Father forgive them, for they know not what they do.'"[46]

Positive Tone as Tenderness, not Levity

The positive tone so crucial for preaching is independent of humor or levity. It must be recognized that natural humor and the levity that it provides, at times, is unavoidable. It just happens and does so naturally, inevitably. In the proclamation of sobering, eternal truths there will be instances where correct, accurate, and helpful expression will be found humorous. Instances of levity brought about by natural humor is not sinful. Natural humor does not require repentance nor is it an abdication of the preaching ministry. Instances of natural humor are neither a problem nor a compulsory matter for a positive tone which is so necessary in preaching.

A positive tone in preaching is not dependent upon making the proclamation of eternal truth an entertainment entity, an attempt to turn preaching into a branch of the entertainment arena. I appreciate the view of the Puritan preacher Richard Baxter when he wrote, "Of all the forms of preaching that I most dislike, I hate that which tickles the audience with many jokes and entertains them with superficial amusement. It is as if they were in a theatrical performance, instead of being awed by the holy reverence of God's character."[47] In agreement with Baxter, such attempts to make preaching entertainment is antithetical to preaching and, therefore, can have nothing to do with the positive tone needed in preaching. Even the very acceptable instances of natural humor and levity do not provide a positive tone.

Levity and triviality are so common in the pulpit one might think it is part of the biblical qualifications of an elder! Many preachers seemingly are aspiring to be entertainers of men rather than being Bible expositors. Pastor Alistair Begg refuted this ailment pointedly when he wrote, "Pulpits are for preachers. We build stages for performers."[48] John Piper lamented that, "Laughter seems to have replaced repentance as the goal of many preachers. . . . Even preachers who bemoan the absence of revival in our day seem locked into a cavalier demeanor in front of a group of people."[49]

The positive tone of tenderness is a result of the painful experience/condition of brokenness in the life of a preacher. Good preaching comes from a broken and tender spirit. Despite his authority and power, Jesus was compelling because he was "gentle and lowly in heart." When Jesus saw the multitudes, he was moved with compassion

46. Moore, *Thoughts on Preaching*, 1861, 81.
47. Baxter, *The Reformed Pastor*, 1665, 20.
48. Begg, *Preaching for God's Glory*, 14.
49. Piper, *The Supremacy of God in Preaching*, 55–57.

on them, because they were scattered abroad like sheep having no shepherd (Matthew 9:36). A Spirit-filled preacher has a tender affection that sweetens every promise and softens every warning and rebuke. Paul could write to the church in Thessalonica that he and his companions "proved to be gentle among you, as a nursing mother cherishes her own children. Having so fond affection for you, we were well pleased to impart to you not only the gospel of God but also our own lives, because you had become very dear to us" (1 Thessalonians 2:7–8).[50]

The authority with which Jesus spoke, distinguishing himself so greatly from the scribes and Pharisees, was not due to a spirit of levity and triviality. Christ sought to lighten the load of people and he did so, but it had nothing to do with laughing with him, but it had everything to do with learning from him. The true pastor, by means of the sermon conclusion, will provide for God's people scriptural substance that will be essential to their spiritual well-being and he will declare it in a manner that will assist them in their compliance to the truth.

Again, as I believe it bears repeating, *"Regardless of the content and tone of the text and the sermon preached from it, in the conclusion of the sermon the content and tone should be positive as correction and remediation become hard targets of the true pastor. In the body of the sermon the true pastor, as a faithful shepherd, feeds God's sheep. In the conclusion of the sermon the true pastor, as a faithful shepherd, tends God's sheep. He desires to tend them. He seeks to correct what is weak, inadequate, and erroneous in their lives. He desires to establish a pathway in the training of their righteousness. He seeks to bind up their wounds. He desires to nurture them. He seeks their healing. God's people need this ministry, a ministry that is in his heart to provide, and the Word of God contains the substance to make this ministry a personal provision."* The application of this paragraph alone, if applied in one's preaching, would go far to correct what is weak and lacking in sermon conclusions.

---

50. Piper, *The Supremacy of God in Preaching*, 100.

3

General Matters about the Sermon Conclusion and Preaching: Part 1

"The preacher's responsibility for the reception of the Word by the hearers is based upon his responsibility to be filled with joy and filled with the Spirit for the appropriate manner of proclamation. This double filling is the appropriate manner of biblical proclamation."

"One of the most crucial considerations about the preacher's manner is the earnestness of his preaching. An earnest preacher may or may not be a passionate preacher, but a passionate preacher is an earnest preacher! One cannot be passionate without being earnest because earnestness is the foundation for passionate preaching, and it is the bedrock of all preaching."

"The earnest preacher has a controlled passion. The passionate preacher has a controlling earnestness. The earnest preacher and the passionate preacher both have a rightful place in the pulpit, while a man without earnestness has no place in the pulpit! Earnestness is essential. Passion is "essential-plus." A preacher may or may not be passionate, but he must be earnest in his preaching!"

"The church has always had preachers of great earnestness. In fact, the early church was blessed to have preachers of integrity, men who turned the world upside down! Unfortunately, today the church is cursed with some preachers, who are not clothed in the garment of earnestness, men whom the world has turned upside down and left in an indecent state for the pulpit! The result of this tragedy is that the church is the weaker for it, in that, it is not the recipient of a vital preaching ministry which only earnest preachers provide. The reproachable indecency of a lacking earnestness is never more obvious than in the conclusion of a sermon—the place where a preacher should be trying valiantly to achieve his purpose for preaching the sermon."

"Add to this the convictions of a preacher who believes that the conclusion is what the sermon is made for and that the conclusion is where he achieves or fails to achieve his purpose for preaching the sermon. When this is the case, you will find a preacher who preaches with greater earnestness in this part of the sermon than any other part of the sermon that preceded it. However, the understanding that the conclusion is what the sermon is made for and that the conclusion is where he achieves or fails to achieve his purpose for preaching the sermon must be convictions the preacher holds and convictions that holds the preacher. If so, he will be found in his sermon conclusion trying to accomplish something! If not, his sermon conclusion will find him trying to accomplish nothing other than ending the sermon."

"Nothing can serve as a legitimate reason for a preacher being other than an earnest preacher, from his sermon introduction to his sermon conclusion. There are reasons for being other than an earnest preacher, but there is no legitimacy in any of them. An equal, if not greater condemnation is reserved for sermon conclusions when they are other than what they should be—the highpoint of the sermon."

"A lack of earnestness in preaching? That's a huge problem! Preachers who prepare and preach sermon introductions and sermon bodies containing sufficient earnestness with sermon conclusions that are woefully lacking in earnestness? That's a tragedy!"

"A preacher who lacks earnestness will be powerless before his hearers and will not be heard attentively, but one who possesses earnestness is listened to with interest, as soon as he begins to preach. His soul is kindled by the significance of his subject. As he continues to preach his sermon, his strength is felt and acknowledged. However, under no circumstances should it be the case that the increasing strength of his earnestness is exhausted before he gets to the conclusion of his sermon. On the contrary, the sermon conclusion should be the culmination of the earnest preacher's strength."

"Nothing short of piety in the preacher, pure Christian character, will make him earnest. Earnestness ought certainly to exist in full strength in anyone who preaches God's Word. As there is a want of earnestness, there must be some inexcusable fault in the state of a preacher's heart. Whatever checks piety in the heart will check earnestness in the pulpit. A man must have purity in his Christian character and daily walk to be an earnest preacher. If this is not the case, that man needs to abandon the pulpit ministry and substantially grow in Christ and develop Christian maturity authenticated by a life of unassailable purity, then, and only then, should he enter the pulpit again. As earnestness can be checked by any and every form of iniquity, earnestness may be strengthened by the means that are fit for ministry."

"There are truly earnest preachers who are personally passionate preachers, that is, they are passionate within their personality and temperament. However, these men

are not comparatively passionate, that is, they do not compare with preachers of personality and temperament who are given to a greater emotional display and/ or physical gesturing in their delivery. Every preacher can be personally passionate in his preaching, that is, passionate according to the natural limitations imposed by his own personality and temperament. One preacher's passion may be another preacher's earnestness, and one preacher's earnestness may be another preacher's passion. This is just the natural and acceptable order of things."

"There is in all enthusiasm an excitement that is unmistakable. A preacher may display enthusiasm and emotion, or enthusiasm and feeling, or enthusiasm and reason. But, in almost every sphere of influence, enthusiasm stands before everything else in moving people. The preacher who is enthusiastic in what he does, and what he believes, and in all the components of his preaching, will generally attract people and carry them with him. If one has the ability to preach and skill to present truth, and is enthusiastic in the proclamation of it, most people will become enthusiastic about the truth proclaimed."

EARNEST PREACHING

A Lack of Earnestness is Ruinous to Preaching

Many things can provide a negative influence on a preached sermon or preaching in general. However, a lack of earnestness is ruinous to preaching! That means, first, if the man in the pulpit is not earnest, he is no preacher! How can a preacher be a man who is not earnest for the things of God, and specifically, how can a preacher be a man who is not earnest in the proclamation of his truth? That means, second, that the man in the pulpit is very much responsible for how the sermon is received by his hearers! This statement does not deny the vital reality that God alone opens the heart of a hearer to receive his Word. It is God who brings to fruition his Word in the lives of men.

The above statements are intended as a reminder that the preacher bears responsibility for how he proclaims God's Word but not for the effective reception of it. However, the manner in which God's Word is proclaimed is a matter that must not be overlooked. In Acts 13:52–14:1, Luke records the preaching of Paul and Barnabas along with other disciples with these words: "And the disciples were continually filled with joy and with the Holy Spirit. In Iconium they entered the synagogue of the Jews together, and *spoke in such a manner* that a large number of people believed, both of Jews and of Greeks." How incredible it is that Luke draws attention to the way they spoke rather than the content of their speaking. *The preacher's responsibility for the reception of the Word by the hearers is based upon his responsibility to be filled with joy and filled with the Spirit for the appropriate manner of proclamation. This double filling is the appropriate manner of biblical proclamation.*

One of the most crucial considerations about the preacher's manner is the earnestness of his preaching. An earnest preacher *may or may not be* a passionate preacher, but a passionate preacher *is* an earnest preacher! One cannot be passionate without being earnest because earnestness is the foundation for passionate preaching, and it is the bedrock of all preaching.

Earnest Preaching Compared to Passionate Preaching

Passionate preaching is earnestness combined with strong emotion. As earnestness is being *strong and firm in purpose, eager and serious*, being passionate is all the preceding plus *having or showing strong emotion*. Passionate preaching has been referred to as a higher earnestness. In a manner of speaking, passionate preaching was thought to be "earnestness-plus" preaching. Notice the clear distinction between earnest preaching and passionate preaching in the following statement: "The *higher kinds of earnestness*, exhibiting themselves in *pathetic tones of voice*, and in a *warm and impulsive eloquence*, cannot be commanded at will."[1] This author had reference to passionate preaching as the higher kinds of earnestness conveyed through elevated means.

Perhaps some well-known preachers representing earnest preaching compared with passionate preaching might clarify the distinction between the two. John MacArthur, Erwin Lutzer, David Jeremiah, D. Martyn Lloyd-Jones, Warren Wiersbe, and Robert Jeffress are/were earnest preachers. Chuck Swindoll, Tony Evans, Alex Montoya, John Piper, Stephen Lawson, Adrian Rogers, and Stephen Olford are/were passionate preachers.

To ascribe earnestness to the former six preachers, but not describing them as passionate, is not a knock against these men any more than ascribing passion to the latter seven preachers is an exaltation of them. There is great admiration for all of them, in that, every one of them is suffused with an unquestionable earnestness in preaching! The preaching of the last seven is marked with an emotional display that is palpable and penetrating which significantly affects how they are heard. To lack a profuse exhibition of emotion in preaching is perfectly acceptable. A less than profuse exhibition of emotion is a fact of one preacher's emotions working through his personality just as a passionate preacher's profuse exhibition of emotions is another preacher's emotions working through his personality. There is no need for an altered personality or a different emotional display for any of the thirteen preachers. The latter seven do not need to become less passionate and the former six do not need to become more passionate. Earnestness is the essential matter! The latter seven are not more earnest than the former six, just as the former six are not less earnest than the latter seven. All are extremely earnest in their preaching though there are differing emotional displays which are discernable.

1. Burgess, *The Art of Preaching*, 1881, italics added, 210.

Earnestness Based on the Preacher's Character and Convictions

Earnestness is based upon the convictions and character of the preacher. Passion is based upon the conviction and character of the preacher accompanied with a higher level of emotion displayed through the preacher's personality. Great emotional display in preaching can be dispensed with, though this would be regrettable. Yet, great earnestness cannot be dispensed with in preaching. The earnest preacher has a *controlled passion*. The passionate preacher has a *controlling earnestness*. The earnest preacher and the passionate preacher both have a rightful place in the pulpit, while a man without earnestness has no place in the pulpit! Earnestness is essential. Passion is "essential-plus." A preacher may or may not be passionate, but he must be earnest in his preaching!

The attempt to distinguish the earnest preacher and the passionate preacher is predicated upon the fact that the terms basically are used interchangeably in homiletical literature. I cannot control how the terms are used nor with what meaning they are given as they are used by others. I only can uphold my distinctions between the concepts as I employ them, yet I will not bring my distinctions to the terms as they are used by others so that I might deal fairly with their writings.

Not a few sermons, composed of good and profitable content, are orphaned by a mode of delivery devoid of earnestness. "Almost every other defect can be easily pardoned, provided that the sermon is so delivered as to leave this impression upon the hearer's mind—'That man says what he means, and means what he says!'"[2] Convictions that hold a man making him truly earnest is what is profitable, even indispensable, in preaching.

It was earnestness in the preaching of George Whitefield that made him such a noteworthy preacher. In Edinburgh, Scotland people would get out of their beds at 5 o'clock in the morning to hear Whitefield preach. A man on his way to the place where Whitefield was to preach met David Hume, the Scottish philosopher and skeptic. Surprised at seeing him on the way to hear Whitefield, the man said, "I thought you did not believe in the gospel?" Hume replied, "I don't, but he does!"[3] What a stellar report of earnestness in preaching. Whitefield was earnest, and people heard him gladly.

The Indecency of a Lack of Earnestness

The church has always had preachers of great earnestness. In fact, the early church was blessed to have preachers of integrity, men who turned the world upside down![4] Unfortunately, today the church is cursed with some preachers, *who are not clothed in the garment of earnestness*, men whom *the world has turned upside down* and left in an indecent state for the pulpit! The result of this tragedy is that the church is the weaker

2. Ellicott, *Homiletical and Pastoral Lectures*, 1880, 130.

3. Macartney, *Preaching without Notes*, 183.

4. Acts 17:1–7. This expression denotes the results of the preaching ministry of Paul and Silas.

for it, in that, it is not the recipient of a vital preaching ministry which only earnest preachers provide.

The reproachable indecency of a lacking earnestness is never more obvious than in the conclusion of a sermon—the place where a preacher should be trying valiantly to achieve his purpose for preaching the sermon. Convictions must be adhered to in preaching. This is true regarding the content of preaching as well as for the process of preaching. Alex Montoya is absolutely correct when he wrote: "Passionate preaching . . . comes from a man who holds the truth he proclaims with deep personal convictions. . . . Men hold opinions, but convictions hold the man. . . . Yet conviction about the truths we preach is what is sadly lacking in our pulpits today. We have too many wishy-washy, half-in, half-out, boneless, spineless preachers in our pulpits today, and a wishy-washy pulpit produces wishy-washy people."[5] Montoya, speaking about the content and the process of preaching with passion, cited a problem that is not only detrimental to preaching, in general, but to preaching effective sermon conclusions, specifically.

When held captive by his convictions about the truth he proclaims, preachers will preach with great earnestness. Add to this the convictions of a preacher who believes that the conclusion is what the sermon is made for and that the conclusion is where he achieves or fails to achieve his purpose for preaching the sermon. When this is the case, you will find a preacher who preaches with greater earnestness in this part of the sermon than any other part of the sermon that preceded it. However, the understanding that the conclusion is what the sermon is made for and that the conclusion is where he achieves or fails to achieve his purpose for preaching the sermon must be convictions the preacher holds and convictions that hold the preacher. If so, he will be found in his sermon conclusion trying to accomplish something! If not, his sermon conclusion will find him trying to accomplish nothing other than ending the sermon.

A Lack of Earnestness as Sin

One author cited four obstacles in delivering a sermon—stupidity, laziness, fear, and sin.[6] The one who is faithful to remove these obstacles from his preaching and his preparation for preaching can become the preacher he was called to be—a man who is serious about speaking for God and, therefore, a man through whom God speaks.[7] If it is true that the obstacles in delivering a sermon are limited to only these four, then a lack of earnestness would have to be related to sin more than anything else. To lack earnestness in preaching God's Word should never happen, generally, and more so in the sermon conclusion, specifically.

Nothing can serve as a legitimate reason for a preacher being other than an earnest preacher, from his sermon introduction to his sermon conclusion. There are

5. Montoya, *Preaching with Passion*, 41.

6. Pearson, *The Preacher*, 197–214.

7. Pearson, *The Preacher*, 214.

reasons for being other than an earnest preacher, but there is no legitimacy in any of them. An equal, if not greater condemnation is reserved for sermon conclusions when they are other than what they should be—the highpoint of the sermon.

I can think of only two good reasons for preachers doing other than their best preaching, their very best preaching, in the conclusions of their sermons. The first reason is the obvious, yet occasional, instance of a horrifying week where the opportunity to do the kind of work to construct an excellent conclusion just was not possible. Every preacher has experienced such weeks. It is not an excuse but rather a sad fact of any preaching ministry. The second reason is the perpetual, yet significant, instance when a preacher is inordinately gifted in his ability to teach, being able to draw out incredible insights, connections, and understanding from Scripture so that no matter how he may conclude his sermon his conclusion cannot compare with the opulent spiritual giftedness demonstrated in the body of the sermon in the exposition of the biblical text. Is this a free pass to the very best Bible expositors, that they are exempt from working hard to produce excellent conclusions? Absolutely not. It is just an honest admission that the best work of an incredibly gifted pastor-teacher will not be found in his sermon conclusions, no matter how intent he is and no matter how much diligence he provides to the work of crafting excellent conclusions. The most arduous attempt to produce effective conclusions cannot rival the effectiveness of opulent spiritual giftedness produced by the Holy Spirit of God.[8]

Additional reasons for not doing one's best work in the sermon conclusion are more than a few, but none of them have merit. A lack of earnestness in preaching? That's a huge problem! Preachers who prepare and preach sermon introductions and sermon bodies containing sufficient earnestness with sermon conclusions that are woefully lacking in earnestness? That's a tragedy!

You may hear a man in the pulpit who possesses a blameless walk with God, a good education, and high intelligence, but he cannot preach well. Why? Despite his erudition, his preaching is dry and lifeless, "because he himself has no vital warmth." He brings to his preaching a heart that never felt one throb of God-borne emotion and lips that have not been "touched with a coal from the altar of God."[9] His preaching is marked by a lack of earnestness, the same lack of earnestness that was indicative of his study of God's Word. The time and effort that was put forth in the study never yielded a work in the preacher's heart, which is a prerequisite for earnest preaching. However,

---

8. John MacArthur is a fitting example of such a preacher. In the thousands of sermons I have heard him preach over a forty-plus year time span, I have never heard him conclude in such a manner that could rival his skillful exposition of biblical texts. Though earnest in the sermon conclusion, when he has one, there is a discernable difference in the degree of excellence exhibited in his exposition of Scripture versus his sermon conclusion. This is not to say that his conclusions are poor or preached poorly because that is not the case. But the best conclusions I have heard from him are dwarfed by his incredible skill and giftedness in explaining God's Word.

9. Porter and Matthews, *Lectures on Eloquence and Style*, 1836, 16.

true earnestness remedies the pulpit of scholastic sophistry and every other vice that is detrimental to preaching.

True earnestness, enriched with scriptural knowledge and warmed with genuine emotion, projects deep interest about a biblical text that must be impressed upon others.[10] A preacher who lacks earnestness will be powerless before his hearers and will not be heard attentively, but one who possesses earnestness is listened to with interest, as soon as he begins to preach. His soul is kindled by the significance of his subject. As he continues to preach his sermon, his strength is felt and acknowledged.[11] However, under no circumstances should it be the case that the increasing strength of his earnestness is exhausted before he gets to the conclusion of his sermon. On the contrary, the sermon conclusion should be the culmination of the earnest preacher's strength.

Earnestness is Impossible without True Piety

A preacher who preaches effectively must be earnest. But, nothing short of piety in the preacher, pure Christian character, will make him earnest. Earnestness ought certainly to exist in full strength in anyone who preaches God's Word. As there is a want of earnestness, there must be some inexcusable fault in the state of a preacher's heart. Whatever checks piety in the heart will check earnestness in the pulpit.[12] A man must have purity in his Christian character and daily walk to be an earnest preacher. If this is not the case, that man needs to abandon the pulpit ministry and substantially grow in Christ and develop Christian maturity authenticated by a life of unassailable purity, then, and only then, should he enter the pulpit again.

As earnestness can be checked by any and every form of iniquity, earnestness may be strengthened by the means that are fit for ministry. Few, if any, would contend with the assertion that every preacher must dismiss the possibility of preaching a sermon "with true, natural, and effective warmth, which he has prepared with leisurely coldness."[13] The relationship between diligent study and earnest preaching does not require much enforcement. This is well understood. But what is not understood *in actual practice* is the vital necessity that prayer has for earnestness in preaching.

Prayer

Prayer, particularly, is essential for earnest preaching. The preaching of an earnest preacher is not limited to dependence upon God to bless his efforts of diligent preparation as he pursues a life of holy living before God and men. In holy living, diligent preparation, and dependence upon God, he must not be remiss to avail himself to the power

---

10. Porter and Matthews, *Lectures on Eloquence and Style*, 1836, 17.

11. Porter and Matthews, *Lectures on Eloquence and Style*, 1836, 17.

12. Porter and Matthews, *Lectures on Eloquence and Style*, 1836, 21.

13. Alexander, *Thoughts on Preaching*, 1864, 32.

and blessing that comes as God's response to fervent prayer. In preparing to preach, we have not prepared diligently until we have prayed fervently about every element of the sermon to be preached! Earnest preaching cannot forgo the blessing and power that is made available only through prayer. The indivisible necessities of preaching and praying must be maintained as indivisible necessities in one's preaching ministry.

Without diminishing time or effort to study in preparing to preach, preachers must abound also in prayer, not quenching one ray of intellect but adding to it the warmth of devotion and the power of God. Preachers must labor as if the salvation of souls depended upon their own unaided energies. Yet, the temporal fitness and the eternal destinies of our hearers hang not only upon our preaching but upon our praying. As preachers, we carry out the purposes of our mission, not only in the pulpit and the study but in the closet. True success in ministry is found only by those who avail themselves to this two-fold dependency in first imploring God to pour out his Spirit upon those to whom we preach, and then beseeching hearers to be resolved in responding to the Word of God. Then, and only then, will it be true that we are honoring his wisdom in the use of the means he has appointed, as well as honoring his power by "confessing our dependence upon his grace" and might.[14]

Earnestness, as "the echo of soul-deep thoughts; the glow of holy fervor,"[15] can warm the hearts of its hearers because it is penetrating and powerful. Such fruitful earnestness cannot be possessed without fervent prayer. An earnest preacher is born out of the labor pains of a praying heart, a heart that is not only dependent but desperate to receive that which only God can provide—*the effect of his working through the preached Word in the lives of his people.*

Spiritual power is conceived in the realization of one's utter unworthiness to preach and one's total dependence on God for everything because the preacher understands that he is unable to produce any spiritual effect in the lives of God's people. Scripture is clear that God despises a proud heart and opposes the proud, but he has promised to honor those who honor him (1 Samuel 2:30).[16]

Powerful preaching is preaching that is honored by God. Powerful preaching is preaching that is accompanied by God's power to impact his Word preached by the preacher upon the hearers.[17] Powerful preaching is the preaching of an earnest preacher aided by God who empowers him. It is said that, "Deep earnestness is the untaught rhetoric of an impressed and loving heart; the fervor of the dying man speaking to dying men."[18] That is why the conclusion should be filled with life, earnestness, and should "inflame the hearts" of the hearers.[19] The fervent words of a dying man, like the

14. James, *An Earnest Ministry*, 1847, 294–95.

15. Moore, *Thoughts on Preaching*, 1861, 88.

16. Montoya, *Preaching with Passion*, 24.

17. Montoya, *Preaching with Passion*, 36.

18. Moore, *Thoughts on Preaching*, 1861, 253–54.

19. Claude, *Claude's Essay*, 1801, 132.

conclusion of an earnest preacher, will consist of content that is worthy of hearing and, perhaps, life-changing to those who hear them.

The very prospect of being used by God as a means by which he might be pleased to change the lives of others should give every preacher pause to see if he is one through whom God may do his work. However, if it is clear that far more might have been done in one's personal walk with God to be filled with the Spirit of Christ, then one must confess his guilt by reason of feeble and ineffectual prayer, and of duplicity in commitment in the keeping of one's own soul as God's ambassador. "The gifts of tongues or of miracles are not essential" to the ministry of preaching in our present-day context, but the unhindered cooperation and power of the Holy Spirit is absolutely necessary for the work of the ministry, especially the ministry of preaching.[20]

If one should receive, as he should, the counsel to be mindful of all of life to be certain we are not personally responsible for a diminished effect of our preaching, shouldn't we be equally concerned about every part of the sermon we preach? Is it beneath the concern of an earnest preacher to be concerned about the conclusion of a sermon he will preach? Is the conclusion of a sermon important enough for his prayerful consideration and heartfelt concern? How can a man be earnest in a work unless he feels its importance to himself and others? How can there be true awakening power where there is a manner of preaching that lacks earnestness? If a conclusion is not a matter of diligent labor in the study and fervent prayer in the closet it will not be a matter of significant effect in the pulpit!

Truth, in the absence of earnestness, will hardly be believed.[21] Furthermore, in the absence of earnestness, the hearers certainly may deny to the preacher the credit of believing his own message. Preachers may fail to see hearers moved by the truth they preach simply because they are destitute of the needed earnestness that unquestionably conveys to their hearers that they believe the truth they are proclaiming.

I believe it would be incredibly irresponsible to discuss the topic of earnest preaching without making the connection that prayer is essential for this kind of preaching to be a reality. In subsequent chapters, nine through twelve, we will consider application and the closing appeals of a sermon conclusion. I believe there is a vital connection that must be made between prayer and selecting from Scripture the biblical references that serve as the foundation for the Scripture-based closing appeals of a sermon conclusion. Specifically, prayer will be discussed as part of the personal price to be paid in preparing effective conclusions. This material closes out chapter nine.

Walking in Truth

There is only one way that truth, rightly interpreted from Scripture and prayed through the preacher's life, can be made more earnest in the soul of a preacher. He must live out

20. Arthur, *The Tongue of Fire*, 1859, 275–76.
21. Burgess, *The Art of Preaching*, 1881, 210.

the truth before he preaches it to others. Austin Phelps provides a compelling case for the preacher being the first and most needy recipient of the truth he is to preach. He writes: "Exhortation should find in the preacher's own soul its most docile hearer."[22] That means he must take to himself the admonitions which he will preach to others. In no other way can he be honest in their utterance. In no other way can preaching secure the advantage so obviously aimed at by God's arrangement in which human nature is made to appeal to human nature.

The principle of sympathy is as true and powerful as the principle of authority. But the wisdom of the system of human instrumentality becomes effective and apparent as the preacher sees himself as a fellow-follower of Christ and a fellow-sinner who needs, just like all others, "the appeals which he aims at other men."[23]

Some preachers have made it their habit never to preach a sermon to others until they have experienced the good of it for themselves. The ultimate earnestness in preaching is dependent upon a preacher's personal application of the truth. Truth must first lay hold of his own heart and mind and be matured in his own soul. Arthur Pierson conveys this in an interesting manner as he wrote, "There is needed a practical rumination, till that which you have cropped in the external pasturage becomes milk in the udder, full and warm. Then it is not grass but milk that you are giving to your hearers."[24]

The value of practicing the truth before preaching it to others is that it allows a preacher to feel what is spoken, which helps him to be a convincing preacher.[25] A text that has not been of personal benefit to us in some way will be communicated with a sense of curtailed excitement and significance. *A bored heart makes for boring preaching!*[26] Yet, an excited, persuaded heart makes for excited, persuasive preaching! Preaching, if it is to be earnest preaching, is not to be an act of proclaiming untried truth. God's truth does not need our seal of approval, it is approved by God. However, our preaching of God's Word is benefitted from our seal of approval on what we preach as those who have experienced what we offer to others. As a stream rises to no higher level than its source, so it is in preaching.

Preaching is speaking God's truth to the whole man, so that it impacts intellect, emotions, affections, conscience, and will. But a preacher can apply truth to others, in ultimate effect, only so far as it has first been applied to himself. God's Word must have as its proclaimer a man backed by a personal experience of living the truth he preaches, thus providing "testimony from the inward life of the preacher."[27]

Think for a moment of what we are doing as preachers if we fail to comply with the truths we are advocating others to comply with in their lives. Is not the reality of

22. Phelps, *The Theory of Preaching*, 1882, 568.
23. Phelps, *The Theory of Preaching*, 1882, 568.
24. Pierson, *The Divine Art of Preaching*, 1892, 29–30.
25. Mather, *Student and Preacher*, 1789, 192.
26. Montoya, *Preaching with Passion*, 50.
27. Pierson, *The Divine Art of Preaching*, 1892, 101.

this hypocrisy? Jesus labeled the scribes and Pharisees as "hypocrites," in part, because they failed to practice what they taught. Recall the opening words of Christ which preceded his eight-fold indictment of the scribes and Pharisees as "hypocrites." Jesus said, "The scribes and the Pharisees have seated themselves in the chair of Moses: therefore, all that they tell you, do and observe, but do not do according to their deeds; for *they say things and do not do them.* They tie up heavy burdens and lay them on men's shoulders, but they themselves are unwilling to move them with so much as a finger" (Matthew 23:3–4).

The lives of the scribes and the Pharisees were a condemning discredit to their teaching. How effective do we think we may be in commending truth to others which we are content to disobey? How earnest are we if we are found appealing to others to do what we are unwilling to do? Surely, we must agree that the condition of personal hypocrisy in directing people to obey what we are unwilling to obey cannot be the foundation for ultimate effectiveness in applying truth. Do we dare compel others to do that which we refuse to do?

An Aspiring Heart

A heart that aspires to do much for God is an earnest heart. An earnest heart makes an earnest preacher. A preacher's love for God's people, his passion to preach for their benefit, and the opportunity of preaching God's Word causes him, not only to be an earnest preacher but to be a persuasive preacher as well. Preaching persuasively can be described as an "affecting, penetrating, interesting manner" arising from strong convictions in the heart of the preacher about the value of the truth he proclaims, and an earnest desire that these truths should make an impact on the lives of his hearers.[28] Such earnestness of heart which desires, seeks, and expects much can be disappointed easily and become the grounds for a rather critical self-reflection. Spurgeon acknowledged this when he said, "My brethren, when you've been at your best, you might have been better. Who among us might not have had greater success if he had been ready to obtain it? . . . We are humbled by the reflection that more might have been done had we been fitter instruments for God to use."[29]

In his classic work, *The Reformed Pastor*, Richard Baxter expressed his scathing indictment of his pastoral and preaching ministry as he wrote:

> I know not what others think, but for my own part, I am ashamed of my stupidity, and wonder at myself that I deal not with my own and with others' souls as one that looks for the great day of the Lord, and that I can have room for almost any other thoughts or words, and that such astonishing matters do not wholly absorb my mind. I marvel how I can preach of them slightly

---

28. Ellicott, *Homiletical and Pastoral Lectures,* 1880, 88.

29. Spurgeon, *An All-round Ministry,* 1900, 164–65.

and coldly, and how I can let men alone in their sins, and that I do not go to them and beseech them, for the Lord's sake, to repent, however they take it, or whatever pains or trouble it should cost me. I seldom come out of the pulpit but my conscience smites me that I have been no more serious and fervent in such a cause. It accuses me . . . it asketh me, "How couldst thou speak of life and death with such a heart?"[30]

As was the case with Baxter, so it is with earnest preachers of any era. We may be convinced only of our desire to be earnest but not the fact of its reality in our preaching. This much can be known and taken to heart—the quality of earnestness in a sermon produces its effect allowing hearers to feel, to perceive, and to be moved. A man's desire to have been more earnest than he was in the pulpit is not a denial of his earnestness. Just because a preacher regrets that he was not more earnest than he was, that does not keep his hearers from being positively impacted by the earnestness he actually conveyed in his preaching.

An Earnest Preacher's Enthusiasm as Depth of Feeling and Genuine Emotion

Some preachers, from natural energy of personality and character, may be more prone to, and better qualified for, a passionate proclamation of Scripture than other preachers. Preachers who are passionate in their preaching are of "a more mercurial temperament than their phlegmatic brethren, who creep while they fly. . . . This is constitutional to a very considerable extent; but it is after all, more of a moral than a natural inability in many."[31] This insight makes a final installment to the previous discussion regarding the earnest preacher compared to the passionate preacher. There are earnest preachers who are *personally passionate preachers*, that is, they are passionate within their personality and temperament. However, these men are not comparatively passionate, that is, they do not compare with preachers of personality and temperament who are given to a greater emotional display and/or physical gesturing in their delivery. Every preacher can be personally passionate in his preaching, that is, passionate according to the natural limitations imposed by his own personality and temperament. One preacher's passion may be another preacher's earnestness, and one preacher's earnestness may be another preacher's passion. This is just the natural and acceptable order of things.

Genuine Emotion

The important role that emotion has in preaching is a well-established given, regardless of the extent of the emotion under consideration. The presence of the preacher's

30. As cited in Hoppin, *Homiletics*, 1883, 438.
31. James, *An Earnest Ministry*, 1847, 220–21.

emotion, not its extent, is crucial. The presence of the preacher's emotion, not its absence, is what matters. In the inaugural address of the Lyman Beecher Lectures on preaching, Henry Ward Beecher argued that a preacher without feeling is no better than a book. According to Beecher, one "might just as well put a book, printed in large type, on the desk were all could read it, and have a man turn the leaves as they are read, as to have a man stand up, and clearly and coldly recite the precise truth through which he has gone by a logical course of reasoning." The cold calculated reasoning must melt somewhere. Somewhere there must be that power by which the man preaching and those hearing are unified. For Beecher, that unifying power was "the power of emotion."[32] The emotion that is truly powerful is emotion that is truly genuine because it is emotion that is stirred by personal interaction with Scripture.

Enthusiasm

Genuine emotion is not emotionalism, or emotion alone. It is the emotions of the preacher vitalized by enthusiasm for the truth to be preached. Enthusiasm is not emotion. Emotion may or may not be accompanied by enthusiasm. There is in all enthusiasm an excitement that is unmistakable. A preacher may display enthusiasm and emotion, or enthusiasm and feeling, or enthusiasm and reason. But, in almost every sphere of influence, enthusiasm stands before everything else in moving people. The preacher who is enthusiastic in what he does, and what he believes, and in all the components of his preaching, will generally attract people and carry them with him.

If one has the ability to preach and skill to present truth, and is enthusiastic in the proclamation of it, most people will become enthusiastic about the truth proclaimed. Mere enthusiasm will do nothing, but enthusiasm in preaching is quite effective. Beecher was of the conviction that enthusiasm was an indispensable element in a man's work among men.[33] Of equal insight and significance was the understanding that all earnestness has a considerable amount of enthusiasm about it, and no man can kindle enthusiasm in the soul of another who has none of it himself.[34]

Depth of Feeling

What an earnest preacher can, and must, present before his hearers is a personal intensity which results from possessing the Word of God and being possessed by the Word of God and the God of the Word, which provide an observable intensity of conviction and emotion.[35] Therefore, the source of earnestness in preaching is an intense

32. Beecher, *Lectures on Preaching*, series 1, 1872, 118.

33. Beecher, *Lectures on Preaching*, series 1, 1872, 121–22.

34. James, *An Earnest Ministry*, 1847, 76.

35. Luccock, *In the Minister's Workshop*, 30.

feeling of the subject-matter of the sermon; having one's mind deeply impressed, and one's heart warmed, with the text to be preached.

For a preacher to possess an appropriate earnestness, it is necessary, that he possess a deep interest in the subject-matter of *every particular sermon*. This means, not a general interest in the great activity of preaching, but a deep interest in the subject-matter of every text he actually preaches.[36] The bearing that emotion has to earnestness in preaching is crucial and must not be misunderstood. The significance of emotion to earnest preaching is captured in the three-fold assessment that: "all men are earnest when they feel;" second, depth of feeling is "the charm of all preaching;" third, without depth of feeling preaching will have little prospect to affect the hearts of its hearers.[37]

Earnest preaching includes a manner and method of delivering a message accompanied by deep feelings and convictions regarding the truth and importance of the message. The Apostle Paul's earnestness was undeniably impassioned and impressive. In Paul's presence, Felix "became frightened," and Festus cried out, "Paul, you are out of your mind! Your great learning is driving you mad!" and Agrippa replied, "In a short time you will persuade me to become a Christian."[38] However, if scriptural truth does not press upon the heart of the preacher, and command and possess it, then the truth will be preached in a matter-of-fact, aloof manner. Earnest preaching is the result of eternal truth imparting "its own intensity to the emotions, to the words, and to the tones of the preacher."[39]

One of the finest bits of insightful counsel regarding earnestness in preaching, understanding its built-in limitations, and a warning for violating the limitations, is found in the following quote from James W. Alexander:

> Every excessive manner over matter hinders the effect of delivery. . . . Where there is more voice, more emphasis, or more gesture, than there is feeling, there is waste, and worse; powder beyond the shot. . . . Every man may be said to have his quantum of animation, beyond which he cannot go without forcework and affectation. Hence, to exhort a young man to be more animated is to mislead and perhaps spoil him, unless you mean to inculcate the cultivation of inward emotion. It is better therefore to let nature work, even though for the time the delivery is tame, than to generate a manner only rhetorically and artificially warm, which is hypocrisy.[40]

The treatment of earnestness in preaching is of utmost importance. Without it, preaching does not exist. Where there is true preaching, there will be earnestness. Yet,

---

36. Spring, *The Power of the Pulpit*, 1848, 126.

37. James, *An Earnest Ministry*, 1847, 136–37.

38. Acts 24:25, Acts 26:24, Acts 26:28.

39. James, *An Earnest Ministry*, 1847, 138–39.

40. Alexander, *Thoughts on Preaching*, 1864, 30.

based upon the personality and temperament of the preacher, true earnestness may be swallowed up by passionate preaching, the subject of the next section.

Three implications of earnest preaching, as they relate to the sermon conclusion, might be pivotal before examining passionate preaching. First, it is in the conclusion that the deepest feeling, the finest insights, and the most solemn and significant personal truths should be found.[41] If a preacher is preaching for a verdict from his hearers to respond to the truth, then he must understand that the conclusion is his last and best chance to affect the outcome. The time reserved for the sermon's conclusion must be worth all that have gone before them. "An English preacher used to say that he cared very little for what he said the first half hour, but he cared a very great deal what he said the last five minutes."[42] Cicero's rule was that the most excellent things were to be reserved for the peroration (conclusion), for the final effort of the speech so that the hearers might be moved.[43]

Second, pathos in the conclusion does not so much consist of greater verbal pitch, pace, projection, and punch, as in a deepened tone of feeling and a concentration of personal and practical instruction from Scripture. The stylistic components of verbal expression may reach a height not encountered in any earlier portion of the sermon, but such is not necessarily the case. What should be evidenced clearly is the preacher's urgency that the truths of Scripture are not only understood but applied in the lives of his hearers.

Third, a preacher's earnestness in the conclusion should evidence his great desire to help his hearers walk according to the truth of Scripture. His earnestness will be related to the insights he will provide to help them to live productive lives in Christ. His desire to do so should be evident to all and questioned by none. Consider the following plea for earnest conclusions:

> Of the importance of the conclusion it is hardly possible to speak too strongly. It ought to be the most vital of the whole, and if the preacher has been gradually warming, and accumulating force as the discourse has advanced, at the conclusion his spirit should be on fire, and impression of his closing passages should be by far the strongest of any. Yet in practice the conclusion is often the weakest part . . . so that, instead of being more concentrated at the end, *his discourse lost itself in a marsh, or ended like the emptying of the pitcher, with a few poor drops and dregs.* . . . The last effort of the preacher ought to be a signal one—like Samson's last achievement against the Philistines. It ought to be the concentration, as with a burning glass, of all the rays that have been collected during the progress of the address. . . . Considerations derived from the

---

41. Hoppin, *Homiletics*, 1883, 442.

42. Etter, *The Preacher and His Sermon*, 1885, 366. Contrary to the quotation above, I believe a preacher should care a great deal about the entire sermon, from the first word to the last! However, the conclusion of the sermon is of great significance and he must apply the greatest care for how he ends his sermon.

43. Etter, *The Preacher and His Sermon*, 1885, 366.

discourse fitted to move the will, conscience, and feelings of the hearer should be pressed with an earnestness that will take no denial. If the understanding has been gained in the earlier parts, the heart and the will must be gained in the latter. . . . The last five minutes of the discourse, in point of real effect, ought to be worth all the thirty or thirty-five that have gone before them.[44]

These assertions about a sermon conclusion are not altered based upon the degree to which a preacher's emotions are displayed through his preaching. In fact, everything to be discovered about a sermon conclusion is in force equally for the earnest preacher as well as the passionate preacher. The requirements for sermon conclusions do not change based upon the personality and temperament of the preacher.

44. Blaikie, *For the Work of the Ministry*, 1873, 124–25. (The italicized portion of the above block quote is uncited material which came from John A. Broadus's classic work *A Treatise on the Preparation and Delivery of Sermons* published in 1870).

4

General Matters about the Sermon Conclusion and Preaching: Part 2

"In the time between the discovery of the Word and the declaration of the Word there is a distillation of the Word in the heart of the preacher. That which was discovered and distilled is declared passionately, according to the degree of distillation in the preacher's heart."

"The concentrated extract of personal holiness in the preacher distinguishes the greatest spiritual success in the pulpit. A lack of holiness is the fatal disease which makes many an able pulpit lifeless. The godlikeness of a man is the essence of eloquence in every sermon. It by no means is an overstatement to conclude that a man's character is the ceiling of the sermon. You cannot preach beyond the level of your character!"

"Passionate and earnest preaching is the preaching of consecrated men, men who love God, men who are sold out to Christ, men whose lives are under the control of the Holy Spirit of God, men who are obedient to his Word. These are the kind of men who are passionate and earnest preachers. But passionate and earnest preachers are not just men of high spiritual caliber, they are men who preach a compelling message in their preaching. It is said that people will listen to a preacher when they sense that he is a man with a message, and they are always looking for such men."

"The passionate preaching of a man who puts his very life into his message preaches a compelling message. A compelling message breaks down opposition, penetrates dullness and indifference, produces conviction, quickens moral sluggishness, and energizes life to God's purposes. 'Nothing would so stir the mass of indifferent, half-hearted, worldly Christianity as the renewed sense of message in the pulpit.'"

"A compelling message cannot be, and it never will be, an unimpassioned intellect talking to intellects about intellectual things. The power of sermons is diminished by an inordinate amount of the intellectual content to the exclusion of the emotive and the volitional elements in preaching. When this is the case, there is a shrinking back from declaring the responsibilities linked to the instructive content, as well as a shrinking back from declaring the applications of truth to the conscience in the forms of direct appeals."

"The understanding that a compelling message must go beyond the intellectual to the emotional and practical is important because the sermon conclusion is dominated by the practical and will weigh-in on the emotional. . . . A compelling message grows 'hotter and hotter from beginning to end. The true way is to have an object and be full of it.' This cannot happen without a sermon conclusion, and an effective sermon conclusion, at that!"

"It is charged that the modern pulpit is remote from life and that much preaching is perfunctory. If this is so, why is it so? The answer is neither profound nor pleasing—because of a lack of conviction in the heart of the preacher that the sermon he has prepared is a compelling message!"

"Some truths of the Word instantly connect themselves with the human soul and fit them as a key fits a lock. Some truths get their connection through the insights of other Scriptures, as these are brought to bear to show their vital relationship in connecting and upholding the truth, just as the stones in an arch uphold one another. But to be able to bring together the vital interconnectedness of God's authoritative and relevant Word requires a knowledge of it and a continual, diligent study of it, so that its vital connectedness can be better understood, better appreciated, and more apparent in preaching. To be able to use cross-references in the application of a passage with precision and accuracy is a tremendous skill in preaching. The incorporation of cross-references wisely selected and rightly connected, can fix a truth deeply in the minds and lives of hearers."

"There are motives which make up The Constructive Motive from which passionate and earnest preaching occurs. The Constructive Motive is a composite of three motives, all of which must be functioning for passionate preaching to result. The three motives are related to the love of God, the love of man, and the love of truth. All three motives must function fully, or the result cannot be passionate preaching, but rather, an imbalanced emotional display in preaching."

"Conviction moves from heart to heart. To kindle a fire in others you yourself must be kindled. The preacher's primary duty for himself is to be moved by, and submit to, the truth to which he desires others to surrender. No man who is totally captivated by

the truth he proclaims can be insincere in his preaching. Not only will he be sincere, but he will be found speaking to the hearts of men as he is captivated by truth."

"Expression is the result of impression. . . . The power of expression will correspond to the depth and breadth of the impression. . . . The preacher's expression of the truth represents the impression of the truth on his heart as conveyed to others through his preaching."

"Emotion in preaching is aroused and unconsciously stored up in the process of preparing to preach. Emotion is stored up as one dwells on the message and prays over it. In the act of preaching, that which was stored up, flares up. This is genuine and noble passion. . . . This is true, especially so, in the sermon conclusion where passion, the greatest passion demonstrated in the sermon, will be found. Force, or emphatic impression, must be an integral part of the content of the conclusion, which must be delivered energetically with a sense of urgency. The congregation must be persuaded that the message will make a very real difference in their lives. Of course, this means that the preacher has prepared a conclusion containing content that can and should make a real difference in the lives of his hearers. . . . The Word of God is to be demonstrable in the body of the sermon as well as the sermon conclusion. The sermon conclusion must not be devoid of the testimony of Scripture."

PASSIONATE PREACHING

Passionate Preaching is Done by a Consecrated Man

Spurgeon was a passionate preacher. He was motivated to be so. In fact, he desired to be more passionate in his preaching as he advanced in years in his preaching ministry. He writes, "In times of great pain, and weakness, and depression, it has come over me to hope that, if I should again recover, I should be more intense than ever; if I could be privileged to climb the pulpit stairs again, I resolved to leave out every bit of flourish from my sermons, to preach nothing but present and pressing truth, and to hurl it at people with all my might . . . putting forth all the energy of which my being is capable."[1] It is amazing to discover that such a passionate preacher, as Spurgeon certainly was, believed himself capable of far more.

The apostles of our Lord were gripped by passion in their preaching. They were Christ's witnesses, proclaiming the way of salvation, calling men to repent, commanding men to denounce other allegiances and come under the rule of Christ. With great abandon the apostles made known the grace of God in Jesus Christ.[2] It should not be surprising that these men were passionate in their proclamation of Christ. After all,

1. Spurgeon, *An All-round Ministry*, 1900, 162.
2. Weatherspoon, *Sent Forth to Preach*, 47–48.

they had sacrificed everything to be his followers. In the absence of Christ, they continued on, even though they did so under the stated word of Christ that they would pay the ultimate price in fulfilling their ministries. But fulfill them they did, because they were consecrated men. They were sold out to Christ. Their lives were "lost causes" for the advance of Christ's Kingdom. If they were anything less than passionate, that would be unthinkable and unimaginable.

Preaching is passionate when it is an expression of God's love through the preacher to his people. God's love is fired in the heart of the preacher in his study as he studies God's Word. God's love is expressed through the heart of the preacher as he preaches God's Word from the pulpit. In the time between the discovery of the Word and the declaration of the Word there is a distillation of the Word in the heart of the preacher. That which was discovered and distilled is declared and is done so passionately, according to the degree of distillation in the preacher's heart. In the words of Alex Montoya, "The simmering of the week boils over in the pulpit on Sunday."[3]

The distillation of scriptural truth in the heart of the preacher is indispensable for passionate preaching to be a reality. The truth of the passage from which the preacher will preach must undergo "change in the heart and mind of the preacher, and present itself in a more contemporary form, with more color of imagination and warmth of passion, before it can impact the hearer with full effect."[4]

As distillation entails producing a concentrated extract through a process of separating that which is distilled from all extraneous matter, so it is in processing the Word of God for preaching. The distillation process in the preacher's heart produces a concentrated extract of pure spiritual distillate, separated out from all things base, worldly, and sinful. In other words, the preacher himself is purified in the process of preparing a message from God's Word. The result being passionate preaching as a purified man of God preaches the God of the Word from the Word of God to the people of God that they may conform to the will of God in their lives.

The concentrated extract of personal holiness in the preacher distinguishes the greatest spiritual success in the pulpit. A lack of holiness is the fatal disease which makes many an able pulpit lifeless. The godlikeness of a man is the essence of eloquence in every sermon. It by no means is an overstatement to conclude that a man's character is the ceiling of the sermon.[5] *You cannot preach beyond the level of your character!*

As part of the distillation process in the preacher's heart, one of the most unfit extraneous matters to be separated out is the preacher's promotion of self. No man can preach passionately while at the same time seeking to promote himself. No preacher can ever attain to full earnestness in the pulpit without thorough "self-abnegation."[6]

3. Montoya, *Preaching with Passion*, 13.

4. Alexander, *Thoughts on Preaching*, 1864, 10–11.

5. Phelps, *The Theory of Preaching*, 1882, 461.

6. Simpson, *Lectures on Preaching*, 1897, 192.

He must be so intent on the message as to lose sight of himself. He must be absorbed in the work of advancing the cause of Christ through strengthening his hearers.

Perhaps the most common extraneous matter that needs to be separated out from a preacher's life is the condition that accompanies what our Lord referred to as the "thorny soil."[7] The worry of the world and the deceitfulness of riches are things that "choke the Word." Though the instruction was given to describe a lack of reception of the Word in the heart of those who hear it preached, the fruitfulness of one who proclaims the Word can be inhibited since he tries to preach from a heart that is unduly affected by the things of the world instead of the Lord. A passionate preaching of sermons will be diminished when there is in the heart of the preacher a passion for, and a satisfaction with, other successes than those of saving sinners and building up believers through the preached Word.[8]

According to Austin Phelps, the most disastrous drain of power in preaching is, the lack of spiritual consecration in the preacher. Powerful preaching is built on, and goes forth from, significant spiritual character in a man. No man can preach powerfully who has not an intense working in his own character. The character of the man, and "an intense unity of purpose" for preaching, is the essence of preaching.[9]

The power of God Himself is the source of power in passionate preaching. The power to preach passionately is not found in books, nor does it come from reading books. It is not transmitted from the teaching of professors or contained in the curriculum of schools. The power to preach passionately is a gift directly from God that energizes one's thoughts, convictions, emotions, and animates one's personality.[10] Passionate preaching, accompanied by the power of God and produced by the presence of God in a purified man of God, distinguishes itself for what it is—an authentic divine encounter.

Imitations of passionate preaching may present themselves but in contrast to the real thing, they will be seen for the fabrication that they are. Phelps was emphatic in his assessment that spiritual integrity, claimed as a requirement to the preaching of an intense theology, cannot be successfully imitated. Integrity in anything cannot be imitated with success in the long run, but nowhere else will "a moral counterfeit be detected so surely as in the pulpit."[11] Drawing close to God has always been the way to be purified from everything that is spiritually debilitating. Drawing close to God has always been the way to be imbued with his empowering presence. In view of such a gracious and available provision, Spurgeon invoked this charge to his students:

7. In Christ's parable of the soils the four soil types represent four conditions of men's hearts as the Word of God is sown among them. I am using Christ's words to indicate the condition of a preacher's life, the life of one who has received the Word but is inundated with worldly things. In this instance, one who is good soil has *become* thorny soil.

8. Phelps, *The Theory of Preaching,* 1882, 473.

9. Phelps, *The Theory of Preaching,* 1882, 457.

10. Simpson, *Lectures on Preaching,* 1897, 208–9.

11. Phelps, *The Theory of Preaching,* 1882, 467.

"Burn because you've been in solemn fellowship with the Lord our God."[12] Passionate preaching is fueled by the power of God flowing through a man unchecked by sinful or worldly things.

Let me say, in what might appear as a significant digression, that in passionate preaching where a man is seen to "burn," to use Spurgeon's term, that the essence of such will be found in a commanding eye-contact of the preacher with his hearers. Not that the totality of the preacher's body will not be taken captive, because it will be, and not that the rest of the preacher's body is unimportant in conveying deep passion, because it is. But the height of passionate preaching is to be seen in a personal, purposeful, persistent, penetrating connection of the preacher to his hearers through eye-contact. Matthew Simpson was of the conviction that the eye has an immense influence over a congregation, as it often speaks the feelings in advance of words. Hearers are anxious not only to hear, but to see, the preacher, and the "power of the eye is one of the great elements of oratory."[13]

Particularly, as we think about passionate preaching with a view to the sermon conclusion, which should be the highpoint of the sermon, the most passionate part of the sermon, and the most personal part of the sermon, eye-contact is at a premium. No other part of the sermon, not even the introduction, demands the preacher's eye-contact with his hearers as does the conclusion. Cotton Mather advised, "Ever conclude with vigor. . . . What I therefore advise you to is, let your notes be little more than a guide, on which you may cast your eye now and then."[14] Finally, Mather insisted that sermon conclusions be lively exhortations to the conscience of the hearers; appeals made and questions put to their consciences with consignments of the work to be done fixed in the wills of the hearers.[15] Passionate preaching sustained through personal, penetrating eye-contact with one's hearers via note-free preaching is essential in the sermon conclusion.

Moreover, passionate preaching is not just crucial for sermon conclusions. It is crucial for preaching, by all preachers wherever they preach. Álex Montoya writes, "Empty churches are due not so much to an absence of ability or a lack of desire to hear the truth as with an absolute boredom brought about by passionless preaching. Our people are screaming at us from the silent, empty pews!"[16] Their screams need to be addressed the only way they should be addressed, with passionate preaching. The sermon conclusion has a significant role to play in adequately silencing the screams of those clamoring for passionate preaching.

12. Spurgeon, *An All-round Ministry*, 1900, 177.

13. Simpson, *Lectures on Preaching*, 1897, 187.

14. Cited in James, *An Earnest Ministry*, 1847, 140.

15. Cited in James, *An Earnest Ministry*, 1847, 141.

16. Montoya, *Preaching with Passion*, 11.

Passionate Preaching is Done by a Consecrated Man with a Compelling Message

Passionate and earnest preaching is the preaching of consecrated men, men who love God, men who are sold out to Christ, men whose lives are under the control of the Holy Spirit of God, men who are obedient to his Word. These are the kind of men who are passionate and earnest preachers. But passionate and earnest preachers are not just men of high spiritual caliber, they are men who preach a compelling message in their preaching. It is said that people will listen to a preacher when they sense that he is a man with a message and that they long to hear and "are always looking for such men."[17] Passionate and earnest preachers preach to people who are blessed to hear them, if the people are looking for men who are absorbed in what they say. Not all hearers look for this, but many do. In fact, some keep looking until they can find such a man. The sad truth is, they must look very hard because such men are not so common.

The passionate preaching of a man who puts his very life into his message preaches a compelling message. A compelling message breaks down opposition, penetrates dullness and indifference, produces conviction, quickens moral sluggishness, and energizes life to God's purposes. "Nothing would so stir the mass of indifferent, half-hearted, worldly Christianity as the renewed sense of message in the pulpit."[18]

A sense of message is the prophetic reality in preaching. How can one preach unless he is sent? How can one preach unless he has a message from God?[19] A message from God will always be a compelling message. The Word of God serves as abiding truth to be received into the heart, and to be intelligently applied to the circumstances of life. In discovering, and living the truth, God's people grow spiritually in the likeness of Christ.[20] The source and the substance of such a message assure that it will be compelling.

No man can be a passionate preacher who does not have a sense of message in the sermon he preaches. Arthur Hoyt raises the question, "What will the sense of message do for the preacher?" In a fivefold way, he answers with the following: a sense of message produces *effective speech*; a sense of message *gives a personal quality to speech*; a sense of message *gives the courage to be true*; a sense of message *sustains the fervor of preaching*; and a sense of message *"is the very secret of influence on the manward side."*[21] A messenger, a preacher who preaches a message in his sermon may be perceived by his hearers as an effective, personal, courageous, fervent, influential preacher who passionately preaches a compelling message.

While a passionate preacher is preaching a message that has captured his own heart, he is "alive and energetic" and moves toward one final great impression. "The truth has found him and moved him" and it might be the case that when he comes

---

17. Hoyt, *Vital Elements of Preaching*, 1929, 272.

18. Hoyt, *Vital Elements of Preaching*, 1929, 287.

19. Hoyt, *Vital Elements of Preaching*, 1929, 274.

20. Hall, *God's Word Through Preaching*, 1875, 179.

21. Hoyt, *Vital Elements of Preaching*, 1929, 282–7.

before his hearers, they will be captured as well, and they will be moved by his message which has so moved him.[22] A compelling message is compelling to the preacher, it will be compelling to some hearers, and may be compelling to many of them. But whether it is compelling to many or few, the nature of a message that is compelling is of a certain order. A compelling message will have an instructive element to it, but it will not be instructive only. It will have strong emotive and volitional components, also.

A compelling message cannot be, and it never will be, an unimpassioned intellect talking to intellects about intellectual things. In fact, the power of sermons is diminished by an inordinate amount of the intellectual content to the exclusion of the emotive and the volitional elements in preaching. Inevitably, when this is the case, there is a shrinking back from declaring the responsibilities linked to the instructive content, as well as a shrinking back from declaring "the applications of truth to the conscience in the forms of direct appeals."[23] Such is not a compelling message but rather an objectionable, heartless form of preaching resulting from the "tyranny of an effeminate taste in the pulpit, which rejects pungent applications of truth to the consciences of the hearers, as being incongruent with the wants and prerogatives of refined society."[24]

Such a tendency toward the domestication of preaching is to the minimization, if not the eradication, of feeling. Yet, vigorous discussion provides a pathway for powerful appeals. Hearers must see that the preacher's exhortation rises from the truth on which it is built. Only then can a preacher "exhort as one having authority."[25]

The understanding that a compelling message must go beyond the intellectual to the emotional and practical is important because the sermon conclusion is dominated by the practical and will weigh-in on the emotional. The sermon conclusion is not more instruction from the text about the text.[26] A compelling message is not a message that is made compelling because of its conclusion. A compelling message is just that, a message, all of it not parts of it, that are compelling. Every sermon trends in some direction and it should take that direction and continue in that direction until it culminates in its proper ending. However, a compelling message grows "hotter and hotter from beginning to end. The true way is to have an object and be full of it."[27] This cannot happen without a sermon conclusion, and an effective sermon conclusion, at that!

22. Breed, *Preparing to Preach*, 1911, 117.

23. Phelps, *The Theory of Preaching*, 1882, 469–70.

24. Phelps, *The Theory of Preaching*, 1882, 471.

25. Phelps, *The Theory of Preaching*, 1882, 564.

26. There will be times when the text contains content that will be used in the conclusion. When such instances occur, this content will not be discussed in the body of the sermon but intentionally skipped so that these matters can be treated in the conclusion. As pointed out already and developed more fully in the subsequent pages of this book, the conclusion will be composed of scriptural insights that are related to, but not part of, the preaching passage.

27. Alexander, *Thoughts on Preaching*, 1864, 22.

It is charged that the modern pulpit is remote from life and that much preaching is perfunctory. If this is so, why is it so? The answer is neither profound nor pleasing—because of a lack of conviction in the heart of the preacher that the sermon he has prepared is a compelling message!

As a preacher searches his own heart and thinks about the needy lives of his hearers, he must be sure that he has a message for them from the Word of God. As heralds, preachers announce the Lord's will. Some truths of the Word instantly connect themselves with the human soul and fit them as a key fits a lock. Some truths get their connection through the insights of other Scriptures, as these are brought to bear to show their vital relationship in connecting and upholding the truth, just as the stones in an arch uphold one another. But to be able to bring together the vital interconnectedness of God's authoritative and relevant Word requires a knowledge of it and a continual, diligent study of it, so that its vital connectedness can be better understood, better appreciated, and more apparent in preaching.[28]

To be able to use cross-references in the application of a passage with precision and accuracy is a tremendous skill in preaching.[29] The incorporation of cross-references wisely selected and rightly connected, can fix a truth deeply in the minds and lives of hearers. "A verse rightly put and rightly repeated, will often fix a truth better than a whole sermon."[30] And if he has a message from God it will be accompanied by the power of God.[31] Anything less than this cannot constitute a compelling message.

Passion is strong feeling which prompts to action. Its compound, compassion, or sympathy, which means to suffer together with another, is a word which was used constantly of the Lord's motive for action.[32] The Lord was a passionate preacher and a compassionate servant. The One who came not "to be served but to serve," did so in everything he did, including his preaching. Much is made of the Lord's miracles and rightly so. They were breathtaking demonstrations of compassion and power, meeting physical needs and demonstrating his deity. There is a tendency to epitomize the Lord's power by means of his miracles, his ability to interrupt the laws of nature at any time in any way he pleased. And many times, we are told of his compassion in working these miracles. But, when *he had to go to Samaria* and he spoke to the woman at the well in the village of Sychar and he stayed several days speaking to the men of that village, resulting in their salvation, this was no less of a demonstration of the power, the passion, and the compassion of Christ than any miracle he ever performed.[33]

---

28. Hall, *God's Word Through Preaching*, 1875, 89.

29. The skillful use of cross-references prevents the error of proof-texting. The conclusion, like every other portion of the sermon, cannot benefit from plucking texts out of their contexts to prescribe a meaning to them they were never intended to have.

30. Hall, *God's Word Through Preaching*, 1875, 98.

31. Davis, *Evangelistic Preaching*, 1921, 33.

32. Bull, *Preaching and Sermon Construction*, 1922, 213.

33. John 4:1–44.

On this occasion, as on every other occasion, he had a compelling message and he proclaimed it. He knew of the needs and had compassion on those in need by responding to them, and in this instance the needed response was the proclamation of truth, the message of salvation in the forgiveness of sins. Jesus commanded a compelling message. He was motivated by compassion for people and had so much passion for the message to be proclaimed that he was willing to suffer significant inconvenience to proclaim it. This is a constant opportunity for those who are called to preach, an opportunity that is worth making the most of, regardless of the cost.

To preach compelling messages passionately and to do so consistently, not occasionally, is anything but convenient. A significant price must be paid to do this. We need to know this, and we need to be willing to pay the price. Spurgeon learned this through the help of his grandfather as revealed by his own words:

> I wrote, many years ago, to my venerable grandfather, and told him of many things that happened to me before preaching—sickness of body, and terrible fears, which often made me really ill. The old gentleman wrote back, and said, "I have been preaching for sixty years, and I still feel many tremblings. Be content to have it so; for when your emotion goes away, your strength will be gone." When we preach and think nothing of it, the people think nothing of it, and God does nothing by it. An overwhelming sense of weakness should not be regarded as an evil, but should be accepted as helpful to the true minister of Christ.[34]

The price to preach compelling messages passionately is expensive, not cheap. This requires us to grow up, pay up, and show up ready to preach a compelling message, and to do so passionately!

Passionate Preaching is Done by a Consecrated Man with a Constructive Motive

Is there a constructive motive from which passionate preaching occurs? Or, perhaps, the better question might be, are there constructive motives from which passionate preaching occurs? And the answer is, yes, and yes. Yes, there are motives which make up The Constructive Motive from which passionate preaching occurs. Yes, The Constructive Motive is a composite of three motives, all of which must be functioning for passionate preaching to result. The three motives are the love of God, the love of man, and the love of truth.

All three motives must function fully, or the result cannot be passionate preaching, but rather, an imbalanced emotional display in preaching. If the love of God is lacking in strong emotional preaching, it will possess and be tainted by a humanistic, humanitarian bent. If the love of man is lacking in strong emotional preaching, it will be tainted by an impersonal, indifferent bent. If the love of truth is lacking in strong

---

34. Spurgeon, *An All-round Ministry*, 1900, 208.

emotional preaching, it will be tainted by a superficial, subjective bent. Though there may be strong emotion in the preaching, if all three motives are not functional then that which is weak—the motive that is lacking—becomes its negative strength, *the hallmark of its imbalance.*

A strong emotional display in preaching is not passionate preaching. Passionate preaching displays strong emotion motivated by the constructive motive which results from a love of God, a love of man, and a love of truth, all fully functioning. Passionate preaching is not strong emotional preaching that is impaired by an imbalance of the three necessary motives. Passionate preaching is dependent upon the three motives like a tripod is dependent upon all three legs. The removal of any one of the three motives is as destructive to passionate preaching as the removal of any leg to a tripod.

The Love of God Motivates Passionate Preaching

To move men, a preacher needs to have a sensitive soul and be a true spiritual man. The prerequisite is to love God with all his heart, and mind, and soul, and strength. This can only be attained by one who is persevering in prayer, and in the contemplation and meditation of Scripture.[35] To love God means that we desire to glorify him, to please him in all that we do in our lives, including the sermons we preach. Passionate preaching motivated by the love of God may be aided by presenting the sermon as an offering to God through the preaching of it. John MacArthur offers valuable instruction for preachers related to the time in between the preparation of their sermons and the time they deliver their sermons. He writes:

> Begin by focusing on the reality that your sermon is an offering to the Lord. Be driven by the truth that the Lord is your highest judge. Then your consciousness will compel you to deliver the truth as a holy offering to Him. This gives you the proper frame of mind for your solemn responsibility. What your colleagues or congregation may think or say is not your major concern. Know that delivering the message the Lord has given you is your service to Him for his satisfaction. That is why Paul charged Timothy "in the presence of God and of Christ Jesus" (2 Timothy. 4:1) to preach the Word. Let your thoughts after preparation and before delivery dwell on the Lord and His response to your expositional offering to Him. In the hours immediately before you preach, face the serious reality that you must deliver up a sacrifice that will be acceptable to the divine author of Scripture.[36]

The love we have for God and our desire that he might be well-pleased with our sermonic sacrifice to him is a tremendous impetus for passionate preaching which includes the sermon conclusion just as much as, if not more than, any other part of the sermon.

---

35. Bull, *Preaching and Sermon Construction,* 1922, 218.
36. MacArthur, *Rediscovering Expository Preaching,* 322–3.

The Love of Man Motivates Passionate Preaching

If the true pastor seeks God's pleasure in his preaching ministry to God's people, being motivated by his love for him, then he must love those whom he loves. "He must seek their good! John asks, 'Whoever has the world's goods, and sees his brother in need and closes his heart against him, how does the love of God abide in him' (1 John 3:17)?"[37] Though the Apostle John speaks specifically of the matter of physical needs, the principle applies to spiritual needs as well. For a pastor to withhold spiritually needed instruction from those who need it is unthinkable. He simply must speak to their needs and do so effectively.

To speak well to men, it is necessary to love them much. However blameworthy, indifferent, ungrateful, and shameful one's hearers may be, it is necessary to love them. That is central to the Christian life and the secret of effective living and preaching which is the eloquence of passion. Our task is "to win men's hearts in order that we may restore them to God." Love finds the way that leads to the heart.[38] This love is modified as being "without hypocrisy" in 1 Peter 1:22; 2 Corinthians 6:6; and Romans 12:9. Brian Borgman speaks to this matter well: "If a man of God must put on a ministerial face, then his love is hypocritical. Effective pastoral ministry must be fueled by a love that is unfeigned, and it can be unfeigned only if it is a gracious and principled disposition."[39]

To exemplify the connection between love for people and preaching passionately because of that love, one must consider the words of the Apostle Paul in Romans 9:1–4 regarding his love for his unbelieving Jewish kinsmen. Paul wrote: "I am telling the truth in Christ, I am not lying, my conscience testifies with me in the Holy Spirit, that I have great sorrow and unceasing grief in my heart. For I could wish that I myself were accursed, separated from Christ for the sake of my brethren, my kinsmen according to the flesh, who are Israelites . . ." Paul's love for his fellow Jews and his desire to see them saved caused him to endure incredible hostility from fellow Jews just days after his conversion on the Damascus road throughout his "first missionary journey."

In fact, just days after his conversion Paul went to the synagogues in Damascus proclaiming that Jesus is the Son of God. Upon proving that Jesus is the Christ throughout many days, the Jews plotted to do away with him, watching the gates day and night so that they might put him to death. Paul narrowly escaped through a hole in the city wall, being lowered in a large basket. In Syrian Antioch, Paul along with Barnabas were set apart by God for the work he called them to—what is now referred to as the first missionary journey. When they reached Salamis, they began to proclaim the Word of God in the synagogues of the Jews. Following this, they go to a synagogue on the Sabbath day in Pisidian Antioch and preach the Word with the result that many

37. Borgman, *My Heart for Thy Cause*, 83.
38. Bull, *Preaching and Sermon Construction*, 1922, 218.
39. Borgman, *My Heart for Thy Cause*, 82.

Jews and God-fearing proselytes begged Paul to preach again on the next Sabbath day. On that occasion some Jews began contradicting Paul and blaspheming. Paul and Barnabas announced to the Jews that they were turning to the Gentiles, with the result that many Gentiles were saved, and the Word of the Lord spread throughout the whole region. The Jews of Pisidian Antioch instigated a persecution against Paul and Barnabas and drove them out of the district. Paul and Barnabas shook off the dust of their feet in protest against them and went to Iconium, where, entering the synagogue of the Jews a large number of people believed. When unbelieving Jews and Gentiles of Iconium attempted to mistreat and stone them, Paul and Barnabas fled from Iconium to Lystra. However, while at Lystra, Jews from Pisidian Antioch and Iconium came to Lystra and stoned Paul thinking they had killed him. The next day Paul and Barnabas go to Derbe. After making many disciples in Derbe, Paul and Barnabas returned to Lystra, Iconium, and Pisidian Antioch to encourage the disciples and appoint elders in the churches.

Out of love for believers, both Jews and Gentiles, Paul and Barnabas put their lives in jeopardy to strengthen the souls of the disciples, encouraging them to continue in the faith. It was Paul's love for lost people to preach the Word of God to them so that they might be saved, as well as his love for fellow believers that they might be strengthened by the preached Word, that caused him to endure so much hostility. This account of Paul's earliest ministry presupposes passionate preaching based upon love for those to whom the preaching is provided. One only has to read Acts 13:16–41, Paul's preaching at the Pisidian Antioch synagogue, to verify his passionate preaching. The unfeigned love of a true pastor for the people of God "will exert influence in both the preparation and delivery of sermons."[40] The true pastor, motivated by an unfeigned love for those to whom he preaches, cannot be guilty of the "take it or leave it" mindset of preaching since he is vitally concerned about the spiritual welfare of believers and unbelievers alike.[41] The sermon conclusion, more than any other part of the sermon, will indicate the concern he has for those who hear him preach, and his concern will be indicated by the content of what he has to say to his hearers in this part of the sermon.

The Love of Truth Motivates Passionate Preaching

To move others, it is necessary to be moved oneself. The preacher must cultivate a strong love of Scripture. Without a passion to discover and submit to God's Word as one's unrivaled guide for faith and practice, the guide for one's life will be self-love. Self-love makes one callous to the feelings of others, producing cynicism, skepticism and disillusionment, leaving "the heart of the preacher a cinder instead of a flaming

---

40. Borgman, *My Heart for Thy Cause*, 85.
41. Borgman, *My Heart for Thy Cause*, 86.

coal."[42] Conviction moves from heart to heart. To kindle a fire in others you yourself must be kindled. The preacher's primary duty for himself is to be moved by, and submit to, the truth to which he desires others to surrender. No man who is totally captivated by the truth he proclaims can be insincere in his preaching. Not only will he be sincere, but he will be found speaking to the hearts of men as he is captivated by truth.

One writer exalted passion in the following way, "It lays hold of the deeps within us and it speaks to the deeps of others."[43] Obviously, if the preacher is not passionate about the sermon he will preach, can he truly believe that those to whom he preaches will find it so? Preaching is a personal message, that is, the preacher's heart is in the message he preaches. As a spring cannot rise higher than its source, the preacher's passion for the message will be greater than any who hears him preach it. The preacher's personal conviction of the value and power of the message must be evident to all who hear. The Bible must control the preacher's life and his character before he can do his best work in preaching Scripture as a messenger of Christ.[44]

Nothing can take the place of personal experience and conviction. An effective sermon does not develop and mature "under the study lamp alone."[45] It derives life and power from the preacher's knowledge and personal experience of the gospel. His preaching goes forth from a life of loving surrender and devoted service to Christ. The best emotional preparation for preaching is made as a preacher reviews his own indebtedness to Christ and warms his heart as he reflects upon the love and loyalty that is due to his Lord. If the grounds for one's love and gratitude to Christ is appraised rightly, the preacher will find his heart tuned to the right emotional mood, then he may be used to kindle in others a similar affection.[46] Yet, regardless of the true pastor's love of God, love of God's people, and love of God's truth, the truth of Scripture itself will assure that some people will be alienated by it as it is proclaimed faithfully. Instead of sensing the fragrant aroma provided by the Word of God, Scripture may be perceived by some as more foul than fragrant. But even as this may be inevitable, the true pastor as a passionate preacher who loves the truth of Scripture understands that this is how it will be with some people, but he has "no right to change the aroma of the message!"[47] Of equal importance, a faithful passionate preacher may find that some are alienated temporarily but as the Spirit of God works in the heart, the fulfillment of Proverbs 28:23 becomes an experiential reality—"He who rebukes a man will afterward find more favor than he who flatters with the tongue."[48]

42. Bull, *Preaching and Sermon Construction*, 1922, 219.
43. Davis, *Evangelistic Preaching*, 1921, 26.
44. Davis, *Evangelistic Preaching*, 1921, 31.
45. Davis, *Evangelistic Preaching*, 1921, 32.
46. Davis, *Evangelistic Preaching*, 1921, 67.
47. Borgman, *My Heart for Thy Cause*, 95.
48. Borgman, *My Heart for Thy Cause*, 96.

The Law of Impression and Expression in Passionate Preaching

Expression is the result of impression. Therefore, an influence must first be exerted by the truth on the heart of the preacher himself, and then through his heart onto the hearts of the hearers. The power of expression will correspond to the depth and breadth of the impression, just as the branches of a tree above the ground corresponds to the expanse of a tree's roots below the ground.[49] Impression, therefore, represents the truth at work in the preacher. The preacher's expression of the truth represents the impression of the truth on his heart as conveyed to others through his preaching.

There is little need for concern about the expression of truth in the pulpit if there has been sufficient impression of truth on his heart in the study.[50] If the conception of truth in oneself is clear and accurate, then its effect on oneself will be deep and powerful. The longer the exposure to the influence of the truth, the deeper and more powerful will be the value of the truth formed in the heart. The power of impression depends upon the work of God in the preacher's heart through his exposure to the Word of God as well as the length of exposure to God's Word. The power of impression determines the power of expression of the Word of God in the pulpit.[51]

Purpose Fosters Passionate Preaching

Preaching toward a verdict safeguards the motive for, and urgency in, preaching. "An urgent preacher is very much a madman. An urgent preacher wants you to know something, to do something, to act responsibly, and to act *now*! Preaching with a verdict in mind is urgent preaching and, naturally, passionate preaching."[52] Such urgency is a requirement for the passionate preaching that must saturate the sermon conclusion. Richard Baxter said, "Nothing is more indecent than a dead preacher speaking to dead sinners the living truth of the living God."[53] The preacher's personality is not a kind of conduit through which the Word is conveyed like water through a pipe. It is more likened to the trunk of a living tree with sap seeping through every fiber. In passionate preaching, where the Word is communicated emotionally, "the personality of the preacher is not dormant or passive." It is displayed fully.[54]

---

49. Pierson, *The Divine Art of Preaching*, 1892, 24.

50. This clashes with the view of many who advocate practicing and rehearsing the sermon. I have never thought a sermon should be rehearsed or practiced. I believe this morphs preaching into a performance mode whereby a preacher prepares himself to perform before hearers. This is not preaching! Preaching is a live event! The preacher instead should give himself to internalize the content of the sermon very thoroughly by praying, thinking, and meditating on the content from the introduction to the conclusion.

51. Pierson, *The Divine Art of Preaching* 1892, 25.

52. Montoya, *Preaching with Passion*, 96.

53. As cited in Lawson, *Famine in the Land*, 125.

54. Macpherson, *The Burden of the Lord*, 16.

Emotion in preaching is aroused and unconsciously stored up in the process of preparing to preach. Emotion is stored up as one dwells on the message and prays over it. In the act of preaching, that which was stored up, flares up. This is genuine and noble passion. Displayed in this way, it brings with it "all the justification that it needs" for approval.[55] This is true, especially so, in the sermon conclusion where passion, the greatest passion demonstrated in the sermon, will be found. Force, or emphatic impression, must be an integral part of the content of the conclusion, which must be delivered energetically with a sense of urgency. The congregation must be persuaded that the message will make "a very real difference" in their lives.[56] Of course, this means that the preacher has prepared a conclusion containing content that can and should make a real difference in the lives of his hearers.

For the conclusion of a sermon to make a real difference in the lives of the hearers, it is to be rigorously, closely, and intensely practical. There should be precise and exacting applications of truth "from which the hearer feels that there is no escaping."[57] A sermon conclusion should be the homiletical equivalent of the bombardment of Fort Pulaski in 1862. In the assault on that fort, seventy cannonballs struck the southeast corner of the fort within a circle, twelve feet in diameter. Down came the flag and up went the white flag of surrender! Of what use would it be to resist such fire? If the guns of Scripture were assembled and pointed in one direction, at the same target, and shot upon shot were hurled, hot and heavy, against the walls of unfaithful, irresponsible, disobedient, sinful citadels in the lives of God's people, many a flag of Satan would be hauled down in the lives of believers.[58]

The overarching effect of a preacher's sermon conclusion should be like many of Solomon's proverbs and the conclusion of the book of Ecclesiastes—to fill our hearts with the fear of God and the formation of obedient lives in preparation to stand before God in judgment.[59] As this is the case, the preacher will have a sense of urgency to get to this part of the sermon so that the purpose of the sermon may be accomplished in the lives of his hearers.

Passionate Preaching is Done by a Consecrated Man with a Correcting Ministry

The correcting ministry of a passionate preacher is on display in the sermon conclusion more clearly than any other portion of the message. There is no place like the conclusion of a sermon for a preacher's passion to be in full force. Additionally, the much-needed ministry of correction is most serviceable in the sermon conclusion.

---

55. Sangster, *The Craft of Sermon Construction*, 148.

56. Brown Jr., Clinard, Northcutt, *Steps to the Sermon*, 123.

57. Moore, *Thoughts on Preaching*, 1861, 141.

58. Pierson, *The Divine Art of Preaching* 1892, 103.

59. Moore, *Thoughts on Preaching*, 1861, 142.

Preaching is the unfolding of a "Thus saith the Lord."[60] For such preaching, the preacher searches the Word, gets the mind of God buried in his heart by prayerful meditation by which it is made to grow and germinate. The Word of God is born into the heart and mind of the preacher. It becomes part of his convictions and affections.

The Word of God is to be demonstrable in the body of the sermon *as well as the sermon conclusion.*[61] *The sermon conclusion must not be devoid of the testimony of Scripture.* The following insight from A. T. Pierson is more applicable to the conclusion than any application of Scripture in a sermon. Pierson wrote: "In the application of truth, the object to be accomplished by the preacher may not always be covered by a single text; and it may be needful besides, to defend, discriminate, limit, and guard from misconception by arraying and arranging the testimony of several texts."[62] Just as a single cable must be composed of multiple strands for it to function properly and possess necessary strength, so a single text may require other texts in combination with it to provide an unquestioned strength and functionality to produce an unmistakable result—the purpose of the sermon accomplished.[63]

Just because the conclusion is the best place for the insightful instruction that is crucial for correction to occur, unfortunately, that does not mean that correction will be a component of the conclusion. It would be an exercise in futility to argue against one author's indictment that, there are preachers, who, whatever may be their topic, never get out of their unfeeling, passionless monotony; "whose highest ambition seems to be that they should be coldly correct, and critically dull."[64] For such men, not even the prime opportunity of the sermon conclusion will make a difference in their preaching. But mark it well, the poorly produced conclusion, just like a poorly constructed sermon, is always the same: it is "a calamity, a wrong, and an offense both to heaven and earth. Furthermore, that which costs a preacher very little may cost his hearers a great deal. Should they come to hear those who are charged with the distribution of heaven's bounty, and, having at their disposal, bread enough to spare, only to spread for them a table of empty husks?"[65] A preacher must never allow himself to think that a sermon conclusion is expendable based upon the good work accomplished in the sermon body. That good work can be and must be optimized by a passionate sermon conclusion providing rich insights and correction to the hearers.

The passion needed in a sermon conclusion should be intensive and extensive. The terms, intensive and extensive passion, are used with reference to the effects of

60 The most accurate, personal, applicable, and insightful declaration of "Thus saith the Lord" begins with an accurate interpretation of the preaching passage but it will inevitably include passages outside the preaching portion so that the text is not handled in isolation of the broader scope of Scripture.

61. Pierson, *The Divine Art of Preaching,* 1892, 99.

62. Pierson, *The Divine Art of Preaching,* 1892, 39.

63. Pierson, *The Divine Art of Preaching,* 1892, 40.

64. Moore, *Thoughts on Preaching,* 1861, 254.

65. Moore, *Thoughts on Preaching,* 1861, 302.

passion brought on the hearer. Passion that is extensive refers to the extent to which passion touches the whole man, powerfully bringing corrective insight into contact with the hearers' minds, convictions, emotions/affections, consciences, and wills. Intensive passion has reference to the depth of impression that passion makes upon the hearer, that is, not making a superficial impression, but impacting man in his essence, to "strike to the very vitals" of a man's being.[66]

If a preacher's mission is to provide a ministry of correction to the lives of God's people in his sermon conclusion, then extensive and intensive passion are in order. In his revision of John Broadus's classic work, *A Treatise on the Preparation and Delivery of Sermons*, J. B. Weatherspoon intensifies Broadus's instruction regarding the sermon conclusion with his words: "Weakness in manner, thought, or words draws the nails instead of driving them deeper. Deep passion, thoughts that burn, strong words are the instruments required, whether the conclusion be a direct drive on the will or an appeal to the heart."[67] V. L. Stanfield's subsequent revision of Broadus supplied additional instruction for the strength of the sermon conclusion as he wrote:

> (I)t is evident that the application concentrates itself, so to speak, in the conclusion. This concluding application requires, even more than the other parts of the discourse, that the preacher should have . . . intense earnestness. Often the claim of the sermon will be articulated in a direct appeal. Prophetic and apostolic preaching were characterized by it. And it is not a good sign that many preachers have lost the unembarrassed urgency of importuning men for God.[68]

A hesitance to appeal directly to hearers spells certain death to the ministry of correction in a sermon conclusion. To make earnest appeals for hearers to conduct themselves in certain ways, or to cease and desist from certain things, is entirely compatible with the ministry of correction in a sermon conclusion.

Three quick insights should be made regarding a passionate preacher's corrective ministry in a sermon conclusion. The intensive and extensive passion needed for, and displayed in, a sermon conclusion intending to bring correction to the hearers suggest the following: it is necessary to provide diversification of emotional appeals; it is necessary to provide exemplification of what life-changes are required and how they are to be enacted; and, it is necessary to provide a strong final statement to the conclusion. Therefore, the ministry of correction is aided by the factors of diversity, depiction, and decisiveness.

---

66. Pierson, *The Divine Art of Preaching,* 1892, 26.

67. Weatherspoon, *On the Preparation and Delivery of Sermons,* 126.

68. Stanfield, *On the Preparation and Delivery of Sermons,* 113.

Diversity and the Ministry of Correction

The conclusion should bring a diversity of emotional appeals to the hearers. There are "three sorts" of emotional appeals that a sermon conclusion can bring to the hearers: the "violent" sort; the "tender" sort; and the "elevated" sort of emotional appeal. Violent emotional appeals consist of—indignation, zeal, courage, firmness against temptations, repentance, self-loathing, etc. Tender emotional appeals consist of– joy, consolation, gratitude, etc. Elevated emotional appeals consist of—admiration of the majesty of God, submission to the ways of providence, longing for the glory of paradise, the expectation of benefits, etc.[69] A conclusion may contain more than one of the three sorts of emotional appeal but there is no reason to seek to provide appeals from more than one sort. The beneficial diversity is found, not in a combination of sorts of emotional appeals, but in the number of appeals found in the sermon conclusion.

A single appeal of any "sort" would not be inappropriate based upon the fact that it is not part of a larger plurality. However, the significant issue is that the rest of Scripture should be consulted to provide insights that would be valuable to provide needed correction. Does Scripture provide only one insight that is helpful to bring needed correction? If so, then one appeal must be appropriate. On the other hand, many times Scripture provides more insights than would be wise to include, thereby, requiring careful selection for what will be included in the conclusion. In total, the conclusion should be composed of "two or three, preferably, but as many as four or five" appeals.[70]

The diversity of appeals, regardless of the sort or number of them, if gleaned from the fertile fields of Scripture, will require two things: diligence and humility. One of the first and most important duties of a preacher is the diligent investigation of truth. If he fails here, he fails significantly. And yet, the diligent investigation of biblical truth is of a very peculiar character. It is not the result of a heartless pursuit. It is not discovered by the mere power of the intellect, or by mental discipline, or by laborious and learned investigation. But to the humble of heart who seek diligently to discover that which can be possessed inconveniently, Scripture yields its riches and imparts its treasures. Therefore, the chief requisite for the discovery of biblical truth is a humble diligence.[71]

Both the truth itself and our hearers must suffer in our hands, unless we approach the composition of the sermon *devoutly*, impressed equally by the solemnity of the message, the value of the souls of our hearers, and our own responsibility.[72]

---

69. Claude, *Claude's Essay*, 1801, *132*. *Claude's three sorts of emotional appeals are rudimentary and, therefore, nominally helpful. A fuller, more helpful understanding of appeals will be discussed in chapter eleven under the heading of Content Types and Delivery Tones in Closing Appeals.*

70. Claude, *Claude's Essay*, 1801, 133. Claude uses the term "reflections" rather than appeals.

71. I cannot improve on the terminology of "a humble diligence" when I think about Solomon's instruction found in Proverbs 2:1–8. Another phrase may be more descriptive, but I cannot supply a better one at present.

72. Burgess, *The Art of Preaching*, 1881, 65.

Therefore, it is imperative to pray two petitions from the Psalms in seeking the Holy Spirit's illuminating work to helpfully discover the closing appeals of a sermon conclusion. The first of the two petitions are for a *wondrous beholding*. Psalm 119:18, "Open my eyes, that I may behold wondrous things out of your law." The second petition is for a *restored joy*. Psalm 51:12, "Restore to me the joy of your salvation, and uphold me with a willing spirit. Then I will teach transgressors your ways, and sinners will return to you."[73] The substance of the closing appeals of a sermon conclusion that concludes well should represent an answer to these petitions. In other words, the content of a sermon conclusion should reflect *joyous proclamation of wonderful truths gleaned from the counsel of Scripture.*

Depiction and the Ministry of Correction

The highest demand is that you supply the people of God with none but "well-beaten oil for the lamps of the golden candlestick."[74] Among all other demonstrations of the well-beaten oil to be supplied to God's people, the sermon conclusion is foremost. The finest of the well-beaten oil is in order for the conclusion since this is the place where the preacher must make an appeal for insightful action based on the matters discussed in the text he has expounded. For Cotton Mather, this required the practice to read the sacred Scriptures in a labored fashion to observe and record the ways and means of godliness. To achieve this necessitates that one "pause upon every verse, and see what lessons of piety are to be learned from every clause."[75] How are they to live, what is required of the hearers to live in a manner that achieves the purpose for the sermon? Well-beaten oil provides appeals to the hearers that will correct in their lives that which is out of line with Scripture.

Again, Mather is Bible-laden as he asserts, "Be careful evermore to preach scripturally; and employ the sword of the Spirit. . . . Pertinent Scriptures, demonstrating and embellishing every article, will well become one who would speak as the oracles of God."[76] As the men of God, who wrote Scripture, were moved by the Holy Spirit in it, and for it; and since the Holy Spirit, at the time of the inspiration made suitable impressions on the affections of these writers, those who preach the Word should strive that the same affections would stir and inflame their souls. Preachers should be restless until they find their souls harmonizing and symphonizing with what the Holy Spirit of God inspired in the biblical writer at the time of his writing.[77] Mather advised: "Be not at rest until you find your heartstrings quiver at the touch upon the

---

73. Burgess, *The Art of Preaching*, 1881, 66–67.

74. Mather, *Student and Preacher*, 1789, 176.

75. Mather, *Student and Preacher*, 1789, 164.

76. Mather, *Student and Preacher*, 1789, 192–93.

77. Mather, *Student and Preacher*, 1789, 165–6.

heart of the writer, as being brought into a unison with it."[78] The result of such unison may be that the hearts of those addressed are inspired with devotion and an affection for godliness.[79]

All of this being very valuable, there is one thing more that is needed, that is, exemplification of what is involved in carrying out the appeal, what it looks like when it is applied. Illustrations of the closing appeals being complied with in life is indicative of a sermon conclusion that is the finest well-beaten oil in the sermon. In getting the appeals across, hearers are more responsive to a preacher who speaks to them clearly, going from the unknown to the known, by using examples with which they are familiar and relate to easily, that depicts for them the essence of the appeals being made to them.[80]

Decisiveness and the Ministry of Correction

Intellectual excitement is relatively without warmth. Intellectual enthusiasm for a proposition which has no special practical relation to those to whom it is being presented rarely has the force of real passion in it. The heating power in the nature of man is in its moral element, that is, how one conducts one's life based upon a biblical doctrine, proposition, insight, etc. Power and impulse come from the moral element. "The desire after practical usefulness is, therefore, indispensable to one who would preach well."[81] We need to understand doctrine and theology in order to understand how biblical truth is to affect how one lives. Doctrine bears implicit practical responsibilities. Every sermon is an unfolding of some doctrinal truth revealed in the Scriptures.[82] Preaching should be the exposition and application of a biblical text(s). The authority of a preacher sent by God is commensurate with an allegiance to, and a correct usage of, the text(s) of Scripture.[83] Ultimately, decisiveness is displayed in showing the practical implications of Scripture to bring correction into the lives of God's people.

As with the first sentence of the sermon introduction, the last sentence of the sermon conclusion should also make a significant impression.[84] The conclusion of a sermon should be marked by earnestness and force. "Close your sermons so that the hearer will say to himself, 'Were I to live a hundred years, I would never forget it.'"[85] The final words of a sermon conclusion should be to the sermon what an exclamation mark is to a sentence. It establishes a decisive declaration about a matter.

78. Mather, *Student and Preacher*, 1789, 166.

79. Mather, *Student and Preacher*, 1789, 194.

80. Parker, *Develop your Powers of Persuasion*, 133.

81. Storrs, *Conditions of Success in Preaching Without Notes*, 1875, 148–9.

82. Montoya, *Preaching with Passion*, 47.

83. Piper, *The Supremacy of God in Preaching*, 41.

84. Chapell, *Christ-centered Preaching*, 247.

85. Simpson, *Lectures on Preaching*, 1897, 153.

Regardless of the quality of the last sentence, the whole conclusion, or even the entire sermon, it must never be forgotten that a sermon will not impress the hearers beyond the character of the preacher as it is known and demonstrated among the hearers. That means, the obedient compliance to the truth of Scripture that a preacher proclaims to God's people must be in his life.[86]

The general matters of preachers and preaching are not incidental to doing excellent work in a sermon conclusion. They are integral. If the one who preaches is not a true pastor, and an earnest, personally passionate preacher, then a declaration of the vital content of a sermon conclusion is substantially lost. In this instance, the six elements of a sermon conclusion to be discussed in this book, though implemented, will provide only nominal improvement to one's preaching. As in constructing a brick wall, there must be bricks and there must be mortar. Mortar without bricks like bricks without mortar, does not a brick-wall make! The elements of a sermon conclusion are the bricks and the true pastor as an earnest and/or passionate preacher is the mortar. Both are essential.

Here is the point of this book—Even a passionate preacher who is a true pastor that supplies little to very little content in his sermon conclusion is problematic. The solution? He needs substance, the significant substance that can be provided by a skillful usage of the six elements of a sermon conclusion to which we will now give our attention.

---

86. Piper, *The Supremacy of God in Preaching*, 101.

5

A Synopsis of the Sermon Structure

"Is there an actual correlation between knowing a conclusion is about to begin and being dismissive about it? "Yes" and "NO"! "Yes," when the hearers know that the preacher has a proven track-record of saying almost nothing in his conclusions. In this instance, hearers will be, and should be, dismissive of a preacher whose conclusions are just a waste of time. This is the result of a negatively trained cause and effect scenario. The hearers make a justified response, auditory indifference, to a preacher's advertisement of verbalized impertinence. But let's not lose sight of the problem. In such a case, the problem is not that the preacher lets the hearers know he is about to conclude. The problem is that the preacher does not know how to effectively conclude a sermon. That is the problem. And until this problem is addressed and corrected, it is a moot discussion to consider the merit or lack of merit in alerting hearers that the conclusion is about to begin. . . . However, the answer is a definite "NO!" when the hearers have been trained positively by a preacher's proven track-record that very significant substance, the most significant substance of the sermon, is provided in his sermon conclusions. In this instance, hearers will not be dismissive of the cue that the highpoint of the sermon is about to begin."

"An expository preacher wants his hearers to understand how they are to respond to the purpose of the biblical text that was expounded. A clear understanding between what has taken place, a biblical text thoroughly explained, and what is about to take place, a challenge to apply the purpose of the text in life, along with biblical insights necessary to do so, is not only appropriate but beneficial for both the hearers and the preacher. What Bible expositor would not want his hearers to understand what are the valid implications of the text which has been expounded? What preacher would seek to withhold strategic, crucial, personal insights needed for them to flesh out the truths of the text in their lives? What Bible expositor would not want to prepare his

hearers to make the most of what is about to come their way as he tells them how the purpose of the exposited text can become truths that are personally fleshed-out in their lives? . . . They should know that they have arrived at the last and most significant part of the sermon."

"Not only is the presence of a synopsis in the sermon conclusion significant, but its placement in the conclusion is most vital when it begins the conclusion of the sermon. A synopsis of the message is a clear and effective means by which hearers can be alerted to the fact that the sermon conclusion is at hand."

"When a synopsis is placed at the beginning of a conclusion, it functions to 'look forward as well as backward.' The backward look clearly establishes for the hearers that the discussion the text received . . . was completed in the sermon body as the text was explained, illustrated, and applied in a point by point fashion. The forward look that the synopsis portends is related to achieving the purpose of the sermon in the lives of the hearers."

"The purpose of the sermon, as announced in the sermon introduction, is predominantly a matter of unfinished business. . . . In the conclusion, the hearers are provided the application, not to specific preaching points found in the body of the sermon, but application regarding the purpose of the sermon. The application of the conclusion addresses how they are to live to accomplish the purpose of the preaching passage. The application of the sermon conclusion will be in the form of the closing appeals which address what the hearers are to do so that their daily living conforms to God's purpose for the preaching passage. By no means is the sermon just about over when the sermon conclusion begins. The crux of the sermon has yet to be accomplished. It is significant that the hearers be given a forward look at the beginning of the sermon conclusion. They need to be directed to what is yet to be discovered even more than what has been discovered."

"The importance of the forward look, of which the synopsis portends, may be more vital as it gives the hearers a sense of anticipation. The sense of anticipation is derived as the hearers understand that the preacher is about to discuss crucial considerations which may enable them to live out the purpose of the sermon in their lives. As valuable as it is for the hearers to have assurance that they have grasped the meaning of the text accurately, it is even more valuable for the hearers to anticipate that they are about to receive the motivation, the benefits, or the ways and means by which they can live out the purpose of the text faithfully."

"As a preacher is concluding his sermon to his hearers, he is much like a lawyer who is presenting his closing arguments to the jurors. As with a lawyer, so with the preacher. He must bring to remembrance the case he is making and each one of the

main points, or arguments, which substantiates the case he is making. But more so for the preacher than the lawyer, it is necessary to state in unbroken succession the structure of the sermon—the propositional statement and each main point—and by compression gain cumulative force."

"The ultimate understanding of a sermon conclusion and the ultimate work to be accomplished in the sermon conclusion is related to the will of the hearers. . . . The assault on the hearers' wills must, of course, take place in the context of a preached message. A synopsis of the preached message provides the validity, necessity, and the integrity for what is said in the conclusion as the hearers' wills are targeted for responding to the purpose of the text in daily living."

"The synopsis establishes the transitional link between what has been discussed, the explanation of the text, and what must be discussed, our necessary response to the purpose of the text in daily life. In other words, the transition is from knowing to doing. This requires persuasion. Persuasion is the crowning impression of a preached sermon—persuasion about the truth of the text and persuasion about what to do, what not to do, how to live the truth about which one has been persuaded. The volitional persuasion about living a certain way in application of the text constitutes the essence of the sermon's purpose. The purpose of the sermon is achieved primarily through the insights disclosed in the sermon conclusion."

IS A SERMON CONCLUSION A COVERT OPERATION?

The starting point for establishing good work in a sermon conclusion in the act of preaching is to establish the fact that the sermon conclusion *is about to begin*. A clear understanding on behalf of the hearers that the sermon conclusion is about to begin is a scenario that some homeliticians decry. The thinking seems to be along this line: the conclusion, as it is delivered, and however it is delivered, needs to be delivered before the hearers know that is about to take place. And, having been delivered, the conclusion should be completed before the hearers realized it had begun.

The need to "take'em by surprise" is the advocated mode of concluding sermons by some who write and teach in the field of preaching. As an example of this, David Buttrick writes about the necessity of a sermon conclusion to establish a "reflective consciousness" but "The trick here is to create a reflective consciousness without tipping off a congregation to the fact that a conclusion is taking place. Any time congregations begin to realize, 'Here comes a conclusion,' they are apt to . . . cease listening."[1] The "sneak attack" has always had its advocates and still has them today. Of course, Buttrick is not alone in this unfortunate and misdirected instruction. The same preference has been advocated in similar prescriptive renditions.

1. Buttrick, *Homiletic: Moves and Structures*, 101.

Consider the following precepts designed to dissuade preachers from providing a verbal indication that the conclusion is about to begin. The following precept is a good one to get the feel for an aversion to overt conclusions: "Do not announce that you are concluding—or not often, and never twice in the same sermon."[2] Additionally, overt conclusions are dissuaded by the instruction that what is termed as a "taboo" is any expressed intention of concluding couched in terms such as "'in conclusion' or 'as we close' or 'finally.' It is best to conclude without announcing your intention."[3] Again, advocacy for covert conclusions is made by the counsel that, "Indeed it may not be wise to let it be known that you are bringing your sermon to a close. Close before your people think about it."[4] Contemplate the following to establish the thought process for concluding a sermon in a covert fashion: "While the conclusion need not take the congregation by surprise, the preacher does not have to give verbal or visual signals that the sermon is nearly done. Nothing psychologically is gained by saying or suggesting, 'I'm almost through. Bear with me a little longer!'"[5]

Formidable persuasion against overt conclusions was produced by the argument that there is no need to tell our congregations that we intend to conclude by using a verbal cue, such as "finally" or "in conclusion." Words such as these "should be used sparingly. In a well-planned sermon, conclusions should conclude without announcing their appearance."[6] One final sentiment is offered for a nonverbal indication for a conclusion's beginning:

> It is best not to announce the conclusion. Let your manner and thought indicate the culmination. If you say, "finally" or "in conclusion" in this culture you have tacitly told everyone to stop looking at you and to glance at their watches. Of course, if the sermon has lulled listeners into oblivion, an announcement can serve as a final, desperate effort to raise the eyelids of those who have abandoned hope for an end.[7]

In all the variety of the above counsel to not verbally indicate the conclusion's beginning, I believe there are some beneficial take-aways *to aid in verbally indicating that the conclusion is about to begin.* I find three points of agreement with the men quoted above regarding a verbal cue that a conclusion is about to begin. They and I agree that these three points must be honored as one verbally indicates one's intention to conclude a sermon. First, the indication to conclude the sermon, as it will be provided in this book, must not be made more than once. Second, such phrases as "finally," or "in conclusion," or "let's bring this to a close" emphasize the wrong thing, set a wrong

2. Sangster, *The Craft of Sermon Construction*, 149.

3. Baumann, *An Introduction to Contemporary Preaching*, 145.

4. Evans, *How to Prepare Sermons and Gospel Addresses*, 1913, 108.

5. Cox, *A Guide to Biblical Preaching*, 187.

6. Robinson, *Biblical Preaching*, 171.

7. Chapell, *Christ-centered Preaching*, 251–2.

tone and, therefore, should be avoided strictly. Third, the net effect of causing people to check their watches, to cause them to think about leaving the worship service rather than causing them to be ambitious about capturing the essence of the sermon which is about to be offered to them, is a major error as it undermines what the entire sermon has been intended to accomplish. These three rays of truth are valuable, indeed, to allow one to proceed to the conclusion with optimal productivity as one indicates as clearly as possible that the conclusion is at hand.

Still, the question I must raise is, why would a preacher desire to handle a sermon conclusion in a clandestine fashion? Is there any merit, any real benefit, in a covert operation of concluding a sermon? The surprise tactic for a sermon conclusion seems to me to be analogous to the situation in which a nurse distracts a young child who is about to receive his first vaccination shot. Once distracted, the doctor "sticks it to him" before he knew what happened or could even suspect what was about to happen. Is a sermon conclusion the sermonic equivalent to a vaccination shot for its hearers? I think not! There is no need to conceal the sermon conclusion! It is the highpoint of the sermon! Why would anyone want to conceal that?

A SIGN THAT THE END IS NEAR

Is there an actual correlation between knowing a conclusion is about to begin and being dismissive about it? "Yes" and "NO"! "Yes," when the hearers know that the preacher has a proven track-record of saying almost nothing in his conclusions. In this instance, hearers will be, and should be, dismissive of a preacher whose conclusions are just a waste of time. This is the result of a negatively trained cause and effect scenario. The hearers make a justified response, auditory indifference, to a preacher's advertisement of verbalized impertinence. But let's not lose sight of the problem. In such a case, the problem is not that the preacher lets the hearers know he is about to conclude. The problem is that the preacher does not know how to effectively conclude a sermon. That is the problem. And until this problem is addressed and corrected, it is a moot discussion to consider the merit or lack of merit in alerting hearers that the conclusion is about to begin. The preacher needs to become effective in concluding his sermons, then he can contemplate the question concerning the advisability of an overt or a covert qualitative conclusion.

However, the answer is a definite "NO!" when the hearers have been trained positively by a preacher's proven track-record that very significant substance, the most significant substance of the sermon, is provided in his sermon conclusions. In this instance, hearers will not be dismissive of the cue that the highpoint of the sermon is about to begin. Why would it be advantageous to withhold insight that such a good thing is about to occur? When the best is about to be offered, who would argue that this must not be made known? That is completely illogical! There will be no dismissiveness to a preacher who is skilled in concluding his sermons when he alerts his hearers that the conclusion is about to begin.

Fortunately, a very capable concluder of sermons, Chuck Swindoll, takes a different perspective about sermon conclusions as "sneak attacks." His view is that a conclusion needs to be apparent. His counsel, in a number of ways, is to the point and is persuasive as he writes, "Your audience should sense when you're beginning your approach (to concluding your message). A well-planned transition will signal the change."[8] The rationale for a clear transition to the conclusion is that it is necessary to satisfy "the audience's desire for a feeling of closure."[9] He makes a case that a good conclusion is overt, not covert. A conclusion cannot bring the satisfaction of closure if it is over before they knew it had begun. In fact, he makes a convincing point as he argues that, "A message without a conclusion feels like someone turning and walking away in the middle of an interesting conversation. A hasty, unplanned final conclusion is rude, leaving the audience feeling abruptly dismissed, like they aren't important to you."[10]

Additionally, Swindoll obliterates the idea that an audience's awareness that a conclusion is about to begin dissipates their interest. In fact, he asserts that he is aware of increased attentiveness as he makes it very certain that he is transitioning to the sermon conclusion. With no intent or methodology to provide a sneak attack on his hearers, but rather just the opposite, he testifies to the anticipation that people can have to a conclusion that is obviously apparent.

> With that clear shift from exposition to application, I usually see people shift in their seats to change posture. If they've been sagging a little, they perk up. If they haven't been taking notes, they will often pull a piece of paper out of a purse or a pocket and prepare to jot down the upcoming points. Some literally move to the edge of their seats or lean forward. . . . (T)heir hearts crave to know "So what?" Their body language urges me to offer some answers.[11]

> The transitions between elements help the audience subconsciously learn your pattern as a speaker so that, when you reach the end, the transition to the conclusion feels just like any other. They will know you're headed for the home stretch, but they stay with you. Very often, when I transition to the conclusion, people unconsciously close their Bibles and assume a different posture; they know we're coming in for a smooth landing (hopefully!).[12]

Chuck Swindoll is, in my opinion, the best concluder of sermons by any preacher I have heard over an extended timeframe. At the time of this writing, I have heard him preach for over forty years. Given that kind of exposure, he has provided consistent

8. Swindoll, *Saying It Well*, 212.

9. Swindoll, *Saying It Well*, 228.

10. Swindoll, *Saying It Well*, 228.

11. Swindoll, *Saying It Well*, 214.

12. Swindoll, *Saying It Well*, 234.

effectiveness in his conclusions. I have heard other preachers do fine work in a sermon conclusion, but their fine work is exceptional work for them, work they seldom achieve. However, for Swindoll, less than really good work in concluding his sermons is atypical and, therefore, only occasional. In reference to Swindoll, an effective conclusion, in my opinion, is a commonplace reality.

Swindoll is not a lone advocate for overtly informing hearers that a sermon is transitioning from the body to the conclusion. The view that it is advantageous to overtly transition to the conclusion is not a new concept but rather a longstanding one. Take for example the following, "As a general rule the preacher does well to let it be known, even in so many words, if necessary, that he is about to conclude his discourse."[13] Many years ago one writer asserted, "Upon the whole, therefore, we strongly incline to a set conclusion, and even to some intelligible information to our hearers, that we are about to enter upon it." A verbal cue for a conclusion acts as "a signal for increased attention."[14] Yet, perhaps no one has weighed in more fully than Ilion T. Jones when he stated this very effective argument:

> A transitional phrase is needed at the beginning of the conclusion as a "bridge word" to tie it to the body the sermon. Without it, the conclusion comes as a surprise, or even a shock, to the congregation. Some think it far better for the congregation to awake suddenly to the fact that the conclusion is not only under way but ending rather than be told it is about to begin. Announcing the conclusion, they feel, is a signal for the hearer to put his mind on getting ready to leave, and therefore a sure way to lose his attention. But there is another side to the question. . . . It was suggested that transitions aid the listener in following more easily the progress of thought and at the same time prepare him psychologically for the next step of the journey. If that be true, there is every reason why he should know that he has arrived at the last lap of the journey. If that lap is interesting it not only holds his attention but brings him to his destination with appreciation, inspiration, and aspiration.[15]

Obviously, there is and has been a split decision about announcing one's intent to transition to the conclusion.

But to the point of overt transitions from sermon bodies to sermon conclusions, I think it needs to be said that, especially in expository preaching where the preacher is doing everything he can to make known, to make clear, the understanding of a biblical text, that the surprise tactic of a sermon conclusion would be inappropriate. What Bible expositor would want his hearers to be confused that what is said in a sermon conclusion is still the exposition of the preaching text?[16]

13. Pattison, *The Making of the Sermon*, 186.

14. Moore, *Thoughts on Preaching*, 1861, 140.

15. Jones, *Principles and Practice of Preaching*, 162–3.

16. There will be times when it may be deemed valuable to intentionally skip a portion of the text, not explaining it in the body of the sermon. This would be done because the explanation will be given

Additionally, an expository preacher wants his hearers to understand how they are to respond to the purpose of the biblical text that was expounded. A clear understanding between what has taken place, a biblical text thoroughly explained, and what is about to take place, a challenge to apply the purpose of the text in life, along with biblical insights necessary to do so, is not only appropriate but beneficial for both the hearers and the preacher. What Bible expositor would not want his hearers to understand what are the valid implications of the text's purpose which has been expounded? What preacher would seek to withhold strategic, crucial, personal insights needed for them to flesh out the truths of the text in their lives? What Bible expositor would not want to prepare his hearers to make the most of what is about to come their way as he tells them how the purpose of the exposited text can become truths that are personally fleshed-out in their lives?

Since transitions aid hearers in following more easily the progress of thought and at the same time prepare them for the next part of the sermon there is all-the-more reason why they should know that they have arrived at the last and most significant part of the sermon. If the conclusion is transitioned to in a vital manner, it will aid them in receiving the greatest benefit from the most important part of the sermon.

THE GATEWAY FROM THE SERMON BODY TO THE CONCLUSION

So, the question is this—How can a preacher establish for his hearers that the exposition of the text has been completed and that the sermon conclusion is about to begin? If, indeed, it is appropriate and beneficial to distinguish between the completed work of the sermon body and the initial work of the sermon conclusion, how can this be done productively? Remember, we want to not employ the unproductive terms of "finally" or "in conclusion" or "let's bring this to a close." How do we avoid these terms and yet make it clear to the hearers that we are about to begin the sermon conclusion? Providing a synopsis of the sermon proposition and each of the main points of the sermon is a means by which the hearers can discern, discern very clearly, that the work of expounding the text has been accomplished and the work of addressing what is necessary to live out the purpose of the text is about to begin.

By synopsis, I mean a restating of the sermon's proposition and each point of main structure.[17] This lets everyone know that what was intended to be discussed in

---

in the conclusion since that portion of the preaching text is uniquely appropriate material with which to conclude the sermon. The explanation of this portion of the text, being provided in the conclusion may become the spearhead of the conclusion as it provides the natural or most beneficial way to conclude the sermon.

17. A synopsis that recaps the Plural Noun Proposition and the main structure provides unsurpassed clarity that a transition from the body of the sermon to the sermon conclusion has occurred. However, in analyzing sermons contained in Scripture, one finds only *the concept of a synopsis* that establishes the gateway to the conclusion, but never in the form of *a reiteration of the main assertions* of the sermon body. Still, the functional transition from the body of the sermon to the conclusion

the body of the sermon has been discussed. Therefore, the exposition of the text has been completed but what remains is to consider what is necessary for every hearer to be able to incorporate the purpose of the exposited text in their lives. This is the role that the sermon conclusion must accomplish.

The synopsis of the sermon placed at the beginning of a sermon conclusion is a very beneficial element. The synopsis becomes a gateway out of the body of the sermon into the sermon conclusion. As such, the synopsis is the verbal indicator that announces the fact that the sermon is transitioning away from the body of the sermon to the conclusion of the sermon. It is the most important transition to this point in the sermon. Therefore, to understand the significance that the synopsis has in a sermon conclusion, we will consider seven insights in the form of "the synopsis *as,*" one insight in the form of "the synopsis *and,*" then one insight in the form of "the synopsis *when.*"

The Synopsis as an Improvement of the Hearer's Grasp of the Sermon

Stating a synopsis of the message at the beginning of the sermon conclusion provides immeasurable help to grasp the complete meaning of the sermon that was preached. R. L. Dabney stated that a good synopsis is "the best expedient for fixing in the hearer's memory" the structure of the sermon, which was the major assertions of the discussion of the text.[18] The significance of the sermon being fixed in the hearer's memory is obvious—If the hearers do not grasp the meaning of the message on the day it is preached then they will never be able to remember the message subsequently.

There is a twofold sense in which the meaning of the sermon may be grasped—on the day it is preached, and the days after its preaching. It is paramount that meaning is grasped by the hearers on the day that the sermon is preached. Every good effect

---

of the sermon is quite apparent and varied in its form. In the sermon on the mount, the transition from the body of the sermon to the conclusion is made in 7:21 by a shift in reference to time, from now to then. Matthew 7:21 reads: "Not everyone who says to Me, 'Lord, Lord,' will enter the kingdom of heaven, but he who does the will of My Father who is in heaven will enter." In Peter's sermon on Pentecost, Peter's transition is found in Acts 2:32 as he brings correction to the identity of himself and the eleven as being witnesses of the resurrected Christ, whom they had crucified. Peter's attestation of their being witnesses of Christ's resurrection compounds and clarifies his initial assertion of the sermon that he and the eleven were not men who were drunk. Stephen's sermon in Acts 7 transitions from the sermon body to the conclusion in Acts 7:51 with his painfully clear transition from Israel's history to the present-day repetition of the same sinful reality of the heart that epitomized the history of Israel. Specifically, Stephen said: "You men who are stiff-necked and uncircumcised in heart and ears are always resisting the Holy Spirit: you are doing just as your fathers did." The Epistle to the Hebrews provides a transition to the conclusion of this epistle/sermon by means of a very general summary of the essence of its content. This transition is found in 12:1–2 with the words: "Therefore, since we have such a great cloud of witnesses surrounding us, let us also lay aside every encumbrance and the sin which so easily entangles us, fixing our eyes on Jesus, the author and perfecter of faith, who for the joy set before Him endured the cross, despising its shame, and has set down at the right hand of the throne of God." There is clear evidence in these biblical sermons of a transition to the content that comprises the conclusion of the sermons.

18. Dabney, *Sacred Rhetoric,* 1870, 173.

acquired through preaching is minimized when the hearers do not understand what the preacher is talking about and what he is saying about what he's talking about. It is crucial that the hearers are brought to a point of good understanding as soon as possible. And if it should be that some hearers are never able to accurately grasp the unfolding of the message as it is preached, how very important it is that they come to an accurate understanding of what was preached at the beginning of the sermon conclusion.

A synopsis of the message stated at the beginning of the conclusion will provide a "safety-net" for this much-needed clarity. As Swindoll writes, "If they haven't captured it (the essence of the sermon) beforehand, they'll need to grasp it in the conclusion."[19] The ability to establish in the conclusion the essence of the sermon in the understanding of the hearers is no insignificant matter. In evaluating sermons preached in seminary preaching labs for thirty-plus years, I can attest to the benefit of providing the synopsis at the beginning of the sermon conclusion. There have been times when the structure of the sermon was unclear and I was lost in the sermon, only to have it clarified by the synopsis at the beginning of the conclusion. The benefit of the synopsis is never as certain as on such an unfortunate occasion as this. The meaning of the phrase, "Better late than never!" has an ultimate validity at such a time as that.

A synopsis that begins a sermon conclusion can help to etch the understanding of the message, though clear on the day it was heard, so well in the minds of the hearers that it can be remembered days after the sermon has been preached. So, whether we are talking about the immediate grasp or even the long-range grasp of the meaning of the message, a synopsis of the sermon is a helpful means by which either one, or both, may be accomplished. A synopsis of the sermon proposition and main points stated in the conclusion of the sermon that clarifies the structure of the sermon and makes the sermon memorable, whether for a day or for many days, is very beneficial. Ian Macpherson was of this persuasion as he wrote:

> There is much to commend . . . a useful summary of the message, the concentrated epitome of its central content! Not only am I in favor of giving one's points at the beginning of the sermon; I also wholeheartedly endorse the practice of going over them again . . . at the end. . . . I do most definitely believe that many discourses would benefit immeasurably in distinctness and decisiveness and, what is more, would be infinitely more rememberable—a by no means inconsiderable matter!—if only those who deliver them would be at pains to recapitulate their points at the close.[20]

Many have written about the benefit of providing a synopsis of the sermon in the conclusion. Not only is the presence of a synopsis in the sermon conclusion significant, but its placement in the conclusion is most vital when it begins the conclusion of the

19. Swindoll, *Saying It Well*, 228.
20. Macpherson, *The Burden of the Lord*, 115.

sermon. A synopsis of the message is a clear and effective means by which hearers can be alerted to the fact that the sermon conclusion is at hand.

The Synopsis as a Crucial Nexus between the Sermon Body and the Sermon Conclusion

Ilion T. Jones lists two of his five component parts of the conclusion as: "a proper transition or connective" and "some reference to the truth just unfolded."[21] What is meant as a synopsis in the sermon conclusion, or in the words of Jones, "some reference to the truth just unfolded," which he also calls a "resume," is a brief restatement of the sermon proposition and the main points of the sermon. As such, a synopsis serves as a nexus between the body the sermon and the sermon conclusion, or what Jones calls a proper transition or connective. The first element of a sermon conclusion—a synopsis—fulfills both functions as it connects the body to the conclusion by reminding them what the sermon was about, as the sermon proposition and each main point of the sermon is stated for the last time.

When a synopsis is placed at the beginning of a conclusion, it functions to "look forward as well as backward."[22] The backward look clearly establishes for the hearers that the discussion the text received, as promised by the preacher in his sermon introduction through the statement of his sermon proposition, was completed in the sermon body as the text was explained, illustrated, and applied in a point by point fashion. The forward look that the synopsis portends is related to achieving the purpose of the sermon in the lives of the hearers.

The purpose of the sermon, as announced in the sermon introduction, is predominantly a matter of unfinished business, in that, the hearers need to be provided a supplement of ways and means by which they can live out the truth of the text that was explained and applied in the sermon. In other words, through the application contained in the sermon body the hearers have been challenged about the implications that each portion of the preaching text has for them.[23] This is done in a point by point fashion progressing through each point of the sermon. The application found in the body of the sermon, consisting of implications of the explained textual truths, relates to what bearing the text has for the lives of the hearers, what they are to do in

---

21. Jones, *Principles and Practice of Preaching*, 162–4. Jones's other three components are significant and listed as: some material designed to drive the truth home and clinch it; some material designed to persuade the hearer to accept the truth and do something about it; and a strong concluding sentence. Jones, *Principles and Practice of Preaching*, 164–5).

22. Jones, *Principles and Practice of Preaching*, 164.

23. See Appendix A in the back of this book for an analysis of application methodology implemented by Jesus in the Sermon on the Mount and the Apostle Peter's sermon preached on the day of Pentecost. The application approaches, moving from doctrinal understanding to the personal ramifications of scriptural truth, are "implications" of specific doctrinal instruction.

response to the truths of the text being preached, and how they are to implement these truths in their lives.

In the conclusion, the hearers are provided the application, not to specific preaching points found in the body of the sermon, but application regarding the purpose of the sermon, the purpose statement which was announced in the sermon introduction.[24] The application of the conclusion addresses how they are to live in order to accomplish the purpose of the preaching passage, not the particular points of the preaching passage. The application of the sermon conclusion will be in the form of the closing appeals. The closing appeals address what the hearers are to do so that their daily living conforms to God's purpose for the preaching passage. The closing appeals address how they are to do what is required of them to accomplish God's purpose for the preaching passage in their daily living. Distinguishing the difference between application and implication yields the following; the application found in the body of the sermon is more implication than application; the application found in the sermon conclusion is application proper; the application in the conclusion is related to the purpose for the sermon; the application in the sermon body is related to the sermon points, the truths of the preaching passage.

Therefore, by no means is the sermon just about over when the sermon conclusion begins. The crux of the sermon has yet to be accomplished. It is significant that the hearers be given a forward look at the beginning of the sermon conclusion. They need to be directed to what has yet to be discovered even more than what has been discovered.

Through the backward look of the synopsis, a major consideration for the hearers' accurate understanding of what was taught has been provided. As W. E. Sangster instructed, "The people must see that it (the preached sermon) is a whole. The unity of the sermon must be clear in its final moments and a grand sense of completeness must lie in their minds."[25] This will be achieved most effectively by a synopsis which begins the conclusion of the sermon.

This synopsis, however, must restate the sermon proposition as well as each main point of the sermon. Without a restatement of the sermon proposition along with the restatement of each main point in the sermon, the hearers will be reminded only of the sermon's diversity and will not be reminded of the sermon's unity. Haddon Robinson is very helpful to establish the significance of this as he insists that the benefit of a synopsis in a sermon conclusion is that it allows a preacher to look "back over the terrain and restate the points covered along the way. In doing this, however, he reviews the important assertions in order to bind them into the big idea (proposition) of the sermon."[26] Again, Robinson is helpful as he asserts that a synopsis that restates only the main points of the sermon is inadequate because the hearers will "leave with

24. For a thorough discussion of sermon introductions, see my book, *How Effective Sermons Begin*.

25. Sangster, *The Craft of Sermon Construction*, 149.

26. Robinson, *Biblical Preaching*, 168.

a basketful of fragments but no adequate sense of the whole. . . . Preachers, like their audiences, may conceive of sermons as a collection of points that have little relationship to each other. . . . An outline is the shape of the sermon idea, and the parts must be related to the whole. Three or four points not related to a more inclusive point do not make a message; they make three or four sermonettes all preached at one time."[27]

An effective synopsis, therefore, must restate the sermon proposition and each of the main points of the sermon as they were clarified through the exposition of the biblical text. The synopsis, then, summarizes the sermon body as it was preached completely. Only as the hearers are satisfied that this has occurred, will they be ready for the conclusion to come.

The Synopsis as Assurance and Anticipation

Not only does the synopsis of a sermon conclusion provide a backward look as well as a forward look, but each of these contain an inherent benefit for the hearers. An accurate understanding of the preached sermon provided by the backward look of the synopsis is significant as it gives the hearers a sense of assurance. The sense of assurance is derived as the hearers understand the discussion promised by the preacher has been delivered and it has been delivered completely.

Yet, the importance of the forward look, of which the synopsis portends, may be more vital as it gives the hearers a sense of anticipation. The sense of anticipation is derived as the hearers understand that the preacher is about to discuss crucial considerations which may enable them to live out the purpose of the sermon in their lives. As valuable as it is for the hearers to have assurance that they have grasped the meaning of the text accurately, it is even more valuable for the hearers to anticipate that they are about to receive the motivation, the benefits, or the ways and means by which they can live out the purpose of the text faithfully.

A synopsis provides assurance and anticipation. A synopsis provides assurance in the form of, "See, I've covered the ground which I proposed." Moreover, a synopsis provides anticipation in the form of answers to the following questions:

- "Okay, but now what?"
- "So what?"
- "What am I supposed to do about that?"
- "How are these things to affect me?"
- "How is all this supposed to change my life?"
- "How can I go from disobedience to this matter to obedience?"
- "How can I possibly live that way?"

27. Robinson, *Biblical Preaching*, 32.

- "What will it take for me to become obedient to God's purpose in my life?"

- "What is necessary for me in order to overcome the hurdles that have kept me, to this point in my life, from obeying God's purpose for this text in my life?"

The synopsis plays a significant role in the hearers' understanding of the content of the sermon but also for their conviction and persuasion regarding the content of the sermon. A brief, condensed restatement of the sermon proposition and each main point, stated in great proximity can provide additional conviction and persuasion about the preceding discussion. In addition, such a brief condensed thumbnail sketch of the sermon proposition and each main point, stated in great proximity, can lay a foundation for conviction and persuasion regarding the application about to be discussed in the conclusion.

Though it is crucial for the synopsis to include a restatement of the sermon proposition and each main point, it is just as crucial to understand that a restatement is just that, a restatement, not a re-preaching or an embellishment of the sermon proposition and main points. In restating the sermon proposition and main points, the preacher briefly provides the hearers with the key thoughts of the preceding exposition. The synopsis in the conclusion "should sound like hammer strokes, not sonatas."[28] How very crucial it is to understand that restatement necessitates restatement only, and nothing more. Nothing more than restatement is needed, and nothing more than restatement will be beneficial.

The significance of the backward thrust is simply for the sake of the forward progression of the sermon. Like the driver of an automobile who finds himself stuck in mud or snow, in order to go forward, he must acquire the momentum gained by putting the car in reverse, accelerating, then shifting the transmission into drive to make the needed forward progress. In preaching, forward progress is aided substantially by a backward thrust of providing a synopsis of the sermon at the nexus of the sermon body and sermon conclusion.

The Synopsis as Compressive Force

The value for a synopsis in the sermon conclusion is that by restating the sermon proposition and main points in a quick, compact progression, the essence of the sermon has a greater impression upon the heart and mind thus providing greater clarity and persuasion for the hearers.[29] Having invested the necessary time to establish each main point by means of expositing the portion of the text from which each point was drawn, the most productive thing that can be done to maximize this time and effort is to give a synopsis of the completed exposition and preaching of the text by

28. Chapell, *Christ-centered Preaching*, 245.
29. Potter, *Sacred Eloquence*, 1868, 308.

restating the sermon proposition and main structure at the beginning of his sermon conclusion.

As a preacher is concluding his sermon to his hearers, he is much like a lawyer who is presenting his closing arguments to the jurors. As with a lawyer, so with the preacher. He must bring to remembrance the case he is making. Each one of the main points, or arguments, substantiates the case he is making. But more so for the preacher than the lawyer, it is necessary to state in unbroken succession the structure of the sermon—the propositional statement and each main point—and by compression gain cumulative force.[30]

Beginning a sermon conclusion with a synopsis of the sermon proposition and main points is universally advantageous. However, the synopsis of the sermon conclusion is uniquely beneficial in expository preaching since the body of an expository sermon consists primarily of careful explanation and argument of the preaching passage in a point by point fashion. Having proceeded in this manner to the end of the preaching passage, it is valuable to restate them all together, "and concentrate their force upon one final effort of conviction or persuasion."[31]

The intention of expository preaching, rightly defined and implemented, is not only to expound the text of Scripture with great care and insight but to do so for the express purpose to clarify persuasively for the hearers how they must conduct their lives in light of the exposition and purposes of Scripture. Only in the conclusion can the ultimate persuasion for life-change be presented since the focus of the conclusion is about living the truth in life rather than understanding the preaching passage of Scripture. So, in expository preaching where the understanding of a biblical text does and should command the utmost consideration, the provision of a synopsis is ultimately beneficial to clarify to the hearers that there is now a movement away from the exposition of Scripture to a movement of challenging the hearers to, and instructing the hearers about, conforming their lives to the truth-claims of the Scriptures.

In sermons containing four or more main points, providing a synopsis at the beginning of the sermon conclusion will provide additional clarity, clarity which will be needed by most hearers, as well as providing the momentum needed to progress through the remainder of the conclusion. Regardless of the number or the nature of the sermon's main points, a synopsis is serviceable, yet in some instances it will be more serviceable than in others.

The Synopsis as a Completed Treatment of the Text

A synopsis clearly establishes that the treatment of the text has been completed as the proposition and main points are presented for the final time in one comprehensive collection. This produces "the finishing stroke that clinches the nails of argument"

---

30. Pattison, *The Making of the Sermon,* 178.

31. Broadus, *A Treatise on the Preparation and Delivery of Sermons,* 1870, 279.

as evidenced through the proposition and main structure. The synopsis most effectively establishes that the text has been treated completely when "it constitutes the beginning of the conclusion; and it is used as a transition from the discussion to the ultimate object of the sermon . . . and the crowning impression at the close."[32]

Though a synopsis often increases the power of a discourse by compressing its substance, thus strengthening the whole argument which allows it to be better understood and remembered, it can accomplish these things because "it is addressed to the intellect more than feelings."[33] The chief intellectual take-away from the synopsis stated at the beginning of the sermon conclusion is the certainty that the text has been considered completely and the completely considered text is clearly comprehended.

The fact that a preacher knows the first thing he will do in the conclusion of his sermon is to restate the sermon proposition and main structure compels him to do good work in constructing these crucial statements.[34] Austin Phelps made this connection between sermon structure and the synopsis of the sermon as he advised, "One of the most valuable single rules for constructing divisions is so to frame them that they can be easily and forcibly recapitulated at the close."[35] The advantage of a well-worded proposition and main points of a sermon comes to view in the synopsis when they are stated in quick succession, without any interruption.

The Synopsis as a Bundle of Established Truths

A synopsis of the main structure of the sermon, when collected and compressed in the conclusion, form a bundle of the "established truths" of the text, which should have been the most persuasive things said by the preacher throughout the sermon.[36] The synopsis of the message stated at the beginning of the sermon conclusion, provides for the hearers the essence of the message which was thoroughly established through the preaching of the sermon.

However, the importance of the synopsis may also be understood by considering what takes place when it is not provided. Without a synopsis in the conclusion, the last point of the sermon will occupy an undue weight in the mind of the hearers and force the weight of the previous ones to be lost partially. Through the means of the synopsis of the sermon found in the conclusion, the unity and diversity of the sermon is not only completely evident, but is equally evident.[37] By means of a synopsis of the sermon found in the conclusion, all the points of the sermon will be presented as a bundle of established truths. Sangster is clear about this as he advised, "It is true

32. Etter, *The Preacher and His Sermon*, 1885, 370.

33. Hoppin, *Homiletics*, 1883, 431.

34. For a detailed discussion of sermon structure, see my book, *How Effective Sermons Advance*.

35. Phelps, *The Theory of Preaching*, 1882, 521.

36. Vinet, *Homiletics*, 1854, 324.

37. Dabney, *Sacred Rhetoric*, 1870, 170.

that . . . a partial summary and application are natural and necessary at the end of each section, but when the conclusion of the whole is reached, it should conclude the whole. The relations of the earlier points must be shortly and skillfully tied up with the last one."[38] Therefore, a synopsis stated at the beginning of the sermon conclusion prevents the last point of the sermon from being emphasized to the negation of the previous points.

The Synopsis as a Pathway to the Will

A synopsis is valuable since final clarity about the message is important in the understanding of the hearers. We never want to discount this. As a carpenter drives a nail with successive hammer-blows, the truth of a sermon "needs to be driven home by the hammer-blows of repetition."[39] Though we should be serious that our hearers have a complete grasp of the essence of the sermon that was preached, we should be even more serious that they receive an accurate understanding of how the passage is to be implemented into their lives. Therefore, the conclusion should not be merely a synopsis of the essence of the text's meaning and essence of the sermon.[40] This is important because a sermon conclusion exists, ultimately, *to call the hearers to respond to the purpose of the sermon* which necessitates a response to what they have heard in *a completed sermon, which necessitates a completed sermon conclusion.*

Through the synopsis in the conclusion, any cognitive deficiencies about the sermon may be remedied, fully and finally. Remediation of cognitive deficiencies is essential so that the hearers can move productively from an accurate meaning of the text to an appropriate application of the text's purpose in their lives. In other words, there must be a movement from cognition to volition. We want them to understand what the essence of the sermon's content was, as a reasonable and rational gateway, so we can move productively to discuss the essence of the sermon in their daily conduct.

The ultimate understanding of a sermon conclusion and the ultimate work to be accomplished in the sermon conclusion is related to the will of the hearers. "An effective conclusion appeals to the will; it prompts the audience to action. That's the primary difference between teaching and preaching. Both provide helpful information, and both suggest ways to apply that new information to life, but as a matter of purpose and emphasis, preaching is all about urging action."[41]

The assault on the hearers' wills must, of course, take place in the context of a preached message. A synopsis of the preached message provides the validity, necessity, and the integrity for what is said in the conclusion as the hearers' wills are targeted for responding to the purpose of the text in daily living. Regarding a sermon conclusion's

38. Sangster, *The Craft of Sermon Construction,* 149.

39. Stott, *Between Two Worlds,* 246.

40. Stott, *Between Two Worlds,* 245.

41. Swindoll, *Saying It Well,* 228.

synopsis, Jean Claude wrote, "The fire of the preacher should blaze here; he should collect the ideas of his whole sermon into this part, as rays collected in the focus of the burning-glass, and inflame the hearts of his auditors."[42] The preacher's fire related to the synopsis of the message should be natural since he is now about to launch into the great work for which he preaches, that is, providing the insights needed by the hearers so that declared truth can be demonstrated truth in their lives.

The Synopsis and the Purpose of the Sermon

A synopsis enables a preacher, by distilling the essence of the sermon in summary form, to impress it upon the memory of his hearers, and make it converge more powerfully to achieve the great object of persuasion. The synopsis serves as a *functional* transition, functional in the sense that it provides a connection between the overall argument of the text made known by preaching the body of the sermon and the ultimate, or crowning, impression to be established in the content of the sermon conclusion.[43] However, the functional transition provided by a synopsis, as significant as it is, is not sufficient to provide the *vital* transition that is needed in a sermon conclusion, which is a separate element to be discussed in the next chapter.

The synopsis establishes the transitional link between what has been discussed, the explanation of the text, and what must be discussed, our necessary response to the purpose of the text in daily life. In other words, the transition is from knowing to doing. This requires persuasion. Persuasion is the crowning impression of a preached sermon—persuasion about the truth of the text and persuasion about what to do, what not to do, how to live the truth about which one has been persuaded. The volitional persuasion about living a certain way in application of the text constitutes the essence of the sermon's purpose. The purpose of the sermon is achieved primarily through the insights disclosed in the sermon conclusion.

So, the synopsis clarifies that the meaning of the text has been disclosed through the explanation of the text, explained point by point through the means of sermon structure, yet, the purpose of the sermon has not been satisfied completely. The synopsis then clarifies what has been accomplished completely and what is still yet to be accomplished—what practical necessities are required for the hearers to live in compliance to the text as it has been expounded.

The Synopsis when the Last Point of the Sermon Doubles as the Conclusion

A sermon should be practical throughout. The truth is presented and applied from beginning to end. And yet, even as this is the case, a more direct application of the

---

42. Claude, *Claude's Essay*, 1801, 132.
43. Kidder, *A Treatise on Homiletics*, 1864, 225.

truth is necessary in the conclusion. It most commonly happens that the consequent duties engendered by the truth explained need greater enforcement to the reason and conscience of the hearers, therefore, additional application is needed in the sermon conclusion. Occasionally, the final point and the final portion of the text to be expounded[44] provides the most significant insights found in the entire canon of Scripture which are necessary to achieve the purpose for the sermon so completely that other references from Scripture are not needed. When this is the reality, a separate sermon conclusion is not needed and should not be attempted.[45] In other words, a great sermon may finish with the final point serving as the conclusion. However, all the elements of a formal conclusion must be accomplished in the last point, in addition to the exposition of the portion of text which comprises the final point of the sermon.[46] When the last point doubles effectively as the sermon conclusion, the restatement of the previous points serve as the synopsis of the sermon structure and the transition to the conclusion in this instance.

A synopsis is beneficial for transitioning clearly and intentionally to the final thrust of the sermon—the conclusion. This is true if the conclusion is of the ordinary instance where it is supplemental to the text that was expounded, or if it is of the occasional instance where the conclusion is composed of the last point of the sermon and the last portion of the text to be expounded. Either way it may occur, a synopsis prepares the hearers to consider the conclusion of the sermon with heightened clarity, awareness, and anticipation.

44. On rare occasions, a portion of the preaching passage other than the final portion will provide the substance for the conclusion. In such instances, this portion will be intentionally skipped, not expounded in the body of the sermon, but is explained and applied in the conclusion.

45. Garvie, *The Christian Preacher*, 1921, 441.

46. Davis, *Design for Preaching*, 193.

6

A Vital Transition to the Conclusion

"The idea of a sermon conclusion needing a vital transition is ludicrous if the conclusion itself is not of a vital nature. What is the value of a vital transition to an insignificant portion of a sermon? How meaningless is that? Because of the low thinking about, and inferior product of, sermon conclusions, a bit of redundancy is in order. It must be understood that a sermon conclusion is not material tacked onto a sermon that has been completed. Without a conclusion, a sermon has not been preached to completion. In fact, the purpose for preaching the sermon has yet to be accomplished in its fullest sense. Without a conclusion, the only thing that has been completed is the exposition of the text. The conclusion is needed to clarify the response to the purpose of the text that has been expounded."

"How unfulfilling would it be if the NFL season ended 2 weeks prior to the Super Bowl with the crowning of the AFC champion and the crowning of the NFC champion? Beyond unfulfilling, this would be bizarre! It would be intolerable! It would be known intuitively that this is not right! Nothing has been finalized! The post-season has not been concluded. The Matter Has Not Been Settled! With great vehemence it would be declared by very many people that this is no way for an NFL post-season to end! Nothing is resolved by having two champions in one year. . . . It is unacceptable for the whole matter to be ended, unresolved! Yet, there is no such demand or insistence for satisfactory endings when it comes to preaching sermons from the Word of God! Week after week, most sermons suffer the repeated fate of unresolved endings! Perhaps, the initial point for making enhancement in the work of concluding sermons is to care as much about sermon conclusions as we do about conclusions to NFL post-seasons! Perhaps the ultimate point for making enhancement in the work of concluding sermons is that the great thing to be accomplished on any Lord's Day is a well-concluded sermon."

"The content composing the vital transition to the sermon conclusion should contain 'the most striking, interesting sentiments possible.' But what makes for the 'most striking, interesting sentiments possible?' The most interesting sentiments possible should be those that are in relation to the purpose of the sermon which, despite all the preaching that has taken place in the body of the sermon, the purpose for the sermon has yet to be accomplished fully. The requirement of the most striking, interesting sentiments possible will be met as a verbal cue such as 'So,' 'But,' 'However,' 'Yet,' is connected to the purpose of the sermon combined with questions and assertions regarding the lives of the hearers."

"A preacher must understand the epic significance of his context in preaching as he transitions to the sermon conclusion. He is at the most important part of the message, yet his hearers find themselves in a state where they are the most fatigued. They are no longer fresh, as they were when the sermon began. Ideally, they have followed the preacher well. They have been engaged in the difficult battle to follow in a focused fashion the explanation of many, and perhaps, very difficult matters of the preaching text. If they are to maximize their opportunity to be a ready recipient of the most significant instruction of the entire sermon, then they will need help from the one who is preaching to them. He simply must help them prepare to receive maximum benefit from the sermon conclusion. The preacher must understand this as his responsibility and fulfill it. A vital transition indicates that very crucial content lies ahead in the sermon conclusion."

MORE THAN FUNCTIONALITY REQUIRED

In the previous chapter we discussed the first of six elements for a sermon conclusion, the synopsis. The synopsis provides a *functional* transition. The kind of transition provided by the synopsis is functional because it serves the necessary task to establish for the last time what the sermon has been about to this point—the understanding of the text through preaching the body of the sermon in a point by point fashion. The synopsis accomplishes a functional transition in that it accomplishes what must be done, that is, to provide understanding that a significant transition is about to take place: a transition away from the body of the sermon to the conclusion of the sermon; a transition away from exposition to ultimate application; a transition away from cognition to volition; a transition away from knowing to doing; a transition away from the essence of the sermon, it's proposition and main structure, to the purpose of the sermon; a transition from living as one has been living to living as one must live according to the revealed canon of Scripture.

The vital transition moves the thought process back to the purpose statement that was announced in the sermon introduction, to return to the purpose of the sermon to make ultimate headway with it. Since the purpose of the sermon is indicative of the ultimate take-away for the hearers, the transition used to bring the hearers back to this most crucial element needs to be more than the functional transition provided by the synopsis. What is needed is the second element of a sermon conclusion—the vital transition; a transition that will bring the hearers to the biblical insights that will facilitate their compliance to the expounded text, thus, thoroughly accomplishing the purpose of the sermon.

Each component of the sermon plays a valuable part for the sermon to be a successful one. However, if each component is to contribute to one unified message, then each component must be linked together by meaningful transitions. As significant as a transition is from the sermon introduction to the first point of the sermon, and from each sermon point to every subsequent sermon point, so a transition from the last point of the sermon body to the conclusion is necessary. In fact, I have argued already that this transition, the functional transition provided by the synopsis linking the sermon body to the sermon conclusion, is the most significant transition that has occurred to this juncture of the sermon. Yet the functional transition must be eclipsed by a more significant transition, the vital transition.

Transitions not only tie the components of the sermon together they also make certain the progression and direction of the message to the hearer. Transitions not only point forward they also relate present matters to the previous discussion. Consistent tiebacks to the sermon's main concepts clue the hearer as to "which thoughts are major, which are minor, and how they relate."[1] The functional transition of the synopsis, given at the beginning of the sermon conclusion, certainly accomplishes this and is, therefore, the most significant transition of the sermon thus far. Yet, it must be understood that it is of penultimate significance. It quickly must be upstaged by the ultimate transition of the sermon—the vital transition. The vital transition transitions from the synopsis of the sermon structure to a reintroduction of the sermon's purpose statement. Regarding the reintroduced purpose statement, questions and assertions will be made regarding it. This is done to clarify the issue at hand, that all that is to be said for the remainder of the sermon will be about achieving the purpose of the sermon in the lives of the hearers.

THE CONCLUSION AS THE SERMON'S SUPER BOWL

The idea of a sermon conclusion needing a vital transition is ludicrous if the conclusion itself is not of a vital nature. What is the value of a vital transition to an insignificant portion of a sermon? How meaningless is that? Because of the low thinking about, and inferior product of, sermon conclusions, a bit of redundancy is in order. It must be understood that a sermon conclusion is not material tacked onto a sermon that has been completed. Without a conclusion, a sermon has not been preached to

---

1. Chapell, *Christ-centered Preaching*, 252.

completion. In fact, the purpose for preaching the sermon has yet to be accomplished in its fullest sense. Without a conclusion, the only thing that has been completed is the exposition of the text. The conclusion is needed to clarify the response to the purpose of the text that has been expounded.[2]

To establish a cultural analogy of a sermon conclusion's relationship to the sermon itself, the analogy most fitting would be that of the Super Bowl to the post-season playoffs. Who in their right mind would declare, or even think, that the NFL Super Bowl is just another football game tacked on to the NFL post-season? Since the conclusion is not tacked onto the sermon it must not appear to the hearers to be such. The best way to establish this as a reality is to provide a synopsis of all the main points of the sermon which have been declared, the functional transition, followed immediately by material which recalls the purpose for the sermon and indicates the ways and means by which hearers can respond to the truth they have heard in the sermon.

Back to the Super Bowl analogy for sermon conclusions. How unfulfilling would it be if the NFL season ended two weeks prior to the Super Bowl with the crowning of the AFC champion and the crowning of the NFC champion? Beyond unfulfilling, this would be bizarre! It would be intolerable! It would be known intuitively that this is not right! Nothing has been finalized! The post-season has not been concluded. The Matter Has Not Been Settled! With great vehemence it would be declared by very many people that this is no way for an NFL post-season to end! Nothing is resolved by having two champions in one year! The two champions must compete against one another and establish a true champion, and thereby, bring the post-season to an effective end, a culminating close, a satisfying solution! It is unacceptable for the whole matter to be ended, unresolved![3] Yet, there is no such demand or insistence for satisfactory endings when it comes to preaching sermons from the Word of God! Week after week, most sermons suffer the repeated fate of unresolved endings!

Perhaps, the initial point for making enhancement in the work of concluding sermons is to care as much about sermon conclusions as we do about conclusions to NFL post-seasons! Perhaps the ultimate point for making enhancement in the work of concluding sermons is that the great thing to be accomplished on any Lord's Day is a well-concluded sermon rather than a well-concluded NFL season on a given Sunday in February!

2. Olford and Olford, *Anointed Expository Preaching*, 171.

3. Such unacceptability is demonstrated by the reality of what is now known fondly as the Super Bowl. What we now refer to as Super Bowl I and II in 1967 and 1968, respectively, were called the AFL-NFL Championship games. The first game to bear the official trademark name "Super Bowl" was what we now refer to as Super Bowl III. The point of having an AFL-NFL Championship game/Super Bowl was to provide a satisfying solution and a culminating close to the professional football season by having the two league champions compete to resolve the question of which league was dominant, at least for that year.

THE NECESSITY FOR A VITAL TRANSITION IS A VITAL NECESSITY

The content composing the vital transition to the sermon conclusion should contain "the most striking, interesting sentiments possible."[4] But what makes for the "most striking, interesting sentiments possible?" The most interesting sentiments possible should be those that are in relation to the purpose of the sermon which, despite all the preaching that has taken place in the body of the sermon, the purpose for the sermon has yet to be *accomplished fully*. The requirement of the most striking, interesting sentiments possible will be met as a verbal cue such as "So," "But," "However," "Yet," is connected to the purpose of the sermon combined with questions and assertions regarding the lives of the hearers.

Transitions provide unity and clarity between the major movements in a sermon which are particularly helpful in preaching. Repetition is a critical tool in preaching. Transitions in a sermon provide the opportunity to repeat the main points of the sermon, thus providing unity and clarity to those hearing the sermon so that they hear a message with its unity and diversity clearly presented.[5] The synopsis provides the needed repetition which effects the clarity essential to a sermon. Yet, much more is needed. And what is needed cannot be accomplished solely by the functional transition of the synopsis. What is needed is a transition to a decisive discussion about what is necessary for the purpose of the sermon to become a personal possession in the lives of those who have heard the sermon.

Clarity and Certainty

Two things are needed very much by the hearers at this juncture of the sermon when transitioning from the body to the conclusion of the sermon: first, clarity that the sermon body has been attended to completely and, therefore, the sermon conclusion has begun by means of the synopsis: second, certainty that the sermon conclusion is of sufficient importance and culminating thrust that it reinvigorates the hearers' interest. The provision of such clarity and certainty is mandatory to enable the hearers to continue following the preacher as he brings them to the section of the sermon of ultimate importance—the sermon conclusion.[6]

The Conclusion's Sermonic Context

A preacher must understand the epic significance of his context in preaching as he transitions to the sermon conclusion. He is at the most important part of the message, yet his hearers find themselves in a state where they are the most fatigued. They are

4. Jones, *Principles and Practice of Preaching*, 163.

5. Olford and Olford, *Anointed*, 170.

6. Olford and Olford, *Anointed*, 170.

no longer fresh, as they were when the sermon began. Ideally, they have followed the preacher well. They have been engaged in the difficult battle to follow in a focused fashion the explanation of many, and perhaps, very difficult matters of the preaching text. If they are to maximize their opportunity to be a ready recipient of the most significant instruction of the entire sermon, then they will need help from the one who is preaching to them. He simply must help them to prepare for, and receive maximum benefit from, the final thrust of the sermon, the sermon conclusion. The preacher must not only understand that this is his responsibility, he must also fulfill it. This only can be done by means of the vital transition.

The Right Cue is Needed

To take seriously the need to provide a synopsis of the sermon by restating all the main points preached in the exposition of the text followed immediately by the vital transition makes obsolete the counterproductive overture that you are concluding the sermon.[7] To preface a transition to the conclusion by words like "Let's wrap this up" or "in conclusion" invite hearers to shut down mentally or may be perceived as the inexcusable admission that, "I know I'm taxing your endurance, but take hope, we're almost done."[8] This is a great liability as it sends the wrong cue to the hearers. What must be communicated at this juncture is something to the effect that the most important part of the message is at hand, that is, helpful instruction as to how what has been explained in the sermon can be lived out in life by every hearer of the sermon. This instruction will be found in the appeals, applications, insights, and guidelines making up the bulk of the sermon conclusion.

What is needed, therefore, is the right cue. There is nothing wrong with the hearers understanding that the sermon conclusion is at hand. The functional transition of the synopsis is a dead giveaway that the body of the sermon has been accomplished completely. Therefore, the sermon conclusion must be at hand. The hearers should have no doubt as to where they are in the context of a preached sermon. Without the functional transition supplied by the synopsis of the sermon, the conclusion comes as a surprise, or even a shock, to the congregation. This transition charts the progress of thought and at the same time prepping the hearers psychologically for the next step of the journey. There is no harm in the hearers knowing that they are starting the last, and best, lap of the journey. And, as it was argued in the previous chapter, "If that lap is interesting it not only holds his attention but brings him to his destination with

---

7. Sangster, *The Craft of Sermon Construction*, 149.

8. Sweazey, *Preaching the Good News*, 101. In fairness, Swindoll uses such phrases often but they do not cause his hearers to shut down. This is a tribute to this preacher as he can be productive by use of that which would be quite unproductive for other preachers. So, it has always been the case, genius can thrive with measures that would spell failure for anyone else.

appreciation, inspiration, and aspiration."[9] It is good that the hearers know they are on the last lap.

It is, however, the preacher's responsibility to make sure the last lap is the best lap of the journey. For the last lap to be the best lap will require that a preacher incorporates closing appeals and a clinching element of persuasion that will be highly instructive, cognitively convincing, and volitionally persuasive, thus making a vital transition an obtainable prospect. Predicated upon the strength of the closing appeals and the clinching element of persuasion, the vital transition to the last lap of the sermon can be crafted with relative ease.

The essence of the right cue that is needed in the vital transition to the sermon conclusion is about the transition from the content of the sermon body, the exposition of the biblical text, to the purpose of the sermon being achieved in the lives of the hearers, establishing the equipping of the hearers for every good work. The right cue being established by the vital transition is not about a sermon that is moments from completion, but how life, lived as it should be lived, is about to be made possible through means of compliance to the closing appeals which are about to be given.

Articulation, Persuasion, and Realization

For a transition to be a vital one, there must be a combining of three factors: articulation of crucial questions and assertions about the hearers' level of compliance or noncompliance in their lives regarding the purpose of the sermon: persuasion that the purpose of the sermon is one that is worth their complete compliance in the lives they are to live; realization that what is about to be presented are the ways and means necessary for the hearers to progress from whatever level of compliance they possess to a more complete compliance, and thus, achieve the purpose of the sermon in their lives. All three factors must be present for the transition from the sermon body to the conclusion to be a vital one. An example is in order.

An Example of Moving from a Functional to a Vital Transition

Suppose the purpose for a sermon is: "For you to become one who faithfully shares the gospel with the non-Christians in your life." And suppose further that you are preaching from a text of Scripture that is composed of the following Proposition and Main Structure: "Three reasons we are to faithfully share the gospel with unbelievers: We are to faithfully share the gospel because we are commanded in Scripture to do so; We are to faithfully share the gospel because Christ exemplifies this as a pattern of ministry and personal fulfilment; We are to faithfully share the gospel because the gospel is the only means by which unbelievers can be saved." With the above purpose,

9. Jones, *Principles and Practice of Preaching*, 162.

proposition, and main structure in mind, let's exemplify the transition away from the body of the sermon to the sermon conclusion incorporating the first two elements of a sermon conclusion—a synopsis and a vital transition.

"So, we've seen from our text this morning 3 reasons we are to faithfully share the gospel with unbelievers." (PNP)

"We are to faithfully share the gospel because we are commanded in Scripture to do so." (I)

"We are to faithfully share the gospel because Christ exemplifies this as a pattern of ministry and personal fulfilment." (II)

"We are to faithfully share the gospel because the gospel is the only means by which unbelievers can be saved." (III)

(The above represents the synopsis of the sermon which serves as the transition, a functional transition, away from the body of the sermon to the sermon conclusion. The following assertions and questions are combined with the purpose statement to form the vital transition)

"Yet, many of you, like many Christians everywhere, know these things and have known them for years but have never, not even once, shared the gospel with an unbeliever!"

"Let me ask you a very important question—'Are you content with that?' 'Are you content with a life of disobedience to the Lord in this matter?'"

"Perhaps you're not content with your disobedience but you prefer it to the prospect of engaging any unbeliever with the gospel of Jesus Christ!"

"On the other hand, perhaps you're very discontent with your disobedience, in fact, you hate it! You are sick of it and you desperately want this to change! Let me assure you it can change and it must change!"

"So, how do we go from disobedience to obedience in sharing the gospel?"

"Why is it that so many Christians find themselves in disobedience in this area of their lives?"

"Is it even possible that you could become faithful in this area of your life as a Christian? I assure you that it is!"

"What are the hindrances that keep us from being obedient witnesses for Christ?"

"Yet, some of you have been faithful in days past to share the gospel with unbelievers, but that is a thing of the past! It is no longer true of you!"

"Why is that? What keeps you from ongoing faithfulness in sharing the gospel with unbelievers?"

"Is it possible for you to recover, and even exceed, your faithfulness of former days? I assure you that it is!"

"So, the question is—'How do we move from disobedience to obedience, or from obedience to a greater level of obedience in our opportunities to share the gospel with unbelievers?'"

"In other words, 'What is necessary for you to become one who faithfully shares the gospel with the non-Christians in your life?'"

"If you are not faithful in sharing the gospel with unbelievers you never will become faithful until you overcome one or more of 5 hindrances that can hold you back!"

"Disobedience in faithfully sharing the gospel results from one, or more, of 5 hindrances common to many believers!"

"These hindrances can, and must, be overcome!"

"Let's understand what these hindrances are and how we can overcome them!"

The content composing the vital transition above contains 11 questions, 12 assertions (underlined), and one admonition (italicized).

You may be wondering if all the above is necessary for a vital transition? The answer is, ABSOLUTELY NOT!!! The above represents an attempt to provide abundant opportunity to get a sense of how questions and assertions are used to provide, what could be sensed as, a vital transition. I believe a handful of questions and assertions are sufficient to reinvigorate interest in the purpose of the sermon. If, having preached the sermon, the hearers have a heart for the matter of being faithful to share the gospel to non-Christians in their lives, then the questions and assertions will be perceived as vital because they address the very thing they are interested in, that is, being faithful to the Lord in the matter of sharing the gospel. Obviously, having preached the sermon, if a hearer is content in one's disobedience to the Lord in this matter, these questions and assertions will possess no vitality at all, except to annoy or chaff the one set on disobedience.

Questions, Assertions, and Admonition to Reinvigorate Interest

The significance of a transition made vital through using questions and assertions regarding the purpose of the sermon is that it indicates to the hearer that very crucial content lies ahead in the sermon conclusion. It indicates that they are about to be provided the ways and means by which very significant matters can be improved upon or resolved completely.

A vital transition supplies to conscientious hearers an avenue through which they can become "doers of the Word rather than mere hearers."[10] What a disservice preachers offer up to conscientious hearers when they end their sermons with a few low-key comments, then dismiss them, rather than equipping them with practical, biblical insights as to how they can live in ultimate obedience to the purpose of the text which was expounded to them. How tragic it is for preachers to refuse to help their hearers to do what they must do, that is, to live according to the truths with which they must comply. What they need is enablement to successfully conduct their lives in the light of the truth they now possess.

10. James 1:22.

Just as the preaching of the passage, hopefully, provided the hearers with a theological upgrade in their comprehension of the Word, *the conclusion, hopefully, will be perceived by the hearers as providing an obedience upgrade, or a faithfulness upgrade in their conformity to the Word.* However, the conformity upgrade must be backed up by significant material. And, if significant material is provided in the conclusion, then it should be prefaced by a vital transition to establish how disobedience can give way to obedience.

7

The Purpose of the Sermon Achieved: Part 1

"Without a specific, passionate purpose for preaching a sermon, a sermon may be a homiletical product, but it cannot be a message! Next, without a specific, passionate purpose for preaching a sermon, the sermon may come to a halt, but its ending cannot constitute a conclusion! Just because a sermon ceases from continuation does not mean that it was concluded."

"A sermon without a purpose will never be a message and a sermon without a purpose will never conclude! A sermon without a purpose, a purpose that is to be achieved in the conclusion, will be an open-ended biblical speech event that comes to a stop! It just ends unceremoniously. It's just a public demonstration of a 'give-up.' It is the homiletical equivalent of a UFC fighter's 'tapout!' It's just the self-evident reality that there is nothing to be gained by continuing. What a sad reality, especially since it is such a common one in preaching. . . . The sad but common practice of 'sermonic give-ups' belies the strategic value that purposeful conclusions provide—sermonic excellence, the kind of excellence that benefits the hearers greatly, in valuable practical ways."

"No amount of effort supplied by a preacher for the cause of preaching an excellent sermon, or a sermon conclusion, can overcome the deficit of preaching to no purpose. Nothing must be allowed to rival the thought process we must have about a sermon conclusion, other than this—Did I achieve what I set out to accomplish? Of course, this pivotal question must be predicated upon the question—Is this purpose aligned with what God has designed to be affected through an appropriate response to this text of Scripture, if accurately expounded?"

"The purpose of the sermon is directly and completely responsible for the content of the conclusion and, therefore, the whole of its preparation. One's method of preparing

and preaching an expository sermon is not going to change based upon how the sermon concludes. . . . But one's method of preparing and preaching the content composing the sermon conclusion will change from sermon to sermon based upon the purpose for preaching the sermon at hand."

"Answer the most basic and most vital of all questions—'Why Preach This Sermon?' Yet, this question, for better or worse, is answered most adequately by the sermon conclusion! There is nothing better than the conclusion to answer that question. Therefore, we must learn to, and be content to, let the conclusion of the message be our authoritative answer to the question, 'Why am I preaching this sermon?' The answer must be specific, practical, and vital. But, are present-day hearers of sermons being exposed to a careful consideration of the importance of a pointed, practical, purposeful conclusion in preaching? The evidence supplied by the overwhelming majority of sermons that are preached today scream in one unified thunderous voice— 'Absolutely Not!' In present day preaching, conclusions, and specifically purposeful conclusions, are just a non-issue, they seldom exist!"

"It was argued very well that, 'The proper design of the conclusion is to appropriately finish a discourse.' This jewel of a statement has meaning well beyond that to which one might quickly assent. 'Finish,' not stop or end or cease to continue, but finish! Furthermore, notice the requirement to 'appropriately' finish. This is a huge consideration."

"The conclusion of a sermon exists for the cause of achieving the purpose of the sermon. Whatever design the preacher brings to the purpose of his message, it 'should be palpable in the conclusion, and . . . should be thoroughly accomplished before its close.' An accomplished purpose of any sermon will be to 'effect changes among the members of God's church that build them up individually and that build up the body as a whole.' Good pastoral preaching helps hearers to grow in the faith and to conform their lives to biblical standards. Practical truth designed to effect changes in how believers live in this world will compose the vital content of sermon conclusions."

"The conclusion must deal with measures that are crucial for one to change from 'as is' to 'as according to Scripture.' If such measures are worth incorporating into one's life, then these measures must come from Scripture. . . . Only as Scripture is being faithfully and accurately interpreted, explained, argued, corroborated, illustrated, and applied by a preacher in his sermon is he actually preaching the Word. Only as one is preaching the Word is one preaching. This is true for the sermon conclusion as well. This portion of the sermon must not be allowed to become part of the sermon if it does not incorporate Scripture. The sermon conclusion is not entitled to special privileges. If the conclusion does not contain Scripture and deal with it in proper fashion, then that conclusion is distinct, different from that which preceded it, that

which constituted preaching."

"God has promised to bless his Word. If a sermon conclusion is intended to be the highpoint of the sermon and is incorporated to be a blessing to God's people, do we dare think we can forego what God has promised to bless and expect him to bless our foolish omission? I trust we can see the futility of such thinking. However, if the conclusion is truly the highpoint of the sermon, could it be such if it does not include choice scriptural insights? Certainly not! The only responsible course is to provide in the conclusion the same valuable content we supply in the body of the sermon—the Word of God. The conclusion should be the highpoint of the sermon and the rich, practical insights of Scripture are what may make the conclusion the highpoint. If one intends to have the conclusion as the highpoint of the sermon, then one must incorporate Scripture in the conclusion."

"The conclusions of sermons found in Scripture demonstrate the use of Scripture to substantiate the closing appeals to the hearers or readers of these sermons. Through Scripture-based closing appeals the previously referenced preachers included in the pages of the Bible provided a means by which the purpose of their sermons could be accomplished in the lives of their hearers/readers."

"As evidenced by sermons found in the New Testament, the use of Scripture in the conclusions of these sermons played a vital role. Scripture used in the conclusion of a sermon supplies profitable instruction, reproof, correction, and training in righteousness. Through the use of Scripture in the sermon conclusion, Scripture will provide the needed content that can make the sermon conclusion the highpoint of the sermon and achieve the purpose of the sermon."

A MATTER OF PURPOSE

The date was Saturday, March 28, 1970. The place was the Welsh-Ryan Arena (then called McGaw Hall) on the campus of Northwestern University in Evanston, Illinois. The event was the 1970 NCAA Division I Wrestling Championships, where the greatest attraction in the history of college wrestling took place at the 142-pound championship match. This event, this time, and this place showcased the last collegiate wrestling match of the legendary grappler, Dan Gable. He had never lost a wrestling match in his life. Never! He had won every one of his 181 matches from the time of his sophomore year at Waterloo West High School in Waterloo, Iowa (64–0) to his undefeated career at Iowa State University where he was 117–0 with one match left to go. Enter Larry Owings. Owings was a sophomore from the University of Washington. Owings was telling everyone personally and publicly, via newspaper and television interviews, that he was going to beat Dan Gable. For example, on the morning of the weigh-in of that historic Saturday, ABC TV's Bud Palmer conducted this short interview with Owings. "Larry, why, particularly with such a successful sophomore season in the Pacific loop at 158 pounds, would you drop to a weight class that will be impossible to win because of Gable's presence?" Palmer asked. Owings's eyes burned as he spoke slowly and concisely, saying, "I'll beat him!" in the most determined tone imaginable.[1] True to his word, he did, 13–11. Larry Owings determined that for the first and only time in Dan Gable's life, when he wrestled his final collegiate match, Gable's hand would not be raised in victory.[2] Years later Dan Gable said, with great humility and even greater insight, "I did not have the focus that Larry Owings had for that match!"[3] That was not an excuse offered for the result of that match, it was the carefully considered cause and effect reality that determined the result of that match. The focus of one wrestler compared to a lack of focus of the other wrestler determined the outcome of the most legendary match in college wrestling history.

The significance of "focus" in wrestling is what I am attributing as a parallel to "purpose" in preaching. And, as important as focus is for wrestling, I am contending that purpose in preaching is even more important. H. C. Brown Jr. emphatically pressed the connection between focus and the purpose of a sermon when he wrote, "In each sermon there should be only one specific purpose, and this purpose should be the center and focus of the preacher's attention from the first word of the introduction through the last word of the conclusion."[4]

Perhaps the greatest enigma of preaching, from my frame of reference, is the common error of a preacher rising to preach without having a passionate purpose for preaching the sermon he is about to preach! The greatest, most telling, price to be paid for this colossal error is discovered in the conclusion of the message. But I must remediate the previous sentence because, as it stands, it is so graciously stated that it is to the point of fabricating falsehoods.[5]

First, without a specific, passionate purpose for preaching a sermon, the sermon may be a homiletical product, but it cannot be a message! Next, without a specific, passionate purpose for preaching a sermon, the sermon may come to a halt, but its ending cannot constitute a conclusion! Just because a sermon ceases from continuation does not mean that it was concluded. Sure, it stopped, but in its stopping, there stands the obvious evidence that nothing particularly was resolved, nothing particularly

1. Google Search article: InterMat Rewind: Gable-Owings.

2. Google Search article: InterMat Rewind: Gable-Owings.

3. Talks at Google: Life Lessons from an Olympic Hero—Dan Gable.

4. Brown Jr., *A Quest for Reformation in Preaching*, 138.

5. I make a distinction between a sermon and a message. Every message is a sermon, but not every sermon is a message. A message is predicated upon a sermon conclusion that contains relevant, practical content that brings correction to erroneous aspects of believers' lives, or content that helps believers to more productively live obediently, through helpful and needed instruction from Scripture, thus achieving the purpose of the sermon.

was remediated, nothing particularly was accomplished, no ultimate enablement was provided.

A sermon without a purpose will never be a message and a sermon without a purpose will never conclude! A sermon without a purpose, a purpose that is to be achieved in the conclusion, will be an open-ended biblical speech event that comes to a stop! It just ends unceremoniously. It's just a public demonstration of a "give-up." It is the homiletical equivalent of a UFC fighter's "tapout!" It's just the self-evident reality that there is nothing to be gained by continuing. What a sad reality, especially since it is such a common one in preaching. The inescapable outcome of a weak, purposeless sermon is the correct deduction by the hearers as they reflect upon the sermon they heard, "I guess it wasn't that important after all."[6]

The sad but common practice of "sermonic give-ups" belies the strategic value that purposeful conclusions provide—sermonic excellence, the kind of excellence that benefits the hearers greatly, in valuable practical ways. One author, writing about sermon conclusions many years ago, expressed very well both the problem and the prospect of providing sermonic excellence in this area of one's preaching, that is, purposeful conclusions. He writes:

> Power in the conclusion is not so much attained by startling words or loudness of voice as by a certain concentration of thought which brings the whole weight of the discourse to bear at a single point, and thus results in a strong and lasting impression. How different is such a result from that of an indefiniteness which loses sight of the main object at the very moment when that object should be made most palpable. . . . To attain the highest excellence in executing the conclusion of the discourse is perhaps the most difficult as well as the most important task of an orator. But the elements of success are within the reach of everyone . . . (if there is) a persevering determination to attain excellence at whatever expense of effort.[7]

No amount of effort supplied by a preacher for the cause of preaching an excellent sermon, or a sermon conclusion, can overcome the deficit of preaching to no purpose. Nothing must be allowed to rival the thought process we must have about a sermon conclusion, other than this—Did I achieve what I set out to accomplish? Of course, this pivotal question must be predicated upon the question—Is this purpose aligned with what God has designed to be affected through an appropriate response to this text of Scripture, if accurately expounded?

Nothing is deadlier than preachers becoming mere mechanics or technicians in preaching. Yet, failures of craftsmanship in the attempt to accomplish one's best possible work in preaching is a certain liability. "In all honesty, we must confess that again and again it is our crudities and undisciplined preparation which stand in the way

6. Fabarez, *Preaching that Changes Lives*, 102.
7. Kidder, *A Treatise on Homiletics*, 1862, 230–31.

of real communication in preaching. To be insufficient is one thing; to be careless is quite another."[8] Carelessness, especially the quenched desire to be a more faithful and productive proclaimer of biblical truth, must be arrested. No other portion of preaching demonstrates carelessness on behalf of preachers as the carelessness demonstrated in sermon conclusions.

Should one continue in pursuing one's call from God to preach if, in the pursuit of this calling, he no longer exercises himself to be a better practitioner of God's calling for him to preach his Word? Without getting sidetracked into the truncated discussion about retiring from the preaching ministry, I believe there is one certain indicator to any preacher that it is time for him to retire, that is, when he is no longer working to become better at what God has called him to do! The church would be better served if one, who thinks he no longer needs to grow as a preacher because he is good enough "as is," were replaced by another who desires to grow as a preacher and preach more effectively. Consider the following argument:

> The greater the music and the musician, the more important an instrument becomes. The artist cannot say, "this is Beethoven's work and there is none greater. It will come through because it is Beethoven." The sheer profundity of the music makes it even more imperative that the instrument be finely tuned. Even more so a preacher cannot say, "But this is the Word of God. Who can frustrate God?" We can! An undisciplined preacher is an untuned instrument. The final confirmation of our claim is to see what God can do with the preacher who has sought to be a finely tuned instrument of God's grace.[9]

So, I must ask, how fine-tuned of an instrument is a preacher if he is content to preach without having a purpose for preaching? Is he not yet undisciplined? Is he not yet unprepared? He absolutely is unprepared, undisciplined, untuned, and, if this is not remedied, he should be unemployed in pulpit ministry!

Effective preaching is a result of many factors. An objective view of preaching effectiveness cannot be the product of one thing. Effective preaching, among its other components, "must be directed by a definite intention to produce a definite result. . . . [W]e must know what we mean to do, and we must put out our whole strength to get it done. We shall preach to no purpose unless we have a purpose in preaching."[10] Such sage thinking about what is required in preaching is consistent with this helpful counsel to those preparing to preach: "As you sit down to prepare your discourse, let your question be, 'What is my purpose in the sermon?' and do not move a step until you have shaped out before your mind a definite answer to that inquiry."[11]

---

8. Bartlett, *The Audacity of Preaching*, as cited in Cleland, *Preaching to be Understood*, 88–89.

9. Bartlett, *Postscript to Preaching*, 40–41.

10. Dale, *Nine Lectures on Preaching*, 1890, 24.

11. Taylor, *The Ministry of the Word*, 1876, 111.

The very notable preacher, R. W. Dale, when addressing the Yale Divinity school in his Lyman Beecher Lectures on Preaching in 1890, rather pointedly said that, "Preaching may seem to be very effective, may attract great crowds, may produce intense excitement, may win for the preacher a wide reputation, and may yet be practically worthless and even mischievous."[12] The kind of preaching which he had in mind was aimless preaching, which is the kind of preaching that fails to understand that a true sermon is meant to do something for people, it is not meant to be listened to, merely. Aimless preaching in all its faults and shortcomings is primarily culpable in that it never sets out to produce any vital, life-changing results. Haddon Robinson laments the tragedy of purposeless preaching with his statement: "Pity the man who fails to understand that his sermon should change lives in some specific way."[13]

Aimlessness and its consequent corruption of the preaching ministry is what set Jay Adams to write his very helpful book, *Preaching with Purpose*. In the introduction of this volume, he established his premise with the following: "If you are of the mind that, on the whole, preaching in America is tolerably good (or, for that matter, even tolerable), then you and I are on such entirely different wavelengths. . . . Men and women (and especially young people) are being turned away from Christ and His church by dull, unarresting, unedifying, and aimless preaching."[14] In a different book, Adams again targets purposeless preaching as he writes: "Unless a preacher knows the purpose of his sermon, all is lost. He himself is lost, the congregation will soon get lost, and the sermon would be better if it were lost."[15] In reference to the importance of discerning the Spirit's purpose for inspiring a biblical text and preaching that purpose he stated that "*nothing* is more fundamental to solid biblical preaching."[16]

In response to the question, "*What is the sermon to do?*" R. W. Dale insisted that "the answer to this question determines the whole method of preparation."[17] Though this statement was well-intended, the statement is too general to be true and valid for expository preaching. An additional phrase, "of the sermon conclusion," is needed at the end of his statement to make it accurate and helpful. "The answer to this question determines the whole method of preparation *of the sermon conclusion.*" Now we're talking. Now the statement is a helpful one.

The purpose of the sermon is directly and completely responsible *for the content of the conclusion* and, therefore, the whole of *its* preparation. One's method of preparing and preaching an expository sermon is not going to change based upon how the sermon concludes. Generally speaking, the gifted servants God supplied the church of Jesus Christ—apostles, prophets, evangelists, and pastor-teachers, all of whom

12. Dale, *Nine Lectures on Preaching*, 1890, 25.
13. Robinson, *Biblical Preaching*, 108.
14. Adams, *Preaching with Purpose*, x–xi.
15. Adams, *Truth Apparent*, 9.
16. Adams, *Truth Apparent*, 9.
17. Dale, *Nine Lectures on Preaching*, 1890, 131.

ministered by means of Scripture, were given by God for the equipping of the saints for the work of service, to the building up of the body of Christ.[18] So today, in the preaching of pastor-teachers, every sermon should purpose to build up the body of Christ and further equip each hearer in one's service. Therefore, exposition of God's Word is always in order, the body of the sermon being the explanation and application of Scripture. But one's method of preparing and preaching *the content composing the sermon conclusion* will change from sermon to sermon based upon the purpose for preaching the sermon at hand. This must be the case since a clearly defined objective is "the test of all the means, the guide of every expansion, the judge of every illustration, the governing principle of every adornment" to be found in *the sermon conclusion*.[19] The sermon conclusion, just like the sermon it concludes, fulfills its unique contribution to equip God's people for the work of service. The unique contribution of the conclusion's equipping ministry is demonstrated in how it accomplishes the specific purpose of the sermon through the closing appeals found in the sermon conclusion.

THE UNASKED QUESTION WHICH YIELDS INADEQUATE ANSWERS AND INADEQUATE RESULTS

The questions "Why am I preaching this passage?" and "What is this sermon to do for the hearers?" are related to the purpose of the sermon to be achieved in the conclusion. These questions require us, force us, to raise and answer the most basic and most vital of all questions—"Why Preach This Sermon?" Yet, this question, for better or worse, is answered most adequately by the sermon conclusion. There is nothing better than the conclusion to answer that question. Therefore, we must learn to, and be content to, let the conclusion of the message be our authoritative answer to the question, "Why am I preaching this sermon?" The answer must be specific, practical, and vital.

This is nothing new. It may sound new but the crucial understanding of the relationship that a conclusion bears to a sermon, as well as the practical intent that a sermon conclusion must have, has a deep taproot in homiletical theory and practice. Consider just one brief assertion to this end: "It has ever been deemed important that a discourse should end well—should leave upon the minds of its hearers one clear, agreeable, powerful impression, an impression tending to a practical result."[20] Wow! I mean, really? Are present-day hearers of sermons being exposed to a careful consideration of the importance of a pointed, practical, purposeful conclusion in preaching? The evidence supplied by most sermons that are preached today scream in one unified thunderous voice— "Absolutely Not!" In present day preaching, conclusions, and specifically purposeful conclusions, are just a non-issue, they seldom exist!

---

18. Paul the apostle writes this in Ephesians 4:11–12.

19. Bull, *Preaching and Sermon Construction*, 1922, 125.

20. Kidder, *A Treatise on Homiletics*, 1864, 222.

The prevailing weakness of concluding sermons necessitates that the conclusion should be in the mind of the preacher from the early hours of his preparation. The question of first importance which he must ask himself is this: "What is my purpose for preaching this passage?" Everything he says throughout the sermon will be supplied, directly or indirectly, to contribute to that purpose, so that it may be achieved fully by the time the conclusion ends. His introduction will look to the conclusion; the various divisions of the sermon body will pave the way to it. The result being that, when the conclusion of the sermon is reached, the content of the conclusion will be perceived and appreciated as the "natural, logical, and we might almost say inevitable" result for which the sermon was destined.[21] And, moreover, the sermon will have become a message that began in the Word of God, caught fire in the heart of the man of God, was passionately and profitably applied to the lives of God's people, and ended with choice insights from the expansive counsel of God's Word.

COMPLETING THE SERMON BY ACHIEVING THE PURPOSE

It was argued very well that, "The proper design of the conclusion is to appropriately finish a discourse."[22] This jewel of a statement has meaning well beyond that to which one might quickly assent. "Finish," not stop or end or cease to continue, but finish! Furthermore, notice the requirement to "appropriately" finish. This is a huge consideration.

So, what constitutes an appropriately finished discourse that a sermon conclusion, if designed properly, will produce? Carefully consider the insight that, the design of the conclusion is to apply to the "grand object" of the discourse.[23] Here is the underappreciated, if not the seldom understood, connection between the sermon's "object," or "purpose," and the sermon's conclusion. The conclusion of a sermon exists for the cause of achieving the purpose of the sermon. Whatever design the preacher brings to the purpose of his message, it "should be palpable in the conclusion, and . . . should be thoroughly accomplished before its close."[24] An accomplished purpose of any sermon will be to "effect changes among the members of God's church that build them up individually and that build up the body as a whole." Good pastoral preaching helps hearers to grow in the faith and to conform their lives to biblical standards.[25] Practical truth designed to effect changes in how believers live in this world will compose the vital content of sermon conclusions.

---

21. Breed, *Preparing to Preach*, 1911, 112–113.
22. Kidder, *A Treatise on Homiletics*, 1864, 223.
23. Kidder, *A Treatise on Homiletics*, 1864, 224.
24. Kidder, *A Treatise on Homiletics*, 1864, 224.
25. Adams, *Preaching with Purpose*, 13.

THE SERMON'S PURPOSE AS THE STRENGTH OF THE SERMON'S UNITY

A sermon conclusion is very effective when, having clearly and vividly explained the main thrust as well as the nuances of the preaching passage through solid proofs and skillful illustration and application, the hearers are then made to see the sermon's purpose being accomplished completely at the "crowning moment"[26] of the sermon, the conclusion. This means that the sermon conclusion, if it becomes the actual crowning moment of the sermon, must "consist of earnest, burning, and zealous exhortation which is to penetrate the most hidden recesses of every heart."[27] Such qualitative exhortation is required if the sermon is to accomplish the intended result "to change every will, and make the triumph of grace complete" in the lives of all who hear the message.[28] What a laudable and worthwhile endeavor to have lives changed through preaching—an outcome that would be more common if sermons concluded effectively.

It was the Apostle Paul's desire that the Corinthian church would "seek to abound for the edification of the church."[29] Paul is clear in his instruction in I Corinthians 14 that such edification would come to them most abundantly through the spiritual means of prophesying. Not speaking in tongues "but especially that you may prophesy" is that which Paul implored them to "desire earnestly."[30] Why? According to Paul, "one who prophesies speaks to men for edification and exhortation and consolation."[31] Edification, exhortation, and consolation should reach their zenith in the sermon conclusion where the purpose of the sermon is achieved by means of changed lives in accordance with God's Word.

Strategic to fulfilling our Lord's Great Commission to make disciples is the necessary function of "teaching them to observe all that I commanded you." This led Jay Adams to write: "Truth observed is the goal or purpose of pastoral preaching. In order to be faithful to his task, therefore, the pastoral preacher must know not only the truth but how to communicate it effectively. Again, he must learn not only how truth should affect life but how to help his listeners knead that truth into life—individually and corporately lived."[32] The corporate and individual kneading of scriptural truth into the lives of the hearers is the unique domain of a sermon conclusion.

It must be kept in mind that the lives of the hearers receiving needed correction in some practical way is indicative of a purposeful sermon conclusion. Moreover, a purposeful sermon conclusion provides the master stroke of unity for the entire

---

26. Potter, *Sacred Eloquence*, 1868, 311.

27. Potter, *Sacred Eloquence*, 1868, 310.

28. Potter, *Sacred Eloquence*, 1868, 310.

29. I Corinthians 14:12.

30. I Corinthians 14:1.

31. I Corinthians 14:3.

32. Adams, *Preaching with Purpose*, 15.

sermon, indicating rather pointedly that the sermonic treatment of the text's exposition was paving the way to arrive at a final destination, the highpoint of the sermon—the sermon conclusion. And, if the conclusion is what it should be, the highpoint of the sermon where its purpose is accomplished soundly, it may well be the crowning moment for some who receive a new lease on life. This new lease on life is due, in no small way, to a sermon that was destined to arrive at a strategic place. That strategic place being a purposeful conclusion that adeptly deals with life, life as it is and life as it should be. To accomplish that, the conclusion must deal with measures that are crucial for one to change from "as is" to "as according to Scripture." If such measures are worth incorporating into one's life, *then these measures must come from Scripture.*

If the above were agreed to, as I trust it would be, the life-change to be achieved in the sermon conclusion must incorporate the Word of God. When Paul commanded Timothy to preach the Word, we cannot think for a moment that what Paul meant Timothy to do was to preach sermons, which at certain points would have intersections with Scripture. Only as Scripture is being faithfully and accurately interpreted, explained, argued, corroborated, illustrated, and applied by a preacher in his sermon is he actually preaching the Word. Only as one is preaching the Word is one preaching. This is true for the sermon conclusion as well. This portion of the sermon must not be allowed to become part of the sermon if it does not incorporate Scripture.

The sermon conclusion is not entitled to special privileges. If the conclusion does not contain Scripture and deal with it in proper fashion, then that conclusion is distinct, different from that which preceded it, that which constituted preaching. By means of an unscriptural conclusion a preacher is no longer preaching. But he is still speaking in an unscriptural conclusion, so what is he doing as he continues to speak? He is simply incorporating rhetorical devices trying to get to a stopping point. The use of rhetorical devices to justify the cessation from speaking is not preaching, and such should not be allowed to constitute a sermon conclusion, in theory or in practice!

It is the Word of God that sets the parameters for what must be understood as preaching. It is the Word of God, all of it, that is profitable for, instruction, reproof, correction, and training in righteousness. It is the Word of God that is used to reprove, rebuke, exhort, with great patience and instruction. The same understanding must be true for the sermon conclusion *if one is still preaching in one's sermon conclusion.* The patient instruction of the Word will be offered to reprove, rebuke, and exhort God's people. This is a requirement for preaching in the sermon conclusion just as it is for preaching in the sermon body. John Piper insists that "good preaching is saturated with Scripture and not based upon Scripture because Scripture is more than the basis for good preaching. . . . (It) does not begin with Scripture as a basis and then wander off to other things. It oozes Scripture."[33] Since the Bible is the instrument of regeneration and sanctification, preaching should consist of Scripture as its raw material and deal

33. Piper, *The Supremacy of God in Preaching*, 86.

with it in every component of the sermon "because it is saturated with it."[34]Achieving the purpose of the sermon by the closing appeals, thus supplying patient instruction through reproof, rebuke, and exhortation, not only keeps the preacher preaching in the conclusion but has him supplying, strongly supplying, unity in the sermon all the way to the appropriate completion of it.

God has promised to bless his Word.[35] If a sermon conclusion is intended to be the highpoint of the sermon and is incorporated to be a blessing to God's people, do we dare think we can forego what God has promised to bless and expect him to bless our foolish omission? I trust we can see the futility of such thinking. However, if the conclusion is truly the highpoint of the sermon, could it be such if it does not include choice scriptural insights? Certainly not! The only responsible course is to provide in the conclusion the same valuable content we supply in the body of the sermon—the Word of God. The conclusion should be the highpoint of the sermon and the rich, practical insights of Scripture are what may make the conclusion the highpoint. If one intends to have the conclusion as the highpoint of the sermon, then one must incorporate Scripture in the conclusion.

AN EXAMINATION OF SERMONS FOUND IN SCRIPTURE

Perhaps, you have failed to see in the preaching of sermon conclusions contained in the Bible the incorporation of Scripture being used productively, making the conclusion the highpoint of the sermon. However, the Bible does demonstrate the use of Scripture in the conclusion of sermons that are included in its pages. Let me show you this in three familiar New Testament sermons. Notice how the Word of God was the insightful substance in the conclusion of these sermons. Additionally, the use of Scripture will be seen also in the conclusion of the epistle of Hebrews. The biblical book of Hebrews is considered widely as an early Christian sermon, amended with the postscript of 13:22–25. This epistle/sermon was to be circulated and read among Hebrew Christians struggling in their faithfulness to Christ.

Matthew 5:3–7:27

The Sermon on the Mount was delivered to a mixed group of people, believers (his disciples) and unbelievers (the multitude). The closing appeals of the conclusion were directed to, and insightful for, his disciples and the multitude. All three of the appeals were directed to the multitude while only the final appeal was directed to his disciples. The conclusion of the Sermon on the Mount begins at 7:21[36] and goes to 7:27. Verses

34. Borgman, *My Heart for Thy Cause*, 141.

35. Isaiah 55:11 is one well-documented promise of blessing God gives regarding his Word.

36. In verses 21–27 the Lord changes the focus of his instruction from now to then, from today to "that day," from what some say to what they will experience, from what some will say on that day to what

24b–27 constitute the clinching element of persuasion and verses 21–24a contain the closing appeals. I find three inferences from the Scripture passage used (Psalm 6:8) in the conclusion that form the basis for three closing appeals that serve to achieve the purpose of the sermon. The purpose of the sermon being: "To enter into the kingdom of heaven by possessing a righteousness that surpasses that of the scribes and the Pharisees." This purpose is drawn from Matthew 5:20 which reads: "Truly, truly I say to you that unless your righteousness surpasses that of the scribes and Pharisees, you will not enter the kingdom of heaven." All three of the closing appeals are clinched persuasively by the illustration of the two builders. The Scripture used by the Lord in his conclusion was Psalm 6:8, a well-known Psalm of David. The Lord took the phrase from Psalm 6:8, "Depart from Me, all you who do iniquity" and rendered it as, "Depart from Me, all you who practice lawlessness." In doing so, Jesus broadened the scope of their sinfulness (from iniquity to lawlessness) which characterized their sinfulness more specifically. He intensified their sinfulness as indicated by the change from "do" to "practice" lawlessness, which more accurately described the character of their lives. Psalm 6:8 was used to bring understanding to all three closing appeals. The appeals made by the Lord were three inferences, all being drawn from Psalm 6:8. The three inferential closing appeals were as follows:

1. Be wise and enter the kingdom of heaven knowing the Lord and doing the Father's will (7:21).

- Compliance to this appeal would provide the departure from their lawlessness established by Psalm 6:8.

- Verse 21 reads: "Not everyone who says to Me, 'Lord, Lord,' will enter the kingdom of heaven, but he who does the will of My Father who is in heaven will enter."

- This statement of Christ provides instruction concerning those who will enter the kingdom of heaven.

- This statement of Christ provides a reproof concerning the belief of many that it is sufficient to possess only a knowledge about the Lord to enter the kingdom of heaven.

- This statement of Christ provides a rebuke that many people do not understand that they do not do the will of the Father in their lives.

2. Don't be foolish and forfeit the kingdom of heaven by doing self-directed works in the name of the Lord (7:22–23).

- Compliance to this appeal would correct the epitome of their lawlessness established by Psalm 6:8.

---

they will be told on that day, from how one does or does not act upon his words in life to how one will fare for eternity based upon one's response to his words. This is obviously the highpoint of the sermon.

- Verses 22–23 read: "Many will say to Me on that day, 'Lord, Lord, did we not prophesy in Your name, and in Your name cast out demons, and in Your name perform many miracles?' And then I will declare to them, 'I never knew you; Depart from Me, you who practice lawlessness.'"

- These statements of Christ provide the instruction that many of those who will not enter the kingdom of heaven are very religious, doing humanly impressive things in the Lord's name.

- These statements of Christ provide a reproof for their assumption that the impressive things they do are sufficient for their entrance into the kingdom of heaven.

- These statements of Christ provide a reproof for their assumption that those who will enter the kingdom can be identified by their ability to prophesy, cast out demons, and perform miracles.

- These statements of Christ provide a rebuke for their assumption their works could negate their lawlessness.

3. The Father's will is to act upon the words of Christ, making one wise in the present and safe in the future (7:24).

- Compliance to this appeal would provide the antithesis of their lawlessness established by Psalm 6:8.

- This statement of Christ provides the instruction that the Father's will is accomplished by those who respond to Christ and his words.

- This statement of Christ provides the instruction that acting upon Christ's words defines wisdom.

- This statement of Christ provides the instruction that acting upon Christ's words provides security.

In this instance, one small portion of Scripture became the driving force of our Lord's appeals in the conclusion of his sermon. Through the reference to Psalm 6:8 in his sermon conclusion, Jesus challenged his hearers to respond to his sermon in a three-fold way according to the inferences advanced in 7:21–24. In doing so, they would be like the wise man depicted in his illustration.

Acts 2:14–40

Peter's sermon on the Day of Pentecost, Acts 2:14–40, was intended to conclude in verses 32–36. Verse 36 finalized what Peter was inspired to say in response to the mockers. Verses 32–36 compose the intended conclusion of the sermon and, as such, it was not only the highpoint of the sermon but was so effective that it generated a question from the hearers which necessitated an impromptu addition, thus expanding the conclusion. Verses 38–40 finalized what he was inspired to say in response to the question of the convicted hearers, "Brethren, what shall we do?" found in verse 37. The Scripture used by Peter in his *intended conclusion* was Psalm 110:1 which reads, "The LORD said to my Lord, sit at My right hand until I make Your enemies a footstool for your feet." I find four closing appeals, each of which were an inferential reproof or rebuke, which Peter makes to his hearers regarding the triumph of Christ over his enemies depicted in Psalm 110:1. The purpose of Peter's sermon is <u>to turn them from mocking the initial fulfilment of Joel's prophesy, to receive the gift of the Holy Spirit by repenting and being baptized in the name of Jesus Christ, whom they crucified but whom God has made both Lord and Christ</u>. For this purpose to be achieved, Peter must show them that David, as great as he was, pales in comparison to Jesus, and like David, they must acknowledge the supremacy of Jesus as the exalted One by God. Peter forwards four appeals to the mockers, each of which is an inference drawn from Psalm 110:1. The four inferential closing appeals are as follows:

1. <u>Jesus, not David, was raised up and exalted to the right hand of God</u> (2:32–33a).

- The verses read: "This Jesus God raised up again, to which we are all witnesses. Therefore, having been exalted to the right hand of God . . ."

- These verses provide instruction that through the resurrection from the dead, Jesus fulfilled Psalm 16:10 in that he was not abandoned to Hades, nor did he undergo decay.

- These verses provide instruction that having been resurrected, Jesus was exalted to the right hand of God.

- These verses provide a reproof for their lack of understanding of the greatness of Jesus, thinking of him only as a Nazarene. ("This Jesus" as a Nazarene refers to 2:22a)

- These verses provide a rebuke for their rejecting of God's attestation of Jesus through miracles, wonders, and signs which God performed through him in their midst. ("This Jesus" as attested by God refers to 2:22b)

2. <u>Jesus, not David, ascended into Heaven, received the promise of the Holy Spirit, and has poured him forth</u> (2:33b–34a).

- These verses read: "and having received from the Father the promise of the Holy Spirit, He has poured forth this which you both see and hear. For it was not David who ascended into heaven . . ."

- These verses provide instruction that to Jesus, not David, the promise of the Holy Spirit was given.

- These verses provide instruction that it was Jesus, not David, who ascended into heaven and is responsible for pouring out the Holy Spirit.

- These verses provide a reproof for their lack of understanding what God was doing in their midst.

- These verses provide a rebuke for their mocking of the promised, demonstrated power of God.

3. <u>David prophesied of Jesus' exaltation over his enemies</u> (2:34b–35).

- These verses read: "but he himself says: The LORD said to my LORD, sit at My right hand, until I make Your enemies a footstool for Your feet."

- These verses provide instruction that David acknowledged Jesus as his LORD.

- These verses provide instruction that David understood that Jesus was the One about whom God promised him that he would have one of his descendants seated on his throne. (This refers to verse 30, which is based upon 2 Samuel 7:12f)

- This appeal serves as a sobering rebuke that their opposition to Jesus only made his exaltation over them a certainty.

4. <u>You are God's enemies having crucified Jesus, the Lord and Messiah</u> (2:36).

- This verse reads: "Therefore let all the house of Israel know for certain that God has made Him both Lord and Christ—this Jesus whom you crucified."

- The "Therefore" of this appeal serves as the great implication of their grievous sin which must silence their mocking and bring about repentance.

- This appeal serves as a severe rebuke that they were not worshippers of God, but they had proven themselves to be enemies of God.

- This appeal serves as a severe rebuke that as Christ's enemies they were destined for certain humiliation.

Again, we find one brief portion of Scripture responsible for the appeals made to the hearers of the sermon. Psalm 110:1 was used to leverage four inferences that served as the basis to end their mocking, to supply insight to replace their ignorance, and to provide conviction for the sin that they committed against the LORD. The purpose of this apologetic-evangelistic sermon was achieved in two stages. First, initial achievement of the purpose of the sermon was obtained through the effective hearing of the four inferential closing appeals as evidenced by the hearers' conviction-filled question— "What must we do?" Second, the purpose of the sermon was achieved completely by their subsequent compliance to Peter's impromptu direct closing appeal of exhortation for them to repent and be baptized. Peter's use of Psalm 110:1 in the conclusion of his sermon was instrumental to reprove and rebuke the mockers as well as to bring them to faith in Christ.

Acts 7:2–53

Stephen's sermon found in Acts 7:2–53 represents the more typical fashion of how Scripture is used in a sermon conclusion. This sermon conclusion is typical in the sense that each closing appeal is substantiated by a different scriptural referent. The conclusion of Stephen's sermon begins at 7:51[37] and goes to 7:53. The closing appeals of this sermon are in the form of direct closing appeals based upon selected scriptural passages. These three closing appeals are direct appeals of indictment. Each one of these appeals served the purpose to prove Stephen's innocence and their guilt. I find the following three closing appeals used by Stephen to rebuke his callous, unregenerate hearers:

1. The Holy Spirit is resisted by you who are stiff-necked and uncircumcised in heart and ears just like your fathers (7:51).

2. The Righteous One of God was murdered by you, just as your fathers killed the prophets (7:52).

3. The Law of God, ordained by angels, is violated by you, just as with your fathers (7:53).

Stephen's purpose in preaching his sermon was to prove that they, not he, were guilty of being blasphemers against Moses and against God. His purpose was achieved through his correct recitation of the history of Israel as well as his accurate depiction of their resisting the Holy Spirit to the point of betraying and murdering the Righteous One of God. Stephen's successful shifting of the sin of blasphemy from himself to his accusers was accomplished through the three closing appeals he made in the conclusion of his sermon. Each of the three appeals were backed by well-known Scriptural events that his accusers would have made quick correlation between the actions of their fathers and themselves.

The first appeal, dealing with their rebellious spirit, is a reference to Exodus 32:1–9, wherein Israel's rebellion was demonstrated in the golden calf idolatry. The second appeal relates to 2 Chronicles 36:15–21. These verses provide a summation of the Southern Kingdom of Judah's refusal to hear God's Word announced through his prophets which he sent to them again and again. Having despised the Word of God and his prophets, God brought upon them a seventy-year Babylonian captivity. The third appeal is a reference to the events found in Exodus 19–20 where Moses went up to Mount Sinai to receive the law from God. These three appeals supported by three passages of Scripture were used by Stephen to achieve the purpose of his polemical sermon—to indict these men who resisted and resented the work that God was doing

---

37. At verse 51, Stephen turns from recounting a brief but comprehensive history of Israel, a past tense laden account, to a scathing indictment, a present tense account, of the sinfulness of his hearers with the words, "You men who are . . ." At this juncture, the sermon definitely reaches its highpoint.

in their midst through his preaching and the great wonders and signs he was performing among the people.

Admittedly, the Scripture references used in these sermon conclusions are not as immediately apparent to twenty-first century Christians as they would have been to first century Jews. This, however, does not mean that they are not there. They are there. Additionally, it should be observed that the use of Scripture in these sermons was to establish implications or applications drawn from the Scripture reference(s) thus constituting the closing appeals of the sermon conclusion. This is the methodology advocated to allow preaching, profitable preaching, to be done in the conclusion to make the conclusion the highpoint of the sermon by presenting related Scripture passages to the preaching text and its purpose, thus indicating from the Word of God how the hearers are to respond to the preached text. It must not be overlooked that the conclusion of a sermon as the highpoint of the sermon is intended to be effective for followers of Christ, primarily, as well as for those who are outside of Christ.

Hebrews 1:1–13:19

The purpose for the sermon known as the New Testament epistle to the Hebrews is composed of two statements, one found in 2:1 and the other in 3:1–2a, which read: "We must pay much closer attention to what we have heard, so that we do not drift away from it. . . . Therefore, holy brethren, partakers of a heavenly calling, consider Jesus, the Apostle and High Priest of our confession; He was faithful to Him who appointed Him." Based upon these explicit assertions, it should rightly be expected for the conclusion of this sermon to enforce a challenge to personally duplicate Christ's faithfulness to the Word of God in everyday Christianity. This expectation is realized as the closing appeals constituted the practical ways such faithfulness was to become a daily reality for those first century Hebrew Christians. The purpose of this epistle/sermon, drawn from verses 2:1 and 3:1–2a, may be expressed as "To pay closer attention to the Word of God and not drift away from it by considering the faithfulness of Jesus to his Father, since he, too, was tempted in the things which he suffered." The "Therefore" of 3:1 is a reference to the previous verse, 2:18, which indicates the temptation and sufferings of Christ. The sufferings of the Hebrew Christians and their temptation to drift from the Word to alleviate their sufferings spoke very directly to the situation of these Jews who professed faith in Christ.

In 12:1–2 we find a transition to the conclusion. Verse 3 reiterates the purpose statement to establish a vital transition through the means of considering Christ so that you do not grow weary and lose heart. I find six direct closing appeals through which every believer in Christ[38] will have the purpose of the sermon/epistle accom-

---

38. This sermonic epistle was written to believers as well as those who were not believers but only thought to be so. The spiritual reality of all would be exposed by their ongoing response to this epistle. The Hebrew hearers and readers of this sermonic epistle would display their true identity as

plished in his or her life if they will comply with the appeals. The six appeals I find in this conclusion from 12:4–13:19 are as follows:

1. <u>Strengthen yourself by means of God's discipline that your paths may be straight</u> (12:4–13).

2. <u>Appropriate God's grace for the pursuit of peace and sanctification</u> (12:14–17).

3. <u>Do not refuse to give obedience to God's Word and gratitude for God's work</u> (12:25–29).

4. <u>Love believers with hospitality and honor from character that is free from greed</u> (13:1–6).

5. <u>Remember the conduct of faithful believers and imitate it</u> (13:7–14).

6. <u>Offer to God the sacrifices that please him</u> (13:15–19).

Each of these closing appeals represent the common form of appeals found in sermon conclusions which are primarily exhortations. As exhortation is the form and content of the closing appeals and the Scriptures from which they are derived, correction and training in righteousness will be the profitable effects provided for believers. Through compliance to the closing appeals, the sermon's purpose can be achieved in the lives of the hearers.

The final six verses of this epistle, 13:20–25, were not part of the sermon conclusion. Verses 20–21 of chapter thirteen contain the benediction to the sermon/epistle. Verses 22–25 of chapter thirteen contains the postscript to the letter—a few matters that were not part of the sermon. Verses 18–24 of chapter twelve, however, contain an illustration which generally contrasts the differences between Zion and Sinai, but more specifically contrasts the excellence of the New Covenant through the blood of Jesus over the terror of the Old Covenant established on Sinai. This illustration serves as the clinching element of persuasion for the entire conclusion of the sermon/epistle.

Each of the six closing appeals were accompanied by Old Testament references. Therefore, each of the six closing appeals satisfy what must be the case, that being, that each closing appeal is based upon a Scripture referent(s). The first closing appeal included a quotation of Proverbs 3:11–12. The second closing appeal included a reference to the account of Esau found in Genesis 25:33f. The third closing appeal included a quotation from Haggai 2:6. The fourth closing appeal included a quotation found in Deuteronomy 31:6, 8 and Joshua 1:5, supplemented with a quotation of Psalm 118:6. The fifth closing appeal included a reference to the sin offering found in Leviticus 4:12, 21; 9:11; 16:27. The sixth closing appeal included a reference to Ezekiel 3:17–21. Each appeal was sanctioned by scriptural support which Hebrew Christians would have recognized readily. Even the clinching element of persuasion,

---

they would be found paying closer attention to the truths they heard, or falling away, drifting from the same truths.

the contrasted differences between Sinai and Zion, was a biblical illustration including the insight from Exodus 19:12 that "If even a beast touches the mountain, it will be stoned." Additionally, Moses' response to the event was recorded as, "I am full of fear and trembling" which was drawn from Deuteronomy 9:19.

The conclusions of sermons found in Scripture demonstrate the use of Scripture to substantiate the closing appeals to the hearers or readers of these sermons. Through Scripture-based closing appeals the previously referenced preachers included in the pages of the Bible provided a means by which the purpose of their sermons could be accomplished in the lives of their hearers/readers.

As evidenced by sermons found in the New Testament, the use of Scripture in the conclusions of these sermons played a vital role. Scripture used in the conclusion of a sermon supplies profitable instruction, reproof, correction, and training in righteousness. Through the use of Scripture in the sermon conclusion, Scripture will provide the needed content that can make the sermon conclusion the highpoint of the sermon. The highpoint of the sermon is attributed in no small way to the fact that the purpose of the sermon is achieved in the conclusion, through the content contained in the conclusion, which is based upon scriptural references.

8

The Purpose of the Sermon Achieved: Part 2

"What should cause the preacher to be passionate in the conclusion will be the provision of content that can redirect the lives of the hearers, the substance contained in the closing appeals, which, if implemented by the hearers, will be life changing, and thus, accomplish the purpose of the sermon."

"The various insights and closing appeals of the conclusion must be related to the sermon's purpose, thus providing for the hearers in the conclusion what was promised to them in the introduction as the sermon purpose was stated. In the conclusion the preacher must do more than restate the purpose, he must press for the accomplishment of the purpose in the lives of his hearers."

"There can be no curtailment in establishing the meaning of the text. But, since the conclusion must not be deprived of necessary time, some peripheral matters of explanation will have to be sacrificed. The required sacrifice being for the best of all causes, time needed to provide content that optimally accomplishes the purpose of the sermon in the conclusion."

"The sermon conclusion is complete when one has accomplished the purpose for the sermon and has accomplished it so fully that . . . the content of the conclusion not only relates to the purpose for preaching the sermon, but it has also achieved it. Achieving the purpose of the sermon in the conclusion is an instance of 'Mission Accomplished!' And 'mission accomplished' in preaching is true preaching efficiency."

"The sermon conclusion . . . draws from other texts of Scripture to show how the purpose of the preaching text is achieved by means of additional passages of Scripture. These additional passages, having practical insights not found in the preaching text but are related to the . . . preaching passage's purpose, provide an extended basis for

informing God's people how they are to live according to God's purposes contained in the completed counsel of Scripture."

"Scripture, in its incredible sufficiency provides an unparalleled resource for supplying biblical responses to biblical instruction. There is nothing like the wisdom gleaned from the Scripture's "whole counsel of God" to inform his people how best to respond to any specific portion of his Word. . . . As this is done, God's intention for the preaching portion of his Word will be fulfilled and it will be accomplished by means of the broader provision of his Word."

"Conclusions vary in specificity versus generality of intent, but the purpose of the conclusion must be directly related to, and dictated by, the intended immediate thrust of the preaching passage and the broader purposes that may be generalized from it. That must always be kept in mind and never violated."

"The sermon's purpose is practical in nature and, as such, it will help hearers to become obedient to things in which there is present disregard or disobedience. Basically, that means changing how life is lived in accordance with the truth of God's Word as understood through the exposition of the text. This being the case, there is a vital responsibility to instruct the conscience by providing the correct motives for doing what the hearers are challenged to do. To fail to address correct motives for doing anything, making any changes whatsoever, is a great error. It is insufficient to instruct people about what they are to do (or not do) without providing the "how" to go about it and the "why" they are to do it. . . . Hearers of sermons must be able to discern that the applications, in the form of closing appeals drawn from Scripture, square with the meaning of the passages from which they were derived and that they match what the broader canon of scriptural teaching records for behavior and conduct."

"We have the Word of God—the Scriptures, and if used in all of the sermon, even the sermon conclusion, preaching will have authority and integrity right up to the final words of the sermon. And, more importantly, we will not be replacing God's Word with man's words and replacing his ways with man's ways."

"The simple bottom-line must be this, who can preach for a verdict if there is no purpose in preaching the sermon? Certainly, one could have a purpose for preaching a sermon though not being zealous to achieve it, but who could preach for a verdict without having a clear, distinct, and definite purpose for preaching the sermon? Preachers who have a purpose for the sermon can preach for a verdict and should do so zealously."

"More than just bringing the sermon to an end, a conclusion must bring the sermon to an ultimate point, a climax, an apex, a crescendo. The ultimate point which the conclusion brings the sermon to is the accomplishment of the sermon's purpose. A sermon that ends without accomplishing a practical objective in the lives of its

hearers causes the conclusion to be weak and the sermon to be pointless. An old whaler, after listening to a discourse which lacked an effective conclusion, made a just criticism in his remark that it 'had no harpoon in it.'"

"What must be done away with is the idea of a purposeless sermon. This must be reckoned as oxymoronic as thunderous silence, pleasant sorrow, virtuous demons, or bright darkness. It must be viewed as folly to think that one can preach a sermon that has no purpose; that one can preach a sermon that calls believers to respond in no way to the truth of Scripture; that one can preach a sermon that reveals God's non-existent design for his Word in the lives of his people.

It must be resolved that a sermon, if it is truly a sermon, will not only have a purpose but the purpose will be achieved optimally by the content that comprises the conclusion. The conclusion must be understood in terms of its design and result. In its design, the conclusion of the sermon is an intensified emphasis on the purpose of the message. In its result, the conclusion of the sermon achieves a thorough accomplishment of the purpose of the message."

A MATTER OF PURPOSE (CONTINUED)

Completing the Sermon by Achieving the Purpose (continued)

The Sermon's Purpose as a Catalyst for Passion

The preacher's desire to see the sermon's purpose accomplished in the lives of his hearers should cause him to be passionate in the conclusion. A passionate conclusion? What a rarity! When there are instances where a sermon conclusion may be exhibited, often it will be discovered that the preacher's passion is spent. Furthermore, what is evidenced by the content of the conclusion is sermonic substance to provide a transition to a shut-down mode.

But, of course, the present-day weakness of sermon conclusions defies what used to be a norm of conventional wisdom for preaching, such as: "One should begin the sermon with the conclusion in view. He should strike the same chord in the conclusion which he did at the beginning, though with tenfold force. If one has this aim, to leave a deep and lasting impression on the heart of the hearers, pathetic and passionate thoughts will be gathered up for the conclusion."[1] Again, it is the desire of the preacher to accomplish the purpose of the sermon that will spearhead passion in the conclusion. Obviously, what should cause the preacher to be passionate in the conclusion will be the provision of content that can redirect the lives of the hearers, the substance contained in the closing appeals, which, if implemented by the hearers, will be life changing, and thus, accomplish the purpose of the sermon in their lives.

1. Hoppin, *Homiletics*, 1883, 437.

Not only will having a purpose to be achieved in the conclusion cause the preacher to be passionate in that portion of the sermon when he gets there, it will supply a hastening spirit for him throughout the sermon since he so earnestly desires to get to this portion of the message. In fact, the entire sermon makes a way for, and provides an impetus to, the closing appeals of the conclusion. And, as this is done, everything contained in the sermon "should hasten to the end."[2]

The Sermon's Purpose Fixed in the Conscience of the Hearers

Just as the introduction prepares the way for the sermon to be heard, the conclusion prepares the way for the sermon to be heeded. Until this is done, a sermon may end but it will have no actual completion. The various insights and closing appeals of the conclusion must be related to the sermon's purpose, thus providing for the hearers in the conclusion what was promised to them in the introduction as the sermon purpose was stated. In the conclusion the preacher must do more than restate the purpose, he must press for the accomplishment of the purpose in the lives of his hearers. And, as he does so, the preacher should "fix it unforgettably in the conscience of the hearer, so that he will not be able to rest until this purpose has been realized in his life."[3] This may be done by examining a life in which this purpose was honored, or a life in which the purpose was set aside and, therefore, the inevitable consequences of its rejection are demonstrated.[4] Such exemplification is one form of what will be referred to as the clinching element of persuasion in a later chapter, chapter seventeen, and will be considered there fully.

The Sermon's Purpose in Preaching Efficiency

A sermon conclusion, more than any other portion of a sermon, should demonstrate the assertion that: "Preaching is always for an object, always aimed at a practical result, never for dalliance with entertaining materials."[5] Regarding sermon conclusions, no other part of the sermon defines itself more definitively, more conclusively. Everything contained in the sermon should point one way, toward the conclusion. Every part of the sermon should contribute, primarily in an indirect way, to the ultimate aim of the sermon which is the sermon's conclusion. The result of this, when this is the procedure for preaching, will be true preaching efficiency.

Efficiency in preaching is not accomplished by denuding the explanation of the text or manipulating the interpretation of the text so that the treatment of the text relates directly to the conclusion. Certainly not. The preaching passage must be carefully

2. Hoppin, *Homiletics*, 1883, 437.

3. Reu, *Homiletics*, 1922, 502.

4. Reu, *Homiletics*, 1922, 502.

5. Phelps, *The Theory of Preaching*, 1882, 456.

expounded, given thorough explanation. Due diligence must be given to establish the meaning of the text in preaching the body of the sermon without attempting to tie it to the conclusion that will follow. In other words, just preach the text as the text!

Additionally, preaching efficiency does not require needless haste to get to the conclusion, nor does it require an attempt to preach the gist of the conclusion in the body of the sermon. The conclusion can wait until it can be appropriately addressed in its proper time and place in the sermon. It does not have to be interjected prematurely. The conclusion can stand a thorough treatment of the preaching passage before it appears in the sermon. That being said, a true desire to achieve the purpose of a sermon should cause a preacher to be more efficient in his preaching.

However, true efficiency means that not everything that could be said to explain the text will be said. Everything that must be said and should be said, will be said. There can be no curtailment in establishing the meaning of the text. But, since the conclusion must not be deprived of necessary time, some peripheral matters of explanation will have to be sacrificed. The required sacrifice being for the best of all causes, time needed to provide content that optimally accomplishes the purpose of the sermon in the conclusion. A soldier in a fire-fight who has a limited amount of ammunition understands the value of the concept that, "Frequency of shot is less to be regarded than efficiency of shot."[6] This principle of efficiency must be judiciously adhered to in expository preaching so that the needed time for an effective conclusion will be available.

A preacher must be efficient to the point that he allows himself sufficient opportunity to conclude well by accomplishing his purpose for preaching that text of Scripture. Therein lies the crucial consideration of the ultimate application of the sermon, the closing appeals contained in the sermon conclusion, through which the achievement of the sermon's purpose is accomplished. It is not enough to be relevant in preaching, though this certainly must be the case. What is required is that a preacher be precise and thorough in the most significant application of the sermon, found in the sermon conclusion, so that he does not leave undone what he is responsible to do for his hearers.

In fulfilling what he is required to do, every sermon conclusion must bear the common component of drawing out the natural and necessary responses to the truth of the passage which was explained, showing the hearers how the meaning of the text can be acted upon in daily living. Until this is done, the sermon is not complete. The sermon conclusion is complete when one has accomplished the purpose for the sermon and has accomplished it so fully that one can obey the counsel, "when you feel no necessity of adding anything, let nothing be added."[7] Yet, the major assertion in the matter is that there is truly nothing more that would be vital to say because the content of the conclusion not only relates to the purpose for preaching the sermon,

---

6. Phelps, *The Theory of Preaching*, 1882, 511.

7. Vinet, *Homiletics*, 1854, 321.

but it has also achieved it. Achieving the purpose of the sermon in the conclusion is an instance of "Mission Accomplished!" And "mission accomplished" in preaching is true preaching efficiency.

If we have thoroughly explained the passage and thoroughly helped God's people to implement God's truth into their lives, we have been efficient in preaching. Accomplishing the purpose for preaching the sermon, and only this, is truly efficient preaching. Necessary explanation and application in the body of the sermon is a given. These simply must be present. And yet more is needed. Spurgeon is of benefit here as he instructed:

> I would add that, in our preaching, *we must become more and more earnest and practical*. . . . [Y]our object is to pierce men's hearts. . . . Your work is to charge home at the heart and conscience. Fire into the very center of the foe. Aim at effect. . . . [I]n the right sense, aim at effect,—effect upon the conscience and upon the heart. Some preachers remind me of the famous Chinese jugglers, who not long ago were everywhere advertised. One of these stood against a wall and the other threw knives at him. One knife would be driven into the board just above his head, and another close by his ear, while under his armpit and between his fingers quite a number of deadly weapons were bristling. Wonderful art to be able to throw to a hair's breadth and never strike! How many among us (preachers) have a marvelous skill in missing! . . . [I]f you want to be the means of saving yourselves and them that hear you, cry to your Lord for faithfulness, practicalness, real heart-moving power. Never play at preaching, nor beat about the bush; get at it, and always mean business.[8]

The business we need to be about, the business that commonly is not attended to, is the business of having a clearly defined purpose for the sermon and achieving that purpose through the content of the sermon conclusion.

The Sermon's Purpose and God's Intention

We must define and achieve the purpose of the sermon, "otherwise the conclusion of every sermon will be an embarrassing anti-climax."[9] However, the purpose for which one preaches must be related to the purpose God designed the text to have in the lives of his people. Determining the Holy Spirit's purpose for a passage "is one of the most important obligations in preaching, and perhaps the greatest of all . . . (and) a failure to do so constitutes an affront to the Holy Spirit."[10] A preacher simply cannot come up with a purpose so that he will not be purposeless in preaching. He must discover,

---

8. Spurgeon, *An All-round Ministry*, 1900, 117–8.

9. Stott, *Between Two Worlds*, 251.

10. Adams, *Preaching with Purpose*, 25.

draw out of the passage as precisely as he can, what God intends for the passage to accomplish in daily living. Alex Montoya put it this way:

> Have a reason to preach. Ours is not just to help them understand the truth but to persuade them to be "doers of the word" (James 1:27). Exposition is not merely explaining truth but expecting people to practice truth! . . . Expositors need to keep these words in mind. We are in danger of making "exposition" the end, in itself, rather than a means to an end. Paul's exhortation to "preach the word!" is more to accomplish an end (i.e., teaching, reproving, correcting, training, and exhorting) than an act for an act's sake! Although exposition is the chief of methodologies, if it has no verdict, no explicit purpose, and no warrant, then it will lack in pathos and urgency. Since every portion of Scripture has a purpose, the expositor must find that purpose and preach that purpose.[11]

Securing a biblical purpose means securing the true meaning and intent of Scripture. This means that the grammatical-historical truth of Scripture has been determined, supplying the meaning of the text, as well as determining God's purpose (the intent) for having the passage written originally, securing the intent of the passage.[12]

Perhaps the foremost advocate for purpose in preaching, Jay Adams, suggests three macro-intentions of a text of Scripture: to inform; to convince (to believe of disbelieve); to motivate to do. Thus, a sermonic purpose is what, specifically, the congregation should learn, believe/disbelieve, or do.[13] In actuality, what is to be learned and what is to be believed and disbelieved will be taken care of in the process of expounding the preaching text. Therefore, the purpose will always be about how one lives in light of what has been learned and what one must believe and disbelieve. This being the case, the purpose of the sermon being achieved in the lives of the hearers will necessitate instruction pertaining to how one is to live according to God's purpose for the preaching passage: what is required so that obedience might be one's personal reality; what are the obstacles to obedience and how one can overcome them; what is necessary for one to maintain obedience once obedience has been initiated, etc.

Adams is emphatic and helpful in establishing the merit of discerning God's intent in a biblical text as he writes:

> There are few deficiencies in preaching quite so disastrous in their effect as the all too frequently occurring failure to determine the *telos* (or purpose) of a preaching portion. The passage, and therefore the Word of God itself, is misrepresented, misused, and mishandled when its purpose has not been determined, with the direct result that its power and its authority are lost. . . . You must never preach on a passage until you are certain you understand why

---

11. Montoya, *Preaching with Passion*, 95.

12. Brown Jr., *A Quest for Reformation in Preaching*, 135.

13. Adams, *Preaching with Purpose*, 31.

the Holy Spirit included that passage in the Bible. When you have grasped His purpose, what He intended to do to the recipient of his message, then—and then *only*—do you have the purpose for your sermon, and then—and then only—do you know what God wants you to do to your listeners through it.[14]

More significantly Adams clarifies the extent of the Spirit's intention for a passage when he supplies the following insights:

> When I speak of the purpose or the *telos* of a preaching portion, I refer to the purpose the Holy Spirit had when he "moved" the writer to pen the words of that passage. That purpose was *broader* than the immediate purpose in the writer's mind when writing to a particular person or church. Paul himself makes this point when he uses Old Testament passages in New Testament contexts:
>
> > Now these events happened as examples for us so that we might not desire evil things as they did (I Cor. 10:6).
> >
> > Now these events happened to them as examples and were recorded as counsel for us who live at this late date in history (I Cor. 10:11).
> >
> > Note also his words in I Corinthians 9:9, 10:
> >
> > It is written in Moses' law, "Do not muzzle an ox when it is threshing." It isn't about oxen that God is concerned, is it? Isn't He really speaking about us? It was written for us, because when the plowman plows and the thresher threshes he should do so in hope of having a share of the crop.
> >
> > Paul himself determined that the *telos* of the Holy Spirit was broader than the situation to which the passage in Deuteronomy 25:4 originally was addressed. He saw that the Holy Spirit's intention in it was *to teach a principle* that was of greater value than when it was originally applied to oxen. . . . So, it must be understood that when I say that the intention of the Holy Spirit must be discovered. I do not mean merely His intention *in its limited application* to an event at the time when the passage was written, but any and all valid applications that He intended to make from any principles that may be generalized from the basic thrust of the passage. . . . The thing to be avoided at all costs is to impose your own purposes on the passage. . . . What you must work for is to make His purpose your own.[15]

To understand that God has an intent for his Word and to discover that intent but not to seek to accomplish this intent in the preaching of his Word is simply an irresponsible handling of Scripture.

The hermeneutical principles of the analogy of faith; Scripture interprets Scripture; progressive revelation; and one meaning—many applications of Scripture; provide additional support for understanding that the Holy Spirit's purpose of a passage is more than a limited understanding for that text alone. This is particularly significant

---

14. Adams, *Preaching with Purpose*, 27.
15. Adams, *Preaching with Purpose*, 27–29.

for the sermon conclusion as it draws from other texts of Scripture to show how the purpose of the preaching text is achieved by the helpful use of additional passages of Scripture. These additional passages, having practical insights not found in the preaching text but are related to the same subject-matter of the preaching passage's purpose, provide an extended basis for informing God's people how they are to live according to God's purposes contained in the completed counsel of Scripture.

The heightened significance of a sermon is accomplished by expressing, as persuasively as possible, the potential merit of the sermon if its purpose is accomplished in the lives of the hearers. This purpose must be stated so that it aligns with the interpretation of Scripture and the needs of the hearers.[16]

The four ways in which the God-breathed Scriptures are stated to be "profitable" in 2 Timothy 3:16; "for teaching, for reproof, for correction, for training in righteousness" provide the means by which the purpose of the sermon may be achieved most effectively. Scripture, in its incredible sufficiency provides an unparalleled resource for supplying biblical responses to biblical instruction. There is nothing like the wisdom gleaned from the Scripture's "whole counsel of God" to inform his people how best to respond to any specific portion of his Word. Furthermore, this is in keeping with how the purpose for the sermon was determined initially, which requires one to "consider as near as possible what God intended in revealing that portion of His word, and then you will be in line with the thoughts of God."[17] As this is done, God's intention for the preaching portion of his Word will be fulfilled and it will be accomplished by means of the broader provision of his Word.

Conclusions vary in specificity versus generality of intent, but the purpose of the conclusion must be directly related to, and dictated by, the intended immediate thrust of the preaching passage and the broader purposes that may be generalized from it. That must always be kept in mind and never violated. The purpose statement, declared in the sermon's introduction, and everything said and done in the conclusion should match. Here is the crucial relationship between the sermon introduction and the sermon conclusion. The sermon introduction introduces the purpose of the sermon and the conclusion accomplishes the purpose of the sermon. The purpose statement reveals what the preacher intends to accomplish in the sermon and depicts the basic destination at which the preacher intends to arrive. The conclusion of the sermon keeps the preacher occupied with material that will help his hearers to be able to practice in their lives what he has been explaining in the preaching text. Jay Adams addressed this well when he wrote, "The conclusion either summarizes, applies, or implements truth, or, as in most instances, does some or all of the above. Surely it is important to preach for results—the results that the Holy Spirit intended when He caused the preaching portion to be written."[18]

16. Brown Jr., *A Quest for Reformation in Preaching,* 136.

17. Simpson, *Lectures on Preaching,* 1897, 136.

18. Adams, *Preaching with Purpose,* 66.

The Sermon's Purpose and Integrity

The sermon's purpose is practical in nature and, as such, it will help hearers to become obedient to things in which there is present disregard or disobedience. Basically, that means changing how life is lived in accordance with the truth of God's Word as understood through the exposition of the text. This being the case, there is a vital responsibility to instruct the conscience by providing the correct motives for doing what the hearers are challenged to do.[19] To fail to address correct motives for doing anything, making any changes whatsoever, is a great error. It is insufficient to instruct people about what they are to do (or not do) without providing the "how" to go about it and the "why" they are to do it. Living according to the truth of God's Word is not simply a matter of doing what one is told to do, even when being told by one who professes to be a true preacher of God's Word. Hearers of sermons must be able to discern that the applications, in the form of closing appeals drawn from Scripture, square with the meaning of the passages from which they were derived and that they match what the broader canon of scriptural teaching records for behavior and conduct.

Living according to God's truth is responding to God, doing what his Word instructs us to do, doing it for the right reasons, and doing it in the right way, in the correct manner. So, therefore, let me clarify what was stated above. In the case of careful expository preaching where the preaching passage has been thoroughly scrutinized, the conscience and motives will have been addressed, even if indirectly, along the lines of the text's explanation. Still, when the closing appeals of the sermon conclusion are composed of insights drawn from the broader scope of scriptural cross references, these passages must be examined and investigated, if necessary, so that the action called for can be understood as a correct usage of those references, that the action called for as well as the motivation for that action are in line with the meaning of the passages used as cross references. However, the references used for the closing appeals in a sermon conclusion should be so straightforward and their connection so obvious that examination and investigation should be necessary infrequently.

Jesus' teaching and preaching implicitly and explicitly declared, "But I say unto you." His proclamations were straightforward, vivid, concrete, and authoritative. Christ's preaching "had singleness of thought and singleness of aim, and everything He said made this known."[20] Christ's teachings in the Sermon on the Mount, which accurately indicated the true purposes of the Old Testament passages used, were in part responsible for the response of the crowds who were astonished as they heard him preach. The astonishing thing about his teaching is that it was accompanied with authority, a characteristic that the scribes and Pharisees lacked.[21] The authority of

---

19. Dale, *Nine Lectures on Preaching*, 1890, 133.
20. Hoyt, *Vital Elements of Preaching*, 1929, 318.
21. Matthew 7:28–29.

God's Word was undeniable in Christ's teaching as he handled Scripture according to its God-given intent.

The Word of God—Jesus Christ, provided perfect instruction in his preaching for what people were to do, how people were to do what he said, and why they were to do so. Though we are not Christ, we have the Word of God—the Scriptures, and if used in all of the sermon, even the sermon conclusion, preaching will have authority and integrity right up to the final words of the sermon. And, more importantly, we will not be replacing God's Word with man's words and replacing his ways with man's ways. Scriptural insights composing the framework of the closing appeals of the conclusion aligns perfectly with the best understanding of what expository preaching is. Expository preaching is "a self-conscious, principled commitment to preaching in such a way that Scripture itself is supplying the main theme, principal headings, and central application" in our preaching.[22] Expository preaching must also include the concept of preaching in such a way that Scripture is used in the sermon conclusion to supply the practical insights for how believers are to live their lives in responsible stewardship of the understanding of the preaching text they have received.

The Sermon's Purpose and the Ministry of Preaching

How well we are convinced about the tragedy of a Christian life, well-lived for many years, that ends poorly. That is truly tragic! Is it really any different with a sermon? Just in case there should be any ambivalence in answering the question, let me answer it rather emphatically—Absolutely Not! A good sermon which is preached well but ends without a conclusion or ends with a poor conclusion is a tragedy. As one author descriptively phrased it, "A weak, draggle-tailed ending often ruins an otherwise useful sermon. Waters which rushed out of the fountain in the introduction, and passed through lovely and awe-inspiring scenery in their course, must not be allowed to dribble away in their end."[23] The conclusion should, as a rule, form the climax of the sermon. Great care is necessary to prevent it from being anything other than the highpoint of the sermon. A conclusion that truly is the climax of the sermon and, as such, motivates hearers to action "demands great concentration of force, blow after blow, falling on the same point."[24] This point upon which all concentration finally falls will be achieving the purpose of a sermon, *the point of all points* in a sermon, the prized object in the crosshairs of the preacher's sermonic scope.

Achieving the purpose of a sermon in the lives of God's people is an unrivaled act of ministry for a preacher in the process of preaching. There is no greater blessing than to be a means used by God in the lives of his people to help them live lives

22. Dever et al., *Preaching the Cross*, from J. Ligon Duncan III's chapter "Preaching Christ from the Old Testament," 39.

23. Bull, *Preaching and Sermon Construction*, 1922, 135.

24. Bull, *Preaching and Sermon Construction*, 1922, 137.

pleasing to him as they walk according to the truth of his Word. What a tremendous thing to be used by God in the sanctification process of his people as he causes them to be more like their Lord, Jesus Christ, as their lives become more obedient to the truth of his Word. No well-intentioned preacher of God's Word seeks for anything less.

Therefore, the conclusion of the sermon is the acid-test for what a preacher is all about in the preaching process, namely, that it is not enough to explain the truth of Scripture. Certainly, truth must be explained but even as this is done, more is needed. Two problems immediately present themselves. The worst of the two being that truth is not actually preached, that is, preaching that does not compare with preaching found in Scripture. Steven J. Lawson addresses this when he opines, "Tragically, most of what passes for biblical preaching today falls woefully short of apostolic standards. . . . Many evangelical ministers have succumbed to delivering secular-sounding, motivational pep talks aimed at soothing felt needs of restless church shoppers or, worse, salving the guilty consciences of unregenerate church members."[25]

But the second problem is also tragic and is more common than the first. This problem is a failure demonstrated by a preacher who, having explained a passage of Scripture, does not help his hearers in their responsibility to conduct themselves according to the ultimate truth of the passage, the purpose of the passage, so that the ultimate truth of the passage, its purpose, may be borne out in their daily living. Learning to implement the truths of Scripture into life is so essential to fulfilling the Great Commission that Jesus designated his future followers as "disciples" or learners. According to Jesus, the apostles were to make disciples, followers of Christ who are learning to incorporate biblical truth into their lives. What was it that these learners are to be taught in order to be the disciples Jesus desires? Disciples are made by "teaching them to observe all that I have commanded you." Personal application of the Word of God is how the Great Commission is fulfilled in the lives of believers.[26]

A preacher, thus inclined, has the same passion that was held by the Apostle John as he wrote in 3 John 4, "I have no greater joy than this, to hear of my children walking in the truth." Such a preacher is cognizant of the same privilege that was held by the Apostle Paul as he wrote in Ephesians 4:12 of the gift of pastor-teachers to the church "for the equipping of the saints for the work of service, to the building up of the body of Christ." Such a preacher has the same perspective that was held by the Apostle Peter as he wrote in I Peter 1:14–16, "As obedient children, do not be conformed to the former lusts which were yours in your ignorance, but like the Holy One who called you, be holy yourselves in all your behavior; because it is written, 'YOU SHALL BE HOLY, FOR I AM HOLY.'" The preceding citation Peter used from the Old Testament suggests and exemplifies that, "We are not to shrink from moral exhortation in our preaching of the Bible, whether from the Old Testament or New, because the preachers of the Old Testament and New, under divine inspiration, do not shrink from bringing

25. Lawson, *Famine in the Land*, 38.
26. Lawson, *Famine in the Land*, 30–31.

the imperatives of God's Word onto the hearts and lives of believers. . . . The gospel does not hesitate to call us to response and responsibility."[27] An unhesitating call for response and responsibility should be more apparent in a sermon conclusion than any other place in the sermon.

The Sermon's Purpose and Earnest Preaching

The subject of earnestness was discussed at some length in chapter three, primarily to compare earnest preaching with passionate preaching. Earnest preaching is being readdressed, just briefly, to establish it with the purpose of the sermon. Again, if you look up the word "earnest" in a dictionary, you find definitions like: "strong and firm in purpose; eager and serious;" or "*intent and direct in purpose*; zealous." Imagine that! Earnestness is linked directly to purpose. The connection between earnestness and purpose is not new in preaching. Many years ago, a very popular preaching book in its day, *On Preaching* by Phillips Brooks, posited these choice nuggets of insight connecting earnestness with purpose: "A sermon exists in and for its purpose. That purpose is the persuading and moving of men's souls. That purpose must never be lost sight of. If it ever is, the sermon flags."[28] Brooks was making the point that purpose must not be lost in a preached sermon. I certainly agree with that. The point I am making is that the concept of purpose in preaching, the entire concept, is a lost reality, not just in the practice of preaching individual sermons but in the theory of preaching and in the comprehensive enterprise of preaching. Preaching has become primarily purposeless. In instances where there is a discernable purpose for the sermon it is often a purpose of the preacher rather than the biblical text.

The lost connection between earnestness and purpose must be rediscovered, then recovery of the connection must be made in preaching. The kind of recovery needed is expressed in the following: "If we are to have a new era of power in preaching, we must have a more definite result, toward which all else moves. . . . (T)he preacher needs the power of an engrossing purpose."[29] The rediscovered connection between earnestness and purpose must be understood well, and then it must become a common practice in preaching. As a preacher's purpose for preaching a sermon becomes more clearly focused, his earnestness in preaching the sermon will be more apparent to his hearers.

Another connection that must be understood better in preaching is that the place in the sermon where the purpose is addressed most fully, is the place in the sermon where earnestness should be perceived most fully by the hearers. Since the purpose for preaching the sermon is achieved by means of the conclusion, this should be the place where the greatest earnestness is demonstrated by the preacher and perceived

27. Dever et al., *Preaching the Cross*, from J. Ligon Duncan III's chapter, "Preaching Christ from the Old Testament," 64.

28. Phillips Brooks, *On Preaching*, 110.

29. Pierson, *The Divine Art of Preaching*, 1892, 23–24.

by his hearers. The conclusion often should be the most fervent and moving part of the sermon since it is designed to secure an appropriate and practical effect for the hearers.[30]

It is by means of the sermon conclusion that we possess the most telling insights about the overall merit of a sermon. Brooks pleaded for preachers to understand the goodness of a sermon by a singular standard which was, "you should think no sermon good that does not do its work."[31] The merit of a sermon used to be tied to achieving the purpose of the sermon along with earnestness in achieving it. Consider the following perspective: "A sermon that has an end to reach, and stops short of it, is a failure as truly as a sermon that reaches its true end and highest impression, and then grows weaker by going beyond its proper close."[32] Neither of these failures should exist in the act of preaching.

In fact, Arthur T. Pierson surmised that in pulpit oratory there are three elements, any one of which may control the message: the text, the subject, or the object (or the end aimed at). If the text rules, the result is an exposition; if the subject rules, the result is a discourse; "if the object to be attained be steadily kept in view, and control the disposition of the parts and the expression in the delivery, we get properly a sermon."[33] Though I find Pierson's distinction of a sermon to be *too exclusively a product of its purpose*, he does provide an understanding of the vital connection between a sermon and its purpose. This is precisely the connection that is absent in preaching today.

Earnestness implies that the truth of the preaching passage has taken full possession of the preacher's mind and has kindled an intense desire in his heart to see the truth of his text fleshed out in the lives of his hearers. Earnestness means that all the faculties of the preacher's mind and heart are captivated in the pursuit of seeing the purpose of the sermon achieved in his hearers' lives. Earnestness urges the preacher onward speedily to accomplish his objective since "the object of an earnest man is never for any long period of time absent from his thoughts."[34]

Another strength of the relationship between a sermon's purpose and earnest preaching is established in the statement that: "Many preachers, when they sit down to prepare a sermon, start like Abraham, who 'went out, not knowing whither he went.' The preacher who has a definite end to reach, rarely loses any of the time which he gives to preparation; he sees in the distance the point to which he has to travel and he either finds or makes a road to it."[35] In other words, an inevitable implication of having

---

30. Ripley, *Sacred Rhetoric*, 1849, 106.

31. Brooks, *On Preaching*, 115.

32. Pierson, *The Divine Art of Preaching*, 1892, 114.

33. Pierson, *The Divine Art of Preaching*, 1892, 22.

34. James, *An Earnest Ministry*, 1847, 42.

35. Miller, *The Way to Biblical Preaching*, 123. Miller attributed this quotation to R. W. Dale, but he did not cite the source from which the quote was taken.

a clear purpose for the sermon provides earnestness to study other texts of Scripture to discover how they aid in achieving the purpose of the passage being preached.

Though purpose is essential in writing as well as in preaching, it is by the very nature of preaching to speak to men directly that should produce greater earnestness in a preacher. Socrates said, "I would rather write upon the hearts of living men than upon the skins of dead sheep."[36] This perspective is one that preachers must possess. Since we speak directly to men about eternal issues there must be a sense of recognizing the profound opportunity before him. He must speak, as Richard Baxter phrased it, "as a dying man to dying men."[37] However, a point of contextual insight only heightens the necessity of passionate preaching to achieve the purpose of the sermon, namely, pastors preach predominantly to men and women who are redeemed. They are new creations in Christ Jesus who are created in Christ Jesus for good works which he ordained that they should walk in them. As such, they will give an account to him for how they have lived their lives in Christ.[38]

The Sermon's Purpose and Preaching for a Verdict

I am indebted profoundly to the sentiments of two men writing many years ago about the absolute necessity of having a very specific purpose for preaching, fundamentally, and preaching for a verdict, functionally. Their sentiments about purpose and verdict are so agreeable to me that it would seem like a grave misgiving not to quote them at length. John Henry Jowett, in his Lyman Beecher Lectures on Preaching (The Yale Lectures) delivered at Yale University in 1912 said:

> I think it is needful, before we go into the pulpit, to define ourselves, in simple, decisive terms, what we conceive to be the purpose of the service. Let us clearly formulate the end at which we aim. Let us put it into words . . . and let us compel ourselves to name and register our ends. Let us take a pen in hand, and in order that we may still further banish the peril of vacuity let us commit to paper our purpose and ambition for the day. Let us give it the objectivity of a mariner's chart: let us survey our course, and steadily contemplate our haven. If, when we turn to the pulpit stair, some angel was to challenge us for the statement of our mission, we ought to be able to make immediate answer, without hesitancy or stammering, that this or that is the urgent errand on which we seek to serve our Lord today. But the weakness of the pulpit is too often this;—we are prone to drift through a service when we ought to steer. Too often "we are out on the ocean sailing," but we have no destination; we

---

36. Kennedy, *His Word Through Preaching*, 11.

37. This quote from Richard Baxter does not come from his well-known work, *The Reformed Pastor*, first published in 1656, but from the book, *Baxter's Poetical Fragments*, 1681, p. 40, lines 7–8, where he writes, "I preached, as never sure to preach again, And as a dying man to dying men."

38. Passages such as 2 Cor. 5:17; Eph. 2:10; and 2 Cor 5:10 bear out these significant truths.

are "out for anywhere," and for nowhere in particular. The consequence is that the service has the fashion of a vagrancy when it ought to be possessed by the spirit of a crusade.[39]

In his book, *The Preacher and His Sermon*, J. Paterson Smyth addressed the significance of purpose in preaching as he wrote:

> Never write a sermon in which you have not a definite, clear aim. I've heard sermons carefully prepared and eloquently delivered, too. But I could not see why the man preached them. I could see no purpose in them, except, perhaps, the purpose of preaching a sermon. One would think no man would be such an idiot as to preach without any definite purpose. But I think some do. It is as if a man were working hard with wood and hammer and nails, and when you ask him what he is working at—what he is making—and he should say, "I'm not quite clear about it; I am only hammering.." . . Never, I say, write a sermon in which it is not perfectly clear to you and to your audience: "This is what I want the people to feel; this is what I want the people to do."[40]

Again, Jowett, speaking beyond the matter of purpose in preaching to the ultimate concern of preaching for a verdict, is very instructive when he pleaded:

> In all our preaching we must preach for verdicts. We must present our case, we must seek a verdict, and we must ask for immediate execution of the verdict. We are not in the pulpit to please the fancy. We are not there even to inform the mind, or to disturb the emotions, or to sway the judgment. These are only preparatives along the journey. Our ultimate object is to move the will, to set it in another course, to increase its pace, and to make it sing in "the ways of God's commandments." Yes, we are there to bring the wills of men into tune with the will of God, in order that God's statutes may become their songs.[41]

I find it appalling that such high-minded and valuable perspectives about preaching are lost almost entirely in preaching today. Yet, in the not too distant past it was widely held that "in analyzing the qualities which make a sermon effective, the first" to be named was "definiteness of aim."[42] If definiteness of aim is the chief characteristic of effective preaching then it certainly follows that: "Every sermon should have a distinct object in view"[43] so that "If anyone should say to you, 'What are you driving at?' you should have no hesitation in answering."[44]

The simple bottom-line must be this, who can preach for a verdict if there is no purpose in preaching the sermon? Certainly, one could have a purpose for preaching

39. Jowett, *The Preacher*, 1912, 147–49.
40. Smyth, *The Preacher and His Sermon*, 1922, 109.
41. Jowett, *Preacher*, 1912, 171–72.
42. Taylor, *The Ministry of the Word*, 1876, 110.
43. Taylor, *The Ministry of the Word*, 1876, 110.
44. Hall, *God's Word Through Preaching*, 1875, 115.

a sermon though not being zealous to achieve it, but who could preach for a verdict without having a clear, distinct, and definite purpose for preaching the sermon? Preachers who have a purpose for the sermon can preach for a verdict and should do so zealously.

The Sermon's Purpose Achieved in the Conclusion

More than just bringing the sermon to an end, a conclusion must bring the sermon to an ultimate point, a climax, an apex, a crescendo. The ultimate point which the conclusion brings the sermon to is the accomplishment of the sermon's purpose. A sermon that ends without accomplishing a practical objective in the lives of its hearers causes the conclusion to be weak and the sermon to be pointless. "An old whaler, after listening to a discourse which lacked an effective conclusion, made a just criticism in his remark that it 'had no harpoon in it.'"[45] Lyman Abbott, in the Lyman Beecher lectures on preaching in 1905 wrote:

> If the minister in preparing a sermon has a definite object in view, all his thinking will naturally concentrate itself on the accomplishment of that object, and the sermon will move with increasing power toward the ultimate result. . . . The sermon should be a river, not a chain. It should be so constructed that every new thought should not only conduct to the ultimate conclusion but should reinforce the considerations previously educed: for the object of the sermon is not merely to convince the understanding, it is to transform life; and its value depends, therefore, not merely upon its logical completeness, but upon its reinforcing power.[46]

Not only should the conclusion be the natural consummation of a sermon in which the purpose of the sermon is achieved on behalf of its hearers but in its progression toward the conclusion the sermon should gather greater depth and force to its completion.

The conclusion, then, is not tacked on to add material to the message. When there is a perceptible conclusion in a sermon, it often seems that it is tacked on. When there is not a clear, stated purpose for preaching the sermon, it will be tacked on. It must be tacked on. Why should it be there at all? If there is no purpose for preaching the sermon then there is no need for the conclusion because there is nothing to be accomplished in the preaching of it. The conclusion clarifies, exhorts, and equips the hearers to respond appropriately to the truth that has been declared. The purpose of the sermon set forth in the sermon's introduction *"becomes the focus of the conclusion. Although applications have been made along the way, now the preacher is seeking to call for the basic response to the total message. The motivating thrust really represents*

45. Burrell, *The Sermon: Its Construction and Delivery*, 1913, 190.
46. Abbott, *The Christian Ministry*, 1905, 212.

the issue, the challenge, the call of the theme and text to the listeners. The purpose of the exposition is to proclaim the truth and to call for the response that the truth deserves and demands."[47]

The content contained in the conclusion of a sermon provides explanation, revitalization, conviction, and motivation, in route to the ultimate pursuit of implementation of the truth in the lives of the hearers. In the words of a helpful analogy, the requirement is "to aim our sermons at a particular target, at the pin instead of at the green."[48] While the valuable functional elements of preaching such as explanation, illustration, application, dialog and argumentation are accomplished throughout the body of the sermon, the formal element of a sermon conclusion is dependent upon revitalization, application, illustration, conviction, motivation, and implementation for it to accomplish what a sermon conclusion is meant to accomplish, and thus, "combat the purposelessness of so much preaching."[49]

The Sermon's Purpose and Preaching for Life-Change

To revitalize is to stimulate, to inspire, to arouse enthusiasm, or to deepen a feeling of awe, respect, or devotion on the part of the hearers. To revitalize is to make consciously vital what has been accepted, previously, as vital. The result of revitalization is one of revival, that is, to revive what was once made alive, but has now grown weak and ineffective in one's life. To revitalize is to "make patent what is latent."[50] For a sermon to be a persuasive one, volitionally persuasive, the hearers must be motivated to implement the truth into their lives. This requires that the appeals called for in the sermon conclusion impact the hearts of the hearers not just their heads, that the closing appeals of the conclusion powerfully arrest their emotions/affections along with their intellects, their consciences, and their wills.

Explanation is necessary to cognitively persuade one's hearers that the truth of God's Word demands a response different than what they have offered previously in their lives, but cognitive persuasion must go beyond explanation. If life-change is the ultimate outcome of a sermon, then the penultimate outcome must be "to establish, to influence, to modify, or to change the beliefs" of the hearers.[51] An appropriate change in life is predicated upon hearers inwardly digesting new insights, accepting a more accurate or precise interpretation, or understanding a cause-effect relationship about biblical truth beyond that which was known previously. Jay Adams is insistent that

---

47. Olford and Olford, *Anointed Expository Preaching*, 171, italics added.

48. Cleland, *Preaching to be Understood*, 95.

49. Cleland, *Preaching to be Understood*, 88. The functional elements of explanation, dialog, and argumentation, may at times be used in the conclusion but not to the extent that they are used in the body of the sermon.

50. Cleland, *Preaching to be Understood*, 90.

51. Cleland, *Preaching to be Understood*, 92.

preaching cannot be separated from life-change. He writes: "We are continually concerned about the lack of change preaching brings about. . . . No wonder so little change takes place; much so-called "preaching" does not require it. . . . True preaching . . . *calls on the congregation for a response that is appropriate to it* (the purpose). It works for change. Preaching that stops short of asking for change that is appropriate to the Holy Spirit's letters to His church is not preaching at all; at best, it is lecturing."[52] Again, Adams is particularly insightful in requiring that preaching must be about change of life but preaching and the life-change that is resultant from it must take place through every genre of Scripture. He writes:

> If there are narrative forms, apocalyptic and letter forms, poetic, proverbial and parabolic forms, etc., then you are going to have to learn to "translate" your material from such a form into a preaching form. After all, you aren't in the pulpit to tell stories, recite poetry, or dictate letters! You are there to preach. Neither are you there to talk about the poetic or proverbial form of the preaching portion; a sermon is not a literary analysis of the Bible! Yet much supposed "exposition" is little more than that. Your form, then, must be verbal, not literary; it must grow out of and conform to the purpose of the portion as this best can be conveyed verbally to a given congregation.[53]

It is hard to imagine a perspective about preaching that could be more relevant and needed than that mentioned above from Adams.[54]

The travel from explanation of Scripture to life-change of believers includes cognition, conviction, affection, and volition. A change in life resolved by a hearer demonstrates a volitional response. The volitional response is the result of revitalized affections. Revitalized affections are predicated upon an upgraded theology due to insightful exposition of Scripture.

A preacher desires to obtain some definite corrective response to the truth of Scripture from his hearers. If his heart is right, he intends to preach for a response that will be life changing, a response to God's Word that is sudden, certain, and sincere.[55] Though legitimate life-change only occurs through explaining, through convincing, and through revitalizing, it is crucial that one never minimizes the result of these means—an improved walk of believers in this world that reflects obedience to God's Word, thus glorifying God. This is the purpose of a sermon, every sermon. The closing

---

52. Adams, *Preaching with Purpose*, 42–43.

53. Adams, *Truth Apparent*, 17.

54. Adams is incredibly insightful and instructive with these words. Having survived the futile and enfeebled efforts of inductive homileticians of the later twentieth century to pervert preaching into a non-proclamational event, the same outcome is being perpetuated presently by conservative evangelicals who mistakenly establish genre, not as a crucial hermeneutical consideration, but as a homiletical convention by which preachers should effectively end up not preaching. The seeds of non-deductive propositional declaration in preaching from all genres of Scripture are being sown again.

55. Cleland, *Preaching to be Understood*, 94. Cleland attributes the response as "specific, seen, and soon."

appeals will furnish the ways and means for this improved walk to become a reality, thus achieving the purpose of the sermon.

There is a need to be extremely definitive about distinguishing what is and what is not a sermon. This will not be the only distinction, but it is a major one—If there is no purpose, there is no sermon! Now, that's incredibly radical for our time and in our day. Actually, this just revitalizes a basic understanding of preaching that was readily accepted in former times. Take, for example, this distinction: "The difference between a sermon and a lecture lies in the fact that while a lecture is chiefly concerned with a subject to be elucidated, a sermon is chiefly concerned with an object to be achieved."[56] In this assessment, a sermon is properly fixed to a purpose but the problem is the assessment of what a non-sermon is—a lecture. This stark distinction, in the long run is not just ineffective, but counterproductive. The deduction must be if it is not a lecture then it must be a sermon. This is disagreeable because it is not true. The stark distinction regarding purpose is black and white. A preacher has a purpose, or he does not. He may not have a purpose, but what ensues in his purposeless venture will be, most probably, other than a lecture. However, it cannot be a sermon! The vast majority of "sermons" one may hear will not be a lecture, in that, they will be sermonic in many ways, with the exception being that they do not possess nor are they controlled by a purpose for preaching the sermon and, therefore, they do not end with a strong, effective conclusion that optimally accomplishes the God-given purpose of the preaching text.[57]

A preacher may preach on a text but, without a purpose for preaching the sermon, the result will not be a textual expository sermon. Likewise, a preacher may preach on a topic but, without a purpose for preaching the sermon, the result will not be a topical expository sermon. Even if, in both cases, there were the formal elements of a sermon—introduction, structure, and a conclusion along with the functional elements of a sermon—explanation, illustration, application, dialog and argumentation, the result in either instance would be other than a sermon. The result would be a demonstration of formal and functional elements applied to a text or a topic which was designed to do nothing.

The intent to do nothing with a text is not a sermon! The intent to do nothing with a topic is not a sermon! A sermon is not a sermon because of the incorporation of formal and functional elements, as crucial as these things are to preach a sermon. A sermon is a sermon when, in taking a text or a topic, formal and functional elements are used *to achieve the purpose for preaching the sermon.* The purpose is declared as part of the introduction, the body of the sermon—the exposition of the text—clarifies the rationale for and means by which the hearers may achieve the purpose of the

---

56. Pearson, *The Preacher: His Purpose and Practice*, 89.

57. The other than a lecture, yet, less than a sermon entity is what I call a "preachment." A preachment may contain many of the formal and functional homiletical elements, but it does not possess a purpose. Preachments are far and away the most common entity produced in preaching.

sermon, but the purpose is achieved optimally, in its fullest and most complete sense, in the conclusion. The conclusion exists only to establish the means by which the purpose of the preaching text can be achieved optimally in the lives of the hearers.

What must be done away with is the idea of a purposeless sermon. This must be reckoned as oxymoronic as thunderous silence, pleasant sorrow, virtuous demons, or bright darkness. It must be viewed as folly to think that one can preach a sermon that has no purpose; that one can preach a sermon that calls believers to respond in no way to the truth of Scripture; that one can preach a sermon that reveals God's non-existent design for his Word in the lives of his people.

It must be resolved that a sermon, if it is truly a sermon, will not only have a purpose but the purpose will be achieved optimally by the content that comprises the conclusion. The conclusion must be understood in terms of its design and result. In its design, the conclusion of the sermon is an intensified emphasis on the *purpose* of the message. In its result, the conclusion of the sermon achieves a thorough accomplishment of the *purpose* of the message. It restates the purpose of the sermon followed by questions and assertions regarding how the truth of the preaching passage can be accomplished in daily life, what it will take for the biblical truth to become optimally operational in one's living. Even in public speaking pedagogy there is the understood relationship of a speech's conclusion, the purpose of the speech, and the outcome of the speech upon the hearers. Consider the following instruction regarding the most productive way to end a speech: "Undoubtedly the best conclusion is one that will remind your audience again of the meaning and purpose of your talk. The more specific and pointed your appeals and recommendations, the more likely your listeners will respond as you wish."[58] Conclusion, purpose, response are a logically and functionally inseparable triad.

The conclusion is "the preacher's last opportunity to impress his purpose upon the hearts of the hearers." When it comes to the result of a sermon conclusion, "The crisis is at hand. The moment of decision is at hand. Furnishing an exacting target for the preacher, the conclusion is the time to bring all things to a harmonious and moving culmination" thus achieving the very purpose for which it was preached.[59] The concept of "the last opportunity to impress" and the concept of "the crisis is at hand" are not understood commonly by preachers as evidenced by their preaching.

According to H. C. Brown Jr., "The time and place to press the purpose on the hearers is the conclusion."[60] By focusing the entirety of the conclusion to the sermon's purpose, the conclusion will have a high degree of unity, vitality, and integrity as a preacher applies and illustrates how the purpose is achieved in the lives of the hearers.[61] The conclusion is the place in the sermon where the hearers come nearest to

58. Reid, *First Principles of Public Speaking*, 171–72.

59. Brown Jr., Clinard, Northcutt, *Steps to the Sermon*, 121.

60. Brown Jr., *A Quest for Reformation in Preaching*, 249.

61. Brown Jr., *A Quest for Reformation in Preaching*, 249.

comprehending the entire sermon at one time. The conclusion is the place where the purpose of the sermon "can be seen at its clearest, felt at its sharpest, and carried back into life where, if anywhere, it must be resolved. The conclusion is the last chance to accomplish the sermon's purpose, whatever that may be."[62]

In preaching for a verdict, that is, some specific life-change, a preacher will naturally postpone the attempt to achieve the purpose of the sermon until the conclusion. And, even though he will have been moving steadily toward achieving the purpose of the sermon throughout the preaching of it, the purpose cannot be achieved before he has completed his conclusion. The thought that the purpose of a sermon could be achieved before the sermon has been completed would be like thinking one could conduct a funeral service for a man who is young and in good health. Such a thought-process is completely unacceptable and bizarre. The clear-thinking response to such weirdness would be, "Who would try to conduct a funeral service for a man who hasn't died?" Sane pastors allow people to complete their course in life before they bury them. The same logic and reason apply to a sermon. A preacher must complete the course of expounding the text, thoroughly and fully, then conduct the final arrangements of the sermon conclusion, that is, the means by which the purpose of the sermon can be achieved most optimally in the lives of many people whose lives vary significantly.

In preaching for life-change, it is apparent throughout the time that the preaching passage is being expounded that important questions remain yet unanswered, significant instruction has yet to be provided, in short, the critical issue is still undecided. Throughout the preacher's sermon, he will have clarified the text and clarified the need for change. But until the conclusion of the sermon has been completed the most practical, helpful, and insightful ways and means necessary for affecting change have not been provided and, therefore, the compliance of the hearers has not been resolved. It is in the conclusion where very important practical questions are answered, significant instruction is given, and, hopefully, the complete compliance of the hearers is resolved. Charles Koller stressed the necessity of a purposeful sermon conclusion: "To the extent that any sermon succeeds, it builds up the reasonable expectation of an answer to questions, problems, and needs which have been set forth. An adequate conclusion is therefore essential. Not less futile than a diagnosis without a remedy, is the rambling discourse which leaves a puzzled congregation asking, 'So what?'"[63]

More specifically, Koller yields 5 insights about a sermon conclusion that will be helpful in having the purpose of the sermon achieved in the conclusion, thereby facilitating life-change for the hearers. These insights are: one, the conclusion should bring the message to a *burning focus*; two, *the object* of the sermon is more important than the subject; three, *to this object* the whole sermon must lend itself, down to the last words of the conclusion; four, the conclusion should appeal to the hearers for *a*

---

62. Davis, *Design for Preaching*, 192.

63. Koller, *Expository Preaching without Notes*, 83.

response in some concrete form; five, throughout the sermon, and particularly in the conclusion, the hearers must be made to feel that the message is a *personal matter.*[64]

The Sermon's Purpose and God's Gospel

The purpose of the sermon that is to be achieved will be directed to believers since pastoral preaching is, first and foremost, about the edification of believers. However, for those who are not in Christ, the message that edifies believers is not a message an unbeliever can respond to. In fact, it's not a message he or she can attend to in their lives outside of Christ. So, when there is nothing left to say to believers, that is, the message for them has been completed, nothing else should be said to them. However, that does not mean that there is nothing more to be said, it just means that the remaining words are directed to a different audience—unbelievers.

The message that unbelievers need to hear is the gospel message which indicates the bad news of their sinfulness before a Holy God and the good news that this Holy God has provided a solution for their sin-problem in the person and work of his Only Begotten Son, the Lord Jesus Christ. This second message, which is part of the sermon conclusion, will be detailed in three later chapters, chapters eighteen through twenty. It is mentioned now to underscore an obvious fact about a sermon conclusion, it is the highpoint of the sermon for believers and it contains the needed message for unbelievers, the message of the gospel, which will be the highpoint of the sermon for the unbeliever.

Therefore, time must be very carefully managed. When it comes to the point of achieving the purpose in the sermon conclusion, even though the content is that which appropriately completes the sermon, a preacher cannot take a long time in saying it and he must not take more time than is necessary to say it.[65] This sage counsel should never be violated.

The Word of God proclaimed to man is always an urgent matter. The brevity of life assures that one's exposure to, and implementation of, God's Word in one's life is of utmost importance. This is true for believers but especially true for unbelievers. What a tragedy if unbelievers could hear our sermons and not be exposed to the supremely urgent message of the gospel. Of lesser significance, a sermon that does not contain the gospel message explaining the salvation of Christ cannot be called "a gospel sermon."[66] A gospel sermon does not mean that "the death of Jesus in the place of sinful men is the announced subject of every sermon, nor even that His name should be in every point that is handled. . . . But what is meant is that the salvation of Christ should be the drift, the center, the substance, the aim—should give the tone

---

64. Koller, *Expository Preaching without Notes,* 84.

65. Simpson, *Lectures on Preaching,* 1897, 131.

66. Borgman, *My Heart for Thy Cause,* 140.

and direction and impulse to every discourse."[67] But more specifically, gospel preaching must include a full declaration of the person and work of Jesus Christ. Without a complete proclamation of Christ's person and work, gospel preaching is not the result of preaching regardless of the intent of the preacher and the number of references made about Christ.

I take great exception with those who think preaching must be edificational or evangelistic, that is, a sermon must be one or the other, it cannot be both. I also find disfavor with the idea that it is a sufficient preaching of the gospel, in an edificational sermon directed to believers, to merely remind them how this message is an implication of the gospel, or how some event or detail in the passage prefigures, foreshadows, or in some form or fashion depicts Christ. The following excerpt presents well what I find artificial and unacceptable:

> Preaching is of two sorts: evangelistic and edificational. Evangelism in the Scriptures is done "out there," where the unbelieving are, not primarily in the services of the church. Of course, the gospel relates to everything else that is preached, and no sermon—even in a basically edificational setting—ever should be preached unless it is related to the good news. But the fact does not mean that in edificational preaching only (or even primarily) the gospel should be preached. In evangelistic preaching, the gospel is dominant; in edificational preaching the focus is on the implications of the gospel for the lives of believers.[68]

Because of what I have conveyed above, I want to carefully suggest what I believe should take place in preaching. Specifically, I will provide seven assertions about preaching the gospel in expository sermons.

One, pastors must edify believers in their preaching. A pastor's task in preaching is to feed God's people with his Word, to nurture them in the faith, to grow them in Christ. A pastor cannot overdo this. He must give himself to this completely, and then give himself to this even more. But when excellent edification has been provided and believers have been edified tremendously, the message of the gospel, commonly, has yet to be declared. *Showing the textual connections to Christ do not equate the gospel message.*

Two, expository preaching is unsurpassed in accomplishing the edification of believers. No kind of preaching results in understanding God's Word like a careful, thorough, detailed, insightful, and relevant explanation of biblical texts, especially when texts are expounded consecutively through entire books of the Bible. But, when the most excellent exposition of any given text has been accomplished the result will be, perhaps, the most definitive word on that passage that has ever been uttered. And though that detailed exposition can be advantageous to clarify truth that relates

---

67. Borgman, *My Heart for Thy Cause*, 140.

68. Adams, *Preaching with Purpose*, 70.

directly or indirectly to the message of the gospel, the gospel is a message that is broader than the text that was expounded so excellently.

Three, unbelievers cannot be edified in their faith. They have no faith to edify. They are outside of Christ. They do not need biblical instruction as to how they can be a more faithful follower of Christ. They are unregenerate. They are not Christ-followers. They are in sin and unbelief. Edification is not their need. They need regeneration, not edification. They cannot be edified in their unbelief. The beginning point of edification for unbelievers is the message of the gospel.

Four, unbelievers are blinded by Satan. Only God can remove the veil that blinds them to the glory of the gospel of Jesus Christ. But when he does remove the veil that blinds unbelievers, he does so in connection with the proclamation of the gospel so that the unbeliever may be saved. Their blindness ends with an effectual hearing of the gospel of Jesus Christ.

Five, unbelievers need to hear the gospel, that is, the complete message of the gospel. A few components of the gospel do not comprise the gospel. How can a portion of anything be the whole of it? The gospel is a message of the person and work of Jesus Christ and the mandated response necessary for an unbeliever to receive the gift of eternal life. An unbiblical understanding of the person and work of Jesus Christ must be eradicated by a complete and accurate biblical declaration of Christ. The Jesus of lost people's speculation cannot save them! Lost people need to be exposed to the Christ of Scripture. Do we not find in Scripture that people were willing to believe in Jesus until he, or an apostle of Christ, declared in greater detail and in fuller proclamation who he was? They were only initially accepting *some truth about Jesus* but ultimately, they rejected him as fuller disclosure was made. A partial understanding of Jesus Christ may be acceptable to many people for whom a complete understanding of him would never be acceptable. In such instances, when a complete disclosure of Christ is made and people reject the full declaration of Christ, these people weren't individuals who were saved and then lost their salvation. They were unbelievers and they remained unbelievers. Faith in Christ is not based upon a partial, subjective, selective acceptance of the person and work of Jesus Christ as presented in Scripture. There are lost people who do not reject everything about Jesus Christ. But this changes nothing. They are still lost and will remain lost until they repent of their sins and believe in the Christ of Scripture, as presented in Scripture, trusting in the finished work that he alone could and did accomplish to redeem sinful men.

Six, a pastor is not the Lord. He does not know the hearts of men. In many assembled churches there exists amid those assembled, lost people, even though they may be members of the church. They are religious but lost, none-the-less. There is a warranted need for gospel proclamation in the services of the local church. Part of a pastor's responsibility is to introduce God's sheep who are not yet in the fold, a segment of those who constitute unbelievers, to the Good Shepherd. Some of God's sheep who are not in the fold are unregenerate church members, religious but lost and not yet in the fold. They are not saved. They will not be saved until they respond in faith to the gospel. The gospel is the message they need to hear. It is Christ that they need to hear about and respond to. It is the message of Christ that must be declared. They must be drawn to Christ. Those who are drawn come to Christ as they respond to the gospel, but the gospel must be proclaimed before it can be responded to.

Seven, to incorporate the gospel message at the end of an earnest expository sermon proclaimed to edify believers would not be a gospel "tack on"—an attempt to tack on the gospel to an expository sermon. Well, exactly, what makes it a tack on? I want to interact in the following paragraphs with some assumptions made by those who disfavor a declaration of the gospel message as part of an expository sermon.

Is the message of the gospel "tacked on" by the fact that it is proclaimed at the end of a message designed to edify believers? There are two things that might be assumed as problematic with this procedure. First, that the gospel appears at the end of the sermon. If that is the problem then don't tack it on, proclaim it in the expository sermon somewhere in the body of the sermon. Don't declare the gospel late in the message, do so sooner rather than later. However, the real problem may be that one may not be inclined to proclaim the gospel anywhere in the sermon—not early in the sermon, not at the end of the sermon, not in the middle of the sermon, not at any point between the first and last word of the sermon. For some preachers, preaching is just not the right time to declare the gospel of Jesus Christ! Second, the assumed problem may be that the sermon was intended to edify believers and was doing so until the end of the sermon where the emphasis switched to the need of unbelievers. Well, is declaring the gospel to unbelievers a bad thing in a context where believers have been thoroughly ministered to? I think not! In this case, transition to the need of unbelievers and "tack on" the gospel!

Is the message of the gospel "tacked on" by the fact that the sermon preached was an expository sermon and was intended to be such—an expository sermon, not an evangelistic sermon? A declaration of the gospel message in the conclusion of an expository sermon is not going to undo the exposition. An expository sermon was designed and delivered. A declaration of the gospel in an expository sermon does not make it other than an expository sermon just like the declaration of the gospel in an expository sermon does not make the sermon an evangelistic sermon. An evangelistic sermon is an entire sermon directed to unbelievers, expounding the tenants of the gospel message with the purpose of the sermon being that sinners will turn to Christ in repentance and faith. Fear not. If a pastor preaches an expository sermon that concludes with a declaration of the gospel message, the expository preacher will not lose his standing as an expository preacher any more than he will have morphed into an evangelistic preacher. So, wherein lies the culpability of a final redirection of effort to speak the greatly needed message of the gospel to those who need it? The message of Christ won't harm your expository sermon. If the culpability of such redirection is that the gospel is preached in an expository sermon, then do not be concerned as you "tack on" the gospel!

Is the message of the gospel "tacked on" by the fact that the preacher understands that his fine expository sermon, which upgrades the theology of believers and strengthens their walk in this world, will not do so for unbelievers so, therefore, rather than providing *no ministry to the lost*, he is willing to provide them with the gospel as opposed to *withholding the gospel from them*? If this is the case, rest easy and "tack on" the gospel!

Is the message of the gospel "tacked on" by the fact that God is not restricted in his ability or design to remove the veil that blinds unbelievers if the gospel message is preceded by an expository sermon? If God is not prohibited in his regenerative work in unbelievers when the gospel message is proclaimed after an expository sermon is preached, then you are not guilty of working against God. Therefore, "tack on" the gospel!

Is the message of the gospel "tacked on" by the fact that an evangelistic sermon is not a required context for the complete message of the gospel to be proclaimed with urgency, earnestness, and passion? The context of an expository sermon is an adequate context in which the message of the gospel can be proclaimed. Let the occasion of an expository sermon be the opportunity you seize, like the Apostle Paul, to boast in Christ. If the glorious message of Jesus Christ is the boast of your life, then boast in Christ with all urgency, earnestness, and passion as you "tack on" the gospel to your expository sermon, regardless of the text which has been expounded!

Is the message of the gospel "tacked on" by the fact that a pastor is quite unlike the Good Shepherd who knows (not assumes, or guesses, or thinks he knows) who is and who is not his sheep and, therefore, would rather give a message that may or may not be needed? If so, then it must be "tacked on!" By the way, how many times have you heard flight attendants on a commercial flight announce emergency safety information regarding the seat belts, oxygen masks, floatation devices, and exit doors before the plane is pushed back from the terminal gate? Well, how many times have you flown? They go over this information before every flight, even though the odds are great that this information will be of no actual use to anyone. Relatively few people ever have to use the emergency safety information on commercial flights. However, *every person has the need to respond to the message of the gospel*. Maybe preachers need to value the message of the gospel more than flight attendants value emergency safety information! Minimally, preachers need to be committed to declare the message of the gospel as much as flight attendants are committed to announce emergency safety information.

Is the message of the gospel "tacked on" by the assumption that if attended to last, then it must be done from insincere motives and done in a perfunctory fashion? If this assumption is true, repent! Then with complete sincerity, integrity, and urgency "tack on" the gospel through an urgent, passionate, and purposeful proclamation of a complete gospel message!

With the gospel message in mind, apply Matthew Simpson's counsel about the urgency of preaching as he writes: "Your sermon may be the last one which some poor sinner may hear before he is summoned to the bar of God. Be earnest in your preparation. Say something which a poor soldier on the battlefield, whose lifeblood is oozing away, or a culprit on the gallows, would wish to hear before dropping into eternity. Do not try to please so much as to do good."[69] How good is it to take the opportunity to preach and deprive unbelievers of hearing the message they must respond to in order to be saved? My personal conviction requires me to answer with, "Not good enough!" Do good, indeed, by preaching the gospel as part of your expository sermon's conclusion!

Preaching a sermon and purposeful preaching both require having a purpose for preaching the sermon. If that is not the case, what is preached will be just another non-sermon, a preachment, that usurps the place of that which should have been preached—a sermon that was effectively concluded by achieving the purpose for which it was intended. As is the case in business, athletics, industry, and every other field, so it is in preaching—preaching which is qualitative is based, at least partially, upon doing the little things that make a big difference. Having a clearly defined purpose and striving strenuously to achieve that purpose is certainly a small thing that truly makes a big difference!

Achieving the purpose of the sermon takes place through the closing appeals of a sermon conclusion. As we shall see in the substance of the remaining chapters, the closing appeals must be personally relevant and persuasively presented to the hearers.

---

69. Simpson, *Lectures on Preaching,* 1897, 151.

9

The Closing Appeals of a Sermon Conclusion:
Part 1

"A confirmation of four insights, among others, are helpful in doing good work in a sermon conclusion. The first insight that is helpful in doing good work in a sermon conclusion has to do with the problem *of the conclusion: the sermon conclusion is the 'most-likely-to-be-neglected aspect of proclamation.' The second insight has to do with the* prescription *for the conclusion: 'the preacher must be at his best in the closing minutes.' The third insight is in relation to the* provision *of the conclusion: to 'conclude with something for everyone—unbelievers and believers, young Christians and mature Christians.' The fourth insight has to do with the* pertinence *of the conclusion, which must answer the question: 'As a result of this message, what changes does God want in my life and the lives of those who hear it?'"*

"A sermon without a conclusion or a sermon with a weak conclusion will have a highpoint but what will that highpoint be if it is not the sermon conclusion? A highpoint of a sermon that is other than the conclusion will be some good thing that was brought out in the body of the sermon . . . But it will be the highpoint of the sermon out of default since there was no conclusion or a weak conclusion that ended it. For the sermon conclusion to exist as the highpoint of the sermon means that the entirety of the conclusion, not just a portion of it, is the highpoint of the sermon. The whole conclusion should contain the richest insights, the most urgent exhortation, the most concrete material, the most interesting expression found in the entire sermon."

"The conclusion is not the natural continuation of the discussion found in the body of the sermon. The conclusion deals with the outgrowth of that discussion. The outgrowth of that discussion is a return to the purpose of the sermon. To deal with the

sermon's purpose in the conclusion is the appropriate outgrowth of the discussion and the natural culmination of the sermon."

"The practice of truth means moving from noncompliance to compliance, which may entail initiation: to start doing what should be done but is not being done; or it may entail cessation: to stop doing what should not be done but is being done. Specific areas of noncompliance must be lifted to the level of consciousness, that is, by using Scripture to 'throw light on the problem' and provide the solution for it. In addition, the practice of truth means moving from a level of compliance to a greater level of compliance which entails correction: to continue doing what should be done but do it in a different way and/or for different reasons; or it may entail simply the encouragement to continue doing the same thing, the same way, for the same reasons. Practicing the truth will be in relation to the practical issues of initiation, cessation, correction, or continuation regarding one's present compliance to biblical truth. To assist believers in their daily compliance of living biblical truth is the function of a sermon conclusion and it speaks to the importance of this perpetually underdeveloped element of a sermon."

"Change is more likely to take place in the areas of one's life that can be accommodated more simply, quickly, and conveniently. Even as such beneficial accommodations are made by those who hear sermons, they need help to make the more difficult accommodations required by Scripture. Obviously, then, specific ways and means for the more difficult areas of compliance to the truth may be the greatest benefit a preacher can provide for his hearers. All of this is to be done to be responsible as far as the work of preaching is concerned. But there is also the need to be responsible in the use of Scripture in preaching. The responsible use of Scripture includes the implementation of it in the closing appeals of the sermon conclusion rather than omitting them from the conclusion. There is nothing that can equal Scripture to provide the ways and means of compliance for believers to Scripture's mandates."

"But, what about the conclusion of the sermon? Are we through hearing from God when the expository preacher moves from the body the sermon to the sermon conclusion? Is the sermon conclusion the time and place where God's people hear from the preacher rather than God? Does the voice of God no longer hold sway in the conclusion of the sermon? If our convictions about the Word of God and preaching are what they should be, we would have to say, "Absolutely Not, and may it never be!" to these questions. But honestly, when it comes to sermon conclusions being depleted of the Word of God we would have to declare, "It often is the case!" How illogical it is that the conclusion, especially if it is as it should be—the highpoint of the sermon, would forgo the counsel of God's Word? If the Word of God is profitable for instruction, for reproof, for correction, and for training in righteousness, why wouldn't a sermon conclusion draw richly from the rich resource of God's Word?"

"The insights of Scripture are definitive and determinative for the Christian life. All other sources of counsel or instruction, at best, may provide suggestive, alternative insights to the Word of God. But what good is it to offer other than what God's Word provides, and why would one even desire to do so? Nevertheless, the sermon conclusion is the place where the richest biblical insights are brought forth in condensed fashion to establish a 'Thus saith the Lord' perspective and prescription for living the Christian life. None other than God can appropriately address how his people are to live and he does so throughout his Word. Because of this, the sermon conclusion should supply a condensed corpus of biblical counsel and instruction, the only counsel fit to accurately address the Christian life."

"Though a lack of effective sermon conclusions depicts our homiletical culture, this weakness of preaching does not merit the right of continuance simply because of its existence. No fault is worthy of the merits of advocacy and continuance. . . . Though the context of our preaching culture is impoverished regarding sermon conclusion effectiveness, preachers do not have to be, and must not be content to be, guardians of that culture. Of course, the opposite is needed. It is imperative for preachers to be ambassadors of a new order of homiletic practice in which the sermon conclusion is routinely effective."

"Powerless preaching 'may at times glow and sparkle . . . but the glow and sparkle will be as barren of life as the field sown with pearls.'"

THE IMPORTANCE OF THE CONCLUSION

"The last effort of the preacher ought to be a signal one—like Samson's last achievement against the Philistines."[1] What a fine quotation. It's captivating, compelling, meaningful, and memorable. But, is it true? Is this how a sermon should end or is this just a pious sounding platitude for preaching? If it is true, why should it be so? Well, I absolutely believe that a preacher's conclusion should be a monumental achievement, like Samson's achievement on the last day of his life against the Philistines. I think the biblical analogy of Samson's effort and a preacher's effort in the conclusion of his sermon is perfectly fitting and that it is without any exaggeration or needless hyperbole. In support of this, let's consider the views of just a few homiletical predecessors who have made significant contributions in the field of preaching. Let's begin with this insight: "The great and only question is, How is the deepest impression to be made by a sermon? It certainly depends very much on the conclusion."[2] Imagine that! The impressiveness of a sermon relegated to the conclusion! Next, consider this: "The conclusion is the crown and culmination of your work throughout the sermon.

1. Blaikie, *For the Work of the Ministry*, 1873, 125.
2. Hoppin, *Homiletics*, 1883, 442.

To go wrong here is to fail in accomplishing the purpose for which you entered the pulpit, the capture of the will in order that the truth expounded may be realized in change of thought and life."[3] That certainly is an attestation of the sermon conclusion's apparent worthiness, accompanied with an inferred warning about the prospect of turning a sermon into an artifact of futility if the conclusion is not an effective one.

Of the three fundamental elements of a sermon, its introduction, its structure and discussion, and its conclusion, the sermon conclusion commonly is championed as the most vital. Consider this estimation of the sermon conclusion's hierarchy: "If the conclusion is poor, it may destroy the impression of the introduction, and do much to neutralize the discussion of the sermon. But if the conclusion is good, it will help to atone for the deficiencies of the first and second, or to heighten preceding excellencies."[4] Thus, the sermon conclusion is granted almost mythical abilities—the ability of the conclusion to become a homiletical Phoenix—to enable the sermon to rise up from the ashes of sermonic ruin and inject new life into a sermon that was destined for death.

One final contribution to the cause of the sermon conclusion's supremacy: "In a word, a forcible conclusion may sometimes save a weak sermon, and a weak conclusion is enough to spoil a strong sermon."[5] And so, in this instance, the conclusion is afforded "game-changer" credentials. And on and on it goes. The conclusion is praised by many as that which is paramount in significance—like water is to life.

As tempting as it is to do so, we must not fixate upon the puzzling question of "How in the world did we get to the place where a sermon conclusion declined in valuation from a sermonic 'big ticket item' to the equivalent to sermonic 'chump-change'?" We must, instead, concentrate our efforts to reassess and reaffirm the importance of the sermon conclusion in preaching. To do this necessitates a confirmation of four insights, among others, that are helpful in doing good work in a sermon conclusion.

The first insight that is helpful in doing good work in a sermon conclusion has to do with the <u>problem</u> *of the conclusion*: the sermon conclusion is the "most-likely-to-be-neglected aspect of proclamation." The second insight has to do with the <u>prescription</u> *for the conclusion*: "the preacher must be at his best in the closing minutes." The third insight is in relation to the <u>provision</u> *of the conclusion*: to "conclude with something for everyone—unbelievers and believers, young Christians and mature Christians." The fourth insight has to do with the <u>pertinence</u> *of the conclusion*, which must answer the question: "As a result of this message, what changes does God want in my life and the lives of those who hear it?"[6] The takeaway from these four instructions for sermon conclusions would be along the lines of the following: *Don't neglect*

---

3. McComb, *Preaching in Theory and Practice*, 1926, Italics added, 73.

4. Etter, *The Preacher and His Sermon*, 1885, 366.

5. Hoppin, *Homiletics*, 1883, 430.

6. MacArthur, *Rediscovering Expository Preaching*, from Mayhue's chapter "Introductions, Illustrations, and Conclusions," 252–53.

the conclusion but be at your best during this part of the sermon, having something significant to say to all who hear you, something so significant that everyone can depart with a changed focus, direction, commitment, or agenda for living. That addresses well the importance of sermon conclusions.

To add to the effort to reassess and reaffirm the significance of the sermon conclusion, there are five reasons why a preacher should give his best effort to the composition and delivery of the sermon conclusion. First, the conclusion gives the final chance to impress the message on the hearers. Second, the conclusion has the best chance to be remembered by the hearers. Third, a lasting impression of the sermon depends most upon the conclusion. Fourth, in the conclusion the hearers are pointed to the definite result that the Word of God is to have upon the lives of the hearers. Fifth, only through the conclusion may the sermon be brought to an *"impressive climax."*[7]

The conclusion ought to be the most vital portion of the whole sermon. In the conclusion the preacher should be possessed by utmost earnestness. Also, the weight, the value, and the impression of the biblical passages composing the closing appeals should be the strongest of any used in the sermon. Yet, in common practice the conclusion is often the unrivaled weakness of the sermon.[8] A weak conclusion, or a sermon that ends with no conclusion, forfeits that which only a sermon that ends well can accomplish, that is, to leave upon the minds of its hearers a powerful impression, an impression necessitating a practical response that accomplishes the purpose for which the sermon was intended.[9] The practical response which is necessary to achieve the purpose of the sermon in the lives of the hearers is parceled out in the closing appeals of the sermon conclusion. A sermon is dependent upon the conclusion for it to end as it should, as the highpoint of the sermon.

A sermon without a conclusion or a sermon with a weak conclusion will have a highpoint but what will that highpoint be if it is not the sermon conclusion? A highpoint of a sermon that is other than the conclusion will be some good thing that was brought out along the way in the body of the sermon; perhaps, an interesting illustration, or an insightful implication of the text, or an incredibly interesting expression that was stated in the sermon, a fine interpretation of a difficult passage, or an awesome upgrade of biblical doctrine, etc. All these good things should happen in a sermon and they should happen throughout a sermon. But they will be the highpoint of the sermon out of default since there was no conclusion or only a weak conclusion that ended it. For the sermon conclusion to exist as the highpoint of the sermon means that the entirety of the conclusion, not just a portion of it, is the highpoint of the sermon. The whole conclusion should contain the richest insights, the most urgent exhortation, the most concrete material, the most interesting expression found in the entire sermon.

7. Sweazey, *Preaching the Good News*, 99.

8. Blaikie, *For the Work of the Ministry*, 1873, 124–25.

9. Kidder, *A Treatise on Homiletics*, 1862, 222.

The conclusion is the natural outgrowth and culmination of the sermon, and as such, the conclusion ought to be the "quintessence of all the proceeds it."[10] The key concept here is that the conclusion is not the natural *continuation of the discussion* found in the body of the sermon. The conclusion deals with *the outgrowth of that discussion.* The outgrowth of that discussion is a return to the purpose of the sermon. To deal with the sermon's purpose in the conclusion is *the appropriate outgrowth of the discussion and the natural culmination of the sermon.*

The sentiment that "a sermon without application is worthless"[11] is one that is shared by many. But what is truer still is that a sermon that ends without amassing significant application in the conclusion is a weak sermon. The conclusion is the most appropriate place for application, application proper, application that is more direct and more comprehensive than the relevant implications of the text brought out in the body of the sermon.[12] Though not addressing sermon conclusions, specifically, the assessment of John Stott regarding application, generally, is more true for sermon conclusions than any other portion of a sermon. Stott writes:

> Too much of our preaching is academic and theoretical; we need to bring it down into the practical realities of everyday life. It is not enough to give an accurate exposition of some passage of the Word of God if we do not relate it to the actual needs of men. This is the fascination of preaching—applying God's Word to man's needs. The preacher should be as familiar with man in his world as he is with God.[13]

Certainly, the practical implications of the preaching text must be brought out in preaching the body of the sermon but that does not nullify the crucial role of the sermon conclusion to detail the ultimate application of the sermon which is directed to achieve the purpose of the sermon in the lives of the hearers.

The high ground to be captured in preaching is for believers to be doers of the Word, having received biblical instruction and motivation to respond to the truth of God's Word. The problem is that many preachers are content if believers are sufficiently informed about truth and motivated to respond to the truth in their lives. Admittedly, this is valuable work that has been accomplished, but it is not all that could and should be done, it is simply the extent to which good preaching commonly is done. However, for believers to go from being productive hearers who understand truth and are motivated to respond to it to become effective doers of the Word, they

10. Etter, *The Preacher and His Sermon,* 1885, 370.

11. I agree that application plays a very valuable role in preaching, but I must separate myself from agreement that an irrelevant exposition of a biblical text is worthless. An insightful understanding of a biblical text cannot be a worthless outcome. But I must follow up with the assertion that an insightful exposition of a biblical text without the declaration of the practical implications or applications of the meaning of the text is not preaching.

12. Kidder, *A Treatise on Homiletics,* 1862, 222.

13. Stott, *The Preacher's Portrait,* 87.

need to know what counsel the Word of God has for them so that they may practice the truth in their lives in a manner that allows them to achieve God's purpose for the text of Scripture preached to them.

Of course, the practice of truth means moving from noncompliance to compliance, which may entail initiation: to start doing what should be done but is not being done; or it may entail cessation: to stop doing what should not be done but is being done. Specific areas of noncompliance must be lifted to the level of consciousness, that is, by using Scripture to "throw light on the problem"[14] and provide the solution for it. In addition, the practice of truth means moving from a level of compliance to a greater level of compliance which entails correction: to continue doing what should be done but do it in a different way and/or for different reasons; or it may entail simply the encouragement to continue doing the same thing, the same way, for the same reasons. *Practicing the truth relates to the practical issues of initiation, cessation, correction, or continuation regarding one's present compliance to biblical truth.* To assist believers in their daily compliance of living biblical truth is the function of a sermon conclusion and it speaks to the importance of this perpetually underdeveloped element of a sermon.

Specificity about compliance and noncompliance is crucial because people change their lives in specific areas and in specific ways, which means that change, needed change, cannot be addressed generically.[15] Additionally, change is more likely to take place in the areas of one's life that can be accommodated more simply, quickly, and conveniently. Even as such beneficial accommodations are made by those who hear sermons, they need help to make the more difficult accommodations required by Scripture. Obviously, then, specific ways and means for the more difficult areas of compliance to the truth may be the greatest benefit a preacher can provide for his hearers. All of this is to be done to be responsible as far as the work of preaching is concerned. But there is also the need to be responsible in the use of Scripture in preaching. The responsible use of Scripture includes the implementation of it in the closing appeals of the sermon conclusion rather than omitting them from the conclusion. There is nothing that can equal Scripture to provide the ways and means of compliance for believers to Scripture's mandates.

The insights of Scripture are definitive and determinative for the Christian life. All other sources of counsel or instruction, at best, may provide suggestive, alternative insights to the Word of God. But what good is it to offer other than what God's Word provides, and why would one even desire to do so? Nevertheless, the sermon conclusion is the place where the richest biblical insights are brought forth in condensed fashion to establish a "Thus saith the Lord" perspective and prescription for living the Christian life. None other than God can appropriately address how his people are to live and he does so throughout his Word. Because of this, the sermon conclusion

14. Edge, *Teaching for Results*, 108.
15. Edge, *Teaching for Results*, 113.

should supply a condensed corpus of biblical counsel and instruction, the only counsel fit to accurately address the Christian life.

In the straightforward manner of John MacArthur, he asserts the following regarding the clarity and significance of Scripture: "How can we truly 'hear Him,' meaning God, unless we go to the place He has spoken—His Word? The only way I can ever be certain about *anything* is to approach every biblical text with a careful, rational, discerning mind to hear and understand accurately what God is saying. Take that away, and what basis is there for certainty about *any* truth?"[16] Any worthwhile expository preacher would concur completely with MacArthur's assertions when it comes to expounding a text of God's Word, that is, preaching the body the sermon. But, what about the conclusion of the sermon? Are we through hearing from God when the expository preacher moves from the body the sermon to the sermon conclusion? Is the sermon conclusion the time and place where God's people hear from the preacher rather than God? Does the voice of God no longer hold sway in the conclusion of the sermon? If our convictions about the Word of God and preaching are what they should be, we would have to say, "Absolutely Not, and may it never be!" to these questions. But honestly, when it comes to sermon conclusions being depleted of the Word of God we would have to declare, "It often is the case!" How illogical it is that the conclusion, especially if it is as it should be—the highpoint of the sermon, would forgo the counsel of God's Word? If the Word of God is profitable for instruction, for reproof, for correction, and for training in righteousness, why wouldn't a sermon conclusion draw richly from the rich resource of God's Word?

The answer to the previous question is that two resolves are missing in a preacher's heart and, therefore, missing in the practice of preaching sermon conclusions. They are: first, and foremost, God's people must hear from God in the sermon conclusion; second, the most definitive and direct hearing from God will be found in the sermon conclusion. Again, MacArthur is insightful, and I want to bring his insights regarding the Word of God in preaching to the sermon conclusion specifically. MacArthur asserts, "the preacher's task is not to be a conduit for human wisdom; he is God's voice to speak to the congregation."[17] The Bible contains all things pertaining to life and godliness (2 Peter 1:3). This declaration establishes the basis of "true relevance."[18] Such relevance needs to be demonstrated in the sermon and no less so in the sermon conclusion. In fact, the sermon conclusion should compose a rich deposit of biblical truth providing specific instruction and motivation for living the Christian life.

16. Dever et al., *Preaching the Cross*, from John MacArthur's chapter "Why I Still Preach the Bible after Forty Years of Ministry," 147.

17. Dever et al., *Preaching the Cross*, from MacArthur's chapter "Why I Still Preach the Bible after Forty Years of Ministry," 143.

18. Dever et al., *Preaching the Cross*, from MacArthur's chapter "Why I Still Preach the Bible after Forty Years of Ministry," 144.

The result of preaching is found in the fruit that the Word of God bears in life. The following is a helpful account of the fruit to be borne out by the Word of God in preaching:

> The Bible was given for behavioral change (2 Timothy 3:16–17). Works must follow faith (cf. the book of James). As a result of our preaching, our audience will *do* something. They will obey. Godliness must result in their lives. That is, the pulpit is not just for disseminating more information, it is a platform from which our hearers are motivated to godliness by example and exposition. They must know what God expects and how they may obey God's mandates from any text of Scripture. Preaching must result in godliness.[19]

Therefore, the preacher is responsible to declare the relevance of Scripture and exhort his hearers to comply with its instruction. More specifically, a preacher is responsible to provide application in the conclusion of his sermon which will answer two crucial questions that must be affirmatively answered in order to produce a good conclusion: "Does the sermon build to a climax?" and "Are there effective closing appeals or suggestions"[20] that are derived from the counsel of Scripture? These two questions, if answered in the affirmative, depend upon addressing the interrogative "how" in the sermon conclusion.

"How" is "the master question" that must be addressed in preaching.[21] "How" is especially beneficial to be raised in the sermon conclusion in which it will be answered by the closing appeals of the conclusion. Believers need to know the "how" of most things germane to the Christian life, with the "how" fitted specifically to their experience and culture. Throughout the sermon the preacher has made his case, developed his proposition, explained his text, indicated some duties and perhaps even demonstrated the blessings for the hearer's compliance to the truth. However, the preacher's often overlooked task is to detail how they are to comply to the truth of the preaching passage in such a manner that will achieve the purpose of the passage/the purpose for the sermon. If the necessary "how" of compliance to the truth to achieve the purpose of the sermon is dealt with (but most times it will not be dealt with), it should be dealt with in the "last movement" of the sermon, that is, the conclusion of the message.[22] The knowledge of how to incorporate the truth of Scripture in the Christian life is the prominent domain of the sermon conclusion. Therefore, it almost always is necessary to deal with the "how" of compliance in the conclusion. However, should a conclusion require a different direction, emphasizing the "why" of compliance or the "what" of compliance—what obstacles we must overcome to continue compliance, even these

19. Richard, *Scripture Sculpture*, 24.
20. Richard, *Scripture Sculpture*, 201.
21. Atkins, *Preaching and the Mind of Today*, 210.
22. Atkins, *Preaching and the Mind of Today*, 211.

emphases will constitute, indirectly, the "how" of compliance to the truth that was covered throughout the body of the sermon.

In his book *Preaching to a Postmodern World*, Graham Johnston makes a case that God's people are no longer content to receive a style of preaching that only provides the implications of what is to be done in the Christian life. Hearers desire more than a directive of what to do. They want to know "why" they are to do it and they want to know "how" they are to do it as well.[23] Again, Johnston is correct and even more helpful when he asserts:

> Preaching should move the listeners beyond a sense of feeling uncomfortable or guilty to a point of decisive action. . . . Thoughtful preaching will always provide the listener with an answer to the question: "How can I respond in either thought or action to what I've heard?" . . . Preaching that makes a difference will direct the listeners to a clear, practical, and focused response for each message.[24]

The response of the hearers to each message is the unique contribution of the sermon conclusion. That is why the sermon conclusion is so important. A sermon that ends without addressing what the hearers are to do and/or how they are to respond to the truth that was preached is a great opportunity of which no advantage is taken. But, when such information is advanced in the conclusion of the sermon, the difference made by its inclusion is not modest but a major difference.

Truth which has been established through careful exposition of Scripture makes connection at three points of contact with reality—personal experience, personal observation, and the experience of others in the past or the present day. It is profitable in the conclusion of a sermon to implement one or more of these three points of contact.[25] To set truth within the daily realities of personal experience is advantageous. When a preacher can say, in effect, "Here's how this truth can be implemented in your life," the hearer's interest perks up.[26]

In his discussion of a preacher as a steward and the different aspects of the faithfulness required of stewards, John Stott finalizes the preacher's stewardship with the following statements: "The expository preacher is a bridge builder, seeking to span the gulf between the Word of God and the mind of man. He must do his utmost to interpret the Scripture so accurately and completely, and to apply it so forcefully, that the truth crosses the bridge."[27] The importance of the sermon conclusion is that it provides the opportunity to address what is most needful to make sure the truth, the overall truth of the preaching passage, crosses the bridge into the lives of the hearers.

23. Johnston, *Preaching to a Postmodern World*, 83.

24. Johnston, *Preaching to a Postmodern World*, 85.

25. Atkins, *Preaching and the Mind of Today*, 216.

26. Miller, *The Empowered Communicator*, 150.

27. Stott, *The Preacher's Portrait*, 28.

A matter of great importance for a sermon conclusion relates to the inevitable reality of humor in the act of preaching God's Word. There is nothing that rivals humor as that which is most detrimental to the work to be accomplished in a sermon conclusion. It is hard to disagree with one man's assertion about the abuse of this, otherwise, natural and winsome attribute of preaching as he wrote:

> Deliver the church from the man who cannot control and sanctify his humor! . . . The trouble with the funny man in the pulpit, the clerical jester, is that the wit is an end, not a means. It is indulged and enjoyed as . . . an undo expression of personal taste and eccentric display, and not the natural expression of a consecrated manhood. And in this spirit humor in pulpit speech becomes essentially immoral.[28]

The blending of humor and a sermon conclusion is a tough combination, least the humor foil the effectiveness of the conclusion. Warren Wiersbe admitted that, "There's a place for wit and humor in the pulpit"[29] as long as it did not become a preventative of two outcomes which must result from preaching: "to send the congregation home awed by the greatness of God, not laughing at the cleverness of the preacher;"[30] and, use humor "not at all in the conclusion of the message when you want people to be serious about obeying God's Word."[31]

However, in addressing the very crucial matter of living life according to God's Word, the experience of all believers, including preachers, is that we have quite a resume of instances where we have failed to comply with the Word of God as we should. With the intent to supply instruction from a personal frame of reference about what is to be done, or how what is to be done should be done, or why what is to be done should be done, there is available material from one's resume of personal failure to provide fit instruction for others from one's failures, some of which will be humorous, not by design, just inevitably. This may provide the most beneficial and sanctified use of humor in the pulpit, which will be insightful for the hearers even though it may be found humorous by many. Yet, a sound point of instruction illustrated from a preacher's personal experience which is inevitably humorous, poses a dilemma. If the inevitably humorous personal experience possesses a threat of foiling the seriousness of obeying the Word of God, then it must not be used in the conclusion. If the inevitably humorous incident's instruction is more instructive than humorous, then it may well be beneficial. Of course, the instruction from a personal frame of reference never replaces Scripture as the basis of instruction found in the closing appeals of a sermon conclusion. The personal frame of reference simply amends the provided biblical

28. Hoyt, *The Preacher*, reprinted, 1912, 367–68.
29. Wiersbe, *The Dynamics of Preaching*, 50.
30. Wiersbe, *The Dynamics of Preaching*, 50.
31. Wiersbe, *The Dynamics of Preaching*, 82.

instruction with concrete exemplification and serves to place a personal imprimatur upon the biblically based closing appeals.

The sermon conclusion is essential to instruct believers with specific, Scripture-based information that informs the hearers about how they are to live so that the purpose of the sermon may be accomplished in their lives. The wisdom found in the Word of God, in precept and example, are to be showcased in the conclusion of a sermon.

DIFFICULTY IN PRODUCING AN EFFECTIVE CONCLUSION

Not every sermon will, of necessity, have a *formal* conclusion. In other words, a sermon may finish with the final point serving as the conclusion and, thereby, not have a formal conclusion. Yet, such a sermon could be, nevertheless, a great sermon. However, for this truly to be the case, all the elements of a formal conclusion must be accomplished in the last point, in addition to the exposition of the portion of text which comprises the final point of the sermon.[32] So then, occasionally, the last sermonic point of the sermon may stand in for the conclusion, but the final point of the sermon will have to double in its function, as a sermon point and sermon conclusion, to close out the sermon appropriately.[33]

The conclusion is not an appendage of the sermon nor is it a contrived way to stop preaching, or simply a means by which the sermon is ended. A past frame of reference for a sermon conclusion provided the following summation of its value in a sermon: "It is the crowning, burning, vital point of the sermon. The best of the man should speak then; it is the moment of supreme impression upon the souls of the audience."[34] Additionally, it was understood that the conclusion provides a culmination of thought and its strongest, most practical insights are demanded by the general purpose of all preaching, a persuasion to holy living.[35] However, the practice of preaching reveals that the end of a sermon is too often accompanied with "flagging interest and wearied powers."[36] This reality, far too evident in preaching, indicates the difficulty of concluding a sermon effectively.

The conclusion is an exacting and perilous part of the sermon, because it is always difficult to finish effectively, that is, to provide substance that will instruct the hearers how to respond to the truth of the text with specific scriptural insight, thus accomplishing the purpose of the sermon in their lives. Though it may be difficult to produce, an effective conclusion is possible for every sermon. There is available content in God's Word to constitute an effective conclusion to every sermon, providing

32. Davis, *Design for Preaching*, 193.

33. Vinet, *Homiletics*, 1854, 322.

34. Hoyt, *The Work of Preaching*, reprinted, 1910, 197.

35. Hoyt, *The Work of Preaching*, reprinted, 1910, 197.

36. Hoyt, *The Work of Preaching*, reprinted, 1910, 198.

the hearers the necessary insights to live as the Word of God requires. If this is not done, a conclusion cannot be effective. If this is done and to the degree this is done, the conclusion will be effective, unless it is encumbered with superfluous, additional material. In this unfortunate instance, the result will be that the "preacher has driven a nail in a sure place, instead of clinching it, and securing well the advantage, he hammers away till he breaks the head off, or splits the board."[37] To conclude a sermon only to have the hearers wishing that the preacher would have finished before he did is an inestimable setback to the whole sermon.[38] One writer summarized this unfortunate error this way, "Some preachers end without completing their thought; others finish what they have to say and then, by a fatal aberration, go on to add a conclusion. In both cases the hearer goes away discontented and unhappy."[39]

Unfortunately, it is a long-standing problem for preachers either to leave unsaid what should have been said to conclude well, or for preachers to say what should have been said only to continue speaking so that they negate the conclusion's productiveness. In reference to the latter error, William Jennings Bryan's mother highlighted this failure of her son in an evening sermon as she told him, "Will, you missed several good opportunities to sit down."[40] Though this error is committed less frequently than the error of not saying what needs to be said in a conclusion, it is tragic if a preacher negates an effective sermon simply because he did not know how or when to stop.[41] Though very important, knowing when to stop, adding no superfluous content, does not constitute the difficulty of concluding a sermon well. Not stopping when one should is a terrible detriment to concluding well. However, the difficulty in concluding a sermon well is unrelated to the imprudent procedure of providing unnecessary content to a sermon conclusion.

The heart of the difficulty in producing good sermon conclusions may be boiled down to a lack of desire to produce a good sermon conclusion and a failure to do the additional work of study, diligent study, to produce qualitative content that would result in a good sermon conclusion. Therefore, the assertion that an effective conclusion is not easy to produce is both true and obvious. Yet, the failure of producing effective sermon conclusions is related to an unfortunate lack of character in a preacher for which he is culpable. The result of producing more effective sermon conclusions must begin with a better understanding of sermon conclusions in preaching but it must ultimately be secured by an increased development of the character of the man who would preach them, that is, the character development of the preacher being demonstrated by an obvious, earnest attempt to be of valuable service to those who hear him

37. Hoppin, *Homiletics*, 1883, 427–28.

38. Blaikie, *For the Work of the Ministry*, 1873, 126.

39. McComb, *Preaching in Theory and Practice*, 1926, 72.

40. Demaray, *An Introduction to Homiletics*, 99.

41. Duduit, editor, *Handbook of Contemporary Preaching*, from Brian L. Harbour's chapter "Concluding the sermon," 222.

preach his sermon conclusion. What must be eradicated is a preacher's lack of character demonstrated by nonexistent or poor conclusions resulting from his disinterest in providing help, practical help, for his hearers to live out biblical truth in their lives.

THE DESIRE TO CONCLUDE WELL

The desire to conclude a sermon well is quite a "catch twenty-two." This absolutely is the starting point to produce effective sermon conclusions and yet very few preachers are willing and able to approach this starting point. There is a cultural and contextual reason for preachers' unwillingness and inability to preach effective conclusions. The reason for this is simply a poverty of preachers' personal experiences in hearing good sermon conclusions. Preachers have so infrequently, if ever, been on the receiving end of an effective sermon conclusion that they have little or no personal ambition for producing such in their preaching. There is just no desire to do for others what has never, or very seldom, been done for them in their own experience of hearing sermons.

There is such a lacking culture of good sermon conclusions, that there seems to be little perceived need for their existence. Our existing homiletical milieu has produced an undeveloped market for effective sermon conclusions. Homiletically speaking, we are like the Sentinelese, the unreached bushpeople of North Sentinel Island, who are an undeveloped market for all things that identify a first-world nation: automobiles—compacts or luxury vehicles; electronic devices—computers or smartphones; clothing—formal or casual. The cause of their underdevelopment is due to the fact that they have not experienced such things and are content to exist without them. Powerful, effective sermon conclusions are so unaccustomed to us that they are not sought after when hearing a sermon and not sensed as absent when they are, indeed, absent. So, are effective sermon conclusions really a crucial matter since those who hear sermons and those who preach them seem content to continue without them? Yes, they are a crucial matter!

Though a lack of effective sermon conclusions depicts our homiletical culture, this weakness of preaching does not merit the right of continuance simply because of its existence. No fault is worthy of the merits of advocacy and continuance. Preachers would do well to remember that sermons have a higher function than being understood, and that no sermon functions as it should which does not "bring the hearer into God's presence and leave him under its holy influence."[42] It is the work of a sermon conclusion, especially, to produce this result. Contentment to preach ineffective conclusions must give way to the desire to conclude a sermon well in the ministry of preaching, a ministry of preaching that seeks to profit its hearers by changed lives who live according to Scripture.

---

42. Blaikie, *For the Work of the Ministry*, 1873, 126.

How regrettable would be the following evaluation of a sermon if only the third part of the criticism were accurate—"This discourse consists of an introduction which might've been spared, a second part which does not deal with the text; and a conclusion which concludes nothing."[43] A valuable introduction followed by a sermon body that has been carefully structured and leads to significant exposition of a passage but is followed by a conclusion which settles nothing as to achieving the purpose of the text in the lives of the hearers must be viewed as unfortunate. Yet, an effective introduction followed by a carefully constructed sermon body which leads to an effective exposition of the preaching passage only to have no conclusion, or a token one, must be viewed for what it is—a tragedy of what could have been but never was! More tragic still is the prospect of preachers who spend a lifetime of preaching well except for their conclusions, never learning to maximize this most important element of a sermon. A. T. Pierson's words serve as great counsel to preachers, especially for their work of concluding sermons, when he wrote:

> Never overlook quality and quantity. It is not how much work you do, but how much good work you do, which is the all-important matter. A little well done rather than a great deal ill done should be the law of life. Any first-class piece of work lasts. . . . A good quality of work has a permanent effect on the workman. It stimulates him to still more successful effort, and something well done encourages him to attempt something that shall be even better done; whereas the effect of careless work is to habituate one to carelessness and make one satisfied with an inferior product.[44]

Though the context of our preaching culture is impoverished regarding sermon conclusion effectiveness, preachers do not have to be, and must not be content to be, guardians of that culture. Of course, the opposite is needed—to be ambassadors of a new order of homiletic practice in which the sermon conclusion is routinely effective. The operative question then is, how does one begin to do far better work in concluding one's sermons and to do so in a routine fashion?

In order to conclude well, a minimal guide for any preacher must be to discover and then declare that which would provide the greatest insight for his own life.[45] If a preacher fails to discover in his study how his sermon conclusion furnishes weighty, personal insights for fruitful Christian living in his own life then he cannot preach a significant sermon conclusion delivered from the pulpit in a corporate venue. The discovery of personal, practicable truth is paramount for preaching effective sermon conclusions. Nothing can replace this. Beyond this irreplaceable necessity, three cognitive convictions about sermon conclusions, when fully possessed, will help one to preach effective sermon conclusions.

43. Pierson, *The Divine Art of Preaching*, 1892, 2.
44. Pierson, *The Divine Art of Preaching*, 1892, 4–5.
45. Vinet, *Homiletics*, 1854, 328.

First, the desire to conclude well will end a preacher's contentment to be engaged only in the discussion of a text. But this will occur only if he understands that it is never the exposition of the text alone which results in preaching, but the personal application of the truth of God's Word which must be considered "the very purpose of preaching."[46] Regarding any sermon, there must be "a reason for its being preached. . . . The fundamental of preaching itself is the accomplishment of a direct and desirable objective."[47]

Second, the desire to conclude well is aided by the understanding that as the preaching of a text/sermon without an introduction would be abrupt and unskillful, so the termination of a sermon without a conclusion would be "awkward and incomplete." The sense of incompleteness being due to the understanding that the aim of preaching a sermon is "to produce a practical determination of the hearer's will"[48] to comply with the closing appeals brought out in the sermon conclusion.

Third, the desire to conclude well must possess the settled understanding that a sermon is a weapon of war but its power in the day of battle must be the test of its merits. "That is a great sermon which has power to do great things with the hearts of men. . . . That is a poor and weak sermon that has no power to deliver men from evil and to exalt them in goodness."[49] In short, it is the desire to discover insights that will make a difference in the preacher's own life, as well as having a desire to minister to people in the act of preaching, to help them in the lives they are living, that will cause a preacher to rise above his culture in preaching sermon conclusions that are effective, not occasionally, but routinely so.

THE PERSONAL PRICE TO BE PAID IN PREPARING EFFECTIVE CONCLUSIONS

The sermon conclusion is so discounted in preaching that it is not a feature, much less a priority, in a preacher's weekly activity of sermon preparation. Since it is the last thing to be done in preaching a sermon, if it is done at all, it often becomes the last thing to be done by preachers in preparing a sermon.[50] As the last thing to be done, it is the thing most likely to be slighted in the competition to command time in the sermon preparation process. This simply must change. If the preparation of a sermon

---

46. Breed, *Preparing to Preach*, 1911, 112.

47. Riley, *The Preacher and His Preaching*, 111.

48. Dabney, *Sacred Rhetoric*, 1870, 169.

49. Beecher, *Lectures on Preaching*, First Series, 1872, 227–28.

50. In preparing a sermon, something must be the last thing to be done. However, the introduction of the sermon rather than the sermon conclusion should be the last thing to be done in preparation. When all is prepared except the introduction, a preacher will not be as prone to leave it unprepared because he will sense more deeply his lack of incomplete preparation and attend to it since he must determine how to begin the sermon. The sermon conclusion is thought to be a more suitable candidate for improvisation.

conclusion is the last thing to be done it risks being marginalized and marginalized often. Effective conclusions do not occur as a last-minute, hasty production. David Breed's words speak to this point when he wrote:

> The conclusion of the sermon is often neglected. This sometimes results not so much from the preacher's desire or intention, but from his lack of time. He has perhaps done all that he should do by way of study, and the sermon has been well prepared up to a certain point; but . . . he failed to find the necessary opportunity for its completion, and therefore the conclusion is crude and unworthy of his theme. . . . Nevertheless, the way in which one dismisses his subject, or seeks to bring it home to the hearts and consciences of the congregation, is the very last thing to be slighted.[51]

A sermon conclusion as the priority in preaching cannot be slighted in preparation, which means, typically, that it cannot be the last thing to be done in preparing a sermon. The result of this, if implemented, means that preachers will have an additional and vastly important component of their sermon preparation process extended every week.

A sermon conclusion as the last thing to be done, or the thing seldom done, must become one of the earlier[52] things to be done in preparing a sermon and this part of the preparation process will require more than a little time. The implications of this are obvious. There will be a price to pay for this sermonic element to become a consistent staple of effectiveness in one's preaching.

Though not speaking of the sermon conclusion specifically, but rather speaking about preaching generally, Charles Spurgeon addressed the inevitable outcome that will be commonplace when the preparation of sermons includes a diligent, time consuming effort to prepare effective conclusions. Spurgeon wrote: "If any man preaches as he should, his work will take more out of him than any other labor under heaven. If you and I attend to our work and calling, even among the few people, it will certainly produce a friction of soul and wear of heart which will tell upon the strongest. I speak as one who knows by experience what it is to be utterly exhausted in the Master's service."[53] Yet, sermon conclusions were not the hallmark of Spurgeon's preaching nor were they prepared days in advance of his preaching. If his conclusions would have been the strength of his preaching, the truth of his assertions in the above quotation would have been intensified.

Though additional time and effort in sermon preparation are necessary to preach effective sermon conclusions, still more is needed. With additional sermon preparation there will be a need for additional heart-preparation as well. Heart-preparation

---

51. Breed, *Preparing to Preach*, 1911, 111–2.

52. "Earlier" does not mean first, or initial. Much must be understood about the preaching text before one should have a first thought about how to conclude a sermon from the passage to be preached. A benchmark for "earlier" would be several days before the sermon is preached. This would provide a radical improvement for the typical preacher regarding his prioritizing sermon conclusions.

53. Spurgeon, *An All-round Ministry*, 1900, 134.

includes internalizing truth, meditating upon truth, and prayer. E. M. Bounds provides a trilogy of assertions that are true and valuable in sermon preparation, in general, but even more so when a new and more intense sermon preparation duty, the duty to work hard to produce an effective sermon conclusion, becomes the norm. Read very carefully the exceedingly beneficial practical wisdom of Bounds when he wrote:

> Even sermon-making—incessant and taxing as an art, as a duty, as a work, or as a pleasure—will engross and harden, will estrange the heart from God by neglect of prayer. . . . Prayer freshens the heart of the preacher, keeps it in tune with God and in sympathy with the people.[54]

We have emphasized sermon preparation until we've lost sight of the important thing to be prepared—"the heart."[55]

> We may make preaching our business and not put our hearts in the business. . . . The closet is the heart's study. . . . Praying gives sense, brings wisdom, broadens and strengthens the mind. The closet is a perfect schoolteacher and schoolhouse for the preacher. Thought is not only brightened and clarified in prayer, but thought is born in prayer.[56]

Sermon preparation has not been completed until there has been the necessary preparation of prayer to prepare the heart of the preacher to preach. A prepared heart is mandatory for a preacher to be prepared to preach a sermon. Bounds's words rightly suggest that the lack of heart-preparation to preach may be an even more egregious failure of a preacher's preparation than slighting the preparation to conclude a sermon effectively. However, the failure to pray regarding any component of sermon preparation could not be greater than the failure to pray about the biblical insights of, the desire to minister to God's people in, and the power of God to be at work through, the sermon conclusion.

Quite honestly, the idea that an additional and stringent component of sermon preparation is needed in preparing to preach may be daunting, if not debilitating, for many to consider. But a feeling of being overwhelmed by what must be done in the preaching endeavor is not, necessarily, a negative thing. Phillips Brooks advocated *realized insufficiency* on behalf of preachers with these words of counsel: "never allow yourself to feel equal to your work. If you ever find that spirit growing in you, be afraid."[57] One's lack of power to affect spiritual results in preaching coupled with the sheer magnitude of what needs to be accomplished in preaching should cause one to pray, and to do so fervently.

54. Bounds, *Power Through Prayer*, 34.

55. Bounds, *Power Through Prayer*, 81–82.

56. Bounds, *Power Through Prayer*, 87–88.

57. Brooks, *On Preaching*, 106–7.

The preface of Puritan preacher Cotton Mather's book on preaching states that "The great design and intention of the office of a Christian preacher are to restore the throne and dominion of God in the souls of men."[58] What preacher of a sound mind would think for one moment that he is sufficient to achieve this? What preacher would believe that he could affect this result through preaching without the power of God producing it as a response to humble, desperate prayer? Not just prayer, but desperate prayer is needed because preaching is a desperate proposition.

God calls a preacher to be a part of that which only the Holy Spirit can do through the preacher. Without the Holy Spirit's empowerment in preaching, preaching is powerless, thus, the need of a preacher's prayerful dependence upon the Holy Spirit to cause preaching to be effective. Once again, E. M. Bounds is persuasive as he indivisibly links the ministries of preaching and praying:

> The character of our praying will determine the character of our preaching. Light praying will make light preaching. Prayer makes preaching strong, gives unction, and makes it stick.... No learning can make up for the failure to pray. No earnestness, no diligence, no study, no gifts will supply its lack. Talking to men for God is a great thing but talking to God for men is greater still. He who has not learned well how to talk to God for men will never talk well and with real success to men for God.[59]

To conclude a sermon with the requisite power and biblical insight that results in God dominating the thrones of men's hearts must not be thought of as a viable prospect without fervent, prayerful preparation.

Much preaching is powerless, and sadly, too few are cognizant of it, just as Samson was when the Spirit departed from him and he was not aware of it.[60] Powerless preaching is such a norm that powerful preaching is neither a common expectation of those who hear sermons preached nor a common aspiration of those who preach them. Why should there be powerful preaching when there is such a wide assortment of less than powerful sermons with which hearers will be satisfied; sermons which are popular, pleasant, captivating, and intellectual? Yet, as Bounds asserts, "the preaching which secures God's end in preaching must be born of prayer.... The preachers who are the mightiest in their closets with God are the mightiest in their pulpits with men."[61]

There is no alternative for the connection between prayerful preaching and powerful preaching. We must become thoroughly convinced that "Colleges, learning, books, theology, and preaching cannot make a preacher, but praying does.... The superficial results of many a ministry, the deadness of others, are to be found in the lack

---

58. Mather, *Student and Preacher*, 1789, iv.

59. Bounds, *Power Through Prayer*, 36–37.

60. Lawson, *Famine in the Land*, 57.

61. Bounds, *Power Through Prayer*, 42–43.

of praying. No ministry can succeed without much praying."[62] The matter is simple and inescapably clear—No man can do the work God has called him to do without calling upon God for the ability to do it, which necessitates being a man of prayer.

And what constitutes being a man of prayer? "No man can be a man of prayer who does not give much time to praying."[63] To consider the concept of concluding sermons as the highpoint of the sermon, a conclusion through which God is pleased to work mightily in the hearts of people, is presumptuous without considering the means for this end, which is prayer—humble, desperate, fervent, dependent prayer.

Preaching lacks spiritual power if it fails to instruct the mind to compel conviction, or if it fails to pierce the conscience to compel contrition, or it fails to impact the emotions to compel the affections, or if it fails to encourage the will to compel resolution. The power that forges man's will into God's is not a human work, but the power of God's grace. "For such power we must wait before Him. . . . No time will be lost for preparation which is spent in that first of all preparations—PRAYER. This is the preparation which prepares. All spiritual power runs back for its source and fountain to this mercy seat!"[64] Prayer, as the ultimate preparation for preaching, is simply too valuable, too necessary, to be skimped. Yet, humble, desperate, fervent, dependent prayer regarding the content and delivery of the content composing the sermon's conclusion will exact a significant upgrade to the time, and effort necessary in one's sermon preparation.

Powerful preaching is costly as it costs the preacher much. The cost of powerful preaching includes denying self, death to the world, and "the travail of his own soul."[65] But this should be neither a surprising nor a limiting factor since it is true that it does "not please God for us to offer Him that which costs us nothing."[66] However, death to self, death to the world, and the travail of soul are definite limiting factors for an undisciplined man, limiting factors that are all too common in the preaching ministry. Gardiner Spring provides a great insight about the diligence of a disciplined preacher as he wrote, "No minister can be diligent without a solemn purpose to be so. Severe toil is not naturally a pleasure; labor was the inflicted curse."[67] As certain as powerful preaching is the product of the costly personal price paid by a preacher, it is more so a product of the gracious provision of God reserved as a response to fervent prayer. Prayer is a preacher's "mightiest weapon" as it draws upon the very power of God Himself, giving "life and force to all."[68] And no part of a sermon is more deserving and more needful of prayer than the sermon conclusion.

62. Bounds, *Power Through Prayer*, 49–50.

63. Bounds, *Power Through Prayer*, 59.

64. Pierson, *The Divine Art of Preaching*, 1892, 143–44.

65. Bounds, *Power Through Prayer*, 22.

66. Spurgeon, *An All-round Ministry*, 1900, 156.

67. Spring, *The Power of the Pulpit*, 1848, 99–100.

68. Bounds, *Power Through Prayer*, 14.

For people to respond to God's Word, God must enable them to do so. God-enabled preaching is preaching that God vitalizes so that his will and Word are received by the hearers.[69] According to E. M. Bounds, powerless preaching "may at times glow and sparkle . . . but the glow and sparkle will be as barren of life as the field sown with pearls."[70] As long as preachers are content to preach glowing, sparkling pearls of sermonic infertility there will be no advancement of power in their pulpit ministries and there will be ineffective conclusions that fail to be the highpoint of the sermons they preach.

The personal price to be paid for effective preaching, and especially for an effective sermon conclusion, must be calculated to include whatever time, effort, and sacrifices are necessary to prepare to preach and to preach effectively, including an effective conclusion that truly will be the highpoint of the sermon. Such a commitment will not be common. It never has been and never will be common, but it is always necessary. If this is not the case in one's preaching ministry, one becomes a legacy to the following lament about preachers who are unwilling to prioritize their preaching ministry:

> The great deficiency in the church of the present age is the want of a spiritual and urgent ministry. . . . This state of things demands sober reflection. . . . Ministers may be pious, able, and evangelical in their views, yet not be *good preachers.* . . . And the reason is, their hearts are not ardently set on preaching, the great object of the Christian ministry; they are drawn from it to other things and contemplate the one thing needful with diminished interest.[71]

A heart ardently set on preaching as the great object of the Christian ministry must be a prerequisite for one to sacrifice the necessary time and effort to achieve sermon conclusion effectiveness.

The general criteria of willingness to pay the price for effective preaching by the means of whatever time, effort, and sacrifices are necessary may be too general to be assessed from week to week in one's preaching ministry. Perhaps some targets of commitment for the necessary time, effort, and sacrifices would be helpful. Test your commitment to pay the price in preparing yourself to preach and continue to do so until the following four commitments become a reality, a weekly reality, in your preaching ministry.

First, "I will not take the opportunity to preach God's Word, and yet be content to do so without the enabling power of the Holy Spirit." Second, "I will not preach a sermon without demonstrating what is *required of God's people,* and what is *required for God's people* to achieve the purpose of the sermon in their lives, thus allowing God to be enthroned in their hearts by responding to God's Word appropriately." Third, "I will not presume to instruct God's people through the closing appeals of the conclusion except by precepts and examples appropriately drawn from God's Word." Fourth, "I will not

69. Bounds, *Power Through Prayer,* 20.
70. Bounds, *Power Through Prayer,* 21.
71. Spring, *The Power of the Pulpit,* 1848, 92–93.

presume to think that the Word of God without the power of God will produce the work of God that is to be done through the ministry of preaching. Therefore, I must pray, and I will pray regardless of the time, effort, and sacrifices necessary to do so."

The unwillingness to sacrifice the necessary time and effort to pray fervently in preparation to preach will position a preacher to fulfill Spurgeon's warning that, "We may discover, after having labored long and wearily in preaching, that all the honor belongs to another builder, whose prayers were gold, silver, and precious stones, while our sermonizings being apart from prayer, were but hay and stubble."[72] What a remorseful depiction of that which must be averted!

Gardiner Spring's instruction is sufficient to encourage, reprove, and correct any preacher regarding his preaching ministry: "No man has rich treasures of thought without great labor. God's blessing is with a devoted minister. The minister who dissipates his time . . . need not be disappointed at his want of power in the pulpit, nor that he is unable to sustain himself in his high vocation."[73] Such great assertions advocate for the necessity of devoted diligence in the ministry of preaching God's Word, a devoted diligence which is prerequisite for preaching effective sermon conclusions!

72. Spurgeon, *Lectures to My Students*, 47.
73. Spring, *The Power of the Pulpit*, 1848, 104.

10

The Closing Appeals of a Sermon Conclusion: Part 2

"There can be no mistaking the fact that when it comes to preaching, how the matter ends, ends the matter! The shadow cast by a sermon conclusion is unmistakable."

"What is said, and how it is said, and the time it takes for it to be said, determines the impact that a conclusion may or may not have upon the hearers."

"The best conclusion should be no longer than what is needed to make a deep impression upon the hearers' consciences, affections, and wills through what is said and how it is said in demonstrating from Scripture what is necessary for the hearers to comply with the purpose of the preaching text in their lives."

"In an effective sermon conclusion, time is always a factor of its success, that is, time spent in the study to discover the most significant insights to be brought out in the conclusion, as well as time spent in the pulpit to deliver these significant discoveries."

"Needed, insightful, practical instruction in the closing appeals of a sermon conclusion will materialize only as there is a commitment to prioritize the necessity of diligent study to discover what God has provided for his people, for them to live as he has revealed in his Word. A noted preacher of past generations was of this opinion and reflected it when he wrote: 'It is my candid opinion that the average sermon has cost the preacher entirely too little mental endeavor. Among the reasons that there are not more great preachers is the fact that there are so few painstaking students. Good preaching is only and ever the product of great study.'"

"The hearers do not need to hear from a preacher who espouses his opinion or the counsel of others as the basis for the ultimate application of the sermon, the closing

appeals of the conclusion. They need to hear from God, which means they need biblical instruction as the basis for the closing appeals of a sermon conclusion."

"So, what constitutes the brevity that is not too brief in a sermon conclusion? Brevity is brief enough when the conclusion includes what must be presented so the hearers can begin to, or more faithfully, achieve the purpose of the sermon in their daily living. . . . A concentrated impression is crucial to a sermon conclusion's success. The requirements for a concentrated impression of a sermon conclusion's content are characterized as; important, practical, definite, and condensed. . . . 'Weight, not bulk of appeal, is the test of value.' . . . What must be avoided is having 'a grain of thought to the bushel of words.'"

"The truth hearers are urged to embrace is found in the closing appeals of the sermon conclusion. Not just the final closing appeal, although this is the most important truth to be embraced, but the hearer's response is directed to each appeal regardless of their number."

"A sermon conclusion that makes a powerful impression on the hearers is predicated upon a preacher completing a two-fold cognitive process, the result of which is key to yielding accurate and precise content the hearers will find significant. The two-fold cognitive process includes: first, that a preacher strongly fix before his mind an exact, detailed understanding of what/how his hearers ought to be in reference to the purpose of the passage achieved in their lives; second, that a preacher conceives as correctly as possible what is the present actuality of the hearers. From these two understandings the content of the conclusion can be incorporated by discovering from Scripture what will provide the most needed solutions to the pre-existing problems of the hearers."

"The closing appeals of a sermon conclusion are not intended to prove, primarily, but to specifically and forcefully direct how hearers are to respond to the sermon's purpose which is to be established in the lives of believers. . . . The closing appeals incorporate specific practical responses which naturally relate to the truth of the passage which was preached but more directly establish how the sermon's purpose may be accomplished in the lives of Christians. Thus, every believer making an appropriate response to the truth of Scripture, will be able to live a more holy life as they walk in greater Christlikeness and obedience to the Word of God."

"Because a hearer often may be moved to do something but doesn't know how to respond, the conclusion must declare specific actions by which the hearers may respond responsibly to the intent of the text/sermon. Such needed insights, spelled out in the sermon conclusion, cause it to be the essence of the sermon. The specific actions to be implemented are contained in the closing appeals. What is mandated qualitatively for the conclusion, as depicted by the closing appeals, is that the conclusion be personal, specific, positive, forceful, and urgent."

"Basically, one of two options should be pursued and at times both may be included. One option is to pursue the solution for the problem of entailment, that is, what does this passage of Scripture entail for my life? What am I to do in response to the truth of this passage to achieve its purpose in my life? The other option is to pursue the solution for the problem of engagement, that is, how do I get started? How do I go from negligence to obedience to the truth that this passage requires of me? This option deals with the dilemma of hearers who know basically what they are to do but don't know how to get started in doing what they are supposed to do."

"The four bases of cognition, conscience, affections, and volition are not optional. Each represents a need the hearers have. These needs must be addressed if the hearers are to respond to a sermon with genuine understanding and commitment. The four bases represent the weighty responsibility borne by a preacher in the conclusion of his message. Rather than seeking to become silent as soon as possible, a preacher needs to be concerned about becoming as helpful as possible to his hearers by addressing these needs for them in his conclusion. The help hearers need from a preacher in the conclusion of a sermon is not that he stops talking but rather he starts saying the most personally significant insights contained in the entire sermon."

CAREFUL PREPARATION NEEDED FOR CONCLUSIONS

Many preachers prepare to fail in their sermon conclusions simply because they fail to prepare their sermon conclusions.[1] This simply is the "Genesis" of the problem of poor sermon conclusions, to which the "Revelation" of the issue is that "conclusions are consistently the weakest parts of sermons."[2] What a dreadful "Genesis to Revelation" account of sermon conclusions this is in preaching!

Preachers consistently prepare introductions for their sermons, ranging from thin to thorough, but very seldom prepare a conclusion of any magnitude, even though the conclusion is more important than the introduction. Yet, the great Greek and Roman orators provided diligent preparation for their oratorical perorations, that is, the conclusions of their speeches. Knowing that the outcome of their oration was dependent upon how they concluded, they gathered up "all their powers for one supreme effort" to end their speeches.[3] However, such effort and preparation to craft sermon conclusions is apparently absent in preaching.

Though there is basic agreement in theory as to what a sermon conclusion is expected to accomplish, there is great consensus that in practice "conclusions are done so poorly that they seldom accomplish what is agreed upon that they should do for

---

1. O'Neal, *Make the Bible Live*, 42.
2. Jones, *Principles and Practice of Preaching*, 160.
3. Broadus, *A Treatise on the Preparation and Delivery of Sermons*, 1870, 277.

those who are hearers of sermons."[4] This assertion alone demands that careful prepa-ration of the sermon conclusion become a reality.

It is quite apparent, based upon the evidence of preached sermons, that preachers have little regard for the way they end their sermons. Woodrow Kroll lamented, "It is accurate to say that the last five minutes of the sermon are the most important part of the entire sermon. Yet how little preparation the conclusion receives."[5] There can be no mistaking the fact that when it comes to preaching, how the matter ends, ends the matter!

The shadow cast by a sermon conclusion is unmistakable. Hear how this is echoed by homiletical icons of recent years. According to Haddon Robinson, the preacher "must work on his conclusion with special care. Otherwise everything comes to nothing."[6] Jay Adams asserted, "Without a good conclusion, the otherwise best ser-mon is a dud. As we've seen, introductions are important; if anything, conclusions are even more important. . . . What you say in the conclusion is what people usually take away with them."[7] Bryan Chapell argues effectively as he reasons, "Because listeners are more likely to remember the conclusion than any other portion of the message, and because all the sermon's components should have prepared for this culmination, the conclusion is the climax of the message."[8] Chuck Swindoll provides a great deal of gravity to the work of concluding a sermon when affirmed that it is a trait of novice preachers "to 'wing' the conclusion, perhaps with the expectation that a good begin-ning and solid middle will send them on a trajectory to a great ending. But you can't fling a message toward the audience like a baseball, hoping it flies close enough to catch. On the contrary, if there's anything you *don't* leave to chance, it's the last thought you leave ringing in their ears."[9]

Of course, the importance attributed to the sermon conclusion is a long-standing fixture in homiletical theory. Many years ago, Alexandre Vinet stated, "The peroration [conclusion] is the mouth at which the discourse discharges itself as the exordium [introduction] is its source, and a river at its mouth is larger, fuller, more powerful, than it is at its source."[10] According to the statements included above, there should be no doubt about the matter. Careful preparation of the sermon conclusion must not be neglected.

As preparation of the sermon conclusion is not neglected but prioritized, two concepts become paramount: sufficient preparation time for the sermon conclusion must be provided; and the closing appeals are the essence of the sermon conclusion,

---

4. Jones, *Principles and Practice of Preaching*, 160.

5. Kroll, *Prescription for Preaching*, 179.

6. Robinson, *Biblical Preaching*, 167.

7. Adams, *Preaching with Purpose*, 65.

8. Chapell, *Christ-centered Preaching*, 244.

9. Swindoll, *Saying It Well*, 227.

10. Vinet, *Homiletics*, 1854, 327–28.

which should be the highpoint of the entire sermon. Another way to understand the all-important preparation of the sermon conclusion is to understand that what is said, and how it is said, and the time it takes for it to be said, determines the impact that a conclusion may or may not have upon the hearers.

The first of two considerations for careful preparation of a sermon conclusion is that time is an important reality for the closing appeals of a sermon conclusion. Time is needed to prepare the closing appeals in preparing the sermon as well as time being needed in the pulpit to deliver the appeals to the hearers. As has been mentioned, nothing can exceed the bad effect of a conclusion that is needlessly protracted, and few things are more frustrating to a hearer than the undue continuance of an indefinite and protracted conclusion. This unfortunate situation represents wasting time. Yet, since the conclusion provides a contribution of ultimate significance, a wise preacher will not allow it to be denuded of necessary substance and the time required to cover this content.[11] However, in the pursuit of doing this one must never be deceived about the matter that "length is no substitute for strength."[12] Additionally, one must never violate the maxim to "exhaust neither your substance nor your audience."[13] The best conclusion should be no longer than what is needed to make a deep impression upon the hearers' consciences, affections, and wills through what is said and how it is said[14] in demonstrating from Scripture what is necessary for the hearers to comply with the purpose of the preaching text in their lives.

In appropriating time wisely for sermon conclusions, it will come as a shock for many to understand and appreciate the viewpoint that, "Conclusions, unlike introductions, are often too short."[15] The reason sermon conclusions are too short has to do with the mismanagement of time due to a faulty perspective about proportionality for the elements of a sermon. Possessing a poor understanding of the vital work of sermon conclusions, preachers develop the bulk of a sermon consisting of the introduction and sermon body allowing only a few hurried sentences for the conclusion, if they have one at all! "Few things could be more self-defeating."[16] The faulty proportionality has to do with mismanaging time in the sense that not enough time is allotted for the conclusion. "Conclusions are often too short. Twenty–five minutes of argument and a phrase or two for the conclusion is disproportionate. Without wasting words, the sermon must receive a masterly finish, and fall with satisfying completeness on the ear and mind of all who have intelligently followed."[17] Clearly a new perspective regarding

---

11. Kidder, *A Treatise on Homiletics*, 1862, 229–30.

12. Macpherson, *The Burden of the Lord*, 156.

13. Pattison, *The Making of the Sermon*, 188.

14. Etter, *The Preacher and His Sermon*, 1885, 383.

15. McCracken, *The Making of the Sermon*, 96.

16. McCracken, *The Making of the Sermon*, 96.

17. Sangster, *The Craft of Sermon Construction*, 141.

sermon conclusions is needed to warrant preachers adjusting their sermon preparation process to strengthen how they conclude their sermons.

An adjusted perspective of the time needed for a sermon conclusion is based upon three factors. First, time is required to successfully stress, persuasively, the need for personal, practical action. Second, time is necessary so that the conclusion may indicate how, that is, the ways and means by which, the purpose of the sermon may be achieved. It is inadequate to suggest that something should be done without showing, specifically, how it can be done. Third, time must be expended to incorporate what effective conclusions include, that is, material to impact the conscience, affections, and volition of the hearers, including an instance that illustrates achieving the purpose of the sermon.[18] Persuasive exhortation, ways and means to incorporate the purpose of the sermon into life, and concrete illustration of the closing appeals applied to life represent the reasons for the three adjustments that must be made in the thinking of preachers regarding their work of concluding sermons so that sufficient time can be allocated for this most important element of a sermon.

Time in the pulpit, preaching time, is needed to provide the content that achieves what should be accomplished in a sermon conclusion. Time in the study, study time, is required to discover the needed content to be preached in a conclusion. Therefore, additional study time is another component of necessary time for a sermon conclusion. It is an unavoidable fact that marshalling more content in a sermon conclusion requires additional time in the study to discover this additional content. David L. Larsen expressed one of the most robust instructions for time allocation to produce effective conclusions when he wrote: "I recommend to my students that they spent two-thirds of their time on the last one-third of their message. At any sales convention or conference, the bulk of the time is spent working on the last five minutes the salesmen's presentations, and for good reason. . . . Recognize the necessity of a prompt and polished ending."[19] In an effective sermon conclusion, time is always a factor of its success, that is, time spent in the study to discover the most significant insights to be brought out in the conclusion, as well as time spent in the pulpit to deliver these significant discoveries.

The second component for careful preparation of a sermon conclusion is the closing appeals. Simply put, the closing appeals of a sermon conclusion are a sermon within a sermon. The weight of the sermon is registered by the closing appeals. The most careful preparation of a sermon should be given to the closing appeals of the sermon conclusion. After accumulating strength for the conclusion from the construction of the main body of the sermon and understanding its bearing upon the purpose of the sermon to be enforced in the conclusion, there needs to be musing upon the whole matter "until it burns deep within, thus, boiling down the sermon to a flashpoint in the soul. At the degree of blood-heat we may begin composition" of the

18. McCracken, *The Making of the Sermon*, 96–97.
19. Larsen, *The Anatomy of Preaching*, 121.

most important component of a sermon, its conclusion.[20] The test of the preacher's mettle is clearly seen in his conclusion. If he is in fact preaching for his hearers' spiritual welfare, he will earnestly seek to "forcibly impress" the implications of the text's purpose upon his hearers so that they leave with the truth in their hearts and have a clear direction about how they can live life in a way that achieves the purpose of the text in their lives.[21]

The preparation involved to produce a sermon conclusion is a vital process undertaken to meet people's needs. The importance of this function of a sermon conclusion cannot be overemphasized. Most notably the conclusion must clarify how the sermon's purpose applies to the hearers. Even as application is found throughout the sermon, special attention should be given to application in the conclusion. More than anything else in the sermon, "the conclusion helps to achieve the sermon objective. It will persuade people to act upon the truth of the sermon. No sermon is complete until you have challenged the hearers to act upon the message they have heard."[22] The closing appeals of the sermon conclusion become the substantive basis for exhortation, the place in the sermon where the most condensed exhortation of the sermon should occur.

A conclusion that provides "how to" instruction demands significant biblical research and discovery to yield specific, concrete ways and means of compliance to optimally achieve the purpose of the sermon in the hearers' lives. Needed, insightful, practical instruction in the closing appeals of a sermon conclusion will materialize only as there is a commitment to prioritize the necessity of diligent study to discover what God has provided for his people, for them to live as he has revealed in his Word. A noted preacher of past generations was of this opinion and reflected it when he wrote: "It is my candid opinion that the average sermon has cost the preacher entirely too little mental endeavor. Among the reasons that there are not more great preachers is the fact that there are so few painstaking students. Good preaching is only and ever the product of great study."[23] The lack of much-needed study by preachers brought an interesting indictment expressed as follows: "Much exhortation from the pulpit is weak, more like the pussyfoot creep than the tiger's sure stride. Frequently exhortation is louder than it is clear. We must not be guilty of the criticism: 'Sir, you raise your voice when you should reinforce your argument.'"[24] There must be no ambiguity about this, the conclusion demands diligent biblical study and research to marshal concrete application contained in the closing appeals!

The concrete application of a sermon conclusion's closing appeals will materialize as the following four procedures are incorporated: one, draw from Scripture the

---

20. Etter, *The Preacher and His Sermon*, 1885, 384.

21. Hoppin, *Homiletics*, 1883, 427.

22. Bryson and Taylor, *Building Sermons to Meet People's Needs*, 108–9.

23. Riley, *The Preacher and His Preaching*, 107.

24. Demaray, *An Introduction to Homiletics*, 96.

necessary insights for compliance to the sermon's purpose; two, reduce the general to the specific; three, name the action or actions that should be taken immediately; four, impress the truths by exhorting compliance with loving yet earnest, relentless thrusts to the wills of the hearers. The call for specificity of the hearers' response is paramount in the sermon conclusion. It is the preacher's responsibility to "describe specific and concrete steps of action" or "specific ways to respond in faith" to the purpose of the sermon by putting scriptural truth to work in their lives. "Most sermons fail at this point, leaving the audience with much about *what* they should do with a little about *how*."[25] In the hierarchy of instruction, "what" is penultimate to the ultimate consideration of "how." Perhaps one of the most grievous perplexities of life is not knowing how to do what we need to do.

The concrete application of specific, practical instruction constitutes the closing appeals of the sermon conclusion which means that the concrete, specific material of the closing appeals should be derived from Scripture. I appreciate the insight and could not agree more fully with the viewpoint of Edwin Mouzon when he wrote: "The most instructive and inspiring preacher is the one who knows his Bible best. . . . The Bible never plays out. There is a timeless element in this book. 'Preaching for the times may draw a crowd for a time, but the people will soon tire of that sort of thing. What they want is 'preaching for eternity.' . . . They need an outlook into the life that is life indeed."[26] Mouzon's point, though timely when written, is far more relevant in our present context than in previous days. The hearers do not need to hear from a preacher who espouses his opinion or the counsel of others as the basis for the ultimate application of the sermon, the closing appeals of the conclusion. They need to hear from God, which means they need biblical instruction as the basis for the closing appeals of a sermon conclusion.

The closing appeals of the sermon conclusion are indicative of content, insightful biblical content. But what must be equally indicative of the biblically based content of the closing appeals is that they are the means by which the purpose of the sermon is achieved in the lives of the hearers. In a word, the sermon conclusion seeks to encourage motivation of the hearers to respond to the closing appeals. According to Chapell, "The primary purpose of the conclusion is motivation. There should be . . . a determined effort to mobilize the will of the listeners to conform to previously specified imperatives."[27] John Stott provides counsel, the wisdom of which may be surpassed only by the folly of its violation, when he mandated that preachers must never issue an appeal without first making a proclamation, as an appeal cannot properly be given before the declaration has been made. Truth must be understood before the hearers are asked to respond to it. On the other hand, preachers *must never preach a sermon without appealing for a response* from the hearers to comply to the purpose

25. McDill, *12 Essential Skills for Great Preaching*, 205.

26. Mouzon, *Preaching with Authority*, 1929, 225–26.

27. Chapell, *Christ-centered Preaching*, 246.

of the sermon in their lives. "It is not enough to teach the truth; we must urge men to embrace it."[28] The truth which hearers are urged to embrace is the truths found in the closing appeals of the sermon conclusion. Not just the final closing appeal, although this is the most important truth to be embraced, but the hearer's response should be directed to each appeal regardless of their number.

CAREFUL PREPARATION YIELDS DIVERSITY IN ASCENDING CLOSING APPEALS

To rightly regard the importance of the closing appeals of a sermon conclusion and to appropriately implement them in the act of preaching requires the proper presentation of closing appeals in ascending order from lesser to greater in reference to importance of insight and urgency for compliance. A sermon conclusion essentially is composed of appeals to which the hearers are to implement in their lives. These appeals will be characterized by diversity. These appeals will be presented in an ascending order of significance from lesser to greater importance. These appeals will be offered in ascending order of urgency for compliance from lesser to greater commitment.

In a word, diversity is the leading concept of a sermon conclusion's content; diversity in the number of appeals, diversity in the importance of the appeals, and diversity in the urgency with which each appeal is offered in a given conclusion. French homiletician Jean Claude codified this in 1778 when he instructed: "The conclusion should be diversified. I mean, we should not be content to move one single Christian passion; many must be touched . . . (I)n order to stir up the passion . . . the conclusion ought to be composed at least of two or three, if not four or five, reflections . . . (T)hese reflections must be placed in prudent order so that the weakest and least powerful may be the first, and the strongest last."[29]

Some think that preaching is designed only to make Scripture understood, so they are content with giving the sense of the text and describing some key implications of the passage. Though these things must be done, a conclusion is not required for these things to be accomplished. But such a simplistic theory of preaching, according to Jean Claude, is mistaken "for preaching is not only intended to give the sense of Scripture but also . . . (to) instruct, solve difficulties, solve unfolding mysteries, penetrate into the ways of divine wisdom and established truths, refute error, comfort, correct, and censure, fill the hearers with an admiration of the wonderful works and ways of God, inflame their souls with zeal, and powerfully incline them to piety and holiness, which are the ends of preaching."[30] It is at the end of the sermon where such ends of preaching are to be accomplished most fully.

28. Olford and Olford, *Anointed Expository Preaching*, 261–2.
29. Claude, *Claude's Essay*, 1801, 133.
30. Claude, *Claude's Essay*, 1801, 2.

The overall result of an effective sermon conclusion is to make a powerful impression on the hearers by a preacher who will "appeal directly to the passions and solidly, yet powerfully, appeal to the conscience and understanding."[31] A sermon conclusion that makes a powerful impression on the hearers is predicated upon a preacher completing a two-fold cognitive process, the result of which is key to yielding accurate and precise content the hearers will find significant.

The two-fold cognitive process includes: first, that a preacher strongly fix before his mind an exact, detailed understanding of what/how his hearers ought to be in reference to the purpose of the passage achieved in their lives; second, that a preacher conceives as correctly as possible what is the present actuality of the hearers. From these two understandings the content of the conclusion can be incorporated by discovering from Scripture what will provide the most needed solutions to the pre-existing problems of the hearers.[32] Of course, a correct understanding of one's hearers and the exact instructions to which they must be exhorted to comply so that needed correction is made and the purpose of the sermon is achieved in their lives, though necessary, is insufficient for sermon conclusion effectiveness. The supernatural power of the Holy Spirit is determinative for the closing appeals of a sermon conclusion to find their mark in the lives of the hearers.

The power of a Spirit-filled preacher is exemplified by the Apostle Peter. Once he was filled with the Holy Spirit, he was an instant enigma. He was the same former fisherman who followed Christ for three years, with the same natural intellect and powers of speech; and yet once he was filled with the Spirit on the Day of Pentecost, a supernatural effectiveness was given to him, the results of which were not only instantly apparent but truly amazing.[33] Not only was the effectiveness of his preaching obvious; the understanding of his hearers, their contrition, their repentance, and their conversion, but the boldness of his preaching being riddled with courageous reproof, rebuke, and exhortation was due to the Holy Spirit's power operating in him. The Holy Spirit was responsible for the results of Peter's preaching and for the manner of his preaching, a manner of preaching which culminated in appealing to his hearers to respond to the truth as he strongly exhorted them with many other words to "Be saved from this corrupt generation."[34]

Exhortation, though free of pressure tactics, involves a sincere and earnest pleading by a preacher for the hearers to act in response to the mandates of Scripture. "Exhortation is the calling of the child back from the edge of a traffic-filled street, the calling of a sleeping man out of a burning house, and the calling back of a young man skating toward thin ice."[35] Exhortation is a justified imploring for one to conduct one-

31. Sturtevant, *The Preacher's Manual*, 1866, 502.

32. Sturtevant, *The Preacher's Manual*, 1866, 503.

33. Arthur, *The Tongue of Fire*, 1859, 89.

34. Acts 2:40.

35. Brown Jr., *A Quest for Reformation in Preaching*, 63.

self in wisdom, the withholding of such pleading to be enacted is not only unjustified but would render the withholder culpable.

In a sermon conclusion that is well-prepared, "there should be the focusing of truth upon the hearer, the suggestion of ways and means of practicing it, and the appeal for action. All of this must be done."[36] The closing words of a sermon conclusion must find the preacher exhorting his hearers to respond to needed Scripture-based closing appeals. Responding to Scripture-based closing appeals defines what the hearers are to do just as exhorting hearers to respond to Scripture-based closing appeals defines what the preacher is to do in reference to a sermon conclusion.

Henry Grady Davis suspected that a preacher who incorporates pointed exhortation in his conclusions is due, in part, not to his zeal "but to the false sense of importance and power it gives him to tell other people what they ought to do."[37] Certainly, urgent exhortation stemming from this motivation would, indeed, be vile. But equally vile is the suspicion that a preacher who exhorts people to action by pointed closing appeals is done because of a corrupt motive on behalf of the preacher rather than from the pure motivation of his zeal to see God's people bring glory to God in living productive lives that comply with the teachings of Scripture. With no hesitation about unwarranted suspicions of a preacher's motives, he must be committed to the ministry of exhortation by means of Scripture-based closing appeals which will constitute a sermon conclusion.

FULLNESS AND BREVITY FOR SERMON CONCLUSIONS

With all due respect for the necessity of brevity, brevity can be a characteristic of a boring sermon. Brevity and boredom are not mutually exclusive. Just as a lengthy sermon can be boring, so a brief sermon can be boring. In either case, *a sermon is boring because of insignificant development of the subject matter in the time taken to preach it*. Insignificant development of the subject matter in a lengthy sermon results in a boring lengthy sermon. Insignificant development of the subject matter in a brief sermon results in a boring brief sermon.

A sermon cannot be spared from being boring simply because it is brief. However, it is certainly true that a boring brief sermon would be more boring if it were of greater length. I love the anecdote of "a preacher with a track record of preaching brief sermons who was a guest preacher for another congregation. Having preached his typical brief sermon he was surprised by the comments of one listener who said, 'That was a very brief sermon.' The guest preacher responded to the listener, 'Well, I believe a sermon ought to be brief rather than boring.' To which the listener replied, 'Yes, but you found a way to be both!'"[38] Brevity is not the solution for a sermon in which its

36. Whitesell, *Power in Expository Preaching*, 115.

37. Davis, *Design for Preaching*, 196.

38. I was not able to rediscover the original source of this anecdote of the preacher with a track

content is depreciated by an insignificant development of the subject-matter. Yet, the preference must be for brevity rather than a lack of brevity in an instance where the text is dealt with in a manner that can only yield boredom as a result of its treatment.

In reference to sermon conclusions, brevity is well understood and must be honored as it is implemented, yet its implementation must be modified to assure a necessary measure of completeness. Arthur Hoyt provided counsel that must not be set aside, especially in preaching a sermon conclusion. His suggestion was: "I would not make a hobby of brevity. The application should be so given as to touch the various minds and conditions of the audience, and to this end something of fullness may be demanded. . . . But not a word more than needed should be given. . . . The truth is hurt by needless exhortation. . . . Happy is the man who knows when to stop; who stops when he gets through."[39] So, what constitutes the brevity that is not too brief in a sermon conclusion? Brevity is brief enough when the conclusion includes what must be presented so the hearers can begin to, or more faithfully, achieve the purpose of the sermon in their daily living. In the words of Stephen and David Olford, "The preacher must avoid rushing or deadening the conclusion. . . . [But rather,] the preacher must seek to clarify, exhort, and invite the response that the truth deserves and demands."[40]

What must be recognized regarding qualitative content and quantitative time in which to preach that content is that revision, ruthless revision, is necessary to reduce the preaching time while maintaining qualitative content. Qualitative content must be understood as density of application in the conclusion's closing appeals which are favorable to a concentrated impression. A concentrated impression is crucial to a sermon conclusion's success.

The requirements for a concentrated impression of a sermon conclusion's content are characterized as; important, practical, definite, and condensed. The following three concepts are helpful to shape the thought process necessary to implement conclusion content that complies with fullness and brevity. "Weight, not bulk of appeal, is the test of value."[41] "Next to the evil of having nothing in the sermon at all, is that of having too much in it; for in neither case does the hearer carry much away."[42] What must be avoided is having "a grain of thought to the bushel of words."[43] However, the major consideration for producing sermon conclusions that are full yet brief is the realization that the sermon conclusion appears in a context where hearers are mentally fatigued which necessitates, absolutely necessitates, concentrated impression of content like no other portion of the sermon.

---

record of preaching brief yet boring sermons. T. Harwood Pattison, page 188, comes close with an anecdote of a preacher who thought brief sermons prevented tediousness.

39. Hoyt, *The Work of Preaching*, reprinted, 1910, 206–07.

40. Olford and Olford, *Anointed*, 194.

41. Phelps, *The Theory of Preaching*, 1882, 507.

42. Taylor, *The Ministry of the Word*, 1876, 113.

43. Taylor, *The Ministry of the Word*, 1876, 116.

CLOSING APPEALS AS THE ESSENCE OF A CONCLUSION

The overall work of a sermon conclusion may involve, to a lesser degree, any helpful process of preaching that may be found in the body of a sermon. It may instruct, illustrate, prove, apply, persuade, or motivate. It may include some, most, or all of them combined and intertwined. In this sense it may be the most complicated element of a sermon, and yet, it "is susceptible of the most varied and ingenious methods of procedure."[44] But, the closing appeals of a sermon conclusion are not intended to prove, primarily, but to specifically and forcefully direct how hearers are to respond to the sermon's purpose which is to be established in the lives of believers. The closing appeals should consist of specific exhortation, exhortation which penetrates the heart, captivates the conscience, energizes the emotions/affections, and subjugates the will to the Word of God. This is the role of a sermon conclusion when it is strictly understood and implemented.[45]

The closing appeals incorporate specific practical responses which naturally relate to the truth of the passage which was preached but more directly establish how the sermon's purpose may be accomplished in the lives of Christians. Thus, every believer making an appropriate response to the truth of Scripture, will be able to live a more holy life as they walk in greater Christlikeness and obedience to the Word of God.[46] Throughout the sermon the preacher is building a case and making progress toward the conclusion. In the conclusion the progress is completed, and the case is culminated so that the appeal to action becomes the gateway of commencement in the hearers' response to the truth of the passage which has been expounded.[47]

The sermon conclusion is the essence of the sermon. It is in the conclusion of the sermon where believers are given biblical instruction that remedies and corrects that which is absent or inadequate in the lives of the hearers. In order to provide this content a preacher must discover or discern what the purpose of the text/sermon is, keeping in mind that it is the necessary response indicated by the closing appeals that will achieve the purpose for the sermon, which will be the basis of "the solution to a problem." Therefore, the purpose for the sermon, as stated in the introduction, provides "the basis for an appeal to action in the conclusion."[48] Specifically, the closing appeals of the sermon conclusion are the means by which the purpose of the sermon is achieved, thus, providing solutions to practical problems encountered commonly in the lives of believers.

Because a hearer often may be moved to do something but doesn't know how to respond, the conclusion must declare specific actions by which the hearers may

---

44. Phelps, *The Theory of Preaching* 1882, 455.

45. Potter, *Sacred Eloquence*, 1868, 310.

46. Potter, *Sacred Eloquence*, 1868, 309.

47. O'Neal, *Make the Bible Live*, 43.

48. O'Neal, *Make the Bible Live*, 43.

respond responsibly to the intent of the text/sermon.[49] Such needed insights, spelled out in the sermon conclusion, cause it to be the essence of the sermon. The specific actions to be implemented are contained in the closing appeals. What is mandated qualitatively for the conclusion, as depicted by the closing appeals, is that the conclusion be personal, specific, positive, forceful, and urgent.[50]

The sermon conclusion is comprised of extremely relevant personal application. Too many preachers do not know how to apply truth forcefully and this is especially true in the sermon conclusion. Ilion T. Jones is helpful to provide correction to this common problem as he defines preaching by three criteria, all of which are pivotal in a sermon conclusion.[51] "Preaching is discussion plus—and that plus distinguishes sermons." Three criteria distinguish the "plus" of a sermon beyond the obligation to provide a careful discussion of a biblical text.

The first criterion of that "plus" is "*to apply the truth.*" Though the application may be distributed throughout the whole sermon it "should be compacted in the conclusion." The second criterion of the "plus" is "*to lay the truth on the hearer's conscience*" so as "to focus the claims of the truth on the moral judgments and wills of the hearers. A sermon is defective until that is done. Every proven and tested truth carries a divine obligation to do something with it. . . . Moralizing, in the sense of laying upon the consciences of the hearers their obligations concerning the truth, has been called the 'consummation of preaching.' That consummation is reached in the conclusion."[52] The third criterion, the last and most important part of the "plus" of preaching, is "*to move the hearers to action.*" Of this criterion Jones was most emphatic as he stated:

> People not only want to know what they ought to do about the sermon, but they expect a preacher to exhort them to do it. The hearers, justifiably, should be disappointed and consider the sermon incomplete, if he fails to do so. The preacher should not permit himself to forget that from beginning to end he is out for a verdict, a commitment, a choice, an action on part of the hearers. Pressure on their wills, an effort to arouse their emotional response, is an integral part of the conclusion. No preacher should ever apologize for an

---

49. O'Neal, *Make the Bible Live*, 43.

50. Brown Jr., Clinard, and Northcutt, *Steps to the Sermon*, 122.

51. Jones, *Principles and Practice of Preaching*, 161–62.

52. I am intrigued that what was the "consummation of preaching" is commonly viewed presently as the corruption of preaching. In the view of some who write in the field of homiletics moralizing is to be strictly forbidden. The result of complying with this unfounded phobia is populating the pulpit with people, who are not preachers, that discuss everything and preach nothing. Non-prophets, not false prophets because there is nothing prophetic about their speaking, who misrepresent God as being satisfied with everything and intent on changing nothing in the lives of his people through the vehicle of preaching. The discussion of these non-preachers seems to have as its chief end, not correction to conform to the requirements of Scripture, but simply to remind believers of the identification, that they are his possession.

endeavoring to move –feelingly move– his hearers to action as he closes his sermon.[53]

If one were to consider Jones's criteria for sermon conclusions to be a reliable means of distinguishing preaching from mere discussion of biblical subjects and texts, one could only conclude that preaching predominantly is non-existent in pulpits today. If this is true, how does the predominance of non-preaching get turned around? What is the starting point by which the needed change from non-preaching to preaching can occur?

The starting point is the use of an explicitly stated transitional phrase by the preacher that depicts, not that the sermon is almost over, but rather that the climax of the sermon, the essence of the sermon, the most significant part of the sermon, is now at hand. Basically, one of two options should be pursued and at times both may be included. One option is *to pursue the solution for the problem of entailment*, that is, what does this passage of Scripture entail for my life? What am I to do in response to the truth of this passage to achieve its purpose in my life? The other option is *to pursue the solution for the problem of engagement*, that is, how do I get started? How do I go from negligence to obedience to the truth that this passage requires of me? This option deals with the dilemma of hearers who know basically what they are to do but don't know how to get started in doing what they are supposed to do.

The first option, *to pursue the solution for the problem of entailment*, provides an answer to the question, "So what?" The hearer who may ask this question may be thinking, "I know that, and I do that. I am not disobedient to that." But this option will pursue how partial obedience or present obedience can become an obedience that is more consistently, more fully, and more responsibly carried out in the lives of believers. The second option, *to pursue the solution for the problem of engagement*, provides an answer to the question, "Now what?" The hearer may be thinking, "I am so completely lacking here that I don't even know how to get started, or where to begin. How do I go about getting this turned around in my life? Where do I start and how do I begin?

The closing appeals of the sermon conclusion evidence the greatest oratorical force found in the message. The closing appeals do not further develop the subject-matter of the text but applies the purpose of the text/sermon in the most natural and practical manner to the hearts and consciences of the hearers.[54] Of course, the ultimate application of the sermon's purpose takes place in the conclusion, and specifically, through the means of the closing appeals, by which the purpose of the sermon is accomplished in the lives of the hearers.

53. Jones, *Principles and Practice of Preaching*, 162.
54. Etter, *The Preacher and His Sermon*, 1885, 376.

FOUR TARGETS OF CLOSING APPEALS—COGNITION, CONSCIENCE, AFFECTIONS, VOLITION

In baseball, LOB is a bitter-sweet designation of players who were "left on base." Through various means one or more players got on base but were stranded there at the end of their half of the inning having failed to cross home plate to score a run. A baseball game is won, not by the team who leaves more men on base, but by the team who gets more men across home plate. No one knowledgeable of baseball is impressed or pleased with the number of players "left on base" as opposed to the number of players who crossed home plate.

In baseball, there is a clear understanding between potential success, men on base, and actual success, men crossing the plate. To press the analogy to preaching, preachers are too content to preach for potential success rather than to preach for actual success. In other words, preachers are thrilled with the potential success of "preaching men on base," that is, making the truth of Scripture clearly understood when actual success is to see men act upon what has been clearly understood from Scripture, that is, "preaching men across the plate." What is needed in preaching is an equivalence to baseball's dictum of "Get'em on, get'em over, and get'em in!" Preaching's aspiration of "Just get'em on base" must be expanded. We need to preach to see hearers "cross the plate," not to see them "left on base." In baseball, a score is made when a player safely reaches all four bases, and so it is in preaching. In the closing appeals of a sermon conclusion there are four bases that must be reached for potential success to become actual success, success at the highest level—changed lives through responding to closing appeals which are based upon Scripture and exhorted by the preacher.

What is necessary in preaching to see men cross the plate? A preacher needs to help his hearers reach four bases in preaching his sermon conclusion—the bases of cognition, conscience, affections, and volition.

The base of cognition answers the hearer's need expressed in the plea, "Help me to understand what I need to know so that I may do what I need to do." A declaration of biblical instruction based upon a scriptural cross reference or cross references is the foundation for the closing appeals of an effective sermon conclusion, which reaches the base of cognition.

The base of conscience answers the hearer's need expressed in the plea, "Help me to understand that what I now know to do is indispensable for me." The base of conscience is reached when hearers realize that what ought to be done needs to begin or needs to be complied with more fully in their lives. "Men must have their sense of right and duty awakened by lively agitation. It is not enough that the intellect be addressed; for the mind may receive knowledge without feeling and moral obligation. It is one thing to be made to understand a thing; another, to be made to feel that a thing ought to be done."[55]

---

55. Etter, *The Preacher and His Sermon*, 1885, 376.

The base of affections answers the hearer's need expressed in the plea, "Help me to understand how what I am to do is affiliated with Christ and the advancement of His Kingdom, and how this will be of benefit to my life of service to the Lord." When conscience has been aroused, it is easier to stir the affections, or the feelings of the hearers to render them responsive to whatever demands the truth makes upon them. The objective in moving the feelings or the affections is that, in so doing, the will may be more effectively moved. The mind may be fully convinced, the conscience made wide-awake, and yet the will unchanged. "If, at this point, we call to our aid the powerful influence of the emotion, we may gain a complete victory over the will of the hearer, which otherwise might be almost gained, but altogether lost."[56] The feelings, that is, the emotions/affections of the hearers must be moved by the force of the closing appeals before the purpose of the sermon can be accomplished in the lives of the hearers.[57] The base of affections is reached when the hearers "buy in" and desire to do that which they know they are to do.

The base of volition answers the hearer's need expressed in the plea, "Help me to understand what I need to do to implement the purpose of the sermon in my life and keep it functioning in my life." To arouse the affections and stop there would render the conclusion incomplete. The ultimate objective of every sermon is that the hearers would make a commitment that changes how they live. The entire effort of the sermon is only preparatory to a stirring of the affections and to a commitment of the will that is necessary to compel the hearers to respond to the closing appeals of the conclusion and, thereby, accomplish the purpose of the sermon in the life of each one who responds to the truth.[58] Therefore, having been persuaded of the true and necessary nature of the sermon's purpose to be lived in the lives of believers, the hearers should be told how to perform those duties necessary to achieve the sermon's purpose in their lives, including whatever insights that may be necessary to overcome the difficulties they will encounter in the attempt to fulfill their responsibilities.[59] The base of volition is reached when the hearers are found doing what they know they are to do.

The four bases of cognition, conscience, affections, and volition are not optional. Each represents a need the hearers have. These needs must be addressed if the hearers are to respond to a sermon with genuine understanding and commitment. The four bases also represent the responsibility, a rather weighty responsibility, borne by a preacher in the conclusion of his message. Rather than seeking to become silent as soon as possible, a preacher needs to be concerned about becoming as helpful as possible to his hearers by addressing these needs for them in his conclusion. The help hearers need from a preacher in the conclusion of a sermon *is not that he stops talking but rather he starts saying the most personally significant insights contained in the entire sermon.*

56. Etter, *The Preacher and His Sermon*, 1885, 376.

57. Etter, *The Preacher and His Sermon*, 1885, 378.

58. Etter, *The Preacher and His Sermon*, 1885, 377.

59. Hoppin, *Homiletics*, 1883, 435.

When the content of the conclusion contains the most personally significant insights of the entire sermon, the closing appeals will be the "expression of a glowing heart."[60] A glowing heart accompanies a sermon conclusion that is the highpoint of the message. Incorporating the content of Scripture in the closing appeals, which impress the purpose of the sermon upon the hearer as well as provide crucial insights necessary to comply to the sermon's purpose, is the best method of concluding a sermon for one's hearers. In addition, incorporating Scripture in the closing appeals is the best means by which a glowing heart may rightly be possessed by a preacher in his sermon conclusion.[61]

The conclusion ought to be the most quickening and impressive part of the sermon, being communicated with intensity, energy, vividness, and urgency. If the sermon conclusion converges toward some great purpose, which it certainly should, and the preacher is what he should be in heart, he should implore his hearers to respond to the demands of Scripture without hesitation and without cessation.[62] To reference again the baseball analogy regarding base runners, in the conclusion of a sermon a preacher is like the third base coach waving a base runner around third base to home plate so that he may score a run. Without a doubt, this is the most urgent time in an entire game for a third base coach since his most important function is to help his players cross the plate and score. For a preacher, as a third base coach, this means he must supply content in his conclusion that is exceedingly relevant to the lives of the hearers. If not, his hearers are destined to be left on base without ever crossing the plate and scoring a run. All baseball analogies aside, this simply means in preaching that the hearers will not receive the most beneficial instruction needed in order to make the most profitable compliance in their lives to the Word of God if Scripture-based closing appeals do not form the content of the closing appeals of a sermon conclusion.

Though much has been clarified about the closing appeals of a sermon conclusion in chapters nine and ten, chapter eleven—The Closing Appeals of a Sermon Conclusion, Part 3—will expand clarification about the closing appeals in relation to the purpose of the sermon, guidelines for closing appeals, prerequisites for closing appeals, content types and delivery tones for closing appeals, the final words of a sermon conclusion, and the necessity of biblical authority for the closing appeals to produce life-change for the hearers.

60. Etter, *The Preacher and His Sermon*, 1885, 381.

61. Etter, *The Preacher and His Sermon*, 1885, 380.

62. Etter, *The Preacher and His Sermon*, 1885, 382.

11

The Closing Appeals of a Sermon Conclusion: Part 3

"A major weakness of sermon conclusions is an absent or inadequate intent to achieve the purpose of the sermon, which may be compounded by content contained in the conclusion that does not establish significant ways and means necessary for the achieving the purpose of the sermon. The failure to provide specific ways and means by which the purpose of the sermon can be achieved in the lives of the hearers is a monumental omission by the preacher."

"A sermon conclusion is about one thing primarily, achieving the purpose of the sermon. In a sermon conclusion the purpose of the sermon is like the hub of a wheel, upon which all the spokes consolidate. Various cross references of Scripture, all related to the subject-matter of the sermon's purpose, are like the spokes of a wheel. Each of the various spokes of the wheel are joined solidly to the hub (the purpose), but no two spokes fasten to the hub at the same place."

"The purpose of the preacher and the preaching text must be accomplished in the sermon conclusion. 'There is no use in gathering hammer and nails if they are never driven in where needed. To fail here, may be to fail altogether.' In the sermon conclusion a preacher should appeal to the hearer's 'heads, their hearts, and their hands.' A sermon conclusion seeks to preclude the misfortune, so far as is possible, that the hearers are left ill-equipped to live out the purpose of the text in their lives. A sermon which makes no spiritual appeal or moral demand is not a sermon since truth is something that must be obeyed. The conclusion is the place in the sermon where rays of biblical truth are 'brought to a focus and made to burn.'"

"When it comes to the wealth of eternal truth that is found only in the Scriptures, the

wisest of preachers will be found incorporating God's Word in his sermons as often as possible, using God's Word as well as possible, and resorting to God's Word as long as possible in his preaching. This is the understanding that mandates making the use of Scripture for the closing appeals of a sermon conclusion a reality."

"To forego a Scripture-rich conclusion which profits God's people by means of instruction, reproof, rebuke, exhortation, and training in righteousness is a lost opportunity that can only be viewed rightly as incalculable. But, again, we are talking about a specifically select, surgically precise, inclusion of Scripture-based closing appeals that establish the most valuable insights necessary to achieve the specific purpose of the preaching passage."

"The heart and life were targeted by Jesus and His apostles in their preaching. By this standard a sermon conclusion should be estimated. Only as a conclusion is adapted to make the hearers feel the power of the gospel and obey its precepts is a sermon conclusion what it should be."

"Four concepts are imperative for preachers to implement in a sermon conclusion if the conclusion is to be the highpoint of the sermon and, thus, it may be found to be of great benefit for its hearers. . . . Prerequisite number one for sermon conclusion excellence is that preachers aim at practical effects. . . . Prerequisite number two is that preachers understand the principles of the human mind. . . . Prerequisite number three is that preachers arrange content for effect in the close. . . . Prerequisite number four is that preachers must exhibit warmth of heart in his closing appeals. . . . As valuable as prerequisites one, two, and three are for sermon conclusion excellence, it must be understood that the absence of exhibited warmth of a preacher's good will toward his hearers will nullify the benefits to be received through these prerequisites. However, by means of a preacher's exhibited warmth toward his hearers, the importance of aiming at practical effects, understanding the human mind, and arrangement of content become spendable currency for the acquisition of sermon conclusion excellence."

"In the conclusion we are no longer preaching the preaching text, and we are not teaching so much in the closing appeals as we are persuading our hearers by means of them. We are addressing ourselves more immediately to the conscience, the affections, and the will, pressing upon the awakened conscience solemn issues. As a preacher gives himself fully to this, if the closing appeals of the sermon conclusion contain instruction that will help them to comply with the mandates of Scripture, the hearers, typically, will be 'prepared to welcome them.'"

"The conclusion's objective is to press the sermon's purpose upon the hearer's cognition, conscience, affections, and will. Once the sermon's purpose has been applied fully to the hearer's soul, the conclusion must be terminated. However, termination

of the conclusion must never be enacted before the purpose of the sermon has been achieved. Thus, the wisdom of prioritizing not only brevity but completeness for the content of the sermon conclusion."

"We understand that the conclusion of a sermon is to be the 'highpoint of the sermon.' Subsequently, we have come to understand that the last closing appeal should be the 'apex of the sermon's highpoint.' But then, there are the final statements that close out the last closing appeal. These statements should be the 'highlight of the apex of the sermon's highpoint."'

"There are five means by which the apex of the sermon's highpoint may be highlighted. These five means include: Returning to material used in the sermon introduction; Repeating the opening phrase used to start the sermon introduction; Reciting a striking passage of Scripture; Registering a profound statement of propositional truth, warning, promise, or encouragement; Rendering a graphic illustration that becomes a clinching element of persuasion. Several of these means may be combined to accomplish the principle of climax. Christ's sermon on the Mount, for example, ended very persuasively through the means of an epic propositional statement of truth, Matthew 7:24, which was followed by an illustration, Matthew 7:25–27, that brought clarity and profundity to what he had stated propositionally."

"Life-change, not behavior modification is what God desires. He has provided his Word to accomplish this. Furthermore, life-change, as valuable as it is, is not the end-product for complying with scriptural truth. Complying with Scripture is, in a word, obedience. As one obeys God's Word, more than life-change results. The ultimate result from obedience to Scripture is Christian maturity, growth in Christ."

CLOSING APPEALS AND THE PURPOSE OF A SERMON

The closing appeals of the sermon conclusion should be "the most practical" bearings of the sermon.[1] Though the closing appeals will be related indirectly to the subject-matter of the sermon developed in the preaching text; the closing appeals must be related directly to the purpose of the text/sermon since they are the means by which the sermon's purpose can be accomplished more fully by those who comply with the closing appeals. Therefore, an obviously logical relatedness of content between the sermon conclusion and the sermon that preceded it is mandatory. As this is so, *the closing appeals will be related to the purpose of the sermon/text more closely than to the subject-matter of the sermon/text.*

For example, the subject-matter of a text and the sermon may be the proclamation of the gospel, in a word, evangelism. But the purpose of the sermon/text may be,

1. Phelps, *The Theory of Preaching*, 1882, 516.

in a word, commitment, the commitment that is necessary for believers to proclaim the gospel message to those who need it. The subject-matter of the purpose of the sermon is commitment, whereas, the subject-matter of the sermon/text is evangelism. The subject-matter of commitment bears a direct relationship to the closing appeals of the conclusion, whereas, commitment bears an indirect relationship to the subject-matter of the sermon/text, which is evangelism. Therefore, the closing appeals will deal with the subject-matter of commitment, what is necessary for believers to be committed in their daily lives to proclaim the gospel to unbelievers. The closing appeals will deal directly with commitment and indirectly with evangelism. The result of this is that the closing appeals will consist of content that constitutes the natural conclusion to the message, content that will help believers to achieve the purpose of the sermon in their lives, that is, the hearers will live lives committed to evangelism.

The strict pertinence of the conclusion's closing appeals to the sermon they conclude and the purpose they achieve constitutes a natural termination of a sermon. Austin Phelps is insightful when he insists that, "Pertinence demands more than logical congruity between a discussion and its uses. Pertinence requires a conclusion that is the natural end of the process to which it leads."[2] The natural process, stemming from the discussion of a text in the sermon that leads to its ending, is the accomplishing of the sermon's/text's purpose in the lives of those who seek to live according to the truth of Scripture. So, in the example above, instruction about evangelism is of little use without insights regarding the commitment necessary to proclaim the gospel to unbelievers.

In a sermon conclusion, "the nexus" of the closing appeals and the discussion advanced in the exposition of the preaching text is not legitimate for the hearer if its relationship is not understood. There cannot be a secret connection, recognized only by the preacher, between the exposition of the text's/sermon's subject-matter and the practical means for the achievement of the text's/sermon's purpose offered in the sermon conclusion. The actual connection, not the possible connection of the sermon's subject-matter to the closing appeals of the sermon conclusion must be recognized by everyone. The hearers have a right to expect that the exhortations or direct closing appeals and/or the inferences or indirect closing appeals found in a sermon conclusion are an actual result of the discussion of the text/sermon they had just heard.[3]

2. Phelps, *The Theory of Preaching*, 1882, 519.

3. Phelps, *The Theory of Preaching*, 1882, 525. Phelps is certainly correct in his insistence that the discussion of the subject-matter in the conclusion must relate to the discussion advanced in the body of the sermon. Phelps thought it best to withhold application from the body of the sermon. Phelps believed the application of the subject-matter of the sermon was to be in the conclusion. Since the application of the subject-matter of the sermon would not take place until the conclusion, the same subject-matter certainly must be the same in the conclusion as in the body, because now application of that subject-matter is to be made. Of what benefit would there be to withhold application of the subject-matter from the sermon body, then withhold application of that subject-matter in the conclusion because the application being made is to a different subject-matter than the one discussed in the body? This would be a bait and switch, pure and simple. It would make no sense to do this. That Phelps

Moreover, the accomplishing of the sermon's purpose through the closing appeals will not only *qualify as the obvious discussion* but accomplishing of the purpose through the closing appeals of the sermon *constitutes the obligatory discussion to be had in the sermon conclusion.*

To incorporate matters that are rightly connected to the discussion will totally miss the point of the conclusion if the closing appeals of the conclusion fail to provide that which must be done in order for the purpose of the sermon to be accomplished in the lives of God's people. In other words, a remote connection is not a sufficient connection for the material that becomes part of the sermon conclusion. The obligatory range of the discussion must ensue in the sermon conclusion and this obligatory range deals with the accomplishing of the purpose of the sermon in the lives of those who hear it.

A major weakness of sermon conclusions is an absent or inadequate intent to achieve the purpose of the sermon, which may be compounded by content contained in the conclusion that does not establish significant ways and means necessary for the achieving the purpose of the sermon. The failure to provide specific ways and means by which the purpose of the sermon can be achieved in the lives of the hearers is a monumental omission by the preacher.

Just as every sermon point in the body of the sermon suggests something in the way of a unique contribution to the sermon,[4] the same principle is true in the sermon conclusion. A sermon conclusion is about one thing primarily, achieving the purpose of the sermon. In a sermon conclusion the purpose of the sermon is like the hub of a wheel, upon which all the spokes consolidate. Various cross references of Scripture, all related to the subject-matter of the sermon's purpose, are like the spokes of a wheel. Each of the various spokes of the wheel are joined solidly to the hub (the purpose), but no two spokes fasten to the hub at the same place.

LEGITIMATE YET FORCEFUL CLOSING APPEALS

The closing appeals of a sermon conclusion must be legitimate, and they must be forceful. Legitimacy of deduction is not the equivalent of force. A perfectly logical inference, though natural, may be feeble in reference to force and insight. What is

---

was in favor of the conclusion being about the application of a subject-matter withheld from the sermon body but reserved for the conclusion is clear. He wrote: "Which is the superior, the continuous application in the body of the sermon, or the compact application at the close? . . . An argument that is incomplete often cannot logically be applied to anything of homiletic use. . . . The compact application at the close is more natural." Phelps, *The Theory of Preaching*, 505. For Phelps, the conclusion was not about targeting the purpose of the sermon for application in the conclusion, but the application of the subject-matter that was not applied in the body of the sermon. Still, Phelps makes some good arguments that are relevant to sermon conclusions in which the sermon's purpose, rather than the sermon's subject-matter is the thing about which application is made.

4. Phelps, *The Theory of Preaching*, 1882, 526.

mandatory for the closing appeals of a sermon conclusion is that they are a legitimate means by which the purpose of the sermon may be achieved in the lives of the hearers. Beyond legitimacy, what is needed is that the inferences found in the closing appeals of a sermon conclusion be found "striking." Though legitimate, closing appeals will be found striking only as they provide needed insights that the hearers have neither realized, nor possessed in their lives to the present time.

The conclusion must contain a carefully selected corps of insights related to the sermon purpose's subject-matter. A conclusion, therefore, should incorporate the strongest inferences found in cross-references gleaned from the wider terrain of Scripture, and only those, which provide the most needed insights, to constitute the closing appeals, thereby making the purpose of the sermon achievable in the lives of the hearers. Therefore, the inferences garnered from scriptural cross-references should always be selected materials, never simply a compilation. A lack of carefully selected references will produce a fault of the sermon conclusion's closing appeals, namely, that they are not the most forceful and instructive appeals of the sermon and, perhaps, not vitally related to the purpose of the sermon. This fault exemplifies "the radical defect" of sermon conclusions, that is, weak closing appeals that do little to achieve the purpose of the sermon.[5]

What is necessary for the closing appeals in a sermon conclusion is that each one makes a specific, unique point of relevance. Austin Phelps made an ingenious observation that is applicable to sermon conclusions when he wrote: "We care little for the genus of anything. We crave species. We do not admire the genus flora: we enjoy elms, maples, lindens, oaks." And so it is with the closing appeals of the sermon con-clusion—species rather than genus quality insights of specific relevance are needed for the achievement of the sermon's purpose. If each inference has a logical connection to fulfilling the sermon's purpose and each one supplies insights necessary to the accom-plishing of the purpose, "they cannot fail to form a forcible conclusion."[6] A forcible conclusion provided by closing appeals selected with wisdom and accuracy from the complete canon of Scripture is what is necessary for the conclusion to end the sermon with true insight and power.

However, power must be understood in reference to purpose. An elephant is powerful for hauling hundreds and hundreds of pounds on his back for many miles. But an elephant is powerless for performing delicate neurosurgery. A neurosurgeon is powerful for performing delicate neurosurgery. But a neurosurgeon is powerless for hauling hundreds and hundreds of pounds on his back for many miles. The ultimate conception of power lies in the ends that a power can serve. As one phrased it rather well when he insisted that, "nothing is weaker than a power that can do everything except what needs to be done."[7]

5. Phelps, *The Theory of Preaching*, 1882, 526.

6. Phelps, *The Theory of Preaching*, 1882, 529.

7. Pearson, *The Preacher*, 108–9.

The effective power of a sermon conclusion is to bring the hearers to a decision—a decision that wins the verdict which God intended for his Word to have in the lives of his people. The conclusion is a very important part of the sermon not only because it makes the last impression on the congregation, but for its practical effect. The purpose of the preacher and the preaching text must be accomplished here. "There is no use in gathering hammer and nails if they are never driven in where needed. To fail here, may be to fail altogether."[8] In the sermon conclusion a preacher should appeal to the hearer's "heads, their hearts, and their hands."[9] A sermon conclusion seeks to preclude the misfortune, so far as is possible, that the hearers are left indifferent to living out the purpose of the sermon or that the hearers are ill-equipped to live out the purpose of the text in their lives.[10] A sermon which makes no spiritual appeal or moral demand is not a sermon since truth is something that must be obeyed.[11] The conclusion is the place in the sermon where rays of biblical truth are "brought to a focus and made to burn."[12] A sermon conclusion should produce a sense of finality. As with a lawyer before jurors, a preacher seeks a verdict from his hearers. The hearers, especially through the means of a sermon conclusion, "should know and feel what God's truth demands of them."[13]

THE NUMBER OF CLOSING APPEALS

The closing appeals of the sermon conclusion could be a single appeal, but for the vast majority of times a conclusion will consist of a plurality of appeals, with the plurality representing more than two, typically, in order to provide the greatest advantage to the hearers. Either necessity, one closing appeal or a plurality of closing appeals, is acceptable as each one is indicative of its own strength.[14] In reference to one closing appeal, there is the power of a singular focus so that an obedient hearer may make a concentrated resolve as was made by the Apostle Paul when he declared, "but one thing I do."[15] However, a plurality of closing appeals exhibits the power of a fruitful variety of practical results, thus providing the hearers with ample resources, ample means, for their response that is indicative of that which God has purposed. Most often, what is needed to assist a congregation of hearers is the disclosure of a plurality of "practical

---

8. Fry, *Elementary Homiletics*, 1897, 125–6.

9. Fry, *Elementary Homiletics*, 1897, 129.

10. Morgan, *Preaching*, 87.

11. Morgan, *Preaching*, 88.

12. Fry, *Elementary Homiletics*, 1897, 124.

13. Robinson, *Biblical Preaching*, 167.

14. Phelps, *The Theory of Preaching*, 1882, 533.

15. Reference is being made to Paul's statement found in Philippians 3:13–14, that he pressed on toward the goal for the prize of the upward call of God in Christ Jesus as he disciplined himself to a life of daily forgetting what lies behind and reaching forward to what lies ahead.

bearings" for their response. A plurality of closing appeals may address one's conscience more completely as it "may be more profoundly moved than if goaded by one."[16]

The tendency for a plurality of closing appeals in the sermon conclusion is that each appeal is more specific, that is, more microscopic than a sermon conclusion consisting of one more general, or macroscopic, closing appeal. A plurality of closing appeals, because they are more specific, form a bundle of more diverse and direct means for responding to the purpose of the sermon. The bottom line, when it comes to the application found in the closing appeals of the sermon conclusion, is this—the closing appeals must do much more than merely resurface or echo the application[17] that was part of the body of the sermon. In fact, it should not resurface anything established in the sermon body regarding application.

The closing appeals must reflect application that is of a new order because it relates to achieving the purpose of the sermon rather than relating to a specific point, or the points of the text that was preached. Obviously then, the application found in the closing appeals of the conclusion will be more general or more specific than the application, that is, the implications of the truths of the text, found in the body the sermon.[18]

CLOSING APPEALS AS AN ASSET FOR THE PREACHER

In his book *Preparing to Preach*, homiletician David R. Breed asks an essential question regarding the sermon conclusion and yet he provides an answer that is not so good, being based on a poor understanding and a disappointing view of sermon conclusions. Breed asked:

> Should the conclusion always take the form of an appeal? By this we mean a personal address to the hearers, urging them to specific action. The answer to this question is, "Not always," and it might be safe to say "Not generally," because if the sermon body has been what it should be, and the preacher has had that solemn purpose in mind in its preparation and delivery, of which we have spoken, then the whole sermon will be of the nature of an appeal, even though it's closing portion be not cast in that exact form.[19]

Breed is correct in his assertion that application should be made throughout the body of the sermon. I certainly agree with and appreciate Breed's major premise that the relevance of biblical truth should be demonstrated throughout the sermon.

16. Phelps, *The Theory of Preaching*, 1882, 533.

17. Again, "application" in the body of a sermon is more precisely the "implications of a specific truth of the preaching text" for the hearers, that is, what this truths means to the lives of the hearers, whereas, the closing appeals of a sermon conclusion constitute "application proper" since these provide what the hearers need to do for the purpose of the sermon to be achieved in their lives.

18. Vinet, *Homiletics*, 1854, 324.

19. Breed, *Preparing to Preach*, 1911, 115.

However, his view regarding no appeal, no personal address, in the conclusion overlooks the fact that the purpose of the sermon is achieved in its ultimate sense only by means of the conclusion, specifically, through the closing appeals contained in the conclusion. These closing appeals will incorporate relevant instruction in the form of application that is more general or more specific than application which was made in the body of the sermon. But the application found in the closing appeals will constitute action that must be enjoined by the hearers if they are to comply with God's purpose for their lives in the fullest sense possible.

Furthermore, since the purpose of a sermon is achieved in life after having heard the sermon, the closing appeals contained in the sermon conclusion prepare the hearers to achieve the purpose of the sermon in their lives as the closing appeals are lived out when the sermon has concluded. The closing appeals of the sermon conclusion contain the much-needed insights, the fine tuning, necessary for the sermon's purpose to be actualized fully in the lives of the hearers. Complying with God's purpose for Scripture is too significant for this not to be dealt with specifically and insightfully in a sermon conclusion which appeals for believers to respond to God's purpose in the lives they are living.

The bottom-line is this, no believer's life is above the need for instruction, reproof, correction, and training in righteousness in the endeavor of living out God's Word pleasingly in a fallen and sin-filled world. God's purposes for his people will not be achieved in the lives of those who resist or reject his Word, or simply fail to respond to his Word in their lives. On the other hand, compliance to, or a greater compliance with, scriptural truth will require a response on behalf of God's people if his Word is not ignored by them. What could be of greater value for a pastor than to be in agreement with God in his desire to see his people live in greater obedience to his Word? So, how could it be anything other than perfectly consistent and productive for a preacher to appeal to God's people to respond to God's truth in ways that will remedy what is disobedient, or lacking complete obedience, in their lives? Closing appeals in a sermon conclusion that provide correction and training in righteousness, especially, for God's people are an asset to them, to say nothing of being an asset to the preacher to help him conclude his sermon productively.

The closing appeals represent the ultimate provision from God's Word which a preacher provides to God's people in his ministry of the Word. In stark contrast to Breed's dismissal of the need for an appeal in the sermon conclusion, Alfred E. Garvie is far more serviceable as he writes, "It may be objected that a sermon should be practical throughout, that the truth should be so presented as to be applied from the beginning to the end. And yet, even if this be the case, a more direct application may be necessary."[20] A more direct application, indeed, will be necessary as the purpose of the sermon becomes the focal point of application proper in the sermon conclusion. This direct application takes place as Scripture references from outside of

20. Garvie, *The Christian Preacher*, 1921, 441.

the preaching text become the bases for the closing appeals and become the source of invaluable insights that will be useful for the hearers to conform their lives to the sermon's purpose.

Having closing appeals in a sermon conclusion that facilitate the hearers' response in a way that fully achieves God's purpose in the lives of his people allows the preacher to be able to end his sermon with a great deal of certainty, knowing that he is through and there is nothing more that needs to be said. Therefore, he is spared from earning the bad reputation of being a very fine preacher in every way but one—he lacks "terminal facilities."[21] Yet, the valuable terminal facilities of a preacher are demonstrated most aptly through closing appeals that provide such significant assistance to God's people that additional instruction is unnecessary. Therefore, well beyond valuable terminal facilities, the closing appeals of the sermon conclusion demonstrate the profitable "purpose-fulfilment facilities" of a preacher who can conclude his sermon well.

Without caring less about any other part of a sermon, it is vital to care a great deal more about the final minutes of sermons. R. W. Dale brings much needed correction for a low view of sermon conclusions by offering as exemplary the concluding work of Jonathan Edwards, who spent the majority of his time getting his guns into position and in the applications of his conclusions he opened fire on the enemy. In contrast to Edwards, according to Dale, "Too many contemporary sermons end without ever firing a shot, or barely firing a shot! Depend upon it, gentlemen, this is a great and fatal mistake."[22]

The crux of the matter regarding significant closing appeals of a sermon conclusion is indicated by the following two maxims upon which Dale insisted: preachers must project the truth into the very depths of the hearers' thoughts and lives so that they cannot but comprehend its practical value and worth; and, preachers must compel hearers to discharge their duty.[23] These maxims reflect the asset which the closing appeals are to a preacher as he concludes his sermons. The asset that the closing appeals are to a preacher is based upon the reality that many people, who are accustomed to reading the Bible and listening to sermons, have a loose grasp of scriptural truth, particularly in the arena of living out the truth they know. They are appreciative of any man who can make their knowledge of Scripture effective and profitable by providing sharpness and clarity for a personally practical response to biblical truth.[24]

God has revealed his Word for certain definite ends, for which a preacher must be preaching, especially so in the closing appeals of his sermon conclusion. But in doing so, no preacher should be surprised by the inevitable, albeit occasional, reality that not everyone will receive gladly the direct and forceful closing appeals of the sermon

---

21. Breed, *Preparing to Preach*, 1911, 116.

22. Dale, *Nine Lectures on Preaching*, 1890, 146.

23. Dale, *Nine Lectures on Preaching*, 1890, 147.

24. Dale, *Nine Lectures on Preaching*, 1890, 149.

conclusion, even though they are graciously offered. In such instances the unfortunate and unavoidable outcome for a preacher will be a personal experience of the expression that, "It is much easier to lose friends than to gain opponents."[25] As long as such an unjustified response to a preacher is based solely upon a hearer's unwillingness to accept a personally needed word of truth, the preacher must understand that this is part of the reality of proclaiming God's truth. But those who do not gladly receive the direct and forceful closing appeals of a sermon conclusion are in the minority. Most people appreciate them and find them beneficial, thus they are a true asset for a preacher in his preaching.

SEVEN GUIDELINES FOR CLOSING APPEALS

Philip Doddridge, in the 1807 publication of his book *Lectures on Preaching and the Several Branches of the Ministerial Office*, provided seven guidelines regarding the content of a sermon which he referred to as "the choice of thoughts." Doddridge was not isolating the sermon conclusion as the target for "the choice of thoughts" nor was he exempting the sermon conclusion from his choice of thoughts guidelines, but they are uniquely appropriate for the conclusion, perhaps more so than any other portion of a sermon.

Adapting Doddridge's choice of thoughts to the sermon conclusion, specifically, yields the following seven guidelines for the closing appeals of a sermon conclusion: 1. *Let the closing appeals be* solid, such as will stand the test of severe judgment; for if they fail to do so they will be despised however they may be adorned. 2. *Let the closing appeals be* useful as to equip, not to amuse the hearers. Ask yourself, will this closing appeal be one that is likely to do good? If not, lay it aside. 3. *Let the closing appeals be* proper to the sermon's purpose by avoiding loose digressions back to the subject-matter of the preaching text and by maintaining a certain and easy connection to what is necessary for correction or training in righteousness in the lives of believers. 4. *Let the closing appeals be* natural in their flow back to the purpose of the sermon, establishing what is essential for the purpose of the sermon to be achieved in the lives of believers. 5. *Let the closing appeals be* new, if possible, being gained by an intensive search of Scripture, thus providing purpose-specific insights for the hearers; by observing the workings of your own heart; and by the general matters of men, in their diversified situations. 6. *Let the closing appeals be* popular, that is, suited to believers in general, not geared only to a subgroup of individuals. 7. *Let the closing appeals be* select, that is, by providing only the most helpful things that will be instrumental for believers to live in compliance to the purpose of the sermon in their lives.[26]

The sermon conclusion, generally, and the closing appeals, specifically, will be aided toward greater effectiveness by incorporating Doddridge's "choice of thoughts" guidelines to the statements and contents of the closing appeals. These guidelines,

25. Dale, *Nine Lectures on Preaching*, 1890, 17.

26. Doddridge, *Lectures on Preaching*, 1807, 53–57, italics added.

though valuable for conclusions, even if they are applied consistently from sermon to sermon, will not produce a sameness, an invariable product, a monotonous cast to the work of concluding sermons. The variety to be found in sermon conclusions from sermon to sermon will be due to the differing substance of content in the conclusions and the differing motivations of a preacher in the use of the content found in the conclusions. This presents the need to understand closing appeals by means of content types and delivery tones in sermon conclusions.

CONTENT TYPES AND DELIVERY TONES OF CLOSING APPEALS

In his 1866 publication of *The Preacher's Manual*, homiletician S. T. Sturtevant advanced, notably, five different *"types"* and four different *"strains"* of closing appeals for sermon conclusions.[27] Sturtevant's five *types* of closing appeals for sermon conclusions included the directive, the appellatory, the remedial, the entreating, and the expostulatory. Additionally, Sturtevant identified four different *strains* in which the appeals of a sermon conclusion may be offered: the encouraging, the consoling, the elevating, and the alarming strain.

Sturtevant's five types of closing appeals for sermon conclusions have reference to the character of the content of the closing appeals whereas the strains of closing appeals refer to the character of the preacher's motivation for, and delivery tone used in the delivery of, the content of the closing appeals.

According to Sturtevant, the "directive" type of appeal supplies directions or actions which the hearers must implement as indicated by the closing appeals of the sermon conclusion. The "appellatory" type is appeals which are accompanied by crucial insights with strong comments and counsels. The "remedial" type of appeal, in the kindest possible manner, proposes instruction by which errors of conduct may be corrected. The "entreating" type of appeal implores the hearers to receive, believe, be, or do in accordance with the instruction/insights indicated by the closing appeals of the sermon conclusion. The "expostulatory" type of appeal supplies earnest reasoning regarding impropriety of conduct, objecting to wrong conduct, and strongly dissuading hearers against continuing in such behavior.

For Sturtevant, the "encouraging" strain of a closing appeal is indicative of encouraging the hearers to act on the implications of the preaching text's purpose as indicated in the closing appeals of the sermon conclusion. The "consoling" strain provides timely words spoken in season by which the hearers may gain comfort regarding the implementation of the closing appeals. The "elevating" strain seeks to raise in the hearers' minds a depiction of worthiness or productivity when carrying out the appeals of the conclusion. The "alarming" strain arouses fear, dread, or anguish in the hearts of the hearers if they do not attend to the closing appeals of the sermon conclusion.

---

27. Sturtevant, *The Preacher's Manual*, 1866, 511–20.

Sturtevant made a significant contribution to sermon conclusion instruction based on his types and strains of closing appeals. However, to process profitably this data more than a century and a half later in a preaching culture that is bereft of sermon conclusion closing appeals, I believe some contemporary acclimation and biblical correlation is in order. Sturtevant's insights need greater clarity and comprehensibility if they are to be helpful in the prospect of providing closing appeals for sermon conclusions in twenty-first century preaching.

It is advantageous to retain the quantitative understanding of closing appeals in the manner of *five* types and *four* strains as provided by Sturtevant. Yet, a clarification provided by an additional strain will aid in greater comprehension and implementation of them. Furthermore, the descriptors "types" and "strains" may be more comprehensible if referenced as "content types" and "delivery tones." Therefore, *we will understand the there are five content types and five delivery tones for the closing appeals of sermon conclusions.*

Three of Sturtevant's five content types of closing appeals, the directive, the appellatory and the expostulatory, are due a renaming. Changing the terminology from directive to "mandating" clarifies the insight that this type of appeal is command-worthy in nature and, therefore, the hearers will be exhorted to comply their lives to the exhortations contained in these appeals. Changing the terminology from appellatory to "advocating" clarifies the insight that this type of appeal is counsel-worthy in nature and, therefore, the hearers will be encouraged to comply their lives to the inferential biblical instruction contained in these appeals. It is advantageous to change the terminology of expostulatory to "condemning." Changing the terminology from expostulatory to "condemning" clarifies the insight that this type of appeal deals with matters that are condemnable in nature. One might discern the essential meaning of "expostulatory" as a remonstrance, or a protesting against what is done or not done, but this is not certain. Therefore, a descriptor of "condemning" not only clarifies the content of this type of closing appeal as containing a remonstrance or protest against what is being done, or not being done, but it clarifies the nature of this content type of closing appeal as being the opposite of the commendatory types of closing appeals.

So, there are four commendatory types of closing appeals which have as their exact opposite the condemnatory type, that is, the condemning type of closing appeal. But what distinguishes the four commendatory types of closing appeals: the mandating type, the advocating type, the remediating type, and the entreating type of closing appeals? These four types are specific, nuanced variations of a closing appeal containing commendable content, either of explicit exhortation or inferential instruction, to be implemented in the lives of believers. The commendable content of these four types of closing appeals, however, varies in the nature of the content and the way it is commended to the hearers.

The <u>mandating content type</u> of closing appeal has as its content *commendatory direct appeals of explicit exhortation which commands or makes certain actions imperative for the hearers.*

The <u>advocating content type</u> of closing appeal has as its content *commendatory indirect appeals of inferential instruction from Scripture composing specific counsel which the hearers are encouraged to implement in their lives.* The implemented counsel will provide training in righteousness for the hearers through their ongoing compliance in living out the biblical truths contained in the advocated counsel.

The <u>remediating content type</u> of closing appeal has as its content *commendatory indirect appeals of inferential instruction from Scripture which seek to bring correction to the lives of the hearers by certain means which will improve, enhance, or purify their current attempts to comply to the teaching of Scripture.* The remediation initially results in correction but ultimately contributes to their training in righteousness.

The <u>entreating content type</u> of closing appeal has as its content *commendatory indirect appeals which implore the hearers to cease and desist from certain actions, or to implore the hearers to initiate certain actions that immediately affect their training in righteousness.* The training in righteousness effected through the entreating type of closing appeals is due to the things that are terminated in a believer's life that should not be present and/or the things that are initiated in a believer's life that were absent but become part of their lives.

An updated rendition of Sturtevant's content types of closing appeals includes four commendatory types of closing appeals: the mandating type; the advocating type; the remediating type; and the entreating type. These are in direct contrast to the condemnatory, that is, the condemning type closing appeal. Each of the five types of closing appeals is based upon differing kinds of content contained in the appeals as well as various intents for each type of appeal.

Sturtevant's four delivery tones for closing appeals were listed as an encouraging tone, a consoling tone, an elevating tone, and an alarming tone. Again, a change in terminology might be helpful to clarify and specify the intent of the preacher by use of the tone employed. These four tones take on greater clarity when understood as an "<u>encouraging</u>" tone, a "<u>motivating</u>" rather than a consoling tone, a "<u>persuading</u>" rather than an elevating tone, and a "<u>dissuading</u>" rather than an alarming tone. Additionally, it is needful to understand a most basic and universal delivery tone as an "<u>exhorting</u>" tone which is an unmistakable part of every delivery tone applied to every content type of closing appeal. Every delivery tone is a nuanced variation of the exhorting delivery tone. However, an urgent and pure exhorting delivery tone, is the essential tone which dominates the mandating content type of closing appeal which is the most basic commendatory type of closing appeal.

A contemporary revision of Sturtevant's five types and four strains for closing appeals yields five content types and five delivery tones for closing appeals. Each content type of closing appeal is combined quite naturally with a certain delivery tone.

The <u>mandating content type</u> of closing appeal, a direct appeal, is controlled by an <u>exhorting delivery tone</u>. The straightforward imperatival exhortations of Scripture-based closing appeals in the mandating content type of appeal require nothing more and nothing less than urgent exhortation for believers to comply with the insights from Scripture that will help them to achieve the purpose of the sermon in their lives.

The <u>advocating content type</u> of closing appeal is accompanied by an <u>encouraging delivery tone</u>. The advocated counsel composing the closing appeals of the sermon conclusion are drawn from scriptural inferences. The inferential instruction from Scripture is offered to hearers in an encouraging delivery tone to aid in their compliance to the biblical counsel which will help them to achieve the purpose of the sermon in their lives.

The <u>remediating content type</u> of closing appeal is assisted by a <u>motivating delivery tone</u>. The need is to correct that which is established in the lives of the hearers, not to start or stop anything but to adjust, refine, enhance, improve that which they are already doing. Therefore, motivation is needed to convince the hearers that the adjustments they are called to make are, and will be, profitable for them. Much of the motivation needed to make the corrections called for in the remediating content type of closing appeals is produced through insights gleaned from Scripture so that the hearers are certain that the corrections, when made, will help them to live their lives in closer obedience to God's Word.

The <u>entreating content type</u> of closing appeal is enabled by a <u>persuading delivery tone</u>. Since the hearers are being addressed to cease and desist from established activities and/or to initiate activity that has not been established in their lives, the preacher will naturally need to implore them, to persuade them to make a difficult and abrupt change in their lives. The changes being called for are based upon scriptural instruction and will be instrumental for the hearers to live their lives in compliance to the purpose of the sermon. The prospect for effective persuasion is related to the benefits of putting off what should not be a part of a believer's life and the benefits of putting on what should be part of a believer's life.

The <u>condemning content type</u> of closing appeal, a direct closing appeal, is consistent with a <u>dissuading delivery tone</u>. The need is for the hearers to terminate, or never initiate, matters that have no place in the life of a believer, shameful and reproachable things that are explicitly forbidden by Scripture. A dissuading delivery tone may be aided and strengthened by indicating that initiating or continuing certain practices are not only a violation of Scripture, but these will bring about fearful, dreadful, and anguishing consequences in the life of a believer.

It is helpful to realize that the mandating and condemning content type closing appeals are direct closing appeals as opposed to indirect closing appeals. The mandating content type of appeal is positive whereas the condemning content type of appeal is negative. Both of these content type closing appeals will be composed of direct exhortations; therefore, they are direct closing appeals. The advocating, remediating, and entreating content type closing appeals will be composed of inferences or inferential instructions that are, therefore, indirect closing appeals. A thorough discussion of direct and indirect closing appeals will be made in chapter twelve, "*Application in a Sermon Conclusion*," but presently it is enough to understand that direct closing appeals take the form of explicit exhortations whereas indirect closing appeals take the form of inferences, or inferential instructions.

A delivery tone that matches the content type of each closing appeal not only makes sense but is indicative of the effect a preacher seeks to accomplish in the lives of his hearers through the means of the content contained in the closing appeals of his sermon conclusion. So much, then, for the contemporary acclimation of content types and delivery tones for closing appeals in a sermon conclusion. But what about a correlation between the "profitable uses of Scripture" in relation to the content types and delivery tones?

Each content type of closing appeal contains a dominant profitable use of Scripture. The Apostle Paul reminded Timothy that all Scripture is profitable for instruction, for reproof, for correction, and for training in righteousness and should be preached as one reproves, rebukes, exhorts, with all patience and instruction.

The mandating content type of closing appeal consists of explicit instruction provided through an exhorting delivery tone. Thus, the profitable use for instruction from Scripture is dominant. The dominant profitable use of Scripture that provides immediate instruction will additionally or subsequently bring reproof, correction, and training in righteousness into the lives of believers.

The advocating content type of closing appeal consists of inferential instruction in the form of advocated counsel conveyed through an encouraging delivery tone. Again, the profitable use for instruction from Scripture is dominant. The dominant profitable use of Scripture that provides immediate instruction will additionally or subsequently bring reproof, correction, and training in righteousness into the lives of believers.

The remediating content type of closing appeal consists of inferential instruction for correction provided through a motivating delivery tone. Thus, the profitable use of Scripture for correction is dominant. The dominant profitable use of Scripture that provides immediate correction will additionally or subsequently bring instruction, reproof, and training in righteousness into the lives of believers.

The entreating content type of closing appeal consists of inferential instruction which the hearers are implored to implement in their lives for training in righteousness through a persuading delivery tone. Thus, the profitable use of Scripture for training in righteousness is dominant since this is the goal of the inferential instruction as well as the immediate outcome of the inferential instruction when implemented in believers' lives. The insights of the inferential instruction, about which the preacher will implore and seek to persuade his hearers to implement in their lives, are the means to this end of training in righteousness. The dominant profitable use of Scripture that provides immediate training in righteousness will additionally or subsequently bring instruction, reproof, and correction into the lives of believers.

The <u>condemning content type</u> of closing appeal consists of explicit instruction that yields reproof provided through a dissuading delivery tone. Thus, the profitable use of Scripture <u>for reproof</u> is dominant, yet this profitable use may be incorporated in such a manner to facilitate rebuke. However, the dominant profitable use of Scripture that provides reproof, whether it does or does not progress to establish rebuke, will additionally or subsequently bring instruction, correction, and training in righteousness into the lives of believers.

In chapter twelve, *"Application in a Sermon Conclusion,"* the matter of direct and indirect closing appeals will be discussed fully. However, since I have made reference to direct and indirect closing appeals in the above paragraphs, I have provided below some examples of direct closing appeals, indirect closing appeals, and a combination of direct and indirect closing appeals in sermon conclusions. The examples below are taken from chapter twelve where these and other examples of closing appeals will be exhibited to clarify direct and indirect closing appeals. They are presented here to clarify an understanding of how content types and delivery tones are used in connection with direct and indirect closing appeals.

1. **Closing Appeals of <u>Direct</u> Address—Purpose related to <u>blessing others</u>**

- Pray for opportunities to be a blessing to others!
- Be diligent to discern every opportunity to be a blessing to others!
- Be a blessing to others as well as you can in each instance!

The closing appeals above are of the <u>Mandating content type</u> as each appeal is an explicit exhortation and is positive in nature. The <u>Exhorting delivery tone</u> will be used.

2. **Closing Appeals of <u>Direct</u> Address—Purpose related to <u>abstaining from evil</u>**

- Do not practice abomination by participating in any evil thing!
- Do not participate in that which appears evil!
- Do not commit evil by violating personal convictions or your conscience!
- Do not be deceived, evil brings detrimental consequences upon yourself and others!

The closing appeals above are of the <u>Condemning content type</u> as each appeal is an explicit exhortation and is negative in nature. The <u>Dissuading delivery tone</u> will be used.

3. **Closing Appeals of <u>Indirect</u> Address—Purpose related to <u>good stewardship</u>**

- Good stewardship is predicated on the lordship of Jesus Christ in your life.
- It is necessary to realize that possessions are the substance of your stewardship.

- Stewardship is a test that lasts throughout your lifetime.

- No believer, including you, is outside of the possibility of being a good steward.

The closing appeals above are of the Advocating content type as each appeal is an inferential instruction establishing counsel to which the hearers will be encouraged to implement in their lives. An Encouraging delivery tone will be used.

4. **Closing Appeals of Indirect Address—Purpose related to being Spirit-filled**

- Only when Spirit-filled will you Joyously boast in the Lord.

- Only when Spirit-filled will you Zealously protect the purity of the church.

- Only when Spirit-filled will you Boldly proclaim unwelcomed truths.

- Only when Spirit-filled will you Wholeheartedly accept what God provides.

The closing appeals above are of the Advocating content type as each appeal is an inferential instruction establishing counsel to which the hearers will be encouraged to implement in their lives. An Encouraging delivery tone will be used.

5. **Closing Appeals of Indirect Address—Purpose related to turning from pride**

- Pride causes you to not walk in the fear of the Lord.

- Your pride will guarantee God's hand of discipline on your life.

- Unless you turn from your pride, you will continue to sacrifice God's fellowship in your life.

The closing appeals above are of the Entreating content type as each appeal is an inferential instruction establishing that which the hearers will be implored to cease and desist from in their lives. A Persuading delivery tone will be used, and persuasion will be needed for the hearers to turn from pride which can easily control their lives.

6. **Closing Appeals of Indirect Address—Purpose related to walking in truth**

- You must love the truth in order to speak it and live it faithfully in your life.

- Lies, deceptions, falsehoods are the essence of betraying God in your life.

- Truth is a belt that girds you and enables you to stand, resisting evil in your days.

These closing appeals are of the Remediating content type as each appeal is an inferential instruction for correcting how the hearers conduct their lives according to truth. The need of the hearers is to be motivated to comply with these insights about truth in their lives. A Motivating delivery tone will be used.

7. **Closing Appeals of Indirect and Direct Address—Purpose related to submitting to authority**

- Your submission to authorities is God's will.

- Your submission to authorities pleases God.

- You Must submit to authorities even if they are ungodly individuals!

- Never submit to authorities who require you to violate Scripture!

These closing appeals are composed of inferential instruction, that is, indirect closing appeals and, also, explicit exhortation, that is, direct closing appeals. The first two closing appeals are inferential instruction regarding submission. Both closing appeals are of the Advocating content type since submission, that which is advocated, is encouraged by two declarative statements about it—it is God's will, and it pleases God. The Encouraging delivery tone will be used for these two closing appeals. The third closing appeal is a positive exhortation, that is, a direct appeal and is, therefore, of the Mandating content type which will be accompanied by an Exhorting delivery tone. The fourth closing appeal is a negative exhortation, that is, a direct appeal and is, therefore, of the Condemning content type closing appeal which will be conveyed in a Dissuading delivery tone.

8. **Closing Appeals of Indirect and Direct Address—Purpose related to forgiving others**

- Become adept at forgiving others, for this is your calling!

- Forgiving others is not to be done based upon your personal convenience.

- Forgiving others allows you to be much like your Heavenly Father.

- The guilty do not need to be forgiven as much as you need to forgive.

- Having forgiven another, have no expectations for the forgiven one to meet.

- Never withhold forgiveness from others since you have been forgiven by Christ!

Every content type is represented in the closing appeals found in example eight, above. The first closing appeal is an explicit exhortation of a positive nature. It is a direct appeal of the mandating content type that will incorporate an exhorting delivery tone. The second closing appeal is an indirect appeal of the entreating content type. This appeal instructs believers to desist from postponing the urgent need of forgiveness. This appeal will accompany a persuasive delivery tone. The third and fourth closing appeals are indirect appeals that provide insights about forgiveness. The insights constitute the counsel advocated—to be like your Heavenly Father, and to provide what you, primarily, and the guilty also need. Closing appeals three and four are indirect closing appeals of the advocating content type and both will be joined to an encouraging delivery tone. The fifth closing appeal is an indirect closing appeal of the remediating content type and will be delivered with a motivating delivery tone. Believers will be enhanced in their forgiveness when they correct their manner of forgiving others, and thus improve it, by expecting nothing in return from the one who is forgiven. The sixth closing appeal is an explicit exhortation of a negative nature. It is a direct appeal of the <u>condemning content type</u> that will be conveyed by a <u>dissuading delivery tone</u>.

As demonstrated with abundant clarity by example eight, above, the closing appeals do not have to be of the same content type and there should be no attempt to have all the closing appeals to be of the same content type. The intent of the closing appeals of a sermon conclusion is not to provide appeals of the same content type but appeals that will most fully work to achieve the purpose of the sermon. Therefore, significant variety will be produced from sermon conclusion to sermon conclusion resulting from the natural and inescapable inclusion of closing appeals of differing content types being expressed through varying delivery tones.

Once again, the imperatival reality of Scripture-based closing appeals becomes apparent as Scripture alone is profitable to accomplish what hearers need and what God desires to be accomplished in preaching. Likewise, it is imperative to realize that "dry conclusions,"[28] whether indicative of the content of the closing appeals or the delivery tone in which the closing appeals are presented, is extremely problematic.

A dry conclusion is a subversive reality indicative of "the barrenness of the preacher"[29] who has failed to get to the heart of what the Bible has to offer as content for the closing appeals of a sermon conclusion. Or, perhaps, the subversive reality of a dry conclusion may be due to a preacher who has failed to take to heart what the Bible has to offer as valuable content for legitimate closing appeals in a sermon conclusion. However a dry conclusion may be perpetrated, either through a failure to consider Scripture's input for the closing appeals of a sermon conclusion or through a failure to regard as valuable what has been discovered in Scripture, it must be viewed as a crime—a crime in which God's people are denied a valuable connection of biblical truth, or a crime in which God's Word is misrepresented as lacking in value. Any way it might happen, a dry conclusion is a symptom of a much greater problem, a problem that exists in the heart of the preacher.

CLOSING APPEALS ARE SPECIFIC TO THE PURPOSE OF THE SERMON

Because the closing appeals of a sermon conclusion are based upon Scripture references, references which contain insights crucial to living out the purpose of the preaching passage, specificity will be a hallmark of each sermon conclusion if there has been adequate time for research and preparation on behalf of the preacher. If the closing appeals are so general that they could conclude a sermon preached from another text, such appeals must be characterized by the term "barrenness" reflecting

---

28. Porter, *Lectures on Homiletics and Preaching*, 1835, 147.
29. Porter, *Lectures on Homiletics and Preaching*, 1835, 146.

"vacuity of thought."[30] The closing appeals of a sermon conclusion must be the scriptural insights that are most helpful to the hearers for their faithful living of the truths of the preaching text for *the accomplishment of the purpose of that text*. This is the measure of the value of the closing appeals of a sermon conclusion.

Just as the value of everything is related to the end to which it is to be applied, so it is with the closing appeals of a sermon conclusion. To a man marooned on a desert island, money is worthless, because he cannot use it. In the possession of a miser, incredible wealth is worthless, because he will not use it. But to a generous man who is a good steward and delights to see how his wealth can be used well, it is valuable because he will use it and do so productively. The same opportunities and outcomes are true of the Word of God. The Word of God is provided by God for it to be actualized in the lives of his people. The contents of scriptural wisdom and insight are not to be stored up for the sake of storing them alone, but for using them. And when it comes to the wealth of eternal truth that is found only in the Scriptures, the wisest of preachers will be found incorporating God's Word in his sermons as often as possible, using God's Word as well as possible, and resorting to God's Word as long as possible in his preaching. This is the understanding that mandates making the use of Scripture for the closing appeals of a sermon conclusion a reality.

The Christian life must be lived according to the insights found in the Word of God. This is essential to living an abundant life in Christ Jesus. No believer is above the need of having one's life more properly focused and more appropriately directed by the counsel contained in God's Word. Since every believer's life is short and destined to be judged by Christ, time and opportunity must not be marginalized by withholding scriptural insights from the closing appeals of a sermon conclusion. As one homiletician put it many years ago, "Life is not so long that its vigor may all be spent getting ready to live."[31] Since the lives of God's people are precious, brief, and accountable to God it is imperative that they be exposed to Scripture at every possible opportunity. And this includes the conclusion of a sermon. Afterall, preaching, to use the expression of William Perkins, "is the flexanima (that which has the power to change minds), the allurer of the soul, by which our self-willed minds are subdued and changed from an ungodly and pagan lifestyle to a life of Christian faith and repentance" with which God is glorified and others are blessed.[32] How unreasonable it is to have access to a flexanimous power and forego it in the preaching of one's sermon conclusion!

No other portion of a sermon bears the responsibility to subdue and change minds and lifestyles like the sermon conclusion. Therefore, to forego a Scripture-rich conclusion which profits God's people by means of instruction, correction, reproof, rebuke, exhortation, and training in righteousness is a lost opportunity that can only

30. Porter, *Lectures on Homiletics and Preaching*, 1835, 146.

31. Porter and Matthews, *Lectures on Eloquence and Style*, 1836, 15.

32. Perkins, *The Art of Prophesying*, published in Latin, 1592, published in English, 1606, 3.

be viewed rightly as incalculable. But, again, we are talking about a specifically select, surgically precise, inclusion of Scripture-based closing appeals that establish the most valuable insights necessary to achieve the specific purpose of the preaching passage.

FOUR PREREQUISITES FOR EXCELLENCE IN SERMON CONCLUSIONS

We have been considering, specifically, the closing appeals of a sermon conclusion for quite a while. At this point, it may be beneficial to broaden the emphasis. Still with a sermon conclusion's closing appeals as a secondary reference, let's consider briefly the broader matter of the sermon conclusion so that we can appreciate how the closing appeals contribute to a conclusion that accomplishes what it is designed to accomplish.

Four concepts are imperative for preachers to implement in a sermon conclusion if the conclusion is to be the highpoint of the sermon and, thus, it may be found to be of great benefit for its hearers. These four concepts to consider are Scripture's outcome, mankind's adaptability, an unfettered motivation in a preacher, and the unquestioned warmth of a preacher. In addressing sermon conclusions, Ebenezer Porter included four prerequisites for excellence in sermon conclusion success.[33] The following four prerequisites are original to Porter.

Prerequisite number one for sermon conclusion excellence is that preachers *aim at practical effects*. This prerequisite is based upon Scripture's outcome as intended by God. In their conclusions, preachers must seek to implement what they understand to be the outcome of the Word of God in the lives of believers. It is commonly understood that, "All Scripture is profitable that the man of God may be perfect, thoroughly furnished for every good work." But more than knowing this intended outcome of the Word of God in the lives of believers, the preacher must be found working in concert with God's intended design for his Word.

A completely equipped individual who is enabled to conduct oneself with excellence in any given circumstance is the outcome of the effect of Scripture in the life of a believer who complies with its precepts and examples. Living a life that demonstrates the "good work" for which a believer is equipped, thoroughly equipped, by God's Word is the bullseye of a sermon conclusion. The temporal value of a correct knowledge of doctrine is its ability "to sanctify the heart and life." The heart and life were targeted by Jesus and his apostles in their preaching. By this standard the worth of every sermon conclusion should be estimated.

Only as a sermon conclusion is adapted to make the hearers feel the power of the gospel and obey its precepts is a conclusion what it should be. A conclusion "which does not reach the hearers as *individuals*, which is not felt to bear distinctly on their

33. Porter, *Lectures on Homiletics and Preaching*, 1835, 147–56.

ignorance, or error, or moral defects, as *individuals*, answers no good end whatever."[34] Another homiletician and preaching professor of the same time period instructed that the conclusion, by means of the closing appeals, should be directed to men's "bosoms and business" being an earnest application of the sermon's purpose, aiming to secure its genuine influence on the hearers' lives.[35]

As Jesus and his apostles sought to impact the hearts and lives of hearers in their preaching, it should not come as a surprise that heart preaching should be a recognizable component of sermon conclusions, especially. In a chapter dealing with *"Heart Preaching"* rather than sermon conclusions, Jerry Vines connects behavioral change, that which is vital to both heart preaching and sermon conclusions, when he wrote: "The preacher who learns to preach from his heart will move men to action. . . . We preach in order to bring men to decision. Our purpose is to change behavior for the better, to bring men to obedience to God, and to lead them to accept the challenge of a Christ-centered life. Heart preaching will help us accomplish those goals."[36] The conclusion is the most strategic place in the sermon for heart preaching.

Prerequisite number two for sermon conclusion excellence is that preachers *understand the principles of the human mind*. The understanding of the human mind that must be recognized is that the more completely a truth is demonstrated, the more fully the conscience is engaged, making the application of truth stronger and the impression of truth more deeply produced in the hearer.[37] The conscience of a hearer is activated by truth that is demonstrated clearly and makes the hearer recognize that it is not honored in his life.

In order to persuade men to make some specific adaptation for a life of righteousness, it is necessary for a preacher to make a deep impression on the hearers by addressing their sense of Christian duty and by proving to them that worthwhile benefits await those who walk in righteousness.[38] In other words, the conscience must be pricked in endeavoring to affect one's recovery of duty and one's adherence to a righteous life. But one's conscience is aroused only through a clear demonstration of one's obligations, obligations which are not being met.[39]

Therefore, a sermon conclusion must facilitate a lively interaction with the conscience of the hearer.[40] But, even more so, by means of its closing appeals the sermon conclusion must provide resolutions for the shortcomings which caused the conscience to be pained. Yet, a lively interaction with the conscience of one's hearers seems to presuppose information that may not be known to the preacher. How can

34. Porter, *Lectures on Homiletics and Preaching*, 1835, 147.

35. Ripley, *Sacred Rhetoric*, 1849, 104.

36. Vines, *A Guide to Effective Sermon Delivery*, 152.

37. Porter, *Lectures on Homiletics and Preaching*, 1835, 148–49.

38. Ripley, *Sacred Rhetoric*, 1849, 106.

39. Ripley, *Sacred Rhetoric*, 1849, 107.

40. Mather, *Student and Preacher*, 1789, 196.

he command such insight to be able to do this? Can this be achieved? Yes, this can be achieved and will be achieved by knowing the heart of mankind, starting with your own heart. Alex Montoya is helpful when he counsels: "Apply the spiritual meat to your own lean soul. . . . Then form a sermon that preaches to you, to your needs, to your weaknesses, and to your desires. You will rarely miss the bull's-eye! I have often been accused of preaching to specific people in my congregation. The truth is, I was preaching to myself. The sermon was primarily for me!"[41] Imagine that! The pathway to better preaching, generally, and better sermon conclusions, specifically, is an honest, detailed understanding of your own shortcomings, the errors of your own way. In the realization that whatever is problematic for you will be a problem, as well, for those to whom you preach. The provision of scriptural remedies to common, practical grievances is a pathway that no preacher can afford to bypass.

Prerequisite number three for sermon conclusion excellence is that preachers *arrange content for effect in the close.* The emphasis here must not be lost. It is not just that preachers must supply content for effect in the conclusions of their sermons but, moreover, they must arrange the content they supply in those conclusions. "An important thought may lose more than half its weight if standing in the wrong place. . . . The skillful preacher knows the entire effect of his discourse depends on the application in the conclusion and the final impression he wishes to make; and he is not ready to begin the writing of a sermon till he has determined how it is to close."[42] Since the closing appeals of a sermon conclusion consists of diversified practical insights, they are far too important a matter to receive anything less than careful preparation. The careful preparation needed includes arranging the closing appeals in the most productive order of presentation.

To provide effective closing appeals, in their statements and content, so that the appropriate response to the sermon's purpose is driven home and fastened in the mind and conscience of the hearers is a difficult thing to do well. To do so may require a man's most serious, taxing, and thoughtful hours of preparation. In the absence of such careful and costly preparation there will be "the vapid and insignificant verbiage which is poured out at the close of sermons (which) originates from the notion that exhortation is a very simple affair, to which anybody is equal at any time."[43] So, effective sermon conclusions are not easily produced, and the content contained in them must be arranged carefully.

But what is the criterion for careful arrangement of the content? The criterion for arrangement of conclusion content is one of ascending order, to start with the most basic or the least strategic content and move to that which is of greater importance. In other words, the final closing appeal should be the most valuable of the important insights contained in the conclusion. To solidify the concept of careful arrangement of

41. Montoya, *Preaching with Passion*, 65–67.
42. Porter, *Lectures on Homiletics and Preaching*, 1835, 151–52.
43. Ripley, *Sacred Rhetoric*, 1849, 104–05.

a sermon conclusion's content, the phrase "highpoint" will be helpful once again. As the conclusion of a sermon should be the highpoint of the sermon, the final closing appeal should be the highpoint of the sermon's highpoint which will be referred to as the apex of the sermon's highpoint. As the apex of the sermon's highpoint, the final appeal should represent the most crucial insight of the entire sermon.

Prerequisite number four for sermon conclusion excellence is that preachers must exhibit warmth of heart in his closing appeals. There is a tremendous communicative power that is transferred when genuineness is combined with the sensibility of a preacher's good will toward his hearers, to which the hearts of his hearers will be inclined to respond. This kind of pathos "is distinguished by its gentle insinuating, melting influence, which silently wins upon the heart, and makes it yield itself to the power that so irresistibly, and yet so delightfully controls its affections."[44] Again, the concept is "heart preaching" referred to in prerequisite one discussed above. In prerequisite one, the target of heart preaching, the practical effects of life-change of the hearers was the consideration. In prerequisite four, the source of heart preaching, the heart of the preacher, is the consideration. Alex Montoya rightly warns: "Our preaching is lifeless because it comes from stony hearts."[45] Unfortunately, that does not end the matter, as the result of this unwarranted grievance on behalf of a preacher is to promote the same type of response from those who hear him—a lifeless one yielded from unaffected hearts.

As valuable as prerequisites one, two, and three are for sermon conclusion excellence, it must be understood that the absence of exhibited warmth of a preacher's good will toward his hearers will nullify the benefits to be received through these prerequisites. However, by means of a preacher's exhibited warmth toward his hearers, the importance of aiming at practical effects, understanding the human mind, and arrangement of content become spendable currency for the acquisition of sermon conclusion excellence.

CLOSING APPEALS THAT ARE WELCOMED BY THE HEARERS

In the conclusion we are no longer preaching the preaching text, and we are not teaching so much in the closing appeals as we are persuading our hearers by means of them. We are addressing ourselves more immediately to the conscience, the affections, and the will, pressing upon the awakened conscience solemn issues. As a preacher gives himself fully to this, if the closing appeals of the sermon conclusion contain instruction that will help them to comply with the mandates of Scripture, the hearers, typically, will be "prepared to welcome them."[46]

44. Porter, *Lectures on Homiletics and Preaching*, 1835, 154.
45. Montoya, *Preaching with Passion*, 57.
46. Moore, *Thoughts on Preaching*, 1861, 139.

However, since resistance to the truth of Scripture is as unfortunate as it is real, the preacher must be possessed by a passion to serve his hearers through the ministry of the Word of God. This he must do. This is that which he is responsible for and that which he can control. And control this he must. The ministry of the Word must go forth whether it is received or not. Nevertheless, it is of significant consolation to know that:

> The preacher who feels an interest in his subject will always be listened to. His hearers may not believe his doctrine; but they will hear. He cannot have an inattentive auditory; the thing is impossible. Those to whom he preaches may complain; they may hear and hate; but they will hear. No preacher can sustain the attention of the people unless he feels his subject; nor can he long sustain it, unless he feels it deeply. He must have fellowship with the truth he utters.[47]

In the prospect of hearers resisting the truth, a preacher must not yield to the temptation to shrink back, to cease from resolving to win a verdict from them on behalf of the truth of Scripture. His fellowship with the truth must be joined to an unrelenting will to see his hearers submit to the prerogative of biblical compliance in their lives.

Resistance to the truth must be assumed as part of the context in which one preaches but it must never become the reason that one shies away from preaching. The reason one preaches is to help people. For some people, those who are resistant to the truth, the best help a preacher can provide them is to overcome their resistance. Overcoming resistance to the truth will not result from a preacher who shrinks back in the presence of resistance, who is willing to abandon the resistant hearer at the point of his greatest need. Gardiner Spring's assertions are significant as he exhorts: "Our sermon should help people. . . . We dare not be like the worthless shepherds of Israel who became the object of prophetic denunciation. They were castigated because they did not have the welfare of God's people as their highest priority."[48] We must understand that not only does God require us to be faithful in the ministry of his Word to his people, but God's people need such faithfulness from us, and we must provide it to them.

Fortunately, those who desire the truth represent most hearers. As tragic as it is for a preacher to shrink back from preaching truth in the presence of resistant hearers, it must be understood as a greater injustice for a preacher to not provide substantial truth to the hearers who greatly desire it. A preacher from days past recorded a note a pastor friend of his received who heard him provide a lecture to one who wanted to hear and needed to hear a sermon. The note read:

> Reverend Brother: I listened very attentively to your clever essay on history this morning and hoped to find some features of a gospel sermon. Was it my fault that I did not find or detect anything in it . . . to impart information needed for practical utilization in the Christian life? You are a minister of the

47. Spring, *The Power of the Pulpit*, 1848, 132.

48. Montoya, *Preaching with Passion*, 62.

Word, which is to make the man of God perfect, thoroughly furnished unto all good works. Pardon these kindly suggestions from one, who, tired of business, goes to church to be helped.[49]

The intention to help God's people, though not the opportunity of the conclusion alone, finds its greatest opportunity in the conclusion of a sermon.

Hearers who hold a high view of Scripture neither take offense to being told how they are to comply with the Bible, nor do they resent being challenged to comply with the mandates of the Christian life, things that are essential in preaching a sermon conclusion. A true conclusion is about personal application in the closing appeals. Not all application should be left to the end, for a text needs to be applied throughout the sermon, but the application found in the sermon conclusion's closing appeals is that which the preacher, by the Holy Spirit's power, will compel his hearers to do.[50]

Haddon Robinson's comments about the necessity of a conclusion's practical instruction are convincing as he writes: "What can people do to act on the Sunday sermon in Monday morning's world? A conclusion can answer that; and if the preacher does not face this question with his congregation, they may not be able to answer it at all. . . . Preaching comes closer to being incorporated into the structures of life when the minister offers practical guidance on how to translate truth into experience."[51] All believers can be benefitted by closing appeals in a sermon conclusion that provide practical instruction in living the Christian life according to Scripture and, specifically, living it in a manner that complies with the purpose of the sermon and the purpose of the text of Scripture that was preached. Most believers desire this from a preacher in his sermon conclusion and the preacher must determine that his hearers will not be disappointed in this regard. As John Piper put it, "Good preaching pleads with people to respond to the Word of God."[52] Hearers responding to the closing appeals are affected, most commonly and predominately, by the final closing appeal.

THE FINAL WORDS OF A SERMON CONCLUSION

It is certain in an effective sermon conclusion that urgency will quite properly be found. The natural rule governing a sermon conclusion is to "place last that on which you choose to rest the strength of your cause."[53] The closing appeals of a sermon conclusion should contain the most significant content and the most urgent communication found in the entire sermon.

49. Pierson, *The Divine Art of Preaching*, 1892, 145–46.

50. Stott, *Between Two Worlds*, 246.

51. Robinson, *Biblical Preaching*, 170.

52. Piper, *The Supremacy of God in Preaching*, 95.

53. Blair, *Lectures on Rhetoric*, 1852, 170.

In the effort to impact the will of the hearers, a preacher must not overlook the all-important final words of, or the last sentence of, the conclusion. It is true that it is extremely difficult to conclude a sermon well. It is, however, an essential part of the task of preaching to conclude with excellence. "And as important are the first words of a sermon, the final words are even more so."[54] Broadus's instruction was that "The last sentence, of whatever it may consist, ought to be appropriate and impressive."[55] More specifically, the final words of the conclusion may be best spent by strongly and vividly portraying how the purpose of the sermon, can be life-changing for the hearers, if they will comply with the truth of the passage which was preached under the direction of the closing appeals of the sermon.[56]

The conclusion must be thought out very carefully in order to bring the sermon to a planned and powerful termination, not only for the hearers but for the preacher as well. In other words, the final words of the conclusion and particularly the final statement must be one that holds such great anticipation for the preacher that he "can't wait to get there" and, having gotten there, there is simply nothing of greater significance he desires to say. Therefore, having asserted such an epic declaration, the preacher simply is not inclined to say anything further. The strategic role that a well-produced final sentence serves is to bring productive impact to the conclusion's closing words, and prevent the preacher from adding unnecessary, additional sentences to the conclusion.

Though a well-prepared last sentence provides a preventative measure against unwarranted words, it cannot guarantee that they will not be forthcoming. A preacher must know thoroughly the thought and even the language composing the last sentence. Therefore, McComb's exhortation is helpful when he wrote: "Know then, where you're going to stop, and let no excitement generated by the act of speaking, no suggestion of a new idea, cause you to change your mind."[57] Through a carefully prepared last sentence of a sermon conclusion, a preacher knows what his final words should be, and they should be his final words!

The conclusion's objective is to press the sermon's purpose upon the hearer's cognition, conscience, affections, and will. Once the sermon's purpose has been applied fully to the hearer's soul, the conclusion must be terminated. However, termination of the conclusion must never be enacted before the purpose of the sermon has been achieved. Thus, the wisdom of prioritizing not only brevity but completeness for the content of the sermon conclusion. The imperatival nature of supplying the disparate concepts of brevity and completeness in concluding sermons is codified by the following: "When the nail is driven home, all after-hammering is superfluous; but if we stop

---

54. Vinet, *Homiletics*, 1854, 326.

55. Broadus, *A Treatise on the Preparation and Delivery of Sermons*, 1870, 288.

56. Broadus, *A Treatise on the Preparation and Delivery of Sermons*, 1870, 287.

57. McComb, *Preaching in Theory and Practice*, 1926, 77.

before we have driven it home, we might as well never have begun to drive it."[58] The well-prepared last sentence of the conclusion is the final touch of the sermon. In terms of the hammer and nail analogy, the final words of the conclusion are the last hammer strike upon the sermonic nail. As this design becomes a reality a most important thing results—the preacher stops when he is done because he knows when to stop since he knows how he planned to stop preaching.[59] Anything added to this final touch is not only counterintuitive, but it will be counterproductive.

In whatever way the preacher prepares the final sentence of the conclusion and all the content of the closing appeals which precede it, the general implication of the conclusion content should be an unapologetic call for a complete commitment to Christ. The sermon conclusion should not be other than what the completed canon of Scripture is about, generally, a complete commitment to Jesus Christ. If this is not being called for, what is the preacher ultimately doing with whatever text he has selected as the preaching passage for the sermon once he has expounded the passage? Christ's disclosure to a would-be follower should be instructive for all who preach in his name, as Edwin Mouzon points out when he wrote:

> A certain man said to Jesus, "I will follow thee, Lord; but first suffer me to bid farewell to them that are at my house." He was not quite ready to make the final break. And Jesus said to him, "No man having put his hand to the plow, and looking back, is fit for the kingdom of God." For the kingdom of God is never for backward-looking men; it is only and always for those whose faces are turned toward the future. Christ calls for full committal to the interest of his Kingdom.[60]

The sermon conclusion is the most demonstrable portion of the sermon where an unmistakable commitment to Christ is called for by a preacher. This is not anything other than a demonstration of devoted diligence on behalf of one who calls God's people to respond as they should to the truth of his Word. This is not the entirety of his devoted diligence, but it is an important part of it. The words of Gardiner Spring are appropriate and compelling: "Diligent devotedness to the duties of his office is one every minister *owes to himself*. He cannot greatly respect himself, nor the office he holds, unless he is a man of exemplary diligence."[61] An ultimate shortcoming in devoted diligence is demonstrated by sermon conclusions that fail to incorporate scriptural closing appeals which allow the conclusion to become the highpoint of the sermon.

One final insight needs to be codified about the final words of a sermon conclusion. Again, the concept of "highpoint" comes into view but in this installment, we will refer to this highpoint as a "highlight." We understand that the conclusion of a

58. Taylor, *The Ministry of the Word*, 1876, 128.

59. Dabney, *Sacred Rhetoric*, 1870, 178.

60. Mouzon, *Preaching with Authority*, 1929, 245.

61. Spring, *The Power of the Pulpit*, 1848, 102.

sermon is to be the "highpoint of the sermon." Subsequently, we have come to understand that the last closing appeal should be the "apex of the sermon's highpoint." But then, there are the final statements that close out the last closing appeal. This (these) statement(s) should be the "highlight of the apex of the sermon's highpoint."

But the question must be asked, "Are there grounds for honing the edge of a sermon conclusion so sharply?" And, if there are grounds for this, how is it to be accomplished? By what means could this become a reality?

There are grounds for the razor-sharp refinement of the final words of a sermon conclusion. The grounds have been provided by homileticians writing long ago as well as in recent days. A few quotes from several homiletical sources will serve to support the concept that the last statements of a sermon conclusion are of great merit. Since persuasion of the hearers is aided when the "principle of climax" is achieved in the sermon conclusion, it is imperative that this principle is dominant in the conclusion and controls the final closing appeal, particularly.

Notice how various authors portray the importance of the principle of climax and the most climactic component being the final statements of a sermon conclusion. D. Martyn Lloyd-Jones wrote, "You must end on a climax, and everything should lead up to it in such a way that the great truth stands out dominating everything that has been said, and the listeners go away with this in their minds."[62] Bryan Chapell contributes the following: "The message that starts with a gripping introduction should end with an even more powerful conclusion . . . (as) the climax of the message. The last sixty seconds are the most dynamic moments in excellent sermons. With these final words, the preacher marshals the thought and emotion of the entire message into an exhortation that makes all that preceded clear and compelling."[63] Austin Phelps comments are without reservation when he wrote: "No art of invention should be despised by a preacher in the effort to throw a spell over an audience by the . . . closing thoughts and the magnetism of the last words."[64] Again, Chapell is helpful as he surmises that the best ending of a sermon conclusion is always with words that "soundly register in the heart."[65] Jacob Fry's words are insightful when he reasoned: "Besides being an important word, the last word should in its sound be one on which the voice of the preacher and the ear of the hearer can rest."[66] Ilion T. Jones believed that the end of the conclusion is to be composed of a very strong sentence, a very personal word from the preacher to his hearers. This strong final sentence, as for all the conclusion, will carry more weight because their pastor is speaking to them and he is "speaking person to

---

62. Lloyd-Jones, *Preaching and Preachers*, 77.

63. Chapell, *Christ-centered Preaching*, 244.

64. Phelps, *The Theory of Preaching*, 1882, 536.

65. Chapell, *Christ-centered Preaching*, 245.

66. Fry, *Elementary Homiletics*, 1897, 133.

person, heart to heart, as their pastor."[67] And Chuck Swindoll suggests that the final words should be the "thought you leave ringing in their ears."[68]

Clearly a case has been made for the importance of the final words that end a sermon conclusion. But what provisions have been suggested by homileticians to affect this important principle of climax? There are five means by which the apex of the sermon's highpoint may be highlighted. These five means include: Returning to material used in the sermon introduction;[69] Repeating the opening phrase used to start the sermon introduction;[70] Reciting a striking passage of Scripture;[71] Registering a profound statement of propositional truth, warning, promise, or encouragement; that is, words that "soundly register in the heart;"[72] and, Rendering a graphic illustration that becomes a clinching element of persuasion.[73] Several of these means may be combined to accomplish the principle of climax. Christ's sermon on the Mount, for example, ended very persuasively through the means of an epic propositional statement of truth, Matthew 7:24, which was followed by an illustration, Matthew 7:25–27, that brought clarity and profundity to what he had stated propositionally.

These five means make it possible to accomplish the principle of climax in the final statements of a sermon conclusion in which the apex of the sermon's highpoint is highlighted with great effectiveness. What is significant for the preacher is his intent to fasten the purpose of the sermon to the lives of his hearers "as one would drive a nail into a plank and clinch it." So, the material of the sermon conclusion's closing appeals must be so pertinent to achieving the purpose of the sermon that they fit the purpose "like a glove fits the hand."[74]

PASTORAL ADVICE OR BIBLICAL AUTHORITY IN THE CLOSING APPEALS

The purpose of a sermon being achieved in the lives of believers will result only as they are given needed assistance, assistance that can help them live according to Scripture. Worldly wisdom cannot do this. The only means of assistance to aid believers in their Christian walk is the Word of God. Scripture is not the best of a variety of options. It

---

67. Jones, *Principles and Practice of Preaching*, 165.

68. Swindoll, *Saying It Well*, 227.

69. Chapell, *Christ-centered Preaching*, 250. Chapell directs one to refer back "to material mentioned in the sermon's introduction. Complete the story, echo an earlier thought, refer to a character or story specifics in a previous illustration, resolve a tension, repeat a striking phrase, refer to the opening problem, or in some other way end where you began."

70. Kidder, *A Treatise on Homiletics*, 1864, 227. According to Kidder, the "principle of climax" may be accomplished in the sermon conclusion when the preacher ends "as he began."

71. Kidder, *A Treatise on Homiletics*, 1864, 227.

72. Chapell, *Christ-centered Preaching*, 245.

73. Jones, *Principles and Practice of Preaching*, 164.

74. Jones, *Principles and Practice of Preaching*, 164.

is the best and only source. It is the best source because it is the only source that can provide God's people with needed insights to live their lives according to Scripture. Scripture alone can supply the means to fulfill its requirements.

Pertinent closing appeals must derive their pertinency from Scripture. No preacher, regardless of his Christian maturity and personal experience, can be the source of the counsel that believers need. Only the Word of God, forming the content of the closing appeals of a sermon conclusion, is a viable solution to remedy or alleviate believers' immaturity revealed by lives that do not comply with Scripture. So, the issue for the closing appeals of a sermon conclusion is this—what is the basis for the final instruction in a sermon for God's people to live lives that are pleasing to him? Will the source for what believers are challenged to do be derived from biblical authority or pastoral advice or worldly wisdom? Anything other than biblical authority will serve as a disservice to God's people. The following excerpt illustrates the demand for biblical authority as the basis of instruction for one's conduct, a demand that every believer should insist upon from those who attempt to instruct them on behalf of God.

> When Bill Hybels visited Sydney in the early 1990s, Australian evangelist John Chapman ('Chappo') was in the audience. Most of us found Bill's talk on Matthew the tax collector riveting, and as best as I can remember it included plenty of practical party tips, given the fact that the tax collector threw a massive Jesus-party and invited all his friends. When Bill invited questions, Chappo raised his hand. "Dear brother," said Chappo, "I'm not meaning to be rude, but I wonder if you could tell us how people are to know when they are hearing God speak through His Word, and when they are just hearing good advice from Bill? Because as far as I could tell, I couldn't spot the difference. As you spoke to us, it all seemed to come with the same authority."[75]

Certainly, there should be a discernable difference between pastoral advice and biblical authority in a sermon where both are being disseminated. But what is the basis for both being offered to God's people? What preacher in his right mind would think that his advice is a sufficient base from which God's people could be appropriately challenged to conduct their lives according to his counsel?

In an instance where a sermon conclusion's closing appeals are based upon pastoral advice/worldly wisdom/human counsel, is the preacher not demonstrating his belief of the Bible's inadequacy to provide needed instruction, inadequate to the point that it must be augmented by something more, something other than Scripture? Only Scripture is profitable to equip God's people so that they may be adequate for every good work. Human counsel cannot do this. Human counsel must not be offered to God's people in addition to Scripture, or in place of Scripture. If so, such would be the grounds of treason against the Word of God. So, a conclusion that has as the basis

---

75. Millar and Campbell, *Saving Eutychus*, from Campbell's Preface, 15.

of its closing appeals anything other than Scripture must be viewed for what it is, a treasonous conclusion.

Complying with human counsel will reorder the behavior of people but that is all it can do. Behavior modification is not the same thing as life-change. The counsel of man is sufficient to affect behavior modification. Scripture is not needed to affect simple behavior modification. Complying to God's Word will result in behavior modification but it will be modified behavior that is due to a change in life. Life-change is the result of one's response to God's Word as one's mind, conscience, affections, and volition are impacted by Scripture and there is a turning from error to compliance with the Word of God in one's life. In such an instance, behavior will be modified but it will the outcome of a far greater work that was done, life-change, which the Holy Spirit accomplishes by means of the Word of God operating in the life of a Christian.

Life-change, not behavior modification is what God desires. He has provided his Word to accomplish this. Furthermore, life-change, as valuable as it is, is not the end-product for complying with scriptural truth. Complying with Scripture is, in a word, obedience. As one obeys God's Word, more than life-change results. The ultimate result from obedience to Scripture is Christian maturity, growth in Christ. A preacher who is in sync with God will be found seeking what he seeks and using what he has provided to accomplish it. Gary Millar makes a strong case for this as he writes:

> When you listen to someone explain the Bible, what do you want to get out of it? I want to know that God has addressed me through His Word. I want to be challenged, humbled, corrected, excited, moved, strengthened, overawed, corrected, shaped, stretched and propelled out into the world as a different person. I want to be changed! And if I'm the one who's teaching the Bible . . . I long for that change to happen in the hearts of those who hear. . . . I want people to be affected. I want to preach in a way that results in change. Real change. Heart change.[76]

God desires that his Word produces life-change for those who hear his Word preached. But the question is, will those who preach his Word also desire this as they preach?

Proclaiming God's truth through Scripture-based closing appeals is done for hearers to act upon the preached Word in such a fashion that the purpose of the sermon will be achieved in their lives, which will insure life-change and Christian maturity. There must be no reticence about this—we preach that life-change and Christian maturity will be a reality in the lives of our hearers. Jerry Vines and Jim Shaddix express this well when they declare: "Every sermon should be intent upon fostering change in the lives of people. The entire message must move toward this purpose. We preach for a response. We are lawyers pleading our Lord's cause. We are calling for a

---

76. Millar and Campbell, *Saving Eutychus*, from Campbell's chapter, "Preaching that Changes the Heart," 27.

verdict."[77] The verdict for which a preacher calls is made clear and composed of the closing appeals of the sermon conclusion.

The very popular speaker, evangelist, and former pastor of the Moody Memorial Church in Chicago—Dr. Alan Redpath, cited two concepts of first importance in preaching, both of which are of singular significance to the sermon conclusion. These two concepts were strategic for what Redpath called the "Terminal Law" in preaching.[78] These two concepts are "the ultimate object in preaching" and "the objective of the message."[79] According to Redpath, "The ultimate object of any sermon is to gain the assent of the will of the congregation. This ('ultimate') objective may be approached along the line of the emotion and the intellect, but it must lead to the intake of the will. In other words, the preacher is concerned about securing a verdict."[80] The second concept is related to the specific objective of a text and, therefore, the sermon preached from it. Redpath believed, "The (specific) objective of the message must be in view all the time. . . . Power in preaching results from a clear objective in view which burdens the heart of the preacher."[81] Significant for Redpath was the requirement that a preacher discover the purpose of the text/sermon as soon as possible. If this did not occur early in his study he may fail to be controlled by the specific objective for the message in his study and his preaching with the result that he may "fail to grapple with the conscience and the will" of the congregation and, thus, fail to preach a sermon.[82]

Redpath's concepts hold tremendous profitability for the sermon conclusion. If the heart of a preacher is truly burdened to see God's people have the purpose of the text/sermon achieved in their lives, then urgently compelling God's people to live according to the specific, selected insights of Scripture-based closing appeals is the only viable remedy to alleviate the preacher's admirable pastoral desire and responsibility. Life-change and Christian maturity not behavior modification is needed, and biblical authority not pastoral advice is the means by which they may be achieved. The authority of Scripture-based closing appeals affecting the hearers' cognition, conscience, affections, and volition is the only sufficient, God-given provision to accomplish what is needed in the lives of his people.

---

77. Vines and Shaddix, *Power in the Pulpit*, 212.

78. Roddy, editor, *We Prepare and Preach*, from Alan Redpath's chapter "Five Principles of Sermon Preparation," 135.

79. Roddy, *We Prepare and Preach*, from Redpath's chapter "Five Principles of Sermon Preparation," 134–5.

80. Roddy, *We Prepare and Preach*, from Redpath's chapter "Five Principles of Sermon Preparation," 134–5.

81. Roddy, *We Prepare and Preach*, from Redpath's chapter "Five Principles of Sermon Preparation," 135.

82. Roddy, *We Prepare and Preach*, from Redpath's chapter "Five Principles of Sermon Preparation," 135.

12

Application in a Sermon Conclusion

"A sermon conclusion that does not bring conviction upon the hearers, that does not provide correction for that which has been a matter of disregard or disobedience, that does not counsel them as to how regard and obedience to the truth can be theirs, that does not console or encourage them as to the blessing that obedience can and will bring to their lives, is not a sermon conclusion that will compel many believers to a new direction in living. The challenge of the closing appeals of the sermon conclusion will most likely fall on deaf ears for most of its hearers. A sermon conclusion that provides a stand-alone challenge through its closing appeals without supplying what is needful for the closing appeals to be complied with, initially and ongoingly, is an ill-fated effort from any preacher."

"A take it or leave it heart attitude on behalf of a preacher is a vulgar reality. It is not sufficient to plainly and accurately declare what should be done by the hearers in response to proclaimed truth. It must matter to a preacher whether Scripture is complied with or set aside. If the preacher finds it acceptable for the truth of Scripture to be disregarded by his hearers, this faulty disposition will control how the truth is proclaimed by him. And that proclamation will be derelict because it reflects the derelict preacher's heart. The preacher must be one who encourages his hearers in the appeals he makes to them. . . . How could he not do this if he is caught up with the reality that truth matters, that it matters for time and for eternity? This reality should be apparent in how the sermon conclusion, especially, is preached."

"If a preacher desires for truth to relate more fully to his hearers, he must require that truth relates more fully to himself. The only way coal becomes a diamond is for it to be subjected to intense heat and pressure over time. Yet, "charcoal quality" conclusions are offered to the body of Christ when preachers do not pay the price of time,

heat, and pressure to secure diamond quality instruction in their sermon conclusions through insightful application derived by thorough, painstaking investigation of Scripture as well as personal reflection and assessment of his own life and past personal experiences."

"Before any preacher can be effective in the pulpit, he must be effective in his study. Before he studies to prepare a sermon for his hearers, he must study the Bible for his own insight and instruction. The truth of the text he will preach must first be a matter of deep personal significance if it is to become a matter of corporate significance, declared publicly. It is therefore a matter of first importance that a preacher be a profitable student of the Word before he attempts to be a profitable proclaimer of that Word."

"The Apostle Peter makes it clear in 2 Peter 1:3–11 that God has provided all things pertaining to life and godliness, granting to us precious and magnificent promises, having become partakers of the divine nature in which we are to grow increasingly. Every sermon preached for the edification of believers should be a preacher's intentional act to be used by God to advance his purposes for his people's spiritual growth and godliness. The sermon conclusion becomes a preacher's choice opportunity to be used by God for his agenda in the lives of his people. You might disagree, thinking, 'No, providing scriptural instruction is the choice opportunity to be used by God to accomplish his agenda in the lives of his people, not providing a sermon conclusion.' And I would agree with this objection if a sermon conclusion were not laden with Scripture-based closing appeals, as it must be. The sermon conclusion for which I am advocating includes the most insightful, instructive scriptural references related to the purpose of the sermon for every sermon preached. Therefore, the sermon conclusion just like the expository sermon which it concludes, is laden with scriptural insight and understanding as the conclusion incorporates the choicest biblical references related to the purpose of the preaching text. In other words, a sermon conclusion should be a biblical capstone to the sermon rather than a movement away from Scripture. More specifically, a sermon conclusion composed of Scripture-based closing appeals is a topical sermonette regarding the sermon's purpose that concludes an expository sermon. . . . The armory of God's Word exists in such abundance that it cannot be exhausted. However, in its unending supply it can go underutilized, if not unutilized. And the greatest incidence of the armory of God's Word being unutilized is in the sermon conclusion."

"Not to be limited to the sermon conclusion but most certainly in the sermon conclusion, selective inclusions from the whole of Scripture should be supplied to provide living truth, truth that answers tough questions and resolves difficult problems believers will have in living out God's Word in their lives. In the instance of a sermon conclusion, the selected Scriptures will answer tough questions and resolve difficult issues that are germane to the achievement of the sermon's purpose. As a preacher uses the Word of God, even in his sermon conclusion, he will be found making the most of his opportunity to preach the Word but, more specifically, he will be doing the most he can do to be helpful to God's people who hear him preach."

"No one should doubt the connection between being a master of one's Bible and conducting, with accuracy and insight, the necessary work of expounding the Bible. Yet, mastery of one's Bible is just as critical in connecting non-preaching text references to one's preaching text to apply and illustrate the truths of the preaching text. But perhaps the greatest dividend of Bible mastery is found in the necessary work of citing the cross-references that contain the insights which will comprise the closing appeals by which the sermon's purpose may be achieved."

"The sermon conclusion will always be about what believers are to do in order for the purpose of the sermon to be accomplished in their lives. Many times, the conclusion will be about how to do what is necessary for the sermon to be accomplished in life. Sometimes, the conclusion will provide a combination of what is to be done along with essential insights for how it is to be done. Whether the content of the closing appeals proceeds along the lines of what is to be done, or how it is to be done, or a combination of both, the Word of God provides the unrivaled content for the purpose of the sermon to be achieved most fully in the lives of God's people."

"Most preachers are better in every other process of sermonizing than in that of applying truth to its practical uses in the sermon conclusion. They may explain clearly, prove adequately, illustrate vividly, draw implications accurately; but not apply truth insightfully where it is needed most in the sermon, the conclusion. This represents a significant challenge to preachers since the conclusion should be the highpoint of the sermon, composed of the most valuable insights of a personal and practical nature, existing to provide practical aid to the hearers in the closing thoughts and last words of a sermon."

APPLICATION IN SERMON CONCLUSIONS

Monday—The Bullseye for a Sermon Conclusion's Application

As is clear from the maxim that "doctrine should be preached practically and duties should be preached doctrinally," the application found in a sermon conclusion will provide truths that will bear immediately upon the conscience,[1] the affections, and

---

1. Since the conscience is a vital part of man's constitution and an important entity to be targeted in the preaching of Scripture, I want to provide a framework of understanding regarding what is meant by the conscience as it will be used in this book. No attempt is rendered to try to settle the varying doctrinal

the will of the hearers so that the purpose of the preaching text may be achieved in the lives of the hearers quite thoroughly as they comply their lives to the closing appeals of the sermon conclusion since these appeals will be based on truths of Scripture references related to the preaching text's purpose. The sermon conclusion should cause the hearer to consider his own implementation, or lacking implementation, of the sermon's purpose in his life. "Jesus often did the equivalent of that. At the end of a discourse often he would say, 'Go, and do likewise.'"[2] Similar expressions were used by Jesus to drive the application to the hearers in a personal and forceful fashion, such as: "Go, therefore . . ." and "Therefore . . ." or "He who has ears to hear, let him hear." Jesus

---

subtleties and interpretations involving the conscience or the soul of man, in which the conscience is a part, according to the predominance of the sources checked. Brief inclusions from three sources are provided to establish an overview of the conscience. Lewis Sperry Chafer in his *Systematic Theology, Volume VII*, pp. 91–93 writes: "Personality seems to express its full scope and inclusiveness when it wills and executes its purpose guided by the intellect and the sensibilities; nevertheless, over and above this manifestation of personality, conscience sits in judgment whether the action be good or bad. . . . (B)eing intuitively aware of each action to the extent of rendering judgment upon the deed suggests the peculiar and elusive character of this faculty. . . . The Bible assumes the presence of conscience in man as a native factor of his being and predicates such limitations of it as to make it a fallible human characteristic. Though subject to weakening through abuse, conscience is presented in the Scriptures as a monitor over human actions. . . . The following general divisions of the subject are suggested: (1) The conscience acts judicially, accusing or excusing (Rom. 2:15). (2) The conscience acts punitively, inflicting remorse and self-punishment. (3) The conscience anticipates future judgments and then acts by way of prediction. (4) The conscience acts socially in judging others (Rom. 14:4; 1 Cor. 8:13). . . . The truth respecting the human conscience is even more complex in the case of a believer. Being indwelt by the Holy Spirit and therefore subject to the mind and voice of the Spirit . . . the Holy Spirit becomes the new Monitor, and the child of God either grieves or does not grieve the Holy Spirit. . . . It is possible that the Holy Spirit works in and through the human conscience when registering His reactions to the believer's thought and conduct. The Apostle thus testified of himself, 'My consciences also bearing me witness in the Holy Ghost' (Rom. 9:1)." Herbert Lockyer in his book *All the Doctrines of the Bible*, pp. 143–44 writes: "Man is a tripartite being, made up of spirit, soul and body. . . . Man's body was formed from the lower elements—the divine Spirit was inbreathed—a living soul resulted from the union of the first two. . . . Man has a body and a spirit, but he *is* a soul. He 'became a living soul.' The infusion of the immaterial spirit into the material frame produced the third possession, a soul . . . Within the soul, there is the mind, the source of knowledge and intelligence (I Corinthians 2:11). . . . There is also the heart . . . the source of love, affection, as well as consciousness (Hebrews 10:22). . . . Then there is the will, giving man the capacity to choose, act or decide. Man's power to choose is both an end, and the means to attain it." William G. T. Shedd in his *Dogmatic Theology*, third edition, pp. 510–11, writes: There are "two faculties of the soul, namely, understanding and will. The understanding is the cognitive faculty or mode of the soul. It comprises the intellect and the conscience. These are percipient and perceptive powers. They are destitute of desire and inclination; and they are not self-determining and executive power. The intellect perceives what ought to be done, and the conscience commands what ought to be done, but they never do anything themselves. They do not incline to an end. They have no love and desire for what is commanded; and no hatred and aversion toward what is forbidden. The intellect neither loves nor hates, neither desires nor is averse. The conscience approves and disapproves; but approbation is not love and desire, nor is disapprobation hatred and abhorrence. . . . The effect of sin upon the cognitive side of the human soul (the intellect and the conscience) is to darken, dim and stupefy, but not radically to change. This fixidness of the understanding is in striking contrast . . . with the mobility and mutability of the will. The will is that faculty or mode of the soul which self-determines, inclines, desires, and chooses in reference to moral and religious objects and ends."

2. Luccock, *In the Minister's Workshop*, 83.

caused his hearers to conclude that they were negligent in a specific way and needed to become obedient by complying with the instruction he had offered them. This is what a sermon conclusion is all about—compelling change in the lives of those who hear.

Halford E. Luccock cited a bit of verse which depicts that what may be the ultimate low in social conversation is a valuable consideration for preaching, especially for a sermon conclusion, namely, a conscious awareness of "Monday." Luccock recited:

> As Tommy Snooks and Bessie Brooks
> Were walking out on Sunday,
> Said Tommy Snooks to Bessie Brooks,
> "Tomorrow will be Monday."[3]

A stringent test for proclaimed truth is, how effective will the truth of the sermon be on Monday? Will it prepare the hearer to stand strong against Monday's worldliness—"the lust of the flesh and the lust of the eyes and the boastful pride of life" (1 John 2:16b)? Will it provide a corrective force upon the hearer's conduct to bring Monday's world more into alignment with Sunday's sermon and with the purposes of The One who rose from the dead two millennia ago on a Sunday morning?[4]

The Test for a Sermon

The test of a sermon is this—does it convince the mind, move the emotions/affections, convict the conscience, and gain a verdict of the hearers' wills so that the biblical truth preached in the sermon becomes the hearers' personal agenda for their daily lives?[5] Furthermore, the sermon conclusion is the specific time and place where the final exam for preaching is administered.

Specifically, the closing appeals of a sermon conclusion represent the preacher's passing or failing the test of the sermon he preached. Beyond that which must be done for effective preaching to be a reality: that is, an effective introduction; clear and accurate statements of theological principle for the main structure of the sermon; thorough and insightful exposition of the biblical text; illuminating illustrations; and challenging and correcting implications of the text to the hearers; a preacher has passed the test on Sunday regarding the sermon he preached *if clear, insightful, Scripture-based closing appeals are provided in the sermon conclusion as the means by which his hearers may achieve the purpose of the sermon in their lives.* Additionally, the same clear, insightful, Scripture-based appeals of the sermon conclusion to which the hearers are compelled to comply become the basis of their passing or failing the test of the sermon on Monday and every day, thereafter.

---

3. Luccock, *In the Minister's Workshop*, 83–84.

4. Luccock, *In the Minister's Workshop*, 84.

5. Davis, *Evangelistic Preaching*, 1921, 44.

As important as preaching is in the responsibilities of a pastor, essentially, he is a fellow Christian. The sermon he preaches to his hearers is a sermon that he too must follow. Preaching a sermon does not provide the preacher a pass for not living the truth he will proclaim, or for not living the truth he has just proclaimed. Of course, just the opposite is true. He is not only responsible to live scriptural truth like every other believer who hears the sermon but is more responsible to do so than anyone else. Understanding this should cause the preacher to take great diligence to discover from Scripture the specific insights that will achieve the purpose and finalize the sermon in a way *that sets for himself a very clear agenda for his personal responsibility to respond to the closing appeals of his conclusion.* His own desire to know exactly how he is to live will force him to discover and declare content that will be strategic for a faithful response to God's Word. Then the preacher can have an understanding how the conclusion may affect his hearers based upon the effect it has had in his life throughout the week, having begun to implement the truths of the closing appeals before preaching them to God's people.

The Effects of a Conclusion's Closing Appeals: Convict, Correct, Counsel, Console, and Compel

The application of the sermon conclusion must do more than merely relate to the purpose of the sermon. The application of the conclusion, regarding the sermon's purpose, should present a change in direction, a new approach, in order to position the hearers for a more responsible and complete manner of complying to the truth they have heard. The approach by which this may be accomplished includes the following: by interrogating the conscience; by exhortation; by revealing what Scripture promises for those who comply with the requirements of God's Word; by warning about disregard or disobedience to God's purposes; by providing the ways and means necessary for compliance to become a personal reality.[6]

As important as the effect of a sermon conclusion is to compel hearers to a new direction in living, it must do more than that alone. In fact, if a preacher does not seek to do more than compel hearers to live differently, it is doubtful that different lives will be the final product achieved by the preacher's sermon conclusion. A sermon conclusion that does not bring conviction upon the hearers, that does not provide correction for that which has been a matter of disregard or disobedience, that does not counsel them as to how regard and obedience to the truth can be theirs, that does not console or encourage them as to the blessing that obedience can and will bring to their lives, is not a sermon conclusion that will compel many believers to a new direction in living. The challenge of the closing appeals of the sermon conclusion will most likely fall on deaf ears for most of its hearers. A sermon conclusion that provides a stand-alone

---

6. Vinet, *Homiletics*, 1854, 324.

challenge through its closing appeals without supplying what is needful for the closing appeals to be complied with, initially and ongoingly, is an ill-fated effort from any preacher.

A take it or leave it heart attitude on behalf of a preacher is a vulgar reality. It is not sufficient to plainly and accurately declare what should be done by the hearers in response to proclaimed truth. It must matter to a preacher whether Scripture is complied with or set aside. If the preacher finds it acceptable for the truth of Scripture to be disregarded by his hearers, this faulty disposition will control how the truth is proclaimed by him. And that proclamation will be derelict because it reflects the derelict preacher's heart. A preacher must be one who encourages his hearers in the appeals he makes to them. It must be natural for him to counsel them about their responsibility to the truth, to compel them to respond to the truth, and to console them in their response to the truth. How could he not do this if he is caught up with the reality that truth matters, that it matters for time and it matters for eternity? This reality should be apparent in how the sermon conclusion, especially, is preached.

The Value of Concluding Application Is Weight Not Bulk

The conclusion is to affect a deep, concentrated impression upon the hearer. Therefore, "weight, not bulk, of appeal" is the measure of value.[7] Because of the context in which the sermon conclusion occurs, late in the sermon when the hearers are mentally weary, bulk of content must give way to weight of content. To the degree that the sermon conclusion is perceived as bulky rather than weighty by the hearers, it will serve only to thwart the result it is intended to achieve on their behalf.

A sermon conclusion exists to apply the sermon's purpose to the lives of the hearers so that it may advance their godliness in everyday life. Therefore, a sermon conclusion is an intellectual matter, secondarily, and a matter of intense practicality, primarily. Consequently, the intense relevance of the sermon is to be observed most appropriately in its conclusion. Preaching that continues to be an intellectual discussion "never giving way to that which is exceedingly relevant is not a sermon, pure and simple."[8] A sermon conclusion is characterized most prominently by the closing appeals it provides to the hearers—appeals to live differently and instruction to help them to do so.

The appeals found in the sermon conclusion should constitute the most intense portion of the sermon and should epitomize persuasive speech. The closing appeals are intended to persuade Christians to comply to the purposes of God's Word which compel them to fulfill their "most critical obligations" as faithful followers of Christ.[9] Therefore, appeals should be very intentional, in respect to their degree of directness.

7. Etter, *The Preacher and His Sermon*, 1885, 372.

8. Phelps, *The Theory of Preaching*, 1882, 455.

9. Phelps, *The Theory of Preaching*, 1882, 542.

This is true for direct and indirect closing appeals. Though not always the case, direct appeals often make use of the personal pronouns "we" and "you" in exhortation.[10] However, the primary usage should be the standardized "you" to the less often use of "we" in expressing the closing appeals. More will be said about the nature of indirect and direct appeals later in this chapter.

Application In The Conclusion For Achieving The Purpose Of The Sermon

There is a sense in which every sermon should have the exact same, ever unchanging purpose—to preach to "the glory of God and the persuasion of each man to live a life submitted absolutely to the will of God," as was the purpose of Puritan preachers who were committed to accomplish such through their preaching.[11] Though this very general purpose for a sermon should never be mitigated, it must be made more specific according to the text to be preached. How is God to be glorified by submitting absolutely to his will in a specific way according to the purpose of the preaching passage? As the instruction of the preaching text is allowed to answer that question, the purpose of the sermon has taken shape dramatically. The pursuit of the ultimately clear and definitive statement of purpose must be enjoined to the point of completion by the preacher in his study, and this is to be done as soon as it can be accomplished.

Having a clear and definite purpose for the sermon cannot be over-emphasized. In a book published many years ago entitled, *The Preacher and His Sermon*, its author, John W. Etter is extremely insightful as he clearly establishes the relationship between the subject of the sermon and the purpose of the sermon. Etter is clear that the conclusion is about the purpose (or the "object") of the sermon more than the subject of the sermon, thereby, avoiding the carelessness of some who fail to distinguish the primacy of the sermon's purpose above the sermon's subject when writing about sermon conclusions. Etter states: "The conclusion consists of the application of the subject to the object of the sermon. That is the supreme purpose for which the sermon was prepared; and a preacher preaching a sermon without application would be like a physician giving to his patient a lecture on general health and forgetting to write him a prescription."[12] The logical ramification of Etter's analogy regarding the function of achieving the purpose of the sermon in the conclusion is that, if a preacher fails to have a purpose for the sermon or if he fails to achieve the purpose in his conclusion, he is essentially practicing malfeasance in his preaching.

No preacher, in speaking on behalf of the Great Physician, should be negligent in prescribing the needed medicine of God's Word to those who desire it and for those who will not thrive spiritually if it is withheld from them. The role of a preacher is to be a good assistant of the Great Physician, that is, he is to be a good Physician's

10. Phelps, *The Theory of Preaching*, 1882, 572.

11. Bickel, *Light and Heat*, 13.

12. Etter, *The Preacher and His Sermon*, 1885, 371–72.

Assistant, and prescribe detailed, specific medicine from the pharmacy of Scripture. This analogy can only be completed if the preacher helps his hearers by supplying them with detailed, specific instruction from Scripture as to how they can live in a way that achieves God's purposes for them in their lives. Achieving the purpose of the sermon is not only the great work of the sermon conclusion but the greatest work to be done in preaching a sermon for the benefit of God's people.

Quite obviously, then, the purpose of the sermon must be a matter that becomes clear to the preacher sooner, rather than later, in his study as he labors in the biblical text. The purpose of the sermon must be understood with great clarity and specificity as soon as it is possible to do so. James Stewart is helpful to make this point emphatic as he writes:

> But for the preacher it is imperative to see the end from the beginning. In every sermon, he must know exactly what truth it is that he is proposing to drive home to the hearers' minds. He must see clearly the objective to which he hopes to lead them. He ought to be able to define it to himself in a dozen words. Without such definiteness of aim, preaching remains self-stultified and ineffectual, and may never touch a single life. With it, the simplest words, taking wings from the Spirit of God, may reach the hidden depths of many hearts.[13]

As is clear from the references above, having and achieving the purpose of the sermon is mandatory for a sermon to be a sermon, and the conclusion of the sermon is crucial for the purpose of the sermon to be achieved most fully in the preaching of it.

Application Made to the Preacher First, Then the Congregation

In the process of preaching and/or hearing sermons preached, it is readily verifiable that application in a sermon increases in strength and relevance when drawn from the preacher's personal experience. A sermon may include instances of the preacher's personal experience, even if these are not revealed as such, and it is often advantageous not to reveal them as such.[14] This will be the case when any preacher searching the depths of his own heart finds identification with the hearts of others and incorporates such instances of affiliation in the sermon. When a preacher understands what probes and arouses his own conscience, he will be serviceable in touching the consciences of others, and his hearers will feel that he is preaching directly to them.

The most effective sermons are those which have impacted the conscience of the preacher. These sermons carry the aroma and exude the vibrance of life to the hearers

13. Stewart, *Heralds of God*, 122.

14. The reason for not revealing that what is advocated, warned against, challenged about, arises from the preacher's personal experience is due to the fact that a preacher could do this with great consistency, that is, in almost every sermon. No congregation will care to hear about, with great consistency, a preacher's personal experiences.

as they reveal the unmistakable experience of humanity in them.[15] Proverbs 27:19 speaks to this matter when it states: "As in water face reflects face, so the heart of man reflects man."

For a man to be a better preacher in the pulpit, it is helpful to be a better student of himself and others in his study. If a preacher desires for truth to relate more fully to his hearers, he must require that truth relates more fully to himself. The only way coal becomes a diamond is for it to be subjected to intense heat and pressure over time. Yet, "charcoal quality" conclusions are offered to the body of Christ when preachers do not pay the price of time, heat, and pressure to secure diamond quality instruction in their sermon conclusions through insightful application derived by thorough, painstaking investigation of Scripture as well as personal reflection and assessment of his own life and past personal experiences.

In preaching, the closing appeals are like the black-velveted display of diamonds and other gemstones by a jeweler to those who are in the market for precious stones. As with the jeweler, the closing appeals in the sermon conclusion is the grand display of the most precious stones of Scripture excavated, cut, and polished by the preacher through a prayerful, diligent investigation of God's Word.

Assimilated Truth in the Heart and the Mind of the Preacher

Before any preacher can be effective in the pulpit, he must be effective in his study. Before he studies to prepare a sermon for his hearers, he must study the Bible for his own insight and instruction. The truth of the text he will preach must first be a matter of deep personal significance if it is to become a matter of corporate significance, declared publicly. It is therefore a matter of first importance that a preacher be a profitable student of the Word before he attempts to be a profitable proclaimer of that Word. Not only must the distinction be made between his initial effort being one of personal concern before it becomes an effort of public concern, but it is of great importance that his efforts, for the sake of personal and public good, be extremely diligent. James W. Alexander wrote about this persuasively as he insisted, "It must be the habit of the preacher to be continually opening new veins, and deeply considering subjects allied to those on which he is to preach" which requires a "perpetual study of the Scriptures" keeping him "continually laboring in this mine. . . . The liveliest preachers are those who are most familiar with the Bible" who provide "scriptural example, history, and figure by way of illustration. . . . Great preachers . . . are always persons whose life is a study of the Word."[16] An effective preaching ministry will never entail less than diligent sermon preparation, but it must include more than that, namely, a personally rich study of Scripture that precedes any attempt to produce a sermon.

15. Simpson, *Lectures on Preaching*, 1897, 146–47.

16. Alexander, *Thoughts on Preaching*, 1864, 12–13.

Yet, it is of great importance how sermons are prepared and preached. The preacher's solemn commission is to preach the Word, and nothing but the Word. This alone fulfills his duty. Yet, among those equally committed to do so, there is a great difference, not merely in the style of preaching, but in the content of it. The difference lies in the varying proportions, insights, and applications in which preachers seek to establish a sound knowledge of biblical truth; including, but not limited to, what they may "omit or touch lightly and charily, and the foreign matter with which they may illustrate, obscure, or encumber" the Word.[17] In essence, a clear, easy to understand, concrete, relevant style of preaching that not only thoroughly expounds the preaching passage but subsequently draws insights from the wider context of scriptural revelation produces a combination of style and substance that cannot be surpassed.

Earnest, Practical Application

Though a preacher must begin his study process by understanding the author's intended meaning for what he wrote, the preacher's task is not completed until he understands what that original intended meaning means in his own culture. Until this is done, a preacher does not yet understand what he needs to know about the truth of the text he will preach. The objective of preaching is not to prepare people to live in a millennium and culture they will never experience, but to live according to Scripture in the time and place they inhabit. As C. H. Spurgeon put it: "*We must become more and more earnest and practical. . . .* We must preach as men *to* men. . . . It is of no use to fire your rifle into the sky when your object is to pierce men's hearts."[18] Scripture provides not just the best source but the only source by which God's people can be addressed authoritatively and most beneficially to live lives that are pleasing to God.

Teaching is primary in a preacher's work. Instruction is so essential that it requires that a preacher be a clear thinking, hard-working theologian in both the doctrinal and practical components of theology.[19] In other words, a sermon should be intensely practical in its overall thrust providing no indication of the alleged dichotomy between the doctrinal and the practical. Such an assumed dichotomy is not only a false one, but:

> (I)t is a diabolical one. The same God-breathed Scripture which is profitable for doctrine is also profitable for reproof, correction and training in righteousness (2 Tim. 3:16). . . . (I)n that preaching, which is certainly doctrinal, there will be rebukes, exhortations, and instructions, (2 Tim. 4:2). It is obvious from Paul's words that he saw no disjunction between the doctrinal and practical. In

---

17. Alexander, *Thoughts on Preaching,* 1864, 195.

18. Spurgeon, *An All-round Ministry,* 1900, 117, italics in original.

19. Davis, *Evangelistic Preaching,* 1921, 25.

fact, the doctrinal is always the foundation for the practical. To put it another way, the indicatives of Scripture lead to the imperatives of Scripture.[20]

Scripture must be applied in such a way that it connects with what the hearers already know, yet, it must surpass this present knowledge to bring correction to what they are doing. Otherwise, it will be so remote from them that they will make no adjustments in their daily activities.

Preaching cannot be remote from life; it must make a vital connection with what the hearers think and do.[21] When the hearers have heard a competent expository sermon they should have been challenged, personally challenged, vigorously challenged, "and given a clear path of repentance, faith, and obedience," along with the means by which correction and obedience can become a reality.[22] There is no other element of a sermon that rivals the sermon conclusion in providing such a clear path for a new and better way of increased faithfulness and fruitfulness in the Christian life.

The mission of Jesus is to the whole life of man, for time and for eternity. He seeks to save men from sin that destroys their temporal lives as well as sin that will damn them for eternity. Yet, this dual mission of Christ is not reflected so commonly in preaching. The gospel message is an offer of new life to those who have yet to receive it, just as much as it is the basis of continuing new life for those who have received it.[23] Yet, based upon the evidence of preached sermons, it would appear that many preachers must believe that expounding a text of Scripture exempts them from the responsibility of proclaiming the message of the gospel, or, more probably, that expounding a portion of Scripture will suffice as having preached the gospel.

Though the purpose for a sermon is achieved in the "obedience of faith" (Romans 1:5), that is, by believers obeying the truth of Scripture in their daily activities of life,[24] this is not a possibility for those who are outside of the faith, who have no faith to which they may obey. Whatever is incumbent for a believer's compliance, according to the purpose of a given text of Scripture, is irrelevant to an unbeliever. The application of any text of Scripture for an unbeliever is never more than, never less than, never other than, their turning to Christ for salvation having repented from sin. The application of any text has not been made fully until it includes the never changing mandate for the sinner to repent of sin and trust in Christ alone for the gift of life that he alone offers. The earnest, practical application of biblical truth lies in the form of compelling believers to comply to the teaching of Scripture as well as compelling unbelievers to repent of their sins and trust in the person and work of Jesus Christ, alone, for their

---

20. Borgman, *My Heart for Thy Cause*, 138.

21. Davis, *Evangelistic Preaching*, 1921, 41.

22. Borgman, *My Heart for Thy Cause*, 139.

23. Davis, *Evangelistic Preaching*, 1921, 42.

24. Davis, *Evangelistic Preaching*, 1921, 43.

salvation. More attention to a gospel presentation as an element of a sermon conclusion will be provided in chapters eighteen through twenty of this book.

Application and Godliness

The great objective in preaching, with respect to Christians, "is to advance them in holy living and godliness."[25] The Apostle Peter makes it clear in 2 Peter 1:3–11 that God has provided all things pertaining to life and godliness, granting to us precious and magnificent promises, having become partakers of the divine nature in which we are to grow increasingly. Every sermon preached for the edification of believers should be a preacher's intentional act to be used by God to advance his purposes for his people's spiritual growth and godliness. The sermon conclusion becomes a preacher's choice opportunity to be used by God for his agenda in the lives of his people. You might disagree, thinking, "No, providing scriptural instruction is the choice opportunity to be used by God to accomplish his agenda in the lives of his people, not providing a sermon conclusion." And I would agree with this objection if a sermon conclusion were not laden with Scripture-based closing appeals, as it must be. The sermon conclusion for which I am advocating includes the most insightful, instructive scriptural references related to the purpose of the sermon for every sermon preached. Therefore, the sermon conclusion just like the expository sermon which it concludes, is laden with scriptural insight and understanding as the conclusion incorporates the choicest biblical references related to the purpose of the preaching text. In other words, *a sermon conclusion should be a biblical capstone to the sermon rather than a movement away from Scripture. More specifically, a sermon conclusion composed of Scripture-based closing appeals is a topical sermonette regarding the sermon's purpose that concludes an expository sermon.*

Application Is Prescribed Godliness

In his first lecture in the Lyman Beecher Lectures on Preaching, Henry Ward Beecher stated: "It seems to me that the highest conception of the sermon is, that it is a prescription for a certain state of things that the preacher knows to exist in the lives of people. A sermon is as much a matter of prescription as the physician's medicine is."[26] And just as a doctor must have certain knowledge of his patient before he would prescribe medication, so it is in preaching. A preacher must know people so well as to be able to bring correction to that which is errant, to equip his hearers with what they lack. In his third lectureship, Beecher implored: "Go to the inexhaustible armory of God, bring back and serve out to the people those armaments which shall make

25. Alexander, *Thoughts on Preaching*, 1864, 196.
26. Beecher, *Lectures on Preaching*, First Series, 1872, 18.

the weak strong, and the strong stronger."[27] The armory of God's Word certainly does not lack anything needed by which his people may receive correction from the error of their way and live lives of godliness. However, the question is, to what degree will God's people be equipped from the fully supplied armory of God's Word? The armory of God's Word exists in such abundance that it cannot be exhausted. However, in its unending supply it can go underutilized, if not unutilized. And the greatest incidence of the armory of God's Word being unutilized is in the sermon conclusion, the place in the sermon to which the armory of God's Word should never fail to be resorted.

SCRIPTURAL APPLICATION IN SERMON CONCLUSIONS

The Bible as the Divine Source to Meet All Men's Needs

Charles Haddon Spurgeon was a preacher who possessed not only a high view of Scripture but a productive view of preaching. His views of preaching and Scripture were brought together as he wrote: "Preach the gospel of our Lord and Savior, Jesus Christ, in all its length and breadth of doctrine, precept, spirit, example, and power. . . . For, the gospel was so divinely compounded as to meet all the evils of humanity, however they may differ from one another. We have only to preach the living gospel, and the whole of it, to meet the whole of the evils of the times."[28] How very insightful. The *living* gospel, the *whole* of it, are choice insights that speak to the matter of using the Bible as it was designed by God to be used.

Not to be limited to the sermon conclusion but most certainly in the sermon conclusion, selective inclusions from the whole of Scripture should be supplied to provide living truth, truth that answers tough questions and resolves difficult problems believers will have in living out God's Word in their lives. In the instance of a sermon conclusion, the selected Scriptures will answer tough questions and resolve difficult issues that are germane to the achievement of the sermon's purpose. As a preacher uses the Word of God, even in his sermon conclusion, he will be found making the most of his opportunity to preach the Word but, more specifically, he will be doing the most he can do to be helpful to God's people who hear him preach. "For it is within the Canon of the Old and New Testament Scriptures that God's present word for men is still to be found and heard. So the faithful steward of God-given revelation must preach the Scriptures, the whole Scriptures and nothing but the Scriptures."[29]

---

27. Beecher, *Lectures on Preaching*, Third Series, 1874, 142.
28. Spurgeon, *An All-round Ministry*, 1900, 104.
29. Stibbs, *Expounding God's Word*, 21.

Knowledge of Scripture in the Closing Appeals

The closing appeals of a sermon conclusion must be derived by understanding how the completed content of Scripture contributes to the sermon's purpose being achieved in the lives of hearers. From the entire canon of biblical revelation content can be amassed, <u>selectively</u>, to bring insights that are truly the wisdom of God to inform his people about the matter of productive and profitable conduct in life. A preacher's collective knowledge of Scripture is valuable when it comes to the closing appeals. However, regardless of the breadth and depth one may possess of scriptural matters, it is always beneficial to do thorough research to discover and/or be reminded of Scripture texts that may be even better than, that is, more precise and insightful than, the ones that readily come to mind. Certainly, the biblical texts that readily come to mind are not to be discounted. They will not be so readily known to some and they may still be the best insights within the completed canon of Scripture. Therefore, Spurgeon's exhortation is profitable as he writes: "Let us be thoroughly well acquainted with the great doctrines of the Word of God and let us be mighty in expounding the Scriptures. . . . For this purpose, you must understand the Word yourselves, and be able so to comment upon it that the people may be built up by the Word. Be masters of your Bibles, brethren."[30]

No one should doubt the connection between being a master of one's Bible and conducting, with accuracy and insight, the necessary work of expounding the Bible. Yet, mastery of one's Bible is just as critical in connecting non-preaching text references to one's preaching text to apply and illustrate the truths of the preaching text. But perhaps the greatest dividend of Bible mastery is found in the necessary work of citing the cross-references that contain the insights which will comprise the closing appeals by which the sermon's purpose may be achieved. As Brian Borgman points out, Scripture plays a strategic role in the application of biblical truth in the lives of believers:

> The inspired Word which is profitable for doctrine is also profitable for reproof, correction, and instruction in righteousness. But how does the inspired Word come to the hearts of men? It comes through preaching; serious and steady preaching. This preaching is to be characterized by reproof, rebuke, and exhortation. Each of these are strong applicatory terms. Therefore, preaching which is not applicatory is not biblical preaching because it is not commensurate with the stated biblical purposes for which Scripture was given. Application belongs to the essence of preaching.[31]

The conclusion, as the highpoint of the sermon, is fit like no other portion of the sermon for exposing the most vital insights from God's Word. These vital, scriptural

---

30. Spurgeon, *An All-round Ministry*, 1900, 36.
31. Borgman, *My Heart for Thy Cause*, 164.

insights form the closing appeals of the conclusion and become the means to achieve, most fully, the purpose of any preaching passage.

Obviously, one of the intentions God has for his Word is for his people to obey it. As we grow in the knowledge of God's Word, this increased knowledge should be demonstrated in lives that are increasingly compliant to the Word that is known better. Part of what it means to accrue an increasing knowledge of Scripture is to understand how other parts of God's Word are helpful in obeying the portion of Scripture that is preached. Increased knowledge of Scripture is not just a matter of knowing what was unknown, not just a matter of knowing what we are to do about what is now known, but an increased knowledge of Scripture is indicated by understanding how we are to do what we now know we are to do. Spurgeon presses the connection of pulpit responsibility with instructing God's people how to conduct their lives according to Scripture: "Fulfill the whole of your commission; 'teaching them,' says your Lord, 'to observe all things whatsoever I have commanded you.' Preach . . . the whole gospel as far as God has taught it to you."[32] As excellent as it is for a preacher to preach the whole gospel as it has been taught to him, it is better if he preaches the Bible *as he has discovered it beyond how it was preached to him.* In other words, to understand how to do what one knows to do is a valuable increase in the knowledge of Scripture, a knowledge that will be helpful for others to know when it is preached to them.

The sermon conclusion will always be about what believers are to do in order for the purpose of the sermon to be accomplished in their lives. Many times, the conclusion will be about how to do what is necessary for the sermon to be accomplished in life. Sometimes, the conclusion will provide a combination of what is to be done along with essential insights for how it is to be done. Whether the content of the closing appeals proceeds along the lines of what is to be done, or how it is to be done, or a combination of both, the Word of God provides the unrivaled content for the purpose of the sermon to be achieved most fully in the lives of God's people. The purpose of a preaching text will be achieved in the lives of the hearers as they comply with an accurate and insightful exposition of the preaching passage, that is, as the hearers comply their lives to an inductive handling of the preaching text, thus, living out the purpose of the preaching passage according to the truths contained in that passage. Moreover, the hearers will be challenged to comply with a deductive handling of the preaching text's purpose as they are challenged to comply their lives to specific related texts of Scripture, scriptural cross-references, related to the purpose of the preaching passage that provide significant ways and means which are vital for achieving the purpose of the sermon in the fullest possible manner. Therefore, achieving the purpose of the preaching passage in its fullest possible manner is based upon complying with the insights found in the preaching passage as well as insights drawn from the wider spectrum of the complete canon of Scripture.

32. Spurgeon, *An All-round Ministry*, 1900, 110.

Using Scripture to Make Application

One must study the Bible as a book for today, as a book of principles which are in operation now because this is the ultimate reality of God's Word.[33] Even as a preacher knows better, he must not handle Scripture like it is a book that does not significantly speak to the realities and circumstances of twenty-first century life. Of course, any legitimate understanding of how Scripture speaks to our day must be discerned through an understanding of how it addressed life for the original recipients. Having understood thoroughly well the intended meaning for the original readers of Scripture, the Scriptures can be found providing ample insight for life and godliness to the present day. In other words, one's aim should be to discover living principles because they are "universally true, eternally true, for all times, for all places, for all persons, whether they lived long ago in Palestine or Arabia, or whether they are living now in Connecticut or China."[34] It is only in this way that the Bible, and the truth it contains, is perceived by God's people as the unrivaled resource to instruct them for living in this fallen world in a way that God approves of, bringing him glory and honor, and providing him with true representation in this world.

The essential, timeless, principles of a text, which furnish the timely, practical teachings of Scripture, are seldom found on the surface of a text.[35] One must dig for them beneath the surface of Scripture as "the miner digs for the ore." In the attempt to find the principles, like a miner, one can extract some valuable material closely connected with what is sought but is less than what is being sought. But when timeless truths are discovered, they must be applied in a way that relates to one's hearers, in a way that they can understand and use in their present, personal, cultural circumstances.[36] Of course, the clarity and perceived usefulness of preached truth is enhanced when the content preached from the pulpit has been vetted through the process of the preacher's doing and living of that truth throughout the week, minimally, if not for years of previous practice of that truth in the preacher's life.[37]

It frequently happens that preachers go into the pulpit with truth that is not digested and with messages that have not matured. Their minds and hearts have not done their work thoroughly, and when they preach there is a good deal of "floating sediment in thought, and cloudiness of words" which impact the minds and hearts of the hearers with the force of a feather.[38] The sermon conclusion must be a proclamation

---

33. Greer, *The Preacher and His Place*, 1895, 145.

34. Greer, *The Preacher and His Place*, 1895, 147.

35. See my book, *How Effective Sermons Advance* for a complete treatment of principlization as it applies to the main structure of an expository sermon. The main points should be statements of theological principle, that is, a full sentence declaration of the truth of a specific portion of the preaching passage which reflects both its doctrine and its relevance.

36. Greer, *The Preacher and His Place*, 1895, 148–49.

37. Greer, *The Preacher and His Place*, 1895, 187.

38. Jowett, *The Preacher*, 1912, 130.

of truth that is vitally related to the lives of Christians, and thus, perceived as weighty and forceful by its hearers. It must relate to life where the relating is significant. In the process of uncovering the Word of God, the Word of God must uncover the preacher himself. The truth he preaches must be truth that exposed him in his daily life, truth that addressed his own circumstances, truth that reproved what was errant in thought and deed, truth that filled what was lacking in his character and conduct "as the in-flowing tide fills the bays and coves along the shore."[39] If the truth to be preached has no pressing urgency to the preacher himself, if it does no work in his own heart, if it offers no sweetened fellowship for his journey in life, "the sermon had best be laid aside."[40] In such an instance, the preacher has failed to understand the significance of the passage.

The fundamental needs of men are the same everywhere regardless of their vastly varied circumstances. And, yet, the recognized varying circumstances must be considered in making application of truth and/or in the framing of our closing appeals in the conclusion. A popular preacher of years past revealed the following as to his method by which his preaching was so serviceable to many people:

> I keep in the circle of my mind at least a dozen men and women, very varied in their natural temperaments, and very dissimilar in their daily circumstances. These are not mere abstractions. Neither are they dolls or dummies. They are real men and women whom I know. . . . When I am preparing my work, my mind is constantly glancing around this invisible circle, and I consider how I can so serve the bread of this particular truth as to provide welcome nutri-ment for all. . . . Our messages must be related to life, to lives, and we must make everybody feel that our key fits the lock of his own private door.[41]

No believer is excluded from the responsibility to live scriptural truth in his or her life. A preacher should help all believers to understand how biblical truth is applicable to them regardless of their varying circumstances.

Just as it is true that no believer is exempt from the necessity to live according to the truth of Scripture, it is equally true that no doctrine of Scripture is exempt from being relevant to living the Christian life. As was suggested earlier in this chapter, there are practical duties for every biblical doctrine and there is a doctrinal basis for every biblical practice. Without implying that the doctrinal bases for Christian conduct are sufficiently explained in present-day preaching, the practical duties of biblical doctrine are more prone to be slighted in preaching. Therefore, it is crucial to get a good, strong hold of doctrine at its "preaching end," to use the expression of Halford Luccock. There is a preaching end of every doctrine, in fact, many of them. If

---

39. Jowett, *The Preacher*, 1912, 135.

40. Jowett, *The Preacher*, 1912, 135.

41. Jowett, *The Preacher*, 1912, 136–37.

a preacher cannot understand the preaching end of a doctrine, one thing is certain, he does not have an essential understanding of that doctrine.[42]

In like manner, the sermon conclusion may demonstrate a preacher's lack of an essential understanding of how the purpose of the preaching text is to be achieved in life. If a preacher cannot lay hold of significant scriptural insights necessary to help believers to accomplish the purpose of the preaching text in their lives, then there is a deplorable cause and effect scenario operating in that preacher's preaching. The deplorable cause is the preacher's failure to productively search the Scriptures to discover the needed insights to assist his hearers to respond as they should. The deplorable effect is that he has failed to get at the most strategic "preaching end" of biblical truth for the most important component of the entire sermon—the sermon's purpose.

> That this cause and effect is truly deplorable is evident since God's Word is applicable to the present day. The nature of God and the nature of man assures the unending relevance of his Word. Because God is immutable in his nature and perfect in his works, his Word is just as valid today as in the moment it was inspired by the Spirit of God. And because the heart of man is the same as it was in the past, his timeless and timely Word may be brought to bear upon the lives of men now, as in the past. Divine truth contains a constant point of contact in, and provides guidance for, the lives of his people.[43] The point of contact of God's Word is personal and its guidance is perfect. These irrefutable realities must become apparent in preaching and they will become apparent in the pulpit if his Word is handled with wisdom and care in the study. The wise and careful handling of Scripture is obligatory to produce expository preaching since: The true expositor or expository preacher must "deliver the goods" at the door of men's circumstances and need. He must discover by God's help how to present and apply the biblical statements in such a way that they become the living, relevant, meaningful Word of God, to the present-day hearer. . . . Also, since the Bible preacher is the divinely-appointed "voice" to give the truth living utterance . . . to make the truth meaningful and urgent in relation to life, if he does not fall into proper line in his ministry, not only is the Word of God not heard, but men are compelled to listen to a disappointing counterfeit.[44]

The fruit of a wise and careful study of Scripture should be demonstrated throughout a sermon but especially so in the closing appeals of the sermon conclusion. As the sermon conclusion consists of Scripture-based closing appeals, God's people will be allowed to hear from God to the very end of the sermon. If, however, the sermon conclusion provides no closing appeals or closing appeals that are not based upon Scripture, the preacher will be stuck with the indefensible supposition

42. Luccock, *In the Minister's Workshop*, 55.

43. Reu, *Homiletics*, 1922, 361.

44. Stibbs, *Expounding God's Word*, 7, 13–14.

that God's purpose for the preaching passage has no practical ramifications for the lives of his people and this irrelevant purpose is attested to by the silence of the whole counsel of Scripture to provide relevant connections that speak to it. *Of course, this certainly is not the case! So, why should there be sermon conclusions that fail to appeal to God's people from the complete canon of Scripture, supplying choice insights in reference to the sermon's purpose being accomplished in the lives of God's people?*

Before considering the nature of indirect and direct closing appeals, let me clarify three presuppositions about the need for Scripture-based closing appeals in a sermon conclusion so that the conclusion may no longer be the Achilles' heel but rather the highpoint of the sermon.

First, <u>perpetuating the problem is never the solution to the problem</u>! The problem is this, sermons with no conclusions, or conclusions that exist but do so without Scripture-based closing appeals that will help the hearers to achieve the purpose of the sermon in their lives if they will comply with these closing appeals. To seek to do nothing about this perpetual and wide-spread problem is irresponsible. No good thing results from doing nothing about a problem. Sermons need Scripture-based closing appeals to allow the purpose of the sermon to be achieved, as fully as possible, in the lives of the hearers.

Second, achieving the purpose of the sermon is accomplished <u>most fully</u> from the aid of scriptural cross references. It must be understood that there is no inference being made that the content of the text is inadequate to accomplish its purpose. <u>That is not the case</u>! However, the prospect for the purpose of every text being accomplished in the lives of the hearers receives robust additional support from its connection to other passages of Scripture.

Third, it may appear as though providing Scripture-based closing appeals to accomplish, most fully, the purpose of the sermon in the sermon conclusion is similar to preaching a topical sermonette at the end of an expository sermon. This is no apparent reality; <u>it is the reality</u>. However, this sermonette comprising the sermon conclusion develops further, not the subject of the text/sermon, but the purpose of the text/sermon. Indirect and direct closing appeals based upon scriptural references from the complete revelation of Scripture provide insights beyond what any single preaching text can provide on its own.

SCRIPTURAL APPLICATION AS THE CLOSING APPEALS

Application as Direct Appeals

It is beneficial to understand the difference between direct closing appeals and indirect closing appeals in sermon conclusions. Unlike the indirect closing appeals composed of inferences, direct closing appeals being composed of exhortation, have very little of the didactic function in them. Because the direct closing appeals are hortatory, they may require the highest skill, in that, they must be preceded by textual exposition that is filled with rich instruction of a cognitively persuasive nature. With a rich cognitively persuasive base of instruction in a sermon that precedes the direct closing appeals of a conclusion, a preacher needs to state the most important exhortations needful for the purpose of the sermon to be accomplished in the lives of the hearers. However, in direct closing appeals it is crucial that a preacher do more than correct and compel but also provide counsel, consolation, and commencement in these closing appeals of strong exhortation. Each of the direct closing appeals, though exhortations, are the required means by which the purpose of the sermon can become a personal reality in the life of every hearer who complies with these direct appeals.[45]

Closing appeals in the form of direct address do not, like inferences, contribute to a substantially fuller development of the sermon's purpose as these are applied to the hearer. Direct address closing appeals are hortatory. Inferences are far more didactic. Inferences impart further information and additional insights in respect to the sermon's purpose, while they address the minds, wills, emotions/affections, and consciences of the hearers. The minor assertion of inferences is that certain things *are to be done*. The major assertion of inferences is in relation to *what is to be done*, and/or *how to go about doing* what is to be done, and/or *why we are to do* what is to be done, and/or *when we are to do and not do* what is to be done. Not so much, however, with the direct address.

Direct address emphasizes the things that are to be done or not done. Nuances related to procedure, sequence, manner, occasion, and motives may be part of the direct address statements, but the major assertion of direct address is *what certainly must be done or what certainly must not be done*. Consequently, a conclusion composed of direct address closing appeals, typically, is briefer than a conclusion composed of inferences. The exhortation of direct address closing appeals "cannot continue long. . . . If the vehemence of exhortation is too prolonged, it defeats itself. If exhortation goes beyond the proper limits, it not only fatigues, but disgusts" the hearers.[46]

Direct closing appeals more directly address the conscience than indirect closing appeals. Generally, direct closing appeals indicate the sense of what the hearers ought to do, or what they ought not do. Direct closing appeals are cast in the imperative mood. Therefore, direct closing appeals bear an echo of Mount Sinai about them.

In the conclusion, a preacher must make the most direct and forceful appeals to the conscience. They cannot be too clear nor too strong, even though they must not be too long. Duty is imperative—the duty of action. It is not understood well enough that, "One will never be a preacher who does not know how to get at the conscience."[47] Preaching must be directed to the intellect, to the will, to the emotions/

45. Hoyt, *The Work of Preaching*, 1905, 200.

46. Shedd, *Homiletics and Pastoral Theology*, 1876, 204–05.

47. Hoyt, *The Preacher*, reprinted, 1912, 232.

affections, and to the conscience, but it is in the battlefield of the conscience that the battle of preaching is won or lost.[48]

Direct Application and Persuasive Appeal

Application in the conclusion "includes, and often especially denotes, *persuasive appeal.* . . . It is very natural that conclusions should often consist of persuasion and entreaty. . . . Such matter must, if given anywhere, be most commonly put at the close . . . (where) it is desirable not merely to enlighten and convince but also to urge and to beseech."[49] Direct closing appeals, though not strongly didactic, are informative enough to enlighten and to convince while accomplishing their primary role to of urging and beseeching. Having been persuaded of the truth and the necessity of a certain duty, the hearer should then be instructed how to perform that duty and how to overcome the difficulties involved in performing it.[50]

Examples of Direct Closing Appeals in Sermon Conclusions

Perhaps some examples of direct closing appeals might prove helpful to understand and to get the feel for their imperatival, hortatory force and how they should be ordered in ascending fashion in a sermon conclusion. In the following examples, just the statements of direct address and the ascendency of the statements are depicted. The scriptural bases for, and the substantive content of, the closing appeals are not included.

1. **Closing Appeals of <u>Direct</u> Address—Purpose related to <u>honoring one's spouse</u>**

- Honor your spouse with words of personal affirmation!

- Honor your spouse by instances of public recognition!

- Honor your spouse by acts of personal service!

- Honor your spouse for his/her use of spiritual gifts in advancing Christ's Kingdom!

- Honor your spouse as a fellow believer in Jesus Christ!

2. **Closing Appeals of <u>Direct</u> Address—Purpose related to <u>blessing others</u>**

- Pray for opportunities to be a blessing to others!

- Be diligent to discern every opportunity to be a blessing to others!

- Be a blessing to others as well as you can in each instance!

48. Hoyt, *The Preacher,* reprinted, 1912, 233.
49. Broadus, *A Treatise on the Preparation and Delivery of Sermons,* 1870, 283–84.
50. Hoppin, *Homiletics,* 1883, 435.

3. **Closing Appeals of <u>Direct</u> Address—Purpose related to <u>evangelizing the lost</u>**

- Make evangelism a personal priority!

- Humble yourself before the eternal need of the lost person!

- Do not fail to present the gospel as Good News as you boast in Christ!

4. **Closing Appeals of <u>Direct</u> Address—Purpose related to <u>abstaining from evil</u>**

- Do not practice abomination by participating in any evil thing!

- Do not participate in that which appears evil!

- Do not commit evil by violating personal convictions or your conscience!

- Do not be deceived, evil brings detrimental consequences upon yourself and others!

The Value of the Closing Appeals to a Sermon Conclusion

The closing appeals of a sermon conclusion, either of indirect inferences or direct exhortations, are responsible in large measure for the sermon conclusion's importance. In the quote that follows, William G. T. Shedd addresses the importance of the sermon conclusion for a variety of reasons. In so doing, he attributes the qualities of "applicatory and hortatory" to a sermon conclusion without attempting to differentiate indirect and direct appeals by these terms. However, all that is stated is serviceable to introduce an appropriate understanding of a sermon conclusion so that this sermonic element can thrive in preaching today. According to Shedd:

> The conclusion is that part of the sermon which vigorously applies the truth. . . . As the introduction is conciliatory and explanatory, the conclusion is applicatory and hortatory. It should, therefore, be characterized by the utmost intensity, and energy. The highest vitality of the oration shows itself in the peroration (conclusion). The onset upon the hearer is at this point. If the man's will is ever carried, if this true effective eloquence is ever produced, it is the work of this part of the sermon.[51]

In fairness to Shedd, he was accurately writing about sermon conclusions as they should be prepared and preached. Unfortunately, the disparity between what should be done and what is done is immense.

Preachers would do well to prepare and preach conclusions that vigorously applies truth and carries the will of hearers. But this would require some things that are not associated with sermon conclusions in preaching as it is done in these days. First, sermon conclusions would have to exist, as opposed to being "missing in action" in

51. Shedd, *Homiletics and Pastoral Theology*, 1876, 196–97.

the battle of preaching. Second, conclusions would have to consist of substantial truth, scriptural truth, since Scripture is both relevant and capable of carrying man's will. Third, conclusions would have to be so vital in substance that it would exact from the preacher his greatest intensity and energy. Fourth, conclusions would have to contain substance that is so accurate and precise that it could direct people in how they are to respond to Scripture in a responsible way. Fifth, conclusions would have to represent the reality that the preacher is preaching for a verdict. That means correction in the lives of the hearers is not optional, they simply must comply. To fail to do so is nothing other than disobedience. In short, a Homiletical Great Awakening is needed regarding the work of concluding sermons, and present-day preachers need this awakening like no others who have gone before them.

Application as Indirect Appeals

The closing appeals of a sermon conclusion are either indirect appeals or direct appeals. In other words, the sermon may conclude, either by *inferences*, or by *direct address*.[52] Both types of closing appeals are directed to the hearers with substantial force, intention, significance, and exhortation. Whether an appeal is direct or indirect is based upon how the appeal's composition is arranged. Closing appeals in the nature of "indirect appeals" being composed of inferences, are referred to, commonly, in older homiletics books by such terms as "lessons" or "uses" or "remarks" or "suggestions." The inferences from which the indirect closing appeals are drawn "should be intensely practical" addressing primarily the conscience and the will through an unfolding of the practical aspects of a truth.[53] The inferences of the sermon conclusion should be those that are conclusive because they are directly related to the purpose of the sermon and its preaching text. As such these purpose related "corollaries" will not only be of practical significance, but they will also promote the dominant thrust of the sermon. Therefore, the text of Scripture from which the sermon was derived is provided crucial insights by which the sermon's purpose is to be accomplished in the hearers' lives.[54]

The Value of Inferential Application in the Conclusion

A sermon should have an inferential conclusion when the principal practical force of the purpose of the sermon is in the inferences from it. Inferences are logical deductions from the substance of a discussion. The real strength of the purpose of a sermon may lie in that which logically and scripturally follows from it. Sermonic purpose statements may make no great impression of themselves when they are stated in

52. Shedd, *Homiletics and Pastoral Theology*, 1876, 197.

53. Hoyt, *The Work of Preaching*, 1905, 199–200.

54. Dabney, *Sacred Rhetoric*, 1870, 172.

sermon introductions, but they do imply, and they will involve, certain truths that are significant and serious.[55] The significant and serious implications of the purpose statement become apparent as they are explicitly addressed in the sermon conclusion's closing appeals.

An accurate exposition of the preaching text prepares the way for the inferences of a sermon conclusion, contained in the closing appeals, to become the means by which the purpose of the sermon is achieved in an ultimate fashion. Through the means of these inferential closing appeals, the sermon's purpose is brought into a greater living contact with the emotions/affections and will of the hearer. By means of inferential closing appeals, the sermon's purpose may become increasingly "persuasive and influential" upon the minds, wills, emotions/affections, and consciences of the hearers.[56]

In the conclusion, application frequently takes the form of indirect closing appeals composed of inferences. So, let's establish four required criteria for the inferences that may make up the closing appeals of a sermon conclusion. First, the inferences that may compose the indirect closing appeals of a sermon conclusion must be legitimate. Legitimate inferences originate from the very heart and substance of any given subject-matter. If suggestions, lessons, uses, or remarks have no vital relationship or connection with the subject-matter of a sermon's purpose, they are not legitimate inferences. Legitimate inferences "are the inevitable offspring" of the purpose of a sermon. The inferences found in the closing appeals of a sermon conclusion must bear an actual and vital relationship to the sermon's purpose.[57] According to Broadus, "nothing should be presented as an inference which does not logically and directly follow from the subject discussed."[58] Though Broadus's statement is true, it requires amendment for it to be optimally insightful. Nothing should be presented as an inference for the sermon conclusion which does not logically and directly follow from the subject discussed *and does not clarify for the hearer what they must do or not do in order for them to respond in a way that achieves the purpose of the sermon in their lives.* A logical connection to the subject, though mandatory, is not the ultimate consideration of legitimate inferences for their usage in the closing appeals of a sermon conclusion.

Certainly, in the conclusion of a sermon all that is discussed should not be a logical departure from the subject-matter of the sermon. Moreover, all that is discussed must be related to the purpose of the sermon, specifically, yet still related to the subject-matter of the sermon, generally. *What is discussed in the conclusion is not intended to advance the understanding of the passage but to advance the needed response of the hearers to the purpose of the passage.* The conclusion of the sermon helps the hearers

---

55. Shedd, *Homiletics and Pastoral Theology,* 1876, 198.

56. Shedd, *Homiletics and Pastoral Theology,* 1876, 199–200.

57. Etter, *The Preacher and His Sermon,* 1885, 373.

58. Broadus, *A Treatise on the Preparation and Delivery of Sermons,* 1870, 281.

understand what they need to do in light of their understanding of the text so that the purpose of the text can be accomplished in their lives.

Of course, the inferences composing the closing appeals of the conclusion, if legitimate, must not only *relate* to the purpose of the sermon but *contribute* to that purpose being achieved in the lives of the hearers. As this is the case, they are legitimate inferences of the purpose of the preaching text, and as such, they reveal the relationship of the preaching text's purpose to this same purpose, or corollaries of it, found in other texts of Scripture.[59] Great care must be given to make certain that the purpose of the scriptural references used to establish the substance of the closing appeals are accurately understood by the preacher and that their inclusion will provide an actual contribution to achieving the purpose of the preaching text. Jay Adams provides this critical warning for the correct use of Scripture by a biblical preacher or counselor:

> [He] must know the purpose of the passage; that is, he must know what God intended to do to the reader (warn, encourage, motivate, etc.) with those words. Then, he must make God's purpose his own in the application of the passage to human needs. But to do this he must develop an exegetical conscience by which he determines never to use a passage for any purpose other than that purpose, or those purposes for which God gave it (often, of course, there are sub *tele* involved in a larger telic unit). This determination will make him faithful not only as an interpreter, but also in his *use* of the Scriptures.[60]

Second, the inferences <u>must be practical</u>. The principal design of an inference is to deduce the "practical matter" out of a given discussion. That means the inferences will relate to the great duties of life and the vital interests of the hearers, things which the purpose of the sermon will not fail to target.[61] However, it is not enough that they are practical. "They should be *intensely practical*." The inferences of the closing appeals should address the whole of man's nature—the mind, will, emotions/affections, and conscience. If the address is done in the most vivid and vital manner possible, it will be due to legitimate inferences related to the sermon's purpose, revealing its vital, practical significance in the lives of the hearers.[62]

Perhaps the most intensely practical form of indirect closing appeal is that which suggests the ways and means for doing what is to be done so that the sermon's purpose may be achieved in the life of a believer. In this type of application in the conclusion, the ways and means consist of suggestions. The term "suggestions" sounds rather tame. On the contrary, suggestions comprise the product of a careful search of Scripture to discover the most important practical means by which the sermon's purpose can be accomplished most fully in the lives of believers. Suggestions are, in fact, inferences

---

59. Shedd, *Homiletics and Pastoral Theology*, 1876, 201.

60. Adams, *The Use of the Scriptures in Counseling*, 26.

61. Etter, *The Preacher and His Sermon*, 1885, 374.

62. Shedd, *Homiletics and Pastoral Theology*, 1876, 202.

that provide the means and methods of practically performing some duty to be done. It is extremely appropriate to end with practical suggestions which provide insight as to how truth may be obeyed in life, thus achieving the sermon's purpose. Many duties of the Christian life are deemed commonly by Christians as that with which they are not able to comply. In such instances, "the most effective application" is to suggest how the duties may be practiced in one's life.[63]

Third, the inferences must be forceful. This means, first, that they should not represent all the inferences that could be drawn, but the best. It is better that they be few, though significantly beneficial, rather than many and, seemingly, "trifling." An all-inclusive compilation of inferences is destructive to a forceful conclusion. This means, second, that inferences gather force by being "homogeneous" and progressing. Inferences are intensified by their obvious relatedness and they acquire an increasing forcefulness by an arrangement of ascending importance.[64]

Fourth, the inferences must establish a cumulative culmination, in that, "the strongest inference should be the last inference." When a conclusion consists of inferences, these should be so arranged as "to move with a more and more irresistible force" and greater significance.[65] That which is necessary in a sermon conclusion, including inferences, is that the conclusion's substance appeals to the consciences, emotions/affections, and the wills of the hearers. For this to be the case, each inference, from the first to the last, "must increase in weight, heat, and life," to make the greatest impression at the close.[66] James Stewart writes: "Aim at a cumulative effect. Keep your most telling points to the last. . . . Never forget you are working for a verdict. You are hoping and praying to leave your people face to face with God in Christ. That goal must never fade from sight. Make the whole sermon an ascent thither. Construct it with that end in view. Fashion it with that deliberate design."[67] The final closing appeal should end with the most impressive statement possible not only to provide the greatest strength to the final closing appeal but to end the sermon to believers with significant force and weighty impression.

The Result of a Sermon Conclusion's Closing Appeals upon the Hearers

Forcefulness and decisiveness should characterize a sermon conclusion, bringing all the appeals of the conclusion into a single burning focus so that the appeals converge upon the hearer's soul "where the feelings and the conscience come together," where the emotions/affections are roused, and the conscience is stirred.[68] The stirring of the

63. Broadus, *A Treatise on the Preparation and Delivery of Sermons*, 1870, 283.

64. Etter, *The Preacher and His Sermon*, 1885, 374.

65. Shedd, *Homiletics and Pastoral Theology*, 1876, 202–3.

66. Broadus, *A Treatise on the Preparation and Delivery of Sermons*, 1870, 282.

67. Stewart, *Heralds of God*, 135.

68. Shedd, *Homiletics and Pastoral Theology*, 1876, 208.

conscience should be about a present lack of compliance to the closing appeals for which the preacher is pressing in his conclusion. The conscience, once stirred, may not be at ease until there has been a commitment to conform to the instruction of the Word of God which has been so forcefully and decisively provided in the sermon conclusion.

It is important that a sermon ends impressively, that is, it should leave upon the hearers' consciences a clear and powerful impression of a practical result that is to become a personal reality in their lives. Those who are exposed to preaching often have long periods of time to intervene before they can specifically apply what they've heard in the sermon. It's impression, therefore, upon their memory and their conscience must be definite and lasting. It is true that a sermon without application is almost worthless but, even more so, it is true that application must have a dominant presence in the conclusion, and it must be there in impressive force.[69]

In the conclusion, all application whether by direct closing appeals of exhortation, or indirect closing appeals composed from legitimate inferences contained in the form of lessons, remarks, uses, or suggestions, should be of high value material that will captivate the conscience and will of the hearer. Most preachers are better in every other process of sermonizing than in that of applying truth to its *practical uses in the sermon conclusion*. They may explain clearly, prove adequately, illustrate vividly, draw implications accurately; but not apply truth insightfully where it is needed most in the sermon, the conclusion. This represents a significant challenge to preachers since the conclusion should be the highpoint of the sermon, composed of the most valuable insights of a personal and practical nature, existing to provide practical aid to the hearers in the closing thoughts and last words of a sermon.[70]

A good conclusion is needed to enforce the moral impression of the whole sermon and thus achieve the purpose of the sermon in the lives of the hearers. Some hearers in a congregation will make appropriate personal application of the sermon for themselves. But that does not nullify a preacher's responsibility to everyone who hears him preach the message as to what must be done to respond to the sermon in a way that achieves the purpose for which it was preached. The preacher must supply the most substantial application of the sermon, by means of the closing appeals of the conclusion, to the consciences, emotions/affections, and wills of his hearers. And this includes those who will derive their own application for themselves from the sermon which was preached. Even in such instances, it is certain that the closing appeals put forward by the preacher will be other than, if not better than, the applications derived by some hearers.[71]

69. Kidder, *A Treatise on Homiletics*, 1864, 222.

70. Etter, *The Preacher and His Sermon*, 1885, 375.

71. Hoppin, *Homiletics*, 1883, 429.

In reference to inferences in a sermon conclusion, there should be weight and wisdom in them for daily living.[72] When the application found in a sermon conclusion is in the form of inferences, the hearers may be persuaded to take specific actions which are legitimate, wise, practical, and valuable because the inferences are associated soundly with the purpose of the sermon.

The conclusion will, for the most part, consist of application and exhortation, application which the hearers will be exhorted strongly to comply with in their lives. Exhortation predominantly appeals to the conscience and to the will so that the hearers might do what they are being directed to do. Application in a sermon conclusion is to be understood along the lines of four considerations. First, the application in a sermon conclusion will be "application proper." More will be said about this in the following paragraphs. Second, the application in a sermon conclusion may be of suggestions for practical guidance (indirect appeals). Third, the application in a sermon conclusion may be of persuasive (direct) appeals of exhortation. Fourth, the application in a sermon conclusion may include a combination of direct and indirect appeals.

Sermonic application, in a general sense, is the application found in the body of a sermon. This kind of application shows how the truth of the preaching passage "relates to the persons addressed, or what practical instructions it offers them, or what practical demands it makes upon them."[73] Thus, general application, the applications found in the body of the sermon, are really the implications of a truth for the hearers of specific portions of the preaching text.

At this point, I believe a distinction might be helpful regarding the general concept of "application" in a sermon. The distinction between "application" in the body of the sermon, and the "application" in a sermon conclusion, is primarily related to the "*direction of relevance*," the "*nature of relevance*," and the "*referent of relevance*" regarding the application.

The application in the body of a sermon is in the <u>direction</u> "*from the text to the hearer*"—codifying how a given truth of a specific portion of Scripture relates to the hearer. The application in the body of a sermon is in <u>nature</u> of "*an implication*." The focus is about how this truth relates to the hearer, indicating what are the implications of this truth in the life of the hearer. The application in the body of a sermon is in <u>reference</u> to "*a specific portion of the preaching text and, therefore, a specific preaching point of the text*."

However, the application in the sermon conclusion is in the <u>direction</u> "*of the hearer to the purpose of the sermon*"—codifying how the hearer relates to the purpose of the entire text/the purpose of the text and the sermon. Additionally, the application in the sermon conclusion is in the <u>nature</u> of "*application proper*," indicating what things are required of the hearer, indicating what is the responsibility of the hearer, indicating what are the things a hearer must do/not do in order for one to be living

72. Hoppin, *Homiletics*, 1883, 434.

73. Stanfield, *On the Preparation and Delivery of Sermons*, 167.

in a way that is true to God's purpose for this text, so that God's purpose for the text is being achieved in one's life. In the application proper of the sermon conclusion, the focus is about how the hearer is to relate to that which is God's purpose. Finally, the application in the sermon conclusion is in <u>reference</u> to "*the totality of Scripture.*" Because the purpose of the preaching text will share this purpose, or a portion of it, or a corollary of it, with other texts in Scripture, various texts can be cited to provide needed insights as to how the hearers of the sermon can accomplish the purpose of the sermon in their lives.

Sometimes application in a sermon conclusion is found in the form of indirect closing appeals called "remarks" meaning that attention will be given to certain noticeable matters associated with the subject-matter of the sermon's purpose. Application in a sermon conclusion composed of remarks require a great deal of caution, in that, when concluding a sermon with remarks, they must be "of a very practical nature" and not digress into additional commentary on the preaching text rather than dealing with the purpose of the sermon.[74] A sermon "should not end without aiming to bring about some practical result, some corresponding determination of the will, state of affections, or course of action" in the lives of the hearers.[75] A sermon conclusion composed of closing appeals in the form of "remarks" runs a risk of not accomplishing what a conclusion is intended to accomplish.

At times, the content found in a sermon conclusion is inappropriate as it consists of thoughts loosely connected with the preaching text, leftovers for which no place was found for discussion when preaching the text. Such inappropriate content in the conclusion produces a scattering in the thought process of the hearers where there ought to be concentration of focus. Additionally, the hearers are caused to consider further treatment of the text rather than being directed to the purpose of the sermon which, in the conclusion, they must focus upon and be drawn into close personal contact.[76] When a sermon conclusion focuses upon the purpose of the sermon, as it should, the leftover material that never found its way into the body of the sermon, being only tangentially related to the text and subject of the sermon, could never qualify as sermon conclusion material because it is not related to the purpose of the sermon. Furthermore, such material lacking a vital connection to the text could never be the highpoint of the sermon, which the sermon conclusion ought to be.

For the sake of clarity, an example of a direct versus an indirect appeal might be helpful. The closing appeal is intended to convey the same basic truth, but the direct versus the indirect form of expressing the same truth provides noticeable distinction. An example of <u>a direct closing appeal would be</u>: "Do not fail to speak the gospel to unbelievers when given an opportunity to do so!" An example of <u>an indirect closing appeal would be</u>: "When given an opportunity to speak the gospel to an unbeliever

---

74. Broadus, *A Treatise on the Preparation and Delivery of Sermons*, 1870, 279–80.

75. Broadus, *A Treatise on the Preparation and Delivery of Sermons*, 1870, 280.

76. Broadus, *A Treatise on the Preparation and Delivery of Sermons*, 1870, 280.

you may, for many reasons, fail to do so." The inference contained in the indirect appeal is in reference to the reasons why a believer may fail to, or fall short of, proclaiming the gospel to unbelievers. As with direct closing appeals, each of the indirect closing appeals is a required means by which the purpose of the sermon can become a personal reality in the life of every hearer who complies with these indirect appeals.

Indirect closing appeals often implicitly intend the meaning of, if not explicitly incorporate, phrases such as: "Unless you . . . ; It is necessary that you . . . ;" "If you . . . then you . . . ;" "In order for you to . . ." However, these forms of expression are not used in all indirect closing appeals.[77] The example of the indirect closing appeal in the preceding paragraph did not use any of these expressions. Direct closing appeals may use expressions such as: "You must . . . ; You cannot . . . ; Do not . . . ; Never . . ." Again, such expressions are not mandatory for direct appeals, though the direct appeal in the preceding paragraph did use the "Do not . . ." form of expression.

Examples of Indirect Closing Appeals in Sermon Conclusions

Perhaps some examples of indirect closing appeals might prove helpful to understand and to get the feel for their inferential, instructional force and how they should be ordered in ascending fashion in a sermon conclusion. In the following examples, just the statements of indirect address and the ascendency of the statements are depicted. The scriptural bases for, and the substantive content of, the closing appeals are not included.

1. **Closing Appeals of <u>Indirect</u> Address—Purpose related to <u>good stewardship</u>**

- Good stewardship is predicated on the lordship of Jesus Christ in your life.
- It is necessary to realize that possessions are the substance of your stewardship.
- Stewardship is a test that lasts throughout your lifetime.
- No believer, including you, is outside of the possibility of being a good steward.

2. **Closing Appeals of <u>Indirect</u> Address—Purpose related to <u>turning from pride</u>**

- Pride causes you to not walk in the fear of the Lord.
- Your pride will guarantee God's hand of discipline on your life.
- Unless you turn from your pride, you will continue to sacrifice God's fellowship in your life.

3. **Closing Appeals of <u>Indirect</u> Address—Purpose related to <u>walking in truth</u>**

- You must love the truth in order to speak it and live it faithfully in your life.

77. Hoyt, *The Work of Preaching*, 1905, 201.

- Lies, deceptions, falsehoods are the essence of betraying God in your life.

- Truth is a belt that girds you and enables you to stand, resisting evil in your days.

4. **Closing Appeals of <u>Indirect</u> Address—Purpose related to <u>being Spirit-filled</u>**

- Only when Spirit-filled will you Joyously boast in the Lord.

- Only when Spirit-filled will you Zealously protect the purity of the church.

- Only when Spirit-filled will you Boldly proclaim unwelcomed truths.

- Only when Spirit-filled will you Wholeheartedly accept what God provides.

Examples of Indirect and Direct Closing Appeals in Sermon Conclusions

Some examples of how indirect closing appeals and direct closing appeals can work together in the same sermon conclusion, showing how the inferential, instructional insights of the indirect appeals complement the imperatival, hortatory force of the direct closing appeals. The appeals are ordered in ascending fashion in each sermon conclusion. The scriptural bases for, and the substantive content of, the closing appeals are not included. The direct closing appeals are underlined.

1. **Closing Appeals of <u>Indirect and Direct</u> Address—Purpose related to <u>pleasing God</u>**

- Unless you are in submission to the Holy Spirit you cannot be pleasing to God.

- Living to please God, will, at times, put you at odds with others—believers and unbelievers.

- Living a life that is pleasing to God does not insolate you from difficulties.

- <u>Not desiring to please God is a sin that you must repent from</u>!

2. **Closing Appeals of <u>Indirect and Direct</u> Address—Purpose related to <u>submitting to authority</u>**

- Your submission to authorities is God's will.

- Your submission to authorities pleases God.

- <u>You Must submit to authorities even if they are ungodly individuals!</u>

- <u>Never submit to authorities who require you to violate Scripture</u>!

3. **Closing Appeals of <u>Indirect and Direct</u> Address—Purpose related to <u>possessing God's peace</u>**

- God's peace is provided by the Holy Spirit of God.

- God's peace is forfeited by walking in the flesh.

- God's peace is possessed by praying about everything and worrying about nothing.

- <u>You must covet and treasure God's peace in your life!</u>

4. **Closing Appeals of <u>Indirect and Direct</u> Address—Purpose related to <u>forgiving others</u>**

- <u>Become adept at forgiving others, for this is your calling!</u>

- Forgiving others is not to be done based upon your personal convenience.

- Forgiving others allows you to be much like your Heavenly Father.

- The guilty do not need to be forgiven as much as you need to forgive.

- Having forgiven another, have no expectations for the forgiven one to meet.

- <u>Never withhold forgiveness from others since you have been forgiven by Christ!</u>

Direct and Indirect Appeals Made to Believers First

James Hoppin provided an axiom which I find advantageous to follow in a sermon conclusion. As one follows through with the intention to address both believers and unbelievers in a sermon conclusion, Hoppin's instruction is helpful to maintain clarity of content, intentionality of purpose, and order of procedure in concluding a sermon when he wrote: "In persuasion we should address those first who are most favorably disposed, and therefore, we should address the converted before the unconverted."[78] However, many will find favor with Daniel P. Kidder's caution, and find it especially relevant, in considering when and how to deal with the need of unbelievers while one is preaching for the edification of believers in an expository sermon. Kidder writes, "*A good motto*" with respect to the various subjects in the practice of preaching is, "*be guided by rules, but not bound by them.*"[79]

Some find it unacceptable to wait to the end of the sermon conclusion to address the lost person's need for salvation. I would agree that, if this is how they think that it is best to proceed, they should do so most definitely and not be bound by a rule to address unbelievers after believers have been addressed fully in a sermon conclusion. As long as a preacher declares the gospel message so that unbelievers may have the opportunity to respond to Christ as their Lord and Savior, that is, by declaring the person of Christ, the work of Christ, and the biblically mandated response for unbelievers to repent and to trust in Christ, alone, for their salvation, the preacher has ministered to the lost effectively, no matter where in the sermon the message of the gospel was declared. Hopefully, however, the rule that the conclusion is to be the

78. Hoppin, *Homiletics*, 1883, 435.
79. Kidder, *A Treatise on Homiletics*, 1864, 221.

highpoint of the sermon is one rule that will find every preacher intensely striving to obey in his preaching!

Preaching in such a manner that the conclusion is the actual highpoint of the sermon is not some high-sounding notion that preachers might want to attempt if they are concerned about being some kind of "artiste" in their preaching endeavor. Such a mindset cannot begin to ascertain the importance of a sermon conclusion. The matter is simply this—to culminate a message so effectively that believers as well as unbelievers receive the most personally compelling content of the entire sermon in its latter minutes. The sermon conclusion is all about the need to send the hearers away with the highest, weightiest, relevant insights of the sermon ringing in their ears, weighing on their hearts, convicting their consciences, empowering their affections, and compelling their wills. The sermon conclusion is all about making sure the hearers leave with a changed agenda for how they are to live the rest of their days.

Haddon Robinson expressed this need of a sermon conclusion very well in an "Expositape" recording I heard decades ago. Robinson had a friend who owned a restaurant in New York City. In a time of recession, Robinson's friend told him about all the measures he had to enact to remain profitable during the very lean financial times. The restaurateur told him, "But there is one thing I will never cut back on—the after-dinner coffee. That is the taste they leave with! That's the taste that determines what they will do, whether they will come back, or not!" The conclusion as the highpoint of the sermon is not a high-sounding notion! It's "the after-dinner coffee!" A sermon conclusion must be offered as such and it must never be cut back on!

How may the "after-dinner coffee" of the sermon conclusion be offered and, yet, be offered in a "cut back on" manner at the same time? The degree to which the hearers are offered a conclusion which lacks in significant personal relevance determines the degree to which the offering was "cut back on." If the highpoint of the sermon is due to the closing appeals of the sermon conclusion, then the closing appeals cannot lack in significant personal relevance!

Significant, personally relevant preaching found in a sermon conclusion will be the subject-matter of the next two chapters. Such preaching is indicative of a preaching pastor. We will understand fully that there is nothing like the sermon conclusion that differentiates the preaching of this kind of preacher.

13

A Preaching Pastor's Personal Relevance in a Sermon Conclusion: Part 1

"What must be experienced in the arena of expository preaching is the relevant preaching of a preaching pastor. The preaching of a preaching pastor is never less than an accurate articulation of theological truth but is always more than just that. The preaching of a preaching pastor goes beyond the foundation that accurate theology provides to establish the relevance of accurate theology in daily living."

"Without a careful processing of a text of Scripture, there is nothing to expound, there is nothing in the way of relevance that can be said. Without an earnest commitment to accurately expound a preaching text there is no reason a man should enter the pulpit in the first place. . . . The problems of the pew deserve consideration only as the Word of God has been explained carefully and thoroughly. Then the problems of the pew must be addressed by the Word of God which provides real solutions to real problems. The attempt to be relevant in preaching is folly if relevance is not the derivative of God's Word being accurately explained and well understood. But when Scripture has been explained with precision and clarity, the relevance of scriptural truth must not be omitted from preaching. Preaching is predicated upon a theological understanding and a practical bearing of Scripture being provided to God's people. It is the theological understanding of Scripture and the understanding of its practical implications that qualifies talking in a pulpit to be the preaching of God's Word."

"The preaching of a preaching pastor, though expository, does not fall victim to that kind of preaching that parades as expository preaching but is not. The counterfeit version of expository preaching is exhibited by preachers who are committed to faithfully explain Scripture 'but are so buried in the text that they are completely divorced from the culture to which they have been called to preach' and thus provide a

preaching that is 'lifeless, dull, and even thoroughly boring.' . . . The preaching pastor, because he is a responsible shepherd, is concerned not only with what God's people understand as correct doctrine but the relevance of correct doctrine which establishes correct conduct for their living out God's Word in life."

"Nothing is more relevant than clear, Scripture-based instruction indicating how God's people can live according to his Word as they humble themselves in glad-hearted submission to their Lord. Nothing should be more prolific in a sermon conclusion than the ways and means by which glad-hearted submission to the Lord can be demonstrated in the lives of his people as they comply their lives with the purpose of the sermon."

"The exhortations of the sermon conclusion's closing appeals become the means by which the verdict, for which a preaching pastor is preaching, can become a reality. This much is certain: no exhortations tendered; no verdict rendered! A tendering of no exhortation is indicative that a preacher is in the pulpit simply to inform his hearers of biblical truth. The weakness of, or the lack of, a sermon conclusion gives testimony of this limited version of preaching in which the hearers are denied a sermon conclusion that will bring them to a verdict. If there is no verdict for which a preacher is preaching, there will be no exhortations composed of direct closing appeals nor will there be any indirect closing appeals in the form of inferences through which the lives of believers are afforded practical instructions by which they can achieve the purpose of the sermon in their lives."

"It is necessary that a preaching pastor exercise every effort, not just to bring his hearers to an unavoidable response, but a response that will win a verdict from them to comply their lives to the necessary provisions of biblical truth so that the purpose of the sermon may be achieved in their daily living. But, a necessary response? Why is it necessary to make a response to the sermon an unavoidable reality? Very many preachers preach without requiring any response to the sermon. This is true of preachers who are not preaching pastors!"

"Preachers who are not preaching pastors have given themselves a freedom by which they clearly make known the meaning of Scripture by means of careful explanation of a text, along with its implications for the lives of his hearers. But when they get to the end of the preaching text, the sermon is done and ministry to their hearers is done. The help they are willing to provide their hearers is to help them understand the text and its implications, and that is it. In other words, the commitment is to help them to know. To help the hearers to respond and help them understand what that response entails is help they are unwilling to provide. The help that is provided falls short of helping the hearers to do, to be about achieving the purpose for the text they now understand. These preachers understand the care they are to provide for their hearers is limited to a cognitive service. But if it is important for them to live the

truth, should not a preacher be concerned about this as well. Even if this is viewed as a 'second mile' service, shouldn't he be willing to provide it?"

"A preaching pastor, in his sermon conclusion, will compel his hearers to respond to the closing appeals. The closing appeals will not be offered for their musing. The closing appeals will be put forward as that which must be done."

"The ministry of a preaching pastor's preaching is more than a service to help his hearers die with of greater knowledge of the Word. A preaching pastor is concerned that they live the Word as well as they can before they die."

"For a sermon to end by putting forth peripheral ambiguities is insulting. It suggests that the lives of God's people are not important enough to a preacher to command the time and effort necessary for him to provide them with helpful, practicable insights for living. This, of course, is an indictment upon the preacher's character and work ethic as it indicates that he neither cares to provide them with the help they need, nor will he require of himself the time and effort to provide it to them."

"A sermon that ends with closing appeals that are nominal or ambiguous is effectively without application, which is like a cadaver, a body without a soul. But, even more to the point, a sermon conclusion without accurate, insightful, biblical application through the means of closing appeals, is like a car without brakes; it will come to an end, but it will do so quite unproductively and unsatisfyingly."

A PREACHER, OR A PREACHING PASTOR? THE CONCLUSION DECIDES!

The first two chapters of this book considered the sermon conclusion and *preachers.* Chapters three and four considered the sermon conclusion and *preaching.* It was established in chapters one and two that the essence of the sermon conclusion regarding preachers was that the sermon conclusion defines, most definitively, whether the man preaching the sermon is, or is not, a true pastor. It was established in chapters three and four that the essence of the sermon conclusion and preaching was that the sermon conclusion provides a true pastor, especially, the unique opportunity to engage his greatest earnestness and passion in preaching the sermon. The combination of those four chapters asserted that the true pastor, seizing the opportunity to fully tend God's sheep, would be found in the sermon conclusion preaching most earnestly to his hearers for the all-important reason why any sermon is to be preached—for life-change, a change that will effect greater compliance to God's Word in the lives of the hearers. Chapters nine through eleven established that the essence of the sermon conclusion, the closing appeals, are responsible for the conclusion being what it should be—the highpoint of the sermon. Additionally, in chapter twelve it was argued that the closing appeals, whether of a direct or indirect nature, are application proper, that is, the closing appeals spell out how the hearers must conduct themselves to achieve the purpose of the sermon in their lives.

This chapter and chapter 14 will bring together chapters one through four with chapters nine through twelve to develop more fully what was implicit in those chapters, namely, that the true pastor is not just a preacher but a preaching pastor. He is a pastor that truly is a preacher and a preacher that truly is a pastor. This is so because his preaching is marked by significant personal relevance in the closing appeals of the sermon conclusion.

The concept of relevant closing appeals cannot be overlooked, assumed to be understood, or taken for granted as a "given" for effective preaching. We must explore this concept which is so instrumental for a preaching pastor and for all who hear him. Because of the kind of man that he is, the preaching pastor's preaching will be marked by the inescapable quality of relevance in his preaching as demonstrated in the closing appeals of his sermon conclusion. This quality of his preaching will not be the only significant characteristic of his preaching. Furthermore, the relevance of his preaching may not be the most pronounced characteristic of his preaching. However, the relevance of his preaching will be a part of his preaching, it will be present in abundant measure, *and it will be the chief characteristic of his sermon conclusions*. It simply cannot be missed. Additionally, because his preaching is indicative of the kind of man and pastor that he is, his preaching will be marked by relevance consistently, not occasionally, in his sermon conclusions.

A PREACHING PASTOR HAS AN APPETITE FOR DOCTRINE AND THEOLOGY

We must understand biblical doctrine and theology in order to understand the basic truths of Scripture and how they impact mankind. Every expository preacher is a theologian, good or bad. In expository preaching a preacher will be unfolding the doctrinal truths of his preaching text. This he must do since every sermon that explains a biblical text will be establishing doctrinal truth. If a sermon does not unfold doctrine, if it does not "explain a tenant of the faith, it is not a biblical sermon."[1] John Piper has wisely captured the important result of any tenant of theology when he writes: "Theology exists for doxology."[2] Every doctrine, once understood correctly, reflects the praiseworthiness of God.

But, just as doctrine provides theological understanding, doctrine also bears implicit personal and practical responsibilities. And just as doctrine rightly understood affords the opportunity to praise God with our lips, it also requires us to praise God with our lives through a responsible stewardship of the doctrinal truths we understand

1. Montoya, *Preaching with Passion*, 47.
2. Piper, *The Supremacy of God in Preaching*, 66.

correctly, being borne out by lives that are lived according to the truth of Scripture. So, just as every expository preacher is a theologian, good or bad, every expository preacher is a relevant preacher, good or bad. The relevance of his preaching is not a moot point, it is not a minor concern, it is not a consideration that can be dismissed.

The relevance of a preacher's preaching is a vital consideration of his preaching just as the correctness of his theology is a vital consideration of his preaching. Admittedly, correctness of theology is of greater significance than the practical response to theology, but both are indisputably important. What must be demonstrated in preaching is accurate theology as the foundation for a practical bearing of doctrinal truth in the lives of believers. In other words, what must be experienced in the arena of expository preaching is the relevant preaching of a preaching pastor. The preaching of a preaching pastor is never less than an accurate articulation of theological truth but is always more than just that. The preaching of a preaching pastor goes beyond the foundation that accurate theology provides to establish the relevance of accurate theology in daily living.

I want to be clear that I am talking about accurate theology first and foremost. Without a careful processing of a text of Scripture, there is nothing to expound, there is nothing in the way of relevance that can be said. Without an earnest commitment to accurately expound a preaching text there is no reason a man should enter the pulpit in the first place. Yet, we must be realistic enough to know that this is not a universal commitment for all who enter the pulpit. But, from the frame of reference of a preaching pastor's preaching of God's Word to God's people, "To miss the point of a passage because we have decided that what we want to say is more important than what God has to say is sinful."[3] This is just how it is, and this will never change. Alistair Begg indicates the error of bypassing Scripture to speak relevantly when he writes:

> Much of what now emanates from contemporary pulpits would not have been recognized by either Alexander or Baxter or Sangster as being anywhere close to the kind of expository preaching that is Bible-based, Christ focused, and life-changing—the kind of preaching that is marked by doctrinal clarity, a sense of gravity, a convincing argument. We have instead become far too familiar with preaching that pays scant attention to the Bible, is self-focused, and consequently is capable of only the most superficial impact upon the lives of listeners. Worse still, large sections of the church are oblivious to the fact that they are being administered a placebo rather than the medicine they need. . . . In the absence of bread, the population grows accustomed to cake![4]

One must never fall victim to the disastrous presuppositions of liberal theologians and preachers who possess a low view of Scripture and an exalted view of the wisdom

---

3. Millar and Campbell, *Saving Eutychus*, from Millar's chapter "Faithful Wound: The Importance of Critique," 116.

4. Begg, *Preaching for God's Glory*, 13–14.

of the world and one's personal experience as the solution for man's problems. It is totally misguided to believe, as the liberal preacher Harry Emerson Fosdick did, that "the secret of successful preaching lies in discussing from the pulpit the problems of the pew."[5] The problems of the pew deserve consideration only as the Word of God has been explained carefully and thoroughly. Then the problems of the pew must be addressed by the Word of God which provides real solutions to real problems.

The attempt to be relevant in preaching is folly if relevance is not the derivative of God's Word being accurately explained and well understood. But when Scripture has been explained with precision and clarity, the relevance of scriptural truth must not be omitted from preaching. Preaching is predicated upon a theological understanding and a practical bearing of Scripture being provided to God's people. It is the theological understanding of Scripture and the understanding of its practical implications that qualifies talking in a pulpit to be the preaching of God's Word.

To preach God's Word is the most accountable activity of a lifetime, that is, to presume to declare what God has revealed in doctrine and duty. We must recognize "the audacity of that claim."[6] It would be an incredibly groundless claim if God has not spoken to us through Scripture. On what authority do we speak when we preach? If we explain and apply the contents of Scripture, "we invoke the authority of God, for He alone could reveal Himself, speak these things, and tell us what we must know."[7] What must be known is an accurate understanding of his Word and an accurate response to that Word in the lives of his people. A preaching pastor champions both, the understanding of Scripture and its response, in his preaching. Since God has spoken, "then the highest human aspiration must be to hear what the creator has said. And though the revelation of God is not merely propositions, it is never less than that."[8] Propositional truth is truth that can be understood and must be responded to. Albert Mohler is helpful as he connects the continuity of God's Word being given by God and his Word being lived in the lives of his people. Mohler suggests that, if God has spoken, then eight realities should frame the lives of God's people:

> First, *if God has spoken, we do know.*
> Second, *if God has spoken, we know only by mercy.*
> Third, *if God has spoken, we too must speak.*
> Fourth, *if God has spoken, then it is all about God, and it is all for our good.*
> Fifth, *if God has spoken, it is for our redemption.*
> Sixth, *if God has spoken, we must obey.*
> Seventh, *if God has spoken, we must trust.*
> Eighth, *if God has spoken, we must witness.*[9]

5. Oxnam, editor, *Effective Preaching*, 1929, from Harry Levi's chapter "Reality in Preaching," 172.
6. Mohler, *Words from the fire*, 11.
7. Mohler, *Words from the Fire*, 11–12.
8. Mohler, *Words from the Fire*, 16.
9. Mohler, *Words from the Fire*, 17–22.

The framework of the preaching pastor's preaching is the extensive continuity between the Word of God, spoken by God, and the living of that Word by his people.

A preaching pastor is not content to know what he is to do in preaching, but he is concerned that his preaching, which labors to provide theological clarity, also establishes the practical responsibilities of Scripture in the lives of his hearers. Gary Millar expresses the heart of a preaching pastor when he writes, "We also need to preach in a way that applies the gospel to their hearts, engaging them with the real issues they face and enabling them to live (by the Spirit) for Jesus. That's what God calls us to do—and that's why I want to know if I've left people cold or even bored. If I've done great exegesis and preached a sermon packed full of insights that has no 'so what' to it, I need to know."[10] The need to know is based upon the fact that an accurate and significant understanding of the theology of Scripture and its relevance is not a target that is easily hit in any sermon. But, for a preaching pastor it is a target that must not be missed!

The preaching pastor's commitments to doctrinal integrity and practical relevance are not shared by all who preach, neither in a single sermon nor throughout a lifetime of preaching. Their prioritizing other things above a text's theological accuracy and relevance not only prevents them from being a preaching pastor but wins for them a title that not only negatively depicts their preaching but is indicative of practices that should disqualify them from preaching. Alistair Begg provides a list of caricatures of true preaching, a variety of "sad situations" which have replaced the preaching pastor as an expositor of Scripture. His list includes:

1. "The cheerleader" who feels his task is to "pump them up" and prepare them for the daunting week that awaits them.

2. "The conjurer" who leaves a congregation declaring, "Wasn't it amazing what he got out of that?"

3. "The storyteller" who has convinced himself that since everyone loves a good story and since people tend to be less inclined to follow the exposition of the Bible, he will develop his gift for storytelling to the neglect of the hard work of biblical exposition.

4. "The entertainer" who fosters the environment in which the people come to sit back, relax, and assess his performance.

5. "The systematizer" who views the text of Scripture merely as the backdrop for a doctrinal lecture.

6. "The psychologist" who has become a purveyor of helpful insights, most of which can be (and often are) delivered without reference to the Bible.

---

10. Millar and Campbell, *Saving Eutychus*, from Millar's chapter "Faithful Wound: The Importance of Critique," 114–15.

7. "The naked preacher" who will "bear all" in the pulpit by sharing faults and foibles in the attempt at authenticity.[11]

The perspective that must not be missed is this, if those who are charged to preach the Bible do not take with upmost sincerity their responsibility to correctly interpret biblical texts and explain their meaning, then how could there ever be a reliable relevant word to God's people from a passage of Scripture that has not received the necessary treatment so that one may correctly assert a "Thus saith the Lord" instruction from Scripture?

The Bible possesses God's authority since it is his Word. As the contents of Scripture are responsibly interpreted then its doctrinal and practical insights provide God's people with a resource for their thinking and living that is pleasing to God. But this results only as the authority of the Bible is understood and honored by those who preach from it. If the authority of Scripture is not honored in the preaching of it, not only will the preaching of it be other than expository preaching, but whatever is articulated in the way of meaning and implications of its meaning must be viewed with a great deal of suspicion. "The absence of expository preaching is directly related to the erosion of confidence in the authority and sufficiency of Scripture."[12] Pastors bear responsibility for the erosion of confidence in the Word of God when they fail to provide a careful examination of Scripture, clearly explaining the meaning of its contents, and applying the meaning to the lives of his hearers. The inevitable result of such unreputable carelessness is that "the Scriptures are neglected and debased and are used only as a springboard for all kinds of 'talks' that are far removed from genuine biblical exposition."[13] As congregations are willing to welcome such mishandling of Scripture, they bear responsibility for their own erosion of confidence in God's Word with which they will distrust anyone who proclaims an authoritative word from it in the form of doctrine and its relevance.[14]

However, the preaching of a preaching pastor, though expository, does not fall victim to that kind of preaching that parades as expository preaching but is not. The counterfeit version of expository preaching is exhibited by preachers who are committed to faithfully explain Scripture "but are so buried in the text that they are completely divorced from the culture to which they have been called to preach" and thus provide a preaching that is "lifeless, dull, and even thoroughly boring."[15] Such preaching is neither expository preaching nor the preaching of a preaching pastor. The preaching of a preaching pastor, being truly expository, unfolds "the text of Scripture in a way that makes contact with the listeners' world while exalting Christ and confronting them

---

11. Begg, *Preaching for God's Glory*, 16–21. This selective list does not include "the politician, the end-times guru, and the hobbyhorse rider."

12. Begg, *Preaching for God's Glory*, 23.

13. Begg, *Preaching for God's Glory*, 24.

14. Begg, *Preaching for God's Glory*, 24.

15. Begg, *Preaching for God's Glory*, 28.

with the need for action."[16] The preaching pastor, because he is a responsible shepherd, is concerned not only with what God's people understand as correct doctrine but the relevance of correct doctrine which establishes correct conduct for their living out God's Word in life.

In his book *The Passion Driven Sermon*, Jim Shaddix provides excellent insight regarding application in expository preaching through his discussion of "transforming lives from the inside out," a transformation which is based upon: "preaching for Christ's character; preaching for Christ's conscience; and preaching for Christ's conduct."[17] According to Shaddix, "Shepherds need to be concerned with the way people think and feel before they worry about the way they act." Therefore, "pastoral preaching must seek to form the mind of Christ in the conscience of every believer."[18] As this is done, a relevant response to the expounded Word becomes "the natural result" of preaching.[19] The conscience alteration and character development established through the exposition of Scripture is productively poised for the personal application of the specific, relevant instruction found in the closing appeals of the sermon conclusion. This is an opportunity of which the preaching pastor takes full advantage.

The relevance of scriptural truth showcased in the closing appeals become the necessary resort of the preaching pastor's preaching. In so doing the preaching pastor sidesteps the error that "is far too common" in preaching, which is to "fail to answer the 'so what?' in the listener's mind."[20] The sermon conclusion's closing appeals serve as the choice means to establish necessary, personal application so that no hearer will fail to understand the relevance, the significant relevance, that the text's purpose has for their lives. An insightfully instructive conclusion prevents the "tragedy that leaves the audience perplexed and unsure of the sermon's relevancy."[21] Moreover, an insightfully instructive conclusion accommodates God's intention for all of his Word since "every part of Scripture was originally written with a pastoral intention—it was meant to be applied. The original authors always intended their audience to think or do something differently as a result of hearing or reading their words."[22] In the sermon conclusion is found the ultimate application of the sermon. The conclusion is "the point that you're driving towards, the reason you're standing to speak, and the lasting impact when you finally sit down."[23] Regardless of the text, the subject-matter of the passage, or the purpose of the sermon, a good conclusion should provide a

16. Begg, *Preaching for God's Glory*, 30.

17. Shaddix, *The Passion Driven Sermon*, 112–17.

18. Shaddix, *The Passion Driven Sermon*, 115–16.

19. Shaddix, *The Passion Driven Sermon*, 117.

20. Begg, *Preaching for God's Glory*, 36.

21. Carter et al., *Preaching God's Word*, 32.

22. Millar and Campbell, *Saving Eutychus*, from Campbell's chapter "So What's the Big Idea?" 72–73.

23. Millar and Campbell, *Saving Eutychus*, from Campbell's chapter "So What's the Big Idea?" 74.

"clarification" or a "heightened vision" of life and how it is to be lived in accordance to Scripture.[24]

Application in the conclusion is necessary to enforce duty to the conscience of the hearers and to supply direct instruction as to how to carry out their duty so that preached truth "may go with them to their homes because of its lodgment in their hearts."[25] As the ways and means to achieve the purposes of biblical texts are lodged in the hearts of God's people and these purposes become part of their daily living as they submit to the will of their Lord, then they can worship God as he desires. John Piper phrased it like this: "if the goal of preaching is to glorify God, it must aim at glad submission to His kingdom, not raw submission."[26] Again, Piper's deductions are sound as he writes, "The only submission that fully reflects the worth and glory of the King is glad submission. Begrudging submission berates the King. No gladness in the subject, no glory to the King. . . . When the kingdom is a treasure, submission is a pleasure. Or to turn it around, when submission is a pleasure, the kingdom is glorified as a treasure."[27] Nothing is more relevant than clear, Scripture-based instruction indicating how God's people can live according to his Word as they humble themselves in glad-hearted submission to their Lord. Nothing should be more prolific in a sermon conclusion than the ways and means by which glad-hearted submission to the Lord can be demonstrated in the lives of his people as they comply their lives with the purpose of the sermon.

Glad-hearted submission to the Lord and his Word is the design, the desire, and the determination of the preaching pastor's preaching in his sermon conclusion. The preaching pastor understands that God's Word is relevant and, as such, it affords a response from his people, for their good and for his glory. He understands that God desires that his people respond to his Word, for their good and for his glory. The challenges of a preaching pastor's closing appeals in his sermon conclusion are the natural resort to accomplish that which is desired by God, needed by man, and is the intent of God's Word in the preaching of it. This is an area of his preaching in which he excels. "Rarely does anyone excel in that which is not thought to be important and is not carried out with enthusiasm."[28] "It is a rule," writes Spurgeon, "to which I know of no exception that, to prosper in any work, you must have an enthusiasm for it."[29] And so it is that a preaching pastor will be found enthusiastically providing relevant closing appeals in his sermon conclusions that allows his hearers to achieve God's purposes for the biblical texts from which he preaches.

24. Davis, *Design for Preaching*, 197.
25. Garvie, *The Christian Preacher*, 1921, 442.
26. Piper, *The Supremacy of God in Preaching*, 25.
27. Piper, *The Supremacy of God in Preaching*, 25.
28. Burgess, *The Art of Preaching*, 1881, 69.
29. Spurgeon, *An All-round Ministry*, 1900, 194.

All that is needed to identify a preaching pastor is to hear his sermon conclusion. Nothing more is necessary because there is nothing like the sermon conclusion that distinguishes whether the man in the pulpit is merely a preacher or a preaching pastor. The sermon conclusion decides this matter clearly, and it does so every time. The characteristic of relevance, highly relevant preaching, is that which will be demonstrated in the sermon conclusion of a preaching pastor and it will be demonstrated from sermon to sermon.

A PREACHING PASTOR IS AWARE OF THE WAYWARD TENDENCIES OF GOD'S PEOPLE

Western culture is a narcissistic culture. This is no slanderous opinion; it is an objective but grievous reality. It is not possible, if God's Word is expounded, for Christians in this culture not to be subject to correction in a specific, thorough, and consistent manner regarding their own narcissistic ways. That this should and must happen is a given because there exists in the body of Christ in western culture the cult of self. The general thrust of biblical truth is violently opposed to this culture. That the Lord and Savior would necessarily empty Himself, "taking the form of a bondservant" and humble Himself "by becoming obedient to the point of death, even death on a cross;"[30] that he would proclaim, "If anyone wishes to come after Me, he must deny Himself, take up his cross and follow Me;"[31] that he would teach those who gave up everything to follow him that, "whoever wishes to become great among you shall be your servant, and whoever wishes to be first among you shall be your slave, just as the Son of Man did not come to be served, but to serve, and to give His life a ransom for many;"[32] such realities strike death blows for coexistence in the cult of self and the body of Christ. Al Mohler suggests that our culture, as a narcissistic culture, is reckoned as such by several facets, all beginning with the word *self*, namely, "self-fulfillment, self-sufficiency, self-definition, self-absorption, and self-enhancement."[33]

A narcissistic culture such as ours should take a strongly favored view of God's Word because it is given to us to bring much needed enhancement to every believer in Christ. In 2 Timothy 3:16 Paul provides four main ways the Scriptures are profitable in preaching. These four ways are germane to doctrinal instruction, and behavioral instruction. Scripture is useful for doctrinal instruction in a positive manner and in a negative manner. Scripture is useful for behavioral instruction in a negative manner and in a positive manner.[34]

30. Philippians 2:7–8.

31. Matthew 16:24.

32. Matthew 20:26–28.

33. Dever et al., *Preaching the Cross*, from Al Mohler's chapter "Preaching with the Culture in View," 80–85.

34. Dever and Gilbert, *Preach*, 53–55.

Teaching and reproof are pertinent to Scripture's doctrinal instruction. To teach is the positive process of instruction. To teach is to explain what the Scriptures mean. The profitable use of reproof, the negative process of instruction, is in the form of a strong disapproval, revealing erroneous ideas about God and his Word.[35]

Correction and training in righteousness are in reference to behavior, thus, providing behavioral instruction necessary to live in accordance with Scripture. Correction is the negative manner of behavioral instruction. Correction is the profitable use of restoring or improving one's behavior. As reproof has to do with confronting doctrinal error, correction has to do with confronting errors of conduct. Training in righteousness is the positive component to correction. Training in righteousness provides the profitable use of establishing disciplines for the development of spiritual character, the practical means by which one's character and conduct become increasingly correct.[36]

No preacher can afford to misunderstand the culture in which he preaches nor can he fail to stringently apply how the biblical truth must be complied to in that culture. A preaching pastor not only understands the culture in which he preaches but he serves his hearers by helping them to understand how they must respond to the Word in their culture so that they can conduct their lives in obedience to the Word.

A PREACHING PASTOR ADDRESSES PEOPLE'S HARDSHIPS AND DIFFICULTIES WITH CONSOLATION

A preaching pastor will not only be relevant in his preaching, but he will make a concerted effort to provide consolation in his preaching to God's people. Just as the relevance of a preaching pastor's preaching emanates from his preaching strength, consolation is provided because of his pastoral propensity, part of that which identifies him as being a true pastor. The consolation that a preaching pastor provides is not only a natural byproduct of his personality, a sanctified personality that is borne out in his preaching by the Spirit of God, but it is also an intended component of his preaching because of his character as a faithful shepherd of God's people.

Effective, popular preachers of the past such as Joseph Parker, Ian Maclaren, and R. W. Dale in their personal practice of preaching, and in their counsel to others about preaching, insisted that consolation must be a part of a preaching ministry. "Parker repeated again and again, 'Preach to broken hearts!'"[37] Maclaren insisted that "The chief end of preaching is comfort. . . . Never can I forget what a distinguished scholar, who used to sit in my church, once said to me: 'Your best work in the pulpit has been to put heart into men for the coming week!'"[38] Dale asserted that "People want to be

35. Dever and Gilbert, *Preach*, 53–55.
36. Dever and Gilbert, *Preach*, 53–55.
37. Jowett, *The Preacher*, 1912, 107.
38. Jowett, *The Preacher*, 1912, 107.

comforted. They need consolation—really need it, and do not merely long for it."[39] In this effort to supply needed consolation in preaching J. H. Jowett confessed that he was never able to amend his ways as he wished. He tried and sometimes had partial success, but the success was only partial. Yet he maintained that "One thing is perfectly clear, the merely dictatorial will never heal the broken in heart or bind up their bleeding wounds."[40] Many preaching pastors may find their preaching deficient or insufficient in consolation. Like Jowett, they may find themselves making a concerted effort to supply consolation in their preaching. But, such recognition and response for the sake of providing what is necessary is laudable, even if one thinks the result of his effort is still less than what is needed. This is the pastoral dimension of the preaching pastor's personality demanding more from him in the ministry of the Word for the sake of God's people.

A CHANGED LIFE IS WHAT THE SERMON CONCLUSION IS ALL ABOUT

The role of consolation is not to incentivize the status quo of hearers but to aid in their encouragement to seek a new status quo, that which is more fully aligned with the requirements of biblical instruction. Consoling hearers is not an impediment to helping people make needed change in their lives, but rather, it is a means by which the needed change may be made more readily and most completely.

The ministry of consolation prepares hearers to be receptive to exhortation, the means by which hearers may change from "as it is" to "as it ought to be" if they will comply with the exhortations found in the closing appeals of the sermon conclusion. Though consolation is a specific type of the more general concept of exhortation, the terms may be used and understood as synonyms, or they may be understood more distinctly as *an encouraging word to hearers for their consolation* versus *a provoking word to hearers for their exhortation.*

Peter's preaching on the Day of Pentecost[41] shows how exhortation and consolation share a reciprocating function of enablement as they work together.[42] When the hearers of Peter's sermon understood the sobering reality of the result of their wicked response to their promised Messiah, "this Jesus whom you crucified," they were rightly convicted. The impact of their sin was registered by the phrase, "they were pierced to the heart." They cried out for a way in which they might, somehow, have their sin remediated. Peter provided exhortation which, if complied with, would bring greater remediation than they sought. They would receive "forgiveness of their sins" if they complied with the exhortation to repent and be baptized in the name of Jesus

---

39. Jowett, *The Preacher*, 1912, 107.

40. Jowett, *The Preacher*, 1912, 108.

41. Acts 2:1–41.

42. The portion of Peter's sermon to which I am referring regarding exhortation and consolation are drawn from 2:36b – 2:39.

Christ. However, Peter provided additional consolation to these convicted sinners in the form of "and you will receive the gift of the Holy Spirit." Even that was not the extent of the consolation Peter provided. He continued to console them further with his words, "For the promise is for you and your children and all who are far off, as many as the Lord calls to Himself." They were being called by God to Himself. Therefore, they would be the unique possession of God as they became the beneficiaries of God's promise, a promise which God had made for them.

Consolation and exhortation were both offered, and both were received by three thousand repentant sinners who were baptized that day and added to the fellowship of believers. Life-change occurred as consolation and exhortation worked together in preaching. The hearers were exhorted and given specific instruction as to how they needed to respond to the message that was preached. In responding to the exhortation, consolation was theirs in great measure along with life-change that would dominate the rest of their days and extend into eternity.

The principal function of the conclusion is to accomplish the purpose of the sermon in the lives of the hearers. Therefore, it must be powerful. The hearers should depart with the conclusion in their minds, as that to which they have resigned themselves to do in obedience to the faith. True sermons call for change and they do so most notably in the conclusion. Since a preacher will challenge his hearers for a verdict, a verdict that is won by responding to the closing appeals of the sermon conclusion, and since the decision-making process takes place at this time, the conclusion should be powerful, and a preacher should prepare his conclusion accordingly.

A preacher, preaching for a verdict resulting in life-change, especially in his conclusion, bears the "biblical obligation to 'urge,' 'persuade,' 'encourage,' and 'authoritatively instruct' the listener to believe and do whatever God commands."[43] Thus, the verdict being sought by a preaching pastor for his hearers is subject to a set of truths, the exhortations of the closing appeals of the sermon conclusion, which must be met for the verdict to be won in their lives. Consolation must be understood by the hearers as a potential reality for them, by the prospect of moving from disobedience to obedience or moving from a lesser to a greater state of obedience, if they will comply with the exhortations provided to them in the closing appeals of the sermon conclusion.

The exhortations of the sermon conclusion's closing appeals become the means by which the verdict, for which a preaching pastor is preaching, can become a reality. This much is certain: no exhortations tendered; no verdict rendered! A tendering of no exhortation is indicative that a preacher is in the pulpit simply to inform his hearers of biblical truth. The weakness of, or the lack of, a sermon conclusion gives testimony of this limited version of preaching in which the hearers are denied a sermon conclusion that will bring them to a verdict. If there is no verdict for which a preacher is preaching, there will be no exhortations composed of direct closing appeals nor will there be any indirect closing appeals in the form of inferences through which

43. Adams, *Preaching with Purpose*, 69.

the lives of believers are afforded practical instructions by which they can achieve the purpose of the sermon in their lives. In his updated and revised edition of John Albert Broadus's classic textbook on preaching, *A Treatise on the Preparation and Delivery of Sermons*, Vernon L. Stanfield insisted that preaching is essentially a personal encounter in which the preacher is making a claim through the truth of Scripture upon the will of the hearer. The bottom-line for preaching is quite simply as Stanfield leveraged it: "If there is no summons, there is no sermon."[44] The preaching pastor's sermons are designed to change the lives of the hearers by means of closing appeals in the conclusion that mandate a verdict from the hearers.

As was discussed in chapter twelve, the closing appeals of a sermon conclusion may be composed of direct appeals, indirect appeals, or a combination of direct and indirect closing appeals. As discussed, the direct closing appeals are exhortational while the indirect closing appeals are more inferential, providing an instructional component regarding the subject-matter of the sermon's purpose, to which all closing appeals pertain regardless of whether they are direct or indirect in nature. In chapter eleven it was established that there are five content types and five delivery tones for closing appeals. The basic type, the commendatory type of closing appeal, is the type of closing appeal which composes most indirect appeals. The commendatory type of closing appeal, though it is not a direct statement of exhortation, does imply an exhortation in the form of "comply with the instruction being offered," and thus, may be understood as an indirect statement of exhortation. So, the closing appeals will be exhortational whether they are direct or indirect exhortations.

Steven J. Lawson is most insightful as he provides six crucial insights regarding the concept of exhortation in preaching. First, the Apostle Paul mandated that Scripture reading be coupled with "exhortation." Exhortation means "to come alongside with the purpose of helping someone who is weak or wayward." Second, when joined with the definite article, "the exhortation" refers to an "applying of the Word in the lives of the people." Third, in synagogue liturgy the reading of Scripture was followed by the exhortation which "was an exposition and application of the Scripture by way of exhortation or encouragement to a certain course of conduct." Fourth, exhortation, in "the form of rebuke, warning, counsel, or comfort" challenges people to apply the truths that were exposed, expecting to be blessed for obedience and to be judged for disobedience to the exhortations given to them. Fifth, the goal of exhortation is to change lives by its power to quicken the conscience. Sixth, exhortation is to produce life-change as it presses for a verdict from an individual.[45] It must be understood and appreciated that direct as well as indirect closing appeals press for a verdict. The verdict is won as a hearer chooses to comply with the closing appeals, whether direct or indirect appeals, so that the hearer may achieve the sermon's purpose in his or her life which results in life-change.

44. Stanfield, *On the Preparation and Delivery of Sermons*, 165.

45. Lawson, *Famine in the Land*, 113–14.

The preaching pastor aspires to see the lives of those to whom he preaches dramatically changed. Puritan preacher Thomas Manton believed that, "The hearer's life is the preacher's best commendation."[46] The adoption of Manton's perspective will bring vitality to the preaching ministry of any preacher who would dare make the cause and effect connection between one's preaching and the effect of his preaching as viewed by the lives of those who hear him preach. For a preaching pastor, his preaching ministry is constantly vitalized because he preaches for life-change through the means of closing appeals that most certainly spearhead his sermon conclusion.

NECESSITATING DECISION TO THE CLOSING APPEALS

In discussing the response hearers make to the exhortations of the closing appeals, referred to commonly as a decision, it is crucial that it is understood what is meant by this concept. I use the term "decision" only because of its common usage, but having done so, I must replace it with concepts that are more certain, namely, a resolve, a choice, a commitment, or a determination. That is a resolve, a choice, a true commitment, or a determination where one accepts an appeal, a precept, an instruction, a command, and will employ whatever is necessary for its accomplishment. The rich young ruler desired to follow Christ. However, he refused to comply to the commands Christ required of him. Therefore, his response included two choices. His primary resolve was that he would not be separated from his wealth. Secondarily, he determined to separate himself from Christ and the salvation he offered.[47]

It is necessary that a preaching pastor exercise every effort, not just to bring his hearers to an unavoidable response, but a response that will win a verdict from them to comply their lives to the necessary provisions of biblical truth so that the purpose of the sermon may be achieved in their daily living. But, a necessary response? Why is it necessary to make a response to the sermon an unavoidable reality? Very many preachers preach without requiring any response to the sermon. That is true and it will continue to be true of preachers who are not preaching pastors!

Preachers who are not preaching pastors have given themselves a freedom by which they clearly make known the meaning of Scripture by means of careful explanation of a text, along with its implications for the lives of his hearers. But when they get to the end of the preaching text, the sermon is done and ministry to their hearers is done. The help they are willing to provide their hearers is to help them understand the text and its implications, and that is it. In other words, the commitment is to help them to know. To help the hearers to respond and help them understand what that response entails is help they are unwilling to provide. The help that is provided falls short of helping the hearers to do, to be about achieving the purpose for the text they now understand. These preachers understand the care they are to provide

46. As cited in Lawson, *Famine in the Land*, 124–25.
47. Beecher, *Lectures on Preaching*, Third Series, 1874, 257.

for their hearers is limited to a cognitive service. But if it is important for them to live the truth, should not a preacher be concerned about this as well? Even if this is viewed as a "second mile" service, shouldn't he be willing to provide it? I agree with Beecher's conviction that those who are "charged with the care of men's souls, should concentrate every influence possible to bring them to an immediate decision."[48] But a commitment to do what is right does not insure that the character qualities needed to keep the commitment are existent. Therefore, to provide for one's hearers understanding about the circumstances or situations that can derail a commitment once it has been made, and ways and means by which such derailing factors can be avoided or overcome is a practical safeguard a preacher can offer to help those to keep commitments they desire to make.[49]

Through the use of application in a sermon conclusion's closing appeals, which detail how the hearers are to respond so that the purpose of the sermon may be achieved in their lives, the hearers can see how the sermon is appropriate, fitting, and suitable for them. Such application shows the hearers how they can live a life that complies with Scripture, please God, benefit others, and experience personal fulfillment. Such application is a logical, and practical extension of the explanation of the text that occurred previously. H. C. Brown phrased it this way: "As explanation presents the message of God's 'then,' so application presents the message of God's 'now.'"[50] Such application, that which is contained in the closing appeals of the sermon conclusion, shows how the hearers can achieve the purpose of the message in their lives, life as it is to be lived in the present, the life they are responsible to live before God. Achieving the purpose of the sermon in life becomes the justification, the why, for the hearer's responding to the closing appeals of the conclusion, a rationale which may be found so crucial that the hearer wants to respond.[51] But whether the closing appeals are found crucial or not so crucial by the hearers, the hearers will be compelled to respond to the closing appeals by the preacher.

A preaching pastor, in his sermon conclusion, will compel his hearers to respond to the closing appeals. The closing appeals will not be offered for their musing. The closing appeals will be put forward as that which must be done. Henry Ward Beecher was most decided in his view that a preacher must, absolutely must, force upon his hearers a choice regarding their response to the sermon. The strength of Beecher's view is palpable when he wrote:

> I think I see one of these *dilettante* men, one of these modern eunuchs of sermons, who sits and walks before his congregation in such a way as not to disturb their equanimity, or to force upon them any considerations which are not agreeable to them.

48. Beecher, *Lectures on Preaching,* Third Series, 1874, 258.
49. Beecher, *Lectures on Preaching,* Third Series, 1874, 258.
50. Brown Jr., *A Quest for Reformation in Preaching,* 60.
51. Brown Jr., *A Quest for Reformation in Preaching,* 62.

... For my part, I do not believe in the manliness of any such mode of preaching the gospel. It comes from the effeminate philosophy of an effete manhood. ... I believe that I have this much right to bombard your hearts as ever Grant had to bombard Petersburg. ... If the man's whole thought ... is of heaven, immortality, and God revealed in Christ, then I tell you he had better be in earnest, or he had better be out of the pulpit.[52]

The ministry of a preaching pastor's preaching is more than a service to help his hearers die with of greater knowledge of the Word. A preaching pastor is concerned that they live the Word as well as they can before they die. Living the Word requires the knowledge of it, in that, one must know in order to do. However, since knowledge of the Word does not necessitate the living of it, that is, one may know and not do, the preaching pastor's preaching in the closing appeals of the sermon conclusion is his best effort to help his hearers live the truth that they now know.

HARD WORK IN THE STUDY IS NEEDED TO WIN A VERDICT IN THE PULPIT

In the legal profession, "Cases are won in chambers."[53] A legal case in a court of law is won by well-marshalled facts and disciplined, strong, convincing, persuasive arguments presented to the jurors with the result that the victorious attorney wins a favorable verdict from the jury. Though jurisprudential cause and effect does not equate the spiritual reality of a preacher winning a verdict from his hearers,[54] it is true that the preaching pastor who seeks to win a verdict from his hearers must prepare himself thoroughly, just as a courtroom attorney who seeks to win a verdict from a jury must prepare himself thoroughly. So, in reference to a preaching pastor's responsibility of thorough preparation to see a favorable verdict won in the lives of his hearers, it too may be said of him that "cases are won in chambers." But the victory to be won by a preaching pastor is a verdict from the hearts of hearers to comply their lives to the exhortations he will provide for them in the closing appeals of his sermon conclusion. And, as with a victorious attorney, if the preaching pastor achieves this victory, it will begin to be won by him in his study.

It is in the study where the preacher must ask on behalf of those who will hear him preach the sermon, "how can this purpose become a functioning reality of daily life?" This question has not been raised in the exposition of the text, because the exposition of the text was the focus of attention. But in the conclusion the purpose of

52. Beecher, *Lectures on Preaching*, Third Series, 1874, 259–60.

53. Jowett, *The Preacher*, 1912, 113.

54. The working of the Holy Spirit of God is responsible for believers responding to and doing the Word and will of God. Paul's confidence in the believers in the Philippian church to "work out their salvation with fear and trembling" was predicated upon the certainty that "it is God who is at work in you, both to will and to work for His good pleasure" (Philippians 2:13–14).

the text becomes the focus. The purpose of the sermon is to clarify what must be lived out in life, beyond simply understanding what the purpose of the text/purpose of the sermon is. Therefore, practical matters about living out the purpose in a fallen world is what will dominate the sermon conclusion. The conclusion must address the purpose of the sermon practically, that is, by exhorting and/or instructing believers about what they must do or not do so that their lives will be able to comply with the text's/sermon's purpose in daily living. The conclusion is intended to clinch the sermon's purpose to the daily lives of the hearers by means of the closing appeals. "For this reason, the preacher should devote more careful and prayerful attention to the close of his sermon than any other portion of it."[55] This counsel, though it might seem overstated, is not without sufficient warrant. If the material offered in the closing appeals is qualitative material, as it must be, then significant time, effort, care, and prayer will be needed to bring to the hearers the most select, significant content from the Word of God that will help them to achieve the purpose of the sermon in their lives.

Two things must be understood about the nature of the content composing the closing appeals of the sermon conclusion: they must be practical, and they must be biblical. Significant, insightful, biblical, practicality is in order. If the closing appeals are not practical, composed of insights that impact life, then the conclusion might provide a rhetorical flourish of some manner, but it will not be serviceable for daily living. A preacher can say something relevant and appropriate, though obvious, about worldwide problems and perplexities. It is harder, by far, to deal with the issues that are our own. It is paradoxical but nevertheless true, that, "in the artillery of exhortation the distant target is easier to hit than the target which lies close to us."[56] But it is the hearers and the issues of their lives in reference to the sermon's purpose that must become the focus of the practical insights addressed in the closing appeals of the preaching pastor's sermon conclusion. "Praised once for preaching a stirring sermon, the famous Scottish Presbyterian pastor Thomas Chalmers, somewhat hotly, brushed aside an intended complement as he lamented, 'Yes, yes,' he said, 'but what came of it?'"[57] What tremendous insight Chalmers had to understand that a sermon is to terminate into practical worth, truth that is to be lived out in the arena of life. But many things are lived out in the arena of life, very much of it is unbiblical. What matters is that the practical *truth of Scripture* is lived out in the arena of life.

The truth of Scripture is what the preaching pastor must challenge God's people to live out in their lives. A preaching pastor does not desire to preach his own message or speak out of his own authority. He preaches with the divine dogmatism of, "Thus saith the Lord!"[58] What is the rationale for the divine dogmatism of a "Thus saith the Lord" approach in preaching, generally, and in the sermon conclusion, specifically?

55. Burrell, *The Sermon: Its Construction and Delivery*, 1913, 188.
56. Berry, *Vital Preaching*, 60.
57. Macpherson, *The Burden of the Lord*, 116.
58. Macartney, *Preaching without Notes*, 182.

For those who wrote the New Testament, and for the Apostle Paul, particularly, spiritual progress was always Christlikeness.[59] The Christian life, in the fullest sense, is an increasing Christlikeness in the lives of God's people. This is the aim of the preaching pastor. Therefore, it is Christlikeness, in contrast to a selfish, temporary, worldly, sensuous, superficial existence that a preaching pastor will challenge believers to pursue by means of the sermon conclusion's closing appeals. Such a pursuit will always be the general thrust of every sermon conclusion, though it will be framed very specifically from sermon to sermon according to the purpose of the sermon. There is only one source that can be a resource for the development of Christlikeness, that is, Scripture. Thus, the substance of the closing appeals must be derived only from God's Word.

Three observations are obvious regarding the lives of people contained within the pages of Scripture. Because of God's working in the lives of people, "they can know, they can feel, and they can do."[60] The doctrine of God, the doctrine of Christ, the doctrine of the Holy Spirit, the doctrine of Scripture, the doctrine of man, the doctrine of salvation, and the doctrine of sanctification converge in the light of these three facts. The value of preaching hinges on the significance of the hearers knowing, feeling, and doing scriptural truth. In preaching, people should be made to know, feel, and do according to the content and instruction of God's Word. Through God's working in the hearts of people through the preaching of his Word, a preacher is working with God so that people can know, feel, and do his Word in their lives. Therefore, what the preaching pastor is committed to provide God's people in the closing appeals of his sermon is a clear grasp of God's purpose and what it will require of them to achieve it in their lives, an accurate feel for the importance of this purpose becoming part of their lives, and a commitment to comply with this purpose in their lives.

Hard work in the study is obligatory to discover from Scripture what is most crucial for believers to move from some degree of obedience to a greater obedience regarding the purpose of the sermon and the text of the sermon. The merit of the hard work will be found in the degree to which the closing appeals are insightful, substantial, specific, and practical. A failure to work hard to discover from Scripture significant insights will produce nominal instruction and exhortation for believers which is as unreasonable and unproductive as "urging people to follow a light they do not see."[61] For a sermon to end by putting forth peripheral ambiguities is insulting. It suggests that the lives of God's people are not important enough to a preacher to command the time and effort necessary for him to provide them with helpful, practicable insights for living. This, of course, is an indictment upon the preacher's character and work ethic as it indicates that he neither cares to provide them with the help they need, nor will he require of himself the time and effort to provide it to them.

---

59. Hoyt, *The Preacher*, reprinted, 1912, 212.

60. Hough, *The Theology of a Preacher*, 1912, 27.

61. Weatherspoon, *Sent Forth to Preach*, 143.

For a sermon to end ambiguously is unfortunate. As John MacArthur has written, "We get nothing from ambiguity except confusion. Clarity is the desired result of a good understanding of the biblical text. If a preacher is not clear to his hearers, it is likely because he is not yet clear in his own mind. That means more diligent study is required. . . . Understanding is the first and most essential point of expositional preaching, because people cannot believe or obey truth they do not understand."[62] This is as true, if not more so, for the sermon conclusion as for any ambiguity found in the body of a sermon. A sermon that ends with closing appeals that are nominal or ambiguous is effectively without application, which is like a cadaver, "a body without a soul."[63] But, even more to the point, a sermon conclusion without accurate, insightful, biblical application through the means of closing appeals, is like a car without brakes; it will come to an end, but it will do so quite unproductively and unsatisfyingly.

If we think of biblical truth as a diamond, then a responsible handling of it requires of us a threefold task. First, we excavate the diamond from its surroundings; this is the investigation process. Second, we cut and polish the diamond to reveal all its glory; this is the interpretation process. Third, we place it in a contemporary setting, like placing a diamond in a ring's mounting so that it may be worn for all to see in the present day; this is the application process.[64] Every stage of handling necessitates hard work. On the one hand, a lack of hard work to provide the final application of the sermon through the means of the closing appeals of the sermon conclusion is to marginalize the hard work provided in the other stages. On the other hand, much is gained when preaching has concrete, personal application with which to conclude a sermon. Moreover, not only must there be application in the conclusion but there must be a "demonstration" of the application.[65]

Through demonstration the preaching pastor makes known to his hearers, by way of concrete exemplification or illustration, how, or the ways in which, or the means by which, the application may become a personal reality.[66] The provision of illustrative material to make the closing appeals demonstratable only adds to the workload of the preacher's task to be as helpful as possible for his hearers. In the final analysis, application may be the most important part of the sermon since it seeks to show the hearer how to respond to scriptural truth and seeks to motivate the hearer to respond to it. A sermon fails unless it provides a bearing on life and a clear demonstration of how biblical truth impacts life.

What must become convictional for a preaching pastor is that it is far better to make application concrete and specific rather than abstract and general. Sermon

---

62. Dever et al., *Preaching the Cross*, from MacArthur's chapter "Why I Still Preach the Bible after Forty Years of Ministry," 148–49.

63. As cited in Perry and Strubhar, *Evangelistic Preaching*, 76.

64. Cleland, *Preaching to be Understood*, 79.

65. Sangster, *The Craft of Sermon Construction*, 143.

66. Sangster *The Craft of Sermon Construction*, 143.

application is strengthened substantially by illustrations which help to make the relevance of the truth clear to the hearers.[67] An illustration that shows how the application works out in life adds impact to a conclusion. But the illustration "must be exactly on target so that listeners grasp the meaning in a flash without explanation."[68] In other words, the illustration demonstrates how the truth is connected to life. And this, too, will be part of the hard work involved to conclude a sermon well.

Hard work is not an end, but it is a very necessary means to the end. What we are trying to help facilitate is beyond our ability to produce. Only God can produce the result of winning a verdict from people regarding their needed response to biblical truth. Yet, the preaching pastor must be faithful to provide relevant, concrete, significant insights from Scripture as that which he will be found exhorting them to comply with in their lives. And for all who render their verdict to comply with the biblical-based closing appeals of a sermon conclusion to which a preaching pastor exhorts them, God wins their verdict. But it is better that God uses our best effort of ministry as opposed to our lack of effort in being graciously used by him. "I marvel sometimes not that preaching is so bad, but that it is not worse," lamented one writing about preaching years ago.[69]

We may echo such grief or be the cause of it when we consider that the abstractness and generalizations of preaching content, which should be concrete, relevant and life-changing, serves more to validate the conduct and vindicate the consciences of those whose lives are not in keeping with the Word of God. Beyond simply agreeing that this should never be done by a preacher, it is incumbent upon preachers to provide the much-needed reproof and correction that should take place in preaching by means of specific exhortation found in the closing appeals of a sermon conclusion. Closing appeals that are life-changing are so because they consist of sufficient concreteness and relevance that afflicts the conscience, inspires the affections, and constrains the volition.

Preaching should be like Paul's epistles written to churches and individuals. Each one was a heartfelt message that was focused, specific, personal, and instructive. Paul's letters to churches and individuals provided remediation to problems and concerns through instruction and exhortation. Paul's communication of spiritual truth was "alive to actual conditions in the churches on the one hand, and to relevant truth on the other, and undertook in every instance to show the meeting point of truth and pressing need. Paul did not preach to Corinth about the heresies of Colossae, nor to Colossae about the corruption and factions of the church at Corinth. No doubt was left about the meaning and demands of faith in relation to life in one's own church or community."[70] Paul's every correspondence was filled with vital information of a

67. Whitesell, *Power in Expository Preaching*, 92.

68. Robinson, *Biblical Preaching*, 168.

69. Farmer, *The Servant of the Word*, 103.

70. Weatherspoon, *Sent Forth to Preach*, 136.

doctrinal and a practical nature. He provided insights that were of inestimable worth for believers' knowing and doing in the Christian life.

Preaching that emulates Paul's ministry of the Word will never be easy to produce. To be able to exhort people to respond to truth that will be life-changing requires coveted content presented in a tone that is unnecessarily offensive. Fortunately, the ministry of exhortation provides significant latitude for the tone in which the content of the exhortation may be delivered and received as a heartfelt communication, allowing the content to be received, potentially, rather than rejected. Since there is no one English word that expresses the range of meaning for the Greek term *parakalein*, it is translated commonly "to exhort," but sometimes the context requires "to beseech," "to entreat," "to comfort," or "to console." In most cases it should be translated to exhort, but even then one must not lose sight of the fact that "the mood or purpose of the exhortation (will be) varying between entreating or challenging to action, and consoling or strengthening in a situation." Regardless of how it may be translated, the implication of exhortation in preaching, in general, and in the sermon conclusion, especially, is that exhortation makes preaching not only a personal encounter but a "heart-to-heart" communication.[71]

But even when exhortation is perceived to be a true heart-to-heart communication intended for the recipients' well-being, it still may be rejected by the hearers simply because of what the exhortation necessitates. That which a preaching pastor, from the best intentions, exhorts hearers to do may be viewed by some as that which is not in one's best interest, not at this time in one's life, not under one's present circumstances, and maybe not at all, under any circumstances. Worse still, the content of well-intended exhortation may be viewed by hearers as that which is not coveted, but irksome, and perhaps even offensive.

Because the exhortation is what it should be, that which is personal, concrete, and specific, it may clearly expose a hearer's life as that which is worthy of reproof or rebuke. Without the spiritual humility to accept the exposure and change as one should, there will be a fleshly rejection of that which is needful. Being concrete and personal, application by way of exhortation may cause trouble because it particularizes. "No one gets too upset by generalities. But when exhortations are applied specifically and personally hearers may be cut to the quick and become angry."[72] A preaching pastor cannot afford to lose sight of the fact that exhortation, in a sense, brings with it a "prophetic" word that exposes misconceptions, prejudices, hidden fears, excuses, and self-protective rationalizations. The inescapable effect of a preaching pastor's preaching may be to provoke some hearers as well as to encourage others.[73]

To understand more fully a preaching pastor's personal relevance in a sermon conclusion, chapter fourteen will consider the following: motivation to act upon the

---

71. Weatherspoon, *Sent Forth to Preach*, 74.

72. Cleland, *Preaching to be Understood*, 55.

73. Read, *Sent from God*, 58.

application in the sermon conclusion; a sermon conclusion's application as a commencement for the hearers; a preaching pastor's relevance in life and preaching; personal relevance and concern for people; the relevance of preaching and illustrative material; and relevance and the hearers' desire to listen and respond.

14

A Preaching Pastor's Personal Relevance in a Sermon Conclusion: Part 2

"Much preaching touches only the surface and shadow of truths rather than the substance of the truths themselves. As a result, preaching does not penetrate the inner parts of the hearers, their affections, their consciences, and their wills. A superficial handling of Scripture has neither a deep insight into, nor a strong grasp of, the hidden value of God's Word. What is said in the pulpit from a shallow treatment of Scripture is true but only superficially so. The result is that the hearers are exposed to superficial truth that fails to motivate them just as it failed to motivate the one speaking to them."

"'We are guilty of the most irrational conceit' if we think that we can preach with interest texts which are uninteresting to us."

"In the process of implementing application by means of the closing appeals, to which the preaching pastor will exhort the hearers to respond, the consciences, affections, and the wills of the hearers become the intended targets for his direct exhortations or indirect inferential instructions. All truth is relevant since every truth generates some necessities for its accommodation in life, requires some ways it must be responded to, and obligates its hearers to do something about it."

"As a preaching pastor intends to be heard and heeded, he will not expound his preaching text without bringing his sermon to an appropriate end. This means that the end of the sermon cannot occur until his hearers have been challenged to comply with Scripture-based closing appeals which constitutes the appropriate response to which he will compel them to respond."

"The preaching pastor's true desire to see his hearers heeding the truth of the closing appeals of the sermon may be accomplished as he productively speaks to the hearers' affections, what they aspire toward, what they desire to do in response to the truth they have heard. If the closing appeals find no room in the arena of the hearers' desires and aspirations, they will make no commitment to what they are being exhorted and implored to do. The most logical biblical pleadings will go unheeded if the exhortations bypass their affections. People are always interested in what they want and may be interested in what they need if they become convinced of the actuality of their need."

"If there is no desire in the hearers' affections to comply with the exhortations of the closing appeals in a sermon conclusion, then every unaffected hearer will walk away from that to which they have been challenged."

"It has been stated that the radio station of every hearer's heart is naturally 'tuned to WII-FM, the call letters of which stand for, What's In It For Me?' Though this would appear only as an indication of the superficial, self-consumed culture of modern western society, of which it certainly is a chief characteristic, it is an attribute of mankind regardless of time, place, or culture."

"Too much of preaching is like a discussion about engines with a mechanic who is dying, and about to die, of inoperable brain cancer. No matter how mechanically accurate and detailed the discussion is, if there is no transition to an accurate, detailed, needed discussion about the mechanic's impending death, his essential reality, then the conversation is irrelevant. Unless the conversation moves from the superficiality of engine technology and performance to the essential consideration of death and eternity, the irrelevant conversation might just as well as never occurred. The relevance that a preacher needs to establish is the connection between the explanation of biblical truth and life as it is being experienced and as it could be experienced by his hearers. The primary concern of the preaching pastor is with what the hearers do because of the explanation and application of Scripture he provides for them."

"The sermon of a preaching pastor is intended to impact the hearts and the lives of his hearers. His concern is for his hearers to receive a scriptural intake of truth from the pulpit as well as a concern that his hearers respond with a scriptural implementation of truth in their lives. The preaching pastor is constrained by a passion to be helpful to his hearers. The help he aspires to provide for his hearers is that through his, explanation, application, argumentation, and illustration, the Word of God will be exalted in their hearts and the Word of God will be exhibited in their lives."

"The apostles' preaching and the preaching of those who followed them involved two priorities: a proclamation of the gospel to unbelievers; and the 'explaining,

instructing, informing, and guiding' of fellow-believers by means of the Scriptures. Both the proclamation of the gospel and the instructing of believers should still be the two priorities of preaching, and both priorities should be accomplished at the highest level in the sermon conclusion."

"There are two issues for a preaching pastor regarding his hearers in a sermon conclusion: an end and a commencement. The end has nothing to do with the cessation of the sermon but an ending of the hearers' present status of obedience to the Word of God. However complete and consistent the obedience is, however rightly motivated it is, it must end. But it ends only to begin, that is, to commence in greater fulness, greater consistency, and in purer motivation."

"If the closing appeals are presented only in the attire of 'should,' 'ought,' and 'must,' a preacher must not be surprised if very few respond to the affectionless appeals. In appealing to the hearers' volition without appealing to their affections, he is working against himself and not working affectively on behalf of his hearers. If he is sincere about seeing his hearers respond to the closing appeals of the sermon conclusion, then he needs to show them the virtue, the benefits, the outcome of responding to the truth so that their affections may be captured for living their lives in accordance to the truth of Scripture."

"People are willing to listen to a preacher who makes it worthwhile for them to do so. Any preacher who finds himself preaching to hearers who seem habitually dull and uninterested should have no misgivings about the source of this problem. The fault is in himself, if his preaching is irrelevant. As such, it will be viewed by his hearers as dull and uninteresting."

MOTIVATION TO ACT UPON THE APPLICATION IN THE SERMON CONCLUSION

The meaningful ministry of motivating hearers to respond to the preaching of God's Word found in the closing appeals of the sermon conclusion requires from the preacher, prayerful personal preparation, significant scriptural substance, and enlivened extemporaneous expression. In order to make sound and forceful application in the body of a sermon or in the sermon conclusion as expressed in its closing appeals, truth first must be understood in its biblical contexts then lifted out of its contexts and shown to be timeless and universal. "There is something powerful about universal, timeless, eternal truth. Such truth lies underneath the surface of all biblical material."[1] The ultimate task in preaching is to find and explain these timeless truths in such a way that they will challenge and motivate hearers to comply with the truth

---

1. Whitesell, *Power in Expository Preaching*, 93.

of Scripture in their lives. Timeless truths are essential for the main points of sermon structure, and for application found in the body of a sermon and in the sermon conclusion's closing appeals.

The significant, personal implications of Scripture do not lie on the surface of texts to be found by indolent preachers, the purveyors of perfunctory platitudes. "You must think, and muse, and meditate, and be alone with God, and let your mind and your soul and your heart play over the teaching till it glows and becomes alive and grips hold of you."[2] In other words, what is required is diligent effort to understand fully the doctrinal and practical bearings of the truths which God has revealed to us.[3]

Much preaching touches only the surface and shadow of truths rather than the essence of the truths themselves. As a result, preaching does not penetrate the inner parts of the hearers, their affections, their consciences, and their wills. A superficial handling of Scripture has neither a deep insight into, nor a strong grasp of, the hidden value of God's Word. What is said in the pulpit from such a shallow treatment of Scripture is true but only superficially so. The result is that the hearers are exposed to superficial truth that fails to motivate them just as it failed to motivate the one speaking to them. E. M. Bounds reckoned this as preaching superficially, preaching the hull of biblical truth. As Bounds phrased it, "The outside is the hull which must be broken and penetrated to get to the kernel. . . . The failure is in the preacher. . . . The deep things of God have never been sought, studied, fathomed, experienced by him."[4] In such instances, the unfortunate reality is that a preacher has precluded himself from being used by God as an instrument to provide a ministry to one's hearers that motivates them to comply with God's Word in their lives. Being motivated to comply with the Word of God in one's life results from the productive work of the Word of God in that individual's life, a result that is so very valuable for the hearer's spiritual growth, for God's glory, and for the hearer's impact in the lives of others.

The preached Word that is found motivating the hearers in the pews, typically, is preached by a man in the pulpit who has been motivated by the Word he is preaching. He was motivated by Scripture in his study when he was studying it and he is motivated by it when preaching it from the pulpit. Charles E. Jefferson wrote: "If you would catch and hold the hearts of men, you must weave your sermon of the very substance of your soul."[5] Though Jefferson's premise is acceptable in a subsequent and secondary sense, the major premise must always be that a sermon should be woven with Scripture, first and foremost. Then, the substance of one's soul may be woven into the sermon but even then, it must be the substance of a soul that is aligned with the Word of God. But how could any of this weaving take place if Scripture is not processed thoroughly by the preacher for his own understanding and for the care of his own

---

2. Smyth, *The Preacher and His Sermon*, 1922, 79.

3. Smyth, *The Preacher and His Sermon*, 1922, 90.

4. Bounds, *Power Through Prayer*, 26.

5. Jefferson, *The Minister as Prophet*, 1905, 59.

soul? "We are guilty of the most irrational conceit" if we think that we can preach with interest texts which are uninteresting to us.[6]

It is true that the man makes the preacher, but God makes the man. Therefore, it must be recognized that preaching is the ministry of a preacher but, more so, it is the exhibited essence of a preacher's life. In other words, "The sermon is forceful because the man is forceful. The sermon is holy because the man is holy. The sermon is full of divine unction because the man is full of divine unction. . . . Everything depends on the spiritual character of the preacher."[7] It is the character of the preaching pastor that compels him to motivate his hearers to comply with the Scripture-based closing appeals to which he exhorts them in his sermon conclusion.

The man in the pulpit who is best suited to motivate his hearers is the man who is the best student of Scripture that he can be. The best student of Scripture that a man can be is one who studies God's Word diligently and is one who is found obeying the instruction of Proverbs 4:23, "Watch over your heart with all diligence, for from it flow the springs of life." The diligent study of Scripture and the diligent watch over his own heart will cause a preacher to become one who is truly wise regarding the ways of human nature and humanity. The failure to do so is sobering. If one does not look well to the purity and depth of the fountain of one's heart, there will inevitably be a dry fountain or polluted channel from which it flows.[8] Such a condition would be catastrophic for any preacher but especially so for a preaching pastor since he seeks to be used by God as an instrument by which God purifies and enriches his people.

Preaching from a text that has gripped the heart of the preacher, a preacher who is preaching for the spiritual benefit of his hearers, will quite naturally desire to provide a highly personal form of expression in the sermon conclusion. In other words, such a highly personal form of expression is produced by extemporaneous preaching. An extemporaneous preaching pastor may be defined as one who, for the most part, knows what he wants to say, but does not know how he will say it. However, even extemporaneous preaching includes some strong, well-worded sentences which have been phrased "to clinch" portions of the sermon, and the sermon conclusion, in particular.[9]

Unless there is extraordinary earnestness in a preacher, a manuscript often comes between a preacher and his hearers. Therefore, in preaching from a manuscript, one must internalize the content of the manuscript so well that one's mind has certain familiarity with what he will say and one's heart is captivated by the truth so that his focus is upon those to whom he is preaching rather than his manuscript.[10] What is

6. Dale, *Nine Lectures on Preaching*, 1890, 122.

7. Bounds, *Power Through Prayer*, 11–12.

8. Bounds, *Power Through Prayer*, 84.

9. Dale, *Nine Lectures on Preaching*, 1890, 152–53.

10. Dale, *Nine Lectures on Preaching*, 1890, 163.

required is that a preacher be a "heart preacher"[11] for only a heart preacher can be a preaching pastor. It is crucial for the sermon conclusion that the preacher be a heart preacher who is a preaching pastor, with or without a manuscript.

The manuscript may be only a slight detriment to a powerful, highly personal communication to the hearers from a preaching pastor. Because the preaching pastor has the truth so much *in his heart* and the people to whom he is preaching are so much *on his heart*, the manuscript has a decreased necessity to command his attention. Furthermore, a manuscript will never be the cause of a heart preacher preaching to his hearers in a powerful, highly personal way.

Prayer, not a manuscript, makes a heart preacher who is a preaching pastor. "Prayer puts the preacher's whole heart into the preacher's sermon; prayer puts the preacher's sermon into the preacher's heart."[12] Such powerful, God-blessed, heart preaching "is not an inalienable gift. It is a conditional gift, and its presence is perpetuated and increased by the same process by which it was at first secured. . . . Direct from God in answer to prayer."[13] A heart preacher is a preaching pastor, with or without whatever liability may come from a manuscript.

An extemporaneous preaching pastor gains an advantage in his preaching style by an increased ease, directness, and vitality of communication. A heightened sensitivity occurs when a preacher engages his hearers with sustained eye contact. A preaching pastor's sustained eye contact demonstrated at the outset of the sermon conclusion communicates, in effect, "I now desire your complete attention and I will give you mine. I speak to you for your personal spiritual benefit. What I have to say is of tremendous value for you and I am concerned that you receive it."[14] A preaching pastor's direct, personal eye contact helps to bring clarity and enlivened communication in the act of preaching, especially in preaching the sermon conclusion.

Extemporaneous preaching prioritizes the ideas to be conveyed more than the words used to convey them. Extemporaneous preaching functions on the principle that if you have a clear command of the ideas you need to communicate, the words will come of themselves.[15] However, the opening sentences, leading lines of thought, and the closing sentences must be carefully composed because "words, like lenses, obscure what they do not enable us to see better."[16] But, perhaps the greatest benefit derived from the additional time and effort to thoroughly internalize the content of the sermon so that it may be preached extemporaneously is this: extemporaneous preaching is at work for the preaching pastor in his sermon conclusion where "in the generous heat which comes from direct eye contact with his audience, he may achieve

11. Bounds, *Power Through Prayer*, 81.
12. Bounds, *Power Through Prayer*, 81.
13. Bounds, *Power Through Prayer*, 102.
14. Borgman, *My Heart for Thy Cause*, 238.
15. Dale, *Nine Lectures on Preaching*, 1890, 168.
16. Dale, *Nine Lectures on Preaching*, 1890, 174.

a boldness both of thought and expression which are rarely achieved at the desk."[17] Boldness of thought and expression is pivotal in the sermon conclusion for a preaching pastor since he seeks to motivate his hearers to comply with the closing appeals so that the purpose of the sermon may be achieved in their lives.

An enlivened, personal communication is so crucial in the sermon conclusion that Ilion T. Jones advised, "Don't once break eye contact with the people. Memorize the entire conclusion. Here, if nowhere else, be completely free from a manuscript or notes. Let nothing divert your attention or the attention of the people from your final effort."[18] In like manner Woodrow Kroll mandated the following: "Memorize the conclusion. This is not a time to be concerned about whether or not you said the right thing. Make sure. Memorize the conclusion so that you can deliver it with power and maximum eye contact. . . . Bring the congregation to a point of decision or action and make that the highest point of the sermon."[19] When a preaching pastor is free from his paper, "he is more likely to experience the freedom of the Spirit in the act of preaching."[20] But more importantly, those who are on the receiving end of the closing appeals of the sermon conclusion may find themselves motivated to comply with the Scripture-based instructions and exhortations with which the preaching pastor has challenged them so personally and powerfully.

A SERMON CONCLUSION'S APPLICATION AS A COMMENCEMENT FOR THE HEARERS

In the conclusion there should be a focusing of the hearers upon the sermon's purpose, the suggestion of ways and means by which the sermon's purpose can be accomplished in their lives, and exhortation for the hearers to respond to the closing appeals of the sermon.[21] People want to know how they should respond to the sermon and will not begrudge the preaching pastor for showing them from Scripture what they are to do nor will they resent him for his exhorting them to do it, at any point in the sermon but especially in the sermon conclusion. Since the preaching pastor preaches for a verdict in the form of a commitment on behalf of the hearers to comply with the closing appeals of the sermon conclusion, strong exhortation from the preaching pastor to the wills of his hearers must be present in the effort to motivate them to respond.[22] The response to which the preaching pastor exhorts his hearers is for a commencement, a beginning point for a life of unprecedented obedience to the Word

17. Dale, *Nine Lectures on Preaching*, 1890, 165.

18. Jones, *Principles and Practice of Preaching*, 167.

19. Kroll, *Prescription for Preaching*, 182.

20. Borgman, *My Heart for Thy Cause*, 247.

21. Whitesell, *Power in Expository Preaching*, 115.

22. Jones, *Principles and Practice of Preaching*, 162.

of God. A commencement is the personal reality for those who respond to the closing appeals of the sermon conclusion.

Application should be distributed throughout the sermon, but it must be condensed in the conclusion. In the process of implementing application by means of the closing appeals, to which the preaching pastor will exhort the hearers to respond, the consciences, emotions/affections, and the wills of the hearers become the intended targets for his direct exhortations or indirect inferential instructions. All truth is relevant since every truth generates some necessities for its accommodation in life, requires some ways it must be responded to, and obligates its hearers to do something about it. Relevant preaching addresses the consciences of the hearers regarding their need to respond to biblical truth, and it appeals to their wills for an appropriate response as the truth requires of them.[23] The hearers' commencement to a new life of obedience to the Word of God is predicated upon their response to the closing appeals through the means of quickened consciences and wills which have been captivated by the Holy Spirit of God and the truth of Scripture.

From the outset of the sermon conclusion several things must not be lost sight of in the process of preaching it. The first is that the preaching pastor intends to be heard and the second is that he intends to be heeded. Just as the preaching pastor will compel a commitment from his hearers regarding the truth he will preach to them, he must first demand from himself this twofold commitment regarding the truth he will preach: "I intend to be heard and I intend to be heeded."

The preaching pastor will not expound his preaching text without bringing his sermon to an appropriate end. This means that the end of the sermon cannot occur until his hearers have been challenged to comply with Scripture-based closing appeals which constitutes the appropriate response to which he will compel them to respond. What the preaching pastor does for his hearers in the sermon conclusion is of utmost importance. He provides for them a possible commencement to a new life of obedience to the Word of God. But this cannot be so unless he is heard. Therefore, the preaching pastor is resolute in his first commitment regarding the sermon conclusion: that he will preach with the intention to be heard by his hearers.

The second resolve of the preaching pastor requires more from him. There is a built-in level of agreeable accommodation for an unheeded hearing which he must resolve himself against. In other words, "If only he is heard, that will suffice." This is the agreeable accommodation from which he must guard himself. The truth is that an unheeded hearing is better only slightly than not being heard. So, beyond being heard, the preaching pastor must resolve to be heeded. The resolve to be heeded requires the preaching pastor to put himself into urgent contact with his hearers through the means of clear, vital, and concrete instruction to the hearers about their commencement of a more faithful obedience to the Word of God.[24]

23. Jones, *Principles and Practice of Preaching*, 161.
24. Ellicott, *Homiletical and Pastoral Lectures*, 1880, 54.

There are two issues for a preaching pastor regarding his hearers in a sermon conclusion: an end and a commencement. The end has nothing to do with the cessation of the sermon but an ending of the hearers' present status of obedience to the Word of God. However complete and consistent the obedience is, however rightly motivated it is, it must end. But it ends only to begin, that is, to commence in greater fulness, greater consistency, and in purer motivation. The issues of the hearers' ending, and the hearers' commencement must be vital concerns for the preaching pastor. He really must be about this in preaching his sermon conclusion. He truly must desire the ending of their status quo and their commencement of a new level of obedience in their lives.

Regardless of the spiritual maturity and the worthy walk of any Christian a preacher may preach to, it cannot be said of that believer what Jesus Christ declared about Himself when he said, "I always do the things that are pleasing to Him."[25] Every believer has room for greater compliance to Scripture in every area of his or her life. Thus, the important matter of an insightful ending and commencement to be facilitated by the content of the sermon conclusion is justified.

The preaching pastor's true desire to see his hearers heeding the truth of the closing appeals of the sermon may be accomplished as he productively speaks to the hearers' affections, what they aspire toward, what they desire to do in response to the truth they have heard. If the closing appeals find no room in the arena of the hearers' desires and aspirations, they will make no commitment to what they are being exhorted and implored to do. The most logical biblical pleadings will go unheeded if the exhortations bypass their affections. People are always interested in what they want and may be interested in what they need if they become convinced of the actuality of their need. The following testimony indicates the significance of the affections in making any commitment in life, no matter how important or insignificant:

> Many years ago, when I was in direct sales selling cookware, I made a presentation to a family that desperately needed my cookware. I had the opportunity to inventory their kitchen utensils while preparing the demonstration meal, and they had nothing. Because their need was so great, I spent nearly two hours attempting to close the sale. The lady and her husband had the same level of intensity in their ability to persevere as I did because they continued to say, "No money, too expensive, can't afford it!" As I was packing my sample case to leave, the husband, his wife, or I mentioned "China." To this day I can still remember the way that dear lady's eyes lit up. She said, "China? Do you sell fine China?" "Yes, ma'am," I responded. "We sell the finest fine China in the whole world!" Less than thirty minutes later, I left that household with an order worth substantially more than the entire set of cookware. Now Think with me. If she couldn't afford the set of cookware she so desperately needed, how could she afford the China she didn't need? The answer is, she *couldn't*

25. John 9:29b.

afford the set of cookware she *didn't want*, but she *could* afford the set of fine China she *did want*.[26]

If there is no desire in the hearers' affections to comply with the exhortations of the closing appeals in a sermon conclusion, then every unaffected hearer will walk away from that to which they have been challenged. The preaching pastor will have been heard but not heeded.

Why is it that a preaching pastor is not heeded if he was resolved to be heeded, when earnestly offering clear, vital, concrete closing appeals, for their good and God's glory? Among other reasons that could be suggested, the answer may well lie in the way in which the closing appeals were not connected with the hearers' desires and aspirations. "In the Word of God, we are forced to deal with the eternal, the holy, the sublime, and the awesome, we dare not arrange them with the pauper's rag of abstraction or the black sackcloth of dullness."[27] Exhorting hearers to do what they have no desire to do will always be adorned in the sackcloth of dullness. If the closing appeals are presented only in the attire of "should," "ought," and "must," a preacher must not be surprised if very few respond to the affectionless appeals.[28]

If a preaching pastor is appealing to the hearers' volition without appealing to their affections, he is working against himself and not working affectively on behalf of his hearers. If he is sincere about seeing his hearers respond to the closing appeals of the sermon conclusion, then he needs to show them the virtue, the benefits, the outcome of responding to the truth so that their affections may be captured for living their lives in accordance with the truth of Scripture.

A PREACHING PASTOR'S RELEVANCE IN LIFE AND PREACHING

A great way for a preacher to be unfaithful in the preaching ministry is for him to preach only the texts of Scripture to which he is obedient. A preacher's preaching ministry must not be directed or dictated by his personal failures or disobedience. Therefore, preachers find themselves preaching texts to which complete and consistent obedience has yet to accompany their lives. No preacher's life is commensurate with his preaching. Every preacher is found preaching a better rendition of biblical truth than his life is found practicing the biblical truth about which he preaches. This,

---

26. Ziglar, *Selling 101*, 39–40.

27. Montoya, *Preaching with Passion*, 135–36.

28. The reader must not misconstrue this author's instruction dissuading exhortations in the form of "should, ought, and must." I am not siding with the effeminate and liberal position of those who think these terms should not be used in preaching, but rather, should be replaced by the word "can." This heresy has, unfortunately, found a home in conservative circles. The imperatives of Scripture must be enforced as such in preaching. What I am saying is that though these terms certainly will and must be used, they should not be used alone, that is, they should be accompanied by instruction and appeals to the affections so that the hearers may desire to do what they should, ought, and must do.

however, is a great prospect for both, personal spiritual refinement and corporate spiritual advancement.

Often a preacher deals with subject-matter to which he knows he is not completely and consistently obedient. This is the reality, not the problem. The problem is that a preacher would find his lack of complete and consistent obedience satisfactory rather than committing himself to change his disobedience by involving himself in that change before he shows others from the Word of God how and why their complete and consistent obedience matters. The willingness of a preacher to disobey that which he will challenge others to be obedient to is a problem, a big problem. Yet, the commitment to and process of making personal change regarding the subject-matter he will be preaching is not only of significant personal benefit, but it affords valuable insights that will be of benefit to those to whom he preaches.

In the process of making change before he preaches to others to do so, he will learn practical matters regarding the needed change that the ones to whom he preaches will need to know. He will experience what the difficulties are, what is helpful to overcome the difficulties, the ways and means by which obedience can be enhanced, etc. In other words, the week before a preacher is in the pulpit, he should be living in a practical Christianity lab regarding the subject-matter of his preaching, that is, the subject-matter of the sermon and its purpose. The result of which may provide "an example of Christ's power in my life and an encouragement to others."[29] But, of even greater significance, this will be in keeping with biblical precept and example. Steven J. Lawson's insights, drawn from the book of Nehemiah about Ezra the scribe and priest, are motivational as he writes:

> *After* he (Ezra) studied the Word and *before* he taught it, he obeyed it. In other words, somewhere between his study and his delivery, the Word was put into practice in his personal life. Here lies a logical, unfolding progression of activities. The second activity ('practice') builds on the first ('study'), and the third ('teach') rests on the first two. Thus, in being quick to obey the moral requirements of the Law of the Lord, Ezra serves as a model for preachers. The expositor must not only practice *what* he preaches, but he must also practice it *before* he preaches. . . . Moreover, Ezra obeyed the Word with the same 'heart' devotion with which he studied it. . . . Ezra, however, was a scribe who *wholeheartedly* kept the word, not with mere external ritual or empty routine, but with a deep internal desire. . . . The Word must be internalized by the preacher before it is passed on to others. His heart cannot be into preaching until his heart is into the Word and the Word is into his heart. . . . The one who brings the Word must bow first before the Word and fully keep it. Selective obedience

---

29. Dever et al., *Preaching the Cross*, (Wheaton, Illinois: Crossway, 2007), from Dever's chapter, "A Real Minister: 1 Corinthians 4," 32.

is *no* obedience. Partial obedience is nothing more than disguised *disobedience*. To be compelling in the pulpit, preachers must be complete in obedience.[30]

Complete and consistent obedience is to be the response of those who hear the Word of God proclaimed just as it is to be the response of those who proclaim it, before and after they do so. A preaching pastor who follows the example of Ezra's integration of the Word of God in his life will be more concerned with his understanding and obeying the Word of God than he will be with his proclamation of it, though the proclamation of God's Word is a great priority in his life.

PERSONAL RELEVANCE AND CONCERN FOR PEOPLE

People naturally appreciate the relevant preaching of a preaching pastor. People are willing to listen to a preacher who makes it worthwhile for them to do so. This is so patently true that any preacher who finds himself preaching to hearers who seem habitually dull and uninterested should have no misgivings about the source of this problem. The fault is in himself. It is rooted in his irrelevant preaching which is viewed by his hearers as dull and uninteresting. Yet, in order to exempt oneself from shouldering such a burdensome grievance, it must be anticipated that "some stupid person may object, that this is making too much of our own human efforts and tell us that God can use very dull sermons to the helping of men's souls. Of course, that is so, and it is very well that it is, for there are certainly plenty of dull sermons to be used."[31] Dull, irrelevant sermons have no right to exist. They should never occur. When they do occur, barring a miracle from God, the impact of a dull, irrelevant sermon upon the hearers will be that they simply are underwhelmed by the insignificance of that which posed as an imposter of preaching.

It is counterproductive to believe that hearers of sermons have the capacity to think well of a sermon, or the preacher of it, that is irrelevant to them. Personal experience underscores the importance of relevance when subjected to a preacher who provides little or no relevance to his hearers in the preaching of what he alone believes is a sermon. The Master of Ceremony of an irrelevant undertaking will be viewed overwhelmingly as "no preacher" and his "no sermon" speech event will be appreciated only as a waste of time by the consensus of his hearers. It has been stated that the radio station of every hearer's heart is naturally "tuned to WII-FM, the call letters of which stand for, What's In It For Me?"[32] Though this would appear only as an indication of the superficial, self-consumed culture of modern western society, of which it certainly is a chief characteristic, it is an attribute of mankind regardless of time, place, or culture.

30. Lawson, *Famine in the Land*, 90–91, 92.
31. Smyth, *The Preacher and His Sermon*, 1922, 63.
32. Ziglar, *Selling 101*, 43.

The ancient Greek and Roman orators understood the importance that relevance had for its citizens even in civil and political proceedings. That is why Cicero's established essentials of oratory were: placere (to interest), docere (to teach), movere (to move).[33] Based upon the accepted value of a preacher to interest, to teach, and to move his hearers in preaching, one homiletician made the connection of relevance in preaching certain as he queried, "How futile is it to attempt to interest, if you do not go on to teach and to move? On the other hand, of what value is it to attempt to move and to teach, if they have no interest?"[34] Yet, it is in the arena of preaching, more than civil or political proceedings, that relevance must be prominent. Prominent relevance in preaching should be an every-sermon-reality based simply upon the nature of Scripture since it is eternally relevant.

R. W. Dale is helpful as he interjected three key assertions about the importance of relevance in preaching as he weds together the connections between relevance, a concern for hearers, a desire to be of assistance to hearers, and fulfilling one's role in preaching. According to Dale, it must not be the case that, while preaching, the hearers fail to understand how what the preacher is saying has any relevance to them. Should this be the case, the hearers should justly realize that they are of little value to the preacher with the result being that such a preacher "will soon have no congregation to preach to."[35] Dale interjected that for one to preach with greater effectiveness "you must care more for men."[36] Finally, Dale believed that for a preacher to preach a sermon without preaching it to help substantially those who hear it is "treachery" to one's hearers and to the Lord.[37] Relevant preaching addresses life so that the hearers cannot but make the connection between what the preacher is talking about and the value that this has for their lives. When this is done and to the degree to which this is done in preaching, the hearers will be interested accordingly to the preacher's sermon.

The valuable distinction relevance makes in a sermon is the difference between a sermon as a homiletical product versus a sermon as authentic preaching. Authentic preaching is never less than a service of ministry intended to profoundly impact the lives of the hearers. "A sermon, though theologically accurate, structurally sound, thoroughly biblical, amply illustrated, and logically agreeable could be a failure as a product of authentic preaching. Why? Because it lacks incarnation; it has never been earthed in the experience of the preacher"[38] and it is not delivered as an act of serving the hearers in the sense of offering them truth meant to bring profitable reformation to their lives. Though, perhaps, attractive in form, it is stillborn as it is cut short from drawing its first breath of life. A sermon that contains life, that is, preaching that

---

33. Smyth, *The Preacher and His Sermon*, 1922, 59.

34. Smyth, *The Preacher and His Sermon*, 1922, 59–60.

35. Dale, *Nine Lectures on Preaching*, 1890, 23.

36. Dale, *Nine Lectures on Preaching*, 1890, 20.

37. Dale, *Nine Lectures on Preaching*, 1890, 22.

38. Read, *Sent from God*, 68.

speaks to the lives of men and is delivered by a man who is diligently seeking to help them through his preaching, will always be the kind of preaching that is desired by people and is the kind of preaching that is worthy of acclaim.

Many things could be said about the preaching of any preacher. As a Professor of Preaching and Professor of Greek, John A. Broadus's preaching could have been characterized by his homiletical richness or the wealth of insights he could provide from the Greek text. However, it was said of Broadus's preaching that, "He interpreted people to themselves" because "he explained to them their own experiences."[39] Such preaching is valued because it is so profitable for the hearers and it is profitable for the hearers because it is relevant, authentic preaching. Ian Maclaren wrote in his book *Cure of Souls*, "The divinity of the sermon is in proportion to its humanity."[40] Maclaren's statement, though overstated and not logically true, does emphasize what was intended by his statement, namely, that it is important that sermons relate to the lives of those who hear them.

Some men's preaching works only to raise a barrier in the hearts of the hearers. The hearers do not find that his preaching intersects with their lives nor do they find his preaching desirable. However, in the hearts of the same people, another preacher establishes a beachhead of life and human experience in his sermon which captivates their hearts and wins a response of attention and interest from his hearers. And because of his ability to relate to his hearers in the preaching of the Word, he may be used to win a verdict for their obedience to the truth.[41] Authentic preaching, being relevant to the lives of its hearers, finds a reception by them in a way irrelevant preaching could never be received by them.

Too much of preaching is like a discussion about engines with a mechanic who is dying, and about to die, of inoperable brain cancer. No matter how mechanically accurate and detailed the discussion is, if there is no transition to an accurate, detailed, needed discussion about the mechanic's impending death, his essential reality, then the conversation is irrelevant. Unless the conversation moves from the superficiality of engine technology and performance to the essential consideration of death and eternity, the irrelevant conversation might just as well as never occurred. The relevance that a preacher needs to establish is the connection between the explanation of biblical truth and life as it is being experienced and as it could be experienced by his hearers. The primary concern of the preaching pastor is with what the hearers do because of the explanation and application of Scripture he provides for them.[42]

A sermon's relevance begins with the clarification of scriptural truth and the implications of the truth in day to day living. But the ultimate test of a sermon's relevance

---

39. Hoyt, *Vital Elements of Preaching*, 1929, 81.
40. As cited in Hoyt, *Vital Elements of Preaching*, 1929, 104.
41. Hoyt, *Vital Elements of Preaching*, 1929, 102.
42. Pearson, *The Preacher: His Purpose and Practice*, 120.

must appeal to the hearers' acceptance of the truth and their obedience to it.[43] Henry Ward Beecher insisted that the business of a preaching pastor is a living work, which is a building work. "If you are to be true preachers, you are to be man-builders."[44] Beecher's conviction was neither weak nor wavering as he explained, "You will be very superficial, you will be very poor in power, unless you are intimately mixed up with the lives of those to whom you preach, and to whom you bring the gospel. . . . Preaching has to be vital and effective; it should derive a great deal of its element from the known life and wants of the men for whom the sermon is a medical prescription."[45] The connection between the requirement of knowing men and the responsibility of building men is a sound one. This connection is advocated and practiced by the best of preachers in any generation. The degree to which this connection is not demonstrated in a sermon determines the degree to which a sermon is irrelevant, and this is true for preaching in any generation. Significant relevance in a sermon is a major component of building up people through preaching.

John Chrysostom, the "Golden-mouth" preacher, was a man with a great heart for, and a wide knowledge of, people. People flocked to him and hung upon his words, not only because of his oratory, but because "he knew them so well, loved them so much, and talked to them about those actual homely facts of daily life which make up the greater part of everyone's existence."[46] This depiction of Chrysostom represents most fully what is characterized by the concept of a preaching pastor. The magnetism of Chrysostom is that he was a student of the Word and a student of life. Chrysostom was saturated with the Scriptures and was determined that his hearers would be taught to base their lives upon the principles of Scripture and was committed to apply Scripture to the concerns of humanity and the matters of day to day life.

The connection between knowledge of Scripture and knowledge of life and humanity is a connection that must be in existence and must increase in the life of a preaching pastor. The failure to perpetuate this dual increase in the life of a preacher will only serve to produce a plateau in his preaching effectiveness. A failure that produces a plateau in preaching is bad but what is worse is a failure that results in a preacher being robbed of preaching effectiveness.

David H. Greer describes the kind of effectiveness that accompanies the preaching of a man who proclaims truth that has been experienced by him. The offering of his preaching ministry is that which has been field-tested in his life. The truth he offers has been vetted by his own experience and he offers to others what he knows will work in their lives as well. Greer specifies crucial cause and effect realities of a preaching pastor as he writes:

43. Pearson, *The Preacher: His Purpose and Practice*, 121.

44. Beecher, *Lectures on Preaching*, First Series, 1872, 21.

45. Beecher, *Lectures on Preaching*, Second Series, 1873, 148–49.

46. Horne, *The Romance of Preaching*, 1914, 143–44.

> I'm sure we have felt as we listen to some men preach that we would like to
> listen to them often. They helped us so much; they inspired us; they seem to
> touch and awaken what was best and purest, what was the divinest in us, and
> to bring out and express it, and to make it, for a time at least, ascendant and
> dominant in us. And why? What was the secret of their power? They may have
> been eloquent in the ordinary sense of the term, or they may not have been.
> They may have been learned and scholarly, or they may not have been. Nor did
> we always agree, perhaps, with what we heard them say. And yet, somehow,
> they always manage to make us feel as though they had a personal message
> for us. And so, indeed, it was a personal message for us, simply because it
> was their own personal message. . . . It may have been some truth which we
> already knew, some very familiar truth; and yet as the preacher preached it,
> it seemed like something new, and to have in it something new. And it did
> have in it something new; it had the preacher in it. He had made the truth his
> own. He had wrought it out, or fought it out, and won it for himself, and it was
> like a piece of himself. . . . He was telling us rather what he, by his own liv-
> ing thought, by his own living experience, had made his very own. It was the
> travail of his soul, and we saw it, and felt it, and were satisfied. . . . As a living
> truth we felt it, not as truth in abstract form, but as in truth in concrete form,
> as truth in flesh and blood. That was his secret and power, or the secret of his
> power. It is always the secret of power.[47]

The presentation of truth that indicates the undertow of a tacit testimonial about the
profitability of truth is always impressive because it is personal to the preacher and
abundantly clear to the hearers. But more importantly, truth that is perceived by the
hearers as holding the greatest power is that which has not only been personally experienced by the preacher but also is understood to be universal truth that is potential
and available for their own experience and benefit.

Substantial proof that the preacher has grown in his essential ability to preach is
evidenced when a hearer can think about a preacher, while the preacher is in the act
of preaching, "How is it that this man knows so well what my life is about? It seems
like he is preaching about me!" For any preacher, to be in command of the common
experiences of his hearers result only from an insightful understanding of Scripture
and a growing knowledge of life and humanity, which allows a preaching pastor to
relate to his hearers' situations, struggles, perplexities, and tendencies in a profitable
way. As a result of such growth in the knowledge of Scripture, life, and humanity,
there will be an emphasis in his preaching upon the concrete over the abstract, and an
emphasis upon the personal over the general.[48] His increased growth in the knowledge of Scripture, life, and humanity prevents him from preaching as irrelevantly, as
abstractly, and as impersonally as he did in former years. The preacher has changed

47. Greer, *The Preacher and His Place*, 1895, 73–75.
48. Berry, *Vital Preaching*, 58–59.

and so has his preaching. Such a change in one's preaching brings with it an increased potential to change the lives of those who are subjected to it in a sermon.

When a preacher possesses the resulting character-qualities of a man who meets the biblical qualifications for a pastor and has developed the ability to relate intimately well with his hearers in his preaching, that man is a preaching pastor. But the ability of a preaching pastor to relate in such a personally profitable way means that he too has experienced the same, or much the same, situations, struggles, perplexities, and tendencies as his hearers. Yet, where a separation may surface between the experience of his hearers and his own experience is that he has "discovered the adequacy of Christ" in his experiences.[49] It is the combination of the depth and breadth of human experiences and a deeper experience of God's working in them which makes a preacher a preaching pastor, not just a fellow sufferer on the difficult pathway of life. More than sharing the same experiences of life, the hearers need to learn from a preaching pastor how he has, and how they can, respond in a correct fashion to the struggles and difficulties of life in accordance with Scripture.

The sermon of a preaching pastor is intended to impact the hearts and the lives of his hearers. His concern is for his hearers to receive a scriptural intake of truth from the pulpit as well as a concern that his hearers respond with a scriptural implementation of truth in their lives. The preaching pastor is constrained by a passion to be helpful to his hearers. The help he aspires to provide for his hearers is that through his, explanation, application, argumentation, and illustration, the Word of God will be exalted in their hearts and the Word of God will be exhibited in their lives. The example of a Christian's life and character is both valuable and observable. It matters tremendously that the example of Christlikeness be demonstrated by believers in a sin-filled, fallen world.[50] But the exemplification of Christlikeness is demonstrated and maintained in the lives of believers only as a result of hearing God's Word, being challenged to implement the truth of Scripture-based closing appeals, and choosing to respond to the truths of Scripture in one's life. Therefore, preaching must provide a certain knowledge of Scripture and challenge the hearers to respond to it. This is what a preaching pastor will do through the closing appeals of his sermon conclusion. And this must not be viewed as something new to be done in preaching. On the contrary, this is simply a continuation of what was done in the preaching of Christ and his followers.

The apostles' preaching and the preaching of those who followed them involved two priorities: a proclamation of the gospel to unbelievers; and the "explaining, instructing, informing, and guiding" of fellow-believers by means of the Scriptures.[51] Both the proclamation of the gospel and the instructing of believers should still be the

---

49. Hough, *The Theology of a Preacher*, 1912, 14.

50. Davis, *Evangelistic Preaching*, 1921, 20.

51. Read, *Sent from God*, 51.

two priorities of preaching, and both priorities should be accomplished at the highest level in the sermon conclusion.

Preaching begins to gain essential traction for the hearers when the precepts of Scripture connect with life as they know it and experience it. Halford Luccock expressed the initiation of preaching to be tied to the points of relevance between the then of Scripture and the now of life. According to Luccock, "It is when we remove the good Samaritan from the Jericho road to Main Street, just around the corner, remove the rich fool from Judea to our own neighborhood in Nebraska or Texas, or move Judas into our own congregation, that the trouble begins; and that is when real preaching begins."[52]

Real preaching is that which addresses the hearers. The more the hearers are addressed by a sermon, the more real the preaching is. The subjectivity of the hearer is a factor of effective preaching that must not be overlooked. Objectively evaluating a sermon as a homiletical product by many criteria yields a far different evaluation from the subjective evaluation of a typical hearer who applies one criterion, the extremely valuable question of, "how does this sermon benefit me?" For the hearers, the only estimation of a sermon that is worthy of consideration is its ability to impact them. In a word, the significant criterion of a sermon is "relevance."

The hearer's desire for relevant preaching underscores the absolute necessity that a preaching pastor be a man who has insight into humanity, beginning with himself. Though there are distinct characteristics among individuals, overall, people are far more alike than they are different. It is certain that what a preacher finds in his own heart exists also in the hearts of others.[53] Therefore, "examine your own heart, and whatever you find there, apply to others, freely. Let your own heart and conscience represent a portion of your hearers, if not the whole of them. If you are affected, others will be also."[54] So then the vital responsibility of a preaching pastor becomes clear. Before preaching the truth of his text, a preaching pastor has the need to wisely assess his own life, his own obedience to the Word of God as he understands it, applying the implications of its truths to himself. Having done this, he will have an uncanny ability to preach to his hearers effectively, demonstrating to them the value of God's Word for their lives. In such a process he will be about the work of explaining how the understanding of Scripture provides much-needed insights to the lives of men. This necessitates him to wrestle not only with the text to find out what it requires of him by what it means, but to wrestle with himself to provide the discipline to apply the truth to his life, and then apply it to the lives of his hearers.

This disciplining of himself to comply with what he has found in the Scriptures allows the "practical value and vital force" of truth to be perceived by his hearers as he

---

52. Luccock, *In the Minister's Workshop*, 156.

53. Taylor, *The Ministry of the Word*, 1876, 36.

54. Taylor, *The Ministry of the Word*, 1876, 38.

preaches to them.[55] As productive as it is for the hearers to grasp correctly the practical value and vital force of truth, these are only a precursor to that which the preaching pastor is seeking to achieve in the lives of his hearers. He seeks for his hearers to understand the practical value and vital force of truth as it is experienced in their lives, thus changing how they live their lives ongoingly in response to the truth.

The knowledge of one's heart in the context of a sound, increasing knowledge of Scripture is the "light of a higher kind" which Spurgeon implored preachers to acquire. The higher kind of light advocated by Spurgeon was the result of a prayerful study of Scripture and its doctrines which are then brought against one's life for a complete, enlightening exposure to determine what may be out of line and what must be corrected. Additionally, Spurgeon exhorted: "We are to study men and our own hearts; we ought to sit as disciples in the school of providence and experience. Some ministers grow fast because the great Teacher chastens them sorely, and the chastening is sanctified; but others learn nothing by their experience, they blunder out of one ditch into another, and learn nothing by their difficulties but the art of creating fresh ones."[56] The self-understanding that is so valuable for a preaching pastor to preach effectively to others requires him to be a good student of the Bible by understanding what God has revealed to man, as well as being a good student of life by understanding what God always has been doing, and what God is doing in the lives of men.

The value of gaining a sound, insightful understanding of the lives of mankind may be diminished due to the faulty presupposition that people are so different that it is not possible to attain such an understanding. Furthermore, people are so different that any sermon preached can only be received by one's hearers with the greatest amount of variance in terms of effectiveness. The recognition that a sermon is not equally relevant, circumstantially, to all who hear it is a given. Therefore, the obvious differences that exist among the hearers cannot be the grounds for a legitimate criticism regarding the relevance of any sermon that is preached. The relevance of a sermon is not based upon attending to the superficial differences that may differentiate the hearers. The relevance of preaching is in reference to a sermon's essential relevance.

Essential relevance is about that which is universal in the lives of people, the relevance of timeless truths, the relevance of scriptural principles that are in force for all people everywhere. These are the things that are the foundation for essential relevance, the true relevance of the sermon. People are superficially, circumstantially, and insignificantly different from one another. But the difference between one man and another man is like "the difference of islands. One island may be richly forested and another apparently barren, but under the sea they both reach down to share the common structure of the Earth, and beneath the hiding waters the binding land belies

55. Montgomery, *Expository Preaching*, 62–63.
56. Spurgeon, *An All-round Ministry*, 1900, 167–68.

their superficial separation."[57] Even in people's seemingly vast differences from one another, relevant preaching is possible because they are so similar in their essential humanity.

It also must be acknowledged that an experience in the life of any preacher does not possess the same value to relate to and enlighten others in equal measure and in like manner. A preacher's experience will intersect with what is of essential relevance, that which is relevant to all. But the specific, subjective, circumstantial realities of his experience that are the present reality shared by some hearers will be of unique relevance to them. These individuals will find his experience essentially and circumstantially relevant to them. Therefore, one's experience of life, as perceived by others, may be likened to "the stern-light of the ship at sea: it enlightens only the track which has been passed over."[58] Therefore, it needs to be acknowledged that for those who are travelling that same track, the enlightenment they may glean from the experiences of one who has gone before them has unique insight to them, and may be perceived as priceless to them.

The valuable characteristic of relevance in preaching is advocated broadly and commended highly. But, how does a sound understanding of Scripture and its doctrines as well as an insightful knowledge of oneself and humanity make its way into a sermon so that preaching becomes relevant? Relevance is the result of scriptural knowledge and the knowledge of humanity applied to several areas of man's life. A sermon, to be effectively relevant, may include more than but must not fail to incorporate the following areas of life:

1. It must reveal the misconceptions of, or make advancements in, the beliefs which the hearers hold. This is the relevance of their affections and volition being applied to cognitive matters which is the basis of their convictions.

2. It must deal with the challenges, the difficulties, the sorrows of the hearers' actual experience, and what could be the hearers' personal, imminent experience. This is the relevance of their affections and volition regarding their conduct.

3. It must confront the hearers' consciences regarding their associations with sin, and their obedience to the faith as those who have been saved from sin. This is the relevance of their affections and volition directing their moment by moment choices.[59]

Relevance increases in prominence as truth is perceived to impact the hearer's understanding, emotions, judgement, and resolve. As the perception of truth deepens in any or in each of these areas, the more relevant the truth becomes to the hearer. As a preacher exhorts his hearers to comply their lives to the truth as it pertains to their

---

57. Pearson, *The Preacher: His Purpose and Practice*, 90.

58. Storrs, *Conditions of Success in Preaching Without Notes*, 1875, 11.

59. Ellicott, *Homiletical and Pastoral Lectures*, 1880, 30.

convictions, conduct, and choices, the relevance of the truth is perceived to possess an increasing profitability for them as they are faithful to comply their lives to the truth in any or in each of these ways.

THE RELEVANCE OF PREACHING AND ILLUSTRATIVE MATERIAL

Illustration strengthens the relevance of truth that is conveyed through the closing appeals of a sermon conclusion. A conclusion should be diversified, in that, several means of enablement should be gleaned from the storehouse of Scripture that will benefit those who desire to live according to the truth as revealed in God's Word. Conclusion diversity is added to and aided as it includes illustrative material. There are diverse ways the illustrative material can be used productively supplying a concrete depiction of the ways and means, the manner, the impact, the results, or the motives for complying with a closing appeal or appeals. Though it is true as the French homiletician Jean Claude wrote many years ago, "Conclusion sometimes delights in examples,"[60] it is truer that conclusions cannot but help to draw strength in relevance through the inclusion of examples. The profitability of illustrative material in a sermon conclusion does not need to be defended. However, the use of illustrative material as a valuable aid of a preaching pastor for the hearer's optimal understanding is an issue that needs to be clarified and encouraged.

The relevance of the closing appeals being vitalized by the vivid imagery provided through illustration may be a precept of preaching that is known and understood by a preacher as good preaching pedagogy. Yet, his failure to practice what he knows is not just a *personal failure in his preaching,* but it becomes a *pastoral failure of his preaching* that minimizes the relevance of the sermon conclusion, the place where relevance counts most. Though there may be other reasons why a preacher would do less than what is needed for relevance in one's preaching, the most egregious would be a lack of pastoral concern on behalf of the preacher so that he is not willing to do all he can to assist his hearers to comply with scriptural truth in their lives.

There is a case to be made for pedagogical consistency to supply illustrative material for the closing appeals of a sermon conclusion simply because concrete truth is more relevant than abstract truth. Therefore, to violate this axiom is self-defeating. Yet, the concrete truths supplied by a preacher who wishes not to violate what he knows to be the best practices of preaching will be offered with the strength of that motive and will be received by the hearers in the power which that motive accompanies. But how can the power of that motive compare with the motive of a preaching pastor who is motivated to help God's people understand, in optimal clarity and relevance, the concrete appeals he brings to them from the Word of God for their personal, spiritual benefit? There simply is no comparison! The good form of a preacher who supplies

60. Claude, *Claude's Essay,* 1801, 133.

illustrative material with his closing appeals will be a benefit that will be perceived by the hearers. But far better, is the reality that the hearers will be perceptive of the heart of the preaching pastor who, in his preaching, is concerned more for their personal, spiritual benefit than merely being concerned to conform to what he knows to be the best homiletical practices.

That which is relatively unknown, or what is abstract must be learned in terms of that which is known, and, therefore, what is concrete. Any progress in understanding must build from one's present experience or from a cognitive process that understands the abstract in light of the concrete. This is the law of learning and this is how understanding takes place. No one is exempt from this law and no one ever outgrows it. For preaching to be understood clearly and for persuasion to be a possibility, the content of instruction cannot be presented in the absence of known truth, truth as it is known by the hearers, nor can the abstract instruction be presented alone, without the concretion supplied by illustration. The content of preaching must intersect with what is known in the hearer's experience, and that which is abstract must be made concrete by illustrative material. Preachers simply cannot afford to set aside this established law of learning. "The power of illustration is a bright light, a new flash, on common knowledge; it lights up familiar truth or translates the unknown forming a sound bond of interest and sympathy."[61] Advancement of understanding cannot be made, optimally, without the concrete insight provided by illustration.

This law of learning is not just a convention of man, but rather it has been established by God. God, Himself, has sanctioned it as one author argued when he wrote: "General revelation teaches that there are God-given laws of learning. One such law teaches that people learn by moving from the known to the unknown. They learn by associating that which they know with that which they do not know, so that they may gain new knowledge. . . . (God) works by and with this natural law of learning, not against it."[62] How unwise it is to be found working against what God has established as a law of learning when preaching his Word for the hearers' increased understanding.

Illustration, the means by which a preacher moves his hearers from the unknown to the known, is crucial for learning and increased understanding. But illustration is ultimately valuable in preaching to help bring persuasion to the hearers about that which they have an increased understanding. Understanding is clinched by an illustration when hearers are cognitively persuaded about an instruction, that is, they not only understand the instruction but are convinced about its veracity. Yet, at a deeper level of learning, understanding is clinched by the use of illustration when hearers are volitionally persuaded by an instruction, that is, they not only understand the veracity of the instruction but are convinced about its value when it becomes a part of one's life.

For the closing appeals of a sermon conclusion, illustration is used to provide cognitive and volitional persuasion. An illustration that is sufficient to provide

61. Hoyt, *Vital Elements of Preaching*, 1929, 97.

62. Borgman, *My Heart for Thy Cause*, 175.

cognitive persuasion about the veracity of a biblical precept is usually inadequate to be volitionally persuasive. This is so because that which clearly is understood to be true does not necessarily motivate a hearer who has a clear understanding of a biblical precept to implement it in one's life. The veracity of an instruction may not be viewed by a hearer as sufficiently valuable to incorporate the instruction into life. The veracity of a biblical precept may be all that it should be, but the value of that precept may be understood as deficient. What is needed is to illustrate the value of the biblical precept in life. Until this is done, there will be sound cognitive persuasion about the veracity of the precept but an unsound volitional persuasion about the precept with the result that there will be no implementation of the precept into life.

Volitional persuasion is, in effect, a cognitive persuasion of the value of that which is known to be true. In other words, the affections of the hearers are won over once they understand the personal value of truth. An appropriate volitional response is conditioned upon, and the outcome of, a successful captivation of the hearer's affections. In an instance where there is a lack of implementing known truth in life, the shortfall is due, not from a lack in the veracity of the instruction, but rather, the shortfall is due to a lack in the value of the instruction, as perceived by the hearers. The additional use for illustration is not needed to show greater truthfulness regarding the instruction but to illustrate with greater understanding the value of the instruction. This is what is missing, and this is what requires illustration, an illustration that will provide volitional persuasion by depicting the value, the worth, the benefit of implementing the instruction in one's life.

Since preaching is about more than cognitive persuasion, alone, but also volitional persuasion, illustrative material that shows the value of the instruction of the closing appeals is needed in a sermon conclusion. Therefore, the verdict being sought through the closing appeals of a sermon conclusion necessitates the use of an illustration for volitional persuasion. An illustration that provides a concrete demonstration of the value that the closing appeals have in life, if implemented, may provide the motivation needed for hearers to respond to the appeals. W. E. Sangster is instructive about the use of illustration in a sermon conclusion when he writes: "Having given the illustration, end! Make the illustration so good that it is utterly unnecessary to add more than a concluding sentence or two afterward—and be glad when it does not even require that."[63] The use of illustration as a clinching element of persuasion is a big-ticket item for a preaching pastor since he cannot do what he desires to do in preaching without it, to see his hearers motivated to live the truth in their lives.

---

63. Sangster, *The Craft of Sermon Construction*, 145.

RELEVANCE AND THE HEARERS' DESIRE TO LISTEN AND RESPOND

In seeking to establish an understanding for the importance of relevance in preaching, I believe there is warrant to distinguish some parameters of relevance in preaching so that my view of the matter will not be equated with others whom, I find embellishing the concept to a degree that forces me to part homiletical company with them. One example, A. W. Blackwood will suffice. A. W. Blackwood was a strong proponent for "life among men" as a "fruitful source of preaching materials,"[64] and especially so, since he viewed preaching as "the interpretation of human life in the light of eternal truth."[65] I certainly agree with Blackwood that "the best preaching . . . is concrete and vivid."[66] I agree with Blackwood that the errors of life and thought of today should find its way into a sermon,[67] but, beyond Blackwood, I believe these should appear only as *targets for rebuke and reproof* so that Christians can be clear about contemporary errors of conduct and thinking which are paraded in a fallen world of sinful men.

Furthermore, I believe Blackwood is guilty of an overstatement to say about the substance of a sermon: "While the warp comes from the Bible, giving strength and firmness to the pattern, the woof comes largely from the life and thought of today."[68] What, I believe, a better understanding of the substance of a sermon is the following: *While the warp and woof of the sermon comes from the Bible so that a text of God's Word is the focus and substance of a sermon which seeks to explain its meaning, this meaning must be leveraged by biblical application and illustration so that earthly conventions, practices, and beliefs can be understood in the light of Scripture.* So, contra Blackwood's view of preaching, I believe preaching is better understood as the interpretation of biblical truth as it is explained, argued, applied, and illustrated so it may be lived out by Christians in a world that stands staunchly against Scripture.

Preachers are God's messengers and are to deliver his message. His message is not conveyed if the meaning, the words, the tones, and the motives of "the Master" are not detected in what his servants say.[69] Therefore, the proper functioning in this role necessitates that a preaching pastor be committed "to teach clearly, convince strongly, and persuade powerfully."[70] Persuasion is predicated upon a design to influence people to live in an altered fashion, or in some way to make adjustments in how they are living. The need to be relevant and to persuade one's hearers regarding life-change can never be the grounds to do anything less than one's best work in explaining the

---

64. Blackwood, *The Fine Art of Preaching*, 61.

65. Blackwood, *The Fine Art of Preaching*, 65.

66. Blackwood, *The Fine Art of Preaching*, 57.

67. Blackwood, *The Fine Art of Preaching*, 57.

68. Blackwood, *The Fine Art of Preaching*, 57.

69. Hall, *God's Word Through Preaching*, 1875, 174.

70. Moore, *Thoughts on Preaching*, 1861, 19.

meaning of Scripture. John MacArthur's words are extremely accurate, and they sound a vital warning about relevance as he writes:

> If you don't have the *meaning* of Scripture, you do not have the word of God at all. If you miss the true sense of what God has said, you are not actually preaching God's Word! . . . Pastors who embrace fads, usually in an attempt to be culturally relevant, inevitably find themselves neglecting the exposition of God's Word, looking for something else, desperately trying to keep up with what is supposedly cutting edge. . . . Sadly, and ironically, in its attempt to achieve cultural relevance, mainstream evangelicalism has become essentially irrelevant. . . . The quest for cultural relevance is contrary to everything Scripture teaches about church ministry. Preachers are called to preach the Word of God, unfiltered by notions of political correctness, undiluted by the preacher's own ideas, and unadapted to the spirit of the age.[71]

With MacArthur's insights regarding relevance in preaching in place, if a preaching pastor intends to bring change in the lives of his hearers, then it must be clear to the hearers that they are not hearing an exposition of a text of Scripture, only, but they are receiving a personal appeal to respond to the truth of Scripture, also. However, a response requires a hearing.

A hearing requires the preaching pastor to command the attention of his hearers. Therefore, the hearers' attention must be secured and maintained throughout the sermon conclusion because there will be no response to a sermon conclusion that is not listened to with personal interest. An inviolable law for sermon conclusions is this: *No interest means no response! If they have no interest, they will not listen. If they do not listen, they cannot respond!*

No ministry can happen through a sermon conclusion in the hearts of hearers who are not attentive. At the beginning of the sermon conclusion there is a crucial need for the preacher as a true pastor, a preaching pastor, to once again interest his hearers for what he is about to provide for them in the conclusion of the sermon. At this pivotal place in the sermon the hearer's interest must be reestablished, and if possible, brought to a higher level than was achieved in the sermon introduction. At this strategic place in the sermon so much is on the line. R. W. Dale wrote: "*If they don't listen, it doesn't matter what you say.* That is a maxim which it will be worth our while to remember, especially if we complete it by adding that, *if people do listen, what you say matters a great deal.* The maxim is obvious enough, yet there are preachers to whom it never seems to have occurred."[72] Unfortunately, preaching showcases preachers who continue to demonstrate ignorance of this maxim.

The context in which a sermon conclusion is preached militates against a significantly attentive hearing of it. A sermon conclusion is preached after the hearers'

71. Dever et al., *Preaching the Cross*, from John MacArthur's chapter "Why I Still Preach the Bible after Forty Years of Ministry," 139–40.

72. Dale, *Nine Lectures on Preaching*, 1890, 35.

optimal attention span has been consumed by the time taken for the sermon introduction and body of the sermon. "Some brain research indicates the first twenty minutes of anything (sermon, meeting, class) is the most optimal time for attention and learning; after that, it goes down precipitously."[73] This is a brutal realization that requires the honoring of some concepts for preaching a sermon conclusion or the conclusion may be dead on arrival in every sermon.

But just as it is important to understand the post-optimal attention context for a sermon conclusion, it is equally important to realize that attentiveness can be recovered, but even more than that, it can be piqued beyond any level possessed earlier in the sermon. At any point in the sermon, it must be understood that the hearers' attentiveness is more the result of good preaching than it is the condition of good preaching. David Breed's comments are valuable, especially when applied to the sermon conclusion. Breed wrote:

> Let no one say, then, as he enters the pulpit, "If the people will listen, I shall preach well." Let him rather say, "If I preach well, the people will be sure to listen." Attention is the first result of good preaching, and when it is thus gained it becomes also the condition. But it must first be gained. . . . And yet it is only a condition to a certain extent . . . because the condition will not long continue if the result does not continuously appear.[74]

The initial part of the sermon conclusion is the time and place in the sermon where the best preaching must begin to take place. As has been argued extensively in previous chapters, the sermon conclusion is to be the highpoint of the sermon. For the sermon conclusion to be the highpoint of the sermon, the hearers will have to be brought to the highest level of attentiveness throughout the conclusion.

A maxim of inestimable worth to the preaching pastor for the sake of preaching a conclusion that might be the highpoint of the sermon is, "It's easy to feed a hungry man." But because of the preaching time required by the preacher to get to the conclusion, his hearers may not be optimally attentive, and they will have had their hunger satisfied, to a degree, by the content of the sermon. Yet, the conclusion is the part of the sermon in which it is crucial for the hearers to be optimally attentive, and substantially hungering for the content of the conclusion. In other words, the preacher finds himself trying to supply needed spiritual food to people, the most of whom, have suffered, to varying degrees, a sated appetite. And if it's easy to feed a hungry man is also true that, "it is difficult to feed a sated man."

Though things do not line up conveniently for a conclusion to be the highpoint of a sermon, that certainly does not mean it is impossible for this to be the case. But it does mean, however, that some things must be understood and incorporated for a

---

73. Kalas, *Preaching in an Age of Distraction*, 134.

74. Breed, *Preparing to Preach*, 1911, 354–55.

preacher to be able to preach a sermon conclusion that helps his hearers to make the most of this crucial opportunity.

So, how can hearers be induced to give attention to the sermon conclusion when the text has been treated fully, the hour is late, the hearers are weary because of the attention given to the exposition of the preaching text, and the hearers' inner clocks commandeer their thought process toward other matters before the sermon conclusion has begun? There are six concepts that function interrelatedly that can overcome the factors that work against a sermon conclusion's effectiveness. These are the concepts; personal, beneficial, curiosity, variety, desire, and expectation. These concepts are valuable and must be incorporated for the sake of securing the interest of the hearers so that the conclusion may be responded to, rather than being unheeded and unheard.

First, is the concept of personal. Fatigued, sated hearers cannot be reinvigorated to a sermon conclusion that is not addressed to them personally. The concerted attention of the hearers is gained, in part, by the intentional use of the word "you" which indicates to the hearers, and helps them to understand, that the closing appeals of the sermon conclusion require a verdict from each individual[75] since every believer is under the authority of Scripture.[76]

Second, and of far greater significance, is the concept, beneficial. Beneficial describes the outcome of the preaching pastor's ability to command attention for Scripture-based closing appeals that are beneficial, worth hearing, and communicated in such a manner that the hearers discern that they are worth hearing, and will be beneficial for their lives.[77] Attentiveness is diligent mental activity. The minds of hearers that are attentive are diligently engaged to acquire information of a crucial kind, that which will be personally beneficial for them. Attentive hearers are those who are diligently engaged in the natural and delightful economic mental effort to acquire that which has been portrayed as important to them.[78] If this, for whatever reason, cannot be accomplished by the preacher then he must not even attempt to conclude his sermon since the attempt would be futile and the time used to conduct the futility will have been wasted.

Third, variety is necessary to reestablish interest for the conclusion.[79] Variety, here, has in view the dramatic difference that comes about through the transition from focusing on the exposition of the preaching text, to a focus on the purpose of the sermon, which is what the sermon conclusion is all about. The preaching pastor must resurface the purpose of the sermon, and through crucial assertions and vital, personal questions being related to the purpose, he indicates to his hearers how

75. James, *An Earnest Ministry*, 1847, 117.

76. Olford and Olford, *Anointed Expository Preaching*, 172.

77. Breed, *Preparing to Preach*, 1911, 362.

78. Breed, *Preparing to Preach*, 1911, 352.

79. Breed, *Preparing to Preach*, 1911, 369.

beneficial it is for the purpose of the sermon to be achieved in their lives. In doing this, the preaching pastor provides his hearers with the necessary component of desire for the content to be declared in the conclusion. With the means of achieving the sermon's purpose being the content contained in the closing appeals, which the preaching pastor will provide to the hearers, they are provided the necessary component of variety—variety that will be realized in the expectation for the content of the sermon conclusion's closing appeals.

Fourth, curiosity plays an essential role in the sermon conclusion. The ability of the hearers to determine that what the preacher has to say in a sermon conclusion is valuable will occur only if they are made curious about what he might say to them. "Curiosity is the parent of attention."[80] Curiosity, or the desire to know so that one may receive personal benefit, is achieved as crucial assertions and vital, personal questions are directed toward the purpose of the sermon, as was discussed in chapter six which dealt with a vital transition to a sermon conclusion. A transition is vital only as the hearers, through the means of crucial assertions and vital, personal questions, are made curious about how the purpose can be achieved in their lives, thus bringing enhancement to their lives as a result. The curiosity cannot be an idle curiosity, which may be on the level of knowing for the sake of knowing, but curiosity on the level of "a need to know." An understanding on behalf of the hearers that they are about to be given truth that is not just applicable to their circumstances, but truth that is life-changing, will create a curiosity which gains their attention and their interest for the closing appeals of the sermon conclusion. In other words, the hearers anticipate that the sermon conclusion will be relevant to their lives and may be life-changing.

Expectation and desire are the fifth and sixth factors needed to reestablish the attention of the hearers for a sermon conclusion. Expectation and desire bear a reciprocal cause and effect relationship to each other. A desire to know needful content creates an expectation for that content, just as the expectation of needful content creates the desire to hear it. The conclusion, therefore, must provide a promise of expectation and desire for the hearers. Since attention cannot be continuously sustained, it must be gathered repeatedly, particularly when transitioning to the sermon conclusion. An increase in the attention and interest of the hearers at the outset of the sermon conclusion will happen only to the extent that the hearers have a desire and expectation for the content of the sermon conclusion which remains.[81] The expectation and desire of the hearers which are fulfilled through the content contained in the closing appeals of the conclusion must consist of truths that are beyond relevance but are composed of application proper.

In relevance, the hearers *understand what a biblical truth has to do with them.* In other words, through relevance the hearers can answer the question, "So what *does this mean for my life*?" The answer to this question is a more general understanding

80. Breed, *Preparing to Preach*, 1911, 366.

81. Breed, *Preparing to Preach*, 1911, 368–69.

of how the truth of Scripture is germane to the lives of believers. But in application proper, the hearers are made to *know their response to* biblical truth. This means that the hearers must *know what the biblical truth requires of them.* In other words, they must be able to answer the question, "So what *am I to do about that?*" The answer to this question is a more specific understanding of how the truth of Scripture is germane to the lives of believers. Application proper is the definitive and thorough knowledge of what is to be done by a hearer in response to biblical truth, and in the context of a sermon conclusion, it is the definitive and thorough knowledge of what is to be done in response to the purpose of the sermon, the response being produced by complying to Scripture-based closing appeals.

The application proper, found in the closing appeals of the sermon conclusion, should be forceful and vigorous. Force or impact must be an integral part of the content and delivery of a sermon conclusion, which means the substantial truths of the closing appeals must be conveyed vigorously, with a sense of urgency. The hearers must feel that the content of the sermon conclusion's closing appeals makes a very real difference in their thinking and they will make a greater difference in their living.[82] Such is the intent for preaching the closing appeals of a sermon conclusion in the ministry of a preaching pastor.

The preaching pastor's knowledge of Scripture, humanity, and the human heart allows him to provide invaluable relevance in preaching a sermon conclusion that may result in life-change, a change in life that is in accordance with God's Word. Using biblical precepts and example, a preaching pastor can reveal to his hearers how they can live life as they have never lived it before, thus demonstrating to them what life-change includes and what it looks like. The best means to depict this is through the use of a biblical illustration of some individual(s) or some event(s) contained in the Old or New Testament. By an insightful development of what the Scriptures contain, the most grievous stumbling blocks and common blind spots of the human race may not only be revealed but remediated. Illustrative material, especially when drawn from the content of Scripture, possesses the ability to be persuasive to believers about all matters pertaining to life and godliness.

Through preaching, God's grace is magnified as the power of his Word is unleashed upon the minds, the consciences, the affections, and the wills of the hearers. Through preaching, every gracious purpose of God is made available to the hearers "whether for understanding, conviction, repentance, conversion, or responding in righteousness."[83] God's gracious purposes for preaching are not exempted from the preaching done in a sermon conclusion. One may argue that they are never more apparent than in a sermon conclusion preached by a preaching pastor. But, the concepts of personal, beneficial, curiosity, variety, desire, and expectation must compose the DNA of the sermon conclusion if it is to gain a hearing leading to a response.

82. Brown Jr., Clinard, and Northcutt, *Steps to the Sermon*, 122–23.

83. Moore, *Thoughts on Preaching*, 1861, 18.

On behalf of the hearers, Scripture informs the ignorant, alarms the careless, arouses the indifferent, convicts the sinful, excites the worldly to holiness, and equips believers for their walk in the faith. The closing appeals of a sermon conclusion will accomplish these affects in the lives of believers if they are based upon the Word of God. God's Word causes Scripture-based closing appeals to be effective in the lives of believers and allows the sermon conclusion to be perceived as relevant by believers. The inviolable law for sermon conclusions, though not forgotten, must be honored: No interest means no response! If they have no interest, they will not listen. If they do not listen, they cannot respond! And if they do not respond it will be from a lack of perceived relevance on behalf of the hearers because the preacher could not interest them in valuable truth, the truths they most needed to know and the truths he most desired to proclaim to them for their spiritual welfare. How tragic is that?

15

Persuasive Preaching in the Sermon Conclusion: Part 1

"God is at liberty to do and work in preaching in a way that he does not commonly work, and in a way that is not as one might expect him to work. God will work as God wills to work! That means that God works as he commonly works, and God works as he uncommonly works, but both the common and the uncommon work are by the design and desire of God."

"A preacher who desires to preach persuasively has limited prospects of knowing to what degree his desire has been championed by God and used in the lives of his people to bring life-change to them. Preachers must be content to be used by God in their preaching as God is pleased to use them which includes the little that can be discerned and the much that cannot be discerned about how they are used by God. This is first and foremost. Beyond this, we can learn what we can about the kind of man God commonly uses to preach persuasively. We can learn what we can about the kind of preaching that God commonly uses to persuade hearers. Applying ourselves fully to do and be what God would have us do and be marks the end of our best effort to preach persuasively."

"From a human perspective, persuasion is the means by which motivation of the hearers occurs in preaching. There are three modes of persuasion used in preaching where persuasion is an outcome of the sermon in the lives of a portion of the hearers. In a word, persuasion is linked to demonstration. 'Persuasion is clearly a sort of demonstration, since we are most fully persuaded when we consider a thing to have been demonstrated.' Applying demonstration to the three modes of persuasion, persuasive preaching might be understood as that which results from demonstrated character of the preacher, demonstrated passion of the preacher, and demonstrated evidences or

proofs used by the preacher in his preaching."

"Persuasive preaching necessitates a man of known integrity, who has deep convictions about the importance of the truth he passionately preaches to those he desires to serve through the Word of God that is carefully and insightfully processed, clearly explained, and relevantly addressed in a proven demonstration of its worth, to which he earnestly compels his hearers to comply with in their lives."

"A preacher of proven character is winsome in his preaching whereas a man lacking character cannot be winsome. However, winsomeness and persuasiveness are not the same. A persuasive preacher will be winsome, and a winsome preacher may be persuasive. Persuasion requires more than winsomeness, but persuasive preaching typically does not result from a preacher and preaching that are not winsome."

"The principal characteristics of persuasive preaching are 'gravity and warmth,' which are not commonly united in preachers. But when they are combined in a man, the union of the two qualities form an 'affecting, penetrating, interesting manner' of preaching that is best described as winsome. This highly attractive quality 'flows from a strong sense in the preacher of the importance of the truths he delivers, and an earnest desire that they may make full impression on the hearts of his hearers.' The inception of the ability to preach winsomely to people is to realize the hearers' great worth to God. The connection between the hearers' worth and a preacher's opportunity to preach to such people will be for him to serve them, to be of help to them ... regarding their need to be reproved, rebuked, corrected, challenged, encouraged, warned of the error of their way, brought to repentance, trained in how to sustain a life of holiness in a sinful world, all of this in addition to being informed of truth they did not know or to deepen the knowledge of the truth that they did know."

"A winsome preacher of character has a strong base from which he may be a persuasive preacher. For preachers, their 'currency' is their character. 'With it, they are solvent; without it, they are bankrupt.' A preacher of demonstrated character will be winsome in his preaching and this is pivotal to persuasive preaching."

"It is hard for the hearers to disengage from a man of character, a winsome man who can sympathize with them, who cares for them and preaches to help them. Such a man, and the preaching ministry he provides to his hearers, stands a good chance of being persuasive to his hearers."

"A lack of compassion for the hearers and a lack of passion for the truth creates a negative effect on preaching. To lack pathos in preaching or to lack compassion for one's hearers is debilitating for preaching, but to lack either one is devastating for persuasive preaching."

"A Spirit-filled preacher cannot but be persuasive, persuasive as God has determined him to be so on that occasion, persuasive as God has designed him to be so in the lives of his hearers. But so great a privilege brings so great a responsibility, to be filled with the Spirit when preaching so that one does not preach in a condition that finds him other than filled with the Spirit. . . . The success which a preacher can have, the success he must have, is linked to his faithfulness, a faithfulness that finds him Spirit-filled. The faithfulness that allows him to be none other than filled with the Spirit is the measure of success for which every preacher is responsible."

"It is crucial that there are no misunderstandings about this point: God persuades hearers with or without the means of a sermon conclusion. But sermon conclusions demonstrate the height of a preacher's character, passion, and content, which are the very things which God commonly uses in preaching that is persuasive. Therefore, the sermon conclusion should be the height of a preacher's concern regarding his ethos, pathos, and logos in preaching and for the prospect to be used by God to preach persuasively."

"Many preachers, if asked, 'What were you trying to persuade us about in this sermon you preached?' would provide a variety of insufficient answers. The worst, and probably the most common would be, 'I wasn't trying to persuade anyone about anything. I was simply trying to . . .' Or 'I was trying to persuade you about the correct way to interpret the often-misunderstood verses of . . .' Or 'I was trying to help you understand the meaning of the preaching passage and its meaning for our lives.' In other words, many preachers not only fail to be persuasive in their preaching, but they may not even understand that they are supposed to be persuasive in their preaching."

PRE-PERSUASION INFLUENCES

A Sovereign God at Work

God is not bound by anything that we might understand as a law of preaching, or principles of preaching, that would cause God to do, or prevent God from doing, what he desires to do and see accomplished in the preaching of his Word. The God of the Word infallibly works through his Word just as he desires to work through it when it is preached, by any preacher, before any hearers, from any portion of Scripture, on any occasion. God is bound only by his infinitely perfect nature, and works in accordance with that infinitely perfect nature, in the preaching of his Word. Therefore, no one can say or think they can know what God will do, what God must do, when God will do it, and for whom he will do what he desires to do in the preaching of his Word. God will do as God desires to do! Every consideration of persuasive preaching must return to this inviolable truth and yield to its relentless domination, or each consideration will be rendered fictitious.

To discuss preaching, in general, or persuasive preaching, specifically, one must make room for the sovereign work of God that may or may not be consistent with what is common in preaching and in persuasive preaching. God is at liberty to do and work in preaching in a way that he does not commonly work, and in a way that one might not expect him to work. God will work as God wills to work! That means that God works as he commonly works, and God works as he uncommonly works, but both the common and the uncommon work are by the design and desire of God. What God does in preaching in the common way is not denigrated because it is common, just like what God does in an uncommon way is not denigrated because it is uncommon. Furthermore, because God works, at times, in an uncommon way does not make the effort to understand what one can about what God is pleased to do in the common way. There are some things preachers can learn about persuasive preaching as it occurs commonly so that he may work with God in persuading his people to live according to his Word. But the Word of God will be persuasive in the lives of those whom he will cause it to be persuasive, whether desired to be such, or attempted to be such, by a preacher.

Let me give a worst-case example of what I mean. Let's say that I hear a "sermon" that, humanly speaking, has no chance of being a persuasive sermon because the preacher is involved in, what might be called a running commentary if one were extremely charitable in one's terminology, but in reality is only a data dump, the unloading of an avalanche of irrelevant textual technicalities. I, and everyone else have no idea of what he is talking about and what he is saying about it. He has not synthesized the text. He is not preaching a sermon. His talking is not preaching, and his content does not bare even trace evidence of a sermon. There is no proposition, no main structure, no substructure. He has no purpose for this non-sermonic speech event. So, there is no verdict for which he is urgently seeking to win in the lives of his hearers. Therefore, there is no conclusion since there is no purpose to come back to in order to achieve it more fully by the aid of Scripture-based closing appeals. Since he is not preaching a sermon but unloading a data dump of information about a biblical text, he, therefore, has no passion as he parses and declines every form in the passage, along with a few excursions to debate the merits for the strengths and weaknesses of various manuscript evidence. Twenty-five minutes into this mind-numbing parade of technical data, the Holy Spirit of God takes an insight of the text and enlightens my thought process about life as I am living it. Being smitten on the basis of an obscure textual detail that has meaningful ramifications for me, I am cognitively convinced of the error of my way as my conscience is pierced, and I am volitionally persuaded to submit to the correction that I know the Word of God requires of me. As a result, my life is marvelously redirected as I am powerfully persuaded to live my life in greater compliance to the Word of God. I was persuaded!

A few people think, "Boy, that was deep! I didn't understand a single thing!" Others are thinking, "That was about as enlightening as an underground cave!" Most people think, "Well, that certainly was a waste of time!" My question to you is this: Was that passionless patchwork of pulpit perplexities persuasive? It was to one person! It was persuasive to me! For about one miraculous minute God provided a divine intervention in the homiletical train wreck and made it rise above the chaos of confusion to redirect one life in a profitable way! But, for everyone else, this became a white-knuckled event that filled everyone with the terrible fear that, like a west Texas dirt road, this thing may have no end! It might just go on and on!

Yet, this hyperbolized depiction of God working in the life of one hearer, seemingly against all odds, is the very thing that God does commonly in the preaching of his Word. God, by his Spirit and through his Word, does what he has designed to do in the lives of whomever he has willed it. So, whether God enlightens and persuades a few hearers individually about matters known only to God and those few hearers or whether God works in the same way in the lives of very many hearers of one sermon, both represent the persuasive work of God in the lives of his people through his Word.

A preacher who desires to preach persuasively has limited prospects of knowing to what degree his desire has been championed by God and used in the lives of his people to bring life-change to them. Preachers must be content to be used by God in their preaching as God is pleased to use them which includes the little that can be discerned and the much that cannot be discerned about how they are used by God. This is first and foremost. Beyond this, we can learn what we can about the kind of man God commonly uses to preach persuasively and we can learn what we can about the kind of preaching that God commonly uses to persuade hearers. Applying ourselves fully to do and be what God would have us do and be marks the end of our best effort to preach persuasively.

Preaching as a Tremendous Privilege

Since God does, and will, work through his Word as he pleases and none can know the full effect of one's preaching in the lives of people, we must learn what we can to help ourselves to be potentially persuasive in our preaching efforts as we are used by God. There are some things that can be learned that influence who one is as a preacher and influence how one prepares oneself to be used by God in persuasive preaching. Spurgeon offers two very general exhortations that must be applied in a preacher's week to week preaching ministry. The first takes up the important matter of one's perspective about the preaching ministry God has provided. Spurgeon provides this helpful encouragement when he wrote: "We shall not, by all their efforts, be induced to cease from building with the few 'precious stones' which the Lord has entrusted to us; nor shall even our brethren, who so admirably pile up the 'gold and silver,' persuade us to hide away our agates and carbuncles. We must each build with such material as we have; if the work be true and honest, we ought neither to censure others nor to condemn ourselves because our labor is after its own kind."[1] One is certainly not being influenced in a profitable way to be a persuasive preacher when he views his preaching opportunity as something to look down upon rather than that for which he is to be grateful. It is not common that a preacher is used by God to preach persuasively in the lives of people when the perspective of his ministry is viewed by the preacher as unimportant.

Again, Spurgeon's wisdom and understanding of common human tendencies are apparent in his exhortation for preachers to exercise diligence in carrying out their preaching ministries. Spurgeon writes: "We must never think, because the particular work we have in hand seems to be insignificant, that therefore we cannot do it, or should not do it, thoroughly well. We need divine help to preach aright to a congregation of one. If a thing is worth doing at all, it is worth doing well. . . . Know your work, and bend over it, throwing your heart and your soul into it; for, be it great or small, you will have praise from God through all eternity if you are found faithful in it."[2] Ever the realist, Spurgeon is insightful to connect the dots between an understanding of one's ministry as a comparatively insignificant ministry and the fallen condition response of supplying a less than diligent effort in fleshing out that ministry. However, providing less than one's most diligent effort in preparing to preach is never the pathway of a persuasive preacher.

Ethos, Pathos, and Logos

Preaching for a verdict is analogous to homiletical hand to hand combat in a preaching ministry. This kind of pursuit is not possible for one who is content to conduct himself in a "going through the motions" approach in preaching. To preach sermons that have a conclusion that is the highpoint of the sermon, that urgently preaches to win a verdict from the hearers for the purpose of the sermon being achieved in their lives by Scripture-based closing appeals, is a real challenge even for those who supply great effort and time to prepare themselves to preach. This will never be done in the life of a preacher who only supplies a casual effort to prepare and preach sermons. It is just not possible for effective conclusions to become a part of his preaching since they require labor beyond that which he is willing to do.

Certain qualities are consistent in preachers used by the Spirit of God in the process of motivating God's people to respond to his Word. The connection between the man, who he is, and his role in persuasive preaching, how he is used by God in the pulpit, is apparent. Persuasive preachers possess common attributes regarding their character. Persuasive preaching is accomplished, in part, because of the kind of man he is. It may be recognizable that the character of the preacher bears a ready reference to the first component of Aristotle's rhetoric of ethos, pathos, and logos. A man's

1. Spurgeon, *An All-round Ministry*, 1900, 63.

2. Spurgeon, *An All-round Ministry*, 1900, 71.

character, ethos, is an extremely valuable component of persuasive preaching. A man devoid of character is destitute in his ability to be persuasive about spiritual truth. Augustine is responsible for taking Aristotle's components of rhetoric and applying them to preaching. From Augustine's adaptation of the insights of Aristotle's rhetoric, the modes of preaching have been attributed as the character of the preacher (ethos), the preacher's passion (pathos), the preacher's competence regarding knowledge of Scripture (logos). Everything contained in this chapter, like anything written about persuasive preaching, can be linked to these three modes of persuasive preaching.

From a human perspective, persuasion is the means by which motivation of the hearers occurs in preaching. Again, there are three modes of persuasion used in preaching that may be viewed as persuasive, that is, where persuasion is an outcome of the sermon in the lives of a portion of the hearers. When persuasion is the outcome of preaching there must be a cause for that effect. In a word, persuasion is linked to *demonstration*. "Persuasion is clearly a sort of demonstration, since we are most fully persuaded when we consider a thing to have been demonstrated."[3] Applying demonstration to the three modes of persuasion, persuasive preaching might be understood as that which results from *demonstrated character* of the preacher, *demonstrated passion* of the preacher, and *demonstrated evidences or proofs* used by the preacher in his preaching.

Within the three modes of persuasion in preaching, the first mode, ethos, depends on the personal character of the preacher. The second mode, pathos, depends on putting the audience in a productive frame of mind. The third mode, logos, depends on the proofs or evidence provided in the sermon for its explanation, illustration, and application of the biblical text.

First, the preacher's ethos or character is of critical importance. "Persuasion is achieved by the preacher's personal character when known to be a man of integrity. We believe good men more fully and more readily than others. . . . It is not true, as some writers assume in their treatises on rhetoric, that the personal goodness revealed by the speaker contributes nothing to his power of persuasion; on the contrary, his character may almost be called the most effective means of persuasion he possesses."[4] A preacher must be a man who is above reproach, to use the biblical terminology for the overarching assertion of what a man must be if he is to serve as an elder in the church, since his hearers provide a built-in resistance to being subjected to the words and influences of one whose conduct is "a living and open contradiction to his preaching."[5] A man lacking character, regardless of the evidences he marshals and the way he presents his content, will scarcely be persuasive to his hearers.

Second, persuasion may come to the hearers, when the speech stirs their emotions in a productive manner. "Our judgements when we are pleased and friendly are

3. Roberts, *The Rhetoric and the Poetics of Aristotle*, 22.
4. Roberts, *The Rhetoric and the Poetics of Aristotle*, 25.
5. Potter, *Sacred Eloquence*, 1868, 285.

not the same as when we are pained and hostile."[6] Therefore, the preacher's pathos, his ability to preach with confidence, conviction, enthusiasm, and passion have a persuasive effect on the hearers and establish the frame of mind on behalf of the hearers so that they may be willing to be persuaded.

Third, persuasion is created through the content of the sermon itself when truth is proven by means of persuasive arguments and demonstrations, that is, proofs and evidences such as examples or illustrations, suitable to the claims being made.[7] The logos or the content of the message must be understood clearly and convincingly through the use of demonstration. The closing appeals of the sermon conclusion constitute the demonstrated means by which the purpose of the sermon can be achieved most fully in the lives of the hearers. Furthermore, the clinching element of persuasion is a demonstration of how the closing appeals are to be understood and incorporated in the hearers' lives.

A sermon conclusion incorporating Scripture-based closing appeals by which the purpose of the sermon may be achieved is formulaic in its design to be a persuasive sermon. The conclusion is to be the highpoint of the sermon and it is the apex of the sermon's persuasive potential. Such understanding is a necessary foundation to make the most of good homiletical counsel such as: "Be much more careful about the end than about the beginning. The introduction is very important. However, the ending is of vital importance. Lead up to it. Make it the strongest, most incisive part of your sermon."[8] The strength and incisiveness which the conclusion must have is based upon the function it should have as being the turning point in the lives of the hearers as they are persuaded to respond by complying their lives to the closing appeals of the conclusion.

Having a purpose for preaching and seeking to win a verdict from the hearers to comply with this purpose in their lives mandates that persuasive preaching is intended by the preacher. The fact that a preacher has closing appeals indicates that the preacher will be appealing to his hearers to respond to the truth of Scripture. This is the attempt to be persuasive in preaching. By virtue that the closing appeals are based in Scripture, significantly strengthens the cause to be persuasive. As a simple matter of design, a sermon conclusion in which a preacher is urgently seeking a verdict from his hearers to comply to Scripture-based closing appeals so that the purpose of the preaching text can be achieved most completely in the hearers' lives depicts the best possible procedure for persuasive preaching. "Persuasion must in every case be effected by working on the emotions of the hearers, by giving them the right impression of the speaker's character, and by proving the truth of the statements made."[9] In other words, persuasive preaching necessitates a man of known integrity, who has deep

---

6. Roberts, *The Rhetoric and the Poetics of Aristotle*, 25.

7. Roberts, *The Rhetoric and the Poetics of Aristotle*, 25.

8. Smyth, *The Preacher and His Sermon*, 1922, 115.

9. Roberts, *The Rhetoric and the Poetics of Aristotle*, 164.

convictions about the importance of the truth he passionately preaches to those he desires to serve through the Word of God that is carefully and insightfully processed, clearly explained, and relevantly addressed in a proven demonstration of its worth, to which he earnestly compels his hearers to comply with in their lives.

A preacher of proven character is winsome in his preaching whereas a man lacking character cannot be winsome. However, winsomeness and persuasiveness are not the same. A persuasive preacher *will be* winsome, and a winsome preacher *may be* persuasive. Persuasion requires more than winsomeness, but persuasive preaching typically does not result from a preacher and preaching that are not winsome.

The principal characteristics of persuasive preaching are "gravity and warmth," which are not commonly united in preachers. But when they are combined in a man, the union of the two qualities form an "affecting, penetrating, interesting manner" of preaching that is best described as winsome. This highly attractive quality "flows from a strong sense in the preacher of the importance of the truths he delivers, and an earnest desire that they may make full impression on the hearts of his hearers."[10] The inception of the ability to preach winsomely to people is to realize the hearers' great worth to God. The connection between the hearers' worth and a preacher's opportunity to preach to such people will be for him to serve them, to be of help to them.

Help is such a broad term it seems almost devoid of meaning but a more narrowly focused term would not be indicative of the great worth which they possess. Help them? Help them in what way? In every possible way! This is the correct response of a man who preaches to people of such infinite worth. Such a response entails more than just informing the hearers of the scriptural meaning of a text and its implications for their lives, though this is valuable help rendered. But some people need to be reproved, rebuked, corrected, challenged, encouraged, warned of the error of their way, brought to repentance, trained in how to sustain a life of holiness in a sinful world, all of this in addition to being informed of truth they did not know or to deepen the knowledge of the truth that they did know.

The character of a preacher is demonstrated, not by refusing to serve as service is needed, but by meeting existing needs in the best way he can. True character will not serve selectively but comprehensively. His heart is into his preaching for the sake of God's people and this makes him credible to his hearers. They cannot be oblivious to his concern for their spiritual welfare for they sense it consistently in his preaching, not in an occasional sermon, but they sense it throughout each sermon that he preaches. His desire to help them is winsome and they are helped by the service of his preaching. Few people would be resistant to such a man because, for the most part, "everyone wants to be helped."[11] It is difficult to reject the preaching of a man who preaches as a service to his hearers to help them. A winsome preacher of character has a strong base from which he may be a persuasive preacher. For preachers, their

10. Blair, *Lectures on Rhetoric*, 1852, 154–55.

11. Maxwell, *Everyone Communicates, Few Connect*, 40.

"currency" is their character. "With it, they are solvent; without it, they are bankrupt."[12] A preacher of demonstrated character will be winsome in his preaching and this is pivotal to persuasive preaching.

A preacher who is ultimately persuasive to his hearers, is a man who demonstrates by his character an affirmative answer to three crucial questions hearers ask intuitively about every preacher they hear: "Do you care for me?," "Can you help me?," "Can I trust you?"[13] Hearers need to know that the preacher is a trustworthy man of character but they want to have as their preacher one who is concerned for them, that he is a man of spiritual strength who can relate to them in their comparative weakness. Spurgeon phrased it well when he states: "The man who grinds out theology at so much a yard has no power over men; the people need men who can feel—men of heart . . . who can sympathize with the timid and sorrowful."[14] To be a persuasive preacher, in so many ways, means that the persuasion comes from the goodwill and winsomeness of a man of character who bears concern for those to whom he preaches for their benefit and spiritual well-being.

A man of such character asserts himself, not just the content, into the message he preaches. This provides a high level of continuity to his preaching. His character is constant. This brings a wealth of richness to every sermon he preaches, which, regardless of the text, the subject-matter, or the content of his sermons, he engages his hearers effectively in his preaching. For preaching to be persuasive the hearers must be engaged by the one preaching to them.

Persuasive preaching is engaging. A persuaded hearer is engaged in the content of proclaimed truth. Persuasive preaching engages the hearer's mind, conscience, emotions/affections, and will in an uninterrupted manner. An engaged hearer may become persuaded regarding the truth or they may not. But the moment a hearer becomes disengaged to the preacher himself, or to his message, at that moment the hearer cuts himself off from the "productive influence of the Word" which terminates the chances for cognitive and volitional persuasion to become a reality.[15]

But the great thing is, it is hard for the hearers to disengage from a man of character, a winsome man who can sympathize with them, who cares for them and preaches to help them. Such a man, and the preaching ministry he provides to his hearers, stands a good chance of being persuasive to his hearers. Martyn Lloyd-Jones indicated a thorn in the flesh of preachers who do not demonstrate proven character and their love for their hearers in their preaching with these words: "The trouble with some of us is that we love preaching, but we are not always careful to make sure that we love the people to whom we are actually preaching. If you lack this element of compassion for the people you will also lack the pathos which is a very vital element

---

12. Maxwell, *Everyone Communicates, Few Connect*, 230.

13. Maxwell, *Everyone Communicates, Few Connect*, 42.

14. Spurgeon, *An All-round Ministry*, 1900, 221.

15. Phelps, *The Theory of Preaching*, 1882, 512.

all true preaching."[16] A lack of compassion for the hearers and a lack of passion for the truth are two problems which may or may not be interrelated. A lack of either one creates a negative effect on preaching. To lack pathos in preaching or to lack compassion for one's hearers is debilitating for preaching, but to lack either one is devastating for persuasive preaching.

For a preacher to enter the pulpit in a condition that has him lacking in confidence, conviction, enthusiasm, and passion is a blueprint for preaching that will most probably leave the hearers disappointed rather than persuaded. Spurgeon's comments regarding those who enter the pulpit without possessing the pathos that is necessary to preach productively are well worth taking to heart. He wrote:

> God's message deserves every fragment of my ability; when I deliver it, I ought to be "all there," every bit of me; none of me should go astray or lie asleep. Some men, when they get into the pulpit, are not there. One said to me, in conversation, "I do not know how it is, but I feel so different when I shut the pulpit door." I answered, "Have the door taken off." . . . Do not some show, by their manner of preaching, that their heart is not in it? They have come to preach, and they will get through what they have to say; but their deepest thoughts and liveliest emotions would come out better at a political meeting. They have not all their wits about them when preaching. . . . Have you never seen such preachers? They are "not there." . . . The Holy Spirit will not bless men of this sort. He spake by an ass once, but that ass showed its sense by never speaking anymore. I know creatures of a similar kind that are not half so wise.[17]

This pathos problem served up to the hearers from a preacher in the pulpit is the final minutes of the same problem which occurred in the preacher's study days before the preaching occasion. He never processed the Scriptures in such a way that gripped his own heart in strong passion and crucial insight. So, when he gets into the pulpit, he can only project to his hearers the same underwhelming influence that his unprofitable study of Scripture had upon his own heart. In such a situation, the problem of the study becomes the problem of the pulpit. This problem will resurface every time the following advice of William M. Taylor is ignored. "If you have no positive convictions, keep out of the pulpit until you get them; and when you get them, they will make for themselves a manly and earnest utterance."[18] Truth that is not persuasive to a preacher is usually truth that is not persuasive through that preacher as he preaches it to others.

A fail-proof way to be enlivened about any text and the subject-matter of any text is to gain a clear and definite understanding of every given truth to be preached is by submitting it to the Supreme Court of spiritual arbitration, which is to view

---

16. Lloyd-Jones, *Preaching and Preachers*, 92.

17. Spurgeon, *An All-round Ministry*, 1900, 344–46.

18. Taylor, *The Ministry of the Word*, 1876, 134.

that subject-matter through the truth as it has been adjudicated in Jesus Christ. Spurgeon's comment hints at this as he wrote, "When we lean our head too much upon the commentary, and too little upon the Savior's bosom . . . we lose the power of our ministry."[19] The implications of a Christ-centered focus related to all truth so that there will be the kind of pathos that is crucial for persuasive preaching is this, the highest level of persuasion is achieved as truth is connected to Jesus Christ. In other words, the zenith of persuasion is reached only as truth is understood fully through the context of Jesus Christ, allowing the truth to fall under the shadow of Christ's wisdom expressed by his words, deeds, and the work he accomplished as well as that which will be accomplished by him.

A man of character is a caring, helpful, trustworthy man. A caring, helpful, trustworthy man demonstrates the character of the preacher horizontally, his character and trustworthiness as he relates to people. It is the horizontal realities that receive much attention and become the prescription for preaching that is powerful, persuasive, and profitable. Phillips Brooks codified powerful preaching, in any and every way preaching can be viewed as such, as preaching done by a man who is possessed by: character; freedom from self-consciousness; respect for people; enjoying his work; gravity; and courage.[20] Brooks, like many others, establish the horizontal realities of a preacher's character as the foundation for preaching that may be persuasive.

The horizontal realities of a preacher's ethos, pathos, and logos are indisputably imperative for persuasive preaching. However, there is a vertical dimension of persuasive preaching, the preacher's fellowship with the Lord, though inferred and understood as part of the preacher's ethos, it needs to be reckoned for its own merit and for its vital role in a preacher's ability to preach persuasively. As James Hoppin stated, "The preacher is only a medium; but he is a true medium between the hearers and Christ."[21] A persuasive preacher is a man of personal holiness, a Spirit-filled believer who is consecrated to Christ, a man who not only desires to separate himself from the snares of this world but is not ensnared by the worldly influences that beset preachers of another sort.

Though a preacher's preaching methodology, his personality, and his spiritual gifts are used by God in preaching, it is a preacher's deep character and devout life which makes him a conduit through whom the power of God flows uninterruptedly in his preaching.[22] The Christ-promised power of the Holy Spirit, which is still available today and just as powerful today as on the Day of Pentecost, is the invisible source of power which, in effect, is the perceptible mantle of the persuasive preacher.[23] "Of

19. Spurgeon, *An All-round Ministry*, 1900, 64.

20. Brooks, *On Preaching*, 54–60.

21. Hoppin, *Homiletics*, 1883, 259.

22. Smyth, *The Preacher and His Sermon*, 1922, 14.

23. Arthur, *The Tongue of Fire*, 1859, 234.

Whitefield, the most effective preacher of his day, it is said, that his preparation for the pulpit seemed to be 'the bathing of the spirit in heavenly influences' . . . which made him the wonder of his times; causing him to communicate such a hallowed impulse to all who heard him, that, even those who were offended at his want of taste, could not resist the fascinating power of his devoutness."[24] However much a preacher may work to prepare himself to preach, and however gifted he may be, it is only by the grace of God alone that any man's preaching is fruitful.[25]

With great privilege comes great responsibility. No greater privilege has been afforded mankind than to preach in a time in which God has made available his Spirit so that no man must preach in a condition that is other than the condition of being Spirit-filled. Without diminishing the value of a preacher's ethos, pathos, and logos, if one is to grasp the most significant insight for persuasive preaching it must be that of being filled with the Spirit.

A Spirit-filled preacher cannot but be persuasive, persuasive as God has determined him to be so on that occasion, persuasive as God has designed him to be so in the lives of his hearers. But so great a privilege brings so great a responsibility, that being, to be filled with the Spirit when preaching so that one does not preach in a condition that finds him other than Spirit-filled. The following counsel regarding a preacher's true responsibility is as encouraging as it is beneficial: "Do not take an exaggerated view of what the Lord expects of you. He will not blame you for not doing that which is beyond your mental power or physical strength. You are required to be faithful, but you are not bound to be successful."[26] Yet, the success which a preacher can have, the success he must have, is linked to his faithfulness, a faithfulness that finds him Spirit-filled. The faithfulness that allows him to be none other than filled with the Spirit is the measure of success for which every preacher is responsible. To the extent this is not the condition from which one preaches, the all too common occurrence for preaching will be demonstrated once again.

This all too common occurrence is the demonstration of a preacher who wields little in the way of a winsome presence and wields little in the way of power to persuade his hearers about the merits of the truth which he seeks to convey to them. This is a lamentable reality, one which Spurgeon is helpful to depict in a cause and effect fashion: "No dew of the Spirit of God is upon him; he does not require it; he drinks from other fountains. . . . He is as weak as he is polished, as cold as he is pretentious; saints and sinners alike perceive his weakness, and by degrees the empty pews confirm it. He is too strong to ask to be strengthened of the Lord, and therefore he is too weak to bless a congregation. . . . His preaching is like a painted fire, no one is either cheered or alarmed by it."[27] To have access to the power of God, to have the opportunity to

---

24. Moore, *Thoughts on Preaching*, 1861, 89.

25. Potter, *Sacred Eloquence*, 1868, 285.

26. Spurgeon, *An All-round Ministry*, 1900, 214.

27. Spurgeon, *An All-round Ministry*, 1900, 206–7.

be used by God in preaching to accomplish what he desires to do in the lives of his people, is a scenario that should find preachers being used by God to bring glory to God as he uses his servants to persuade his people to live lives that more fully comply to his Word.

As any preacher is enabled to preach persuasively, it will be God who does the persuading work. God uses his human instrument's ethos, pathos, and logos, as he is filled with the Spirit, to accomplish the results intended by him. This is how God commonly works in preaching.

The implications of how God commonly works in preaching are three. The first implication is that God is to be praised for what he does in accomplishing his will through the preaching of his Word. The second implication is that preachers are to be responsible stewards regarding their character, their passion, and the content of the sermons they preach. The third implication is that preachers must preach in the fulness of spiritual power made available to them by being men who are consecrated to Christ and filled with his Spirit.

It is crucial that there are no misunderstandings about this point: God persuades hearers with or without the means of a sermon conclusion. But sermon conclusions demonstrate the height of a preacher's character, passion, and content, which are the very things which God commonly uses in preaching that is persuasive. Therefore, the sermon conclusion should be the height of a preacher's concern regarding his ethos, pathos, and logos in preaching and for the prospect to be used by God to preach persuasively.

CODIFIED TRUTH AND A PERSUADED PERSUADER

Persuasion as the Main Thing

In preaching, as well as in many other endeavors, it is easy to lose sight of the crucial essence of what is to be done with the result being that lesser things usurp the place of the ultimate objective to be achieved. And in preaching as well as other endeavors, the ultimate objective to be accomplished cannot become a reality until lesser but important things are completed first. However, any of the lesser but important things pose a potential risk of becoming the new bullseye, a redirected objective for all efforts to accomplish. In other words, a means to the end may become the end. But the accomplishment of the redirected objective is only an insufficient achievement because it is less, and will always be less, than what is the true ultimate objective.

The potential prospect of opting for a redirected objective is particularly true in the preaching of Scripture. Many preachers, if asked, "What were you trying to persuade us about in this sermon you preached?" would provide a variety of insufficient answers. The worst, and probably the most common would be, "I wasn't trying to persuade anyone about anything. I was simply trying to . . ." Or "I was trying to persuade you about the correct way to interpret the often-misunderstood verses of . . ." Or "I was trying to help you understand the meaning of the preaching passage and its meaning for our lives." In other words, many preachers not only fail to be persuasive in their preaching, but they do not even understand that they are supposed to be persuasive in their preaching. Certainly, the last two responses targeting the correct interpretation of misunderstood verses, or the meaning of a text and its meaning for our lives are things that must be done. These things must be done so that the ultimate thing to be done may be achieved. Preaching requires that these things be accomplished but these things do not constitute the bullseye, the ultimate objective to be accomplished.

The requisite work of diligent labor, in the study and in the pulpit, to correctly interpret and clearly explain the Scriptures are prerequisite means by which the ultimate objective of preaching may be accomplished, that being, to persuade the hearers to life-change in a specific manner according to the requirements of Scripture. Wilbur M. Smith wrote, "I know of no quick road to worthwhile preaching. It is hard work. . . . Unless our souls are painfully exercised and we know what it is to wrestle with God and to contend with principalities and powers, we will never be able to move the souls of others."[28] In the preaching of many preachers they never discover the ways in which believers must change their lives, much less to commit themselves to persuading their hearers to implement life-change.

What is involved in the process that moves the hearer from ignorance of the truth, or disobedience of known truth, to the understanding and implementation of the truth in one's life includes: codification—I see how and why it is true; confirmation— I sense it is truly required of me and needed in my life; conviction— I sorrow that my life has not been in keeping with it; conformation—I submit myself to compliance to it; continuation—I set myself to stay at it regardless of the difficulties I encounter. The preacher must be involved in this process for his own life. He must become the first person persuaded to make changes in his life before he compels his hearers to do the same. In other words, the preacher must be a persuaded persuader.

God's design for the usage of his Word in preaching is not realized fully if preachers are not diligent "to open its meaning, to confirm its facts, to apply its principles, to deduce its lessons, to illustrate its harmony with other parts of our revealed system, and, generally, to exhibit it in its entire adaptation to the moral and intellectual nature of man."[29] Changed lives is the ultimate objective of the Word of God in the ministry of preaching. Compelling hearers to life-change is the ultimate role to be carried out in the process of preaching God's Word to his people. Therefore, the irreducible responsibilities of preaching are to teach clearly through the explanation of Scripture, to convince strongly through corroboration by the Scriptures, and to persuade

---

28. Roddy, editor, *We Prepare and Preach*, from Wilbur Moorehead Smith's chapter, "No Set Rules," 168.

29. Moore, *Thoughts on Preaching*, 1861, 24.

powerfully through application and illustration from the Scriptures,[30] with the most powerful persuasion and most personally pointed application being found in the closing appeals of the sermon conclusion.

Preaching must gain a vital entrance for biblical truth, week after week, to people who possess an existing knowledge of Scripture ranging from slight to significant. Furthermore, preaching must function to provide milk to the weak and meat to the strong, as well as establishing what is not known and re-enforcing what is already known among believers. Perhaps, the best way these functions can be attained week after week in a vital way is to for truth to be "presented in new combinations." The most accessible way new combinations of truth may be presented is by means of the closing appeals of the conclusion, each drawn from Scripture, providing an endless diversity in how Scripture profitably relates to itself.[31]

Obviously, this entails a painstaking effort for any preacher to search the Scriptures and draw from them selected references that become the basis to compel his hearers to life-change through the closing appeals of the sermon conclusion. Such diligent effort must not become a preventative factor for a preacher to fulfill the ultimate objective to persuade God's people for life-change since no preacher should exempt himself from the commitment of the Apostles of Christ who declared, "but we will devote ourselves to prayer and the ministry of the Word."[32]

Devotion to the Word must never be trivialized to become a concept or a slogan for the preaching ministry but rather a weekly reality of it in one's preaching. Unless a preacher can truly claim that he has gifts and powers that are above Christ's Apostles, then he must be devoted to prayer and the ministry of the Word as they were, or even more than they were. The present-day continuum of the apostolic devotion must be for the same results sought by the apostles in their preaching, to see the lost converted to Christ and for believers' compliance to the Word of God to be established in their lives more fully. Both results are the urgent pursuits of the sermon conclusion.

The apostolic devotion to prayer and the ministry of the Word must be directed to the additional effort of persuading hearers to respond to the Scriptures in their lives. The apostolic resolve must be directed to the purpose the apostles had for their preaching, that it would be persuasive in the lives of their hearers, unbelievers and believers alike. Otherwise, the only result will be preaching that is based upon a greater devotion and diligence directed to refinement and enhancement of sermonic minutiae that still leaves undone what the greater diligence needs to supply, sermon conclusions that are rich in instruction from the Scriptures persuading the hearers to needed life-change. Spurgeon identifies such wasted diligence in preparing sermons that are none the better for the misdirected effort. Spurgeon's reproof regarding a destructive diligence in sermon preparation is beneficial as he writes:

---

30. Wilkins, *Ecclesiastes*, 1718, 6.

31. Moore, *Thoughts on Preaching*, 1861, 25–26.

32. Acts 6:4.

Sermons which are studied for days, written down, read, reread, corrected, and further corrected and amended, are in great danger of being too much cut and dried. You will never get a crop if you plant *boiled* potatoes. You can boil a sermon to a turn, so that no life remaineth in it. . . . Give us sermons and save us from essays! Do you not all know the superfine preacher? You ought to listen to him, for he is clever; you ought to be attentive to his words, for every sentence of that paper cost him hours of toilsome composition; but somehow it falls flat, and there is an offensive smell of stale oil. . . . So long as the life of the sermon is strengthened by preparation, you may prepare to the utmost; but if the soul evaporates in the process, what is the good of such injurious toil? It is a kind of murder which you have brought upon the sermon which you have dried to death.[33]

What is called for is a more diligent effort in sermon preparation that prepares a sermon conclusion to be the highpoint of the sermon as well as the apex of persuasion compelling believers to comply to Scripture-based closing appeals resulting in life-change. Hearers who are persuaded to comply more fully to the truth of Scripture as exhorted by a persuasive, persuaded preacher is the missing but needed ministry of the sermon conclusion in present-day preaching.

It's said that the great actor Charles Laughton was attending a Christmas party with the family in London. During the evening the host asked everyone attending to recite a favorite passage that best represented the spirit of Christmas. When it was Laughton's turn, he skillfully recited Psalm 23. Everyone applauded his performance, and the process continued. The last participant was an adored elderly aunt who had dozed off in a corner. Someone gently woke her, explained what was going on, and asked her to take part. She thought for a moment and then began in her shaky voice, "The Lord is my Shepherd, I shall not want . . ." When she finished, everyone was in tears. When Laughton departed at the end of the evening, a member of the family thanked him for coming and remarked about the difference in the response by the family to the two recitations of the Psalm. When asked his opinion on the difference, Laughton responded, "I know the Psalm; she knows the Shepherd."[34]

And so it is in preaching. A personal knowledge of what one preaches about will be superior preaching, and it will be a significant advantage for preaching persuasively. In reference to persuasive preaching, the content of the sermon conclusion's closing appeals must be that which the preacher knows intimately, regards highly, and is offered to his hearers with the greatest interest that they will be used by God to redirect their lives in a significant manner.

---

33. Spurgeon, *An All-round Ministry*, 1900, 346–48.
34. Maxwell, *Everyone Communicates, Few Connect*, 62–63.

A Persuaded Preacher

To move people effectively, a preacher must know his subject-matter, but he must have more than a cognitive understanding of that subject-matter. The knowledge must be his by personal conviction and experience. That which persuades people to make life-change is more than information that has been accrued by diligent study, as necessary and valuable as that is. Truth that persuades hearers to the point that it becomes a part of their lives, commonly is proclaimed to them by a man who owns the truth he proclaims. The truth he declares is accompanied by the conviction and experience of a persuaded persuader.

John Maxwell's statement is helpful to clarify the importance of a preacher's convictions about and practicing of the truth he preaches. "If I try to communicate something I *know*, but do not *feel*, my communication is dispassionate. If I try to communicate something I *know*, but do not *do*, my communication is theoretical."[35] Even when the knowledge being provided is well-beyond what may be common knowledge, there remains the vital necessity that the knowledge be of deep personal conviction to the preacher so that he feels the truth and has some personal experience with the subject-matter about which he preaches. Dispassionate, theoretical truth is too accurate a description of that which is prevailingly predominant in preaching. This is precisely the kind of truth that is most unfit for persuasion.

Since persuasion requires instruction regarding that which is to be believed and lived, the substance about which hearers are persuaded matters greatly. The Word of God must be the sole source and substance of that which preachers persuade God's people regarding their faith and practice. Augustine believed that preachers preach with greater or less wisdom according to their proficiency in the Scriptures, a belief that is irrefutable. But scriptural proficiency is not accrued by merely reading and memorizing passages of Scripture, but by correctly understanding them, discovering insights about them, and being able to connect them profitably to one another, thus, allowing a preacher of scriptural proficiency to incorporate and connect biblical references in significantly productive ways. Specifically, proficiency in the Scriptures wields great value in the ability to access biblical truths for their appropriate and insightful inclusion in the closing appeals of a sermon conclusion.

Proficiency in the Scriptures is *the tremendous asset* for a preacher. A certain hinderance to proficiency in the Scriptures arises from the thinking of a preacher that he has already obtained it. The truth is, any preacher has gained some proficiency in the Scriptures, but for all he has gained there is the capacity to gain that much more, many times over. The great need is to gain greater enlightenment about that which a preacher thinks he knows. The need is for preachers to stop being impressed with what they know and become hungry to discover what they don't know about what

---

35. Maxwell, *Everyone Communicates, Few Connect*, 49.

they know. It is only when this becomes a reality that a preacher can be enlightened to the extent that he can bring significant spiritual enlightenment to his hearers.

Nothing is more exhilarating for a preacher and more infectious for the hearers, than the discovery of new insights, deeper understanding, or wider implications of a truth one has known for a long time. One instance of how new insights, deeper understanding, and wider implications of biblical truth can be afforded is through the use of Scripture-based closing appeals that provide the ways and means by which the purpose of the sermon can be possessed in the hearer's daily living. The weekly opportunity to discover how the content of the completed canon of Scripture can insightfully connect to the purpose of the sermon's achievement in life is a way that proficiency in the Scriptures can be an ongoing reality for the preacher and for those who hear him.

The weight and force of one's preaching is equal to one's convictions about that which he preaches. In the absence of convictions, preaching is theoretical and "destitute of real life."[36] William Ward Ayer writes:

> The preacher must be possessed by the message. Some preaching is like an old mother hen pecking and clucking. She finds a grain of corn, breaks it with her bill, and gives small portions to her brood. The food has never become a part of her. . . . Much preaching is like that. . . . The message may be orthodox, practical, and helpful, but it is obvious that the preacher is giving something that has never become a part of him. In this lies its ineffectiveness. In contradistinction I would present as an example old "Bossy" who feeds her calf that which she has first eaten, digested, and providentially turned into rich milk. In other words, she gives of herself. How much more effective much of today's preaching would be if the word that is given forth had first richly dwelt in the preacher, if he had entered into the experience, and could speak out of a warm heart by his fellowship with God! If only he could say with the disciples, "I speak what I do know!" John tells us that "the Word was made flesh." So it is in preaching, the Word must be made to live, before it is effective. Nothing is more effective than personal conviction. God still speaks out of "the bush that burns with fire." This is the first requisite of the man behind the message.[37]

The proclamation of truth which has made a moral impression on the preacher may make the same impression on behalf of some of the hearers. But the truth to be proclaimed must have made an impression on the one who proclaims it.

The Moral Impression of Truth

In every part of a sermon where there is a moral impression made in connection with a subject-matter, the impression becomes that which the hearer must attend to, that

36. Burgess, *The Art of Preaching*, 1881, 392.

37. Roddy, editor, *We Prepare and Preach*, in William Ward Ayer's chapter "My Method of Preparation," 16–17.

which the hearer must resolve in one way or another. As a hearer receives an indelible impression of a truth's connection to life, the hearer is forced to respond to it since a decision has become an inescapable matter.[38] As the sermon conclusion is directed to win a verdict from the hearers, it is the part of the sermon that is most fit for, and amenable to, a connection of truth and moral impression. Of course, it is incumbent upon the preacher to understand and articulate the vital connection that truth has to the hearers' lives so that a moral impression becomes an existing reality upon the consciences of the hearers in a sermon conclusion. Though this can and should take place, it is quite observable that such connection infrequently takes place due to conclusions that are non-existent or contain insufficient content when they are incorporated in a sermon. Mark Dever writes:

> Why does the postal service exist? What do we pay mailmen to do? Do we pay them to write letters to us and put them in our mailboxes? No. We pay them to deliver faithfully the message of someone else. The mailman has been entrusted with other people's messages to us. The same is true for ministers and their ministries. We are not to invent the message but to faithfully deliver God's message to his people. That is our calling, which means that we are called as ministers only insofar as we present God's message to His people.[39]

To Dever's point, and beyond the point he was making, preachers are to deliver God's message and in so doing preachers are to deliver the fulness of God's message, not just a portion of it. What kind of mailman would deliver three of five items of mail intended for a given mailbox? There is no reasonable and reputable understanding for withholding what should have been delivered.

Yet, sermons are preached in great numbers which deliver little or nothing by way of the sermon conclusion, the sermon's highpoint and the apex of persuasion. The common reality is that conclusions are non-existent, and when they exist, they are neither the highpoint of the sermon nor are they persuasive. God's mailmen are more than occasionally guilty of withholding that which was intended to be delivered, with the result that God's people are deprived of what they should have received.

Through solid instruction and argumentation backed by deep personal conviction of the preacher, the feelings of the hearers are conditioned subtly toward persuasion "which thus appears to come in as a natural consequence of what has been said." Insightful instruction and demonstrated argumentation supported by personal experience "is doubly necessary when we know our hearers entertain dispositions, which are anything but favorable to our purpose."[40] Significant skill in demonstrating truth is never more necessary than when preaching to people who are committed to understandings and practices that are contrary to Scripture. Demonstrated truth is

---

38. Storrs, *Conditions of Success in Preaching Without Notes*, 1875, 150.

39. Dever et al., *Preaching the Cross*, from Dever's chapter, "A Real Minister: 1 Corinthians 4," 19.

40. Potter, *Sacred Eloquence*, 1868, 300.

required for persuasion. "The mediocre teacher tells. The good teacher explains. The great teacher demonstrates."[41] A persuasive preacher is so because of the proofs and evidences he provides cause him to be so clear in his preaching that people cannot refute his claims. All that remains is their willingness to align their lives with convincing truth.

Instruction Precedes Persuasion

That which often is misunderstood is the relationship between preaching that is powerful to persuade and preaching that is rich in instruction. Insightful instruction is always the means by which persuasion may become the end. Long-standing homiletical counsel that continues to reward its practitioners is found in the following: "Alarm the conscience if you can, move the emotion if you can, persuade the will if you can, but whatever you do, you must teach."[42] To state it simply, persuasion cannot occur without instruction that is proven to be true, seen to be beneficial, and clearly understood by the hearers. The veracity and beneficial nature of any instruction cannot be ascertained until there has been substantial understanding on behalf of the hearers. "People are persuaded not by what we say, but by what they understand" is a precept that one desiring to preach persuasively cannot afford to overlook.[43]

Understanding is so crucial that it cannot be minimized. Every good result from preaching occurs after understanding has been secured in the minds of the hearers. Nothing will suffice to fill the void that is left by an absence of understanding when it is not secured. Spurgeon was adamant about this as he wrote:

> I fear that we are more deficient in heat than in light; but, at the same time, that kind of fire which has no light in it is of a very doubtful nature, and, is not from above. Souls are saved by truth which enters the understanding, and so reaches the conscience. How can the gospel save when it is not understood? The preacher may preach with a great deal of stamping, and hammering, and crying, and entreating but the Lord is not in the wind, nor in the fire;—the still small voice of truth is needed to enter the understanding, and thereby reach the heart. People must be taught.[44]

Though a persuaded hearer is one who has been on the receiving end of significant instruction, instruction does not equate persuasion. Persuasion is dependent upon instruction, but persuasion is not the result for all who receive substantial instruction. "You may teach a man the holiest truths, and yet leave him a wretched man. . . . Did the mere truth suffice to renew, there are towns, districts, and countries where all would

41. Maxwell, *Everyone Communicates, Few Connect*, 210.
42. Moore, *Thoughts on Preaching*, 1861, 20.
43. Maxwell, *Everyone Communicates, Few Connect*, 165.
44. Spurgeon, *An All-round Ministry*, 1900, 169–70.

be saints."[45] Persuaded hearers are always a portion of a larger group of those who were instructed in a manner that should have persuaded all of them, but it failed to do so.

Instruction is what a preacher can and must do while persuasion is that which the preacher is motivated to do, attempts to do, and hopes to do in the lives of all who hear him even though it will not happen that all are persuaded. Yet, even among those who were persuaded, as he hoped all would be, he was not responsible for their persuasion any more than he was responsible for those who were not persuaded, if he was urgently attempting to persuade them with clear, demonstrated, beneficial instruction. Preaching is a means God uses in the work that he does to make persuasion a reality for everyone who is persuaded through preaching.

It is understood that regardless of the truth that is proclaimed, regardless how well-intended was the one who proclaimed it, regardless of how well the truth was presented clearly, and demonstrated to be beneficial, not all will be persuaded to comply to the truth. But those who are persuaded are so because they comprehend that compliance to the Word of God is far more acceptable, is of far greater benefit, is of much greater importance than continuing to live in relative indifference to God's Word. But those who are persuaded desire to understand how the truth will be life changing, that the truth will make a very real difference in their lives, a difference that is not nominal but meaningful. They need for preaching to make the beneficial reality of complying with the truth demonstrable. "If we cannot show that our Christian faith really works for the enrichment, the unifying and the energizing of life, it may be as pretty as a gorgeous sunset and yet have no real grip on lives."[46] What people want and need to know is how compliance to the truth will impact them.

Since compliance to the truth will impact the lives of the hearers, this needs to be demonstrated to them. It has been said that "'The cure for dullness in the pulpit is not brilliance, but reality.' That is a great word to keep in front of your eyes, especially at a time when we are slain all day long by the assertion . . . that preaching is dull."[47] Preaching that is irrelevant is dull. Irrelevant preaching will always be dull. Most hearers greatly appreciate a preacher who can preach the truths of Scripture and relate them to their life experience, their situations. Such a preacher will never be dull. Hearers of sermons remember little of what a preacher says but "they will always remember how you made them feel."[48] Bored, is how hearers feel when listening to a dull preacher who is irrelevant. And being made to feel bored because of the irrelevance of one's preaching is that which hearers will not forget.

Codified truth in a persuaded persuader's sermon conclusion entails: that the bullseye for preaching remains the bullseye, which is to persuade the hearers to life-change; that the preacher is a persuaded persuader; that the basis of persuasion is

---

45. Arthur, *The Tongue of Fire*, 1859, 170.

46. Oxnam, editor, *Effective Preaching*, from Luccock's chapter "Reality in Preaching," 18.

47. Oxnam, *Effective Preaching*, Luccock's chapter "Reality in Preaching," 17.

48. Maxwell, *Everyone Communicates, Few Connect*, 65.

biblical instruction; that the moral impression of the preacher may become the moral impression of the hearers; that persuading the hearers is the completed intention in communicating God's message; and that insightful instruction is mandatory for persuasive preaching to become a reality. But what are the most crucial components of insightful instruction in sermon conclusions so that persuasion may be the result in the lives of the hearers?

Seven Crucial Components Mandatory for Persuasion

The sermon conclusion must incorporate seven most crucial components that check confusion and promote clarity so that persuasion may become a reality for the hearers. Even if it is true that, "Few sermons demand the entire attention of the listener. . . . An intelligent listener does not need more than half his mind half the time actually to follow the argument of a quite soundly reasoned sermon,"[49] it is prudent to make sure everything is done for the hearers so that they may easily follow the sermon conclusion. Since they can be persuaded only by what they understand, it is necessary that they are able to follow along with the content of the conclusion without any confusion. Therefore, the cognitive clarity of the hearers is a macroscopic starting point at which seven smaller understandings regarding the persuasion of the hearers must be grasped by a preacher and implemented in his preaching.

The first crucial component of persuasion for the hearers in the sermon conclusion is that they *must understand that the conclusion exists to focus upon the purpose of the sermon*, to discover what is necessary for that purpose to be accomplished in the hearers' lives. If there is one thing above all else that the hearers must understand it is that the conclusion is all about achieving the sermon's purpose. As is true for any part of a sermon, preachers who communicate effectively establish "the point before their listeners start asking, 'What's the point?'"[50] When it comes to the conclusion, the hearers must suffer no confusion regarding what is about to take place. Closing appeals will be provided as the means by which the sermon's purpose can be achieved in the lives of believers.

If the conclusion becomes the highpoint of the sermon and the apex of persuasion for the hearers, they must understand that as valuable as it was for them to understand the exposition of the preaching passage it is even more important that they understand what they need to do in response to the purpose of that text in their daily living. Therefore, they should expect that, in the conclusion of the sermon, the preaching will not be directed to teaching so much as to *persuading* them to comply with direct, straightforward, Scripture-based inferences and/or exhortations which they are to respond to by implementing them in their lives. As preachers, we will be exerting ourselves to impact the conscience, the affections, and the will; pressing

49. Atkins, *Preaching and the Mind of Today*, 220.
50. Maxwell, *Everyone Communicates, Few Connect*, 157.

upon them their "solemn responsibility to live according to God's Word."[51] Preaching methodology in the sermon conclusion will demonstrate the conviction that the purpose of preaching is to persuade the hearers in some specific manner of life-change "to make them better;" to furnish them with biblical counsel that will cause their lives to conform more fully to biblical truth.[52]

The second crucial component of persuasion for the hearers in the sermon conclusion is there *must be a provision of discernable movement from the beginning to the end of the conclusion.* Specifically, discernable movement makes clear the development of the closing appeals. The enablement of the hearers to track the closing appeals is a factor for clarity, understanding, and interest in the sermon conclusion. As a sermon conclusion is progressing in an anticipated manner, the hearers are encouraged to go along with the progress as it is made.[53] The movement that carries the hearers along is the advancement of thought the preacher provides through the connection established between the sermon's purpose and the closing appeals which are the means for achieving the sermon's purpose in the hearers' lives. It is critical that this advancement of thought must progress throughout the conclusion without getting bogged down in any portion of the conclusion.

The third crucial component of persuasion for the hearers in the sermon conclusion is that the hearers *must know what to anticipate as to the number of closing appeals.* Regardless of the number of closing appeals, it is of great advantage for them to know what to anticipate. The best way to track with the closing appeals as they are provided is to understand how many will be provided. Since the corpus of the closing appeals constitutes what is necessary to achieve the sermon's purpose in daily life, the hearers must not suffer confusion about what all is necessary for their compliance to the Word of God in daily living. So, if it is the case that four closing appeals constitute the hearers' compliance, they are well served to understand that four closing appeals are to be clarified in their hearing.

As miscommunication thrives in the presence of assumptions, preachers must assume nothing and clarify much. In the effort to help hearers track accurately the closing appeals being presented in serial fashion, it is counterproductive to assume that everyone is accurately tracking them. Therefore, repetition is quite serviceable to keep the hearers abreast of what they most need to know, so that there is no confusion about what all they need to do to comply fully for the achievement of the sermon's purpose in their lives.

The value of repetition is conveyed in the assertion that, "The first time you say something, it's heard. The second time, it's recognized, and the third time, it's learned."[54] The concern of being too clear is simply the grounds for unnecessary caution. Every

51. Moore, *Thoughts on Preaching*, 1861, 139.

52. Blair, *Lectures on Rhetoric*, 1852, 154.

53. Atkins, *Preaching and the Mind of Today*, 223.

54. Maxwell, *Everyone Communicates, Few Connect*, 161.

time repetition is made, someone who was suffering confusion gains clarity. But the clarity gained through repetition is essential for truth to be learned so that what is learned can become personal truth, thus establishing learned truth at its highest level. As one writer graphically advised, "preach like fencers with their foils off," in that, preachers should be direct, pointed, and surgically precise both in the manner and matter of their preaching.[55]

In the manner and matter of preaching, that which is preached must become personal to the hearers if it is to be truth that is borne out in their lives. "A rapier and even the household pin" are both effectively pointed weapons to command the undivided attention of those to whom they are applied in a personal way.[56] Truth that is borne out in daily living is truth that is personal, pointed, and clearly understood. Repetition is a crucial component in helping hearers to practice understood truth.

The fourth crucial component of persuasion for the hearers in the sermon conclusion is that the hearers *must understand the rationale for why they will be exhorted to comply to Scripture-based closing appeals.* Through the conclusion, a verdict from the hearers is sought, a verdict from the hearers that brings each hearer to a personal commitment to comply with the closing appeals of the sermon conclusion. The content of the closing appeals and the manner of exhortation rightly depicts the essence of preaching found in the conclusion as "forceful." The forcefulness of the preaching found in the sermon conclusion is only as it must be since the substance of what is said is weighty as the appeals are drawn from the Word of God. Therefore, "having something weighty to say, and in the determination to make yourself clearly understood," forcefulness will be a natural byproduct of the preaching that takes place in the sermon conclusion.[57]

The forcefulness of the preaching found in the sermon conclusion is only as it must be since the urgency of what is said by way of exhortation demands a response of compliance or non-compliance to Scripture, causing the preacher to be "at white heat" in his thought process and at "truest eloquence" in preaching in the sermon conclusion.[58] The forceful preaching of a sermon conclusion is appropriately explained by James Hoppin when he wrote:

> There are many who will preach from what they carry in their heads; few, very few, speak from their heart, from their bowels of charity. . . . This true emotion is (sensed through) a strong will to attain a proposed end. . . . The radical difficulty with men is not so much a perversion of the reason as of the will. Men are more willful than they are irrational. Here the preacher is to direct his

55. Black, *The Mystery of Preaching*, 1924, 129.
56. Black, *The Mystery of Preaching*, 1924, 129.
57. Behrends, *The Philosophy of Preaching*, 1890, 223.
58. Behrends, *The Philosophy of Preaching*, 1890, 223.

main assault. . . . He is to aim at immediate results. He is to persuade men, not next year, nor tomorrow, but today.[59]

Therefore, the closing appeals to which the hearers are exhorted to comply their lives to, if not based upon Scripture and backed by the preacher's conviction, are "worse than fruitless. They react against the speaker."[60] Any Scripture-based exhortation which fails to challenge the will and excites no enthusiasm of the affections has not been presented in its full measure of truth. Its meaning has dissipated and its importance has not been captured. Any exhortation that is based upon biblical truth understood fully and correctly "is at once a spur" of reproof and/or rebuke.[61]

Hearers must understand that there is much to be done in the Christian life as directed by God through his Word. This requires of preachers a willingness to supply exhortation, and even warnings through Scripture-based closing appeals. Preachers are not only to direct but compel hearers to conduct their lives according to the truth of Scripture. No believer is guilty of knowing too much of the Word of God, but all believers know far more than they faithfully practice of biblical truth, so that, the head is far more advanced than the heart. The corrective to be found in preaching the sermon conclusion is "to persuade, to entreat, to beseech" in reference to living the truth that is known.[62]

The ramifications of a preacher urgently exhorting hearers to comply with Scripture-based closing appeals which, if done, result in life-change and a fuller obedience to the Word of God in their lives. This means that the sermon conclusion cannot be dull, and it will be forceful as it should be. "A dull preacher of a past generation said to his congregation, 'If you cannot keep awake without it, when you feel drowsy, why don't you take a pinch of snuff?' At the close of the service one of his hearers gave this shrewd but good-natured reply: 'I think the snuff should be put into the sermons.'"[63] There will be no lack of "snuff" in a preacher who is urgently preaching to win a verdict from his hearers for the cause of their compliance to the Word of God in their lives. As a preacher is doing this, he cannot be dull, uninteresting, or impassionate. He, however, will be sincere, forceful, and very possibly, persuasive.

What then might compose the "snuff" of the closing appeals that would cause the preacher to be earnest, if not passionate, in challenging the hearers and at the same time that which the hearers would recognize as that to which they must be attentive? Regarding the innumerable things which might be said about the many biblical texts and their purposes, is it possible that they could all be significant? The answer is, they can be absolutely significant! Here is why. The primary means of exciting emotional

---

59. Hoppin, *Homiletics*, 1883, 254–55.

60. Kidder, *A Treatise on Homiletics*, 1864, 225.

61. Brown, *The Art of Preaching*, 1926, 68.

62. James, *An Earnest Ministry*, 1847, 87.

63. Bryan, *The Art of Illustrating Sermons*, 15.

interest of a hearer is by relating the content to be provided as that which satisfies their desires and values.[64]

There are three basic satisfactions that closing appeals can provide to the hearers.[65] First, the content contained in the closing appeals may be directed to satisfying a given need that is not being satisfied or the removal of that which prevents the satisfaction of this need. Second, the content contained in the closing appeals may be directed to satisfying a given need better or more thoroughly than is presently being satisfied. Third, the content contained in the closing appeals may be directed to the continued satisfaction of a given need against that which could bring it to an end. Any one of these three basic satisfactions will be perceived with interest by the hearers as they recognize the connection between the satisfaction of spiritual desires and values by means of the closing appeals if they are complied with by the hearers. In other words, the affections of the hearers will be productively met by their compliance to the closing appeals offered in the sermon conclusion.

The fifth crucial component of persuasion for the hearers in the sermon conclusion is that the closing appeals to which the hearers are exhorted to comply *must be made concrete and not left as abstract*. It is said that, "You must be able to see something clearly in your mind before you can say it clearly with your mouth."[66] If true, this may account for the ambiguity that is too common in preaching, but, more importantly, this is key to clear communication for the crucial content of the closing appeals of the sermon conclusion. The preacher must be able to depict in his own understanding what it looks like to comply with the exhortations he will provide to his hearers. His ability, or lack thereof, to supply a concrete illustration of what he is exhorting his hearers to do will determine the degree to which he can proclaim truth clearly, and to what degree he will be clear to those who hear him. An exhortation that is not combined with illustration will be abstract, and it will lack the power that is furnished by concretion.

Many people grasp an idea sufficiently, well enough to incorporate it in their lives, only when it is presented to them in a concrete fashion. This should not become for preachers a regret but should establish for them what their responsibility is to preach in a manner that will be most helpful to their hearers. It is a given, it is nonnegotiable that "understanding is developed more fully in the average mind by a picture than by an idea. There is a fine Arab proverb which says, 'He is the best speaker who can turn the ear into an eye.'"[67] Moreover, a preacher turns the ear into an eye equipped with the clearest vision when he incorporates the ultimate use of illustration in preaching, to show an idea "*in action*."[68] This entails illustrating how a truth was complied with or not complied with in the life of a person or people as recorded in Scripture.

64. Minnick, *The Art of Persuasion*, 226.

65. Minnick, *The Art of Persuasion*, 215.

66. Maxwell, *Everyone Communicates, Few Connect*, 163.

67. Black, *The Mystery of Preaching*, 1924, 120.

68. Black, *The Mystery of Preaching*, 1924, 121.

The sixth crucial component of persuasion for the hearers in the sermon conclusion is that there *must be an expectation of the preacher that God will accomplish a persuasive work in the lives of his people.* Nothing is lost to the preacher because he cannot know what God does in the lives of his people through the preaching of his Word. However, very much is lost to a preacher if he does not expect God to work, or thinks God will not work, in the lives of his hearers as he preaches God's Word. As one could rightly anticipate, Spurgeon is compelling in his convictions about the expectancy a preacher should have for God to work through the preached Word. Spurgeon writes: "We expect to take fish in our nets, and to reap a harvest in our fields. Is it so with you, my brethren? Let it be more so. . . . So pray and so preach that, if there are no conversions, you will be astonished, amazed, and broken-hearted. . . . Believe your own doctrine! Believe your own Savior! Believe in the Holy Ghost who dwells in you!"[69] The following words of Spurgeon depict both, the kind of thinking that is detrimental to preaching and the kind of thinking that is advantageous for preaching:

> Some preachers evidently do not believe that the Lord is with their gospel, because, in order to attract and save sinners, their gospel is insufficient, and they have to add to it inventions of men. Plain gospel preaching must be supplemented,—so they think. . . . A man said to me, "You told the dead sinner to believe." I pleaded guilty, but told him I would do it again. He said, "I could not do it, I should feel that it was of no use to do so." I answered, "Possibly, it might be of no use for you to do it, for you have not the necessary faith; but, as I believe that God bids me do so, I deliver the message in the Name of the Lord, and the dead sinners believe and live." I do not trust in the dead sinner's power to live, but in the power of the gospel to make him live.[70]

Spurgeon's frame of reference was the expectancy of God to work in the lives of unbelievers for conversion not just the expectancy for God to work in the lives of believers for their sanctifying growth in Christ.[71]

But God is just as able and just as faithful to use his Word in the lives of believers and unbelievers alike. Preachers must understand that in the work of regeneration or in the work of sanctification, God is able and willing to work, and God will work through his Word as he has determined to do so. In the instance of God working in the lives of his people to comply with the closing appeals of the sermon conclusion that are based in Scripture, there must be nothing but complete confidence that God will certainly do so! Steven J. Lawson is encouragingly to the point, "One God-called man armed with one God-sent message, committed to one God-prescribed

---

69. Spurgeon, *An All-round Ministry*, 1900, 187.

70. Spurgeon, *An All-round Ministry*, 1900, 388–89.

71. Spurgeon expected God to work in the lives of believers as they heard the Word of God in preaching. However, the quoted reference captured his expectancy for God to work in the lives of unbelievers in hearing the gospel.

method—preaching—is *always* sufficient for *any* situation."[72] Exhorting God's people to comply to appeals based on precepts and examples drawn from God's Word is certainly a situation for which a preacher can always be sufficient.

The seventh crucial component of persuasion for the hearers in the sermon conclusion is that there *must be an urgent ministry being enacted in the delivery of God's Word to his people from the preacher.* The incredible difference that becomes dominant in the conclusion of the sermon is the kind of ministry that is taking place in preaching. In the body of the sermon, the profitable ministry of explaining the text of Scripture is prominent. That is what the preacher urgently seeks to do in that part of the sermon. But, as of the conclusion, the ministry of preaching shifts from explanation to application; from the knowing to the doing; from comprehending the meaning of the text to complying to the purpose of the text; from understanding how the text contributes to the comprehensive knowledge of Scripture to seeing how the comprehensive knowledge of Scripture contributes to inform how one is to live in light of its wisdom; from equipping hearers with the knowledge of God's Word to equipping hearers with the wisdom to live the Word of God in their lives.

Every preacher who is cognizant of this dramatic transition of ministry in the conclusion, and engages it, will complete it by means of urgency in delivering the content of the conclusion. "To feel properly is therefore the surest way to speak effectively."[73] Persuasive preaching is a byproduct of a man who is serious about ministering to God's people effectively. Being a persuasive preacher is the reality for a preacher who is engrossed to win a verdict on behalf of his hearers that will result in their enhanced spiritual formation and daily living that is of greater obedience to biblical truth.

The Eloquence of Persuasive Preaching

The eloquence of persuasive preaching is produced through vital insight into biblical truth which precedes the empowering of the Spirit to speak persuasively. There must be spiritually "anointed eyes" before there is a spiritually "anointed tongue."[74] The eloquence of persuasive preaching is proclaimed through one who has discovered God's truth and preaches to convince and persuade because "he is himself convinced and persuaded."[75] The eloquence of persuasive preaching and self-consciousness cannot coexist. The preacher who is Spirit-filled forgets himself and experiences "the free flow of God's power through him." A persuasive preacher "habitually cultivates this holy engrossment, for the sake of the divine endowment and enduement."[76] Any preacher might preach an occasional persuasive sermon. Persuasive preaching, though it is

72. Lawson, *Famine in the Land*, 62.
73. Burgess, *The Art of Preaching*, 1881, 187.
74. Pierson, *The Divine Art of Preaching*, 1892, 109.
75. Pierson, *The Divine Art of Preaching*, 1892, 110.
76. Pierson, *The Divine Art of Preaching*, 1892, 112.

persuasive one sermon at a time, is persuasive week after week because of the kind of man the preacher is, because of the understanding he has about preaching to which he is committed, and how he prepares the sermons he preaches as well as preparing himself to preach them.

The Candor of Persuasive Preaching

An important quality about a persuasive preacher is his candor. Candor, the ability to correctly address the hearers' lives and the willingness to do so is essential to the persuasive preacher. "There are certain virtues which may be called professional virtues. No man can be an efficient soldier without courage; though he may be efficient as a soldier without honesty. No man can be an efficient merchant without honesty; though he may be efficient as a merchant without courage. Candor is the professional virtue of the minister. He cannot be truly successful without it. He must have convictions and the courage of his convictions."[77]

The candor that is so significant for persuasive preaching is more than the honest, straightforward depiction of the reality of Christian living in a fallen world but, more importantly, the insightful provision of scriptural truth that remediates that which must be corrected. The ability and willingness to correctly address the need for improvement and supply scriptural remediation to that which must change, in no small way gives persuasive preaching its carrying power, that which may be described by the hearers as "the breath of the Almighty."[78] From the hearers' perspective persuasive preaching is accompanied by the impression that they are being personally addressed by God.

Hearers who are persuaded through preaching are aware that God is speaking to them just as they understand that the one preaching to them has heard from God. Unless the preacher's own soul has been moved by the truth of Scripture, no one else's will be. Unless the preacher has delighted in the voice of the Lord in his study, no one will delight in the sound of his voice in the pulpit. Whenever a preacher burns with God's message and delivers it as well "as a good singer sings, or a good writer writes," people will hear him well.[79] "The indifference of the people to preaching is due to the fact that the preaching is indifferent."[80] People appreciate hearing a preacher who says what he means and means what he says, especially when what he says is from God's Word and he says it in the power of the Spirit and what is said is said for God's glory and for their benefit.[81] People are appreciative of persuasive preaching!

---

77. Abbott, *The Christian Ministry*, 1905, 219.

78. Calkins, *The Eloquence of Christian Experience*, 1927, 144.

79. Calkins, *The Eloquence of Christian Experience*, 1927, 144.

80. Calkins, *The Eloquence of Christian Experience*, 1927, 144.

81. Calkins, *The Eloquence of Christian Experience*, 1927, 143.

16

Persuasive Preaching in the Sermon Conclusion: Part 2

"Without cognitive persuasion there cannot be any appropriate volitional persuasion. Cognitive persuasion is, therefore, a tremendous service of ministry to God's people but persuasion must not end there. God is concerned not just about what his people believe but also with how they live in light of what they believe."

"Since there is a divergence between one's theology and one's living out one's theology, there will always exist the need for preachers to be persuasive in their preaching—cognitively persuasive as well as volitionally persuasive."

"God has granted to his people his Spirit and his Word to direct, guide, and empower them in a life that complies with his Word. This is why preaching should be so saturated and suffused with Scripture, not only in the sermon conclusion but especially in the sermon conclusion. The sermon conclusion should supply Scripture-based closing appeals through which, if complied with in the lives of believers, provides the training in righteousness that matures them in Christ, thus strengthening and developing their character. Scripture is key to produce persuasion."

"The supernatural means of the Scriptures are the only means by which believers may be appropriately and accurately directed in volitional persuasion. Anything other than the supernatural means of the Word of God and the Holy Spirit of God working in the lives of people will result in their manipulation which may produce behavioral change that cannot affect character, and thus, the behavioral changes will be short lived. Persuasive preaching is not about manipulation of people for short term behavioral change but for a miraculous work of life-change and character development which God alone can and does do, but only through the 'instrument' of his

Word and only through the 'agent' of his Spirit."

"Preachers are to preach for life-change providing exhortations to this effect, but they must impact the hearer's cognition, conscience, affections, and volition through the sanctioned means of Scripture which is profitable for instruction, reproof, correction, training in righteousness as a preacher reproves, rebukes, exhorts, with great patience and instruction."

"The most strategic place for persuasion of the affections and volition is at the end of each point of a sermon when the persuasion of the cognition and conscience have been completed. 'Its peculiar place, however, is in the peroration or conclusion of the sermon.' The obvious implication for persuasion in preaching is that the sermon conclusion is of paramount importance. The degree to which a sermon is found to be persuasive is determined primarily by the conclusion."

"In reference to the hearer's perspective, the difference between motivation and manipulation is the difference between desire and drudgery. The difference lies in the state of the hearers' hearts. Motivation causes people to respond to God's Word out of joy and enthusiasm. However, a convinced mind regarding the truth of God's Word combined with an unmotivated heart may respond to the truth from a constrained conscience alone—the reality of 'oughtness,' in which there is no joy, only drudgery. Because of compliance to the truth compelled by the oughtness of the conscience without the strength produced by joy and enthusiasm, obedience to the truth will be inconsistent, half-hearted, and short-lived. . . . So long as we do nothing but explain and reason, we may have convinced the mind about truth, but we have not persuaded the hearer by means of the conscience, affections, and volition. The understanding may be convinced, but the mechanism for a personal response to the truth may not be compelled in the least."

"I believe it is important to understand that, in preaching, a preacher can only provide incentives, positive and/or negative, legitimately drawn from the Word of God for his hearers to respond to the truth of God's Word. He must not manipulate, and he cannot even motivate his hearers. . . . If he were to think clearly and accurately about the biblical means by which God's Word can be applied and/or the benefits of such application in the lives of hearers, this would not be motivation. This would be providing incentivization legitimately drawn from the Word of God. And certainly, the preacher should incentivize a correct response to God's Word from the Word of God. However, the Holy Spirit of God, and only the Holy Spirit, can truly motivate."

"Just as the sufficiency of Scripture is essential, so is the primacy of Scripture essential to persuasive preaching. In other words, persuasive preaching is contingent upon the Word of God being proclaimed without compromise. To be a persuasive preacher

does not require one to avoid any aspect of truth. But rather, the exact opposite is necessary. A requirement for a persuasive preacher is that he is too committed to the truth of God's Word to curtail it to avoid condemning the consciences of his hearers. In fact, the consciences of the hearers must suffer conviction if they are moved to a 'serious and radical change of life.' The conscience of the hearer must suffer disruption as a precursor of persuasion, if it is to occur. And, for those who suffer conviction but respond with grace seeking to remedy the error of their way, they can only have a grateful respect for a sincere, courageous preacher who is intent upon the welfare of his hearers. Preached truth must have its effect upon the conscience if it is to be a persuasive word. 'Speaking the truth in love' is the DNA of persuasive preaching and it will never be less than that."

"Thomas Potter writes, 'It is one thing to convince a man that he ought to change his life; it is another to persuade him to make this change. . . . There are many preachers who know how to prove the Christian doctrine and to convince the intellect, but comparatively few who know how to move the heart and persuade men to practice what is preached."'

VOLITIONAL PERSUASION

The Basis for Persuasive Preaching

The words of a wall plaque read, "I practice daily what I believe. Everything else is religious talk."[1] The proposed wisdom contained in the words of the plaque, though well intended, is false wisdom. Neither the positive nor the negative assertion is accurate as the positive is an overstatement, while the negative is an understatement of reality. The positive assertion is that one's practice and beliefs are the same. This is an overstatement. They are not. Every believer's beliefs are greater than their practice of them and all believers fail to live fully what they certainly do believe. The negative assertion is that what one fails to practice may be a violation, but it violates only the insignificant matter of religious talk. This is an understatement. Every believer's practice reflects, to some degree, a lack of compliance to the Word of God. Believers are the same in this sense—we practice what we most desire to do whether it is in compliance or non-compliance to the Word of God. What we think we believe but don't practice represents either our deepest deceptions or our highest aspirations. We need to know which is true because our deceptions need reproof and correction, but our aspirations need encouragement and exhortation.

The gap between what believers hold true with conviction, and their compliance to those truths, practically and consistently, provide a crucial basis for persuasion in preaching. Persuasive preaching ensues from a real, Christ-like concern for people in

1. Smith, *Real Evangelism*, 81.

which personal compliance of divine truth is prioritized so that there might be from God's people a desire to submit to the divine obligations of Scripture so that their confession of truth and their compliance to truth is consistent.

Some preachers, though not fully persuasive in their preaching yet concerned for people, prioritize ideas, organized thought, doctrinal systems from Scripture, so that their hearers discern the cognitive correctness of what they hear and, therefore, gain a feel for the cognitive "strength of their preaching but are not moved by it."[2] To the degree that such preachers are able to establish an accurate understanding of what one should believe from the Word of God they are persuasive in their own right but they may be this, and only this—cognitively persuasive.

Without cognitive persuasion there cannot be any appropriate volitional persuasion. Cognitive persuasion is, therefore, a tremendous service of ministry to God's people but persuasion must not end there. God is concerned not just about what his people believe but also with how they live in light of what they believe. A preacher can, by the force of his own passion being expressed through his entire personhood, by his gestures, his voice, his eyes, and his words, impact his hearers "with the same sentiments and feelings with which he has been so deeply penetrated."[3] Though more than this is needed for persuasive preaching to be the result of a man's preaching, the preacher's passion for the truth he proclaims will always be a vital element of the kind of preaching that results in volitional persuasion.

Since there is a divergence between one's theology and one's living out one's theology, there will always exist the need for preachers to be persuasive in their preaching—cognitively persuasive as well as volitionally persuasive. The success of preaching is due to its provision of a theological upgrade but also an obedience upgrade through preaching that supplies greater doctrinal understanding and incorporates greater practical adherence to scriptural truth. The reality is this, doctrinal understanding is more quickly comprehended than it is consistently lived out. The typical believer's orthodoxy exceeds one's orthopraxy. Preaching must be committed to seek the advancement of practical consistency among those who hear and are responsive to biblical truth. Spiritual truth works in the lives of believers "as light works upon vegetation" in that the cause and result of growth is certainly occurring even if it cannot be quantified, yet without such imperceptible increments, "there is no growth."[4]

It would be damaging to preaching for a preacher not to understand the primacy of practicing scriptural truth and for him not to be committed to challenge, exhort, and provide insights and instruction crucial to his hearers so that they might be able to live lives of greater practical integrity through the means of his volitionally persuasive preaching. A preacher is not in full agreement with God regarding his design for preaching if he thinks that preaching need not include insight and instruction about

2. Hoppin, *Homiletics*, 1883, 254.

3. Potter, *Sacred Eloquence: or the Theory and Practice of Preaching*, 1868, 273.

4. Phelps, *The Theory of Preaching*, 1882, 518.

how believers are to live their lives in greater practical consistency to the doctrinal truths they understand.

Scripture contains truth that formulates what must be understood as well as truth that instructs believers how to live their lives consistently in a manner that complies with the teaching of the Word of God and pleases the God of the Word. There is a need for preaching to be strong in cognitive and volitional persuasion, not in one only, but in both. In the life of every believer there is room for and need of growth in what is to be understood and what is to be done regarding the truths of Scripture. No matter how well a preacher may do in either arena of cognitive or volitional persuasion, the strength in either one does not nullify the need of the other. William Arthur's comments are helpful to understand this rightly. He wrote:

> Every power has its own sphere. The strongest arm will never convince the understanding, the most forcible reasoning will never lift a weight, the brightest sunbeam will never pierce a plate of iron, nor the most powerful magnet remove a pane of glass. The soul of man has separate regions, and that which merely convinces the intellect may leave the emotions untouched, and that which merely operates on the emotions may leave the understanding unsatisfied, and that which affects both may yet leave the moral powers uninspired. The crowning power of the messenger of God is power over the moral man; power which, whether it approaches the soul through the avenue of the intellect or the affections, *does* reach into the soul . . . and the result of its action is . . . subsequent and moral fruit. Power which cleanses the heart, and produces holy living, is the power of the Holy Ghost. . . . It (the power of the Holy Spirit) strikes deeper into human nature than any mere reasoning or pathos.[5]

Since Scripture is profitable to make the man of God adequate for every good work and preaching includes reproving, rebuking, and exhorting in addition to instruction, it is not a stretch to understand that Scripture is to be the basis of content for the doctrinal and behavioral development of God's people.

Scripture as the Instrument of Persuasion

All the days of the temporal lives of believers present the temptation and opportunity to not comply to the Word of God as they know it and have convictions about its veracity and need of compliance to it. Yet, "mere conviction never carries a point of practical moral conduct. Deeper than the judgment, deeper than the feelings, lies the seat of human character, in that which is the mystery of all beings and of all things, in what we call their 'nature,' without knowing where the nature lies, what it is, or how it wields its power. . . . To turn nature belongs to the Power which originally fixed

---

5. Arthur, *The Tongue of Fire*, 1859, 105–06.

nature."[6] The needed power for believers to live lives that are consistent with the will of God expressed in his Word, resides with God, Himself. But God has granted to his people his Spirit and his Word to direct, guide, and empower them in a life that complies with his Word. This is why preaching should be so saturated and suffused with Scripture, not only in the sermon conclusion but *especially in the sermon conclusion.*

The sermon conclusion should supply Scripture-based closing appeals through which, if complied with in the lives of believers, provides the training in righteousness that matures them in Christ, thus strengthening and developing their character. Scripture is key to produce persuasion. Only Scripture possesses the power to make the needed changes in believers' lives. Nothing less than the value and worth of Scripture could serve as the grounds for believers to submit and commit themselves to the rigorous process of implementing change, continuing with its demands and requirements, sticking with it to the point of spiritual maturity and character development. Only Scripture ranks as that which is sufficient enough for believers to command that which will be for them a rigorous process. The objective of persuasive preaching, life-change, many times is an arduous process, one which has been compared to the process of making candles, which entails melting, molding, and making hard.[7] Only Scripture wields the might and the merit to make this a reality for believers.

To be reminded of the power of God's Word, consider the amazing suddenness and sharpness of the conviction experienced in the hearts of the thousands who responded to Peter's sermon preached on the Day of Pentecost. Though these unbelieving individuals were naturally opposed to what God was doing in their midst, they were converted by means of the Word of God and the Spirit of God working in them. These people went from being mockers to beggars, begging for the help that might redeem them from the error of their way. God's work in these individuals is evidenced further, and even more dramatically, by the decisive and steadfast change demonstrated in their lives as they were baptized, added to the church and were devoted to the Apostles' doctrine, fellowship, prayer, and in the breaking of bread. By the power of God, they had been made new creations in Christ Jesus. They possessed a new nature "by supernatural means," the only means by which man's nature can be changed.[8]

The supernatural means of the Scriptures are the only means by which believers may be appropriately and accurately directed in volitional persuasion. Anything other than the supernatural means of the Word of God and the Holy Spirit of God working in the lives of people will result in their manipulation which may produce behavior modification that cannot affect character, and thus, the behavior modification will be short lived. Persuasive preaching is not about manipulation of people for short term behavior modification but for a miraculous work of life-change and character development which God alone can and does do, but only through the "instrument" of

6. Arthur, *The Tongue of Fire,* 1859, 112.

7. Griffin, *The Mind Changers,* 4.

8. Arthur, *The Tongue of Fire,* 1859, 130.

his Word and only through the "agent" of his Spirit.[9] As cognitive and volitional persuasion are understood rightly, two mandates are thrust upon a persuasive preacher.

First, he must incorporate the Word of God in his sermon conclusions and he must trust in the Spirit of God to make the Word effective in the lives of people. Second, he must expect God to work by means of his divinely ordained instrument and agent. "If no supernatural power is expected to attend the Gospel, its promulgation is both insincere and futile."[10] The very intent of preaching persuasively is, in actuality, a faith proposition. Incorporating the Word of God in Scripture-based closing appeals, trusting and expecting that the Spirit of God will accomplish his work in the lives of the hearers is befitting for any preacher and is central to the act of preaching. G. Campbell Morgan's words are convincing when he instructed, "The aim of every sermon is stirring the human will. . . . A discourse which makes no spiritual or moral appeal or demand is not a sermon. Truth is something that must be obeyed. . . . How important this part (the conclusion) of the sermon is I think can hardly be over-stated. Preach for a verdict. It is no use talking reality to the crowd unless we show them it is for them."[11]

Of great importance for persuasive preaching is the understanding that those who are persuaded by the instrument of God's Word and by the agency of God's Spirit will apply themselves to an intensive and immediate response to the truth. This type of response is the verdict for which one preaches. God's persuasion does not produce a response in the nature of, "I think I might kinda, sorta try this" or "I think, perhaps, maybe in the future I should give this a shot." Such a response is only a nonresponse, indicative that persuasion has not occurred. A lack of persuasion leaves the hearers in a state where they depart "untouched, unwounded, and uncomforted. Somehow the sermon must penetrate their hearts and move their sluggish wills. Somehow the listeners, varied as their needs are, must go away resolved to translate what they've heard into immediate and practical action."[12]

It is not enough to persuade the hearers about the legitimacy of the closing appeals, in other words, that they now bear personal, certain understanding regarding the truth claims of the Bible. Beyond their recognition that biblical truth has legitimate claims upon their lives, the hearers must be persuaded that these legitimate claims upon their lives *must be fulfilled* in their lives. Beyond persuading the hearers that truth must be fulfilled in their lives is persuading the hearers to *commit to fulfilling* these truths in their lives. In the words of Austin Phelps, "Appeals should be aimed ultimately at the executive faculty of the soul. . . . 'What will you do about it?' is a question which the pulpit always asks. . . . An assembly of worshipers need to be brought, by appeal, to

9. Arthur, *The Tongue of Fire*, 1859, 174.

10. Arthur, *The Tongue of Fire*, 1859, 174.

11. Morgan, *Preaching*, 88–89.

12. Roddy, editor, *We Prepare and Preach*, from Stott's chapter "Stewards of God," 183.

the test of executive action."[13] The closing appeals of the sermon conclusion constitute the test of executive action which must be met for persuasion to be a reality.

The Sermon Conclusion as the Test of Executive Action

Preaching in the sermon conclusion must focus, ultimately, upon the will of the hearers for obedience to the Word of God, taking up the duties that belong to the Christian life, entering into the activities that belong to a servant of Christ. There must be an emphasis placed upon obedience, a submission to the truth. The critical point of preaching is to reach the conscience of the hearers with the truth of Scripture, to impact their affections so that they desire to comply with scriptural truth, and to persuade the will of the hearers to action. Obedience is the life of spiritual knowledge. Life is a growth; when obedience or the life of spiritual knowledge ceases to grow, decay begins. Growth, development, gain in the life of spiritual knowledge is by using it, by obeying that which is known.[14] Preaching must be about more than providing additional information, or new insights about that which is known already, as important as these are to preaching. Preaching must contend for the compliance of the truth in the lives of God's people.

Spiritual growth and health must be understood in terms of faithfulness to what is known, to be good stewards of truth as it is known, not only in the necessity to amass more knowledge. The ultimate purpose of a conclusion is to focus the claims of scriptural truth on the moral judgments and wills of the hearers since all of God's Word carries a divine obligation for his people to comply with it.[15] The concept of divine obligation is that which must compel a preacher regarding his sermon conclusion and persuasive preaching in the conclusion of a sermon. In a sermon conclusion containing Scripture-based closing appeals providing choice insights and instruction regarding how the purpose of the sermon can be achieved most effectively in the lives of the hearers, the matter before the hearers is one of compliance or noncompliance. Persuasive preaching makes it impossible for the hearers to misunderstand that a verdict of non-compliance to the closing appeals of the sermon conclusion is nothing but disobedience to God's truth.

The Affections As The Key To Persuasion

In all honesty and with no motive to minimize a hearer's response to not comply with the Scripture-based closing appeals of a sermon conclusion, they do so because they are not inclined to compliance. This lack of being inclined to comply with truth,

13. Phelps, *The Theory of Preaching*, 1882, 540–41.
14. Hoyt, *The Preacher*, 1912, 232–33.
15. Jones, *Principles and Practice of Preaching*, 161.

though regrettable and certainly the response of the hearer, may represent a failure on behalf of the preacher who failed to supply information that would affect how compliance and noncompliance will impact their lives. In other words, he failed to provide information that might impact the hearer's affections. He failed to provide truth that would, prospectively, cause them to desire to comply with the truth. What the preacher failed to do, and probably failed to understand, is that "Persuasion is . . . the influencing of the will by appealing to the passions. Always supposing a due foundation of clear instruction and solid proof, persuasion, therefore, is the fruit of a successful appeal to, and moving of, the passions of the human heart."[16] The passions are those affections of the soul which are awakened at the site of some good object, by which the will is drawn to embrace, or some bad object, from which the will is compelled to flee. Thomas Potter is as clear as he is convincing when he argued that:

> *Truth* is the object of the intellect, *good* that of the will. Man never places an act except for the attainment of something which really is, or, which he rightly or wrongly conceives to be a good; something which will conduce to his happiness, to the perfection of his nature, and the development of his being. To make me *believe*, it is enough to show me the truth. To make me *act*, you must show me that the action will answer some end. Now, nothing can be an end to me which does not gratify some passion or affection in my nature; and, therefore, in order to induce me to attain that end, you must necessarily appeal to the passion or affection which is to be gratified by its attainment. . . . There is no persuasion without an appeal to the passions.[17]

The war to win a verdict from the hearer's volition is won on the battlefield of the affections. Much persuasion is relegated to truth that seeks to win a verdict from the hearers by reaching the mind and the conscience so that hearers are made to understand what the truth is and what is to be done/not done in response to the truth. In other words, there is an accurate realization of the oughtness of one's life, what ought to be done or what ought not to be done, based upon the truth as it is known. Yet, this overlooks the reality that the affections "are at the center of volition." These "must be reached" in order for a person to respond, "in a meaningful way," by being touched where he is motivated," in the affections.[18]

People tend to "do what they desire to do" and do not do what they "don't want to do or don't choose to do."[19] Persuasion is the result of "a process of vitalizing old desires, purposes, ideals or a process of substituting new desires, purposes, ideals in

16. Potter, *Sacred Eloquence*, 1868, 269.

17. Potter, *Sacred Eloquence*, 1868, 270–71.

18. Sleeth, *Persuasive Preaching*, 60.

19. Lewis, *Speech for Persuasive Preaching*, 108.

the place of the old ones."[20] Hearers must be able to discern from Scripture how life-change can and will work for their greater good.

There is a greater understanding that is needed regarding the affections as the prime mover of the volition. Genesis 3:6 is very insightful. Notice the three-fold victory over Eve that appears after the word "was" in verse six. The verse tells of the successful persuasion Satan had over Eve as she saw that the tree <u>was</u> "good for food" and it <u>was</u> a "delight to the eyes" and it <u>was</u> "desirable to make one wise." She is poised to be volitionally persuaded because Satan has impacted her affections. Notice how her affections were impacted. The tree is no longer thought to be good for death, but it is thought now to be good for food. The tree for the first time was a delight to her eyes. She now wanted, coveted the forbidden fruit. She never delighted in it before. But she did as of verse six. She desired the wisdom that the fruit was promised to provide to her if she would partake of it. She believed there was wisdom to be gained by eating the fruit and she wanted to be in possession of that wisdom. In a word, Eve was "persuaded" to disobey God's command. She was persuaded because of the deceptive assault on her affections. From the beginning we can see the instrumental means of appealing to the affections to persuade. Genesis 3:6b provides the report of the successful persuasion of Eve by Satan as it says, "she took from its fruit and ate." Yet, the victory of Eve's volitional persuasion was rooted in verses four and five, but it began in verse one.

In verse four the serpent came to *the woman*. Genesis 2:16–17 says that God told *the man* (Eve had yet to be created) that from any tree of the garden he could eat, freely, but from the tree of the knowledge of good and evil he could not eat, for in the day that he ate from it he would surely die. Adam clearly told Eve about the tree once she had been created because she was able to report to Satan well enough that she knew that eating from this tree had been forbidden by God. Yet, it was *to Adam* that God gave the expressed restriction about the tree of the knowledge of good and evil. Eve knew about the restriction that had been placed upon the fruit of the tree in the middle of the garden, but Adam knew it more certainly than Eve. So, it was as Genesis 3:1 reports that Satan came *to Eve* to persuade her to partake of the forbidden fruit. The first demonstration of Satan's craftiness was *to persuade Eve rather than Adam*. This speaks to the role that the certainty of knowledge has in the persuasion process. Adam's knowledge being more certain than Eve's did not keep him from eating the fruit, for he did eat, but he did not eat as Eve did. Eve ate because she was persuaded to do so, or as Paul distinguished the difference between Adam's and Eve's participation in disobeying God's command regarding the forbidden fruit, "And it was not Adam who was deceived, but the woman being deceived, fell into transgression."[21]

Eve's deception was the result of Satan's persuasion of her to enter into disobedience. Adam disobeyed. But his disobedience was not by means of deception, the result

20. Lewis, *Speech for Persuasive Preaching*, 111.

21. I Timothy 2:14.

of Satan's persuasion. Adam did what he should not have done on his own volition, without his affections being directly persuaded as Eve's affections were. Adam and Eve understood well enough what they were not to do. And this knowledge was backed by the consequence of suffering death in the day of their disobedience, should they choose to disobey.

One might think there could be no way that Adam and Eve would ever disobey God. They walked with God in perfect fellowship. They had the joy of obeying the Word of God in their lives. They had no shortage of food from many trees from which they could eat freely. And there was just one tree that they needed to not eat from and it was clearly identified so that they could not accidentally eat from this tree—they had sound protection from, and a clear warning about, this tree with its forbidden fruit. But enter the tempter and the choice to disobey God became reality.

We will understand persuasion well if we understand that the temptation to do evil is the same in process, in its antithesis, as the persuasion to do good. The persuasion process includes the components of; *whatness*, the cognition of what truth is; *oughtness*, the consciousness of conviction that what is true ought to be done; *wantingness*, the affection to gain what is not possessed or to maintain what is possessed; *willingness*, the commitment to do what one chooses to do. In other words, the persuasion process incorporates the cognition, the conscience, the affections, and the volition.

Cognition matters. What is known, the degree of knowledge, the depth of knowledge is a factor in persuasion. Conscience matters. What one knows well and holds with conviction is a factor in persuasion. Affections really matter. What one begins to understand as valuable, as desirable, as beneficial, as advantageous, comprises the affections which are pivotal in determining one's choices. But one's affections are influenced by the conscience and cognition. Knowledge and convictions about the truth contribute to what is deemed desirable, what is coveted.

The understanding of persuasion must not omit the insights available in verses four and five. Two things are observed which must be recognized because they are vital to the persuasion process. Verse four is a clear and decisive dismissal of the certain consequence God had established for eating the forbidden fruit. Significant to the process of persuading Eve to disobey God was the instruction of Satan that the proposed threat of death was not true. "You surely will not die!" was a cognitive assertion that had to be offered and received or persuasion to disobey God would not have happened, most probably. How effective could the persuasion to disobey God be if Satan would have offered this, "God certainly is correct. If you eat of this fruit you will die. But . . ." The persuasion to disobey God would have been crippled. The adverse consequence had to be dismissed as a reality. The implication of this is crucial to persuasion in preaching. Some are quick to think that a preacher's instructing hearers of negative ramifications for their actions is unloving, unkind, fearmongering, or coercive. Sowing and reaping is an abiding principle. What one does or does not do matters. Satan's dismissal of the negative consequence of death for eating the forbidden fruit was a necessary factor to persuade Eve to disobey God. Cognition and conscience matter in the process of persuasion.

Verse five provides insight that is valuable to understand regarding persuasion. Satan's direct challenge of the veracity of God's stated consequence could not stand alone. It needed to be joined with changing Eve's convictions about God's character of trustworthiness. Satan's angle was to discredit God, to call into question his goodness, his truthfulness, and his motives for saying what he said. Genesis 3:5 says, "For God knows that in the day that you eat from it your eyes will be opened, and you will be like God, knowing good and evil." The objective was to disarm her conscience by altering her convictions about God and his Word. If Eve believes that God said what he said to keep her from experiencing life most fully, that God is holding out on her, that God does not have her best interest as a priority then why should she have any reservations about doing other than what he said? Eve's conscience was now free to do what she wanted to do.

The sad reality of Satan's successful volitional persuasion of Eve so that "she took from its fruit and ate" occurred because of the work that had taken place in her cognition, conscience, and affections. The same process is involved in the volitional persuasion of believers to comply with the Word of God in their lives. The cognition, conscience, and affections cannot be bypassed but must be addressed through the Word of God for there to be successful volitional persuasion to comply with what the Word of God instructs.

Previously in this book, reference has been made to cognitive persuasion and volitional persuasion. These terms may now be understood in reference to the cognition, conscience, affections, and volition in the following way. Cognitive persuasion pertains to the cognition and conscience, primarily. Volitional persuasion pertains, primarily, to the affections and volition. Life-change, the result being sought in preaching, requires that preaching impacts the hearers' cognition, conscience, affections, and volition. Seeking to see lives changed only by addressing the volition, the will of the hearers, must be viewed as the inadequate reality that it is. Satan's first words to Eve were not an exhortation to her volition, "Eat of this fruit!" but instead, he begin to impact her cognition with the question of Genesis 3:1, "Indeed, has God said, 'You shall not eat from any tree of the garden?'" Preachers are to preach for life-change providing exhortations to this effect, but they must impact the hearer's cognition, conscience, affections, and volition through the sanctioned means of Scripture which is profitable for instruction, reproof, correction, training in righteousness as a preacher reproves, rebukes, exhorts, with great patience and instruction.

Persuasion, in part, is the result of how preached truth powerfully appeals to the hearers to motivate them to live in greater obedience to Scripture, thus becoming to them the word of life. Through persuasion, the hearers' wills are swayed, and their moral affections are increased, so that they "not only hear and understand, but yield and obey." Or, according to Augustine's perception of persuasion, "the preacher should seek 'to bend men to action.'"[22] The most strategic place for persuasion of the affections and volition is at the end of each point of a sermon when the persuasion of the cognition and conscience have been completed. "Its peculiar place, however, is in the peroration or conclusion of the sermon."[23] The obvious implication for persuasion in preaching is that the sermon conclusion is of paramount importance. The degree to which a sermon is found to be persuasive is determined primarily by the conclusion. Thomas Potter expressed this in the following:

> There is no part of the discourse which requires to be more skillfully managed and more carefully studied than the conclusion. This is, indeed, the decisive moment, the last assault which is to decide the victory. In spite of our explanations, in spite of our reasoning, it may be that our hearers still hang back, unable to deny the force of our arguments, and yet unwilling to make the generous sacrifices which God demands at their hands. It is in these concluding and decisive moments that we are to bring the full weight of our zeal, of our love, of our ardent desire for the advancement of their best interests, to bear upon the hearts of our hearers. . . . Hence, the conclusion is, above all other parts of the discourse, the place for the appeal to the passions.[24]

For the closing appeals of the sermon conclusion to be persuasive they must be related to the affections of the hearers. If not, the persuasiveness of the preacher will be limited to challenging the hearers to do what they ought to do rather than challenging them to do what they ought to do *and what they desire to do*.

The Strength and Length of the Closing Appeals

Care must be exercised regarding the closing appeals between the strength of the appeals being made and the length of time in making the appeals. The stronger the emotive nature of the appeals, the briefer they must be.

Under the influence of strong emotive exhortation, the souls of the hearers are "in a state of violence" and, therefore, the appeals must not be protracted. "Prolonged feeling, when strong, is contrary to nature. The stronger any emotion is the more brief is its duration."[25] Therefore, the final minute of the conclusion may be suited best to carry most productively the strongest passion in the sermon. This was the advice of G. Campbell Morgan as he wrote, "The last sixty seconds are the dynamic seconds in preaching. . . . Make that last sixty seconds, as we are able, distinct and intense with all the power of our message."[26] In the conclusion, relative brevity is in order since the

22. Hoppin, *Homiletics*, 1883, 252–53.

23. Potter, *Sacred Eloquence*, 1868, 304.

24. Potter, *Sacred Eloquence*, 1868, 305–06.

25. Potter, *Sacred Eloquence*, 1868, 302.

26. Morgan, *Preaching*, 89–90.

will must be gained or lost through clear, practical, urgent, and straightforward closing appeals which need no involved argumentation or lengthy explanation.[27]

Since the conclusion is the place for direct address and personal appeal which are related to the purpose of the sermon, the conclusion is quite naturally the place for an appeal to the hearers' cognition, conscience, affections, and volition.[28] The conclusion should excel in persuasion by means of the closing appeals aimed at the mind, conscience, affections, and will of the hearers. In the conclusion, if anywhere, the whole man should be influenced by a preacher fired with the force of the truth developed in the closing appeals "glowing" with light and heat.[29]

Synchronization of the Intellectual Mode and the Emotional Mode

Since a preacher preaches simultaneously from two modes, the intellectual mode and the emotional mode, every time he preaches, it is important that both modes communicate the same thing, that is, what is communicated intellectually is supported emotionally. Though this is what should occur, this may not be the situation.[30] When the two modes are not in sync, what is communicated in the intellectual mode is canceled by the lacking support from the emotional mode. "When the intellectual and emotional modes are at variance with each other, people instinctively choose the emotional message and disregard the intellectual."[31] This must never be a reality in the sermon conclusion since the intended result of all preaching, especially the conclusion, is to produce a practical determination of the hearer's will to comply with the truth of Scripture in daily life. As the aim in preaching is "the transformation" of the hearers, "to persuade people to think, and to act in a certain way" there must be no dissonance between what is said intellectually and emotionally.[32] To this end, the truths of the closing appeals should be so compiled, arranged, and delivered as to galvanize the whole sermon into one effect. It is the conclusion, then, which "twines" everything together, compelling the persuaded hearer to fulfill the mandates of God's Word in his or her life.[33]

In reference to the hearer's perspective, the difference between motivation and manipulation is the difference between desire and drudgery. The difference lies in the state of the hearers' hearts. Motivation causes people to respond to God's Word out of joy and enthusiasm. However, a convinced mind regarding the truth of God's Word combined with an unmotivated heart may respond to the truth from a constrained

27. Potter *Sacred Eloquence*, 1868, 307.

28. Hoppin, *Homiletics*, 1883, 437.

29. Dabney, *Sacred Rhetoric*, 1870, 176.

30. Stevenson and Diehl, *Reaching People from the Pulpit*, 73.

31. Stevenson and Diehl, *Reaching People from the Pulpit*, 73.

32. Luccock, *Communicating the Gospel*, 125.

33. Dabney, *Sacred Rhetoric*, 1870, 169.

conscience alone—the reality of "oughtness," in which there is no joy, only drudgery. Because of compliance to the truth compelled by the oughtness of the conscience without the strength produced by joy and enthusiasm, obedience to the truth will be inconsistent, half-hearted, and short-lived. In this case, an unmotivated believer trying to comply to the truth of Scripture feels manipulated by the Word of God.

What is needed is to supply what is sorely lacking, the necessary insights to understand fully, convincingly, why it matters that the truth of Scripture is obeyed and how it is beneficial to comply with the truth. "It is one thing to convince a man that he ought to change his life; it is another to persuade him to make this change. . . . There are many preachers who know how to prove the Christian doctrine and to convince the intellect, but comparatively few who know how to move the heart and persuade men to practice what is preached."[34] The previous quotation establishes a reason why sermon conclusions, even when they are existent, are prone to be less than what they should be.

So long as we do nothing but explain and reason, we may have convinced the mind about truth, but we have not persuaded the hearer by means of the conscience, affections, and volition. The understanding may be convinced, but the mechanism for a personal response to the truth may not be compelled in the least.[35] "Earnestness is demanded, but with some, it is rather the earnestness of the head, than of the heart; the labored and eloquent effusion of the scholar . . . rather than the gush of the hallowed feeling of him who watches for souls, as one that must give account. . . . (B)ut the heartless declamations of the pulpit orator will do for some, though it has little tendency to do anything more than please the intellect."[36] What must be understood is this, persuasion does not follow as a matter of course from a rightly informed mind and a conviction of the conscience. Again, these absolutely are mandatory but volitional persuasion is a subsequent work that still must be affected once the conscience has been convicted. Therefore, persuasion necessitates a different sort of skill than is needed to explain truth.[37]

"Feeling is the soul of eloquence" and it is the pathos of feeling, the passionate expression of that feeling about the truth as it is communicated through thoughts, words, and expression that a preacher makes tremendous headway in gaining the "noblest victories over the hearts of our hearers."[38] It is at this point that many preachers are doomed from being volitionally persuasive in their preaching because they are adept at discovering the truth, but they feel little of the truth they discover. The feelingless way they processed the truth in the study is duplicated in their preaching in the pulpit, to the effect that those who hear them preach are not moved by the unmoved preacher.

34. Potter, *Sacred Eloquence*, 1868, 264–65.
35. Moore, *Thoughts on Preaching*, 1861, 69.
36. James, *An Earnest Ministry*, 1847, 249.
37. James, *An Earnest Ministry*, 1847, 97–98.
38. Potter, *Sacred Eloquence*, 1868, 268.

The feelings, emotions, or passions are part of the affections, that which is crucial for volitional persuasion to occur. However, it is important to understand that the affections are not under the immediate influence of the will. For example, it is one thing to know that I am to be deeply grateful to God. It is another thing to be deeply grateful to God.[39] The affections are not under the will, but the affections may influence the will. For example, I may be grateful to God out of compliance to the command to be so, or I may be grateful to God out of the desire to do so and to express my gratitude to God. Either instance finds my volition complying with what is required of me from Scripture. However, the instance of my being grateful to God out of response to his profound goodness is preferable to my being grateful to God only out of obedience to a command in his Word. I will be grateful to God to the extent that I desire to be grateful to God, out of oughtness or out of wantingness. I may be obedient to Scripture because I ought to be, or I may be obedient to Scripture because I want to be.

However, it is important to understand the merit of doing as one ought to do, all affections aside, just as it is important to understand the demerit of doing as one desires to do, all conscience aside. Therefore, it is important to understand the role that affections may have on the volition to move one from disobedience to obedience. In the instance of my potential disobedience to God in the matter of gratitude, it may not be enough for me to know that I should be grateful to God if I do not desire to be grateful. A lack of affection regarding gratitude to God may overrule my conscience, which knows I ought to be grateful to God, so that I choose not to be grateful to God. I choose to be ungrateful and will be ungrateful to God because my affections are not as they should be, even though I know that what I want to do and am doing is not right. I will be ungrateful to God, knowing it is not right, simply because it is what I desire to do, or put a bit more acceptably, because I lack the desire to be grateful to God. Furthermore, I will continue to be ungrateful to God until my affections have been changed.[40] If, however, my affections are changed, then my will can be changed. As in this hypothetical example, so it is for many people, that persuasion for one to move from disobedience to obedience cannot bypass the affections.

In seeking to move hearers from disobedience to obedience, a preacher is wise to appeal to the affections of the hearers so that they may be found living in obedience to Scripture because they desire to do so even more than they know they ought to do so. The unfortunate reality is that most believers will not practice obedience in some matters unless, or until, they desire to do so. The fact that they ought to comply with Scripture in some matters is insufficient to compel their obedience. Until they are convinced about the benefit of their compliance to God's Word, they simply will continue to be disobedient to the Word of God in their lives.

---

39. Potter, *Sacred Eloquence*, 1868, 277.

40. This personal example of ungratefulness to God is purely hypothetical and is offered only as an exemplary means to understand the manner in which the process of volitional persuasion is conditioned upon the affections.

Persuasion from the Hearer's Perspective

A couple of core characteristics of basic human nature cannot be disregarded when seeking to serve hearers by helping them to respond to Scripture as they should, in ways that will benefit them. These core characteristics of basic human nature are neither honorable nor flattering, but they are almost universally true so it would be unwise to pretend that they did not exist. "Ninety-nine out of a hundred are mirror-minded, being interested morning, noon, and night in their own personal lives."[41] And, perhaps, even less impressive is this, "People will not usually exert themselves beyond the point of absolute necessity and they will not act unless they are prodded."[42] People are interested in that which benefits them and it is the prospect of receiving a benefit that serves as an effective prod to action. An appeal to the passions of the hearers is strengthened when a preacher depicts a scene, circumstance, or occurrence, in which the affections of the hearers he seeks to excite are necessary for a biblically correct response to occur, or when a biblically correct response increases the sought after affections as a natural outcome. In so doing, the preacher is presenting scenarios in which the affections he desires to excite are viewed by the hearers as valuable; either as the winsome means for appropriate conduct by believers, or as the winsome outcome of appropriate conduct by believers.[43]

In order for the closing appeals presented in the sermon conclusion to be viewed as persuasive by the hearers, each appeal must pass three criteria: it is true; it is appropriate or fit; and it is profitable or beneficial.[44] Unless the hearers are convinced of the truthfulness of what they are exhorted to do, they should not and must not do it. Unless the hearers are certain about the fitness or propriety of doing what they are exhorted to do, they will not do it. And, unless the hearers are compelled to see the profitability or benefit of doing what they are exhorted to do, they will not do it because they are not motivated to do so. The hearers must feel compelled to comply to the closing appeals "with zeal and ardor" if they are to be volitionally persuaded to cease from doing what they are doing or to begin doing what they have not been doing.[45] For the sake of effective, appropriate persuasion, the affections are the "means of determining the will and stimulating to corresponding action."[46]

Life-change requires that understanding, conviction, and motivation be provided to the hearers. As Haddon Robinson phrased it, "Directly or indirectly the conclusion answers the question, So what? What difference does this make? And the people face another question: Am I willing to allow God to make that difference in my

41. Parker, *Develop Your Powers of Persuasion*, 32.

42. Parker, *Develop Your Powers of Persuasion*, 32.

43. Potter, *Sacred Eloquence*, 1868, 276.

44. Blair, *Lectures on Rhetoric*, 1852, 166.

45. Blair, *Lectures on Rhetoric*, 1852, 168.

46. Broadus, *A Treatise on the Preparation and Delivery of Sermons*, 1870, 284.

experience?"[47] If their affections have not been moved, in addition to their cognition and conscience having been properly provided for, their lives will reveal the answer to the question which is—they are not willing! In order to be volitionally persuasive in preaching, preachers must do far more than to appeal to their hearers with strong, well-intentioned, exhortations to make significant change in their lives. Warren Wiersbe was indicating the critical nature of the hearers' affections when he designated "The best conclusion is one that . . . makes obeying the truth so attractive and Jesus so worthy of obedience."[48] Such attractiveness and worthiness, if these are indicative of the hearers' hearts, are so because their affections have been appropriately impacted by the preacher in his sermon conclusion.

As important as it is for preachers to understand what they must do to preach persuasively, it is beneficial to possess adequate understanding about those who are hearers of sermons. People hear sermons through differing personal contexts which predispose them to be receptive to what they hear or to varying degrees to be resistant to what they hear. In other words, some hearers will be resistant to what they are challenged to do because of various stumbling blocks in their character or their situation in life that militate against their compliance to the truth. Therefore, such hearers may view their compliance to the truth "as a threat to their worldview, or culture, or family unity, or personal self-esteem, or sinful way of life, or economic lifestyle." In understanding that such stumbling blocks exist, there is a need to "persuade by argument (anticipating and answering people's objections), or by admonition (warning them of the consequences of disobedience), or by indirect conviction (first arousing a moral judgment in them and then turning it upon themselves, as Nathan did David), or by pleading (applying gentle pressure of God's love)."[49] God's people are disobedient to the truth for some reason or reasons. These must be portrayed so that they may be viewed for the vice that they are.

As unfortunate as it is, preachers must understand the reality that there will always exist some people who, seemingly, are unpersuadable people. As far as he can tell, they seem impervious to change so that the truth seems to have no impact upon these icons of changelessness. Cotton Mather provided an encouraging word when he wrote: "Go on to do as well as you can what you have to do. Let not the crooked things that cannot be made straight encumber you."[50] Certainly, such people should not cease to be prayed for since they must be prayed for. Certainly, such people should not cease to be appealed to in preaching, for they must be appealed to as well. However, they may have need to be converted, to be saved, to be born again, to become a disciple of Jesus Christ, rather than to be persuaded to comply to scriptural truth designed for

47. Robinson, *Biblical Preaching*, 167.

48. Wiersbe, *The Dynamics of Preaching*, 83.

49. Stott, *Between Two Worlds*, 253–54.

50. Mather, *Student and Preacher*, 1789, 247.

believers. The rationale to include a presentation of the gospel message as the final part of a sermon conclusion will be the subject of chapters eighteen through twenty.

The Sermon Conclusion and Vitality

The crucial need to persuade believers to life-change by means of the closing appeals of the sermon conclusion must be understood as the ultimate work to be accomplished in preaching. But this work will not be accomplished if the subject-matter of chapter six is not taken care of, the need to make the transition to the conclusion of vital one. Ramesh Richard is correct, "If the inception of a sermon conclusion seems unimportant to them, the hearers will not give the attention needed to profit from what will be offered to them."[51] A sermon conclusion that is effective to persuade unbelievers to repent of their sin and believe in Jesus Christ, trusting in his finished work on their behalf for their salvation or to persuade believers to comply with the closing appeals so that the purpose of the sermon may be fully accomplished in their lives must be a sermon conclusion that is heard well by the hearers. This necessitates that the sermon conclusion be a vital one, one which begins and continues in vitality.

A PERSUADED PERSUADER IN THE PULPIT

Persuasive Preaching Is A Holy Thing

Sermon conclusions must be controlled by the power of the last impression. In order for a conclusion to make a lasting impression, it must be perceived by the hearers as persuasive. A persuasive conclusion making a lasting impression on the hearers must include direct scriptural exhortation, vivid material to clinch the purpose of the sermon, and a strong closing sentence that may echo in the minds of the hearers.[52] A lasting, last impression is representative of the kind of conclusion that may be persuasive in the hearers to motivate them to comply with the closing appeals and thus effect life-change.

Technically, I believe it is important to understand that, in preaching, a preacher can only provide incentives, positive and/or negative, legitimately drawn from the Word of God for his hearers to respond to the truth of God's Word. He must not manipulate, and he cannot even motivate his hearers. If he were to require a response of his hearers, that is, in some way force his hearers to respond, this would be manipulation. And, of course, this has nothing to do with what a preacher rightly should do in the closing appeals of his sermon conclusion. If he were to think clearly and accurately about the biblical means by which God's Word can be applied and/or the benefits of such application in the lives of hearers, this would not be motivation. This would be

---

51. Richard, *Preparing Evangelistic Sermons*, 132.

52. Abbey, *Communication in Pulpit and Parish*, 178–79.

providing incentivization legitimately drawn from the Word of God. And certainly, the preacher should incentivize a correct response to God's Word from the Word of God. However, the Holy Spirit of God, and only the Holy Spirit, can truly motivate.

Additionally, the Holy Spirit may motivate some of God's people without usage of any of the biblical means offered by the preacher in the conclusion. Instead, the Holy Spirit may illumine the mind and motivate the heart of some believers by bringing to their minds biblical texts known to the hearer but not referenced by the preacher. Either way, it is the Holy Spirit and not the preacher who motivates God's people to respond to God's Word. The preacher should be content to be responsible for discovering from God's Word the most "appealing carrots and effective sticks" to incentivize God's people to respond to his Word. And should God's people respond to what the preacher challenges them with from the Word of God, it will be God not the preacher who motivated them to respond.[53] From a human perspective only, without consideration of God working by his Spirit, by his Word, and through the preacher, one may think about persuasion as that which is autonomous, as that for which the hearer is responsible for producing, along the lines of, "Whenever people take action, they do so for their reasons, not yours or mine."[54] But, it is far better to realize that God deserves all credit for the correct response to his Word because he, Himself produced it in the heart of the one who responded wisely. Most believers recognize a need for improvement in the daily pursuit of taking up their cross and following Christ. In hearing a preacher who can relate valuable insights and needed corrections to them to achieve this, they will be attentive to what he has to say from the Word of God.[55]

Though change, per say, is not a welcomed prospect for many people, it is through the realization that change is necessary to live a life of greater obedience to the Word of God that allows believers to be open to understand what it may entail for them. And, furthermore, hearers expect those who preach to them to challenge them regarding such change. Few, however, would insist upon the requirement for it as former President Abraham Lincoln supposedly did. The following anecdote reveals what the former President of the United States believed was a preacher's duty in proclaiming biblical truth.

> President Abraham Lincoln, an incredible communicator, was known during the Civil War to attend a church not far from the White House on Wednesday nights. The preacher, Dr. Gurley, allowed the president to sit in the pastor's study with the door open to the chancel so he could listen to the sermon without having to interact with the crowd. One Wednesday evening as Lincoln and a companion walked back to the White House after the sermon, the president's companion asked, "What did you think of tonight's sermon?" "Well," Lincoln responded, "it was brilliantly conceived, biblical, relevant, and well presented."

53. McDonough, *Keys to Effective Motivation*, 73.

54. Maxwell, *Everyone Communicates, Few Connect*, 43.

55. Maxwell, *Everyone Communicates, Few Connect*, 102.

"So, it was a great sermon." "No," Lincoln replied. "It failed. It failed because Dr. Gurley did not ask us to do something great."[56]

The conclusion is the element of the sermon where, if something great is to be required of the hearers, it should be made known in the conclusion. But, as a rule, sermon conclusions are of little importance for the greater part of the sermons delivered every Sunday.

Commonly, as a sermon nears its end the typical hearer is more concerned about departing from the preaching service than being concerned about applying the instruction offered in the sermon to one's life. Though this ought not to be the case, it will continue to be so until preachers determine that their conclusions will be delivered with "the distinct intention of gaining the assent and affecting the will of his hearers."[57] As John Broadus phrased it, "What we want in the conclusion is something which appeals to the affections and the will" through closing appeals that "increase in weight, heat, and life, so as to make the greatest impression" on the hearers.[58] The cumulative effect of the closing appeals should provide persuasion for life-change in accordance to the purpose of the sermon.

To whatever extent the hearers' interest has been secured in the sermon, it should be strengthened in the conclusion to the point of persuading them to comply with the closing appeals and thus achieving the sermon's purpose in their daily living.[59] "The conclusion is that part of the sermon which vigorously applies the truth" since the conclusion is applicatory and hortatory. It should, therefore, be characterized by the utmost intensity, and energy. "The highest vitality of the sermon shows itself in the sermon conclusion. If the hearers' wills are ever carried, it is the design of this part of the sermon to achieve it. Therefore, the prospects for actual persuasion of the hearers probably will not occur if the conclusion "is lame."[60] In preaching for results, that is, preaching for a verdict that will result in changed lives for God's glory, the interest of the hearers must be elevated for the content of the conclusion.[61]

Christlikeness is the Objective of Persuasive Preaching

Targets for application include that which must start, that which must stop, that which must be corrected, that which must be improved upon methodologically, that which must be improved upon motivationally in the lives of the hearers. The purpose for the sermon is the main consideration of the conclusion. A preacher should seek to win a

56. Maxwell, *Everyone Communicates, Few Connect*, 205.

57. Burgess, *The Art of Preaching*, 1881, 385.

58. Broadus, *A Treatise on the Preparation and Delivery of Sermons*, 1870, 282.

59. Burgess, *The Art of Preaching*, 1881, 386.

60. Shedd, *Homiletics and Pastoral Theology*, 1876, 197.

61. Black, *The Mystery of Preaching*, 1924, 165.

verdict, or endeavor to win it, and "this is what we do in a proper conclusion."[62] There is one great general purpose in preaching which is to make men and women Christ-like. Every sermon should seek to achieve some particular purpose, in a particular way, of that one great general purpose for preaching.[63]

To the extent that the preacher fails to preach for the accomplishment of the purpose of the sermon, to that same extent the sermon will fail to be appropriately persuasive. An effective sermon conclusion is one in which the purpose of the preaching text "is fitted to life;" challenging "the minds and hearts and wills of the hearers with all the concentration of force which the preacher can muster. At this point weakness is unpardonable."[64]

The most consistent extension of apostolic preaching seeks for conversion and for the perfecting of holy lives among those converted. Such preaching "casts light on all the varied interests of human life and all the aspects of human character; on everything, in fact, where there can be a right and wrong, and where responsibility is incurred by the moral choices of rational beings. The final object of preaching, then, is edification." Preaching for edification "is to build up the soul in righteousness and true holiness. It is the work of soul-culture. It is the formation and completion of Christian character."[65] The earnestness of a preacher, in part, is the result of "the pressure of the message on our own heart, our feeling of urgency." An earnest spirit is just "the glow of an inner flame," kindled and fanned by an occasion of the specific purpose of a preaching text contacting the specific needs of the hearers.[66] Conclusions very naturally should consist of persuasion and entreaty since the hearers must be enlightened and convinced about the value of the closing appeals for their lives, but they also need to be urged to comply with them.[67]

There is a degree to which a preacher's desire to see his hearers transformed by the Word of truth is contagious. The internal conviction, urgency, and purpose of a preacher adds an affecting influence to his words, his looks, his gestures, and his whole manner, which exerts itself upon the hearers.[68] It has been suggested that, "If you can't put fire into your sermon, put your sermon into the fire." Preaching may be likened to fireworks or dynamite. They both make noise, but fireworks, at best, may have the power to amuse while dynamite accomplishes a significant purpose.[69] "The preacher is an advocate. He wants his truth to effect changes in the lives of those who hear him. . . . The whole person is the object of the influence of the sermon; but the

62. Montgomery, *Preparing Preachers to Preach*, 102.

63. Montgomery, *Preparing Preachers to Preach*, 103.

64. Davis, *Principles of Preaching*, 1924, 217.

65. Hoppin, *Homiletics*, 1883, 257.

66. Black, *The Mystery of Preaching*, 1924, 172.

67. Broadus, *A Treatise on the Preparation and Delivery of Sermons*, 1870, 284.

68. Kidder, *A Treatise on Homiletics*, 1864, 226.

69. McEachern, *Proclaim the Gospel*, 30.

will is the point of attack in the conclusion where the deep feeling and the expression of the preacher's earnestness is in its most complete form."[70] Thus, the conclusion is vigorous in manner as well as vital and vivid in matter.

The first condition of a sermon or any part of the sermon that is found, on behalf of hearers, to be interesting is "a fused unity of interest for both preacher and congregation." A preacher may be in deep earnestness with what has little interest for his hearers. "A preacher will never be on fire with a message unless it gets hold of him entirely." However, though they will feel the preacher's passion, the hearers will not respond to truth that is not demonstrated as valuable to them.[71] "No matter how good your medicine is under competent analysis, if you cannot induce the people to take it, it will not do them any good."[72] The pathos of a preacher, among other things, allows him to connect with the feelings, desires, wishes, fears, and passions of his listeners.[73] Therefore, the passion of the preacher in the sermon conclusion is a passion for his hearers to understand the significance that the closing appeals can have for their lives so that they can live in greater obedience to the Word of God and, thus, experience greater fulfillment and fruitfulness as believers.

Sympathy for People is Prerequisite for Persuasive Preaching

"Passion is powerful. It supersedes mere spoken words."[74] "The simplest man with passion is more persuasive than the most eloquent without it."[75] A preacher is a man with a message on fire. It is the message, burning in his heart, that begets the heat. He is in dead earnest, and "earnestness creates enthusiasm and passion."[76] Persuasiveness, to a degree, is the byproduct of enthusiastic earnestness. Vernon Stanfield writes, "Some men preach in what I call 'the key of gee whiz,'" and conclude their sermons in this manner. When a preacher realizes that the destinies of human souls are at stake, he cannot preach so half-heartedly. The concern of a preacher's heart shows in his delivery.[77] We must recognize that, "unless we are enthusiastic ourselves, all our efforts to inspire that quality in others will be failures."[78] A lack of enthusiasm was viewed by C. H. Spurgeon as one of four marks of the absence of being fitted to preach. Prospective students to Spurgeon's pastors College were denied entrance on the basis of four criteria which rendered them "not naturally *fitted to preach*." These were: "a

70. Davis, *Principles of Preaching*, 219.

71. Atkins, *Preaching and the Mind of Today*, 221.

72. Brown, *The Art of Preaching*, 1926, 68.

73. Maxwell, *Everyone Communicates, Few Connect*, 202.

74. Maxwell, *Everyone Communicates, Few Connect*, 212.

75. Black, *The Mystery of Preaching*, 1924, 107.

76. Black, *The Mystery of Preaching*, 1924, 132.

77. Stanfield, *Effective Evangelistic Preaching*, 24–25.

78. Burgess, *The Art of Preaching*, 1881, 391.

low state of piety; a want of enthusiasm; a failure in private devotion; and, a lack of consecration."[79] So, as Spurgeon reckoned, that some men are not fitted to preach, some men, though fitted to preach, are not fitted to be persuasive preachers because they lack a sympathetic nature toward others.

> Persuasion is a subtle, spiritual element; it has to do more with the temper and tone of the man than with what he says; it is essentially personal, coming from the contact of mind with mind, the spirit with spirit. Some men are antipathetic to you; they constantly antagonize and so rarely influence you, though they may speak the truth. And they may take this attitude toward a large part of their audience. The very sight of some men is a benediction. They are like the sunlight upon the landscape, making it beautiful and also fertile for any good seed that may be sown in its soil. . . . The truth itself and the way it is spoken all bear relation to the personality of the preacher and so have to do with the winning or repelling of men.[80]

A persuasive preacher is one whom the hearers discern quite clearly that he seeks for their souls to prosper and he is sympathetic toward them.

A persuasive preacher is one who recognizes the spiritual needs of his hearers as well as the sufficiency of the Scriptures to meet those needs. For one to be a persuasive preacher "there must be a real sympathy with men" which means that there will be a sympathetic understanding of the difficulties of faith, including its doubts, denials, temptations, and failures. "Some of our brethren have great influence over men, and yet others with greater gifts are devoid of it; these last do not appear to get near to the people, they cannot grip them, and make them feel. There are preachers who, in their sermons, seem to take their hearers one by one by the buttonhole, and drive the truth right into their souls, while others generalize so much, and are withal so cold, that one would think they were speaking to dwellers in some remote planet, whose affairs did not much concern them."[81] Greater spiritual gifts cannot diminish the tragedy of a preacher who is not concerned deeply about the people to whom he preaches. This must be reckoned as the most irksome reason for a preacher's lack of persuasiveness in his preaching. It must be realized as an essential reality that preaching cannot be detached from loving the people for whom the sermon is intended. Spurgeon is insightful regarding this essential reality as he writes:

> Assuredly, we must abound in love. It is a hard thing for some preachers to saturate and perfume their sermons with love; for their natures are hard, or cold, or course, or selfish. We are none of us all that we ought to be, but some are especially poverty-stricken in point of love. . . . Love is power. The Holy Spirit, for the most part, works by our affection. Love men to Christ; faith

79. Spurgeon, *An All-round Ministry*, 1900, v.

80. Hoyt, *The Work of Preaching*, 1905, 259.

81. Spurgeon, *An All-round Ministry*, 1900, 43.

accomplishes much, but love is the actual instrument by which faith works out its desires in the Name of the Lord of love. . . . You will never preach well unless you are enamored of it: you will never do well in any particular charge unless you love the people . . . and I'm sure that, until we heartily love our work, and love the people with whom we are working, we shall not accomplish much.[82]

The preacher who, by the inclination of his personality, is not given to a warm demeanor toward others, must out of sheer compliance to the commands of Scripture understand that his role in preaching requires of him to preach as a means to love God's people and, therefore, he must be motivated to do so in the exercise of his ministry. John Hall is quite convincing as he makes connection between the preacher's demeanor toward his hearers and his ability to persuade them in his preaching. Hall stated:

> Good preaching should be *persuasive*. The motives, pleas, arguments, and appeals of the Bible should be presented in such a way as to lead men to move in the desired direction. Young preachers expect that reason so cogent as they can state it will command the assent and corresponding action of men. But, in point of fact, men are not thus uniformly moved. Men must be not only reasoned with, but they must be convinced of your goodwill toward them. . . . The tone of the voice, the expression of the face, the attitude of deference, or of imperious authority assumed toward them—all these have their influence. A remorseless logic, clear and is irresistible by a logician, will be set at defiance by many a human heart that would be influenced by a tone of tenderness in the voice.[83]

In order, however, for love to be effectively demonstrated in preaching there must be the pre-existing reality of a thorough going renunciation of self. "Self-renunciation is the root of all excellence. . . . In the Christian ministry, it is self-sacrifice that gives real excellence and glory to our work. When self-interest disappears, and only Christ is seen, then will be our highest success . . . in the moving of our fellow-men."[84] Only as a preacher sets aside every semblance of self and prioritizes the spiritual welfare of his hearers is he fully capable of providing the kind of preaching that his hearers may perceive as loving and may find persuasive.

Persuasive Preaching is Dependent upon a High View of Scripture

The persuasive preacher is one who holds a high view of God's Word and presents it as a more than sufficient remedy for man's needs. As such, the life of no man is beyond the remediating or redemptive power of God's Word. Such a theological conviction about Scripture's sufficiency is vital to persuasive preaching.[85]

---

82. Spurgeon, *An All-round Ministry*, 1900, 192–93.
83. Hall, *God's Word Through Preaching*, 1875, 171–72.
84. Taylor, *The Ministry of the Word*, 1876, 21–22.
85. Hoyt, *The Work of Preaching*, 1905, 260–61.

Just as the sufficiency of Scripture is essential, so is the primacy of Scripture essential to persuasive preaching. In other words, persuasive preaching is contingent upon the Word of God being proclaimed without compromise. To be a persuasive preacher does not require one to avoid any aspect of truth. But rather, the exact opposite is necessary. A requirement for a persuasive preacher is that he is too committed to the truth of God's Word to curtail it to avoid condemning the consciences of his hearers. In fact, the consciences of the hearers must suffer conviction if they are moved to a "serious and radical change of life."[86] The conscience of the hearer must suffer disruption as a precursor of persuasion, if it is to occur. And, for those who suffer conviction but respond with grace seeking to remedy the error of their way, they can only have a grateful respect for a sincere, courageous preacher who is intent upon the welfare of his hearers. Preached truth must have its effect upon the conscience if it is to be a persuasive word. "Speaking the truth in love" is the DNA of persuasive preaching and it will never be less than that.[87]

The Motives for Persuasive Preaching Are Found in Christ

Persuasive preaching is that which exalts Christ, preaching that makes much of him. Though not spoken by Christ in reference to the pulpit, Jesus provided a great component of persuasive preaching when he declared, "And I, if I be lifted up from the earth, will draw all men unto Me."[88] As it is true and necessary on behalf of sinners to look to Christ alone for their salvation, as they understand that he is the One who was crucified on the cross, having their sins commuted to him who became sin, upon whom God poured out his wrath for sin, who shed his blood and died on that cross, was buried and rose from the grave on the third day victorious over sin so that everyone who believes in him may share in his victory over sin and death. It is equally true that for those who have received the gift of eternal life have the power of the Spirit indwelling them and the instruction of the Scriptures available to them so that they can live life in a manner that is, indeed, Christ-like.

The prospect of Christ-like living is the attractiveness, the magnetism, the power of persuasive preaching. Persuasive preaching is not merely a man speaking winsomely, convincingly, and powerfully to others about specific life-change needed by them. An effective proselytizer of any cult may accomplish as much. Persuasive preaching is Christian preaching in that Christ is the One to whom all Scripture has reference, directly or indirectly, and Christ is the One for whom our lives are to honor and whom our lives are to follow. Christ is not incidental to persuasive preaching. Christ is that which motivates persuasive preaching in its proclamation and in its reception. Christ personifies righteousness, establishes what it means to live according to truth,

86. Hoyt, *The Work of Preaching*, 1905, 263.
87. Hoyt, *The Work of Preaching*, 1905, 263.
88. Pierson, *The Divine Art of Preaching*, 1892, 100.

demonstrates the purest and most sacrificial love, exemplifies the most productive life of service, defines what it means to live an abundant life, and satisfies perfectly his Father's will and good pleasure. In Jesus Christ one finds "the persuasive motives of the Gospel."[89]

89. Hoyt, *The Work of Preaching*, 1905, 266.

17

Persuasive Preaching in the Sermon Conclusion: Part 3

"The hearers desire to learn from one who is a practitioner of truth, not just from one who is a proclaimer of it. The experiencing of the truth he proclaims provides much in the way of developing his heart for a persuasive preaching of the Word."

"For those who are the recipients of persuasive preaching, not those who are exposed to it but those who are moved by it, they are on the receiving end of a 'baptism of fire,' a personal experiencing of the divine work of God in their lives through his Word and his Spirit. A divine intervention is needed in men's hearts, for preachers themselves and for their hearers. Without God's work of providing an effective hearing, a preacher will be found by his hearers to be, not just unpersuasive, but lifeless and without power."

"In preaching as in other forms of communication, there are two instruments of self-expression: the voice of the one speaking and the actions of the one speaking. The voice finds the ear. The face and gestures find the eye. The soul may flash upon the face the light of its thought and passion, and motion may deepen and enforce them. Persuasiveness is aided by the preacher in whom all the personal components of expression unite, who preaches from the whole man."

"In order to possess the earnestness required to be a persuasive preacher, one must possess 'an intense perception and appreciation of the end for which he preaches,' that is, to show from Scripture how his hearers may become the beneficiaries 'of some definite spiritual good.' The persuasiveness needed to accomplish this is aided by his intense desire to see that his hearers are helped through the means of his preaching."

"The internal convictions of a preacher produce external manifestations in his preaching. It is quite discernible when a preacher is deeply impacted by biblical truth, and personally affected by it. It is a great fault for preachers to 'endeavor to acquire the art of persuading men before they have learned what they have to persuade them of.' What is crucial for persuasive preaching is for the preacher, 'not only to appreciate, but to feel' the significance of the truth he preaches. This motivates him to have his hearers to feel the truth as he feels it, to respond to the truth as he has responded to it, and for the truth to impact their lives as it has impacted his life. If a man has a limited capacity to feel the truth, to the same degree he has limited prospects of being a persuasive preacher."

"For preaching to wield 'great power over mankind,' it must be either by the preaching of 'extraordinary men,' or by the preaching of 'ordinary men with extraordinary power.' Persuasive preaching of the ordinary man, to the extent that it is so, is the preaching of a man that is 'imbued with . . . the operation and power the Spirit.'"

"A preacher, as a persuader, prepares the hearts of everyone who hears him to decide for or against the truth he has taught. The hearers may fail to make the decision they should make but, decide they must. They are forced to do so. Why? Because they were the recipients of the teaching of a persuader. A persuader teaches so that his hearers may do, not just hear and understand. And, because he teaches so that they may do, he challenges them to respond to the truth. He forces the decision upon them. He will not allow them to hear the truth then walk away without being called upon to respond to it. A preacher who is persuasive in his preaching brings his hearers to a commitment. He requires of them to make a choice about their compliance or noncompliance to the truth."

"Any considerations about a preacher's preaching style or his gifts for preaching, though important considerations, are almost moot points when it comes to the matter of what is to be done in a sermon conclusion. Any preacher's style and spiritual gifts provide specific strengths and advantages in concluding a sermon, but it does not change anything regarding the necessity of a conclusion in a sermon. A sermon conclusion is not the prerogative for those who have the gift of exhortation, etc. The important functions of a sermon conclusion are to be fulfilled regardless of the man who preaches it. A preacher's style and gifts do not cause him to be effective or ineffective in a sermon conclusion. The power of God working through the preacher's gifts and style cause him to be effective in the conclusion as in any other part of the sermon. As one man expressed it, 'Just as you can find all types of preachers who are imbued with divine power, so you can find every type of preacher who is destitute of it.' Every preacher is positioned to bring the power of God, as it uniquely works in him, to his preaching in a sermon conclusion. As every preacher does so, the results

will not be the same since God determines the results of every preacher's preaching, but every preacher should be found in the sermon conclusion seeking to persuade his hearers to respond to God's truth in their lives."

"It must not be lost upon the preacher that in his sermon conclusion he is very much like a lawyer in his closing arguments. Therefore, the preacher's sermon conclusion is the climax of his persuasive appeal to his hearers to win a verdict from them for their compliance to the truth of Scripture to be lived out in their lives. How foolish it would be for a lawyer to fail to maximize the strategic opportunity for his closing appeals to the jurors and appeal earnestly for a verdict from them. Such folly only escalates for a preacher's failure to seize his opportunity to win a verdict from God's people for the practice of the truth in their lives. If a preacher is truly preaching for a verdict in his sermon conclusion, then he will be vigorous in manner, according to his preaching style, personality, and temperament, as well as vital and vivid in matter."

"Any design other than limited and lofty content for the sermon conclusion is a design that will be met with failure. The failure will be attributed to offering substance that did not persuade them to act upon necessary truth, substance that did not provide for them the means by which compliance to truth could be made, or substance that did not help them to defeat "the obstacles which hinder them" from living according to the sermon's purpose."

A PERSUADED PERSUADER IN THE PULPIT (CONTINUED)

In considering a persuaded persuader in the pulpit, we have discovered that persuasive preaching is a holy thing, Christlikeness is the objective of persuasive preaching, sympathy for people is prerequisite for persuasive preaching, persuasive preaching is dependent upon a high view of Scripture, and the motives for persuasive preaching are found in Christ. We will consider three additional concepts regarding a persuaded persuader in the pulpit: the heart is crucial for persuasive preaching, persuasive preaching flows from extraordinary power, and persuasion as a god given enablement. This chapter will wrap up our consideration of persuasion as we detail the clinching element of persuasion.

The Heart is Crucial for Persuasive Preaching

The heart makes a persuasive preacher. A persuasive preacher may be described as a preacher who understands the eternal majesty of God's Word, being personally captivated by it, who possesses a deep compassion for his hearers, who commends the hearts and the minds of God's people to himself and the Word he proclaims. Many hearers are burdened, weary, struggling, dispirited, and they crave the insights and encouragement brought to them by one from whom flow the love and the Word of God.[1] "A minister who handles the Word of God as one who has tried and proved it, is known at once by his congregation."[2] Those who hear the Word of God proclaimed are interested in what the preacher knows from the Word that may be of benefit to them and just as significant to the hearers is their interest in what the preacher has experienced in his life in connection to the Word he preaches to them. The hearers desire to learn from one who is a practitioner of truth, not just from one who is a proclaimer of it. The experiencing of the truth he proclaims provides much in the way of developing his heart for a persuasive preaching of the Word.

To preach God's Word as needed truth, as practical truth, is the foundation of persuasive preaching. This provides perceptible conviction regarding the truth of the message preached and its importance to the hearers. For those who are the recipients of persuasive preaching, not those who are exposed to it but those who are moved by it, they are on the receiving end of a "baptism of fire,"[3] a personal experiencing of the divine work of God in their lives through his Word and his Spirit.

A divine intervention is needed in men's hearts, for preachers themselves and for their hearers. Without God's work of providing an effective hearing, a preacher will be found by his hearers to be, not just unpersuasive, but lifeless and without power.[4] William Arthur's musing about the infrequency of God's Word being persuasively proclaimed and received are not without interest. Arthur asks:

> What are the hindrances? Is it because, as many would seem to think, that nothing is so difficult to obtain as the grace of the Holy Spirit? We often hear it said, all effort must be unsuccessful without the blessing of God, without the accompanying power the Spirit; and the tone used indicates that it is therefore proper not to look for any great results, as if the accompanying power of the Spirit was the only thing not to be counted upon. . . . The power of the Holy Spirit is freer than any of God's other gifts, because it is the one which cost Him most, and which blesses His children most, that this gift is ever at hand.[5]

A necessary precursor for persuasion to occur is that the hearers understand and feel the truth as the preacher understands and feels the truth. Obviously, there is the pre-existing state of the preacher's weighty understanding and significant feeling for the truth about which they need persuasion.

In preaching as in other forms of communication, there are two instruments of self-expression: the voice of the one speaking and the actions of the one speaking. The voice finds the ear. The face and gestures find the eye. The soul may flash upon

1. Hoyt, *The Work of Preaching*, 1905, 268.

2. Spurgeon, *An All-round Ministry*, 1900, 113.

3. Hoyt, *The Work of Preaching*, 1905, 270.

4. Hoyt, *The Work of Preaching*, 1905, 270–71.

5. Arthur, *The Tongue of Fire*, 1859, 313–15.

the face the light of its thought and passion, and motion may deepen and enforce them. Persuasiveness is aided by the preacher in whom all the personal components of expression unite, who preaches from the whole man.[6] Spurgeon's counsel regarding the heart of the preacher is appealing as he wrote, "Brothers, I beseech you to keep to the old gospel, and let yourselves be filled with it, and then *may you be set on fire with it!* When the wick is saturated, let the flame be applied. Fire from heaven is still the necessity of the age. . . . May God himself, who is a consuming fire, ever burn in you as in the bush at Horeb! All other things being equal, that man will do most who has most of the Divine fire."[7] Balaam would speak only the Word of God, in that, he would not deviate from it.[8] However, this was of little virtue because his heart was radically different than God's. Balaam was totally without the divine fire that one who speaks for God should rightly have. It is exceedingly grievous to apply analogically Balaam to present day preaching which would have men saying what should be said but saying it devoid of the divine motives and divine fire. What is so grievous is the reality that a "Balaam-like" preaching ministry is so widespread.

An essential prerequisite for one who moves others in his preaching, is to be deeply moved himself, authentically inspired by the content he will preach. He must feel and strongly express that about which he is so deeply persuaded. "Cicero said of his ability to move hearers, 'I candidly confess that I owe my success much less to my own efforts than to the force of the passions which agitate me when I speak in public and which carry me out of myself.'"[9] The passions Cicero referenced were directed toward political concerns, issues about the state. Is it not true that divine truth, matters that determine the productivity of people's lives for time and eternity, should merit and result in preaching that is persuasive and passionately so? Certainly, this is true. Thomas Potter provides a series of arguments to remediate the lacking passionate persuasiveness in preaching which stems from the heart of the preacher.

> Let us first feel in our own hearts those sentiments with which we seek to animate in them. How shall I soften others if my own words prove that I myself am unmoved? How shall I inflame the hearts of my hearers if I myself am cold? How shall I draw the tears from their eyes if my own are dry? It is impossible. You cannot kindle a conflagration without fire. . . . And the reason of all this is very plain. When the preacher is profoundly penetrated with, and moved by his subject, his interior emotion imparts to his words, his looks, his gestures, his whole bearing, a warmth and feeling which exercise an irresistible influence upon his hearers.[10]

---

6. Hoyt, *The Work of Preaching*, 1905, 331.

7. Spurgeon, *An All-round Ministry*, 1900, 126.

8. Numbers 22–24.

9. Potter, *Sacred Eloquence*, 1868, 286.

10. Potter, *Sacred Eloquence*, 1868, 286–87.

Your words must be inflamed . . . by the "interior warmth and feeling of your soul." They must spring from the heart rather than from the mouth. It has been beautifully said that it is the heart which appeals to the heart, the tongue only speaks to the ears.[11]

> Earnestness creates earnestness in others by sympathy; and the more a preacher loses and is lost to himself, the more does he gain his brethren. . . . What is powerful enough to absorb and possess a preacher, may claim attention on the part of his hearers. On the other hand, anything which interferes with this earnestness is still more certain to blunt the force of the most cogent argument conveyed in the most eloquent language.[12]

In order to possess the earnestness required to be a persuasive preacher, one must possess "an intense perception and appreciation of the end for which he preaches," that is, to show from Scripture how his hearers may become the beneficiaries "of some definite spiritual good."[13] The persuasiveness needed to accomplish this is aided by his intense desire to see that his hearers are helped through the means of his preaching.

The internal convictions of a preacher produce external manifestations in his preaching. It is quite discernible when a preacher is deeply impacted by biblical truth, and personally affected by it. It is a great fault for preachers to "endeavor to acquire the art of persuading men before they have learned what they have to persuade them of."[14] What is crucial for persuasive preaching is for the preacher, "not only to *appreciate*, but to *feel*" the significance of the truth he preaches. This motivates him to have his hearers to feel the truth as he feels it, to respond to the truth as he has responded to it, and for the truth to impact their lives as it has impacted his life. If a man has a limited capacity to feel the truth, to the same degree he has limited prospects of being a persuasive preacher.[15] However, every preacher, if he is a responsible man of God who lives a life of purity, if he is committed and devoted to prayer, if he lives a life of vital detachment from the world, if he possesses a burning zeal for the glory of God and a heart that aches for the salvation of lost souls, then such a man cannot be other than a winsome preacher, and because of that, to a significant degree, a persuasive preacher as well.[16] In fact, the most magnetic characteristic of any preacher, and which is achievable by every preacher, is a "sweet, pious, and affectionate effusion of the heart which is full of God" which provides a portion of persuasiveness in preaching.[17]

11. Potter, *Sacred Eloquence*, 1868, 288–89.

12. Potter, *Sacred Eloquence*, 1868, 290.

13. Potter, *Sacred Eloquence*, 1868, 291.

14. Moore, *Thoughts on Preaching*, 1861, 67.

15. Potter, *Sacred Eloquence*, 1868, 293.

16. Potter, *Sacred Eloquence*, 1868, 294.

17. Potter, *Sacred Eloquence*, 1868, 299.

Persuasive Preaching Flows from Extraordinary Power

For preaching to wield "great power over mankind," it must be either by the preaching of "extraordinary men," or by the preaching of "ordinary men with extraordinary power." Persuasive preaching of the ordinary man, to the extent that it is so, is the preaching of a man that is "imbued with . . . the operation and power the Spirit." As this is the case, the hearers will wonder, how it could be that the preaching of such an ordinary man could produce such extraordinary effects? "They cannot discover the source of his power; and it is precisely this fact which intimates that it is spiritual."[18] Spurgeon's words are as terse as they are compelling when he wrote, "The man whom God uses for quickening is the man who is himself quickened."[19]

A preacher must first experience in his own heart that which may become a reality in the hearts of his hearers. William M. Taylor emphasized this as he wrote, "If we would illuminate others, we must have light in ourselves; and if we would kindle the flame of piety in the hearts of others, we must take the 'live coal' with which we do so, from the burning 'altar' of our own spirit. . . . If we be ourselves uninterested, how can we expect to interest others? If we be ourselves insincere, how can we hope to bring others to the faith? If we be ourselves cold, passionless, and dull, how can we expect to arouse others to enthusiasm?"[20] Persuasive preaching occurs in a context where there is an impression perceived by those who are persuaded, "that something very great is at stake. . . . Lack of intensity in preaching can only communicate that the preacher does not believe or has never been seriously gripped by the reality of which he speaks—or that the subject matter is insignificant."[21] Of course, this is not the condition of a preacher who is used by God to preach persuasively. A persuasive preacher preaches in the power that began to fill him in his preparation to preach. This power of God is perceptible by the hearers and, for some, they experience this power as a persuasive power to commit themselves to comply with the instruction that has worked so strongly in them.

Persuasive preaching flows from the extraordinary power of God working in the lives of people to result in new understanding, commitment, motives, and life-change that can only be attributed to God Himself, a work that he accomplishes through his Word and by his Spirit. A persuasive preacher is rightly motivated in his preaching. He desires to be an instrument in the hand of God, the One who works persuasively in the lives of men. Being rightly motivated arrests any attempt to be presumptuous in his preaching, that is, to incorporate in his preaching things that are sure to antagonize those whom he desires to be persuaded. In other words, it is consistent with

18. Arthur, *The Tongue of Fire*, 1859, 98–99.

19. Spurgeon, *An All-round Ministry*, 1900, 191.

20. Taylor, *The Ministry of the Word*, 1876, 25–6.

21. Piper, *The Supremacy of God in Preaching*, 103.

a preacher's right motives and appropriate procedure in preaching for him not to be a stumbling block to his hearers in his preaching.

It is not defensible for a preacher to be a personal liability in the pursuit to see hearers' lives transformed through the preaching of the Word. What follows are some things that a preacher should understand and implement in his preaching so that he will not be working against himself in the process of ministering to God's people through his Word. Paul Bull provides ten criteria that is helpful for preachers to not become a personal liability through their content and manner in their effort to persuade their hearers to act upon biblical truth.

- Be careful not needlessly to arouse prejudices by carelessness of speech and manner.

- Do not touch on points which you know to be irritating, unless it is your duty to deal with them.

- Avoid allusiveness, the habit of alluding to side issues.

- Begin by emphasizing those aspects of the subject on which you think the congregation will agree with you. This creates an atmosphere of consent.

- Make the best of men—people are more ready to accept rebuke when full credit has been given to them and justice has been done to their good qualities.

- You're most likely to persuade men to agree with you if you begin by agreeing with them.

- Make a wise use of suggestion. If you suggest that a man will disagree with what you are going to say, you create the atmosphere of the opposition you wish to avoid. If on the other hand you suggest that "we shall all be agreed on this point," you place the burden of disagreement on each individual. He has to make a deliberate mental effort to disassociate himself from the supposedly universal agreement.

- Remember that conviction is caught not taught. In proportion as love, faith, and zeal burns fervently in your own heart they will communicate to others.

- Sterilize yourself against the controversial spirit. The man who enters a pulpit expecting opposition creates what he expects. If your heart and words and tone of voice are conciliatory you create an atmosphere of conciliation.

- No art of persuasion can be of any value unless it is at every moment penetrated by the illuminating light and power of the Holy Spirit. Form the habit of constantly seeking and being dependent upon the Holy Spirit of God. Prayer and the Holy Spirit's power are the secrets of persuasion.[22]

---

22. Bull, *Preaching and Sermon Construction*, 1922, 209–10.

The power of God to persuade hearers to comply their lives to the truth of his Word is not diminished because a preacher endeavors not to be an obstacle to his hearers responding as they should.

Persuasion as a God Given Enablement

Though a preacher is to be a teacher, he is to be more than a teacher, much more. He is to be a persuader in his preaching, one who is able to exhort in sound doctrine and to refute those who contradict the truth.[23] Therefore, as a persuader, he prepares the hearts of everyone who hears him to decide for or against the truth he has taught. They may fail to make the decision they should make but, decide they must. They are forced to do so. Why? Because they were the recipients of the teaching of a persuader. A persuader teaches so that his hearers may do, not just hear and understand. And, because he teaches so that they may do, he challenges them to respond to the truth. He forces the decision upon them. He will not allow them to hear the truth then walk away without being called upon to respond to it. A preacher who is persuasive in his preaching brings his hearers to a commitment. He requires of them to make a choice about their compliance or noncompliance to the truth.

In preaching, the absence of its effects is conclusive evidence of an absence of power from which the effects would have been realized. The mind cannot but recognize the presence of intellectual power. The emotions cannot resist the stirring that is created within them. And the conscience cannot be prevented from registering the weight that is thrust upon it.[24] The power of preaching is felt by those exposed to it, even if a correct response is never forthcoming from its hearers.

Any considerations about a preacher's preaching style or a preacher's gifts for preaching, though important considerations, are almost moot points when it comes to the matter of what is to be done, what is to be sought, in a sermon conclusion. Any preacher's style and spiritual gifts provide specific strengths and advantages in concluding a sermon, but it does not change anything regarding the necessity of a conclusion in a sermon. In short, a sermon conclusion is not the prerogative for those who have the gift of exhortation, etc. The important functions of a sermon conclusion are to be fulfilled regardless of the man who preaches it. A preacher's style and gifts do not, cannot, and will not cause him to be effective or ineffective in a sermon conclusion. The power of God working through the preacher's gifts and style cause him to be effective in the conclusion as in any other part of the sermon. As one man wisely expressed it, "Just as you can find all types of preachers who are imbued with divine power, so you can find every type of preacher who is destitute of it."[25]

23. Moore, *Thoughts on Preaching*, 1861, 28.

24. Arthur, *The Tongue of Fire*, 1859, 235–6.

25. Arthur, *The Tongue of Fire*, 1859, 258.

Every preacher is positioned to bring the power of God, as it uniquely works in him, to his preaching in a sermon conclusion. As every preacher does so, the results will not be the same since God determines the results of every preacher's preaching, but every preacher should be found in the sermon conclusion seeking to persuade his hearers to respond to God's truth as God enables the preacher to do so. So, the critical issue is, not a man's style and gifts, but whether God's enablement is allowed to work through the preacher's efforts to win a verdict from his hearers in the conclusion of the sermon.

In the conclusion of the sermon a preacher "should exert himself to the utmost to bring about an immediate decision."[26] The vital issue in a sermon conclusion is not the preacher's spiritual gifts, personality, or temperament but his willingness to challenge his hearers in reference to making a commitment to comply their lives to the closing appeals of the sermon conclusion. John Stott minces no words in establishing the reticence of preachers to do what they should do in preaching the sermon conclusion, that is, mounting an assault on the hearers' wills.

> We are out to storm the citadel of the will and capture it for Jesus Christ . . . whether evangelizing or teaching does not matter. The appeal is the final thing. Now citadels cannot be stormed without the use of violence. Nor can human hearts and wills. If a hardened heart is to be broken, it is not stroking but striking that must do it. . . . It is just here that many of us are weak. We would not be comfortable in using these metaphors of "storming," "striking," and "hitting." They are altogether too violent, too bellicose, for our mood. . . . In consequence, we . . . seldom if ever press home a point which demands decision.[27]

What is important is that the preacher, regardless of his temperament, personality, and spiritual gifts, employ them to persuade the hearers to respond to God's Word in their daily living.

A forfeiture of the spiritual enablement for persuasive preaching will always exist when there is a belief that one's hard work and good intentions in preaching are sufficient to produce this necessary result from one's preaching. This is simply one's unbridled unbiblical belief in one's ability to do what God alone can do through his preached Word. Such unbiblical belief will be evidenced by the limited role of, or the absence of, prayer.

Unless it is other than a token activity that shouldn't be omitted, prayer is the dependent begging of a beggar, that is, a preacher seeking God to enable his Word in the lives of those who hear the sermon. To recognize the existence and the extent of one's unbiblical unbelief in one's sufficiency to produce spiritual results in preaching, "Simply ask ourselves how long, how often, how importunately, have we waited at the throne of the Savior for the outpouring of the Spirit? Let our closets answer. The eyes

26. Burrell, *The Sermon: Its Construction and Delivery*, 1913, 192.

27. Stott, *Between Two Worlds*, 248.

of the Lamb . . . have noted. Oh, is it any wonder that oftentimes we have been power-less, and oftentimes have had but 'a little strength?'"[28] By virtue of the fact that God works through his Word and he has made available to his people prayer, the means by which his people can avail themselves of his enablement to achieve his will, then preaching should be the unrivaled cause for the most fervent and incessant praying. And, as this is the case, the results of such fervent and incessant praying would be demonstrated in preaching that is accompanied by a supernatural enablement in the preacher and in those who hear the preaching of such a preacher. George Whitefield is representative of this kind of preacher and preaching. Gardiner Spring writes the following about the preaching of Whitefield and the effects of Whitefield's preaching on those who heard him.

> It is said of the preaching of George Whitefield that, in intensity of feeling, he had no equal. He enchained his auditory by his intense interest in his subject. A ship-carpenter once remarked, that "he could usually build a ship from stem to stern, during the sermon; but under Mr. Whitefield he could not lay a single plank." It is of themselves ministers should frequently complain, rather than of their hearers; it is they who are cold and inanimate. A drowsy pulpit makes an inattentive and drowsy congregation. . . . I have often asked myself why it is that a congregation assembled for the worship of God is, for the most part, less interested in a discourse from the pulpit, than a jury are interested in an argument from the bar! It is not because the bar is always more eloquent than the pulpit, though it often is so; nor is it altogether because the pulpit speaks of unearthly things, and the bar of things earthly. It is mainly because the speaker and hearers in the courts of law speak and hear with the view of coming to a present decision on the subject submitted to their consideration. This *responsibility rests upon them*, and they may not be listless. Let but the thought be present to the mind of the preacher and the hearers, that in the progress and at the close of his discourse *decisions* are to be made that will affect the destiny of man, for weal or for woe, through interminable ages, and this listless hearing, and this insensate preaching, will exist no longer.[29]

A lack of spiritual enablement is not the result of fervent and dependent praying! From a human perspective, it would appear that in the preaching of Whitefield there was no loss of spiritual enablement on behalf of the one preaching and on those who heard him preach.

It must not be lost upon the preacher that in his sermon conclusion he is very much like a lawyer in his closing arguments. Therefore, the preacher's sermon conclusion is the climax of his persuasive appeal to his hearers to win a verdict from them for their compliance to the truth of Scripture to be lived out in their lives.[30] How foolish

28. Arthur, *The Tongue of Fire*, 1859, 316.

29. Spring, *The Power of the Pulpit*, 1848, 132–3.

30. Davis, *Principles of Preaching*, 1924, 219.

it would be for a lawyer to fail to maximize the strategic opportunity for his closing appeals to the jurors and appeal earnestly for a verdict from them. Such folly only escalates for a preacher's failure to seize his opportunity to win a verdict from God's people for the practice of the truth in their lives.

If a preacher is truly preaching for a verdict in his sermon conclusion, then he will be vigorous in manner, according to his preaching style, personality, and temperament, as well as vital and vivid in matter. In the attempt to persuade his hearers, the preacher should present specific rather than general precepts and examples of truth.[31] Persuasive preaching "convinces the intellect, stirs the heart, and quickens the conscience of the hearer, so that he is moved to believe the truth which has been presented to him, or to take the course which is been enforced upon him."[32] Persuasive preaching accomplishes these things because it is God who provides the enablement of his Word to be powerful in the lives of those who hear it.

Having heard a sermon, the hearers may esteem it greatly even though it produced no particular resolve of their wills for personal action. And many preachers would be thrilled to preach such sermons every time they preach. However, a sermon that may not be esteemed may be persuasive because it "stirs the hearers, by pressing conscience, rousing passion, and urging home something to be done."[33] It must be the case that preachers are thrilled to preach sermons that God uses in the lives of his people, even if God's people never esteem these sermons highly nor highly esteem the preachers who preach them.

The Word of God assures us that, "The fear of man brings a snare, but he who trusts in the LORD will be exalted" (Proverbs 29:25). The element of preaching and the place in the sermon that is most susceptible to the vice of fearing man in the pulpit, is the sermon conclusion. The closing appeals of the sermon conclusion require a preacher to "set forth the truth of God" while he seeks to enforce upon his hearers "that which is right in the sight of God."[34] Only a fearless man is the kind of man who can conclude a sermon with conviction, insight, and winsome yet straightforward exhortation. The fearlessness of the preacher needs to be demonstrated in speaking to the spiritual needs of all men—the needs of believers and unbelievers. Therefore, as the conclusion should be the most fervent and moving part of the sermon, it aims to secure two results: persuading fellow believers to a heightened practice of righteousness in some specific manner according to the instruction of God's Word; and persuading lost men to be personally reconciled to God by faith in Jesus Christ.[35]

But, just as a preacher must have no fear of man in his preaching, he must have a great fear about providing too much content in his sermon conclusion. Limited

31. Kidder, *A Treatise on Homiletics*, 1864, 226.
32. Taylor, *The Ministry of the Word*, 1876, 107.
33. Porter, *Lectures on Eloquence and Style*, 1836, 30.
34. Taylor, *The Ministry of the Word*, 1876, 139.
35. Ripley, *Sacred Rhetoric*, 1849, 106.

content is the first of two considerations that must be honored regarding the content to be included in the sermon conclusion. Since the effort of the sermon conclusion shifts to drive home the purpose of the sermon to the hearts of the hearers and achieve this purpose in their lives, only the scriptural insights most needed for the hearers to achieve the purpose in an optimal fashion must be included. Surpassed only by the fear of misinterpreting Scripture, the provision of too much content in his conclusion is the thing a preacher is well justified in fearing, least, by his zeal and indiscretion, he makes improbable the very thing he most desires to do.

In the closing appeals of the sermon conclusion, a preacher's attempt to achieve the purpose of the sermon exhaustively will be counterproductive as nothing is more detrimental to persuasion than unnecessary thoroughness. To achieve the purpose of the sermon in a thorough manner is fine but to be unnecessarily thorough is destructive. If a preacher is unwilling to impose limitations on the content to be incorporated, he must be willing to suffer the lessened force of his conclusion.[36]

The second consideration of the content of the conclusion is that it must be significantly valuable content. Since the conclusion is the part of the sermon, "*par excellence*," where the closing appeals to the hearers must impact their conscience, emotions/affections, and wills, this content must reign supreme in quality.[37] It must be the best that Scripture has to offer, and it must be scriptural content that impacts every dimension of the hearers' humanity.

Content that is unsurpassed in qualitative insight is that which is to be included in the conclusion of a sermon. Though the intent of his question was designed to warn against a different threat to preaching, Spurgeon's question is extremely appropriate in reference to the sermon conclusion as he asked, "Do we not fail in our preaching, in our very ideal of what we are going to do, and in the design we set before us for accomplishment?"[38] Any design other than limited and lofty content for the sermon conclusion is a design that will be met with failure. The failure will be attributed to offering substance that did not persuade them to act upon necessary truth, substance that did not provide for them the means by which compliance to truth could be made, or substance that did not help them to defeat "the obstacles which hinder them" from living according to the sermon's purpose.[39]

---

36. Blair, *Lectures on Rhetoric*, 1852, 156.
37. Potter, *Sacred Eloquence*, 1868, 284.
38. Spurgeon, *An All-round Ministry*, 1900, 360.
39. Bull, *Preaching and Sermon Construction*, 1922, 200.

THE CLINCHING ELEMENT OF PERSUASION

Illustration as a Means of Preaching Persuasively

Just as the conclusion of the sermon must bring the sermon to a focus, an illustration is needed to bring focus to the sermon conclusion. "[T]here is no method of touching both heart and mind more effectively than by leaving a vivid picture."[40] An illustration plays a useful role to bring clarity and weight to the closing appeals of a sermon conclusion. In hearing or reading a powerful conclusion to a sermon, a staple component of such will be that it ends with an appropriate and effective illustration.

The typical hearer is quickened in interest when an illustration is given. As there is no possibility of preaching persuasively to the hearers apart from interest, the use of illustration is a critical element of persuasion. A vivid illustration of truth revitalizes interest. Illustrations are beneficial, not only to clarify thought, but to establish or reestablish a level of interest on behalf of the hearers, without which, persuasion is impossible.[41] J. B. Weatherspoon phrased it rather bluntly, "Illustration is a psychological necessity."[42] Illustration, because of its concrete imagery, is a most legitimate instrument of persuasion. In fact, it is an indispensable instrument.

The minds of all the hearers, by the time the conclusion of the sermon begins, will be to varying degrees sluggish. The minds of some hearers will be fatigued to the degree that they cannot listen productively except by the means of the clarity and vitality which only illustrations provide. Additionally, there are some who, at any point in the sermon, are helped little by abstract argument but who comprehend truth well when it is offered "in that concrete form" by way of illustration.[43] Such individuals need significant help if they are to benefit from the most crucial component of the sermon. It would be counterproductive for a preacher to deprive his hearers of that which is needed to help his hearers respond to the closing appeals of the conclusion.

Ultimately, preaching must address the experience of people. Therefore, effective preaching "is direct, near, intimate, and deals always with the realities of daily experience."[44] Furthermore, effective preaching that is helpful to its hearers because it brings "the realities of eternal life upon the realities of daily life."[45] It is at this point where sermons commonly fail because they do not focus on the specific "spiritual situations in which men and women find themselves."[46] Biblical flesh and blood scenarios are best used to apply truth and depict it concretely. Since they personalize

---

40. Bryan, *The Art of Illustrating Sermons*, 171–72.

41. Riley, *The Preacher and His Preaching*, 114.

42. Weatherspoon, *On the Preparation and Delivery of Sermons*, 196.

43. Dale, *Nine Lectures on Preaching*, 1890, 48.

44. Calkins, *The Eloquence of Christian Experience*, 1927, 131.

45. Calkins, *The Eloquence of Christian Experience*, 1927, 131–32.

46. Calkins, *The Eloquence of Christian Experience*, 1927, 132.

truth and integrate a specific circumstance of life and its consequences, "they can pack an emotional wallop" that applies the purpose forcefully.[47]

Of all the uses of an illustration in the sermon, arguably the most valuable use of an illustration is to persuade to action. And though illustrative material is valuable in every part of the sermon, the portion of a sermon that profits most from illustrative material is the sermon conclusion. A sermon that does not persuade the hearers to act upon the purpose of the sermon has failed its major objective. The most effective of all illustrations used in a sermon discourse should be the final one. It should, by its content and emotional character, compel the hearers' determination to comply with the closing appeals "prescribed by the preacher."[48] An apt illustration is a powerful means to foster conviction. In this respect an illustration can be used effectively at the close of the message to draw together the closing appeals of the sermon in a vital way to persuade the hearers to do what Scripture demands of them. A final illustration is an excellent way to clinch the hearers' understanding of truth and to enable their decision to respond to the truth. "Thus, conviction is often brought about by what has been called the 'sledgehammer of illustration.'"[49]

The most important use of illustrations in a sermon is to provide a basis for conviction and persuasion regarding the "appeal for action" which is designated by the closing appeals of the sermon conclusion. What is particularly useful is a reference to a "Bible character" whose actions represent an appropriate response being called for by means of the sermons closing appeals. Likewise, an illustration from an individual contained in Scripture who failed to take the appropriate action and suffered the consequences is an excellent possibility.[50] Through the use of Scripture to depict a historic, true-life account of one's actions provides the sermon hearers with the advantage of visualization, an opportunity to benefit from the wisdom or folly of those who are found in Scripture. The merit of such visualization is that it "projects a congregation into the future and pictures a future situation in which they might apply what they have learned. Visualization must be probable enough so that anyone could imagine himself in the situation before it takes place."[51] A biblical flesh and blood scenario helps in the visualization process because it depicts a scene that has occurred already, it reveals what obedience and disobedience looks like through the perspective of another's or others' lives. They depict the circumstances, situations, pressures, struggles, rationales, and motivations for the conduct to which one commits. They present the outcomes of obedience or disobedience and what consequences one can anticipate for one's response to the truth. There is no other resource made available to preachers that can rival the trustworthy content found in the Word of God by which

47. Adams, *Preaching with Purpose*, 67.
48. Riley, *The Preacher and His Preaching*, 124.
49. Kroll, *Prescription for Preaching*, 171.
50. O'Neal, *Make the Bible Live*, 44.
51. Robinson, *Biblical Preaching*, 170–71.

the hearers of sermon conclusions can be clearly and convincingly challenged to respond to scriptural truth.

Illustration as a Means of Preaching Effectively

One of the most helpful precepts for preaching has been codified by the phrase to "turn the ear into an eye." Though an illustration is useless when there is a need for clear explanation and argumentation, upon the completion of these, providing an illustration of truth furnishes "images which make one see as well as hear." As this is done, not only is the comprehension of the truth greater, but the memory of that which is comprehended will be retained more fully.[52] In addition to helping the hearers to understand the truth, "you must make them see it."[53] The graphic, concrete, visual understanding of Scripture must be offered to the hearers if one is truly concerned about the hearers' grasp of biblical truth.

All that is unfamiliar or unknown is clarified by an analogy of that which is familiar by common experience. That is the function of an illustration. In the absence of illustration, some hearers will find spiritual truths too uncertain and unclear for them to comprehend it meaningfully, and none will obtain the understanding they could have been afforded if illustration had been supplied.[54] Illustrations in preaching epitomize the learning process of understanding a new thing by means of its being likened to something which is known already.[55] This learning process is just as true in the context of preached sermons as in any other context. Therefore, without good illustrations a sermon is "virtually worthless."[56] This position taken by Faris D. Whitesell is less harsh than it is true because so much is sacrificed in the absence of illustrative material in preaching. An illustration may do one or more of the following: "gain interest, throw light on the subject, clarify the subject, make truth vivid, strengthen argument, bring conviction, aid persuasion, make for lasting impressions, appeal to all classes of people, and help to make a good conclusion."[57] To Whitesell's point taken to the sermon conclusion, even the application found in the closing appeals, though relevant, are abstract until they are joined to illustrative material that depicts what is being called for in the closing appeals. Illustrative material composing the clinching element of persuasion, indeed, is helpful to make the conclusion effective.

Abstract preaching divides a congregation, in that, some are capable of following abstract thought well, but others are not so equipped. Illustration, however, communicates to everyone in the congregation. Through the use of illustration "you are

52. Luccock, *In the Minister's Workshop*, 113–14.

53. Dale, *Nine Lectures on Preaching*, 1890, 176.

54. Jeffs, *The Art of Sermon Illustration*, 19–20.

55. Hoyt, *The Work of Preaching*, 1905, 242.

56. Whitesell, *Power in Expository Preaching*, 75.

57. Whitesell, *Power in Expository Preaching*, 75–76.

bound to see that everybody gets something every time. You will scarcely be able to do it in any other way than by illustration."[58] What an incentivized imprimatur for the illustrative material of the clinching element of persuasion in a sermon conclusion, especially.

Though important, illustrations can be incorporated into sermons, or their conclusions, needlessly. As in a dark room with its shades drawn, one shade lifted brings in abundant light but "after the room is well lighted the added effect of one or two more windows means little or nothing, except glare."[59] When used wisely, illustrations give force to truth because they provide greater distinctness and vividness to ideas. Vividness is strength, impacting the sensibilities of the hearers. The hearers of sermons "*feel strongly only as they see vividly.*"[60] Truth that is sufficiently persuasive to produce life-change must be truth that is concrete, truth that bears the strength of vividness.

Illustration cannot substitute for thought. And though illustrations "may have argumentative force of their own, they are but assistants to clear thinking."[61] Every worthwhile sermon conclusion must contain solid biblical truth in the form of the closing appeals. The closing appeals must be brought to light through the concreteness and vividness of illustrative material composing the clinching element(s) of persuasion. The illustrative material of the clinching element(s) of persuasion must make the closing appeals concrete and vivid but provide persuasion to the hearers to comply their lives to these Scripture-based exhortations.

Yet, unfortunately, "Some preachers indeed are too proud to express their thought in pictorial form. They deal in foggy abstractions. . . . You may feel what they mean; you never see what they mean. . . . They offer us hints and glimmerings and glimpses of the truth, but they never give us an open view of it. How gratifying it would be to their hearers if . . . they were to light up their meaning with a graphic illustration!"[62] The unfortunate truth captured by the previous quote is precisely the kind of thing that cannot take place in a sermon conclusion. The hearers must understand with the greatest possible clarity what is being called for in the closing appeals of the sermon conclusion. Illustrationphobes will never do other than second-rate work in a sermon conclusion. It is not possible for them to do better since they are set against what is needed for them to do better work, the use of illustrations. Ian Macpherson's argumentation is compelling enough to bring reform to one who fails to appreciate and incorporate illustrations in their preaching. Macpherson argued: "Shouldn't the Master's use of illustration in preaching be the supreme example for all? He made free and frequent use of living figures of speech, metaphor, simile, analogy, parables. Let it

58. Hoyt, *The Work of Preaching*, 1905, 251.

59. Bryan, *The Art of Illustrating Sermons*, 16.

60. Hoyt, *The Work of Preaching*, 1905, 245–47.

61. Bryan, *The Art of Illustrating Sermons*, 27.

62. Macpherson, *The Burden of the Lord*, 105.

not be beneath your dignity to do what Jesus did."[63] Christ's flesh and blood scenarios, drawn from Scripture and outside of Scripture, included Moses' brazen serpent, Jonah's deliverance, the people upon whom fell the Tower of Siloam, Pilate's mingling the blood of the Galileans with the blood of their own sacrifices, to cite just a few.[64]

A well-chosen illustration is an essential element for the effectiveness of a sermon conclusion. The iconic masterpiece of this is the conclusion of Christ's Sermon on the Mount. Jesus' sermon conclusion ended with an illustration of two houses, a house that was built on a rock which stood firm when the floods came and the rain descended and the winds blew and beat upon it, and another house that was built upon the sand and collapsed when the same storm came against it. Though this illustration was not drawn from a historical event or a biblical citation but was purely from Christ's imagination, the point must not be missed that Christ was compelled to graphically depict the significance of his hearers' response to his sermon. Also, it should be appreciated that "Imagination, no less than reason, is God's gift"[65] and it has every right to be used in preaching, and all the more so in the sermon conclusion.

Illustrative material wields the power by which uncertainty is made certain so that persuasion may result in the lives of those who understand what they must do to live according to the truth of Scripture. "Preaching must represent truth, as far as language can do so, in living forms. . . . The best preachers have been masters of illustration."[66] The history of preaching attests to the merits of preachers who were skilled in the use of illustrative material. Effective preaching impacts the lives of those who hear it because, "Life responds to life, and enthusiasm to enthusiasm."[67] Personal illustrations, especially, and illustrations drawn from Scripture which have stirred the preacher, himself, possess potential for an enthusiastic hearing to his preaching.

Persuasion of the hearers is aided when the "principle of climax" is achieved in the sermon conclusion. This may be accomplished when the preacher ends "as he began" or incorporates "a striking passage of Scripture" as a clinching element of persuasion.[68] A very effective way of concluding a sermon is to refer back "to material mentioned in the sermon's introduction. Complete the story, echo an earlier thought, refer to a character or story specifics in a previous illustration, resolve a tension, repeat a striking phrase, refer to the opening problem, or in some other way end where you began."[69] When a sermon conclusion incorporates a return to an illustration or major component found in the introduction of the sermon, the hearers will be

---

63. Macpherson, *The Burden of the Lord*, 106.

64. Macartney, *Preaching without Notes*, 57–8.

65. Hoyt, *The Work of Preaching*, 1905, 241.

66. Hoyt, *The Work of Preaching*, 1905, 243.

67. Greer, *The Preacher and His Place*, 1895, 85.

68. Kidder, *A Treatise on Homiletics*, 1864, 227.

69. Chapell, *Christ-centered Preaching*, 250.

made aware that the conclusion completes what the sermon started out to do.[70] Of course, dealing with the purpose of the sermon, stated in the sermon introduction, and achieved in the conclusion enacts the principle of climax in every sermon.

The best ending of a sermon conclusion is always with words that "soundly register in the heart."[71] As to importance, the last statement of the sermon should be one which echoes in the minds of the hearers.[72] No amount of toil should be despised by a preacher in the effort to provide the hearers with persuasive closing thoughts by the "magnetism of the last words."[73] The end of the conclusion is to be composed of a very strong sentence, a very personal word from the preacher to his hearers. This strong final sentence, as for all of the conclusion, will carry more weight because he, as a true pastor, is imploring them "person to person, heart to heart," as one who seeks their temporal wellbeing and their eternal good.[74] What is significant for the preacher regarding an effective conclusion is his intent to fasten the truth of the passage to the lives of his hearers "as one would drive a nail into a plank and clinch it." However, the illustrative material must be pertinent to clinch the closing appeals to the minds and hearts of the hearers and persuade them to act upon the appeals. Therefore, the illustration(s) must be an apt depiction of what is to be done, so that fits the truth of the closing appeals and the purpose of the sermon "like a glove fits the hand."[75]

Those who are persuaded by preaching are persuaded by means of truth understood as they have not understood it before, and by truth that accompanies conviction as they have not known before. This equates cognitive persuasion. But volitional persuasion requires a fuller working of truth in the hearers' lives. In addition to this important and initial means of persuasion, volitional persuasion results as the hearers are moved by truth that is valued as it has never been esteemed before, and by truth that they must respond to in a fashion as they have never done before. Unchanging truth, truth that cannot change, now has a meaning that it never had for them before and because of the value they now hold for the truth, their lives must comply with truth, seemingly of a new order, truth of great personal value. Because of their persuasion regarding truth, their lives as lived formerly are not commensurate to the truth as they now hold it, as it is now understood and appreciated. Truth that is valued differently necessitates living differently because of its newly discovered worth. Those who are persuaded to respond to the closing appeals of a sermon conclusion become persuaded only after they have been appealed to on the basis of truth "they already

70. Sweazey, *Preaching the Good News*, 103.

71. Chapell, *Christ-centered Preaching*, 245.

72. Fry, *Elementary Homiletics*, 1897, 133.

73. Phelps, *The Theory of Preaching*, 1882, 536.

74. Jones, *Principles and Practice of Preaching*, 165.

75. Jones, *Principles and Practice of Preaching*, 164.

know" and "examples with which they are familiar."[76] This is the beginning of the persuasion process without which volitional persuasion cannot result.

Volitional persuasion, a commitment to life-change in some specific way, is caused by known truth that has been added to significantly, by means of additional understanding, additional conviction, and additional value. The closing appeals and clinching element(s) of persuasion are incorporated to provide each of these additional upgrades to the hearers. A particular case in point, that is, a biblical flesh and blood scenario or a personal illustration, is effective to register in the affections of the hearers. An allusion to some individual in some particular circumstance is a must in the conclusion. And in the close of the conclusion, "nothing is more impressive and moving than (the reading or quoting of) a feeling, solemn passage of Scripture."[77]

Illustration as a Means of Preaching Biblically

Scripture contains "the most vivid, dramatic, arresting material" a preacher can use for illustrative content since the Bible depicts truth in life and provides the significant quality of concrete understanding to the preacher's necessary but abstract explanations and arguments. "That is what people respond to, the concrete, the specific."[78] What people need and what Scripture has to offer provide a connection that must be made in determining the content of a sermon conclusion. A. T. Pierson expressed this well in these words, "The Holy Scriptures are the feathers which carries the divine arrow straight to its mark."[79]

A preacher ought to be "soaked in life" that he might communicate truth in terms of human experience. The conclusion of each sermon is worthy of being preserved and "verified in daily life."[80] However, a preacher who lived a hundred lifetimes could not accrue the life experiences recorded in the pages of Scripture. Therefore, no preacher can afford to bypass the wisdom contained in the Bible to address how believers are to live faithfully in their lives.

In his classic preaching text, *A Treatise on the Preparation and Delivery of Sermons*, John Broadus argued that Scripture was "the best of all the sources of illustration"[81] materials for four reasons: "The Scriptures present materials of illustration suited to every legitimate subject of preaching;" "The (scriptural) material is to some extent familiar to all, and thus the illustration will be readily intelligible;" "[T]his material will be much more impressive than any other, because of its sacredness, and its known and felt relationship to ourselves;" and "[T]he frequent use of Scripture illustration serves

---

76. Parker, *Develop Your Powers of Persuasion*, 133.

77. Hoppin, *Homiletics*, 1883, 439.

78. Luccock, *In the Minister's Workshop*, 152–53.

79. Pierson, *The Divine Art of Preaching*, 1892, 33.

80. Hoyt, *Vital Elements of Preaching*, 1929, 103.

81. Broadus, *A Treatise on the Preparation and Delivery of Sermons*, 1870, 228.

to revive and extend the knowledge of Scripture among the hearers."[82] Quite obviously, there is a difference between the greater familiarity of Scripture of the typical Christian in 1870 as compared to the lesser familiarity of the typical Christian today. Therefore, though his second reason is not as credible now as it was then, his fourth reason, "to revive and extend the knowledge of Scripture among the hearers," takes on greater necessity and credibility for hearers today as compared to those hearing biblical illustrations in the nineteenth century. But I could not agree more with Broadus's conclusion that, "Every preacher should most diligently draw from this source."[83]

The best conclusion is accompanied by an illustration that puts the message in a living form, that is, a flesh and blood depiction of the truth. This is the ultimate illustration. It embodies the truth, it sets it before the mind of the hearer, and every component of the hearer is affected by an understanding of truth that cannot be ignored.[84] As the expression goes, "We shall never fight the battles of Heaven to any purpose with arms forged in Hell."[85] The greatest relevance of this expression related to preaching is that application, in the form of the closing appeals of the sermon conclusion, comes from the Word of God, not the wisdom of the world, and that the biblical application in the closing appeals are illustrated from Scripture. "'I believe, therefore I speak' has always been the law of preaching."[86] A preacher's believing and preaching in a sermon conclusion should demonstrate a robust faith as evidenced by the inclusion of Scripture-based closing appeals to which the hearers are exhorted to respond. A sound belief in the sufficiency of Scripture recognizes that Scripture is the best resource, the unrivaled resource, to help him do all that a preacher needs to do in preaching.

The sermon conclusion is no exception to the need of Scripture for its vital content for the closing appeals and, perhaps, even for the clinching element of persuasion. Personal experience is an effective testimony of scriptural truth, but no man's experience is diversified enough to illustrate sufficiently the truths of Scripture. And no preacher's experiences, no matter how numerous and varied, can be the authoritative basis by which the lives of believer's are challenged to replicate. Scripture, however, is the sufficient resource to provide ample illustration of all truth in practical experience. "The Bible is a rich storehouse of illustration for the preacher. As a truthful record of man's life, special record of his religious experience, the treasured experiences of many centuries, no other source of illustration for the preacher could be so varied, apt, and telling."[87]

Dawson C. Bryan's assessment of the Bible is one that expresses its commendable nature that mandates its dominant usage in the sermon conclusion. Bryan wrote, "The

---

82. Broadus, *A Treatise on the Preparation and Delivery of Sermons*, 1870, 228.

83. Broadus, *A Treatise on the Preparation and Delivery of Sermons*, 1870, 228.

84. Hoyt, *The Work of Preaching*, 1905, 203.

85. Dale, *Nine Lectures on Preaching*, 1890, 193.

86. Hoyt, *The Preacher*, reprinted, 1912, 14.

87. Hoyt, *The Work of Preaching*, 1905, 252.

Bible is . . . the truthful and tested record of life experiences. Its resources are inexhaustible and, because of the sacred associations which cluster around them, it has power to persuade which is absent from any other materials. No other source is the equivalent. . . . The Bible is always contemporary."[88] Scripture, besides having much to offer in the way of illustrating biblical truth, when used to illustrate biblical truth increases the hearers' knowledge of the Word of God and continues to establish the essential authority for preaching.[89] Scripture can completely furnish "the raw material" for sermons, not just the texts to be preached. The predominant substance of our preaching should be content derived from Scripture. The Bible contains the truths to be preached, and the content with which to illustrate and apply scriptural truths to the lives of God's people.[90]

Since preachers are continually preparing sermons, he should naturally become increasingly alert to the incidents and events contained in Scripture and experienced in his life which will help him present his messages more interestingly and forcefully. This is called a "homiletical mind" where one's attention not only naturally but by active interest is directed to anything and everything which will give clarity to his sermons.[91] The continual, perpetual, daily reading of Scripture engaged with a homiletical mind is an unsurpassed resource and opportunity to soak oneself in scriptural knowledge and life experience that will be valuable in preaching, generally, and for concluding sermons, specifically.

88. Bryan, *The Art of Illustrating Sermons*, 92.
89. Bryan, *The Art of Illustrating Sermons*, 98.
90. Dale, *Nine Lectures on Preaching*, 1890, 118.
91. Bryan, *The Art of Illustrating Sermons*, 91.

18

Proclaiming Christ in a Sermon Conclusion:
Part 1

"The most crucial consideration of deep preaching is the proclamation of the person and work of Jesus Christ to those who are not believers. Everything other than this that may be heard from a pulpit, though truly profound content for believers, is shallow content for unbelievers as it is other than that to which they can respond and need to understand. They need Jesus Christ. They need the salvation that he alone can provide them but they must understand who he is and what he has done so that they may repent of their sins and trust in the Christ whom they now understand as revealed in the Word of God."

"The fact that many people think they are Christians when they are not is an understood reality, and a tragic one. But this tragedy is only compounded when the gospel is not proclaimed on the occasions when people who are deceived about their lack of salvation are present, in the preaching services of the church."

"Expository preaching, regardless of Testament, text, or occasion should be 'evangelistic' in that, expository preaching should not forgo the proclamation of the gospel."

"There are various elements of the person and work of Christ that some people do not accept and will not believe. Yet, to offer unbelievers an incomplete gospel is to assure them a continued separation from God for time and for eternity. The message of the gospel of Jesus Christ is to be proclaimed and, in its proclamation, it is not to be compromised or negotiated. . . . Every component of the person and work of Jesus Christ is one that represents a barrier to some unbelievers as something to which they will not consent. A cosmetic gospel, a gospel that has removed features which might be a detraction, or a politically correct gospel, a gospel that affirms all and offends

none, is not the gospel and such non-gospel substitutes should be preached."

"Gospel-centered preaching without a complete, condensed, clear declaration of Christ's person and work being made in a sermon conclusion without an immediate exhortation for unbelievers to respond to him in repentance and faith is not gospel-centered enough! A preacher must be gospel-centered in preaching the body of his sermon and be gospel-complete in preaching the end of his sermon conclusion!"

"The absence of the gospel message in preaching stands on its own merits, if there are any merits on which preaching may stand in light of such a profound omission. There is no rationale that dignifies this omission. Not even a commitment to excellence in expository preaching, an extremely praiseworthy thing, can be permitted a pass if it fails to declare a clear, complete, condensed proclamation of the gospel of Jesus Christ to those who are lost and desperately need to hear this message."

"The need is for preachers to understand that some to whom they regularly preach are religious but lost people. They are deceived regarding their spiritual state. What they need is to respond to the message of the gospel, which necessitates their hearing of it. Their hearing of it is dependent upon one who is committed and desirous to proclaim it, and to do so with sincerity and urgency. The need is for expository preaching pastors to recover or obtain a passion to see deceived religious people be converted and become followers of Jesus Christ."

"Many expository preachers are blind to the fact that their preaching does not contain the message of the gospel. This must change. In all their successful efforts to make connections from their text to some truth about Jesus Christ, as laudable is the effort and as profitable is the connection, it is less than the message of the gospel and in pointing out such connections, they have yet to declare the complete, condensed, clear message of the person and work of Jesus Christ along with an exhortation for unbelievers to repent of their sins and trust in Christ alone for their salvation."

"Can a preacher truly say, 'The reason why I don't proclaim the message of the gospel in my preaching is because of God's monopoly on my life?' Is God to be credited for the omission of the gospel in one's preaching?"

"A sympathetic urgency to proclaim the message of the gospel should be unsurpassed by an expository preacher since he is absorbed in the study of the profound temporal and eternal blessings which belong to believers but are not experienced by those outside of Christ. Such disparity between believers and unbelievers should incite expository preachers to be just as devoted to preach the gospel to unbelievers as he is to expound the Scriptures to believers."

"A preacher cannot preach effectively to the lost without including the message of the

gospel and the gospel message will not be included in preaching without a heart for the lost, to see them converted. As this is the case, there will be a proclamation of the gospel message and an appropriate appeal for the lost to respond to the gospel. Yet, an appropriate appeal preceded by faithful proclamation of Christ's person and work is infrequently observed even in evangelistic preaching, and unfortunately, is a foreign precept in expository preaching."

"Many preachers today cannot even be convinced that appealing to sinners to turn to Christ, having proclaimed Christ, is something that they need to do in preaching! The lack of passion to see Christ exalted for his profound humility to die and be raised from the dead to provide sinners with a victory over their sin, as well as the lack of passion to see sinners repent of their sins and turn to Christ in faith and receive the gift of life, must be seen for what it is—a very poor commentary regarding the heart of the preacher. We are quick to be concerned about the heart of the preacher when it keeps him from effectively edifying believers, and rightly so. . . . Yet, the preacher's heart is crucial in the intent to see unbelievers converted just as it is in the intent to see believers edified."

It is relatively safe to say that believers desire other than shallow preaching but rather believers desire preaching composed of greater depth. But what is the greater depth that is desired? What does it mean to provide preaching that consists of greater depth? For some, "deep" preaching is the kind of preaching that always provides the listener with new information, providing them with something they did not already know. "Give me more knowledge! Tell me something I didn't know!" is the mantra of folks who deem deep preaching as more information.[1] Certainly, I would agree with the desire of such people in their quest to encounter this kind of "deep" preaching. A preacher handling any text from the ocean of God's Word only to provide the same thimble-full of living water will justly perpetuate the error of shallow preaching and will intensify the desire of his hearers to be exposed to preaching that is far more informative.

For others, regardless of the quantity and quality of new information, "deep" preaching must be personally practical. "Information isn't the goal, transformation is!" represents the perspective of these people.[2] And, again, I certainly can champion the perspective of these believers. Any preacher providing new insights and deeper understanding of a biblical text, yet, without providing the wider personal and practical implications of such knowledge from the passage will always fail to provide "deep" preaching in the minds of these people.

Ultimately, however, beyond the information and application that produces the deep preaching sought after by believers, preaching is to declare the person and work of Jesus Christ, the gospel. For unbelievers it is the message of the gospel alone that

1. Wax, *Gospel-Centered Teaching*, 11.
2. Wax, *Gospel-Centered Teaching*, 14.

"transcends" the preaching of greater information and application to furnish the deep preaching of the gospel of Jesus Christ, the only message needed by unbelievers.[3]

The most crucial consideration of deep preaching is the proclamation of the person and work of Jesus Christ to those who are not believers. Everything other than this that may be heard from a pulpit, though truly profound content for believers, is irrelevant content for unbelievers as it is other than that to which they can respond and need to understand. They need Jesus Christ. They need the salvation that he alone can provide them, but they must understand who he is and what he has done so that they may repent of their sins and trust in the Christ whom they now understand as revealed in the Word of God.

EVANGELISTIC PREACHING IS NOT AVERSE TO EXPOSITORY PREACHING

In a preaching ministry, preachers are not simply to edify believers in the knowledge of Scripture as they "reprove, rebuke, and exhort with all long-suffering and doctrine" but they must never be negligent to make known to the lost man "the way of salvation."[4] A sermon preached in a worship service of assembled believers is to be both expositional, predominantly, and evangelistic, ultimately. "All preaching worthy of the name is evangelistic" so that at least a part of the sermon is specifically intended for the conversion of those who are not disciples of Jesus Christ. But since most congregations are composed of those who in varying degrees of maturity and commitment are already followers of Christ, not all of the sermon is intended to be preaching that is aimed to bring the lost person to faith in Christ through the proclamation of the gospel.[5]

It is only an assumption, and an unwise one at that, that everyone assembled in a preaching service is a true follower of Christ. An intentional, earnest presentation of the message of the gospel for those who may be deceived about their true relationship with Jesus Christ is just as worthwhile as the exposition of Scripture for the edification of believers. "The point is you never know who is unsaved" writes Bailey E. Smith. In the twelve years previous to the publication of his book, *Real Evangelism*, Smith documented a staggering report of 106 pastors' wives, 93 pastors, 111 staff members, and 88 deacons who were converted through his crusades.[6] The fact that many people think they are Christians when they are not is an understood reality, and a tragic one. But this tragedy is only compounded when the gospel is not proclaimed on the occasions when people who are deceived about their lack of salvation are present in the preaching services of the church.

---

3. Wax, *Gospel-Centered Teaching*, 17–18.

4. Taylor, *The Ministry of the Word*, 1876, 97.

5. Coffin, *What to Preach*, 1926, 157.

6. Smith, *Real Evangelism*, 164.

The preacher is simply a herald, and the irreducible core of his message is the proclamation of the free gift of eternal life in the forgiveness of sins through the person and work of Jesus Christ. It is always a mistake, however, if a pastor's weekly messages from the pulpit to believers is intended, mainly, for the unconverted, if the salvation of lost people is a pastor's ultimate purpose in preaching. As this is the case, preaching prioritizes converts but neglects to make disciples of those who have already been converted. When the priority of preaching is to minister to those who are unbelievers, providing the message that they need as the dominating substance of the sermon, it fails to edify those who have been converted "and it cannot long hold those whom it does not reach." Though it offers milk, it offers "no meat for strong men."[7]

Expository preaching, regardless of Testament, text, or occasion should be "evangelistic" in that, expository preaching *should not forgo the proclamation of the gospel*. Gary Millar, in providing a good eight-fold assessment of expository preaching, makes a great inclusion in his final component of expository preaching, that it is evangelistic. Expository preaching according to Millar includes the following:

1. Expository preaching does justice to the biblical material which makes it clear that God works through His Word to change people's lives.

2. Expository preaching acknowledges that it is God alone, through the Spirit, who works in people's lives, and that it is not our job to change people through clever or inspiring communication.

3. Expository preaching minimizes the danger of manipulating people, because the text itself controls what we say and how we say it.

4. Expository preaching minimizes the danger of abusing power, because a sermon driven by the text creates an instant safeguard against using the Bible to bludgeon (or caress) people into doing or thinking what we want them to do or think.

5. Expository preaching removes the need to rely on our personality.

6. Expository preaching encourages humility in those teaching.

7. Expository preaching helps us to avoid simple pragmatism. . . . Conversely, working through the Bible week by week will force us to cover subjects that we wouldn't choose to address in a million years. In other words, expository preaching is the simplest, longest-lasting antidote we have to pragmatism.

8. Expository preaching drives us to preaching the gospel . . . that is, to spell out what God has already done for us in the death and resurrection of his Son, and then move from that grace to what God asks and enables us to do.[8]

---

7. Behrends, *The Philosophy of Preaching*, 1890, 14.

8. Millar and Campbell, *Saving Eutychus*, from Millar's chapter "Preaching that Changes the Heart," 40–41.

Millar's necessity for the preaching of the gospel is to provide a rationale of remembrance to believers regarding the benefits they possess to provide a basis for their response to expounded truth.

Though I believe Millar's point is valuable and would agree it should be preached to motivate believers to respond to preached truth because, being new creations in Christ Jesus, they can do so. However, the point I am making is this, *the necessity for preaching the gospel is for the sake of those who are unconverted*, knowingly, or unknowingly so. Therefore, expository preaching is not to forgo the message of the gospel being proclaimed to unbelievers in a sermon that is devoted to mature believers through their understanding of biblical texts.

THE UNKNOWN VALUE OF A SERMON

People are essentially the same today as they were in the days of the great revivals, and in the era of the apostles. The means by which God transforms the innermost depths of man's moral and spiritual life, the proclamation of the gospel, is still used by him.[9] The Apostle Paul preached to everyone "the unsearchable riches of Christ." The message of the gospel as preached by Paul was a message of immeasurable worth, need, and glory. The unsearchable riches of Christ not only described the substance of Paul's gospel message but doubled as the significant provision which may be appropriated by unbelievers. For Paul, the most sinful of mankind could be saved on the basis of repentance and trust alone in the person and work of Jesus Christ. Because of the unsearchable riches of Christ, the sinfulness of the worst sinner is no match for the sinlessness of the Savior. As with Paul, the unsearchable riches of Christ afford the most winsome light and heat in the confident proclamation "that the crown of life can be brought to the most bespotted, and the pure white robe to the most defiled."[10] Paul was always ready and quick to proclaim the gospel in any circumstance even though the likelihood of seeing sinners converted were slim. As it was for the Apostle Paul, it is true for preachers today that the gospel offered in clarity and passion will be rejected by many lost people.

There are people who refuse to acknowledge that faith in Christ is the only way to everlasting life, and that unbelief will end in everlasting destruction. Such persons possess a deeply rooted hostility to the authority of Christ that demands that they, like all unbelievers, repent of their sins.[11] There are various elements of the person and work of Christ that some people do not accept and will not believe. Yet, to offer unbelievers an incomplete gospel is to assure them a continued separation from God for time and for eternity.

---

9. Dale, *Nine Lectures on Preaching*, 1890, 184.

10. Jowett, *The Passion for Souls*, 1905, 8.

11. Dale, *Nine Lectures on Preaching*, 1890, 198–99.

The message of the gospel of Jesus Christ is to be proclaimed and, in its proclamation, it is not to be compromised or negotiated. R. W. Dale warns: "We shall never make men Christians by suppressing and throwing into the shade those parts of the Christian revelation which especially provokes their hostility. Truth which men regard as incredible, truth which men resent . . . is precisely the truth which men most need to hear, and which is likely to produce the deepest moral impression."[12] Every component of the person and work of Jesus Christ is one that represents a barrier to some unbelievers as something to which they will not consent.

A cosmetic gospel, a gospel that has removed features which might be a detraction, or a politically correct gospel, a gospel that affirms all and offends none, is not the gospel and such non-gospel substitutes should not be preached. However, though the gospel contains more than a few elements that will be unacceptable to lost people, this must be anticipated, but one cannot know how the Holy Spirit of God is working in the lives of an unbeliever through the preached Word. Therefore, the complete uncompromised gospel must be proclaimed and let God do his work in the hearts of lost people.

PREACHING AND TEACHING IN THE EARLY CHURCH

The distinction between the concepts of "preaching" and "teaching" as practiced by the early church and referred to in the New Testament need to be recognized. C. H. Dodd, in his book, *The Apostolic Preaching*, provides careful distinction between the terms. According to Dodd:

> "It pleased God," says Paul, "by the foolishness of the Preaching to save them that believe." The word here translated "preaching," *kerygma*, signifies not the action of the preacher, but that which he preaches, his "message," as we sometimes say.
>
> The New Testament writers draw clear distinction between preaching and teaching. . . . Teaching (*didaskein*) is in a large majority of the cases ethical instruction. Occasionally it seems to include what we should call apologetic, that is, the reasoned commendation of Christianity to persons interested but not yet convinced. Sometimes, especially in the Johannine writings, it includes the exposition of theological doctrine. Preaching, on the other hand, is the public proclamation of Christianity to the non-Christian world. The verb *keryssein* properly means "to proclaim." A *keryx* may be a town crier, an auctioneer, a herald, or anyone who lifts up his voice and claims public attention to some definite thing he has to announce. Much of our preaching in the church at the present day would not have been recognized by the early Christians as *kerygma*. It is teaching, or exhortation (*paraklesis*), or it is what they called, *homilia*, that is, the more or less informal discussion of various aspects

12. Dale, *Nine Lectures on Preaching*, 1890, 201.

of Christian life and thought, addressed to a congregation already established in the faith. The verb "to preach" frequently has for its object "the Gospel." Indeed, the connection of ideas is so close that *keryssein* by itself can be used as a virtual equivalent for *evangelizesthai*, "to evangelize," or "to preach the Gospel." It would not be too much to say that wherever "preaching" is spoken of, it always carries with it the implication of "good tidings" proclaimed.

For the early church, then, to preach the Gospel was by no means the same thing as to deliver moral instruction or exhortation. While the church was concerned to hang on to the teaching of the Lord, it was not by this that it made converts. It was by *kerygma*, says Paul, not by *didache*, that it pleased God to save men.[13]

Certainly, a pastor's foremost responsibility is to expound the Scriptures to believers so that they may continue in the ongoing work of being made disciples. Having completed this ministry for the believers, a preacher must not negate his ministry to unbelievers but he must absolve himself of his full responsibility in preaching by providing the message of the gospel, the person and work of Jesus Christ, to the unbelievers. Ian Macpherson was of this viewpoint as he argued:

> Were Christianity just a set of dogmatic propositions, a collection of theological theories, it may suffice to win an intellectual assent to it and to leave it at that. But no. You dare not do so. For, if the content of your preaching be personal, there can be but one adequate and appropriate response to it from those to whom it is addressed—a response of acceptance of the Christ it seeks to convey. When you have persuaded your hearers to do that, your work is done, your ordeal over: your burden has become their blessing.[14]

Key to Macpherson's argument was that proclaiming Christ to those who have yet to become his followers must be a burden in the heart of the preacher. Without a burden for the lost, a preacher will not avail himself of the opportunity to address this need even in a context of a preaching service.

An additional insight must be understood regarding the preaching of the early church is that the Old Testament was the source material to authenticate the proclamation of Jesus Christ. "Is the Old Testament moving towards Jesus? Yes, it is. Do I want people to walk away with a fresh sense of the power and grace that God has given us in Christ every time I open the Old Testament? Yes, I do. Is Jesus visible in every verse of the Old Testament? No, he isn't. If we pull back the camera far enough, eventually Jesus will come into view as the fulfillment of all that is going on. But sometimes we have to pull back quite a long way to see that."[15] Through the use of Christ-references,

13. Dodd, *The Apostolic Preaching*, 7–8.

14. Macpherson, *The Burden of the Lord*, 44.

15. Millar and Campbell, *Saving Eutychus*, from Millar's chapter, "Why Preaching the Gospel is so Hard," 83–84.

that is cross references that relate directly or indirectly to Jesus Christ, there can be from any passage being preached a legitimate way to bring Jesus into the exposition of the passage as the ultimate explanation and meaning of the text. Tony Merida provides a much-needed word when he writes:

> We must avoid Christ-less sermons. Often expositors miss the forest of the Bible (God's redemption in Jesus) for the trees (a particular passage). According to some hermeneutical plans, we could preach through the book of Nehemiah verse by verse, yet never mentioned Jesus—and the sermon would be classified as expository! . . . No Jewish rabbi should be able to sit comfortably under our preaching from the Old Testament. Expositors should work hard at finding the redemptive connections within the text and make a grace-filled application of it.[16]

Merida's words provide a helpful correction in expository preaching.

To expound a passage so that the authorial intent of the passage is understood and not corroborate how the meaning of the passage relates to Christ is culpable. However, dealing with a text as a means to speak of Jesus Christ without ever establishing the meaning of the passage is culpable as well. Understanding the meaning of a text, honoring the text for having a meaning, then relating how the meaning of the text relates to Christ, and how the meaning of the text can become a legitimate means by which a preacher can make insightful declaration about Jesus Christ is always appropriate. This is a need in expository preaching since the meaning of the text often is not related to Jesus Christ by the expository preacher. The motivation of C. H. Spurgeon will pay dividends to expositors who work hard in providing the meaning of their preaching passages. Spurgeon is reported once to have said to a young preacher:

> Don't you know, young man, from every town and every village and every hamlet in England, wherever it may be, there is a road to London? So, from every text of Scripture there is a road to Christ. And my dear brother, your business is, when you get to a text, to say, "now, what is the road to Christ?" I have never found a text that did not have a road to Christ in it, and if ever I do find one, I will go over hedge and ditch but I would get at my Master, for the sermon cannot do any good unless there is a savor of Christ in it.[17]

A thoroughly explained passage of Scripture is well suited to make, not a doubtful and strained connection, but a sound and significant connection to Jesus Christ. The question, at this point, is about how much the preacher wants to declare about Christ once he has made that relationship between Christ and the text's meaning.

---

16. Merida, *Faithful Preaching*, 14.

17. Millar and Campbell, *Saving Eutychus*, from Millar's chapter "Why Preaching the Gospel is so Hard," 86–87. This commonly attributed quotation of Spurgeon appears in his 1859 sermon "Christ Precious to Believers" as Spurgeon quoted the Welsh pastor from whom the expression originated.

The declaration of Christ from any text is rewarding and edifying for the believer and may be illuminating to the unbeliever. Though expository preaching will always be more than, it must not be less than, the proclamation of the gospel message of Jesus Christ. Robert Mounce's insights are in good form when he wrote:

> The ultimate test of the genuineness of preaching is, Does it really convey the saving action of God? . . . True preaching is an event that effectively communicates the power and redemptive activity of God. . . . To be genuinely relevant it (preaching) must be addressed to man's ultimate spiritual need. . . . It must deal with sin and offer salvation. Only preaching of the Gospel is preaching that is truly relevant. . . . If preaching be the extension in time of God's great redemptive act, then not only *may* we preach the *kerygma* today, but we *must*.[18]

In addition to this, for the sake of the unbeliever, I believe presenting a full presentation of Christ's person and work at the end of a sermon conclusion provides a complete, condensed, clear declaration of who Christ is and what he has done so that sinners can be forgiven of their sin and no longer be God's enemy having become his child in possession of the free gift of eternal life. This need exists and this message needs to be proclaimed in a complete, condensed, clear manner followed by an opportunity to respond to this message.

I am arguing for the message of the gospel to be preached to unbelievers at the end of a sermon conclusion in which the sermon itself was clearly connected to Christ. I couldn't agree more with Trevin Wax when he wrote, "It is critical for us to not assume most people know who God is, what he is like, and what he is done for us. We need to be clear in what we teach, with a laser-like focus on Jesus Christ our Savior."[19] Some reservation, however, is warranted for the following caution: "Sometimes teachers and preachers decide that the way to be gospel-centered is to tack on a gospel presentation to the end of a message. . . . But if we're not careful, by tacking on a bullet point presentation to the end of our talks, we can communicate that the gospel doesn't have much to do with everything else we've been talking about. In other words . . . the gospel seems disjointed from the rest of your sermon."[20] If the motive and method of the preacher while preaching the sermon was devoid of establishing the relationship of the text's meaning with Jesus Christ, then speaking of Christ in the conclusion of the sermon may truly seem disjointed. But it does not have to be so, and it will not be so when the motive of the preacher is more than to simply relate the meaning of the text to Jesus Christ, but in addition to present him, his person and work, in a complete, condensed, clear declaration to which they are challenged to respond to the message of the gospel so that unbelievers may receive the free gift of eternal life.

18. Mounce, *The Essential Nature of New Testament Preaching*, 155–56.
19. Wax, *Gospel-centered Teaching*, 57.
20. Wax, *Gospel-centered Teaching*, 41.

The point I am making is that gospel-centered preaching without a complete, condensed, clear declaration of Christ's person and work being made in a sermon conclusion is not gospel-centered enough! Furthermore, even when a conclusion contains a complete, condensed, clear declaration of Christ's person and work, without an immediate exhortation for unbelievers to respond to him in repentance and faith, this too constitutes preaching that is not gospel-centered enough! The preaching of the gospel cannot be gospel preaching if it is separated from the content of the gospel, the person and work of Jesus Christ, or if it is separated from the requirement of the gospel, repentance toward God and faith in Jesus Christ. The preaching of the gospel cannot forgo the declaration of who Jesus Christ is and what he has done so that sinners may be saved from their sins, nor can the preaching of the gospel forgo the exhortation for sinners to repent of their sins and trust in Christ alone for their salvation from sin.

True gospel-centered preaching will be urgent preaching because "the love of God and the nature of lost people demand it."[21] A preacher must be gospel-centered in preaching the body of his sermon and be gospel-complete in preaching the end of his sermon conclusion! When the message of the gospel, a complete, condensed, clear declaration of Christ's person and work is made in the sermon conclusion, Wax's assertion is ultimately true as he writes: "[U]nless we bring people back to the gospel, we are not offering anything distinctively Christian. . . . We may be commenting on Christian Scripture, pulling out good points of application, and offering solid information. But it's the gospel that makes our teaching distinctively Christian. It's the gospel that separates our study from mere moralistic suggestions."[22] Amen, to a very good word.

James W. Thompson registers three insightful reminders about the preaching process before establishing the Apostle Paul as a very appropriate model for our preaching in a post-Christian culture.

> First, as a result of the pluralism of our society, the preacher may never assume that the entire congregation has already been converted. Second, the listening audience is always composed of Christians who are at different stages of Christian experience and perhaps people who possess only a non-Christian experience. Third, evangelistic preaching is the task of every preacher. This preaching model has too often been ignored in the preaching tradition of Europe and North America. The close interrelationship between *kerygma* and *paraklesis* in Paul is forgotten both in the tradition of evangelistic preaching that focuses on the initial response of the listener and in the preaching tradition that offers instruction and comfort. The Pauline model that combines evangelistic and pastoral preaching remains a helpful model in our own culture.[23]

---

21. Armstrong, *Evangelistic Growth in Acts 1 & 2*, 69.

22. Wax, *Gospel-Centered Teaching*, 78.

23. Thompson, *Preaching Like Paul*, 60.

Paul's preaching of the gospel involved both an authoritative proclamation of a message and an authorized appeal to respond to the message announced.[24]

In 2 Corinthians 5:20, Paul addresses his preaching ministry and includes elements of his preaching that were pivotal for the conversion of lost people. Paul's perspective is helpful for expository preachers, especially. Paul declared, "Therefore we are ambassadors for Christ, as though God were making an appeal through us; we beg you on behalf of Christ, be reconciled to God." It is in the sermon conclusion, when preaching is not only continuing to occur but when it is at its peak, where preaching must include for unbelievers an authoritative announcement from a King to which there is this exhortation requiring an imperative response: "Be reconciled to God through Jesus Christ!"

The conclusion completes the sermon, a sermon composed of two messages each intended for hearers with different needs. The message for believers is for them to respond to the closing appeals of the sermon conclusion which will help them to achieve the purpose of the sermon in their lives. The message for unbelievers is for them to respond in repentance and faith to the person and work of Jesus Christ which has been proclaimed to them in a complete, condensed, clear manner. Among other things, a conclusion "invites the audience to obedience."[25] If done with integrity, a preacher in his sermon conclusion appeals for every person in the audience to respond in obedience. Obedience on behalf of believers entails obedience to the implications of the gospel, resulting in the maturity of their Christian walk. Obedience on behalf of unbelievers entails obedience to the message of the gospel, resulting in the beginning of their Christian walk.

ABSENCE OF THE GOSPEL

The absence of the gospel message in preaching stands on its own merits, if there are any merits on which preaching may stand in light of such a profound omission. There is no rationale that dignifies this omission. Not even a commitment to excellence in expository preaching, an extremely praiseworthy thing, can be permitted a pass if it fails to declare a complete, condensed, clear proclamation of the gospel of Jesus Christ to those who are lost and desperately need to hear this message. When the renown Scottish pastor, expository preacher, and Greek scholar William Robertson Nicoll was forced to retire from pastoral ministry because of lung disease, he moved to the South of England in 1886. While recovering from his illness, he attended the services of various churches in south England. Though he was impressed that the preachers he heard were "well educated and sincere men who delivered thoughtful and carefully prepared sermons" he could not refrain himself from the criticism of their preaching

24. Thompson, *Preaching Like Paul*, 55.

25. Richard, *Scripture Sculpture*, 131.

ministries that, "Not one of them would have converted a titmouse!"[26] Well, there you have it! Conversion requires the gospel message to be proclaimed. If it is not proclaimed, many great things could be said about the sermon, and they would truly be good if one is a believer, but for an unbeliever, *they have been denied the message they needed to hear.*

As is typical of Spurgeon, he has a uniquely insightful viewpoint for anything pertaining to preaching. The absence of the gospel in preaching did not fail to garner the wrath of the most quotable one. Spurgeon wrote, "I have marveled at the way in which certain persons avoid preaching the gospel when they profess to be doing it. They get a text which you think must cut into the conscience, and they contrive to speak so as neither to arouse the careless nor distress the self-confident. They play with the sword of the Spirit . . . instead of thrusting the two-edged sword into the hearts of men, as soldiers do in actual combat. . . . He may expect one day to be crowned with shame for such a crime."[27] David H. C. Read suggested that a helpful measure to remedy a reticence to proclaim the gospel might be secured if part of the Apostle John's description about the ministry of John the Baptist were placarded on every preacher's pulpit where he can see them and be reminded that what was true of the Lord's forerunner should be true for him as well: "'He was not himself the light: he came to bear witness to the light.'"[28] But, the bearing witness to the light by many present day preachers would probably be less than proclaiming the person and work of Christ. Bearing witness to the light would simply mean the preaching that they commonly deliver which is bereft of the proclamation of Christ's person and work and the appeal to repent from sin and trust in the finished work accomplished by Christ for their salvation. Therefore, the placard would probably only serve to signify to the preacher that he has been a witness to Christ in his gospel-less sermon.

The Scottish preacher, Robert Murray McCheyne, held this conviction, "I had rather beg my bread than preach without success." And success, for McCheyne, meant winning men to Christ.[29] Such urgency to see lost people won to Christ is necessary to assure that the message of the gospel is proclaimed in every sermon. One man's well-intentioned admonition would very effectively leave many pulpits vacated when he admonished, "If there be anything under the sun in which a man has a keener interest than in . . . open(ing) the door into that life, the life with Christ in God, to them who are without, let him not stand in a Christian pulpit."[30] The requirement of such a great desire to see the lost won to Christ would significantly depopulate pulpits.

The need is for preachers to understand that some to whom they regularly preach are religious but lost people. They are deceived regarding their spiritual state. What

26. McCartney, *Preaching Without Notes*, 9.

27. Spurgeon, *An All-round Ministry*, 1900, 148–9.

28. Read, *Sent from God*, 38.

29. Hoppin, *Homiletics*, 1883, 253.

30. Coffin, *What to Preach*, 1926, 187–8.

they need is to respond to the message of the gospel, which necessitates their hearing of it. Their hearing of it is dependent upon one who is committed and desirous to proclaim it, and to do so with sincerity and urgency. The need is for expository preaching pastors to recover or obtain a passion to see deceived religious people be converted and become followers of Jesus Christ.

What is missing, what is needed, so that expository preachers will be sure to provide preaching that includes a complete, condensed, clear message of the gospel? How does this get turned around? In general, it starts with the realization that there is a lacking, an incompleteness of a preacher's preaching, that has no right to continue. There needs to be the realization of a blind man, that is, a blind man possesses an understanding that his friends who have sight live their lives with something that he himself does not have.[31] Without such a realization of the common expository preacher, that his preaching, as good as it is for believers in helping them to mature in their faith, does not provide that which is needed by some of his hearers because they need the message of the gospel. However, many expository preachers are blind to the fact that their preaching does not contain the message of the gospel. This must change.

In all their successful efforts to make connections from their text to some truth about Jesus Christ, as laudable is the effort and as profitable is the connection, it is less than the message of the gospel. In pointing out such connections, they have yet to declare the complete, condensed, clear message of the person and work of Jesus Christ along with an exhortation for unbelievers to repent of their sins and trust in Christ alone for their salvation. Once this general realization has been grasped and there is a desire for this to be corrected, there needs to be three areas of increasing development that mark the life of the preacher for him to continue to provide excellent expository preaching for the maturity of believers coupled with the message of the gospel for those who are not in Christ.

First, there must be an increasing consecration to God for the work God has called the preacher to do in a preaching ministry. King David prayed, "Create in me a clean heart, O God, and renew a steadfast spirit within me. Do not cast me away from Your presence and do not take your Holy Spirit from me. Restore to me the joy of Your salvation and sustain me with a willing spirit. Then will I teach transgressors Your ways; and sinners will be converted to You" (Psalm 51:10–13). The situation could not be more opposite than a murderous, adulterous king and an expository preacher who does not include the gospel message in his preaching. The meaning of David's plea to God from his personal context is well understood. But how does what David wrote, from his context, have implications for preachers who fail to provide the message of the gospel in their preaching? Just as the heart of David, from which he committed adultery with Bathsheba and had Uriah killed, was not right before God and was not fitting for a king who was to have oversight of God's people, expository preachers need to examine their hearts to discover how it is that they can absent the message of the

31. Orr, *The Faith That Persuades*, 89.

gospel in a context of preaching God's Word to people he is given oversight of, and for whom he cannot be certain of their regeneration.

Just as David desired and knew he needed the presence of God's Spirit, the joy of his salvation, and a willing spirit in order to instruct transgressors and have a role in sinners being converted to God, so it is with the expository preacher. He must be filled with the Spirit who indwells him, and he must be filled with the joy of his salvation and desire this joy to become a possession of those who do not have it.

The spiritual preparation of personal sanctification is an absolute necessity for the appropriate consecration for effectiveness in a preaching ministry.[32] God's monopoly on a preacher's life is a crucial factor of a man's preaching. "When Dwight L. Moody was being considered by a minister's group for a third crusade in a particular city, someone objected, 'Why get Moody again? Does he have a monopoly on God?' Said another pastor in reply, 'No, but God has a monopoly on Moody.'"[33] So, can a preacher truly say, "The reason why I don't proclaim the message of the gospel in my preaching is because of God's monopoly on my life?" Is God to be credited for the omission of the gospel in one's preaching? Absolutely not! But, however, the preacher must shoulder blame for omitting the gospel, "the power of God for salvation,"[34] from his sermon.

Second, there must be an increasing appreciation for and urgency to proclaim the gospel to others. As Paul was seeing the Ephesian elders for the last time, he testified to them, "But I do not consider my life of any account as dear to myself, so that I may finish my course and the ministry which I received from the Lord Jesus, to testify solemnly of the gospel of the grace of God" (Acts 20:24).

The gospel of the grace of God may be the most conspicuous thing missing in the preaching of the typical preacher's sermons. The following anecdote of a Baptist preacher's proclamation of the gospel of Jesus Christ would be desirable if it were actual rather than anecdotal. He said: "When I was 30 years of age, I said there is nothing *better than* the gospel. After I preached a little while longer, and when I reached the age of 40 and the years of my life were stealing away, I said that there is nothing *as good as* the gospel. I became 50 and there were empty chairs at home and the gravediggers had done service for the family, I said there is nothing *to be compared with* the gospel. When I reached the age of 60, I could see life behind me and Heaven before me, I said to myself there is nothing *but* the gospel."[35] A growing appreciation for the gospel, if that is the reality for a preacher, should be demonstrated in his preaching.

Martin Luther said of his preaching, "I preach as though Christ were crucified yesterday; rose again from the dead today; and is coming back to earth tomorrow."[36]

---

32. Morriss, *The Sound of Boldness*, 25.

33. Smith, *Real Evangelism*, 109.

34. Romans 1:16b.

35. Purtle, "The Psychology of Evangelistic Preaching," 62, published PhD Dissertation.

36. Smith, *Real Evangelism*, 114.

A commitment to an urgent proclamation of the gospel message, not to replace expository preaching but to accompany it, is what is needed.

Third, there must be an increasing sympathy for the lost and a deepening grief regarding their lostness. Consider Paul's grief over the lostness of his Jewish kinsmen. "I am telling the truth in Christ, I am not lying, my conscience testifies with me in the Holy spirit, that I have great sorrow and unceasing grief in my heart. For I could wish that I myself were accursed, separated from Christ for the sake of my brethren, my kinsmen according to the flesh" (Romans 9:1–3).

Expository preachers, in particular, must not be unsympathetic to the state of the lost who may be seated before them and proclaim to them they message they need to hear.

> A preacher went a day early to a prison where he was to preach to familiarize himself with the facilities. The warden showed him the building where the inmates would gather to hear him preach the next day. He noticed as they walked inside two chairs draped in black to the right of the podium a distance from where every other person would be gathered. He asked the warden about the chairs draped in black and he was informed that the two men who would sit in those chairs would be put to death in the electric chair at 6:30 a.m. the next day after he preached. The preacher asked, "My sermon will be the last sermon those men ever hear?" The warden replied, "Yes, it will be their last. They will be dead less than 10 hours after your sermon!" The preacher went home and got alone with God. In tears, the preacher repented for the sermon he had planned to preach and resolved instead to preach the Gospel with the promise of everlasting life and forgiveness through a bloody cross.[37]

Shortly before the end of Paul's life he wrote to Timothy, "For this reason (suffering hardship for the gospel) I endure all things for the sake of those who are chosen, so that they also may obtain the salvation which is in Christ Jesus and with it eternal glory" (2 Timothy 2:10). Paul's passion to see the lost saved is undeniable. "Someone once said to William Booth, founder of the Salvation Army, 'I understand your evangelism program is the very best.' He responded, 'No, it could be better.' 'What could be better, General Booth?' they insisted. Booth responded, 'If all of my soldiers could spend just 5 minutes in hell that would be the best training for soul-winners.'"[38]

How very true is the wise adage, "a man must not only know what to say; he must have a vehement longing to get up and say it."[39] A sympathetic urgency to proclaim the message of the gospel should be unsurpassed by an expository preacher since he is absorbed in the study of the profound temporal and eternal blessings which belong to believers but are not experienced by those outside of Christ. Such disparity between

37. Smith, *Real Evangelism*, 180–81.

38. Smith, *Real Evangelism*, 171.

39. Coffin, *What to Preach*, 1926, 187.

believers and unbelievers should incite expository preachers to be just as devoted to preach the message of the gospel to unbelievers as he is to expound the Scriptures to believers.

Jesus' instruction in Luke 16 regarding the rich man and Lazarus, among other things, provides five insights that must be remembered by the expository preacher who would preach effectively for the sake of the lost: one, those who are lost will spend eternity in utter torment without mercy (not even one drop of water could be applied to the rich man's tongue in order to assuage his torment); two, the lost, while still living, are bound for eternal torment and are given the testimony of Scripture, alone, to warn them ("send Lazarus to my father's house—for I have five brothers— in order that he may warn them"); three, the lost will not be saved from eternal torment unless they are warned of this and respond to the truth ("warn them, so that they will not come to this place of torment"); four, the response of the lost which prevents them from entering into the place of eternal torment is repentance ("No, Father Abraham, but if someone goes to them from the dead, they will repent"); five, the only sufficient power to produce the persuasion to repent is brought about by hearing the Word of God ("If they will not listen to Moses and the Prophets, they will not be persuaded even if someone rises from the dead"). A preaching service in which followers of Christ are being edified through the exposition of God's Word is the optimal opportunity to proclaim the message of the gospel to those who are unregenerate.

A preacher cannot preach effectively to the lost without including the message of the gospel and the gospel message will not be included in preaching without a heart for the lost, to see them converted. As this is the case, there will be a proclamation of the gospel message and an appropriate appeal for the lost to respond to the gospel. Yet, an appropriate appeal preceded by faithful proclamation of Christ's person and work is infrequently observed even in evangelistic preaching, and unfortunately, is a foreign precept in expository preaching. Contrast this to the mindset of the fervent proclaimer of Christ, Puritan preacher Richard Baxter, as he would reproach himself with the following, "How could'st thou speak of life and death with such a heart? Should'st thou not weep over such a people, and should not thy tears interrupt thy words? Should'st not thou cry aloud and shew them their transgressions and entreat and beseech them as for life and death?"[40] Baxter was broken because he was not more fervent, passionate, and urgent in his appeals for sinners to turn to Christ.

Many preachers today cannot even be convinced that appealing to sinners to turn to Christ, having proclaimed Christ, is something that they need to do in preaching! The lack of passion to see Christ exalted for his profound humility to die and be raised from the dead to provide sinners with a victory over their sin, as well as the lack of passion to see sinners repent of their sins and turn to Christ in faith and receive the gift of life, must be seen for what it is—a very poor commentary regarding the heart of the preacher. We are quick to be concerned about the heart of the preacher when

---

40. As cited in Stott, *The Preacher's Portrait*, 58.

it keeps him from effectively edifying believers, and rightly so. We would be quick to agree with Stott about the matter of having a well-prepared heart for the task of preaching as he writes:

> The preparation of the heart is of far greater importance than the prepara- tion of the sermon. The preacher's words, however clear and forceful, will not ring true unless he speaks from conviction born of experience. Many sermons which conform to all the best homiletical rules yet have a hollow sound. There is something indefinably perfunctory about the preacher of such sermons. The matter of his sermon gives evidence of a well-stocked, well-disciplined mind; he has a good voice, a fine bearing, and restrained gestures; but somehow his heart is not in his message.[41]

The preacher's heart is crucial in the intent to see unbelievers converted just as it is in the intent to see believers edified. Richard Baxter also provides the much-needed means for conviction and correction for expository preachers who desire to be true heralds of God when he writes:

> The work of conversion is the first and most vital part of our ministry. . . . As long as there is a strong probability that there are several in our congregation who are in this category (who have need to be truly born again), we should la- bor with all our might on their behalf. . . . Just as Paul's spirit was stirred within him when he saw the Athenians so addicted to idolatry, I am so moved by the plight of the unconverted. It seems to me that he who will let a sinner go to hell simply by not speaking to him gives less place to hell than the Redeemer of souls does. So, whoever you pass over, do not forget the unsaved. I say it again. Focus on the great work of evangelism, whatever else you do or leave undone.[42]

What must not become acceptable in the thinking of a preaching pastor is for him to think that doing excellent service in expounding Scripture for the edification of believers permits him to be negligent in his service to unbelievers by withholding from them the proclamation of the gospel of Jesus Christ. When Jesus defended his ministry of proclaiming truth to tax-gatherers and sinners and eating with them, he told the Pharisees and the scribes three parables which revealed the heart of God for sinners and the love he had for them. Such a heart and such a love for sinners the scribes and Pharisees neither possessed nor could they rationalize in their thinking. Jesus began by saying:

> What man among you, if he has a hundred sheep and has lost one of them, does not leave the ninety-nine in the open pasture, and go after the one which is lost, until he finds it? And when he has found it, he lays it on his shoul- ders, rejoicing. And when he comes home, he calls together his friends and his

41. Stott, *The Preacher's Portrait*, 76
42. Richard Baxter, *The Reformed Pastor*, 1665, 73.

neighbors, saying to them, "Rejoice with me, for I have found my sheep which was lost!" I tell you that in the same way, there will be more joy in heaven over one sinner who repents, than over ninety-nine righteous persons who need no repentance.[43]

It was Christ's love for lost people that caused him to separate Himself from the established practices of the religious leaders regarding their indifference toward sinners. Indifference toward those who are not believers is reflected in the context of preaching as preachers fail to provide to unbelievers the message of the gospel. Furthermore, preachers indicate the absence of their desire to see sinners saved from sin when they fail to include the message of the gospel and to do so with sincerity, urgency, and passion as Christ, himself, did.

Again, it is Richard Baxter who provides needed insight for the fervent proclamation of Christ to the unconverted in our preaching.

> If you give the holy things of God the highest eloquence of words, and yet do so coldly, you will contradict by your manner what you say of the matter. It is indeed a kind of contempt to speak of great matters without the appropriately great affection and fervency that they deserve. If we are commanded, "whatever our hands find to do, do it with all our might," then certainly such a work as preaching for the salvation of men should be "done with all our might!" Alas, how few there are to do so![44]

Baxter does good service by pointing out that the manner of our preaching as well as the matter of it is significant. However, the matter of the gospel message and the manner of its proclamation must be viewed as that which is of the highest priority, and that which must be proclaimed in completeness and earnestness. A perfunctory and lackadaisical proclamation of the person and work of Jesus Christ in reference to the salvation of the lost is both a reproach to the Lord and to the lost who are in need of him.

Leighton Ford, in his book *The Christian Persuader*, suggests four general characteristics of Peter's sermon found in Acts chapter two that are instructive for expository preachers in addressing lost people in the conclusion of their sermons. Three of the four characteristics can be incorporated in every sermon conclusion. Peter's preaching on the Day of Pentecost appealed to the Scriptures as authoritative; it centered on Jesus Christ; it brought conviction upon and concern to the hearers; it called for an immediate and definite response.[45]

The conviction brought upon the unbelievers is that which a preacher would like to see but that which he cannot accomplish as this is the work which the Holy Spirit alone does. However, the other three are always in the preacher's control and these should surface in the conclusion of every sermon. An expository preacher's faithful

---

43. Luke 15:4–7
44. Baxter, *The Reformed Pastor*, 1665, 56.
45. Ford, *The Christian Persuader*, 95.

proclamation of scriptural truth includes the declaration of the person and work of Jesus Christ, the message of the gospel, the message needed by those who are not Christians. An assembly of people in a preaching service represents a tremendous opportunity for believers to be edified in their faith through the exposition of Scripture and for unbelievers to be converted as they respond to the message of the gospel.

We have considered briefly the fact that evangelistic preaching is not averse to expository preaching, the unknown value of a sermon, preaching and teaching in the early church, and the absence of the gospel in preaching. In the next two chapters we will consider the basic presuppositions of evangelistic expository preaching, the gospel message to be preached to the unconverted in the conclusion, that there is nothing preliminary to repentance, and we will clarify the person and work of Jesus Christ.

19

Proclaiming Christ in a Sermon Conclusion: Part 2

"There are only two types of people who hear sermons. There are those who possess salvation and those who do not! As the message is addressed primarily to Christians, they should be exhorted to respond, even if there is a special word for the unbelievers who need to respond in repentance and faith in Jesus Christ. What is of utmost importance is that people should only be exhorted to respond to what has been proclaimed clearly. This includes believers and unbelievers. Just as believers should be exhorted to obey the truth that has been explained to them, so unbelievers should be exhorted to respond to Christ who has been proclaimed to them. But this also requires the prerequisite reality that the person and work of Christ has been clearly declared so that unbelievers can respond to Christ as he has been made known to them."

"Proclaiming the message of the gospel at the end of the sermon conclusion resolves several questionable procedures which commonly are integrated into preaching. First, the message of the gospel is preached in the sermon in a complete, condensed, clear manner as opposed to the sermon ending without the gospel message having been proclaimed. . . . Second, the appeal for unbelievers to respond to the preached gospel in repentance and faith is made so that those responding can make immediate inquiry about their response to the gospel and be informed promptly about baptism as a public proclamation of their faith in Christ. Third, proclaiming the message of the gospel at the end of the sermon conclusion ends the needless procedure of making one's faith in Christ public through the means of responding to an altar call rather than the biblical means of being baptized as a public attestation of repentance and faith in Christ."

"Sermons need a conclusion, a conclusion that renders a verdict to every hearer of the sermon according to the needs of each hearer, whether lost or saved."

"An either/or conviction regarding the intended recipients of a sermon conclusion is not an inescapable reality, it is just a self-imposed reality for many based upon needless and faulty presuppositions regarding sermon conclusions. Once the erroneous presuppositions are surrendered, there is room to adopt a both/and conviction regarding the recipients of a sermon conclusion that can meet the needs of believers and unbelievers alike."

"The conclusion <u>must be directed</u>, not should be directed, <u>to both</u>, not to but one class in the audience. This corrects the most artificial presupposition about preaching a sermon conclusion, that is, some people matter, they are being preached to, while others do not matter, they are not being preached to! Those for whom the sermon conclusion is not directed, they may overhear what is being said to the people who matter, but an overhearing is all they will get because they don't matter! There will be no word intended for them! They have great need for a most significant message, but they will not get it! The established practices for concluding a sermon do not allow them to be addressed! Though their souls are in peril of eternal torment in hell, it is better that they go to hell than it is to proclaim to them in the sermon conclusion the message that might transform them for time and eternity!"

"Should it (the sermon conclusion) be directed to believers or unbelievers? It can and should be directed to both. The sermon conclusion should be devoted to believers, dealing with them to complete the message to them without interruption. Afterwards, uninterrupted attention can be given to the unbelievers by fully proclaiming to them the person and work of Jesus Christ and appealing to them to respond to the gospel of grace in repentance and faith."

"The significance of this second message, the message of the gospel which ends the sermon, must not be depreciated. . . . Christ is to be made known, as well as the good news that salvation is possible because of what he has done. Who he is, according to Scripture, and what he has done, as revealed in Scripture, must be made known to those who do not know him and are not in possession of the salvation that he alone brings to those who repent of their sin and trust in the finished work he has accomplished. . . . The error of the lost must be warned against as well as imploring the lost to seize the solution to the error of their way. Omitting these crucial responsibilities in one's preaching is foolish."

"Unbelievers need a preacher who will not overlook their need or disrespect them by not addressing their need, but cares for them by informing them of what they need to know and do."

"'Converting sinners is God's role. Communicating the gospel is yours.' This is what preaching must do, proclaim the gospel, in the context of expository preaching or

in the context of preaching that is other than expository! Why should there be any reticence about heralding the good news of salvation in a preaching context? But for whatever reasons, reticence exists."

"An expository sermon should include evangelistic preaching. At any point in the sermon, when the focus of the content being declared focuses upon the person and work of Jesus Christ so that those outside of Christ can know who he is and what he has done so that sinners can be saved from their sins, that portion of the sermon is evangelistic. Evangelistic preaching, wherever it occurs in a sermon, becomes an exposition of the person and work of Jesus Christ."

"Evangelistic preaching requires a clear declaration of the person and work of Christ as a starting point, but it must also call the lost to respond to the message of the gospel. In other words, a sermon which has become evangelistic needs to continue in evangelistic completion which requires the preacher 'to preach persuasively for an immediate verdict.' Unbelievers should be compelled either to receive or to reject Christ at the end of every message preached."

"Within the sermon, at some point there should be, an unfragmented, full and complete disclosure of the person and work of Jesus Christ along with a demand for the biblically mandated response of repentance toward God and faith in Jesus Christ for salvation."

BASIC PRESUPPOSITIONS OF EVANGELISTIC EXPOSITORY PREACHING

Though more could be added, recognition should be given to seven presuppositions regarding Christian preaching, the preaching that occurs when believers assemble for worship. To summarize what this preaching consists of, the concept of evangelistic expository preaching is offered. One, preaching is God's chief instrument of saving man. Two, Christian preaching must be evangelistic. Three, the pulpit is the preacher's greatest opportunity to evangelize. Four, people not in Christ are lost. Five, the gospel is still the power of God for salvation.[1] Six, the Great Commission requires proclamation and preaching that makes disciples, which necessitates *kerygma*, initially, and *didache*, ongoingly. The making of disciples predicates the conversion of sinners since baptism is part of what is necessary for a disciple to be made. Being baptized is how unbelievers make public their repentance and faith in Jesus Christ, the positive response to hearing the preaching of the gospel of Christ. So, the making of a disciple entails a sinner hearing the gospel of Jesus Christ, evangelistic preaching, and responding to the gospel in repentance and faith. Then, the baptized convert is made a disciple in an ongoing fashion as he is taught to observe all things Christ's disciples have been

---

1. Stanfield, *Effective Evangelistic Preaching*, 12–16.

commanded, which is Christian instruction. Seven, Christian preaching, preaching to believers for their edification and maturity of the faith, "should incorporate an evangelistic twist. Always turn the messages some point toward an appeal to the unsaved in the audience. . . . All Bible preaching issues forth into evangelism. Regardless of the Bible content of your message, the subject should include an evangelistic appeal."[2] Despite the wise counsel provided by Vines and Shaddix to culminate as sermon with an evangelistic twist which includes an appeal to respond to the gospel, this is not how the typical expository sermon ends.

INCLUDING THE GOSPEL MESSAGE TO THE UNCONVERTED IN THE CONCLUSION

A preacher's exhortations in the sermon conclusion place everyone under the sentence of the Word. There are only two types of people who hear sermons. There are those who possess salvation and those who do not! "As the message is addressed primarily to Christians, they should be exhorted to respond, even if there is a special word for the unbelievers who need to respond in repentance and faith in Jesus Christ. What is of utmost importance is that people should only be exhorted to respond to what has been proclaimed clearly."[3] This includes believers and unbelievers. Just as believers should be exhorted to obey the truth that has been explained to them, so unbelievers should be exhorted to respond to Christ who has been proclaimed to them.[4] But this also requires the prerequisite reality that the person and work of Christ has been clearly declared so that unbelievers can respond to Christ as he has been made known to them.

An "invitation may be used, as Peter used it, in the evangelistic message, as a part of its conclusion."[5] Jay Adams's words are serviceable in two respects. First, the invitation is a declaration which compels the unbeliever to respond to the gospel message in repentance and faith. This does not necessitate an altar call which, if incorporated, is provided after the sermon has been completed but is not part of the sermon or its conclusion. Of course, the altar call is not a requirement for an invitation that compels the lost to repent and place faith in Christ alone as part of the preached sermon. Additionally, if the lost are compelled to respond to Christ in repentance and faith, the gospel message declaring the person and work of Christ must precede the invitation for them to respond.

Second, the conclusion of the sermon is usually the most convenient and best opportunity to provide the consolidated, complete declaration of the gospel message. Then those who are interested to respond to the gospel message and/or those who

2. Vines and Shaddix, *Power in the Pulpit*, 218.
3. Olford and Olford, *Anointed Expository Preaching*, 172.
4. Olford and Olford, *Anointed Expository Preaching*, 172–73.
5. Adams, *Preaching with Purpose*, 76.

have questions can be addressed personally, only minutes after the appeal for them to respond, when the service has concluded. In using Paul and Barnabas as an example, Jay Adams suggests, "To invite inquirers to remain afterwards to talk further, therefore, seems quite proper" since in Acts 13:43 Paul and Barnabas spoke to many who remained after the synagogue meeting had ended and urged them to continue in the grace of God.[6]

Proclaiming the message of the gospel at the end of the sermon conclusion resolves several questionable procedures which commonly are integrated into preaching. First, the message of the gospel is preached in the sermon in a complete, condensed, clear manner as opposed to the sermon ending without the gospel message having been proclaimed. Alfred Garvie addressed this omission pointedly as he wrote: "There is an *expository preaching*, in which the scholarly interest is allowed to predominate, and the preacher seeks only to inform and instruct regarding the Bible without any practical purpose or evangelistic appeal. It is altogether doubtful whether the ambassador of Christ has any right to be content with doing this only. . . . All Christian preaching should make *patent* the *latent* Gospel of the Bible."[7]

William M. Taylor acknowledged the tendency for preachers to grow decreasingly concerned about providing the gospel message to the lost through the years of one's preaching ministry. "[Y]ou will be most apt to set yourself in the beginning of your career, to secure the conversion of sinners; while, perhaps, as you advance in your work, you may be tempted to run into the other extreme, and preach only to those who are already in the church. But in neither case will there be a 'right division' of the word of truth; and your aim ought to be, on every occasion, to give to each 'his portion in season.'"[8] Second, the needful appeal for unbelievers to respond to the preached gospel in repentance and faith is made so that those responding can make immediate inquiry about their response to the gospel and be informed promptly about baptism as a public proclamation of their faith in Christ. Third, proclaiming the message of the gospel at the end of the sermon conclusion ends the needless procedure of making one's faith in Christ public through the means of responding to an altar call rather than the biblical means of being baptized as a public attestation of repentance and faith in Christ.

Sermons need a conclusion, a conclusion that renders a verdict to every hearer of the sermon according to the needs of each hearer, whether lost or saved. In his book *Preaching with Passion,* Alex Montoya provides seven "ends of preaching." The first of the ends of preaching is, "We should strive to convert the sinner." According to Montoya, "Every sermon should have the gospel. It should end at the cross and the empty tomb. . . . Mimic the biblical preachers. Aim at forming Christ in the

6. Adams, *Preaching with Purpose,* 75.

7. Garvie, *A Guide to Preachers,* 1911, 108–09.

8. Taylor, *The Ministry of the Word,* 1876, 95.

lives of your people. Keep the end in mind, *always!*"[9] This is excellent counsel for preaching, provided by an excellent expository preacher and a consistent proclaimer of Christ, although this counsel is commonly set aside by expository preachers and non-expository preachers as well.

There has been, and still is, a long-standing disagreement about whether the substance of the sermon conclusion should consist of the proclamation of the gospel. This disagreement does not have to continue for perpetuity, but I have no doubt that it will. An either/or conviction regarding the intended recipients of a sermon conclusion is not an inescapable reality, it is just a self-imposed reality for many based upon needless and faulty presuppositions regarding sermon conclusions.

Once the erroneous presuppositions are surrendered, there is room to adopt a both/and conviction regarding the recipients of a sermon conclusion that can meet the needs of believers and unbelievers alike. The following includes three quotations that include presuppositions that can and should be dismissed so that the sermon conclusion may be the highpoint of the message for everyone who hears it, whether believer or unbeliever. I have italicized the portion of the quote in which correction and adjustment must be made in a preacher's thinking about and practice of concluding sermons. Additionally, I have underlined the portion of the quote which must be strenuously maintained in a preacher's thinking about and practice of concluding sermons.

> The question arises whether the conclusion by direct address should refer to both classes of hearers, the regenerate and unregenerate. . . . In laying down a general rule, we would say in answer to the question, that *the conclusion should be directed to but one class in the audience.*[10]

> *If the object is to edify the Christian, or to enforce a particular duty*, the conclusion must be faithfully devoted to this object. We have no right to divert the drift of the discourse at its terminus, or to cripple the final impression, by deserting the subject for the sake of addressing the sinner.[11]

> *If the conclusion is directed to both the believer and the unbeliever* it is important that we "address those first who are most favorably disposed, and therefore, we should address the converted before the unconverted.[12]

The correction for the italicized portion of the first quotation is that the conclusion "must be directed," rather than "*should be directed.*" It is uncalled for to cast the intent of a sermon conclusion to a "should be" proposition rather than a "must be" reality.

---

9. Montoya, *Preaching with Passion*, 63–64.

10. Shedd, *Homiletics and Pastoral Theology*, 1876, 209–10.

11. Etter, *The Preacher and His Sermon*, 1885, 383.

12. Hoppin, *Homiletics*, 1883, 435.

The quotation requires an additional refinement to assert that the conclusion is intended to appeal "to both," rather than "to but one" class in the audience. This corrects the most artificial presupposition about preaching a sermon conclusion, that is, some people matter, and they are being preached to while others do not matter, and they are not being preached to.

Those for whom the sermon conclusion is not directed, they may overhear what is being said to the people who matter, but an overhearing is all they will get because they don't matter! There will be no word intended for them! They have great need for a most significant message, but they will not get it! The established practices for concluding a sermon do not allow them to be addressed! Though their souls are in peril of eternal torment in hell, it is better that they go to hell than it is to proclaim to them in the sermon conclusion the message that might transform them for time and eternity! This depicts that the one group that does not matter is the unbelievers.

If, however, the one group that does not matter is believers, the conclusion is reserved for proclaiming the gospel to the unbeliever while believers are left to overhear the gospel directed to the unsaved and they, as believers, are given no message that will help them to achieve the purpose of the sermon in their lives. Intentionally excluding either believers or unbelievers in the conclusion of a sermon lacks in the arenas of ethics, calling, responsibility, logic, and the provision of profitability for a group of people that need to be addressed by the Word of God.

The error of the second quotation is found in its making conditional that which is a given regarding a sermon conclusion, to edify the believer, to enforce a particular duty by instructing them and exhorting them to comply with Scripture-based closing appeals so that they may achieve the purpose of the sermon in their lives. The quotation begins, "*If* the object is to . . ." which should be, "Since the object is to . . ." or "Because the object is to . . ." so that the purpose of a conclusion does not become conditional but remains a given. It is true that the conclusion must be devoted, not just *directed*, but devoted to the believers to conclude the sermon for them. The sermon has been devoted to their edification, and the conclusion simply completes this devoted intention on their behalf. And it is true that to divert or drift away from the discourse in the conclusion would be counterproductive, and the deserting of the substance of the conclusion to address the unbeliever should never be done.

However, proclaiming the message of the gospel to the unbeliever in a sermon conclusion does not need to interrupt the message being completed to believers. Furthermore, the importance of the lostness of the unbelievers, as vital as this is, does not warrant an interruption of the message devoted to believers. The importance of the lostness of the unbeliever is such that it requires its own focus, so that the state of the unbeliever can be focused upon uninterruptedly and the gospel can be proclaimed in its fulness and the unbeliever can be exhorted to repentance and faith in response to the message devoted to them and their great need of salvation.

The error of the third quotation again is found in the conditional "If" rather than "Since" or "Because." "<u>Since the conclusion is directed to both the believer and the unbeliever it is important that we should address the converted before the unconverted</u>." It just makes sense to finish the work in the conclusion that began with the introduction and continued throughout the body of the sermon, expounding the Word of God to the people of God for their edification. Having accomplished this completely, without suffering any interruption, then the focus can be given to the unbelievers by preaching to them the sermon that they need to hear, the message of the gospel, which will terminate the sermon.

In summary, the recovery of appealing to the unconverted in the conclusion, as was formerly done in preaching still has merit, especially if offered with the affection that is consistent with the gospel of grace. James Hoppin makes a case for this when he wrote, "The old method of direct appeal to the impenitent, at the close of the sermon, might . . . be deeply effective."[13] He continues, "As a suggestion in closing a sermon, let the preacher be *kind* in his words and manner, even to the wickedest and worst. In the moment of the most burning rebuke and denunciation, let the affectionateness of the gospel glow."[14] The sermon conclusion does not have to be an either/or proposition, that is, should it be directed to believers or unbelievers? It can and should be directed to both.

The sermon conclusion should be devoted to believers, dealing with them to complete the message to them without interruption. Afterwards, uninterrupted attention can be directed to the unbelievers by fully proclaiming to them the person and work of Jesus Christ and appealing to them to respond to the gospel of grace in repentance and faith.

A further inducement to including the gospel message in the conclusion of a sermon is supplied by John Stott's insistence for, and sequence of, proclamation then appeal in preaching. Stott is insistent that a true herald of God must always couple together proclamation and appeal. Therefore, one of two errors could be made by a preacher which would prohibit him from being a true herald of God, from doing other than true biblical preaching. According to Stott:

> First, we must never issue an appeal without first making the proclamation. . . . Evangelistic preaching has too often consisted of a prolonged appeal for decision when the congregation has been given no substance upon which the decision is to be made. But the gospel is not fundamentally an invitation to men to do anything. It is a declaration of what God has done in Christ on the cross for their salvation. The invitation cannot properly be given before the declaration has been made. Men must grasp the truth before they are asked to respond to it.[15]

13. Hoppin, *Homiletics*, 1883, 441–42.

14. Hoppin, *Homiletics*, 1883, 443.

15. Stott, *The Preacher's Portrait*, 55.

Second, Stott asserts, "we must never make the proclamation without then issuing an appeal.

. . . We are to find room for both proclamation and appeal in our preaching if we would be true heralds of the King. . . . I am simply saying that proclamation without appeal is not Biblical preaching. It is not enough to teach the gospel; we must urge men to embrace it."[16] Proclamation then appeal. Both are imperative but neither should be supplied in absence of the other.

More than arguing that the message of the gospel be proclaimed in preaching, particularly at the end of the sermon conclusion, the significance of this second message that ends the sermon must not be depreciated. "One of the most important things we do when we stand to preach is *herald the good news of Jesus Christ*."[17] Christ is to be made known, as well as the good news that salvation is possible because of what he has done.

Who he is, according to Scripture, and what he has done, as revealed in Scripture, must be made known to those who do not know him and are not in possession of the salvation that he alone brings to those who repent of their sin and trust in the finished work he has accomplished. "Just as Christian preaching should edify believers in Christ, it also ought to call those who do not yet believe to do just that. We should preach to evangelize."[18] The error of the lost must be warned against as well as imploring the lost to seize the solution to the error of their way. Omitting these crucial responsibilities in one's preaching is foolish.

Mark Dever and Greg Gilbert are insistent that evangelistic expository preaching should be the norm and they provide insight regarding the rationale for such:

> Your sermons should never be forty-five-minute morality lessons or best practices for living a better life. They should drive forward to the good news that King Jesus saves sinners through His life, death, and resurrection from the grave. In fact, we think that in every sermon you preach, you should include at some point a clear and concise presentation of the gospel. Tell people how they may be saved![19]
>
> The main message we need to apply every time we preach is the gospel. Some people do not yet know the good news of Jesus Christ. . . . They need to be informed of the gospel. They need to be told. . . . Such people need to be urged to believe the truth of the good news of Christ. And, too, people may have heard and understood but may be slow to repent of their sins. They may not even doubt the truth of what you're saying; they may simply be slow to repent

---

16. Stott, *The Preacher's Portrait*, 57.

17. Dever and Gilbert, *Preach*, 57.

18. Dever and Gilbert, *Preach*, 57.

19. Dever and Gilbert, *Preach*, 96.

of their sins and to turn to Christ. For such hearers the most powerful application you can make is to exhort them to hate their sins and flee to Christ.[20]

People who are lost need a preacher who, having experienced the conversion they are in need of, will not overlook their need, will not disrespect them by not addressing their need, but will care enough for them to inform them of what they need to know and do.

Ramesh Richard provides a faithful reminder as he writes, "converting sinners is God's role. Communicating the gospel is yours."[21] This is what preaching must do, proclaim the gospel, in the context of expository preaching or in the context of preaching that is other than expository! Why should there be any reticence about heralding the good news of salvation in a preaching context? But for whatever reasons, reticence exists.

Perhaps some reticence can be curtailed by supplying what Ramesh Richard calls a postscript to an expository sermon. Richard says, "We can add a postscript, and evangelistic appendix, to almost any sermon, but that doesn't make the sermon evangelistic. Such a sermon includes an evangelistic ending—and I encourage pastors to seek creative and customary ways to conclude sermons with an evangelistic twist."[22] Richard's assertion about the addition of an evangelistic postscript fits my contention that evangelistic endings are authoritative and effective when they are supplied "not as afterthoughts but as postscripts. In fact," contends Richard, "you'll preach a mini-evangelistic sermon at the end of a regular sermon."[23]

An expository sermon should include evangelistic preaching. At any point in the sermon, when the focus of the content being declared focuses upon the person and work of Jesus Christ so that those outside of Christ can know who he is and what he has done so that sinners can be saved from their sins, that portion of the sermon is evangelistic. Evangelistic preaching, wherever it occurs in a sermon, becomes an exposition of the person and work of Jesus Christ, as William M. Taylor makes clear:

> To call upon men constantly to "come to Christ" or to "believe in the Lord Jesus Christ" without at the same time telling them who Jesus is, and what it is to come to him, and believe on him, is the merest mockery. . . . If, therefore, we would be effective preachers, we must be ready to give an answer to him that asks us, "Who is Jesus, that I may believe on Him? and what was there in his dying that has any relation to me?" . . . It is not believing on Christ as I have shaped him for myself, rather believing on the Christ that is set before me in the gospel, that saves me; and so it is of immense consequence that I should have a right view both of his person and work.[24]

---

20. Dever and Gilbert, *Preach*, 115.

21. Richard, *Preparing Evangelistic Sermons*, 11.

22. Richard, *Preparing Evangelistic Sermons*, 76.

23. Richard, *Preparing Evangelistic Sermons*, 115.

24. Taylor, *The Ministry of the Word*, 1876, 83–85.

The indistinct manner of attempting to address the lost person's need of salvation is problematic in the vagueness of proclaiming Christ. "Men have been pled with to 'accept Christ' without being told what that means." Furthermore, what it is made to mean "is scarcely what the New Testament means by being 'found in Christ.'"[25] The inclusion of such vagaries in refence to Christ is not evangelistic preaching.

Evangelistic preaching requires a clear declaration of the person and work of Christ as a starting point, but it must move on to call the lost to respond to the message of the gospel. In other words, a sermon which has become evangelistic needs to continue in evangelistic completion which requires the preacher "to preach persuasively for an immediate verdict." Unbelievers should be compelled either "to receive or to reject Christ at the end of every message we preach."[26] Steve Gains is as specific as he is emphatic when he states, "People should be allowed to decide about Christ at the moment the gospel is presented."[27] The Apostle Paul could not have been clearer in his declaration that it is by the foolishness of preaching that unbelievers are saved. Foolish preaching, that is, preaching that saves, therefore, contains the gospel, a gospel that is responded to. It is the hearers' responsibility to respond to the gospel and it is the preacher's responsibility to provide the gospel and to provide the appeal to the unbeliever to respond in repentance and faith.

In 2 Corinthians 4:5 the Apostle Paul says of his preaching, "For we preach not ourselves, but Christ Jesus as Lord." The Lordship of Jesus Christ is the basis for the application of every exposition of Scripture. Preaching Jesus Christ as Lord, the name given him because of his humility to go to the cross, Philippians 2:5–11, must never be unsure. Yet, how can he be preached as Lord without being preached as Savior? There are preachers with whom making an appeal to unbelievers in the conclusion "is never wanting." It is, indeed, unavoidable, and . . . it has place in all sermons." The gospel separates the hearers into two groups "of which conversion is the separating line."[28] It is by responding to the gospel that the unconverted are converted, and yet, this requires a gospel that is proclaimed.

The indignity of preaching which fails to proclaim Christ is borne out well by Cotton Mather's words: "I beseech you, let not the true bread of life be forgotten, but exhibit as much as you can of a glorious Christ to them." How reprehensible it is for men to "preach as if they were ashamed of making the glories of Jesus" part of their sermons "and so rarely introduce Him, as if it were an indecent stoop to speak of Him!" . . . The Holy Spirit of God forever aims at nothing more, than what our Savior has declared

25. Coffin, *What to Preach*, 1926, 161.

26. Fasol [et. al] *Preaching Evangelistically*, in Steve Gaines's chapter "The Setting of the Evangelistic Sermon," 15.

27. Fasol [et. al] *Preaching Evangelistically*, in Steve Gaines's chapter "Preparing the Evangelistic Sermon," 58.

28. Vinet, *Homiletics*, 1854, 325.

in that word, "He will glorify Me." The "Holy Spirit withdraws from the ministry, which has in it little concern to glorify Him, and it is therefore an unsuccessful ministry."[29]

Perhaps, Mather's most helpful insight is found in his encouragement, "Be a star to lead men unto their Savior, and stop not till you see them there. . . . Set yourself above all things, to glorify the Christ of God . . . that He may be exalted, and be extolled, and be very high."[30] The failure to proclaim the glories of Christ's person and work, and the failure to implore lost people to receive that which they desperately need must be viewed as a profound error in preaching. Ending a sermon by declaring the gospel and appealing to unbelievers to respond in repentance and faith in Christ glorifies him, ministers to the lost at the point of their need and completes that which a preacher is responsible to do.

NOTHING PRELIMINARY TO REPENTANCE

In examining sermons in the New Testament, one can discern the cause, the intent, and the result of the sermons that were preached. No sermon in the New Testament was proclaimed simply to supply the meaning of a biblical passage, though an understanding of a biblical referent(s) was always provided. But more than this, there was always something the hearer(s) would be expected to do having had the truth declared to them. In other words, the sermons were preached to facilitate change in behalf of the recipients of biblical truth. And so it is today.

Preaching is to change the lives of those who hear it, and the preacher is to appeal to his hearers to make such change as is required by Scripture. "It is not enough to stir emotion and instruct our people; we must also call them to action. . . . Our sermons are to *do* something. They are to make a difference in our listeners. They are to constitute a call to become different persons from what we are."[31] Change is to result in the lives of all who hear Scripture proclaimed to them, and this is true of believers and unbelievers. Believers are to respond as required by the truth of the Scripture in some specific way that will impact their *sanctification* as they *more completely align* their lives to the revealed Word of God. Unbelievers are to respond in repentance and faith to the Christ of Scripture to secure their *salvation* as they *initially align* their lives to the revealed Word of God. However, no sermon is to be preached with an intended result that all will leave as they arrived.

William M. Taylor makes an invaluable argument for the inclusion of the gospel message in a pastor's weekly preaching ministry. He writes:

> The truth is, that the Gospel is related to everything which affects the happiness and the holiness of men; and its minister not only may, but ought to

29. Mather, *Student and Preacher*, 1789, 180–81.
30. Mather, *Student and Preacher*, 1789, 183.
31. McEachern, *Proclaim the Gospel*, 99.

show its relations to these things in his discourses. Only let him see to it that . . . he uses the cross as his lever, and then while his discourses are helpful to believers, they will at the same time be the means of awakening and converting sinners. There is a way of getting at the hearts and consciences of the unconverted, even when we are furnishing guidance and encouragement to the true Christian; and on the other hand, we may deal with sinners in such a way as shall also stimulate and quicken saints. Indeed, if we care to study true wisdom here, we shall aim at having in every sermon a word for every hearer.[32]

Though Taylor's insights here are valuable and true, they fall short of what must be done in reference to unbelievers. Providing a word for unbelievers that may truly get to their hearts and consciences while providing guidance to believers is less than what must be done for the lost person. It is the gospel message of Jesus Christ that the lost person must hear and respond to. Therefore, within the sermon, at some point there should be, an unfragmented, full and complete disclosure of the person and work of Jesus Christ along with a demand for the biblically mandated response of repentance toward God and faith in Jesus Christ for salvation.

But, a biblically mandated response? Is repentance necessary for the lost person to be saved, to be born again, to become a true follower of Jesus Christ? Unfortunately, there is not a complete, emphatic, affirmative consensus on this point. Without going into the extensive debate over this issue, I believe, along with many, that repentance is absolutely necessary. A handful references to this effect might be serviceable. H. C. Brown states it plainly. "The gospel calls for repentance. The gospel is good news in that men may repent and be saved."[33] Leighton Ford cites three imperatives as summarizing Christ's appeal to lost men: Repent; Believe the Gospel; Follow me.[34] In reference to repentance he writes, "To repent not only means that I acknowledge I have sinned, not only that I am sorry about it, but that I change my mind about sin, and about God, and about myself—I am ready for God to change my life, and to leave my sin."[35] As in the preaching of the Apostle Paul, people should be called upon to repent of their sins and believe in Jesus Christ. R. Alan Streett's comments are insightful regarding the place repentance had in Paul's preaching and for the role repentance must have in preaching for the salvation of unbelievers. According to Streett:

> Repentance he (Paul) described as being "toward God." Since man's sin is basically an act of rebellion against the divine Sovereign of the universe, he is called upon to show repentance toward Him. Faith, on the other hand, is specifically directed toward God's only begotten Son. It is on the basis of Christ's death and resurrection that God is able to extend mercy and forgiveness to sinful man. Only when the sinner recognizes this and trusts Christ alone to

32. Taylor, *The Ministry of the Word*, 1876, 99.

33. Brown Jr., *A Quest for Reformation in Preaching*, 141.

34. Ford, *The Christian Persuader*, 130.

35. Ford, *The Christian Persuader*, 131.

save him can he be reconciled to his heavenly Father. Repentance toward God and faith in the Lord Jesus Christ are the two steps every person must take to be saved. For this reason, every invitation should call upon hearers to take these required steps.[36]

True faith includes repentance. That the terms repentance and faith are used interchangeably at times can be clearly seen by comparing John 3:16 with 2 Peter 3:9. John indicates that "whosoever believeth in him should not perish." Peter, on the other hand, makes repentance the requirement for not perishing: "the Lord is not . . . willing that any should perish, but that all should come to repentance." Therefore, to believe in Christ carries with it the idea of repentance, and the call to repentance implies a turning in faith to Christ. Repentance and faith are two sides of the same coin. This reciprocal relationship is seen in 1 Thessalonians 1:9 where Paul reminds his readers, "ye turned to God from idols." Before one can turn to God (faith), he must first turn from idols (repentance). Repentance and faith are two aspects of the same action. Together they form the process known as conversion.[37]

Austin Phelps is clear in representing repentance as the necessary, initial, and indivisible response of the unbeliever who is converted to Christ.

The fact is a very significant one that impenitent men are never exhorted in Scripture to anything preliminary to repentance. But one thing is the center of all biblical appeals to the ungodly; that is repentance and faith,—a complex yet a single act. Nothing short of this is deemed worthy of mention by inspired preachers to the unconverted. . . . The one thing is the only thing on which the attention of the awakened conscience is riveted in biblical persuasion of the impenitent. . . . An impenitent soul is at a dead-lock until impenitence ceases.[38]

John Piper identifies the essential evil of sin that mandated from God the extreme measure of his only begotten Son's death as the payment price so that a sinner can be released from their debt of sin. Piper writes:

It horribly skews the meaning of the cross when contemporary prophets of self-esteem say that the cross is a witness to my infinite worth, since God was willing to pay such a high price to get me. The biblical perspective is that the cross is a witness to the infinite worth of God's glory, and a witness to the immensity of the sin of my pride. What should shock us is that we have brought such contempt upon the worth of God that the very death of his Son is required to indicate that worth. The cross stands in witness to the infinite worth of God and the infinite outrage of sin.[39]

36. Streett, *The Effective Invitation*, 40.

37. Streett, *The Effective Invitation*, 46–47.

38. Phelps, *The Theory of Preaching*, 1882, 543–44.

39. Piper, *The Supremacy of God in Preaching*, 32.

The outrage of sin warrants, not the continuance in, but a repentance from sin. The assertions above affirm the crucial matter of repentance.

However, not only is repentance necessary but it is important to understand that for the lost person to be saved there is nothing that is preliminary to repentance. For the unbeliever, the reality of their conversion begins with repentance, if it indeed occurs. As C. H. Dodd put it, "The *kerygma* always closes with an appeal for repentance, the offer of forgiveness and of the Holy Spirit."[40]

Nothing precedes repentance, that is, there is nothing prior to repentance that a lost person needs to do for conversion. Of course, repentance is a response to the truth that is clearly understood: all unbelievers are separated from a Holy God because of their sin. The removal of the veil that blinds unbelievers of the glory of Christ exposes the sinfulness of the sinner leading to the desperate condition of desiring forgiveness of sin by the One who died and rose again to provide a victory over death and sin for those who seek it. John Angell James establishes the significance of repentance and of the knowledge of sin that produces it.

> Repentance toward God is no less included in the apostolic ministry, than faith in our Lord Jesus Christ; and a sinner cannot repent of his transgressions against the law, which he has violated, if he know it not: for "sin is the transgression of the law;" and "by the law is the knowledge of sin." No man can know sin without knowing the law: and herein appears to me to be one of the prevailing defects of modern preaching: I mean the neglect of holding up this perfect mirror, in which the sinner shall see reflected his own moral image. . . . (M)en will care little about pardon, until they are convinced of sin. . . . Law without the gospel will harden, as the gospel without the law will only lead to carelessness and presumption: it is the union of both that will possess the sinner with loathing of himself, and love to God.[41]

Though strategic in the declaration of Jesus Christ, the Lord and Savior of sinners from sin, the knowledge of the unbelievers' sinfulness before a Holy God is an element of the gospel proclamation that is proclaimed more fully than the declaration of the sinner's need to repent and trust in Christ alone for their salvation. My argument is not that the knowledge of sin is over emphasized, because it is not. My argument is that the solution to the problem of man's sinfulness, repentance and trust in the finished work accomplished by Jesus Christ, is not fully declared.

> It is Jesus whom we solemnly preach for he is the message—a message that is momentous in the highest degree! Belief in him is life! Otherwise, there is only death! Men are sinful! They are to be blamed for it, and to be shown their sin! And they are to be taught, to be shown the way of forgiveness and life, that they may receive it and walk in it. We cannot, indeed, too eagerly or too frequently

40. Dodd, *The Apostolic Preaching*, 23.

41. James, *An Earnest Ministry*, 1847, 83–85.

cry, "Come to Jesus." But to make this call intelligent and emphatic, we must assign scriptural reasons. We must not scruple to say, "Come! For you have sinned. You are guilty. If you do not, you will die; for the wages of sin is death."[42]

The declaration for sinful men to seek the solution for their sin problem is that which is communicated commonly when the gospel is intended to be proclaimed. And, certainly, the name of Jesus will be used as the One in whom the lost person's sin problem may be remedied.

But much knowledge about who Jesus is and what he has done, as revealed in Scripture, is presupposed by preachers as that which is well understood by lost people. It is as though lost people hold a biblically correct Christology and soteriology, therefore, all they need to do is to do what they have yet to do, "believe in Jesus." Furthermore, unless they are an acknowledged atheist, the unconverted may be prone to think that they don't even need to believe in Jesus since there has never been a time when they did not believe in him. But how Jesus Christ, alone, can save sinners is understood with as much perception as the understanding that Jesus is responsible for salvation like he is responsible for Christmas and Easter.

As far as many lost people understand, the Jesus of their speculation saves lost people, however he does so. Can lost people be saved by the Jesus of their imagination, or are they saved by Jesus as he is revealed in Scripture? Are they to trust in Christ, alone, on the basis of their lack of understanding of what he did, or are they to trust in Christ, alone, on the basis of their faith in what he did as revealed in Scripture? Their lack of understanding of the person and work of Jesus Christ, as revealed in Scripture, is what must be declared to them so that they might understand and respond in faith to him and to the completed work which he, alone, could do and has done.

So, what does the lost person need to understand about Jesus Christ, who he is and what he did so that an unbeliever can trust in him for salvation, all according to that which is revealed in the Bible? In other words, what needs to be declared about Jesus Christ so that a lost person may trust in the Christ of Scripture rather than the Jesus of their imagination or the Christ of their misinformation?

There are six components of Christ's person and four components of his work that are the irreducible, essential core of understanding about Christ so that one will not hold a fictitious or cultic belief about him. Before the person and work of Christ is detailed, there are six basic certainties, worthy of mention, that must be understood as we declare these biblical, propositional truths about Christ. Each of these six basic certainties have been referenced various times in the preceding chapters of this book. The purpose in briefly reintroducing them again is to provide a context and rationale for the declaration of the person and work of Jesus Christ in the sermon conclusion for the prospective salvation of lost people who have heard the sermon.

---

42. Hall, *God's Word Through Preaching*, 1875, 60–61.

20

Proclaiming Christ in a Sermon Conclusion: Part 3

SIX BASIC CERTAINTIES IN THE PREACHER'S CONVICTIONS

Though there may be more than what I am about to offer, there are six basic certainties that are sufficient to cause one to be faithful in proclaiming the gospel in the preaching services of the church, even as the edification of believers is the reason for the preaching service. In my mind and heart, the following six basic certainties serve not only as convictional realities but will be the basis of my resolve to proclaim the gospel of Jesus Christ to those who attend my preaching. I believe that these six certainties may work to bring resolve to others to proclaim the gospel to unbelievers in a context of a preaching service intended to expound a text of Scripture for the edification of believers.

First: The proclamation of Jesus Christ as the only way by which sinful humanity can have access to God is the unparalleled declaration in any sermon.

Humanity's greatest problem is the issue of sin in their lives. The knowledge of how a sinner can be delivered from its bondage for time and delivered of its penalty for eternity is a declaration that must not be omitted from a preached sermon. The declaration of Christ's person and work to an unbeliever is akin to introducing unbelievers to the Lord, introducing one in great need to One whom can provide great help to the one in need. As in the case where a mutual friend seeks to have two friends who do not know each other become friends, he is zealous to introduce them to one another. And so, he does, but this is all he can do. He cannot make the introduction become a friendship. Once the introduction has taken place a friendship may become a reality, or it may not. The mutual friend can be responsible for the introduction, but

429

he cannot be responsible for what becomes of the introduction. Because the mutual friend seeks to make the introduction, not out of social courtesy but out of vital necessity, he will not only do so but do so with enthusiasm and thoroughness. And so it is as a preacher introduces Jesus Christ to unbelievers. Phillips Brooks captured this reality in preaching the gospel to unbelievers with these words:

> The salvation of men's souls from sin, the renewing and perfecting of their characters, is the great end of all. But that is done by Christ. To bring them, then, to Christ, that he may do it, to make Christ plain to them, that they may find Him, this is the preacher's work. But I cannot do my duty in making Christ plain unless I tell them of Him. . . . I must keep nothing back. All that has come to me about Him from his Word, all that has grown clear to me about His nature . . . becomes part of the message that I must tell those men whom He has sent me to call home to Himself.[1]

A preacher must be committed to fulfill his responsibility in preaching to proclaim Jesus Christ to unbelievers so that they may be saved from their sins but in doing so he must have an unshakeable confidence that God will work in the lives of the hearers as God wills to do so.

C. H. Spurgeon had great confidence in the fact that God works through his Word to bring the elect to a saving knowledge of Christ. "I preach with a living certainty, knowing the God has a people whom Christ is bound to bring home, and bring them home He will. While He will see the distress of His soul, His Father will take delight in every one of them. If you get a clear view of that, it will give you backbone and make you strong."[2] A preacher should desire to see sinners introduced to Christ with an introduction, a declaration of the gospel, that is not only clear but one that rightly represents the eternal worthiness of the Lord. This declaration should be made with the greatest confidence that God will accomplish the work he has designed to do in the preaching of his Word. In so doing, a preacher fulfills his responsibility and satisfies that which he, himself, desires to do.

Second: The proclamation of Jesus Christ as the only way by which sinful humanity can have access to a holy God is so important that its declaration demands a verdict from unbelievers.

As with any offering, the offering of the gift of life by Jesus Christ, is one that is either accepted or something that is other-than-accepted. Regardless of how the other-than-accepted reality is viewed, whether as rejection, postponement, further consideration, etc., it is other than the only verdict hoped for. Though it is wrong to attempt to force a positive verdict, it is not wrong to make a verdict a non-option. The greatness of the offering of eternal life, if refused, must register on the heart of one who would reject it. If this is the reality of what is happening there should be the cognizant

---

1. Brooks, *The Joy of Preaching*, 103.
2. Spurgeon, *Holy Spirit Power*, 154–55.

affect for its occurrence. In his preaching, John the Baptist "pinned them down with a definite choice. Either they would signify their repentance by going under the waters of Jordan . . . or they would not."[3] The offering of salvation by grace alone, through faith alone, in Christ alone is an offering that demands a verdict from unbelievers.

Salvation, as offered in Jesus Christ, is a finished work and a free gift. But an unbeliever's receptivity of that which is offered by Christ involves a necessary response since salvation is appropriated personally. Thus, the proclamation of the gospel includes a personal "summons of repentance" and trust in Jesus Christ.[4] "The gospel is the royal announcement," writes Trevin Wax, "that . . . calls for a response: repentance (mourning over and turning from our sin, trading our agendas for the kingdom agenda of Jesus Christ) and faith (trusting in Christ alone for salvation)."[5] A preacher must not feel free to withhold the declaration of Christ to unbelievers and he must not feel free to exempt unbelievers from a verdict of response to the offering of Christ. Just the opposite is true. Preachers, with great joy, should anticipate the declaration of the eternally glorious provision of salvation made available through Jesus Christ.

Spurgeon is convincing as he makes the case for why the joyous glorification of Christ must be proclaimed. He writes: "The Holy Spirit . . . comes to glorify Christ. If we want to be in accord with Him, we must minister in a manner that will glorify Christ. If it is not distinctly my aim to glorify Christ, I am not in accord with the aim of the Holy Spirit, and I cannot expect His help. We would not be pulling the same way. Therefore, I will have nothing of which I cannot say that it is said simply, sincerely, and only that I may glorify Christ."[6] Ending a sermon that glorifies Christ through the proclamation of who he is and what he has done so that sinners may be saved from their sins is an unbeatable way to end any sermon! What believer could truly make the case, or should even attempt to do so, that a glorious retelling of the good news of the gospel of Jesus Christ is an inadequate way, or a less than the best way, to end a sermon?

Third: Though a changed will is the ultimate target in preaching, and may become the outcome of a preached sermon, it is not in the power of the preacher to change the will of a hearer.

A preacher may affect a hearer's mind, conscience, and emotions/affections with the content that is preached, but the Holy Spirit alone is responsible to engage the will of the hearer. "Preaching doesn't consummate in belief unless the Holy Spirit draws people, awakens the hearers' hearts, and influences their will to believe."[7] This does not mean that the preacher should not do all he can do in the process of preaching to affect the wills of his hearers. As this is understood, the instruction of R. Allen Street is

3. Read, *Sent from God*, 77–78.

4. Garvie, *A Guide to Preachers*, 1911, 166.

5. Wax, *Gospel-Centered Teaching*, 39.

6. Spurgeon, *Holy Spirit Power*, 161.

7. Richard, *Preparing Evangelistic Sermons*, 43.

appropriate and in keeping with a preacher's sincere intentions. Street writes: "A man can be moved to action if his mind can be convinced the action is reasonable, and if his heart can be convinced that the action is necessary. You must, therefore, bring your hearer to the point where he says, 'I can be saved (mind). I must be saved (emotions). I will be saved (will).'"[8] The gospel must be declared and in its declaration a preacher must clarify by explanation the scriptural, propositional truths that compose the gospel. But what he must not attempt to do is to proclaim a simple gospel. "The clamor for a *simple* Gospel is a stupid and lazy demand."[9] Simplicity has nothing to do with the gospel in its content or presentation.

The gospel is far too complicated for geniuses to comprehend, unaided by the Holy Spirit. Without the Holy Spirit removing the veil that blinds the minds of unbelievers, the message of the gospel is incomprehensible. Regardless of intellectual acuity, it makes no sense, or to use the expression of the Apostle Paul, it is foolishness. The necessity for the understanding and reception of the gospel is the supernatural work of regeneration, the work of God removing the spiritual blindness, the condition suffered by every lost individual. God does this and does this easily, without any help of man to try to make it understandable in the effort of simplifying the gospel. The message of the gospel is the power of God for salvation. It does not need to be manipulated by man. Without the regenerating work of God no one can, no one will, no one ever has understood the gospel and responded to it in repentance and faith.

With God's necessary work of regeneration removing the veil from the eyes of a lost person hearing the gospel, not the simple gospel or a partial gospel, the gospel is comprehended and responded to in repentance and faith. The intention behind such clamor for a simple gospel is for a partial gospel. How partial the partial gospel is will depend upon the subjective standard of each partial gospel advocate. This attempt to partialize the gospel stems from the tenant(s) of the gospel message that the partial gospel advocate rejects, finding it/them totally disagreeable and will not allow it/them to be part of the gospel proclaimed by him. Such folly warrants the prohibition of Lloyd M. Perry and John R. Strubhar when they wrote, "As ministers of the gospel, we dare not depend on natural means to produce supernatural results."[10] The Holy Spirit of God's convicting the world of sin, righteousness, and judgment as the Father draws those who come to the Son in response to the proclamation of the gospel is the supernatural work which preachers must rely upon for the supernatural result of salvation to occur.

Complete reliance upon the Holy Spirit to do the work only he can do in the hearts of unbelievers is the preacher's responsibility, one which supplies the faithful preacher benefits for having fulfilled his responsibility. The testimony of evangelist Leighton Ford affirms this as follows:

8. Streett, *The Effective Invitation*, 159.
9. Garvie, *The Preachers of the Church*, 1926, 210.
10. Perry and Strubhar, *Evangelistic Preaching*, 18.

If I may add a personal word, I have discovered that faith in God's sovereign grace and salvation has helped me in two basic attitudes toward my evangelistic work. For one thing, it has kept me from losing heart, from pessimism. Only the sovereignty of God is sufficient ground for preaching to a verdict. Otherwise, evangelism is a hopeless task. . . . But this confidence in God also guards us from self-dependence. . . . There is a great danger in the success status psychology of our day. The pressure to produce results . . . leads to trusting in techniques and manipulation, and brings the danger of leading people into premature, abortive decisions before they have really faced up to the meaning of the Gospel and the demands of the Christian life. The last state of this person is often worse than the first. God holds me responsible for "faithful evangelism," not for success. Therefore, I may plead, but never coerce.[11]

The Holy Spirit removes the veil from unbelievers and draws them to Christ according to the will of the Father. Our role, as it has been established by God, is to proclaim the gospel in clarity and completeness.

Fourth: Though a changed will is the ultimate target in preaching, and may become the outcome of a preached sermon, the penultimate targets of the mind, conscience, and emotions/affections are neither rendered insignificant nor are they to become the ultimate targets in preaching.

The mind, conscience, and emotions/affections are the pathways to the will. The will cannot be changed without these penultimate pathways being affected beforehand. Therefore, it is necessary to seek to affect these pathways with the content of a sermon. However, it is of greater necessity neither to seek to affect these pathways as an end in themselves, nor to shy away from affecting these pathways in the effort to impact the will of the hearers. Evangelist Billy Sunday had the right mindset in his statement that, "They tell me I'm rubbing the cat's fur in the wrong direction. If I'm rubbing the cat's fur in the wrong direction, let the cat turn around."[12] Sunday sought to win the lost to Christ. He was not reticent to disturb unbelievers in their lostness in the hope that they may be won to Christ. He was reticent to seek to win them to Christ without their suffering any disturbance for their lostness.

Of special concern is the emotion of fear being introduced in the hearts of the hearers. There are people who believe that it is an inappropriate response of repentance and faith if it is accompanied by fear. But further reflection would render this false. One reference is sufficient to do the job. The writer of the book of Hebrews recorded in Hebrews 11:7, "By faith Noah, being warned by God about things not yet seen, in reverence[13] (fear) prepared an ark for the salvation of his household, by

11. Ford, *The Christian Persuader*, 121–22.

12. Morriss, *The Sound of Boldness*, 103.

13. The word translated "fear" or "reverence" is neither phobos nor deilia, but eulabeia. Eulabeia is found in Heb. 5:7 as the "godly fear" or "peity" of Christ, from which his prayers and supplications arose and were heard by the Father. In Heb. 12:28 "reverence (eulabeia) and awe" constitute the manner with which of our service to God is acceptable to him. Eulabeia, "godly fear, marks that careful

which he condemned the world, and became an heir of the righteousness which is according to faith." Faith responding to the Word of God is no less faith even as it is accompanied by fear. Therefore, a fear filled response in faith to the Word of God "is always appropriate!"[14] The emotions/affections, including fear, are not to be shied away from but must be viewed as a crucial component of preaching. "Human nature in all its prevailing features, tastes, necessities, and enjoyments, is the same in the king and in the peasant; in the savage and the sage. All men are susceptible of emotion, as well as capable of reasoning; and all men love to feel, as well as to think. . . . A sermon, however intellectual it may be, which has nothing that impacts the affections, and causes the hearers to feel, is sure to be disappointing and dissatisfying to them."[15] Just because the emotions/affections of the hearers are impacted does not mean they will be changed to align with the truth of Scripture, but their wills will not be changed if their emotions/affections have not been impacted in the preaching of the Word.

As unbelievers are impacted by the Word of God the effect will always begin with the sinfulness of the unbeliever. Jesus told his disciples that the promised Holy Spirit would "convict the world of sin, righteousness, and judgment" (John 16:8). The unbeliever will only find Christ's sacrifice as glorious if they recognize their sinfulness before a righteous God who will judge them for their sin. That the proclamation of an unbeliever's sinfulness will be recompensed by eternal torment is not fearmongering but the necessary reality which must be understood with conviction if an unbeliever desires the good news of salvation in Christ. The person and work of Jesus Christ will not be glorious to unbelievers who do not suffer the painful conviction of their sin before a Holy God. In fact, this glorious declaration will only be viewed as irrelevant to them. The person and work of Jesus Christ is a glorious message, a message which must be introduced by the declaration of the sinfulness of all unbelievers. Spurgeon is, again, helpful as he revealed his pattern of proclaiming Christ when he wrote:

> I want to make a man feel his sins before I dare tell him anything about Christ. I want to probe into his soul and make him feel that he is lost before I tell him anything about the purchased blessing.[16]

> It is our duty to preach Jesus Christ to even self-righteous sinners, but it is certain that they will never accept Jesus Christ while they hold themselves in high esteem. Only the sick will welcome the physician. It is the work of the

---

and watchful reverence which pays regard to every circumstance in that which it has to deal," Fritz Rienecker and Cleon Rogers, *Linguistic Key to the New Testament*, 679. W. E. Vine, in his *An Expository Dictionary of New Testament Words* renders eulabeia as "godly fear," 85. How unreasonable it is to think that unbelievers, convicted by the Spirit of God because of their sinfulness before a Holy God, could respond in faith to the gospel yet do so from a personal state that is free from fear!

14. Morriss, *The Sound of Boldness*, 102.

15. James, *An Earnest Ministry*, 1847, 79–80.

16. Spurgeon, *Holy Spirit Power*, 23.

Spirit of God to convince men of sin, and until they are convinced of sin, they will never be led to seek the righteousness that God gives by Jesus Christ.[17]

A preacher will be negligent if he fails to present Jesus Christ other than how he is revealed in Scripture. But a preacher will be culpable, as well, if he fails to declare the reality of mankind as they are presented in the Word of God, sinners who cannot save themselves and desperately need a Savior.

Fifth: Because the Holy Spirit uses Scripture, that which was inspired by him, to affect the conversion of sinners and the sanctification of believers, preachers should prioritize a focused explanation and exhortation of Scripture in preaching to believers and unbelievers, alike.

How crucial it is that a preacher never forgets that what is preached in preaching is not so much a sermon, but rather, it is the Word of God that he preaches in his sermon. How tragic it is when a preacher loses sight of the fact that the "what" of his preaching is the Word of God, which is preached through the vehicle of the sermon. Not a sermon but Scripture "is a sword; it is a two-edged sword; it pierces; it divides soul from spirit. Things which no human analysis ever separated, it analyzes, and holds up to the eye of conscience."[18] Preachers must focus on the Word of God and make much of Christ in their preaching, otherwise, they have abandoned that which God purposed to use and promised to exalt.

It is a certain indication that Scripture is not the focus of a preacher's preaching if he finds himself having to incorporate Scripture in the sermon he preaches, less the Scriptures be nominalized or left out altogether. However, a preacher is always on target when he has to supply great effort to be sermonic in the process of preaching the Scriptures. There is always a tendency to drift away, ever so subtly, from that which should be a priority, from that which should be one's focus. "I love the story of the sophisticated Englishman who visited Brazil and approached a man of the Amazon region reading a Bible. The gentleman from London said, 'Ha! In England we've out-grown that book.' The former cannibal looked up into the ashen face of that man and said, 'Sir, had we outgrown the Bible here, I would have eaten you yesterday.'"[19] Not much good can come from the preaching of a man who has lost the conviction that the Bible is the eternal Word of God, that it is the believer's guide for faith and practice of the faith, and that it must be explained clearly and practically to impact the lives of the hearers.

Sixth: Evangelistic preaching should occur in a sermon that is not intended to be an evangelistic sermon.

An expository sermon geared to edify and robustly build up believers in their Christian lives is not an exception nor an exemption from evangelistic preaching. An

17. Spurgeon, *Holy Spirit Power*, 89.
18. Phelps, *The Theory of Preaching*, 1882, 559.
19. Smith, *Real Evangelism*, 52.

expository sermon, like any other sermon, is just the context in which evangelistic preaching occurs. An evangelistic sermon, an entire sermon purposed to declare the person and work of Jesus Christ which will culminate in a summons for sinners to repent from their sins and trust in Christ for their salvation, is certainly evangelistic preaching. Yet, evangelistic preaching may also be the reality of an expository sermon where a text of Scripture is carefully explained and applied for the believers' sanctification. But the expository sermon becomes evangelistic preaching at any place in the sermon where the emphasis shifts from the edification of believers to expounding the person and work of Jesus Christ to unbelievers so that they may respond to the gospel in repentance and faith. Obviously, evangelistic preaching will be limited to a portion(s) of the expository sermon rather than the entirety of the sermon. But even an expository sermon must not exclude evangelistic preaching in at least one portion of it.

Evangelistic preaching does not require an evangelistic sermon for its reality. Ramesh Richard is helpful to differentiate an evangelistic sermon from evangelistic preaching. "(E)vangelistic preaching is the public proclamation of the Good News of eternal salvation found in the person and work of the Lord Jesus Christ so that any unbeliever may embrace him as the only God who saves sinners."[20] But just as clarifying and more crucial to a correct proclamation of the message of the gospel is the injunction that there can be no substitute for and no omissions from the person and work of Christ.[21] But what establishes the person and work of Christ from which there must be no omissions? Though there are numerous additions that could be included, ten components will be suggested as essential to establish a clear and comprehensive proclamation of Jesus Christ, thus, establishing the bases upon which the hearers will be compelled to respond in repentance and faith. A preacher must be faithful to unbelievers to help them to understand who Jesus is and what he did so that sinners, enemies of God can become righteous children of God, if they are willing to respond in repentance and faith in Jesus Christ as he has been proclaimed according to the Scriptures.

It is the message of the gospel in which the person and work of Jesus Christ is declared that makes that portion of the sermon in which the gospel is proclaimed evangelistic, technically evangelistic. A sermon at some point must be evangelistic, but never technically evangelistic! What makes a declaration of the person and work of Jesus Christ technically evangelistic? Any sermon can become technically evangelistic when the right truths about Jesus Christ are declared, the message is as it should be, but the motive is not pure because the preacher is not seeking to glorify Christ, and the manner of the proclamation is corrupt because it is declared without joy. The right motive and manner are essential for a sermon to contain evangelistic preaching that is not technically evangelistic. Therefore, the right motive and manner must never be absent in the proclamation of the gospel.

20. Richard, *Preparing Evangelistic Sermons*, 73.

21. James, *An Earnest Ministry*, 1847, 79.

The right motive and manner must accompany the proclamation of the good news regardless of the consequences of its proclamation, as Spurgeon was certain to clarify as he wrote: "If our Lord and King is exalted, then let other things go whichever way they like. If He is exalted, never mind what becomes of us. We are pygmies, and it is all right if He is exalted. God's truth is safe, and we must be perfectly willing to be forgotten, derided, slandered, or anything else that men please. The cause is safe, and the King is on His throne. Hallelujah! Blessed be His name!"[22] With the right motive and manner of the proclamation understood, let's consider the components that are essential to the right message to be proclaimed, that which composes the declaration of Christ's person and work.

TEN ESSENTIAL COMPONENTS IN THE PREACHER'S DECLARATION OF JESUS CHRIST

So, what are the ten essential components in the preacher's declaration of Christ's person and work that provides unbelievers with an undisputable realization of God's promised Savior and Lord as he is revealed in Scripture? A clear and complete declaration of the person of Jesus Christ must include the following: Jesus is God, Jesus is man, Jesus was born of a virgin, Jesus is sinless, Jesus is God's exclusive offering for the forgiveness of sins, and Jesus is God's perfect, eternal offering for the forgiveness of sins. A clear and complete declaration of the work of Jesus Christ must include the following: Jesus was a substitutionary sacrifice for sinners, Jesus made atonement for sin through his shed blood, Jesus died on the cross, and Jesus rose from the grave on the third day victorious over sin and death.

For each of these ten essential components of the declaration of Christ's person and work, roughly half a dozen to a dozen biblical references will be cited below to support the essential nature of each of these components. It goes without saying that many more references could be cited and those that are cited were subjectively cherry-picked from the many verses that are available which support the truth of each component of Christ's person and work. Surely, it will be the case that the reader will think that references which were not cited should have been cited. Of course, in every instance the reader is correct, and I am culpable for not including them since I am seeking to provide only a sampling of that which could be provided.

The biblical references for each component of Christ's person and work are provided as that which is indicative of what Scripture reveals about Jesus Christ. From these and other biblical references, declaration about Christ can be made regarding each component. Not all the biblical references for each component of Christ's person and work are to be incorporated in proclaiming Christ, but rather, with differing selected references from sermon to sermon, a biblically clear and complete declaration

---

22. Spurgeon, *Holy Spirit Power*, 167.

of Christ will be made with variety. Which references and how many references for each component of Christ's person and work which are to be incorporated in each sermon conclusion will be at the discretion of the preacher as he is led by the Holy Spirit. Each biblical reference presented below is taken from the New American Standard Bible.

The Person of Christ

Jesus is God

John 8:56–58 "Your father Abraham rejoiced to see My day, and he saw it and was glad." So the Jews said to Him, "You are not yet fifty years old, and have You seen Abraham?" Jesus said to them, "Truly, truly, I say to you, <u>before Abraham was born, I am</u>."

John 5:17–18 But He answered them, "<u>My Father is working</u> until now, and I Myself am working." For this reason therefore the Jews were seeking all the more to kill Him, because He not only was breaking the Sabbath, but also was <u>calling God His own Father, making Himself equal with God</u>.

John 1:1–3 <u>In the beginning was the Word, and the Word was with God , and the Word was God</u>. <u>He was in the beginning with God</u>. All things came into being through Him, and apart from Him nothing came into being that has come into being.

Hebrews 1:1–3 God, after He spoke long ago to the fathers in the prophets in many portions and in many ways, in these last days has spoken to us in His Son, whom He appointed heir of all things, through whom also He made the world. And <u>He is the radiance of His glory and the exact representation of His nature</u>, and upholds all things by the word of His power. When He had made purification of sins, He sat down at the right hand of the Majesty on high,

Hebrews 1:10–12 And, "<u>YOU, LORD, IN THE BEGINNING LAID THE FOUNDATION OF THE EARTH, AND THE HEAVENS ARE THE WORKS OF YOUR HANDS</u>; THEY WILL PERISH, BUT YOU REMAIN; AND THEY ALL WILL BECOME OLD LIKE A GARMENT, AND LIKE A MANTLE YOU WILL ROLL THEM UP; LIKE A GARMENT THEY WILL ALSO BE CHANGED. BUT YOU ARE THE SAME, AND YOUR YEARS WILL NOT COME TO AN END."

Hebrews 13:8 <u>Jesus Christ is the same yesterday and today and forever</u>.

Revelation 1:8 "I am the Alpha and the Omega," says the Lord God, "who is and who was and who is to come, the Almighty."

Revelation 5:11–13 Then I looked, and I heard the voice of many angels around the throne and the living creatures and the elders; and the number of them was myriads of myriads, and thousands of thousands, saying with a loud voice, "Worthy is the Lamb that was slain to receive power and riches and wisdom and might and honor and glory and blessing." And every created thing which is in heaven and on the earth and under the earth and on the sea, and all things in them, I heard saying, "To Him who sits on the throne, and to the Lamb, be blessing and honor and glory and dominion forever and ever."

Luke 5:21–25 The scribes and the Pharisees began to reason, saying, "Who is this man who speaks blasphemies? Who can forgive sins, but God alone?" But Jesus, aware of their reasonings, answered and said to them, "Why are you reasoning in your hearts? Which is easier, to say, 'Your sins have been forgiven you,' or to say, 'Get up and walk'? But, so that you may know that the Son of Man has authority on earth to forgive sins,"—He said to the paralytic—"I say to you, get up, and pick up your stretcher and go home." Immediately he got up before them, and picked up what he had been lying on, and went home glorifying God.

John 5:22 "For not even the Father judges anyone, but He has given all judgment to the Son,"

1 Timothy 3:16 By common confession, great is the mystery of godliness: He who was revealed in the flesh, Was vindicated in the Spirit, Seen by angels, Proclaimed among the nations, Believed on in the world, Taken up in glory.

Mark 14:61–62 But He kept silent and did not answer. Again the high priest was questioning Him, and saying to Him, "Are You the Christ, the Son of the Blessed One?" And Jesus said, "I am; and you shall see THE SON OF MAN SITTING AT THE RIGHT HAND OFPOWER, and COMING WITH THE CLOUDS OF HEAVEN."

Jesus is man

Isaiah 9:6–7 For a child will be born to us, a son will be given to us; And the government will rest on His shoulders; And His name will be called Wonderful Counselor, Mighty God, Eternal Father, Prince of Peace. There will be no end to the increase of His government or of peace, on the throne of David and over his kingdom, to establish it and to uphold it with justice and righteousness from then on and forevermore. The zeal of the LORD of hosts will accomplish this.

Matthew 1:1 The record of the genealogy of <u>Jesus the Messiah, the son of David, the son of Abraham</u>.

Luke 1:30–33 The angel said to her, "Do not be afraid, Mary; for you have found favor with God. And behold, <u>you will conceive in your womb and bear a son, and you shall name Him Jesus. He will be great and will be called the Son of the Most High; and the Lord God will give Him the throne of His father David; and He will reign over the house of Jacob forever, and His kingdom will have no end."</u>

John 1:14 And <u>the Word became flesh, and dwelt among us, and we saw His glory, glory as of the only begotten from the Father,</u> full of grace and truth.

John 1:18 No one has seen God at any time; <u>the only begotten God who is in the bosom of the Father, He has explained Him.</u>

John 3:16 For God so loved the world, that <u>He gave His only begotten Son</u>, that whoever believes in Him shall not perish, but have eternal life.

Philippians 2:6–8 who, although <u>He existed in the form of God</u>, did not regard equality with God a thing to be grasped, but <u>emptied Himself, taking the form of a bond-servant, and being made in the likeness of men</u>. Being found in appearance as a man, He humbled Himself by becoming obedient to the point of death, even death on a cross.

Colossians 2:9 For <u>in Him all the fullness of Deity dwells in bodily form,</u>

Hebrews 2:14 Therefore, <u>since the children share in flesh and blood, He Himself likewise also partook of the same, that through death He might render powerless him who had the power of death</u>, that is, the devil;

Hebrews 2:17 Therefore, <u>He had to be made like His brethren in all things, so that He might become a merciful and faithful high priest in things pertaining to God, to make propitiation for the sins of the people.</u>

Hebrews 2:18 For since <u>He Himself was tempted in that which He has suffered, He is able to come to the aid of those who are tempted.</u>

Jesus was born of a virgin

Genesis 3:15 And I will put enmity between you and the woman, and between your seed and <u>her seed; He shall bruise you on the head, and you shall bruise him on the heel."</u>

Isaiah 7:14 Therefore the Lord Himself will give you a sign: "Behold, <u>a virgin will be with child and bear a son, and she will call His name Immanuel."</u>

Luke 1:34–35 Mary said to the angel, "How can this be, since <u>I am a virgin?"</u> The angel answered and said to her, "<u>The Holy Spirit will come upon you, and the power of the Most High will overshadow you; and for that reason the holy Child shall be called the Son of God."</u>

Matthew 1:18 Now the birth of Jesus Christ was as follows: when His mother Mary had been betrothed to Joseph, <u>before they came together she was found to be with child by the Holy Spirit.</u>

Matthew 1:24–25 And Joseph awoke from his sleep and did as the angel of the Lord commanded him, and took Mary as his wife, but <u>kept her a virgin until she gave birth to a Son; and he called His name Jesus.</u>

Romans 1:3 concerning <u>His Son, who was born of a descendant of David according to the flesh.</u>

Galatians 4:4 But when the fulness of time came, <u>God sent forth His Son, born of a woman,</u> born under the Law,

Hebrews 10:5 Therefore, when He comes into the world, He says, "SACRIFICE AND OFFERING YOU HAVE NOT DESIRED, BUT <u>A BODY YOU HAVE PREPARED FOR ME."</u>

Jesus is sinless

Luke 1:35 "The Holy Spirit will come upon you, and the power of the Most High will overshadow you; and for that reason <u>the holy Child shall be called the Son of God."</u>

Mark 1:23–24 Just then there was a man in their synagogue with an unclean spirit; and he cried out, saying, "What business do we have with each other,

Jesus of Nazareth? Have You come to destroy us? I know who You are—the Holy One of God!"

John 6:68–69 Simon Peter answered Him, "Lord, to whom shall we go? You have words of eternal life. "We have believed and have come to know that You are the Holy One of God."

Mark 15:25–26 It was the third hour when they crucified Him. The inscription of the charge against Him read, "THE KING OF THE JEWS."

Acts 3:14–15 "But you disowned the Holy and Righteous One and asked for a murderer to be granted to you, but put to death the Prince of life, the one whom God raised from the dead, a fact to which we are witnesses."

2 Corinthians 5:21 He made Him who knew no sin to be sin on our behalf, so that we might become the righteousness of God in Him.

Hebrews 4:15 For we do not have a high priest who cannot sympathize with our weaknesses, but One who has been tempted in all things as we are, yet without sin.

Hebrews 7:26 For it was fitting for us to have such a high priest, holy, innocent, undefiled, separated from sinners and exalted above the heavens;

1 Peter 1:18–19 knowing that you were not redeemed with perishable things like silver or gold from your futile way of life inherited from your forefathers, but with precious blood, as of a lamb unblemished and spotless, the blood of Christ.

1 Peter 2:21–22 For you have been called for this purpose, since Christ also suffered for you, leaving you an example for you to follow in His steps, WHO COMMITTED NO SIN, NOR WAS ANY DECEIT FOUND IN HIS MOUTH;

1 John 3:5 You know that He appeared to take away sins; and in Him there is no sin.

Jesus is God's Exclusive Offering for the Forgiveness of Sins

Genesis 22:7–8 Isaac spoke to Abraham his father and said, "My father!" And he said, "Here I am, my son." And he said, "Behold, the fire and the wood, but where is the lamb for the burnt offering?" Abraham said, "God will provide for

Himself the lamb for the burnt offering, my son." So the two of them walked on together.

Exodus 12:3–7 they are each one to take a lamb for themselves, according to their fathers' households, a lamb for each household. . . . Your lamb shall be an unblemished male a year old; you may take it from the sheep or from the goats . . . then the whole assembly of the congregation of Israel is to kill it at twilight. Moreover, they shall take some of the blood and put it on the two doorposts and on the lintel of the houses in which they eat it.

Isaiah 53:7 He was oppressed and He was afflicted, Yet He did not open His mouth; Like a lamb that is led to slaughter, And like a sheep that is silent before its shearers, So He did not open His mouth.

John 1:29 The next day he saw Jesus coming to him and said, "Behold, the Lamb of God who takes away the sin of the world!"

John 14:6 Jesus said to him, "I am the way, and the truth, and the life; no one comes to the Father but through Me."

John 10:7, 9 "Truly, truly, I say to you, I am the door of the sheep. . . . I am the door, if anyone enters through Me, he will be saved, and go in and out and find pasture."

John 11:25 "I am the resurrection and the life; he who believes in Me will live even if he dies,"

Acts 8:32–35 Now the passage of Scripture which he was reading was this: "HE WAS LED AS A SHEEP TO SLAUGHTER; AND AS A LAMB BEFORE ITS SHEARERS IS SILENT, SO HE DOES NOT OPEN HIS MOUTH.." . . "Please tell me, of whom does the prophet say this? Of himself or of someone else?" Then Philip opened his mouth, and beginning from this Scripture he preached Jesus to him.

1 Corinthians 5:7 Clean out the old leaven so that you may be a new lump, just as you are in fact unleavened. For Christ our Passover also has been sacrificed.

1 Peter 1:18–19 knowing that you were not redeemed with perishable things like silver or gold from your futile way of life inherited from your forefathers, but with precious blood, as of a lamb unblemished and spotless, the blood of Christ.

Revelation 5:11–12 Then I looked, and I heard the voice of many angels around the throne and the living creatures and the elders; and the number of them was myriads of myriads, and thousands of thousands, saying with a loud voice, "Worthy is the Lamb that was slain to receive power and riches and wisdom and might and honor and glory and blessing."

Revelation 5:13–14 And every created thing which is in heaven and on the earth and under the earth and on the sea, and all things in them, I heard saying, "To Him who sits on the throne, and to the Lamb, be blessing and honor and glory and dominion forever and ever." And the four living creatures kept saying, "Amen." And the elders fell down and worshiped.

Jesus is God's Perfect, Eternal Offering for the Forgiveness of Sins

John 1:29 The next day he saw Jesus coming to him and said, "Behold, the Lamb of God who takes away the sin of the world!"

John 6:51 "I am the living bread that came down out of heaven; if anyone eats of this bread, he will live forever; and the bread also which I will give for the life of the world is My flesh."

Hebrews 5:8–9 Although He was a Son, He learned obedience from the things which He suffered. And having been made perfect, He became to all those who obey Him the source of eternal salvation,

Hebrews 7:27 who does not need daily, like those high priests, to offer up sacrifices, first for His own sins and then for the sins of the people, because this He did once for all when He offered up Himself.

Hebrews 9:12 and not through the blood of goats and calves, but through His own blood, He entered the holy place once for all, having obtained eternal redemption.

Hebrews 9:14 how much more will the blood of Christ, who through the eternal Spirit offered Himself without blemish to God, cleanse your conscience from dead works to serve the living God?

Hebrews 9:25–28 nor was it that He would offer Himself often . . . but now once at the consummation of the ages He has been manifested to put away sin by the sacrifice of Himself.

And inasmuch as it is appointed for men to die once and after this comes judgment, so Christ also, <u>having been offered once to bear the sins of many</u>, will appear a second time for salvation without reference to sin, to those who eagerly await Him.

Romans 5:8–10 But God demonstrates His own love toward us, in that while we were yet sinners, <u>Christ died for us</u>. Much more then, having now been justified by His blood, we shall be saved from the wrath of God through Him. For if while we were enemies we were reconciled to God through <u>the death of His Son</u>, much more, having been reconciled, we shall be <u>saved by His life</u>.

Romans 6:9–10 knowing that Christ, having been raised from the dead, <u>is never to die again</u>; death no longer is master over Him. For the death that He died, <u>He died to sin once for all</u>; but the life that He lives, He lives to God.

Romans 6:23 For the wages of sin is death, but the free gift of God is <u>eternal life in Christ Jesus our Lord</u>.

Romans 8:38–39 For I am convinced that neither death, nor life, nor angels, nor principalities, nor things present, nor things to come, nor powers, nor height, nor depth, <u>nor any other created thing, will be able to separate us from the love of God, which is in Christ Jesus our Lord</u>.

1 John 2:25 <u>This is the promise which He made to us, eternal life</u>.

The Work of Jesus Christ

His Substitutionary Sacrifice

Hebrews 7:27 who does not need daily, like those high priests, to offer up sacrifices, first for His own sins and then for the sins of the people, because <u>this He did once for all when He offered up Himself</u>.

Hebrews 9:13–14 For if the blood of goats and bulls and the ashes of a heifer sprinkling those who have been defiled sanctify for the cleansing of the flesh, how much more will the blood of Christ, who through the eternal Spirit <u>offered Himself without blemish to God, cleanse your conscience from dead works to serve the living God</u>?

Hebrews 9:26, 28 <u>but now once at the consummation of the ages He has been manifested to put away sin by the sacrifice of Himself</u>. . . . so Christ also, having been offered once to bear the sins of many, will appear a second time for salvation without reference to sin, to those who eagerly await Him.

Hebrews 10:10 By this will we have been sanctified through the offering of the body of Jesus Christ once for all.

Hebrews 10:12 but He, having offered one sacrifice for sins for all time, SAT DOWN AT THE RIGHT HAND OF GOD,

Romans 8:3 For what the Law could not do, weak as it was through the flesh, God did: sending His own Son in the likeness of sinful flesh and as an offering for sin, He condemned sin in the flesh,

2 Corinthians 5:14–15 For the love of Christ controls us, having concluded this, that one died for all, therefore all died; and He died for all, so that they who live might no longer live for themselves, but for Him who died and rose again on their behalf.

2 Corinthians 5:21 He made Him who knew no sin to be sin on our behalf, so that we might become the righteousness of God in Him.

1 Peter 2:24 and He Himself bore our sins in His body on the cross, so that we might die to sin and live to righteousness; for by His wounds you were healed.

1 Peter 3:18 For Christ also died for sins once for all, the just for the unjust, so that He might bring us to God, having been put to death in the flesh, but made alive in the spirit; Matthew 27:46 About the ninth hour Jesus cried out with a loud voice, saying, "MY GOD, MY GOD, WHY HAVE YOU FORSAKEN ME?"

His Shed Blood

Matthew 26:28 for this is My blood of the covenant, which is poured out for many for forgiveness of sins.

Acts 20:28 Be on guard for yourselves and for all the flock, among which the Holy Spirit has made you overseers, to shepherd the church of God which He purchased with His own blood.

Romans 3:25 whom God displayed publicly as a propitiation in His blood through faith. This was to demonstrate His righteousness, because in the forbearance of God He passed over the sins previously committed;

Romans 5:9 Much more then, <u>having now been justified by His blood</u>, we shall be saved from the wrath of God through Him.

Ephesians 1:7 In Him we <u>have</u> <u>redemption through His blood</u>, the forgiveness of our trespasses, according to the riches of His grace

Ephesians 2:13 But now in Christ Jesus you who formerly were far off <u>have been brought near by the blood of Christ</u>.

Colossians 1:20 and through Him to reconcile all things to Himself, having made <u>peace through the blood of His cross;</u>

Hebrews 9:12 and not through the blood of goats and calves, but <u>through His own blood, He entered the holy place once for all, having obtained eternal redemption</u>.

Hebrews 9:20 saying, "THIS IS <u>THE BLOOD OF THE COVENANT</u> WHICH GOD COMMANDED YOU."

Hebrews 9:22 And according to the Law, one may almost say, <u>all things are cleansed with blood, and without shedding of blood there is no forgiveness</u>.

Hebrews 10:19 Therefore, brethren, <u>since we have confidence to enter the holy place by the blood of Jesus,</u>

Hebrews 13:12 Therefore Jesus also, <u>that He might sanctify the people through His own blood</u>, suffered outside the gate.

Hebrews 13:20 Now the God of peace, <u>who brought up from the dead the great Shepherd of the sheep through the blood of the eternal covenant</u>, even Jesus our Lord,

1 John 1:7 but if we walk in the Light as He Himself is in the Light, we have fellowship with one another, <u>and the blood of Jesus His Son cleanses us from all sin</u>.

Revelation 1:5 and from Jesus Christ, the faithful witness, the firstborn of the dead, and the ruler of the kings of the earth. <u>To Him who loves us and released us from our sins by His blood</u>

His Death on the Cross

Acts 2:23 this Man, delivered over by the predetermined plan and foreknowledge of God, you nailed to a cross by the hands of godless men and put Him to death.

Acts 3:15 but put to death the Prince of life, the one whom God raised from the dead, a fact to which we are witnesses.

Acts 5:30 The God of our fathers raised up Jesus, whom you had put to death by hanging Him on a cross.

Romans 5:10 For if while we were enemies we were reconciled to God through the death of His Son, much more, having been reconciled, we shall be saved by His life.

Romans 6:10 For the death that He died, He died to sin once for all; but the life that He lives, He lives to God.

Philippians 2:8 Being found in appearance as a man, He humbled Himself by becoming obedient to the point of death, even death on a cross.

Hebrews 2:9 But we do see Him who was made for a little while lower than the angels, namely, Jesus, because of the suffering of death crowned with glory and honor, so that by the grace of God He might taste death for everyone.

Hebrews 2:14 Therefore, since the children share in flesh and blood, He Himself likewise also partook of the same, that through death He might render powerless him who had the power of death, that is, the devil;

1 Peter 3:18 For Christ also died for sins once for all, the just for the unjust, so that He might bring us to God, having been put to death in the flesh, but made alive in the spirit; Revelation 1:17–18 When I saw Him, I fell at His feet like a dead man. And He placed His right hand on me, saying, "Do not be afraid; I am the first and the last, and the living One; and I was dead, and behold, I am alive forevermore, and I have the keys of death and of Hades."

His Resurrection

Acts 13:29–30 When they had carried out all that was written concerning Him, they took Him down from the cross and laid Him in a tomb. But God raised Him from the dead;

Romans 4:24–25 but for our sake also, to whom it will be credited, as those who believe in Him who raised Jesus our Lord from the dead, He who was delivered over because of our transgressions, and was raised because of our justification.

Romans 6:4 Therefore we have been buried with Him through baptism into death, so that as Christ was raised from the dead through the glory of the Father, so we too might walk in newness of life.

Romans 8:11 But if the Spirit of Him who raised Jesus from the dead dwells in you, He who raised Christ Jesus from the dead will also give life to your mortal bodies through His Spirit who dwells in you.

Romans 10:9 that if you confess with your mouth Jesus as Lord, and believe in your heart that God raised Him from the dead, you will be saved;

1 Corinthians 15:12–14 Now if Christ is preached, that He has been raised from the dead, how do some among you say that there is no resurrection of the dead? But if there is no resurrection of the dead, not even Christ has been raised; and if Christ has not been raised, then our preaching is vain, your faith also is vain.

1 Corinthians 15:54 But when this perishable will have put on the imperishable, and this mortal will have put on immortality, then will come about the saying that is written, "DEATH IS SWALLOWED UP in victory. O DEATH, WHERE IS YOUR VICTORY? O DEATH, WHERE IS YOUR STING?"

2 Corinthians 1:9–10 indeed, we had the sentence of death within ourselves so that we would not trust in ourselves, but in God who raises the dead; who delivered us from so great a peril of death, and will deliver us, He on whom we have set our hope. And He will yet deliver us,

Ephesians 1:19–20 and what is the surpassing greatness of His power toward us who believe. These are in accordance with the working of the strength of His might which He brought about in Christ, when He raised Him from the dead and seated Him at His right hand in the heavenly places,

Colossians 2:12 having been buried with Him in baptism, in which <u>you were</u> <u>also raised up with Him through faith in the working of God, who raised Him</u> <u>from the dead</u>.

1 Thessalonians 1:10 and to wait for His Son from heaven, <u>whom He raised</u> <u>from the dead, that is Jesus</u>, who rescues us from the wrath to come.

Hebrews 11:19 He considered that <u>God is able to raise people even from the</u> <u>dead</u>, from which He also received him back as a type.

1 Peter 1:21 who through Him are believers in God, <u>who raised Him from the</u> <u>dead</u> and gave Him glory, so that your faith and hope are in God.

The essential components of the person and work of Jesus Christ are clearly and prolifically embedded in Scripture. Though the declaration of Christ's person and work declared in the conclusion of a sermon for the salvation of the lost by the incorporation of the references above will not be belabored, it must be a clear, Scripture based declaration. And because of the many biblical references supporting each of the essential components of Christ's person and work, the proclamation of Christ can be varied from sermon to sermon through the use of different passages clarifying the same, never to be omitted, essential components of Christ's person and work.

It is only the Christ of Scripture that saves sinners. The Jesus of the lost person's imagination, misinformation, or personal preference cannot save anyone. No preacher should assume a correct, biblically accurate Christology to be possessed by a lost person. The good news of salvation through Jesus Christ is a message that is too important for a preacher to allow it to stand obscured by falsehoods held by lost individuals, and it is too important for it to be withheld from his preaching. The message of the gospel of Jesus Christ is the only message some hearers can be profited by because it is the message they have yet to hear and/or respond to.

A sermon conclusion should be the most insightful, practical means of helping believers to live their lives more consistently with the Word of God. And a sermon conclusion should be the most insightful, personal message by which unbelievers can be saved by the God of the Word as they hear about the Word incarnate and are compelled to repent of their sins and trust in him, thus beginning a life with meaning that will last for time and throughout eternity. But poor conclusions or sermons that forgo conclusions deprive all who hear sermons of that which is most needful for them and that which is most beneficial to them. No sermon is to be preached for the deprivation of the hearers, but this is the result of preaching that exempts a well-prepared conclusion, and the deprivation of the hearers happens every time such conclusions are withheld from them.

In the introduction of this book, the words of Ilion T. Jones were quoted to establish the necessity for a treatise on sermon conclusions. In the perspective of Jones,

"Conclusions are consistently the weakest parts of sermons. Far too many sermons ravel out at the ends. Every poor conclusion is a lost opportunity, because there the sermon should come to its final climax, there its main purpose should be achieved, there the preacher's supreme effort should take place. More attention should therefore be given to the problem of how to make conclusions effective."[23] It is the opinion of this writer that, however true Jones's perspective of weak conclusions may have been in the twentieth century, the important work of concluding sermons effectively has, if anything, only gotten weaker in the intervening years. I have written this book in a humble attempt to strengthen the work of concluding sermons effectively, hopefully for many years in the future of preaching.

23. Ilion T. Jones, *Principles and Practice of Preaching* (New York: Abingdon Press, 1956), 160.

Appendix A

The following analysis of application methodology is an attempt to codify how a transition was made from instruction to the personal implications of the instruction. What follows is a list of 30 general principles for making application. These principles can be utilized to move from instruction to implications of instruction for innumerable subject-matters and texts. These general principles of application methodology can be used in any part of the sermon-the introduction, the body, or the conclusion of the sermon.

1. Depict present state vs. future state realities which commonly are not understood/appreciated. (Matthew 5:3–12)

2. Present God's <u>intended design</u> for believers along with <u>warning</u> of <u>violating</u> that design. (Matthew 5:13)

3. Present God's <u>intended design</u> for believers along with <u>encouragement</u> for <u>fulfilling</u> that design. (Matthew 5:14–16)

4. Provide <u>convincing argument</u> for the <u>reasons</u> why people <u>fail</u> to keep the Word of God in their lives. (Matthew 5:17–19)

5. Defend the <u>inviolable condition</u> of an unsurpassed <u>righteousness</u> for all who enter the kingdom of heaven. (Matthew 5:20)

6. Point out how <u>attitudinal manifestations</u> of sin render one <u>culpable</u> before God. (Matthew 5:22a)

7. Establish the <u>connection</u> between our <u>actions</u> and the <u>consequences</u> of our actions in this life and in the life to come. (Matthew 5:22)

8. Establish the <u>connection</u> between our <u>actions</u> and the <u>motives</u> for our actions. (Matthew 5:23–26)

9. Depict <u>comparative</u> case scenarios for <u>how</u> a truth is <u>fleshed out</u> in life. (Matthew 5:22)

10. <u>Warn</u> against <u>non-compliance</u> to God's Word by demonstrating how <u>supposed</u> compliance is actually non-compliance. (Matthew 5:21–22)

11. <u>Warn</u> against <u>non-compliance</u> to God's Word by demonstrating the <u>repercussions</u> of non-compliance. (Matthew 5:21–22)

12. Doctrinal <u>instruction</u> must be <u>established</u> very firmly before any practical <u>instructions</u> are given. (Matthew 5:23a)

13. Provide <u>ways</u> in which commonplace <u>inadequate</u> conduct may become conduct that is <u>in keeping</u> with God's design. (Matthew 5:23–24)

14. Present <u>remedial</u> steps of <u>correction</u> for the occurrence of sin. (Matthew 5:23b-25)

15. Present <u>preventative</u> measures so that God's standard can be <u>realized</u>. (Matthew 5:25–26)

16. Offer <u>true-to-life</u> situations depicting <u>how</u> a given instruction applies. (Matthew 5:22–26)

17. Show <u>cause/effect</u> scenarios regarding an <u>action</u>. (Matthew 5:28)

18. Provide sin <u>reduction/restriction</u> measures. (Matthew 5:29a, 30a)

19. Demonstrate <u>how</u> sin can be committed <u>indirectly</u>. (Matthew 5:28b)

20. Demonstrate <u>how</u> sin may be brought upon <u>others</u> because of one's <u>actions</u>. (Matthew 5:32)

21. Give <u>reasons</u> for complying to a <u>negative</u> command. (Matthew 5:36)

22. Give <u>reasons</u> for complying to a <u>positive</u> command. (Matthew 5:37)

23. Provide a series of <u>ways/means</u> in which a command can be <u>fulfilled</u>. (Matthew 5:39–41)

24. Give a <u>rationale</u> with <u>reasons</u> for complying with a command. (Matthew 5:43–48)

25. Show how honorable <u>actions</u> are negated by dishonorable <u>procedures</u> and dishonorable <u>motives</u>. (Matthew 6:1–18)

26. Offer <u>encouragement/motivation</u> to act upon instruction through a projection of <u>well-being</u> based upon one's actions. (Matthew 7:24–25)

27. Offer <u>encouragement/motivation</u> to act upon instruction through a projection of <u>devastation</u> based upon one's actions. (Matthew 7:26–27)

28. Show how <u>incorrect suppositions</u> about God's <u>workings</u> in the world are made because Scripture is not understood. (Acts 2:15–21)

29. Show how one may be <u>opposing God</u> as one <u>carries out</u> one's beliefs and convictions. (Acts 2:22–24)

30. Show how one may <u>experience</u> God's working yet <u>fail</u> to appropriate the <u>benefit</u> of God's working in one's life. (Acts 2:32–33)

Bibliography

Abbey, Merrill R. *Communication in Pulpit and Parish*. Philadelphia: Westminster, 1973.

Abbott, Lyman. *The Christian Ministry*. Boston: Houghton, Mifflin, 1905.

Adams, Jay E. *Preaching with Purpose*. Phillipsburg, New Jersey: Presbyterian & Reformed, 1982.

———. *The Use of the Scriptures in Counseling*. n.p.: Presbyterian and Reformed, 1976.

———. *Truth Apparent*. Stanley, North Carolina: Timeless Texts, 1982.

Alexander, James W. *Thoughts on Preaching*. Carlisle, Pennsylvania: Banner of Truth, reprint, 1988.

Awbrey, Ben. *How Effective Sermons Advance*. Eugene, Oregon: Resource Publications, 2011.

———. *How Effective Sermons Begin*. Fearn, Ross-shire, Great Britain: Mentor, 2008.

Aristotle, *The Rhetoric and the Poetics of Aristotle*. New York: Random House, 1984 edition, *Rhetoric*, translated by W. Rhys Roberts.

Armstrong, D. Wade. *Evangelistic Growth in Acts 1 & 2*. Nashville: Broadman, 1983.

Arthur, William. *The Tongue of Fire: or the Power of Christianity*. London: Hamilton, Adams, and Co., 1859.

Atkins, Gaius Glenn. *Preaching and the Mind of Today*. New York: Round Table, 1934.

Bartlett, Gene E. *Postscript to Preaching*. Valley Forge, Pennsylvania: Judson, 1981.

Baumann, J. Daniel. *An Introduction to Contemporary Preaching*. Grand Rapids: Baker, 1977.

Baxter, Richard. *The Reformed Pastor*. Portland, Oregon: Multnomah, abridged ed., 1982, first published in 1656.

Beecher, Henry Ward. *Lectures on Preaching*. Boston: The Pilgrim Press, Three volumes in one, n.d.

Begg, Alistair. *Preaching for God's Glory*. Crossway. Wheaton: Illinois, reprint, 2011.

Behrends, A. J. F. *The Philosophy of Preaching*. New York: Charles Scribner's Sons, 1890.

Berry, Sidney M. *Vital Preaching*. London: The Camelot Press, 1936.

Bickel, R. Bruce. *Light and Heat*. Morgan, PA: Soli Deo Gloria, 1999.

Black, James. *The Mystery of Preaching*. New York: Revell, 1924.

Blackwood, A. W. *The Fine Art of Preaching*. Grand Rapids: Baker, 1976.

Blaikie, William G. *For the Work of the Ministry*. Birmingham, Alabama: Solid Ground, 2005, first published in 1873.

Blair, Hugh. *Dr. Blair's Lectures on Rhetoric*. New York: W. E. Dean, 1852, Nabu Public Domain Reprints.

Borgman, Brian. *My Heart for Thy Cause*. Fearn, Ross-shire, Great Britain: Mentor, 2002.

Bounds, E. M. *Power Through Prayer*. Chicago: Moody, paperback edition, 1979.

Breed, David R. *Preparing to Preach*. New York: George H. Doran, 1911.

Broadus, John Albert. *A Treatise on the Preparation and Delivery of Sermons*. New York: A. C. Armstrong and Son, twentieth edition, 1893.

Brooks, Phillips. *The Joy of Preaching*. Grand Rapids: Kregel, 1989.

———. *On Preaching*. New York: The Seabury Press, 1964.

Brown, Charles Reynolds. *The Art of Preaching*. New York: MacMillan, 1926.

Brown, Jr., H. C. *A Quest for Reformation in Preaching*. Waco, Texas: Word, 1968.

Brown, Jr., H. C., Clinard, H. Gordon, Northcutt, Jesse J. *Steps to the Sermon*. Nashville: Broadman, 1963.

Bryan, Dawson C. *The Art of Illustrating Sermons*. New York: Abingdon-Cokesbury, 1938.

Bull, Paul B. *Preaching and Sermon Construction*. New York: Macmillan, 1922.

Burgess, Henry. *The Art of Preaching and the Composition of Sermons*. London: Hamilton, Adams, 1881.

Burrell, David James. *The Sermon: Its Construction and Delivery*. New York: Revell, 1913.

Buttrick, David. *Homiletic: Moves and Structures*. Philadelphia: Fortress, 1987.

Calkins, Raymond. *The Eloquence of Christian Experience*. New York: MacMillan, 1927.

Carter, Terry G., et al. *Preaching God's Word*. Grand Rapids: Zondervan, 2005.

Chapell, Bryan. *Christ-centered Preaching*. Grand Rapids: Baker, 1994.

Claude, Jean. *Claude's Essay on the Composition of a Sermon*. Cambridge: M. Watson, 1801.

Cleland, James T. *Preaching to be Understood*. New York: Abingdon, 1965.

Coffin, Henry Sloane. *What to Preach*. New York: Henry H. Doran, 1926.

Cox, James W. *A Guide to Biblical Preaching*. Nashville: Abingdon, 1976.

Dabney, Robert L. *Sacred Rhetoric*. Carlisle: Pennsylvania, The Banner of Truth, 1979.

Dale, R. W. *Nine Lectures on Preaching*. London: Hodder and Stoughton, 1890.

Davis, Henry Grady. *Design for Preaching*. Philadelphia: Fortress, 1958.

Davis, Ozora S. *Evangelistic Preaching*. New York: Revell, 1921.

———. *Principles of Preaching*. Chicago: The University of Chicago Press, 1924.

Demaray, Donald. *An Introduction.to Homiletics*. Grand Rapids: Baker, 1974.

Dever, Mark, et al. *Preaching the Cross*. Wheaton, Illinois: Crossway, 2007.

Dever, Mark and Gilbert, Greg. *Preach*. Nashville: Broadman & Holman, 2012.

Dodd, C. H. *The Apostolic Preaching*. New York: Harper & Brothers, 1962.

Doddridge, Philip. *Lectures on Preaching and the Several Branches of the Ministerial Office*. London: Richard Edwards, 1807.

Duduit, Michael, editor. *Handbook of Contemporary Preaching*. Nashville: Broadman, 1992.

Edge, Findley B. *Teaching for Results*. Nashville: Broadman, 1956.

Ellicott, C. J. *Homiletical and Pastoral Lectures*. New York: A. C. Armstrong & Sons, 1880.

Etter, John W. *The Preacher and His Sermon: A Treatise on Homiletics*. Dayton, Ohio: United Brethren, 1885.

Evans, William. *How to Prepare Sermons and Gospel Addresses*. Chicago: Moody, 1913.

Fabarez, Michael. *Preaching that Changes Lives*. Eugene, OR: Wipf and Stock, 2005.

Farmer, Herbert H. *The Servant of the Word*. New York: Charles Scribner's Sons, 1942.

Fasol, Al [et. al]. *Preaching Evangelistically*. Nashville: B & H, 2006.

Ford, Leighton *The Christian Persuader*. New York: Harper & Row, 1976.

Fry, Jacob. *Elementary Homiletics*. Philadelphia: The General Council Press, second edition, 1909.

Garvie, Alfred E. *A Guide to Preachers*. Hodder And Stoughton: London, 1911.

———. *The Christian Preacher*. New York: Charles Scribner's Sons, 1921.

———. *The Preachers of the Church*. London: James Clarke, 1926.

Greer, David H. *The Preacher and His Place*. New York: Charles Scribner's Sons, 1895.

Griffin, Em. *The Mind Changers*. Wheaton, Illinois: Tyndale, 1977.

H. Jeffs, *The Art of Sermon Illustration*. London: James Clarke, n.d.

Hall, John. *God's Word Through Preaching*. Grand Rapids: Baker, reprinted, 1979, first published in 1875.

Hoppin, James M. *Homiletics*. New York: Funk & Wagnalls, 1883.

Horne, Charles Sylvester. *The Romance of Preaching*. New York: Revell, 1914.

Hough, Lynn Harold. *The Theology of a Preacher*. New York: The Methodist Book Concern, 1912, second reprint, 1915.

Hoyt, Arthur S. *The Preacher*. New York: Hodder & Stoughton, reprinted, 1912.

———. *The Work of Preaching*. New York: Hodder & Stoughton, reprinted, 1910.

———. *The Work of Preaching*. New York: Macmillan, 1905, New Edition with New Chapters, 1936.

———. *Vital Elements of Preaching*. New York: Macmillan, 1929.

James, John Angell. *An Earnest Ministry*. Carlisle, Pennsylvania: The Banner of Truth, 1993.

Jefferson, Charles Edward. *The Minister as Prophet*. New York: Grosset & Dunlap, 1905.

Johnston, Graham. *Preaching to a Postmodern World*. Grand Rapids: Baker, 2001.

Jones, Ilion T. *Principles and Practice of Preaching*. New York: Abingdon, 1956.

Jowett, John H. *The Preacher: His Life and Work*. New York: Harper & Brothers, 1912.

———. *The Passion for Souls*. New York: Revell, 1905.

Kalas, J. Ellsworth. *Preaching in an Age of Distraction*. Downers Grove, IL: IVP, 2014.

Kennedy, Gerald. *His Word Through Preaching*. New York: Harper & Brothers, 1947.

Kidder, Daniel P. *A Treatise on Homiletics*. New York: Eaton & Mains, rev. ed., 1892.

Koller, Charles W. *Expository Preaching without Notes*. Grand Rapids: Baker, 1962.

Kroll, Woodrow. *Prescription for Preaching*. Grand Rapids: Baker, 1980.

Larsen, David L. *The Anatomy of Preaching*. Grand Rapids: Baker, 1989.

Lawson, Steven J. *Famine in the Land*. Chicago: Moody, 2003.

Lewis, Ralph L. *Speech for Persuasive Preaching*. Ann Arbor, Michigan: LithoCrafters, 1973.

Lloyd-Jones, D. Martyn. *Preaching and Preachers*. Grand Rapids: Zondervan, 1972.

Luccock, Halford E. *Communicating the Gospel*. New York: Harper & Brothers, 1953.

———. *In the Minister's Workshop*. New York: Abingdon-Cokesbury, 1944.

MacArthur, John. *Rediscovering Expository Preaching*. Dallas, TX: Word, 1992.

Macartney, Clarence E. *Preaching without Notes*. New York: Abingdon-Cokesbury, 1946.

Macpherson, Ian. *The Burden of the Lord*. New York: Abingdon, 1955.

Mather, Cotton. *Dr. Cotton Mather's Student and Preacher*. London: R. Hindmarsh, 1789.

Maxwell, John C. *Everyone Communicates, Few Connect*. Nashville: Thomas Nelson, 2010.

McComb, Samuel. *Preaching in Theory and Practice*. New York: Oxford University Press, 1926.

McCracken, Robert J. *The Making of the Sermon*. Harper & Brothers: New York, 1956.

McDill, Wayne. *12 Essential Skills for Great Preaching*. Nashville: Broadman & Holman, 2nd edition, revised and expanded, 2006.

McDonough, Reginald M. *Keys to Effective Motivation*. Nashville: Broadman, 1979.

McEachern, Alton H. *Proclaim the Gospel*. Nashville: Convention, 1975.

McLaughlin, Raymond W. *Communication for the Church*. Grand Rapids: Zondervan, 1968.

Merida, Tony. *Faithful Preaching*. Nashville: B&H, 2009.

Millar, Gary and Campbell, Phil. *Saving Eutychus*. Kingsford, Australia: Matthias Media, 2013.

Miller, Calvin. *The Empowered Communicator.* Broadman & Holman, 1994.

Miller, Donald G. *The Way to Biblical Preaching.* New York: Abingdon, 1957.

Minnick, Wayne C. *The Art of Persuasion.* Boston: Houghton Mifflin, 1957.

Mohler, R. Albert. *Words from the fire.* Chicago: Moody, 2009.

Montgomery, R. Ames. *Expository Preaching.* New York: Revell, 1939.

Montoya, Alex. *Preaching with Passion.* Grand Rapids: Kregel, 2000.

Moore, Daniel. *Thoughts on Preaching.* London: Hatchard, 1861.

Morgan, G. Campbell. *Preaching.* Grand Rapids: Baker, fourth reprinting 1980.

Morriss, L. L. *The Sound of Boldness.* Nashville: Broadman, 1977.

Mounce, Robert H. *The Essential Nature of New Testament Preaching.* Grand Rapids: Eerdmans, 1960.

Mouzon, Edwin. *Preaching with Authority.* Garden City, New York: Doubleday, Doran, 1929.

O'Neal, Glenn F. *Make the Bible Live.* Winona Lake, IN: BMH, 1972.

Olford, Stephen F. and Olford, David L. *Anointed Expository Preaching.* Nashville: B & H, 1998.

Orr, J. Edwin. *The Faith that Persuades.* New York: Harper & Row, 1977.

Oxnam, G. Bromley, editor. *Effective Preaching.* New York: Abingdon, 1929.

Parker, Paul P. *Develop your Powers of Persuasion.* London: The New English Library, 1963.

Pattison, T. Harwood. *The Making of the Sermon.* Valley Forge: Judson, 1941.

Pearson, Roy. *The Preacher: His Purpose and Practice.* Philadelphia: Westminster, 1962.

Perkins, William. *The Art of Prophesying.* Carlisle, PA: Banner of Truth Trust, reprinted, 2011, published in Latin, 1592, published in English in 1606.

Perry, Lloyd M. and Strubhar, John R. *Evangelistic Preaching.* Chicago: Moody, 1979.

Phelps, Austin. *The Theory of Preaching: Lectures on Homiletics.* New York: Charles Scribner's Sons, 1882.

Pierson, Arthur T. *The Divine Art of Preaching.* London: Passmore and Alabaster, 1892.

Piper, John. *The Supremacy of God in Preaching.* Grand Rapids: Baker, 1990.

Porter, Ebenezer and Matthews, Lyman. *Lectures on Eloquence and Style.* Andover, MA: Gould and Newman, 1836, reprinted, Memphis: General Books, 2010.

Porter, Ebenezer. *Lectures on Homiletics and Preaching.* London: R. B. Seeley and W. Burnside, 1835.

Potter, Thomas J. *Sacred Eloquence: or the Theory and Practice of Preaching.* New York: Fr. Pustet, fifth edition, 1903.

Purtle, Perry D. "The Psychology of Evangelistic Preaching." PhD. Dissertation for National Christian University, August 1971.

Read, David H. C. *Sent from God.* New York: Abingdon, 1974.

Reid, Loren. *First Principles of Public Speaking.* Columbia, MO: Artcraft Press, second edition, fourth printing, 1967.

Reu, M. *Homiletics.* Chicago: Wartburg, 1922.

Richard, Ramesh *Scripture Sculpture.* Grand Rapids: Baker, 1995.

———. *Preparing Evangelistic Sermons.* Grand Rapid: Baker, 2005.

Riley, W. B. *The Preacher and His Preaching.* Wheaton, IL: Sword of the Lord, 1948.

Ripley, Henry J. *Sacred Rhetoric.* Boston: Gould and Lincoln, fourth ed., 1859.

Robinson, Haddon W. *Biblical Preaching: The Development and Delivery of Expository Messages.* Grand Rapids: Baker, 1980.

Roddy, Clarence Stonelynn, ed. *We Prepare and Preach.* Chicago: Moody, 1959.

Sangster, William E. *The Craft of Sermon Construction.* Grand Rapids: Baker, reprinted, 1974.

Shaddix, Jim. *The Passion Driven Sermon*. Nashville: Broadman & Holman, 2003.

Shedd, William G. T. *Homiletics and Pastoral Theology*. New York: Scribner, Armstrong, eighth edition, 1876).

Simpson, Matthew. *Lectures on Preaching*. New York: Nelson and Phillips, 1897.

Sleeth, Ronald E. *Persuasive Preaching*. New York: Harper & Row, 1956.

Smith, Bailey E. *Real Evangelism*. Nashville: Thomas Nelson, 1999.

Smyth, J. Paterson. *The Preacher and His Sermon*. New York: George H. Doran, 1922.

Spring, Gardiner. *The Power of the Pulpit*. Carlisle, Pennsylvania, Banner of Truth, 1848.

Spurgeon, Charles H. *An All-round Ministry*. Carlisle, Pennsylvania: The Banner of Truth, reprinted, 1986).

———. *Holy Spirit Power*. New Kensington: PA, Whitaker House, 1996.

Stanfield, Vernon L. *Effective Evangelistic Preaching*. Grand Rapids: Baker, 1965.

———. *On the Preparation and Delivery of Sermons*. San Francisco: Harper & Row, 1979.

Stevenson, Dwight E. and Diehl, Charles F. *Reaching People from the Pulpit*. New York: Harper & Row, 1958.

Stewart, James S. *Heralds of God*. Grand Rapids: Baker, reprint, 1972.

Stibbs, Alan M. *Expounding God's Word*. Grand Rapids: Eerdmans, reprinted, 1961.

Storrs, Richard S. *Conditions of Success in Preaching Without Notes*. New York: Dodd, Mead, 1875.

Stott, John R. W. *Between Two Worlds*. Grand Rapids: Eerdmans, 1982.

———. *The Preacher's Portrait*. Grand Rapids: Eerdmans, 1961.

Streett, R. Alan. *The Effective Invitation*. Old Tappan, New Jersey: Revell, 1984.

Sturtevant, S. T. *The Preacher's Manual*. London: Reeves and Turner, fourth edition, 1866, historical reproduction by BiblioLife.

Sweazey, George E. *Preaching the Good News*. Englewood Cliffs, New Jersey: Prentice-Hall, 1976.

Swindoll, Charles R. *Saying It Well*. New York: FaithWords, 2012.

Taylor, William M. *The Ministry of the Word*. Grand Rapids: Baker, reprinted, 1975.

Thompson, James W. *Preaching Like Paul*. Louisville, Kentucky: Westminster John Knox, 2001.

Vines, Jerry. *A Guide to Effective Sermon Delivery*. Chicago: Moody, 1986.

Vines, Jerry and Shaddix, Jim. *Power in the Pulpit*. Chicago: Moody, 1999.

Vinet, Alexandre. *Homiletics: or the Theory of Preaching*. New York: Ivison & Phinney, 1854.

Wax, Trevin. *Gospel-Centered Teaching*. Nashville: B & H, 2013.

Weatherspoon, Jesse Burton. *On the Preparation and Delivery of Sermons*. Nashville: Broadman, 1944.

———. *Sent Forth to Preach*. New York: Harper & Brothers, 1954.

Whitesell, Faris D. *Power in Expository Preaching*. np: Revell, 1963.

Wiersbe, Warren W. *The Dynamics of Preaching*. Grand Rapids: Baker, 1999.

Wilkins, John. *Ecclesiastes*. London: Black-Swan, 1718, Gale ECCO Print Editions.

Ziglar, Zig *Selling 101*. Nashville: Thomas Nelson, 2003.